International Business

DATE DUE

Student:

To help you make the most of your study time and improve your grades, we have developed the following supplement designed to accompany Taoka/Beeman: *International Business: Environments, Institutions, and Operations:*

Study Guide 0-06-500086-2
By Don R. Beeman and Donald G. Howard

You can order a copy at your local bookstore or call HarperCollins Publishers directly at 1-800-782-2665.

International Business

ENVIRONMENTS, INSTITUTIONS, AND OPERATIONS

George M. Taoka
University of Toledo

Don R. Beeman
University of Toledo

HarperCollins*Publishers*

338.88
T171i

Photo Credits

Page 75, AP/Wide World; page 76, Scott Foresman; page 89, Greenberg, Monkmeyer; page 140, Scott Foresman; page 183, Herwig, Stock, Boston; page 199 © 1985, Menzel, Stock, Boston; page 204, © 1984, Menzel, Stock, Boston; page 221, AP/Wide World; page 225, Photo Researchers; page 259, Scott Foresman; page 297, Rapho, Photo Researchers; page 298, Franken, Stock, Boston; page 357, AP/Wide World; page 392, Franken, Stock, Boston; page 417, Grant, Picture Cube; page 446, Southwick, Stock, Boston; page 483, © 1982, Spragens, Jr., Photo Researchers; page 498 (top), Conklin, Monkmeyer Press; page 498 (bottom) Hayman, Stock, Boston; page 537, Cheney, Stock, Boston.

Sponsoring Editor: Debra Riegert
Project Editor: David Nickol
Design Supervisor: Lucy Krikorian
Text Design: Caliber Design Planning, Inc.
Cover Design: Edward Smith Design, Inc.
Cover Illustration: Imtek Imagineering/Masterfile
Photo Research: Mira Schachne
Production Administrator: Paula Keller
Compositor: Ruttle, Shaw & Wetherill
Printer and Binder: R. R. Donnelley & Sons Company
Cover Printer: New England Book Components, Inc.

INTERNATIONAL BUSINESS: Environments, Institutions, and Operations

Library of Congress Cataloging-in-Publication Data
Taoka, George M.
    International business: environments, institutions, and
operations / George M. Taoka, Don R. Beeman.
        p.   cm.
    Includes bibliographical references.
    Includes index.
    ISBN 0-06-046568-9
    1. International business enterprises.   2. International finance.
3. Financial institutions, International.   I. Beeman, Don R.
II. Title
HD2755.5.T4   1991
338.8'8—dc20   90-49862
                                                                        CIP

90 91 92 93   9 8 7 6 5 4 3 2 1

Professor Taoka would like to dedicate this text to the entire Taoka family both in the United States and in Japan for a lifetime of love and support.

Professor Beeman would like to dedicate this book to his mother, not merely because she literally started it all, but primarily because it was on her knee and at her side that he learned all of the things he ever REALLY needed to know: how to work without forgetting how to play, how to get joy out of giving, and how to care deeply. So, Colleen Beeman Kuhn, this book is for you.

Contents in Brief

Contents in Detail

CHAPTER

2

Theories of International Trade and Investment 38

PART TWO

The International Environment for International Business   57

CHAPTER

3

International Agreements to Minimize Conflicts   58

CHAPTER

4

Foreign Exchange   82

CHAPTER

5

The International Monetary System and the Balance of Payments   106

CHAPTER

6

International Business and the Role of Financial Institutions   136

PART THREE

The Intranational Environment of International Business   163

CHAPTER 7

Commercial Policies and Instruments for Protection 164

Introduction   165

History of Commercial Policies   166

CHAPTER
8

Geographic Environment   196

CHAPTER

9 Political and Legal Considerations in International
Business   218

PART FOUR

 **Functions of International and Multinational Firms
317**

CHAPTER
12
**Strategies and Structures of International Firms
318**

CHAPTER

13 Modes of Entry and Forms of Involvement for Exploiting International Business Opportunities 352

CHAPTER
16

CHAPTER
17

International Financial Management   462

CHAPTER
18

International Supply Strategies: Production and Sourcing   494

CHAPTER
19

Human Resource Management   516

PART FIVE

Trends and the Future of International Business
577

CHAPTER
21

Prospects for the Future of International Business
578

Preface

GUIDING PRINCIPLES

The world of business has changed dramatically in the last 20 years. Total world trade and investment has been increasing at an enormous rate. The United States has gone from being the world's greatest creditor nation to the largest debtor nation. Imports provide competition for nearly 70 percent of all U.S. goods. In fact, it could be agrued that domestic business no longer exists and that all business is international business.

To prepare our future managers for these new challenges, colleges of business are increasingly requiring that their students take an introductory course in international business. Thus, as authors of this text, we felt it important to write a book that offers a new relevance for a broader range of students. We have tried to meet these new demands by writing a text that is as meaningful for students whose future employers are predominately domestic firms facing foreign competition in the United States as for those who will work for a global manufacturer, multinational bank, or export management company. To accomplish this objective, we utilized the input of dozens of professors, international business executives, and students.

PURPOSE AND SCOPE

We have written this text for an introductory course in international business to be taken in the junior or senior year of an undergraduate business program or in the first year of an MBA program. It presumes only that knowledge which would be covered in sophomore-level courses in a business program: basic economics, accounting, and management or organizational behavior.

We had three goals for this text. First, we have tried to create a text with greater breadth of topic coverage than competitive texts while maintaining substantial conceptual depth and a standard text length. Second, we have sought to make the text highly readable and "student friendly"—a text that could be understood by the typical university student and yet present a challenge for the superior student. Finally, we have tried to provide the student with a sense of the importance and excitement of international business.

It took all of the authors' combined 60 years of experience to meet these objectives. George Taoka's more than 40 years of university and corporate experience and Don Beeman's 20 years of experience in academia and industry provide life to the material in this text.

ORGANIZATION

In Part One, we provide a historical background (Chapter 1) and discuss the theoretical foundations (Chapter 2) of international business. Although these considerations are often treated in a cursory manner in other textbooks, we believe that students cannot adequately understand the world of international business without this historical, societal, and theoretical foundation.

Parts Two and Three cover the *inter*national and the *intra*national environments of business. Part Two analyzes the international institutions and other external factors that influence commercial activities among nations and the operation of firms. In this section we include both standard and unique topics. Among the standard topics are the IMF, balance of payments, foreign exchange, the World Bank, AID, and so forth. The somewhat unique topics include explanations of informal governmental agreements, immigration, the law of the sea, and international commodity agreements. In Part Three we discuss the environmental factors within countries that impact commerce and the operation of firms.

In our opinions, the heart of any textbook on international business is its analysis of the strategic management of international firms. We discuss these topics by business function in the nine chapters of Part Four. Each of these chapters offers breadth and depth of coverage that we believe are superior to other texts. Our overall focus for this section of the text is to show students how to manage a firm strategically to enhance global competitiveness. Part Five offers our views and interpretation of the major trends that are at work today and also of the future of international business.

SPECIAL CONTENT FEATURES

Although the text is organized in a manner that will be familiar to the experienced instructor, there are several features that are unique to this text or unique in terms of the depth of coverage.

In these turbulent times, it is easy for a text to become rapidly out of date. This text is as current as any text can be on contemporary issues, for example: Europe 1992, Eastern European and Soviet liberalization, the debt crises of many LDCs, and the rise of Pacific rim, newly industrialized countries (NICs). Due to the enormous importance for international business of several highly contemporary issues, we have discussed and analyzed a variety of these contemporary issues throughout the text.

Pacific Rim Economies Japan and the newly industrialized countries of the Pacific rim have proven to be formidable competitors for U.S. firms the world over; therefore, we have emphasized the development and operations of these economies and their global firms.

Multinational Firms Multinational firms have become the dominant force in global business and are increasingly establishing manufacturing investments in the high-growth markets of the developing world.

New Technologies New technologies, especially those relating to computers, are revolutionizing the way we communicate, produce goods, and market. As a result, global competitiveness among firms and nations is increasingly being impacted by their ability to develop and implement new production, marketing, and communications technologies. Therefore, we have made this a thread that weaves through this text.

Eastern Europe and the USSR Eastern European countries have asserted their political independence from the USSR and are shifting to more open and market-oriented economies. This major and very contemporary trend is not only discussed in this text but also analyzed in terms of its impact on Western economies and global business.

The International Debt Crisis Latin American economies especially are stagnating under the weight of external, long-term debt, while American banks stand on the verge of bankruptcy if those nations default. We have included a substantial discussion of this situation because we believe that it is of critical importance not only to the economic development of Latin America but also to the economic well-being of the United States.

Protectionism and Subsidization Despite numerous bilateral and multilateral agreement among nations, many nations still subsidize their firms in an attempt to create competitive advantages or erect protectionist barriers against the firms of other nations. We believe that subsidies and protective barriers will present major problems and decision situations for both corporate executives and government officials during the decade of the 1990s.

Geography The well-documented weaknesses of American students in understanding world geography is not only important in its own right but is also symptomatic of an ethnocentric narrowness that inhibits the global competitiveness of U.S. firms. For this reason we have included an entire chapter on geography.

In addition to extensive treatment of contemporary issues, we believe that a text needs to be operationally focused. A business education and a business text must offer the student more than knowledge about a subject; it must also teach the student how to make managerial decisions. We believe that the operational, decision-oriented nature of the chapters of Part Four of this text represent a very special feature of this text. Furthermore, for some extremely important topics we believe the coverage in many texts is markedly insufficient. The following are some examples of these critically important topics.

An Operational Focus Utilizing our corporate experiences both as full-time managers and as consultants, we have written chapters that do not merely talk about a topic but rather teach the students how to manage each of the business functions from a global perspective. For example, some texts present information about exporting, international marketing, or international finance but do not provide the student with the necessary skills and knowledge to make managerial decisions. This text is operationally focused with the intention of creating international managers.

International Sourcing and Production In the competitive wars that are raging between U.S. and Japanese firms, the American firms have for nearly two decades been operating at a distinct disadvantage in the arena of production and yet many texts still treat this topic in a very cursory manner. We believe that international sourcing and production are a major strength of this text.

International Strategies The increasing levels of global interdependence and the development of globally competitive industries have necessitated the development of worldwide strategies. Our Chapter 12 gets to the heart of both research and practice for the development of worldwide strategies in both global and multidomestic industries.

Other Key Advantages of This Text Several other topics are treated with greater depth in this text than in others with each topic being handled in a separate chapter: forms of international involvement; exporting, importing and trade financing; transportation and logistics; international financial management; and international taxation and accounting.

PEDAGOGY

Our pedagogical goals were to present the materials in a manner that would interest and excite the student as well as provide information, and to assist the professor so that he or she would have more time to enhance the course with additional information and would not have to spend more time clarifying the text. The following features help attain these goals.

Learning Objectives and Outline of Topics Although these are relatively standard features, they are useful in that they target the student's thinking and orient the student to the materials that are to be covered.

Margin Comments These serve to summarize and reinforce key facts, concepts, theories, or techniques that have been presented while the material is still fresh in the student's mind. Furthermore, they allow the student to do a quick skim review of a chapter once it has been completed.

Global Insights The boxed Global Insights present current and real-world illustrations of concepts or theories that have been presented, immediately following the presentation. As a result, students do not have to hunt for an example or wonder whether the theory has any real-world validity.

Full Color Map Portfolio This portfolio visually acquaints students with world geography in terms of where U.S. competitors and markets are located.

Maps, Charts, Graphs, Photographs, and Figures These enhance the written material by providing a visual summary of the most important concepts of the book.

Chapter Summaries These, along with the text matter, Global Insights, and margin comments, reemphasize the important points of the chapter.

Key Terms, Concepts, and Glossary To help the student learn the often confusing vocabulary of international business, we have listed the key terms and concepts at the back of each chapter and provided a comprehensive glossary at the conclusion of the text. The student can test his or her understanding of the key terms and concepts immediately after reading a chapter.

Review Questions The review questions at the end of each chapter are intended to test the student's understanding of the most important topics from the chapter as well as to challenge the student to apply the theories of the chapter in a managerially relevant manner.

Chapter Cases At the end of each chapter we have presented a case that requires the student to use the concepts of the chapter to understand and to react to a realistic situation. For each case we have listed questions to facilitate class discussion.

Notes, References, and Selected Readings The notes and references are presented so that the student or instructor can look up the source of the information provided in the text. The selected readings provide students and instructors with both a chapter-specific reading list and the literature foundation for individual research papers.

Integrative Cases Integrative cases are provided at the end of the text. Each case covers several aspects in the operation of a multinational firm. These are intended to allow for the integration of materials presented in several different chapters of the text as well as to expose the student to some of the complexities of the real world of international business.

SUPPLEMENTS

We believe that one of the major weaknesses of many textbooks is that someone other than the authors have written the Instructor's Manual, Test Bank, and so forth. We are personally responsible for all instructor support materials. We have also not used graduate students to write questions. This was done because we believe that limited or poorly developed support materials make the professor's job substantially more difficult and make the text less useful.

Instructor's Manual The Instructor's Manual includes a presentation on how to use this text in a 15-week semester system and 10-week quarter system. For each chapter, the manual summarizes the learning objectives and gives a detailed chapter outline. The manual also provides the instructor with detailed teaching notes, the answers to the chapter review questions, solutions for the end-of-chapter cases and the case questions, and a chapter glossary. This chapter glossary is provided to eliminate the need for the instructor to seek terms in the end-of-text glossary. The Instructor's Manual also presents detailed solutions for the integrative cases, including examples of appropriate analyses.

Texts often become less valuable to professors because student organizations develop files on the cases in the text. To minimize this problem, we have included additional cases, with questions and solutions, as part of the Instructor's Manual.

The manual also includes suggestions of topics for, and sources of, guest lecturers. This is intended to facilitate the work of an instructor in selecting outside speakers. In addition, topics for term papers are suggested. Finally, the Instructor's Manual lists a variety of films and videotapes that can be used to enrich the class.

Overhead Transparencies The supplemental materials also include transparencies for key figures from the text as well as transparencies that are not based on text figures.

Test Bank The Test Bank for this text provides four types of questions and answers: true-false, multiple-choice, fill-in, and short essay questions. We have developed substantially more questions than found with most international business texts; approximately 100 questions are provided for each chapter.

Harper Test The Test Bank is also available on the highly acclaimed, computerized test-generating system called Harper Test. It is important to note that this system has full word-processing capabilities that allow for customizing tests, scrambling questions, and adding new questions. It is available for use on IBM and some compatible computers.

Study Guide Written by Don Beeman and Donald Howard of the University of Akron, this helpful manual offers summaries and outlines for each chapter, key terms, self-test questions, case summaries and cases for self-study, a special case analysis guide, and an overview of career possibilities.

HarperCollins Business Video Library Adopters may select videos from the HarperCollins library of business videos, including *Future Forum*, a Wall Street Journal production that features Peter Jennings leading a panel of experts through an hour-long discussion of worker loyalty, entrepreneurship, management responsibility, financing, job security, the role of government in business, America's position in the competitive global economy, and other topics of interest.

ACKNOWLEDGMENTS

The authors would like to express their deep appreciation to the large number of people who have made this text possible.

The following reviewers whose criticism and suggestions helped enhance and improve each draft of this text also deserve a special note of thanks: Philip D. Grub, George Washington University; Gary Hannem, Mankato State University; Rose Knotts, University of New Orleans; David Lei, Southern Methodist University; John E. Mack, Salem State College; and Rosalie Tung, University of Wisconsin. One of these reviewers was with us through all of the drafts and played such an important role that he almost qualifies as a coauthor. So, to Professor David Lei, we express our deepest respect and appreciation.

Finally, we need to acknowledge several other individuals for their assistance: Professor Emeritus Robert Hansen, University of Toledo, for his contribution to the chapter on international accounting and taxation; Professor Lee Thuong, University of Toledo, for his assistance and guidance on the international transportation and logistics chapter; and George Ghareeb (Vice President of the International Division, Ohio Citizens Bank) for assistance on the section pertaining to financing international trade.

George M. Taoka
Don R. Beeman

About the Authors

GEORGE M. TAOKA

George M. Taoka (Ph.D., Columbia University) is Professor Emeritus of International Business at the University of Toledo. Professor Taoka has taught at the University of Toledo for nearly four decades, including courses in international business, international economics, import/export management, and economic geography. An excellent teacher, Dr. Taoka has twice been selected as outstanding teacher at the University of Toledo by the University and by Alpha Kappa Psi business fraternity.

Dr. Taoka has specialized in U.S. international trade and the economic development of Pacific rim nations. He has published in journals such as the *Journal of International Business Studies*. Additionally, Professor Taoka was the recipient of a Ford Foundation Grant in International Business at New York University and a Canadian Studies grant from Canadian Embassy.

Dr. Taoka has consulted with numerous firms and public organizations including the Champion Spark Plug Company, Owens Illinois, Toledo Scale, and with the Toledo Board of Education. He also served as an economic advisor to Sanseido Publishing Company of Tokyo, Japan.

DON R. BEEMAN

Don R. Beeman (DBA, Indiana University) is a Professor of International Business and Business Policy/Strategy at the University of Toledo. He is currently serving his second term as director of their International Business Institute (IBI).

Selected as the outstanding professor in the University of Toledo's MBA program, Professor Beeman has also been a Visiting Professor at the Netherlands School of Business and a Presidential Fellow at the American Graduate School of International Management (Thunderbird).

His current research interests include reinvestment strategies of U.S. corporations abroad and strategies for U.S. firms in import-impact industries. He has published in such journals as *Management International Review, Business Horizons, The Journal of Business Strategy,* and *The Journal of Business and Economic Perspectives.*

He has consulted for several multinational firms on various topics: international capital allocation, the strategic management of foreign subsidiaries, and cross-national mergers. His clients include Owens-Illinois, Dana World Trade, and Mather Metals (now a division of NHK of Japan).

Dr. Beeman is a member of the International Management Division of the Academy of Management, serving as membership chair and editor of the research round-up. He is active in the Academy of International Business.

International Business

*P*art One of this text is composed of only two chapters, but it covers an immense amount of material that will provide the foundation for the remainder of the text. Chapter 1 deals in substantial depth with the development and importance of world trade, investment, and the multinational firms from the beginning of recorded history to the present; Chapter 2 explains the theoretical foundations for both international trade and international investments.

Chapter 1 provides the student with a chronological explanation of both trade and investment. This chapter not only affords the student an opportunity to come to understand the nature and magnitude of trade across history but also explains the factors and historical occurrences that enhanced or impeded the further development of trade and investment. Despite the attention paid to the periods prior to 1900, a substantial portion of this chapter addresses trade and investment in this century. The impact of the three traumatic events during the first half of this century—World War I, the Great Depression, and World War II—are analyzed and explained. Finally, the explosion of world trade and investment in the post–World War II period is illustrated and explained. Chapter 2 presents a brief but thorough explanation of the major theories of international trade and investment.

The Nature, Importance, and Bases for International Business

1

The Development and Importance of World Trade, Investment, and the Multinational Firm (MNF)

- Understand the history and development of world commerce

- Learn how different commercial policies affect international business

- Describe the reasons for the tremendous growth and importance of international trade and investments

- Understand the factors affecting the development of world trade and investment from 1900 to the present

- Learn the relationship between exports and national income

- Understand the nature and magnitude of U.S. trade, the reasons for the current U.S. trade imbalance, and the impact of exports and imports on various sectors of the U.S. economy

- Explain the importance, types, purposes, and patterns of U.S. foreign investments

- Understand the geographic and sectoral distribution of foreign investments

THE DEVELOPMENT OF TRADE, INVESTMENT, AND THE MULTINATIONAL FIRM THROUGH 1900

Prehistoric Period (to 1500 B.C.)

Recent anthropological studies of primitive societies and their trading traditions provide us with some clues as to the nature of prehistoric trade. Thurnwald concludes that the earliest form of trade was one-sided, directed toward the acquisition of goods, and in the form of an expedition or adventure. It was a long-distance extension of traditional hunter-gatherer behavior. This one-way movement probably evolved into two-sidedness when resistance was encountered. Objects were not allowed to be carried away without something being left in exchange.[1] One of the interesting trade traditions emerging from this resistance was silent trade. Although it was once quite prevalent on the islands of the Pacific and in other areas of Asia and Africa, it is no longer a common practice. Even Herodotus, the ancient Greek historian, mentions silent trade. In silent trade, deliverers would leave objects in a clearing and then hide. Others would come along and leave other articles in exchange for what they took. A pygmy tribe, the Akka of central Africa, practiced silent trade out of fear of stronger parties.

Among some primitive peoples, bartering was a common practice. Specific objects were exchanged for other objects. The Lango and Oambo tribes of southwest Africa bartered corn for meat; the Masai exchanged cows for oxen. These clearly represent economic reasons for trade. The Mafuru tribe of south New Guinea exchanged dogs' teeth for pigs. Since the length of the string of dogs' teeth was equated in value to the size of the pig, this system could be viewed as a transition stage between a barter and a money system. Indeed, when an "exchange rate" was set at 200 dogs' teeth for a pig, dogs' teeth became a form of money.

In many primitive societies, trade was conducted more for social reasons than for economic ones. Trading trips were a time for reestablishing social bonds with neighboring groups.

In addition to the current trading practices of primitive societies, historical data can also be examined. In Australia, flat stones and red ochre have been discovered 800 kilometers (about 500 miles) from their sources, indicating that the natives traveled great distances to obtain these goods. Artifacts from Asia have been discovered in Mexico, suggesting that goods were even transported over large bodies of water to their destination. Along the desert routes of north Africa, it is known that camel caravans were used to transport such products as dates, wool, and garments to the civilizations of the Tigris-Euphrates region, Babylonia, and Assyria in exchange for such luxuries as olive oil and spices.

Before the birth of Christ, the ancient Chinese were engaged in trade with India and the Baltic regions of northern Europe. The round trip on the overland route between China and Europe took about two years, so the products being traded had to be sufficiently valuable (e.g., silk, brocade, jade) to withstand the high transportation costs and could not be perishable. Legend has it that green tea was shipped from China to Europe, but it arrived as black tea—because of the fermentation and the subsequent drying of the product.

Trade during prehistoric times was probably as much social as economic in motive.

Ancient Period (1500 B.C. to A.D. 500)

International trade as we know it today probably had its earliest beginnings in the Mediterranean area between 2500 and 1500 B.C. Foremost among the early traders was the island of Crete, located in the eastern Mediterranean. Such luxuries as paintings, sculptures, gems, ivory, and fabrics were shipped to Egypt, Sardinia, and the centers of population along the Aegean Sea. The decline in importance of Crete as a trading nation was followed by the rise of Phoenicia. Located along the eastern shores of the Mediterranean, cut off from the interior by the mountains, and helped by the abundance of shipbuilding materials, Phoenicia developed skilled shipbuilders and navigators. Phoenicia was the dominant trading state during the period between 1500 and 1000 B.C. The Phoenicians established colonies along the Black Sea, the Mediterranean Sea, the north coast of Africa, and as far as the Straits of Gibraltar. Of these, Carthage on the north coast of Africa became the most important trading center, exchanging such items as

International trade originated in the eastern Mediterranean between 1500 and 1000 B.C.

gold, silver, iron, brass, glass, and purple dye for ivory, ebony, textiles, utensils, dried fish, grains, fruit, and slaves.

The dominance of Phoenicia gradually faded with the rise of Greece as a great maritime and trading nation. Geographic location and terrain forced Greece to turn to the sea for its livelihood. Built-in advantages such as the abundance of shipbuilding materials, a long coastline with excellent harbors, and a central location facilitated the development of Greece as a prosperous trading nation. Colonies were founded to carry on trade with major centers of population, again a nascent form of investment. Trade centers were established in Central Asia and India, while Carthage remained a dominant trading center. Commodities that could withstand the high cost of transportation were the only goods traded. Thus, manufactured goods of metal or clay, along with wool, wine, and olive oil were exchanged for grain, slaves, and luxury goods.

With the decline of Greece, Rome became all-powerful. Rome's interests, however, lay in political domination rather than trade. "Pax Romana," peace through the court of law and later through the use of military force, was something totally new to the provinces that emerged under the Roman Empire. Unintentionally, "Pax Romana" created an environment conducive to the development of trade and the growth of international business. Commerce developed rapidly and extended from Egypt to Britain and from Spain to Persia (Iran), with trade links as far as China.

Commerce grew rapidly under the Greeks and Romans because of the establishment of trading centers and the implementation of stable laws and administration.

Administrative corruption and military adventurism led to the deterioration of societal values, the weakening of the Roman Empire, and its eventual downfall in A.D. 476. The chaos of wars and invasions by barbaric tribes from the north replaced the order and constancy of Roman rule. Most of the Western world remained in disarray for 500 years.

Middle Ages (A.D. 500 to 1500)

The Christian church completed its rise to political and economic dominance with the crowning of Charlemagne as the Emperor of the Romans in 800. Monasteries were established in the areas dominated by the church; however, trade was stifled because commerce was considered irreligious. Profits and interest were condemned. To further discourage trade, business taxes were levied against merchant traders, leaving what little trade existed to the clergy, who were exempt from taxes. Despite its lack of support for trade, the church's domination did provide the stable environment in which business and trade would later flourish.

The rise of feudalism gained impetus with the breakup of the empire of Charlemagne in 814. For mutual protection, people lived in groups on land owned by lords, giving rise to largely self-sufficient feudal manors. Trade was limited to such necessities as salt. Centralized control was replaced by the decentralization of feudalism.

The church continued to control the political and financial spheres.

Ironically, it was the church-sponsored Crusades that were directly responsible for the rebirth of international trade in the Western world. These contacts with the Arab world resulted in an exchange of customs, ideas, and products; indeed, the Crusaders found that the "infidels" had a more highly developed civilization than their own. Comforts and luxuries such as carpets, furniture, beds, silks, perfumes, sugar, and spices were already in use in Egypt, Syria, Arabia, India, and China. The result of this exposure was an irrepressible demand for these products in Europe.

The wealth, power, and authority of the church increased, while feudalism declined in importance. The church accumulated the property of those knights who did not return from the Crusades. At one time the church owned one third of the land area of western Europe. Nevertheless, the seeds of trade had been planted and even the church could not stop it.

The Crusades introduced new customs, ideas, and products to the Western world and resulted in the rebirth of international commerce.

Towns that had sprung up near the monasteries for protection became important centers for trading and, relatedly, manufacturing. Individuals engaged in similar work organized into associations or guilds. Craft guilds exercised monopolies in their respective crafts, while merchant guilds controlled the industry and trade of the towns. Strict regulations were adopted by these guilds for self-benefit. The craft guilds remained important until small factories replaced the independent craftsmen many centuries later.

The Crusades aided in the growth of a number of Italian cities on the Mediterranean, such as Venice, Pisa, Genoa, and Florence, as they became suppliers of provisions for the fleets (Figure 1.1). After the Crusades, these cities continued to trade with the Arab world. Competition among the different cities for financial reward and influence became so keen that it often took the form of military action against each other.

As commerce between the Orient and Europe expanded, these Italian cities became increasingly important. Today, certain merchant families such as the Peruzzi and Medici in Italy and the Fuggers in Germany can trace their financial and political powers to this period. These and other wealthy merchant families eventually controlled both government and finance. Commercial agreements were made and trade concessions were obtained from other centers throughout the known world. Trading privileges were often restricted to the townspeople. Duties were levied on "imports" to protect "domestic" producers. "Exports" of items of limited supply, such as foodstuffs, were often prohibited. Central market places were established to protect consumers from sellers. Thus, commercial policies were developed, not dissimilar to those in existence today. This period also marked the emergence of market economies and international trade.

Unlike the Italian cities, those in northern Europe were less competitive and more cooperative. Cities joined together to form a commercial association called the Hanseatic League. Together, their wealth, military power, and political influence enabled them to dictate to feudal lords and even princes on matters dealing with commerce and politics. They negotiated commercial treaties and regulated trade, cleared the seas of pirates,

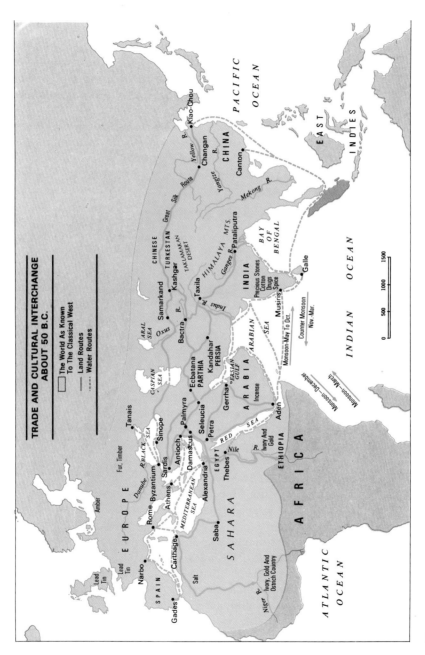

Figure 1.1   Trade and Cultural Interchange to India and the Orient About 50 B.C.

and, in general, provided an environment for the rapid growth of international commerce and regional enterprise.

This period of shifting political power bases in Europe resulted in a tenuous set of relationships. Although the church remained strong, its power was balanced by the last remnants of feudalism, the merchant and craft guilds, and the alliances of cities. It was in this environment that the nation-states as we know them today began to take shape. Very rapidly the nation became the dominant political and economic institution. Nevertheless, this dominance was maintained only by keeping happy the church, merchants, craftsmen, and the nobility. In modern terminology the nation-state was a coalition government wherein no one group was strong enough to threaten the whole. Over many centuries the nation became more powerful, and the other pillars of the society became less powerful.

The power of the church was offset by guilds, feudal nobility, and the city-states, resulting in coalitions that were to become nations.

Colonial Period (1500 to 1900)

With the decline in power of the Mongols in Asia and the fall of Constantinople (now Istanbul) in 1453, the important overland routes to the Orient came under the control of the Turks. The flourishing overland trade between Europe and the Far East was cut off. Thus, it became essential for the trading nation-states of Europe to find alternative routes.

Portugal and Spain led the way in financing expeditions to seek a water route to India and the Orient. Columbus sailed westward in 1492 expecting to reach India, but "discovered" America instead. Vasco da Gama sailed around the Cape of Good Hope to India in 1498. Magellan circumnavigated the globe in 1552.

These and other discoveries had an immediate effect on world trade. Commerce shifted westward from the Italian cities. Water transportation almost completely replaced overland transportation. Products that had not previously been exportable because of the extremely high cost of land transportation now became available at reasonable prices. Luxuries were no longer the only items entering trade. Products such as sugar, textiles, tea, and coffee from the Middle East and Asia, and tobacco, sugar, and other products (especially gold and silver) from the Americas became available in Europe.

With the strengthening of the nation-state, the position of the church steadily weakened. This movement was accelerated by one of the most significant events in the history of the Western world: the Protestant Reformation. The Catholic church had become corrupted. Bribery was commonplace, and wealth and opulence abounded in Rome. The church had evolved into a social, political, and economic organization of immense size and power, but in the minds of many of its members it had lost its position as a religious institution. This difference of opinion and the resulting frustrations found their voice in Martin Luther who nailed his list of grievances on the church door, leading to the development of a new faith—Protestantism.

Protestantism was based upon individualism, self-determination, and an effort-reward linkage. The divisiveness also served to launch reform within the Catholic church. This reform took the church away from politics and back into religion, and eventually led to the Referendum Novarum in which the Catholic church legitimated profits.

With the Reformation, the separation of church and state, the passing of feudalism, and the decline in importance of the cities, national governments came into supremacy. England, with its superior political and military organizations, became the dominant power in western Europe. Simultaneously, political and economic weaknesses resulted in the relative decline in importance and influence of Spain and Portugal.

England, the Netherlands, France, and Belgium established colonies for the monetary benefit of the mother countries. High taxes were levied and duties were imposed on products from the colonies. Other regulations were adopted to control commerce and to protect domestic industries. Only when such policies failed did these countries turn to trade as a means of accumulating wealth. The bulk of this trade was carried on by government-chartered companies that were granted monopolistic trade privileges in different geographic areas. These chartered companies often used unscrupulous methods, even force, for economic gain. Of the many companies that received charters, the Hudson's Bay Company (British) is still in existence, but its main function is restricted to merchandise retailing. It is interesting to note that the activities of these companies were a combination of both investment abroad and trade facilitation.

Many organizations to facilitate commerce were developed during this period. Joint stock companies or corporations provided an alternative to the individual proprietorship and partnerships. Furthermore, they provided a source of funds for foreign investments and trading facilities. Stock and produce exchanges provided a central meeting place for buyers and sellers. Modern banks replaced the medieval goldsmiths. Marine insurance got its start in Lloyd's Coffee House in London, and middlemen of various types appeared to meet the specialized needs of trade.

Largely as a result of the influence of eighteenth-century free-trade economists (Adam Smith, David Ricardo, and others), the restrictive trade and protectionist policies gave way to free trade. For example, in 1849 England abandoned the Corn Laws that had been passed to protect domestically produced grain. Along with free trade came economic competition and interdependency among nations. International trade was dominant, and international investments existed almost exclusively to facilitate trade.

The Italian city-states lost economic power initially to Spain and Portugal, which were later displaced by the free-trade nations of northern Europe.

Foreign Investments Prior to 1900

Foreign investments are not a recent phenomenon although the methods of investment and the policies to regulate foreign investments have become much more sophisticated in recent years. Centuries ago, citizens and merchant trading companies made foreign investments through direct participation in various types of commercial enterprises. The Medicis (of Florence, Italy) and the Fuggers (of Augsburg, Germany) were the forerunners of modern financial institutions. They had financial interest in mines, industries, fleets of merchant ships, and other types of economic activities in many countries during the fifteenth and sixteenth centuries.

In the seventeenth century, financial institutions of Amsterdam were primary investors in foreign commercial and industrial enterprises. These were followed by financial institutions of Paris in the eighteenth century, of London in the nineteenth century, and of London, New York, Paris, and Berlin in the early years of the twentieth century.[2]

There is no doubt that capital provided by foreign financial institutions and international agencies contributed to the more rapid development of the basic industries and infrastructure among the less developed nations. The United States, for example, was almost completely dependent upon foreign capital for the development of its infrastructure and basic industries during much of the nineteenth century.

Foreign direct investment on a large scale by U.S. multinational corporations is a relatively recent phenomenon; however, the beginnings of the international activities of these corporations can be traced to the middle of the last century.

WORLD TRADE AND INVESTMENTS: 1900–WORLD WAR II

Trade Fluctuations Through the Great Depression

It was not until after World War I (1914–1917) that the existing national barriers became serious impediments to world commerce. Economic cooperation and interdependency during the war years were replaced by economic warfare during the immediate postwar period. Nations shifted production from military goods to civilian goods with predictable results: overcapacity and falling prices. This was especially true with agricultural production. The United States, feeling that its agricultural industry was threatened by imports, passed the highest tariff in the history of the country—the Fordney-McCumber Tariff Act of 1922. Other nations retaliated with similarly restrictive measures, resulting in depressed economic conditions. Fortunately, economic development and technological progress during the 1920s did much to aid in the recovery from the post–World War I recession. This was followed by the boom of the late 1920s, especially in the stock market, until the crash in 1929, which ushered in the Great Depression. This complete collapse in economic activities affected western Europe even more severely than the United States.

As a result of the Depression and global protectionism, world trade declined by more than 40 percent between 1929 and 1931. In 1934 total world trade amounted to only $23.3 billion, or about one-third of the 1929 figure of $68.6 billion. By 1938, although the Depression had subsided, total world trade was still only $27.7 billion, only 40 percent of the 1929 level.[3] This major decline in world trade can be attributed to decreases both in the volume of trade and in price levels.

There is no doubt that national policies were largely responsible for the length and persistence of the Depression of the 1930s. Again, nations sought relief by keeping out foreign goods. As unemployment in the United States reached 25 percent, Congress adopted an isolationist commercial policy through the passage of the Hawley-Smoot Tariff Act in 1930. The reasoning behind the passage of this act was that if competitive imports were restricted, Americans would be forced to purchase domestically produced goods. As the demand for goods increased, production would have to be increased. Increased production would stimulate investments to increase productive capacity, increasing employment. Additional jobs would lead to increased income and additional spending, which would further increase demand and output—thus an upward spiral of employment and prosperity. Slogans such as "Buy Now Under the Blue Eagle" represent additional attempts to stimulate the purchase of domestically produced goods rather than foreign goods, which were higher-priced due to the tariffs.

Unfortunately, that logic was as faulty in 1930 as it is today. Congress failed to realize that a large segment of the United States economy depended upon foreign markets. As other countries retaliated, markets for American agricultural products and manufactures were cut off. The loss of jobs from retaliatory tariffs was almost immediate. To add to the seriousness of the problem, the absence of foreign goods caused domestic prices to escalate.

The severity of the Depression of the 1930s can be attributed in part to the economic nationalism and the protectionist policies adopted by nations.

During the Great Depression, the United States realized that protectionism would not solve its economic problems, and it became one of the first countries to take action to solve the problem. In 1934, Congress passed the Reciprocal Trade Agreements Act, which authorized the president to enter into trade agreements with foreign countries.[4]

World Trade from the Depression Through World War II

As World War II drew near, world trade again declined, erasing the slow recovery that had been occurring since the Depression. During World War II, economic warfare temporarily took a back seat to economic cooperation. The United States contributed to the maintenance of world trade and to the war effort through lend-lease shipments of war materials to its allies. These shipments amounted to almost 80 percent of U.S. exports in 1943 and 1944 and were the most important components of world trade during the war years. Fortunately for the Allies, the German warships plying the North Atlantic were unable to prevent most of the supplies from reaching Europe.

Additional progress toward intergovernmental cooperation to stimulate trade was made even before the end of World War II with the establishment of the International Monetary Fund (IMF) and the International Bank for Reconstruction and Development (World Bank, or IBRD) in 1944. (See Chapter 6 for a more detailed discussion.) The stated objective of the IMF was to facilitate expanding and balanced growth of international trade. This would be achieved by aiding nations that had balance-of-payments difficulties so that they would not resort to protectionist measures or competitive devaluations of their currencies. The IBRD was established to revive international investments. The establishment of these institutions was followed by the signing of the General Agreements on Tariffs and Trade (GATT) in 1948. The nations that signed the GATT agreement consented to modifying their existing duties and restrictions to permit the freer flow of goods among nations.

With the reconstruction and recovery of the countries of western Europe and Japan during the immediate post–World War II period, the United States found itself in the enviable position of being a seller in a seller's market. As a result, the United States racked up large trade surpluses. Pent-up consumer demand resulted in a dramatic increase in U.S. trade and a steady growth in total world trade for the next 25 years. The United States contributed toward this growth of trade through the Marshall Plan and other forms of transfer payments that were used to purchase U.S.-made goods. Between July 1945 and December 1957, foreign assistance provided by the United States totaled $97,283 million.[5]

From 1900 through World War II the United States went from free trade to protectionism and back to free trade.

To ease the problem of a deficit balance of payments among its trading partners, the United States encouraged imports of foreign goods and adopted various measures to create claims against the United States. Firms in western Europe and Japan did not hesitate to take advantage of this open and accommodating market.

Growth of the Multinational Enterprises and Foreign Investments: 1900 Through World War II

During the early years of the twentieth century, foreign capital flowed rapidly into the United States so that by 1914, foreign investments totaled $7 billion, making the United States the leading debtor nation in the world. At the same time, rapid development of the U.S. economy resulted in the generation of sufficient capital that the country became a leading source of capital for less developed countries. By 1914, $4 billion had flowed out of the country, primarily to Latin America.[6]

At the outset of World War I, U.S. participation primarily took the form of logistical support for the Allies. Shipments of military and related supplies were financed through direct government loans and the revenues from the flotation of Liberty Bonds. After the end of the war, reconstruction and rehabilitation of the war-devastated areas required additional capital. Thus, foreign indebtedness to the United States increased rapidly during the war years, transforming the country from the greatest debtor to the second greatest creditor nation in the world. The direction of the flow of U.S. funds also changed during this period. Europe replaced Latin America as the major site of U.S. investments.

Portfolio investments dominated American private foreign investments after World War I. These continued to increase until the stock market crash in 1929. The major outlets for these investments were Latin America, Canada, western Europe, the Middle East, and Africa (see Figure 1.2).

Total long-term investments (U.S. government loans, commercial loans, and private foreign investments) that had amounted to $1,246 million in 1928 fell to $661 million in 1929 and $30 million in 1932.[7] This precipitous drop was due to the worldwide Depression of the 1930s. Wholesale defaults by governments on their World War I debts were accompanied by increasing defaults by foreign companies portfolio investments made by U.S. nationals. This was especially true among the Latin American countries.

Investments abroad continued at a slow pace in the 1930s as the depressed economic conditions lingered on. The slowdown was due in part to the desire on the part of countries to institute economic measures that would get them out of the Depression. They believed that multinational firms, with their global outlook, might interfere with their efforts to imple-

Figure 1.2   U.S. Investments by World Region (1929)
Source: U.S. Department of Commerce, *American Direct Investments in Foreign Countries*, 1940.

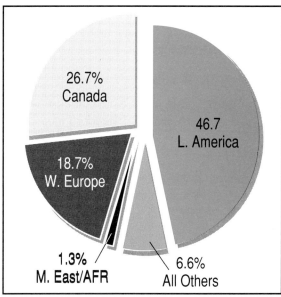

ment these policies. Many of these nations had adopted measures advocated by J. M. Keynes in his economic treatise, *The General Theory on Employment, Interest and Money.* Keynes argued that a nation could emerge from the Depression if the government adopted a policy of deficit financing and if the central bank followed a cheap money policy to encourage capital investments. Furthermore, he advocated a policy of economic nationalism to result in the adoption of barriers to imports and restrictions on the inflow of foreign capital—that is, barriers to foreign investment.

It is, therefore, somewhat ironic that the widespread adoption of barriers, primarily in the form of tariffs, led to the growth and development of the multinational firm (MNF) as we know it today. Small firms were the primary losers when trade was restricted because they lacked the resources to circumvent these protective measures. For larger firms, exporting was only one approach to international business operations. Thus they adopted a more diversified approach to servicing world markets. They looked upon these governmentally imposed restrictions as a condition of business and then made their decision accordingly (see Table 1.1).

This is not to imply that the large firms invested abroad only to avoid trade barriers. In fact, by the turn of the century, some corporations were already making foreign direct investments in both production and distribution facilities; nevertheless, most large corporations were still investing abroad primarily for the extraction of raw materials.

Foreign direct investments increased rapidly after 1945. As in the 1930s, this rapid growth can be attributed to the widespread adoption of trade barriers as nations drifted toward protectionism and the development of regional economically integrated units. Foreign investments provided the primary avenue for reaching these markets. This rapid expansion of foreign investments has led to the dominant role that multinational corporations currently play in international business.

TABLE 1.1 **Corporate Strategies in Response to Trade and Investment Barriers**

Country Policies	MNF Strategies
No trade or investment restrictions	Export or invest as economics dictate
Restrictions on imports; no restrictions on investments	Licensing agreements, joint ventures, or wholly owned direct investments depending upon the economics of the market
Restrictions on imports and wholly owned or majority owned foreign investments	Licensing agreements or minority position joint ventures

TRADE IN THE POST–WORLD WAR II PERIOD

In the postwar period, world trade increased dramatically. One contributing factor was the increase in the number of countries as former colonies gained their independence in Africa, Asia, and Latin America. Population growth, from 2.2 billion in 1940 to approximately 5 billion in 1985, also placed unprecedented demand upon nations to import the necessities of life. Since world trade is measured in terms of value, the rapid increase in prices since World War II (worldwide inflation) is reflected in the growth of trade. Manufactured goods, many of which are highly technical and carry a high per-unit value, dominated trade.

In addition, the exhaustion of many scarce and increasingly expensive natural resources of industrialized nations has forced these nations to turn to foreign sources for such commodities. Greater affluence has resulted in an increased demand for luxuries and other nonessential items from abroad. The developing nations increased the import of capital equipment for their own industrialization as well as basic necessities.

The rapid growth of trade in the postwar period can be traced to the need for reconstruction, pent-up consumer demand, worldwide inflation, and increasing interdependence among the economies of industrialized nations.

The phenomenal growth in world trade, from $40 billion in 1913 to nearly $5 trillion in 1987, is an increase of nearly 12,000 percent, occurring mostly in the last 25 years. Figures 1.3 and 1.4 graphically present the level of world trade for the periods 1913 to 1938 and 1950 to 1987.

Country Groups and World Trade

Industrialized Countries

Most important in world trade are the industrialized countries. Contrary to popular belief, trade takes place largely among the advanced industrialized nations. The exchange of raw materials and crude foodstuffs from the less developed countries for manufactured goods of the more developed nations is not nearly so important. Figure 1.5 illustrates the relative percentages of the trade of industialized nations that goes to other industrialized nations, non-oil-producing developing nations, oil-producing developing nations, and communist nations.

This dominance of trade among industrialized nations is not a recent phenomenon. During the period 1911–1913, the 18 leading industrial nations of the world were the United States, Canada, Australia, Japan, New Zealand, Austria, Belgium, Denmark, Finland, France, Germany, Italy, Netherlands, Norway, Spain, Sweden, Switzerland, and the United Kingdom. During those years this group accounted for 68.5 per cent of total world trade.[8] Since 1976, this same group plus Iceland and Ireland accounted for approximately two-thirds of total world trade. Despite changes in the world economy, the share of world trade controlled by the industrial nations has remained relatively constant.

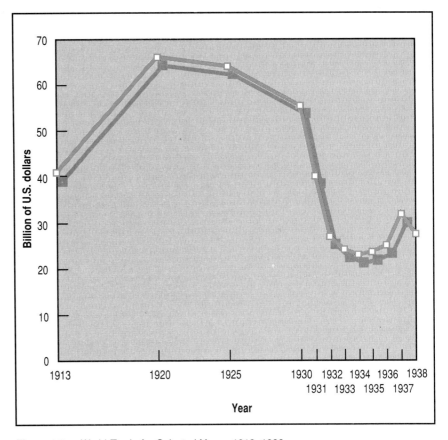

Figure 1.3   World Trade for Selected Years, 1913–1938
Source: W. S. Woytinsky and E. S. Woytinsky, *World Commerce and Government Trends and Out-looks* (New York: The Twentieth Century Fund, 1955), p. 39.

Trade among the industrial countries themselves reflects a number of factors. These countries have a higher per capita income. Various manufactured products are in great demand throughout the industrialized world. Many of the industrialized nations are also major producers of primary products. Exports create the necessary foreign exchange to pay for the desired imports.

About two-thirds of the world's trade is conducted by the more highly industrialized nations.

Less Developed Countries

Most less developed nations are dependent on the export of raw materials, crude foodstuffs, and semiprocessed goods to pay for their imports. The export of manufactured goods from the less developed countries is generally limited to less sophisticated, more labor-intensive goods. Thus, most of these countries have difficulty earning the necessary foreign exchange to

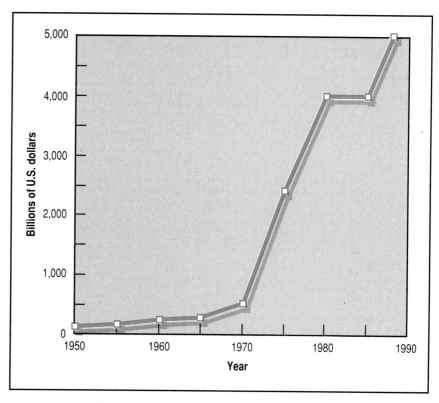

Figure 1.4   Total World Trade, 1950–1957
Source: International Monetary Fund, *Supplement on Trade Statistics,* Supplementary Series No. 4,
1982, pp. 2–3; *Direction Trade Statistics Yearbook,* 1989.

service their debt obligations, pay for capital imports, and import the necessities for their rapidly growing populations.

Trade between industrialized countries and the non-oil-producing developing countries of Africa, Asia, Europe, the Middle East, and the western
hemisphere were relatively stable during the period 1976 to 1987. The non-
oil-producing developing countries accounted for between 15.0 to 20.3
percent of the total imports of the industrialized countries. They also purchased between 14.9 and 18.7 percent of the total exports of industrialized
countries.

Trade with the 13 oil-producing and exporting countries of OPEC—
Algeria, Ecuador, Iran, Indonesia, Iraq, Kuwait, Libya, Nigeria, Oman,
Qatar, Saudi Arabia, the United Arab Emirates, and Venezuela—was not
so stable. These nations accounted for 16.2 percent of all imports by industrial countries in 1976, but only 5.2 percent in 1987. In 1976 OPEC countries purchased 8.4 percent of all exports from industrial nations but only

The OPEC cartel allowed member nations to amass large quantities of foreign exchange by controlling sup- ply and prices of crude oil. The oil glut of the last few years has eroded this monopolistic position.

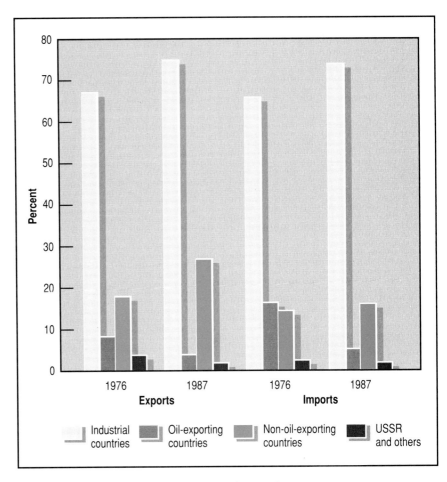

Figure 1.5   Trade of Industrial Countries by Country Groups
Source: International Monetary Fund, *Direction of Trade Statistics Yearbook,* 1989.

3.7 percent in 1987. These significant changes are the result of fluctuations in the world market prices of crude oil and the weakening of the OPEC cartel.

Trade with and Among Communist Bloc Nations

Trade between the communist nations and the free world countries has always been small, usually only about 3 percent. Several reasons account for this lack of trade. First, communist bloc countries, especially the Soviet Union, have preferred to trade among themselves following a policy of regional self-sufficiency. Second, they have restricted imports of goods produced domestically. Third, they have sought to conserve supplies of hard currencies and gold. The only exception to these limitations occur when Western nations are prepared to supply credits to pay for the communist bloc nations' imports. Regarding exports to Western nations, the paucity of trade stems from the fact that, except for raw materials, these nations have little of what the free world wants. This is especially true for manufactured goods, which are generally of inferior quality.

Overall the trading philosophies of the West and the East are very different. Western nations want to sell more than they buy; Eastern bloc nations want to buy more than they sell, especially when credits are available to finance the purchases.

For national security reasons, sales by U.S. companies of high technology products that are in great demand by the communists are subject to licenses or are prohibited. Since the state decides what is to be imported, few consumer goods are imported by communist countries despite great demand for them. The new economic and political policies of Gorbachev seem to suggest a fundamental alteration in trading objectives toward more trade, a greater emphasis on consumer goods, an openness to Western investments, and the associated intracompany sales form of trade.

Until the last several years trade among communist bloc nations has been more for political than economic reasons. In fact trade between the USSR and the nations of Eastern Europe has essentially been an extension of Soviet foreign policy. The Soviets sold raw materials below world market prices, even if it meant selling below cost. They purchased manufactured goods above world market prices despite inferior quality. This kept civil unrest low by keeping employment high, reduced contact with the West, and kept the linkages with the Soviet Union strong.

Beginning in 1987, the Soviets began allowing the nations of Eastern Europe to open their economies to the West. This economic and later political opening reached such a level that by 1989 most of the communist governments were removed from office and replaced by democracies. The nations' economies were forced to begin to function as open markets. The effect was inflationary pressures and the need for credits from western governments to finance seriously needed imports. To date, the response from western governments would seem to be insufficient to meet the needs of these peoples; however, the citizens have shown a great willingness to tolerate economic hardships in return for political freedom.

Trade between the communist countries and the free world is relatively limited due in large part to the communist countries' desire for economic self-sufficiency.

Although the Soviet policy of using trade as a tool of political policy seems to have changed with regard to the nations of Eastern Europe, the same can not be said regarding the Baltic Republics. The Lithuanian declaration of independence has been met by trade sanctions. The Soviets have cut off supplies of crude oil and other energy and have threatened to charge Lithuania world market prices for all imports. What occurs in Lithuania will have major political and economic consequences for both the U.S.S.R. and the nations of Western Europe.

Exports and National Income

One measure of the importance of international commerce to a country is the relationship between exports and national income. Table 1.2 shows this relationship for selected industrial countries between 1960 and 1985. For most countries exports are becoming an increasingly important contributor to national income. Even for the United States, exports as a percentage of national income were nearly twice as important in 1980 than in 1960, although exports are still relatively less important for the United States than for most other countries.

Exports as a percentage of national income vary among nations. Recent figures indicate that exports are becoming increasingly important to a nation's economic welfare.

Importance of Foreign Trade to the United States

Although the absolute amount of U.S. international trade is large, it has, until recently, received little attention. The general public views international trade as important only to nations with limited resources. Even elected officials seem to believe that the implementation of protectionist trade policies will hurt other nations more than the United States. Only after other nations retaliate does Congress realize that foreign commerce is essential for the economic welfare of the country—but memories seem to be short. In spite of bitter lessons from the past, calls for protectionism surface whenever an economic slowdown occurs, as in 1974–1975, 1981–1982, and 1984–1986.

TABLE 1.2   **Exports as a Percent of National Income**

Country	*1960*	*1970*	*1980*	*1985*	*1988*
Belgium	35.9%	48.2%	65.8%	73.0%	64.4[a]
Denmark	36.7	30.0	36.9	33.3	29.06[a]
Germany	21.8	25.2	26.1	33.3	30.5
Sweden	22.9	26.8	34.3	28.8[b]	28.8[b]
Japan	10.4	13.1	18.9	15.4	11.3[a]
Canada	20.1	26.6	32.9	32.9	22.4
United Kingdom	21.8	24.4	31.8	30.1[c]	n.a.
New Zealand	25.5	24.6	31.8	35.2	23.25[a]
Italy	13.1	17.2	18.7	20.3	20.1[d]
France[e]	15.3	16.8	23.1	25.1[c]	20.16
Australia	15.7	17.0	19.8	18.4	16.6
United States	4.8	5.9	9.3	6.1	7.38

[a] 1987.
[b] 1984.
[c] 1986.
[d] 1985.
[e] Based upon exports as a percent of GDP.
Source: IMF, *International Financial Statistics 1985, 1989*.

U.S. Share of World Trade

Even though exports and imports make up a relatively small part of the national income of the United States, the total value of foreign trade is larger than that of any other nation. In 1987, the United States accounted for 17.5 percent of the world's imports and 10.6 per cent of the world's exports (down from 18.2 percent in 1955). This decrease in exports was largely due to the increase in the foreign trade activities of the industrialized countries and the newly industrialized countries of the Pacific Rim, and the decrease in imports by the oil-exporting nations. As these Asian countries seek new markets abroad, the U.S. share of the world's exports is likely to decrease even further. Relatedly, as other nations seek a greater share of the U.S. market, a further deterioration of the U.S. trade balance is likely.

Although the United States is largely self-sufficient, it is still the world's leading trading nation.

Exports and the U.S. Economy

For some industries, the abundance of natural resources and the large domestic market created a lack of interest in international commerce. Firms considered export markets only for selling surplus production. As a result, few firms specifically designed or adapted their goods for sale abroad. Even when the U.S. Department of Commerce began programs to increase exports, many firms ignored them. It must be noted, however, that industries such as agriculture, transport equipment, nonelectric machinery, and basic manufactures have for many years been dependent upon foreign markets to take a sizable portion of their output. In spite of governmental efforts to improve export competitiveness and the substantial international involvement by selected industries, U.S. exports continue to be a relatively small percentage of GNP, between $5\frac{1}{2}$ and $9\frac{1}{2}$ percent since 1975.

Exports and the Merchandise Trade Balance

Exports are essential because nations do not have an unlimited supply of gold or foreign exchange to pay for imports. This is true of any nation, regardless of the degree of its economic self-sufficiency. At some point, even the wealthiest nation will be hard-pressed to pay for imports if it continues to run a negative balance of trade.

Since 1971, with the exception of 1973 and 1975, the United States has had a negative trade balance. The value of imports has generally increased at a more rapid pace than that of exports, with the deficits exceeding $100 billion annually since 1984 and a record of about $150 billion in 1987. This rapid deterioration in the trade balance can be traced to several factors. The United States is no longer self-sufficient in petroleum, and an increase in the price of crude petroleum is immediately reflected in the value of imports. For example, total imports of petroleum increased from $4.30 billion in 1972 to $7.55 billion in 1973, based solely upon OPEC price increases. U.S. imports of petroleum jumped to $26.12 billion in 1974 and have remained at a high level every year since.

Another reason for the inability of the United States to eliminate the negative balance of trade is a deterioration in the country's sales of manufactured goods abroad, and increased purchases of foreign manufactured goods by U.S. consumers and corporations. Foreign producers design products specifically to meet the tastes of the American consumer. Automobiles provide such an example. The Japanese spent years studying comsumer tastes before entering the American market. In 1983, about one-third of the deficit in the merchandise trade balance of the United States was due to the deficit with Japan.

The fact that the United States is running a deficit in the trade of manufactured goods makes the overall trade deficit all the more alarming. The United States has long ranked first among nations in the export of manufactures. During the period between 1976 and 1986, the U.S. share of world exports of manufactured goods has fluctuated widely, increasing from 18.8 percent in 1976 to a high of 20.6 percent in 1981, and then falling to a low of 14.1 percent in 1986. With the increase in the value of the dollar after 1981, U.S. goods became more expensive in terms of foreign currencies, leading to a decline in exports.

Several other factors were responsible for the recent decrease in exports. Many countries with huge foreign debts found it increasingly difficult to import while attempting to service these obligations. The incomplete recovery from the worldwide recession of 1981–1982 adversely affected sales abroad. Leading manufacturers from other countries also experienced similar difficulties.

Regardless of the deficit, imports are indispensable for the economic well-being and the high standard of living of the United States. Coffee, cocoa and chocolate, bananas, tea, cashew nuts, and pepper are some of the imported foodstuffs that we take for granted. Many minerals and raw materials critical to American industry and essential for national security are available only from abroad. Strategic minerals such as manganese, tin, chromite, tungsten, industrial diamonds, graphite, platinum, mercury, cobalt, nickel, and petroleum are produced domestically in quantities insufficient to meet the needs.

The United States is the world's leading supplier of manufactured goods, but sales are inadequate to keep pace with the increasing imports.

Markets for U.S. Exports and Sources of U.S. Imports

U.S. Trade with Industrialized Nations   The most important markets for U.S. exports are other industrialized countries, chiefly Canada, Japan, the United Kingdom, and West Germany. These four countries account for 35 to 40 percent of U.S. exports and approximately half of U.S. imports. Canada is the largest export customer and Japan the largest import supplier (see Figure 1.6).

The leading markets for U.S. manufactured goods are Canada, Japan, the United Kingdom, and West Germany. Japan has replaced Canada as the largest source of U.S. imports.

U.S. Trade With Non-Oil-Producing Developing Nations   Prior to 1975, trade with the non-oil-producing developing nations was largely one-sided. The United States exported more than it imported, but that has changed in the last 15 years. The percentage of total U.S. exports that went to non-oil-

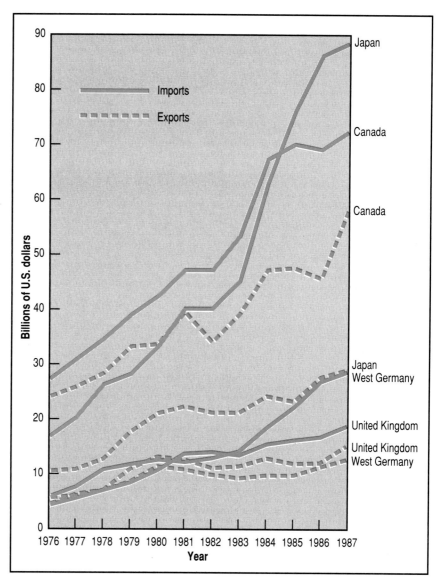

Figure 1.6 U.S. Exports and Imports with Selected Industrial Countries
Source: International Monetary Fund, *Direction of Trade Statistics Yearbook,* 1989.

producing developing countries continued to increase through 1981, peaking at 31.8 percent. Since then, the percentage of exports to these nations has continued to fall (28.8 percent in 1987).

Despite annual fluctuations, imports from these countries have increased steadily over those 15 years. Although U.S. imports from these nations first exceeded exports in 1977, the trade balance was negative for

Increasing U.S. imports from non-oil-exporting developing countries reflect the rapid development of the countries in the Pacific Basin.

seven of the next nine years and was more than $80 billion in 1987. This is largely due to the rise of the newly industrialized countries (NICs) of the Pacific Rim, the so-called New Japans: Singapore, Hong Kong, Taiwan, and South Korea.

U.S. Trade With Oil-Producing Developing Nations   Exports of manufactured goods to the 13 oil-exporting countries fluctuated between a high of 11.1 percent in both 1977 and 1978, and a low of 4.2 percent in 1987. As a group, these countries represent a significant market for U.S. products; however, their purchasing power is clearly tied to oil revenues as indicated by the decrease in imports since 1983. It is also worth noting that the value of U.S. exports to the OPEC nations has remained a relatively small percentage of the value of imports from those nations. As might be expected, Saudi Arabia is the most important market in the Middle East for U.S. goods.

Because of its dependence on petroleum, U.S. imports from the oil-exporting countries constituted a relatively large percentage of total imports between 1975 and 1981. The most important suppliers of petroleum to the United States are Saudi Arabia, Nigeria, Venezuela, Indonesia, Algeria, and the United Arab Emirates. Imports from the OPEC nations have resembled a roller coaster ride, from approximately 2.0 percent of total imports in 1973 to 23.5 percent in 1977 and then down again to only 5.1 percent in 1986 and 5.7 percent in 1987. These wide fluctuations are due less to changes in the market for crude oil than to political instability of the OPEC cartel.

U.S. imports from OPEC tend to fluctuate with the changes in the price of crude petroleum.

World Investments and the MNF: World War II to the Present

Prior to World War II Britain was the leading investing nation; after the war the United States took over the leadership from Britain. This change of dominance occurred for three reasons. First, to finance its war efforts, Britain had to liquidate many investments. Second, many British-controlled interests, such as the railroads in Argentina, were nationalized. Third, the United States had capital over and above what was required domestically.

Following the war many nations began to restrict free trade; military cooperation was replaced by economic competition. In spite of international efforts such as the establishment of the GATT, protectionism grew, and exporting became increasingly difficult. The barriers to trade included tariffs (taxes on imports), quotas (limits on the quantity of imports), and nontariff barriers (regulations and controls that penalize imports). These barriers were justified as protecting infant industries and easing balance-of-payments difficulties. The major results of these protectionist policies were the encouragement of foreign investment by capital-rich nations such as the United States and the discouragement of trade.

A second major trend of the postwar period was experimentation with economic integration: the European Economic Community (EEC), the European Free Trade Association (EFTA), the Latin American Free Trade Association (LAFTA), and so forth. The European Economic Community, established in 1957, provides an excellent example of how economic integration stimulates foreign direct investment. Trade barriers were minimized among member nations, while common external tariffs were adopted. These enabled firms producing within the Community to reach all the markets and made it difficult for firms producing outside to compete effectively. Thus, the establishment of the Common Market presented both a problem and an opportunity for international business: heightened external trade barriers and minimal trade restrictions for firms operating within the Common Market. The immediate effect of the Common Market was an inflow of capital by foreign corporations to set up production facilities.

Faced with the rising trade barriers and pockets of economic integration, many corporations altered their international strategies to emphasize foreign production and deemphasize exporting in both developing and industrialized nations. Caterpillar Tractor's investment in Britain in 1950 provides an excellent example. The British government placed severe restrictions on the outflow of dollars even for the purchase of imports to be sold in the country. To hold on to its market, Caterpillar established a British production subsidiary.

By 1960 foreign investment, once a by-product of trade, had become an integral part of international business and was well on its way to bcoming the dominant form of international business activity.

Types and Purposes of Foreign Investments

Foreign investment is the acquisition of assets in one country by firms, institutions, governments, or individuals of another country. These investments can be classified as foreign direct investments (FDI) or indirect (portfolio) investments.

Direct investments, made primarily by business firms with the objective of control, are usually in the areas of manufacturing, marketing, distribution facilities, or properties (oil fields, mines, plantations, and so forth). Investments may also include service activities such as financial, accounting and legal services, or repairs for products or equipment.

Indirect investments are generally made for reasons of short- or medium-term profits rather than managerial control. The IMF defines three types of indirect investments:

1. Equity investments—the purchase of an ownership position in a foreign corporation or partnership that does not also include an active role in management

2. Private debt investments—the purchase of foreign bonds and other debt instruments for reasons of profit

3. Intergovernmental transfers—government loans that are made for political reasons (infrastructure development, the purchase of military supplies, relief, and so forth)

The most common definition of foreign indirect investment is the first above. (For a further discussion of direct and indirect investments see Chapter 2.)

Foreign Investment Policies of Governments

The rapid increase of foreign direct investment in the past 25 years and the impact of major investments on small nations have resulted in a variety of governmental policies. Some seek to control the investor while others attempt to attract new investments. Most less developed nations recognize that FDI from major industrialized nations is an important source of capital, technology, and managerial know-how, and have adopted policies and incentives that encourage and facilitate FDI:

1. Favorable tax rates to encourage the inflow of foreign capital

2. Tax holidays that exempt locally earned income from taxation for several years

3. Guaranteed repatriability of profits and equity

4. Free land

5. Infrastructure improvements

Overall relations between multinational firms and less developed countries have improved substantially in recent years.[9]

Because of the differences in economic goals among nations, foreign investment policies vary. Brazil encourages foreign investments because the inflow of capital will help to reduce its debt burden. Taiwan encourages high technology investments but discourages investments that compete with local businesses. Saudi Arabia is eager for joint ventures that supply technical, managerial, and marketing know-how but not those in service industries. Hong Kong is an investor's paradise because it encourages all types of investments.

West Germany is an example of a highly developed country that encourages and facilitates foreign direct investment. Although the U.S. national government does not actively encourage FDI, the U.S. market is one of the easiest to enter. The only major restrictions pertain to national security or arise when investors are from a country with which the United States does not have diplomatic relations.

Pattern and Direction of Investments

Direct Investments

Multinational corporations from Europe, Japan, and the United States dominate world FDI. The new direct investments (excluding reinvested earnings) by multinationals from the United States, the EEC, and Japan for the period 1968–1972 were 93 percent of the world total (58.3, 31.5, and 3.2 percent). When total foreign direct investment (new investments plus reinvestments) is considered, the respective figure becomes 95 percent (62.5, 30.1, and 2.3, respectively.)[10] Despite the dollar value of world FDI having nearly doubled for the period 1973–1976, the new FDI from these nations remained essentially unchanged (92.7 percent), and total FDI grew to 96.4 percent of world total. The annual average foreign direct investment, including reinvested earnings, increased from 15,498 billion SDR in the 1968–1972 period to 28,731 billion SDR in the 1973–1976 period.[11] (An SDR—Special Drawing Right—is a unit of value created by the IMF for deposit into a nation's IMF account that could be used among members to finance intermember transactions. During the late 1960s and early 1970s, one SDR equaled $1 U.S.)

Table 1.3 shows the *net* direct investment positions of the major investing nations, 1976–1986. (The net investment position of a nation is the difference between the total value of all foreign investments by that nation less the total value of all foreign investments in that nation.) Between 1976

TABLE 1.3   **Net Foreign Direct Investment Position of Selected Nation: (1976–1986) (Billion SDR)**

	1976	*1978*	*1980*	*1982*	*1984*	*1986*
United States	−6.57	−6.53	−1.83	+17.92	+38.04	+58.23
United Kingdom	−3.35	−4.14	−5.88	−4.02	−21.84	−19.44
France	−1.42	−1.51	−2.38	−2.58	+5.10	−5.83
West Germany	−2.13	−2.89	−3.14	−2.99	−6.72	+13.38
Canada	−0.754	−2.11	−2.84	−0.38	+1.97	+9.87
Japan	−1.72	−1.89	−1.84	−4.10	−49.02	−111.80
Belgium/Luxembourg	−0.304	−0.44	−0.16	−0.06	−2.24	−5.84
Netherlands	−0.666	−0.87	−1.02	−1.23	−4.34	−7.64
Switzerland	—	—	—	−3.98	+0.41	N/A
$/SDR	$1.15	1.25	1.30	1.10	1.03	1.17

Note: A negative value means that the total value of a nation's investments abroad exceed the total value of investments by foreign nationals in that nation.

Sources: IMF B/P Statistics, Vol. 35 Yearbook, Part I, 1984.
IMF B/P Yearbook, Vol. 38 Yearbook, Part I, 1987.

and 1979, the United States increased its dominance in foreign direct investment. The U.S. position peaked in 1979 (not shown on table) with a net foreign direct investment position of 10.35 billion SDR ($13.352 billion). Beginning in 1980, the trend reversed. Although U.S. firms continued to invest abroad, these foreign investments were increasingly offset by investments made in the United States. In 1980 the net U.S. foreign investment position declined to 1.83 billion SDR ($2.379 billion). By 1981, the United States no longer had a greater value of investments abroad than foreign nationals had in the United States—in other words, the country became a debtor nation. This investment deficit has gotten progressively larger: 1982 +17.92 billion SDR ($19.712 billion), 1984 +38.04 billion SDR, and 1986 +58.23 billion SDR. (Note: A positive figure here means that more funds have been invested in the United States than the United States has invested abroad.) Stated somewhat differently, claims by foreigners on U.S. assets exceed U.S. claims on assets abroad. After 70 years as a creditor nation the United States is once again the world's greatest debtor nation. The five most important investors were Great Britain, the Netherlands, Japan, Canada, and West Germany.

The United States is an attractive site for foreign direct investment for several reasons. One, the economic recovery of the United States from the recession of 1981–1982 was faster than that of most other industrial countries. Second, the United States has very few restrictions on the operations of businesses. Third, the United States is one of the most politically stable nations in the world. Fourth, the U.S. market is one of the largest and best markets for foreign products.

Indirect Investments

Indirect investments include bank deposits, corporate stocks and bonds, treasury securities, and so forth. Unlike direct investments, which are primarily determined by long-term economic considerations, indirect investments are largely influenced by short-term factors. During the early 1980s, the United States was also an attractive site for indirect investments because of high interest rates. When one considers that 80 percent of all assets owned by foreign nationals in the United States are indirect or portfolio investments, one begins to realize the extent of the effects that relatively small changes in a nation's interest rates could have.

Since 1986 U.S. interest rates have been declining. As a result demand for U.S. dollars has also declined and the dollar has weakened relative to most major world currencies.

Geographic Distribution of U.S. Foreign Direct Investments

Following World War II, several major changes occurred in U.S. foreign direct investments. First, U.S. investments shifted away from the developing nations, especially Latin America because of its political and economic instability, and toward industrialized nations. Between 1950 and 1970 U.S. direct investment in Latin America decreased from nearly 40 percent of the U.S. total direct investment to less than 20 percent. Investments in Canada remained relatively steady, at 30.5 percent in 1950 and 29.2 percent in 1970. American investments in the Middle East and Africa decreased from 8.5 to 6.5 percent for the same years, also in part because of political and economic instability.

There are several reasons for the shift away from investments in less developed countries (LDCs). The first was the increase in restrictive economic policies by LDCs including restricted operations and ownership, exchange controls, and limits or taxes on repatriations. Many of these nations blamed their economic problems (rampant inflation, shortages of foreign exchange, deficits in the balance of payments, unemployment, and so forth) on uncontrolled foreign investment. A second reason for the decreasing importance of investments in LDCs was the U.S. government's withdrawal of support for direct investments abroad. The U.S. government attempted to influence the International Bank for Reconstruction and Development and the Export Import Bank to withhold loans from nations refusing adequate compensation for nationalizations. Relatedly, the Overseas Private Investment Law of 1974 required investors to shoulder a greater part of the foreign political risk.

A second major change occurred in U.S. direct foreign investment during the 1968–1976 period. There was a relative decrease in U.S. investments and an increase in Japanese investments, while investments by EEC firms remained relatively stable. In absolute amounts, the United States accounted for about one-half of all new foreign investments, but Japan was becoming a major competitor.

The third significant change in U.S. direct investments abroad took place during the 1970s and 1980s. During this period, the reinvestments of locally generated earnings for building the stock of investments abroad became more important than new investment capital. From 1965 to 1984, reinvestments by U.S. firms exceeded new foreign direct investments by more than 200 percent.

The decrease of U.S. direct investments in the developing countries has in part been replaced by an increase of Japanese investments, especially in Asian LDCs. Japanese investments in that area increased from 16.5 percent of total region investments in 1968–1972 to 32.3 percent in the 1973–1976 period. In South and Central America, Japanese investments increased from 11.5 percent to 18.3 percent for those same years. In contrast, Japan's investments in all of Europe during this period dropped from 30.1 to 9.5 percent and from 29.5 to 6.9 percent in the EEC nations. This dramatic decrease was due largely to nontariff barriers aimed at Japanese manufactured goods. While most industrialized nations are investing less in developing nations, Japan is increasing its investments in those nations.

THE RECIPROCAL RELATIONSHIP BETWEEN TRADE AND INVESTMENT

Trade among nations creates opportunities for foreign direct investment, and investment results in increased trading opportunities. Since large investments, especially those associated with major manufacturing facilities, require large quantities of capital, they can be carried out only by large firms or collections of firms. The consequence has been the development of the multinational firm. Although the trade barriers of the postwar period resulted in an initial wave of foreign direct investments by U.S. firms, it may be more correct to attribute the development of multinational firms to the free-trade actions of nations in the 1960s and 1970s.

Investment in Middle East oil production serves as a good example of this reciprocal relationship between trade and investment. Investment in this region by large oil firms to increase production capacity resulted in increased exports. These exports provided the funds to purchase capital and consumer goods. The import of capital goods created further opportunities for capital goods exports to this region as well as investment opportunities in areas as diverse as oil refineries and hotels. The import of these consumer goods resulted in an increase in standard of living, and thereby additional consumer goods demand.

THE SOCIETAL IMPACT OF INTERNATIONAL COMMERCE

The preceding sections described the relative importance and dimension of international commerce for the world as a whole, for groups of nations, and for specific countries, especially the United States. No mention was made of the impact of trade on the various sectors within the economy.

Corporations

Producers within a country are concerned with international trade to sell their products and to purchase raw materials. Foreign trade has been described "as the balance wheel of American prosperity".[12] Many firms and industries are more dependent upon foreign markets than the national ratio of exports to national income would suggest. It is not unusual for domestic sales levels to be only sufficient to cover a firm's costs, so exports, although small, are essential for the firm's profits.

Producers are not only concerned about international trade as it relates to their own exports but also as it pertains to imports with which they must compete. In many industries, the United States has lost its competitive advantage to foreign competitors. This is reflected in the decreasing U.S. share of the sales of manufactured goods both at home and abroad.

Equally important to U.S. firms are the imports of primary products and semifinished goods. Many raw materials that are essential in the manufacturing process must be imported. Component parts are often imported in spite of their domestic availability because of cost or quality consideration. The idea of international outsourcing for a lower cost is nothing new, but outsourcing because of the inferior quality of domestic goods is indeed a recent and alarming situation.

As an alternative to international outsourcing to foreign firms, many U.S. firms have invested abroad in component parts manufacturing operations. These "off-shore" investments have created new profit opportunities for U.S. corporations but have also caused problems of dislocation for certain segments of the U.S. economy. Despite the objections of organized labor, the facts suggest that if U.S. firms did not invest abroad they would essentially be locked out of many profitable markets and would operate, even domestically, at a cost and quality disadvantage.

Relatedly, as the international activities of U.S. firms have expanded, various service firms have established branches abroad to assist those firms with their financial, insurance, accounting, legal, transportation, consulting, and other needs. Thus, a new and lucrative field has opened up in the area of international business.

Labor

Labor generally supports exporting but opposes foreign direct investments and the importation of competitive goods. Thus, their interest in international business is generally negative.

Labor argues that when multinational enterprises invest abroad, they do so at the expense of jobs in the United States. They assume that if such investments had not been made abroad, they would have been made in the United States. What organized labor fails to acknowledge is that because of issues of cost and quality, American products would be excluded from foreign markets and U.S. firms would be unable to compete effectively domestically. To retain their share of markets both here and abroad, firms must have foreign operations. Additional production capacity in the United States would be of little value since there would be no market for the output. In many cases investments abroad actually create more jobs in the United States than they cost. The jobs lost are generally low-skill manufacturing or assembly jobs, while the ones created are in administration, communication, development, and so forth.

Harvey and Kerin found that only 8 percent of what is produced abroad is brought back to the United States and much of this is brought back for additional processing.[13] Only 4 percent of total sales by U.S. affiliates abroad are made to the United States and these sales constitute less than 1 percent of total U.S. imports. Thus, there is little truth in the accusation that American multinationals flood the domestic market with cheap goods produced abroad using cheap labor. Furthermore, most U.S. direct investments are made in western Europe and Canada, where wage rates are not low.

Although the position of organized labor seldom considers the employment impact on businesses directly involved with importing and exporting, these activities make a significant contribution. Employees of import and export intermediaries, financial institutions, transportation companies, and many other firms are directly dependent on international trade for their jobs. Lionel H. Olmer, Under Secretary of Commerce for International Trade, estimated that every $1 billion of exports creates 25,000 new jobs.[14]

Consumers

Were it not for imports, consumers would have to do without many products that most people take for granted. Imagine having to start the day without a cup of coffee, tea, or cocoa or without bananas for your cereal. Various other fruits and vegetables are imported from the tropics and subtropics, and many other products come from abroad during the off-seasons. Other articles that enrich the lives of many are imported. Precious stones, works of arts, and the latest in fashions are just a few of these. Imports provide everyone with a variety of products that are available only from abroad.

Imports also benefit consumers in other ways. Foreign competition is often the major factor in keeping domestic prices low and product quality high. There has been great concern in the United States during the past decade regarding the number of Japanese cars being sold. While these imports have had obvious negative effects on employment, they have kept car prices relatively low by creating increased competiton for consumers' money. Furthermore, these imports have forced the major U.S. automakers to improve not only the quality of their products but also the efficiency of their production processes.

Taxpayers

Customs duties, as a percentage of U.S. revenues, have risen from 1.3 percent in 1975 to 1.7 percent in 1987. The billions of dollars collected annually are important in reducing the overall deficit of the federal government.

International trade affects not only the country as a whole but also each sector of that economy.

SUMMARY

The history of the development of trade can be divided into several major periods. During the prehistoric period, there was little two-way trade. Beginning with the ancient period, there is evidence of the exchange of goods for economic reasons. Crete and Phoenicia conducted both exports and imports. With the decline of those countries, Greece became the center of commerce.

Although the Romans were not primarily concerned with commerce, trade continued to grow because of their skill in establishing law and order.

After the fall of the Roman Empire, the Christian church became the dominant economic and political force of the period. Unintentionally, the church played a major role in the growth of international trade by sending the Crusading armies to recapture the Holy Lands. This contact with the more highly developed cultures of the Arab world resulted in continued trade with that region. The Italian city-states became commercial centers for this trade.

The closing of the overland routes to the Orient resulted in the search for a new water route to India and the Far East. Explorers sailed westward and ended up discovering the New World, causing a shift of commerce westward. This was accompanied by the rise of nations that chartered companies to go on trading missions. New territories were colonized and exploited in the name of the mother country. Nations adopted liberal trade policies in their relation with other countries, resulting in the rapid growth of world trade.

From the beginning of the twentieth century, and especially after World War I, the commercial policies of nations became increasingly protective. Periodic attempts were made to reduce these protective measures, but economic conditions within countries and pressure from special interest groups prevented any major reductions. The global crisis of the Great Depression only compounded the protectionism. The result was a substantial drop in total world trade. Only the urgent needs of a world at war (World War II) and the dire demands of a world trying to recover from war were able to get governments to take the steps necessary to reestablish a form of free trade. The United States passed the Reciprocal Trade Agreements Act, the IMF was established, the World Bank was set up, and the first GATT agreement was signed.

During this same period, foreign investment was beginning to grow. Immediately prior to World War I large amounts of European capital began to flow into the United States in the form of indirect investments. At the same time U.S. firms were making extraction, agriculture, and distribution investments in less developed countries.

Since the end of World War II, there has been a tremendous increase in world trade. This increase can be attributed to a number of factors: increases in the number of countries, the world population, the volume of goods entering trade, the worldwide increase in prices, the increased importance of manufactured goods in trade, and increasing affluence in the industrialized nations of the world. Trade increased among industrial countries rather than between the developed and less developed countries. The single major exception to this was the growing importance of trade with oil-exporting countries.

The leading trading nation is the United States but it is being challenged by the countries of western Europe and Japan. Despite being the world's greatest exporter, the United States is also the world's greatest importer resulting in a negative balance of trade and a deficit in the nation's balance of payments. Reducing imports is not likely because many sectors of the economy are increasingly dependent upon foreign goods.

Prior to World War II, Great Britain was the leading investor nation in the world, but the cost of financing the war and the nationalization of many of its foreign holdings ended Britain's dominance. The United States with its abundance of capital replaced Great Britain as the leading investor nation.

Multinational corporations invested abroad when they found it increasingly difficult to export. As welcome as these investments were initially, many countries feared the possibility of foreign political and economic domination and were concerned about becoming dependent upon multinational firms; therefore, many countries have adopted regulations regarding the amount of foreign ownership, degree of managerial control, and types of business enterprises. With these changes, LDCs became less attractive for foreign direct investments and highly developed countries became more attractive.

During the last decade, the United States has become an attractive site for foreign investments, as reflected in the net inflow of foreign capital. The United States became a debtor nation for the first time since 1917. There is no doubt that the continued attractiveness of the United States and other industrialized countries as an outlet for foreign investments results primarily from the favorable investment climate: minimum government regulations, political and economic stability, favorable rates of returns, and so forth.

Given the reciprocal nature of trade and investments, these investments influence the magnitude and direction of foreign trade. Both investment and trade have an impact on different sectors of a nation's economy. Those looking upon these effects as being favorable cite the benefits to labor as additional jobs are created. Others decry the loss of jobs as multinational firms establish operations abroad. Consumers benefit from the availability of a greater variety of goods of better quality at lower prices. Business firms profit from both foreign and domestic markets. Local, state, and federal governments gain from the additional tax revenues. These and other sectors of the economy are directly or indirectly affected by foreign investments and trade.   □

KEY TERMS AND CONCEPTS

Barter	**Economic nationalism**
Cartel	**Feudalism**
Creditor nation	**Import quota**
Crusades	**International trade**
Currency depreciation	**Labor-intensive industries**
Debtor nation	**Lend-lease shipments**
Direct investments	**Less developed country (LDC)**
Exchange controls	**Multinational corporation (MNC)**

Multinational firm (MNF)	Portfolio or indirect investments
OPEC	Silent trade
Pax Romana	Special Drawing Right (SDR)

REVIEW QUESTIONS

1. What is meant by silent trade?
2. Why did trade first develop in ancient Crete and Phoenicia?
3. What were some of the natural trading advantages of Greece?
4. Why did trade develop rapidly under the Romans even though they were not inclined toward it?
5. What were the Crusades? How did they help in the growth of international commerce?
6. What role did the Italian city-states play in the development of trade?
7. Explain the reasons for the growth of the multinational enterprises after World War II.
8. Why did trade decline sharply during the Depression of the 1930s?
9. Why is trade among industrialized nations greater than trade between developed and less developed nations?
10. Explain the decrease in the U.S. share of world trade despite an increase in the absolute value of U.S. trade.
11. Briefly describe the impact of foreign trade on the United States.
12. Explain why the United States has become a "debtor nation."
13. Explain the foreign investment policies of the United States. Are these likely to continue? If so, why? If not, why not?
14. What are some of the major reasons for the outflow of capital from the United States since World War II?
15. What are the implications of the decrease in U.S. investments in the LDCs, especially Latin America?

NOTES

1. Richard Thurnwald, *Economics of Primitive Communities* (London: Oxford University Press, 1932).
2. Paul V. Horn and Henry Gomez, *International Trade Principles and Practices* (Englewood Cliffs, N. J.: Prentice-Hall, 1959), p. 257.
3. Horn and Gomez, p. 385.
4. The continuing belief in free trade policies is reflected in the renewal of this act a total of 13 times. Following its expiration in 1967, Congress did not extend this presidential authority until the passage of the 1974 Trade Act.

5. U.S. Department of Commerce, *Statistical Abstract of the U.S.*, 1965, 86th ed., p. 861.

6. Horn and Gomez, p. 257.

7. Ibid.

8. IMF, *Direction of Trade Statistics Yearbook 1985*, p. 2.

9. "The Welcome Mat: Third World Nations Still Count Investment After Indian Tragedy," *Wall Street Journal*, December 21, 1984, pp. 1, 12, and 13.

10. Kredietbank *Weekly Bulletin*, No. 39, October 20, 1978.

11. Donald A. Ball and Wendell H. McCulloch, Jr., *International Business: Introduction and Essentials* (Plano, Texas: Business Publications, Inc., 1982), p. 29.

12. Horn and Gomez, p. 29.

13. Michael G. Harvey and Roger A. Kerin, "Multinational Corporations versus Organized Labor: Divergent Views on Domestic Employment," *California Management Review*, Spring 1976, p. 7.

14. *Business America*, May 14, 1984, p. 4.

REFERENCES AND SELECTED READINGS

Arpan, Jeffrey S., and David A. Ricks. "Foreign Direct Investment in the U.S., 1974–1984." *The Journal of International Business Studies* 17:3 (Fall 1986).

Ball, Donald A., and Wendell H. McCulloch, Jr. *International Business: Introduction and Essentials*. Plano, Texas: Business Publications, Inc.: 1982.

Behrman, Jack N. "Transnational Corporations in the New International Economic Order." *The Journal of International Business Studies* 12:1 (Fall 1981).

Board of Governors of the Federal Reserve System. *Federal Reserve Bulletin*. Monthly.

Boddewyn, J. J., Marsha B. Halbrisch, and A. C. Perry. "Service Multinationals: Conceptualization, Measurement, and Theory." *The Journal of International Business Studies* 17:3 (Fall 1986).

Business America. May 14, 1984.

Czinkota, Michael. "International Trade and Business in the Late 1980's: An Integrated U.S. Perspective." *The Journal of International Business Studies* 17:1 (Spring 1986).

Dymsza, William A. "Trends in Multinational Business and Global Environments: A Perspective." *The Journal of International Business Studies* 15:3 (Winter 1984).

Fisk, George Mygett, and Paul Skeels Peirce. *International Commercial Policies*. New York: Macmillan, 1925.

Harvey, Michael G., and Roger A. Kerin. "Multinational Corporations versus Organized Labor: Divergent Views on Domestic Employment." *California Management Review* (Spring 1976).

Horn, Paul V., and Henry Gomez. *International Trade Principles and Practices*. Englewood Cliffs, N.J.: Prentice-Hall, 1961.

IMF. *Direction of Trade Statistics Yearbook*. 1985.

IMF. *International Financial Statistics Yearbook*. 1983.

IMF. *Supplement on Trade Statistics*, Supplement on Trade Statistics. 1982, 1983.

Johanson, Jan, and Jan Erik Vahlne. "The Internationalization Process of the Firm—A Model of Knowledge Development." *The Journal of International Business Studies* 8:1 (Fall 1977).

Keegan, Warren J. "International Competition: The Japanese Challenge." *The Journal of International Business Studies* 15:3 (Winter 1984).

Kredietbank. *Weekly Bulletin*, No. 39 (October 20, 1978).

Lecraw, Donald J. "Performance of Transnational Corporations in Less Developed Countries." *The Journal of International Business Studies* 14:1 (Spring/Summer 1983).

Ricks, David A., and Michael R. Czinkota. "International Business: An Examination of the Corporate Viewpoint." *The Journal of International Business Studies* 10:2 (Fall 1979).

Robinson, Richard D. "Background Concepts and Philosophy of International Business from World War II to the Present." *The Journal of International Business Studies* 12:1 (Spring/Summer 1981).

Root, Franklin R. "Some Trends in the World Economy and Their Implications for International Business Strategy." *The Journal of International Business Studies* 15:3 (Winter 1984).

Thurnwald, Richard. *Economics in Primitive Communities*. London: Oxford University Press, 1932.

United Nations. *Yearbook of International Trade Statistics 1975*, Vol. I. New York: United Nations Publishing Service, 1976.

U.S. Department of Commerce. *Business America* 8:2 (January 21, 1985).

U.S. Department of Commerce. *Overseas Business Reports*. U.S. Foreign Trade Annual, 1976–1982.

U.S. Department of Commerce. *The Multinational Corporations: Studies on U.S. Foreign Investments*. Washington, D.C.: author. 1973.

U.S. Department of Commerce. *Statistical Abstract of the U.S.* Annual.

Woytinsky, W. S., and E. S. Woytinsky. *World Commerce and Governments, Trends and Outlooks*. New York: The Twentieth Century Fund, 1955.

2

Theories of International Trade and Investment

- Explain the theories of absolute, comparative, and equal advantage in a barter economy and a money economy

- Explain the factor proportions or endowments theory of trade

- Learn the differences between natural and acquired advantage

- Explain the effects of foreign exchange fluctuations on international trade

- Explain how the product life cycle theory affects trade

- Provide an understanding of the major theories of foreign direct investment: interest rate differential, monopolistic or oligopolistic advantages, product life cycle, risk reduction, market potential, and other theories

OUTLINE OF TOPICS

I. Introduction

II. Foreign trade theories
  A. Classical theories in both barter and money systems: absolute advantage, comparative advantage, and equal advantage
  B. Factor proportions or endowments theory
    1. Natural advantage
    2. Acquired advantage
    3. Other factors influencing trade: profit margin, rate of exchange, transportation and handling charges, tariffs and quotas, delivery time and schedules, credit terms and quantity discounts, and political factors
  C. Product life cycle theory and trade

III. Foreign investment theories
  A. Direct investment theories: interest rate differentials, monopolistic/oligopolistic advantages, product life cycle of international investments, risk reduction, market potential, and organizational behavior
  B. Miscellaneous reasons for foreign investments

IV. Summary

INTRODUCTION

The two most significant components of international business are international trade and international investments. It is, therefore, important that theories explaining these two phenomena be well understood. This chapter explains the theoretical foundations of trade and investment in a nonmathematical and nongraphic manner. The student interested in either approach should consult any standard international trade or economics text.

FOREIGN TRADE THEORIES

Classical Theories of Trade

Although the practical advantages of international trade were long understood, a theoretical explanation was not available until Adam Smith wrote *Wealth of Nations* in 1776. Smith argued that productivity differences among countries created advantages for one country over another. To capitalize on these advantages a country should specialize in that product for which it has the greatest production efficiency. Country A might be more efficient in the production of wheat than sugar and vice versa for country B; therefore, A should specialize in wheat, B should specialize in sugar, and they should trade for the commodity not locally produced. This, Smith asserted, would benefit each party. The logic of this explanation is presented in the following sections.[1]

Absolute Advantage

Absolute advantage exists in the situation described above: A is more efficient in the production of wheat, and B is more efficient in the production
of sugar. Using labor as the standard of value, Table 2.1 illustrates a barter
example of the gains from trade under conditions of absolute advantage.

In the example, the production of 10 bu. wheat requires 1 day's labor
in the United States but two days' labor in Cuba; therefore, the United
States is more efficient in the production of wheat. On the other hand, it
takes 2 days' labor to produce 5 lb. sugar in the United States, but only 1
day's labor in Cuba; therefore, Cuba is more efficient in the production of
sugar. Logic dictates that the United States should specialize in the production of wheat and Cuba in the production of sugar. Trade will be profitable because, in terms of labor input, 10 bu. wheat is equal in value to $2\frac{1}{2}$
lb. sugar in the United States, but in Cuba 10 bu. wheat equals 10 lb.
sugar. The ratio between wheat and sugar is 4:1 in the United States and
1:1 in Cuba.

Consider the effects of trading wheat for sugar and sugar for wheat. A
merchant takes 10 bu. of wheat to Cuba and exchanges it for 10 lb. sugar
since the exchange rate between sugar and wheat is 1:1. If the 10 lb. sugar
are brought back to the United States, it can be exchanged for 40 bu. wheat
since the rate of exchange is 4:1. Thus, a profit of 30 bushels of wheat is
earned. If the 40 bushels of wheat are then taken to Cuba, they can be
exchanged for 40 lb. sugar. The 40 lb. sugar can be exchanged for 160 bu.
wheat in the United States. Thus, each transaction results in a profit. The
point to be remembered is that in a situation of absolute advantage (assuming no barriers to trade), it is beneficial for both countries to specialize and
to trade.

For those having difficulty visualizing the labor theory of value, money
wages can be substituted for units of labor. If one day's labor costs are
assumed to be $5.00 in both the United States and Cuba, then product
costs can be used in place of labor days (see Table 2.2).

In the United States, the cost to produce 10 bu. wheat is $5.00 (50
cents per bushel) but in Cuba the cost to produce 10 bu. wheat is $10.00
($1.00 per bushel). The reverse is true in the costs for producing sugar.
This example shows that the United States can produce wheat at half the

TABLE 2.1   **Barter Under Conditions of Absolute Advantage**

		Labor Input	
		United States	Cuba
10 bu. wheat		1 day's labor	2 days' labor
5 lb. sugar		2 days' labor	1 day's labor

TABLE 2.2   **Absolute Advantage in a Money Economy**[a]

	Wheat	Sugar
United States	10 bu. = $5.00 ($0.50/bu.)	5 lb. = $10.00 ($2.00/lb.)
Cuba	10 bu. = $10.00 ($1.00/bu.)	5 lb. = $5.00 ($1.00/lb.)

[a] *1 day's labor = $5.00.*

cost of Cuba, while Cuba can produce sugar at half the cost of the United States. The cost differences denote the differences in efficiency.

Comparative Advantage (Barter Economy)

Would specialization and trade be profitable if one country were more efficient than another in the production of both commodities? David Ricardo expanded on the idea of specialization and trade by developing the theory of comparative advantage. Using the labor theory of value, the following example (see Table 2.3) describes a condition of comparative advantage. In terms of labor input, the United States is more efficient than Japan in the production of both wheat and wool cloth; however, the efficiency rate varies for each product. The United States is 2.5 times more efficient than Japan in the production of wheat (10 bu. versus 4 bu.) but is only twice as efficient in the production of wool cloth (4 yd. versus 2 yd.).

Since the United States is comparatively more efficient in the production of wheat than wool cloth, it should specialize in the production of wheat, let Japan specialize in the production of wool cloth, and then trade wheat to Japan for the wool cloth needed. The following illustrates the gains from that type of trade. A merchant takes 10 bu. wheat to Japan and sells it for 5 yd. cloth (assuming no transportation charges or barriers to trade). The merchant returns with the 5 yd. cloth and exchanges it for 12.5 bu. wheat, indicating a profit from the transaction of 2.5 bu. wheat. Similarly, a Japanese merchant will be able to export 2 yd. cloth to the United States, where it can be sold for 5 bu. wheat. If the Japanese merchant had sold the cloth in Japan, the sale would have brought only 4 bu. wheat; therefore,

TABLE 2.3   **Barter Economy Under Conditions of Comparative Advantage**

	1 Day's Labor	
	Wheat	*Wool cloth*
United States	10 bu.	4 yd.
Japan	4 bu.	2 yd.
Relative efficiency: United States/Japan	2.5:1	2:1

a gain (profit) of 1 bu. wheat was earned from trade. Thus, under conditions of comparative advantage, specialization and trade will be profitable for both parties.

Equal Advantage

Equal advantage exists when one country is more efficient than a second in the production of two or more products, and is more efficient by the same production ratio (see Table 2.4). In this example, the United States is twice as efficient as Japan in the production of wheat and twice as efficient in the production of wool cloth. If the United States specializes in the production of wheat and sells the wheat in Japan, 8 bu. can be exchanged for 4 yd. cloth. The 4 yd. can be brought back to the United States and exchanged for 8 bu. wheat. This will result in no gain since the ratio between wheat and cloth production is the same in both countries. Thus, there are, theoretically, no reasons for specialization and trade under conditions of equal advantage.

Comparative Advantage (Money Economy)

To make the example more realistic, Table 2.5 illustrates comparative advantage using money and total factor costs rather than labor days to determine the cost of production.

If the total factor inputs are $10 per day in both countries then the 10 bu. wheat produced in the United States will cost $1.00 per bushel and the 4 yd. of cloth will cost $2.50 per yard. The comparable costs in Japan would be $2.50 per bushel for wheat and $5.00 per yard for cloth. A merchant will see immediately the possible profits that could be made from the sale of both products in Japan.

Assume that an American merchant is able to acquire 80,000 bu. wheat in the United States for $80,000, and 40,000 yd. cloth in the United States for $100,000. The merchant decides to export these goods for sale in Japan. The sale of wheat will result in $200,000 (80,000 × $2.50), and the sale of the cloth will yield $200,000 (40,000 × $5.00). The result for the merchant will be profits of $120,000 on the sale of the wheat and $100,000 on the sale of the cloth. If money is free to flow from one country to another the

TABLE 2.4 **Barter Economy Under Conditions of Equal Advantage**

	1 Day's Labor Input	
	Wheat	*Wool cloth*
United States	8 bu.	4 yd.
Japan	4 bu.	2 yd.
Relative efficiency: U.S./Japan	2:1	2:1

TABLE 2.5   **Comparative Advantage in a Money Economy**[a]

	Wheat	*Wool Cloth*
United States	10 bu. @ $1.00/bu.	4 yd. @ $2.50/yd.
Japan	4 bu. @ $2.50/bu.	2 yd. @ $5.00/yd.

[a] Total input costs $10/day.

merchant will take the proceeds from these sales back to the United States and begin the process again.

It would seem that this process could go on forever with merchants from the United States continuing to sell wheat and wool cloth in Japan, bringing the proceeds of the sales back to the United States, and amassing huge fortunes. Actually, as trade continues, the relative prices in each country will begin to change until it is no longer profitable to continue the trade. For example, assume that both countries are on the gold standard, that gold coins circulate as money among the countries (this will eliminate the problem of foreign exchange), that the total money supply of each country is $1,000,000, and that there are no barriers to trade or transportation costs. The sale of both wheat and cloth to Japan will result in an inflow of $400,000 of gold into the United States, thus increasing its total money supply to $1,400,000. Japan, on the other hand, loses $400,000 of its money supply. With an increase of the U.S. money supply by 40 percent, factor prices will rise by 40 percent to $14.00 per day, while those in Japan will fall by 40 percent to $6.00 per day. In the United States, the cost of wheat is now $14.00 for 10 bushels ($1.40 per bushel) and cloth is $14.00 for 4 yards ($3.50 per yard). In Japan the cost for wheat is now $6.00 for 4 bushels ($1.50 per bushel), and for cloth the cost is $6.00 for 2 yards ($3.00 per yard), as shown in Table 2.6.

Under these conditions, the export of both wheat and cloth has resulted in the inflow of money to the United States and an increase in input costs. In Japan, the imports of the two products and the resulting outflow of

TABLE 2.6   **Effects of Change in Money Supply on Input Cost Structures**

	Wheat	*Wool cloth*
United States	10 bu. @ $14.00 ($1.40/bu.)	4 yd. @ $14.00 ($3.50/yd.)
Japan	4 bu. @ $6.00 ($1.50/bu.)	2 yd. @ $6.00 ($3.00/yd.)

money has resulted in a decrease in input costs. Thus, the product of greatest efficiency in the United States (wheat) remains lower priced but the product of least efficiency (wool cloth) becomes higher priced than in Japan. The flow of revenues from the trade has changed the condition of comparative advantage to one of absolute advantage. The United States will continue to export wheat, but Japan will now find it profitable to export cloth. Under the new terms of trade, the United States will save 50 cents per yard by purchasing cloth in Japan, and Japan will save 10 cents per bushel by purchasing its wheat in the United States. In reality, the loss or gain in money supply will occur over a long period of time rather than in a single transaction. The problem could be made more realistic by considering different currencies with fluctuating exchange rates, tariffs and trade barriers, transportation costs, and other factors affecting costs and prices; however, the omission of these factors does not detract from the fundamental reality of the way trade and money flows affect the input cost structures of nations and thereby future trade.

The classical theories of absolute, comparative, and equal advantage under barter and money economies demonstrate the benefits of specialization and trade.

Factor Endowments or Proportions Theory

The theory of comparative advantage and the subsequent modifications were the generally accepted explanations of international trade until 1933, when the factor endowments or factor proportions theory was introduced by Eli F. Hecksher and Bertil Ohlin. This theory proposed that a country with a relative abundance of a particular factor would be able to produce, at lower costs, goods using that factor, and would become an exporter of those products. For example, the United States with its abundance of capital should produce and export capital-intensive goods, while less developed countries with an abundance of labor should produce and export labor-intensive goods.

It was believed that empirical evidence would support the factor proportions theory. Such evidence was made available when the input-output statistics of the United States were published in the mid-1950s. Wassily Leontief broke down U.S. exports and imports into their labor and capital components, expecting to provide support for the factor proportions theory. What he found was that American exports embodied more labor and less capital than did American imports. Because the results were antithetical to the Hecksher-Ohlin theory, the findings are called the "Leontief Paradox."

In an attempt to restore the creditability of the Hecksher-Ohlin theory, Leontief reconciled his findings by stating that the United States was indeed a labor-abundant country in terms of the particular skills of its labor. Thus, many high-technology products exported from the United States were intensive in highly skilled labor, while imports were simple manufactured goods that were produced using older or more simple technologies.

Neither the earlier trade theories nor the Hecksher-Ohlin theory gave much consideration to the possible substitution of international factor movements for international trade. This omission was probably due to the fact that most factors of production such as land, labor, and capital were considered immobile for political, economic, or cultural reasons. In reality, various production factors do move among nations as a substitute for international trade. Foreign direct investment is the movement of capital abroad rather than the use of this factor in the production of goods for export. Some countries that have an abundance of labor relative to capital do not export labor-intensive goods, but rather permit labor to go abroad to work. Mexico, for example, permits migratory workers to go to the United States to harvest seasonal crops.

Natural and Acquired Advantages

In spite of its shortcomings, the factor proportions theory is still of value in explaining world trade; however, it must be expanded to include both natural and acquired advantages.

Natural Advantages   A country that is amply endowed with certain resources will have the natural advantage of being able to produce products requiring those resources at lower costs. For example, a nation endowed with certain minerals will have a cost advantage in the production of goods requiring those minerals. Similarly, soil and climatic conditions are natural resources that produce advantages in agricultural production and commercial grazing. Lumbering is more important in areas with pure stands of softwoods like the Pacific Northwest than in areas of widely scattered hardwoods like the Amazon Basin (see the Global Insight). Even strategically located waterways can provide a nation with transportation advantages.

Countries that are endowed by nature with mineral resources, rich soils, favorable climate, natural waterways, and so forth have natural competitive advantages in producing and marketing goods.

Acquired Advantages   Some nations are able to produce certain products at lower costs because of advantages that have been acquired through their own efforts. The accumulation of capital and the acquisition of certain skills, education, technologies, and national physical facilities (infrastructure) are all examples of acquired advantages. These acquired advantages often overcome some natural disadvantage and provide a basis for trade. One of the best examples of a country that is able to compete effectively in many economic activities by overcoming the lack of natural advantages is Japan.

Japan is a country that has few natural resources. Because it is very mountainous, only about 19 percent of the land area is arable. The population (121 million) is concentrated along the coastal areas and some inland valleys, making Japan one of the most densely populated countries in the world. One of Japan's few natural resources is the sea.

By means of acquired advantages, Japan has become one of the most highly industrialized nations in the world. This has been accomplished in part by continuously increasing production efficiency. Public and private funds finance research. Japan has one of the highest personal savings rates in the world, so capital is accumulated for investment in a variety of projects.

More efficient operations and lower costs of production can result from acquired advantages.

Plants are regularly modernized, enabling firms to produce at costs that are frequently lower than those of competitor nations. Many jobs that are routine, high precision, or hazardous are done by robots. These and other activities have enabled Japan to make technological progress and to acquire an international advantage in numerous industries. This is especially true in old-line industries such as steel and automobiles.

Product Life Cycle Theory and International Trade

The well-known domestic product life cycle provides a basis for understanding the development of international trade. The domestic product life cycle suggests that a new or substantially modified product will go through five stages: introduction, rapid growth, competitive turbulence, maturity, and decline (see Figure 2.1).[2] This theory does not address export sales directly but serves as a foundation for understanding the development of exports.

As Figure 2.1 depicts, the leveling-off of the domestic market for a product and the rapid decline in the market price generally occur almost simultaneously in the competitive turbulence phase of the product cycle. Price competition occurs because of an increase in industry-wide production capacity, usually as a result of an increased number of competitors. The result is a situation wherein supply equals demand and the same amount of money is bidding for an increasing quantity of goods. At this point foreign markets begin to be viewed as a means for firms to continue to expand sales and to maintain acceptable profit margins.

This exploitation of the export markets usually occurs in three steps. First, firms export to technologically, culturally, linguistically, or economically similar markets because the product will need little modification in design, packaging, or promotion. Second, firms export to other advanced industrialized nations despite a lack of similarity. These exports tend to be successful only to the extent that product and promotion adaptations are successful. Finally, exports flow to less developed nations. For industrial

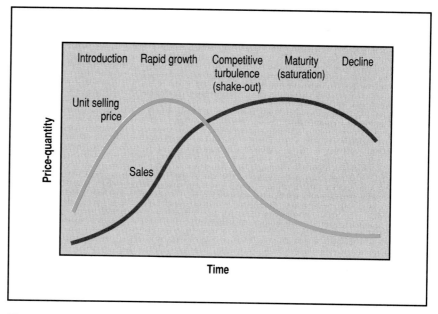

Figure 2.1   Product Life Cycle

goods these exports are often made to subsidiaries of the domestic corporation.

It is typical for foreign production to begin during the competitive turbulence stage of the product life cycle. This production may result from foreign licensing agreements or direct manufacturing investments by firms from the inventing nation, or may result from product development by foreign firms. Foreign production usually begins in advanced industrialized nations and later spreads to less developed countries. The result of the foreign production is that the nation in which the product was originally introduced will ultimately become a net importer of the product. For example, the United States has become a net importer of black-and-white televisions and transistor radios.

The product life cycle is of such significance for understanding international trade and export potential that some nations use it as a component for national industrial planning. For example, the Ministry of International Trade and Industry of Japan (MITI) defines "Sunrise" and "Sunset" industries in terms of the product life cycle and uses these classifications for helping to determine subsidies or tax grants.

Under the product life cycle theory, export markets are exploited when competition reduces the profitability in the domestic market.

FOREIGN INVESTMENT THEORIES

International business is not limited to exports and imports; it also includes the international flow of capital. These capital flows include both the purchasing of foreign stocks and bonds for investment purposes (indirect investments) and the establishing of foreign operations (direct investments).

Various theories have been advanced to explain why a firm chooses to go beyond its national boundaries to conduct its business operations. Some explanations are nothing more than an extension of domestic theories, while others provide new insight into the reasons for foreign investments. The following sections cover some of the principal theories.

Interest Rate Differentials

The classical theory asserts that international capital movements are due to the differences in the rates of interest among countries.[3] Funds will flow from areas of abundant capital where interest rates are low to areas of capital scarcity where interest rates are higher. Although often advanced as a theory of foreign direct investment, this theory is more appropriate for explaining indirect or portfolio investments.

Monopolistic-Oligopolistic Advantage Theory

This theory states that a multinational corporation (MNC) will invest abroad because of monopolistic or oligopolistic advantages due to any of several reasons. The advantages are assumed to overcome the disadvantages faced by the MNC when it goes to an unfamiliar foreign market.

Some of the most common foreign direct investment theories are of this type. Each variant of the monopolistic-oligopolistic advantage theory places emphasis on a different factor but the general thrust is the same: The MNC possesses an exploitable factor that creates a monopolistic or oligopolistic advantage abroad or that will develop into an advantage if the firm invests abroad.

Market Imperfections

Multinational corporations invest because imperfections exist in some market for the factors of production, thus resulting in favorable conditions for the firm's products. These imperfections include such factors as technology, capital, labor, raw materials, and management superiority.[4] The cost of some factors of production in the recipient country might be substantially below the cost in the investor's home country, enabling the firm to exploit this imperfection through investment. Taking advantage of this lower factor cost and then exporting the product back to the home market will give the firm an advantage over competitors. Thus, one might expect firms from developed countries to invest in developing countries where they can utilize the lower labor or raw material costs even if no substantial market exists in that country. This occurs so frequently that it has a name: *Off-Shore or Platform Production*. The hand manufacture of baseballs in Haiti for export to the United States is but one example of thousands that could be cited.

Firms may invest abroad for any of the following reasons: lower costs (including labor, raw materials, energy, capital, and so forth), greater labor skill or productivity, more advanced technology, a well-developed infra-structure and support services, and superior managerial know-how. Any of these could provide the investing firms with advantages in their home or third-country markets.

Intangible Capital

A multinational corporation often invests abroad because it is in possession of some intangible asset that allows for the profitable differentiation of the firm's products.[5] Intangible capital generally refers to technical and other competencies that enable the firm to differentiate products to fit local needs while maintaining production economies or synergy among goods produced globally. Such technological advantages are more often the property of large corporations; therefore, direct investments precipitated by intangible capital will generally be undertaken by larger firms. Caves, pulling together differentiated products and large size, theorizes that the MNC is "apt to operate primarily in market structures of differentiated oligopoly."[6] When a smaller firm is in possession of such an advantage, it will usually export or enter into licensing agreements because of the high fixed costs of direct investment.[7]

Trademark or trade name identification can also represent an intangible asset that allows a firm to exercise a monopolistic advantage in its foreign direct investments. Consider the universality of the trade name *Coke* or the nearly universal recognition of *Mickey Mouse*.

From this theory, one can conclude that the foreign manufacturing investor is likely to be a large firm that (1) adapts its basic product to specific markets; (2) prefers markets wherein a few large firms dominate; and (3) uses its financial, managerial, and technical ability to maintain a monopolistic or oligopolistic market structure.

Internalization and Multiplant Operations

Buckley and Casson's internalization theory suggests that firms internalize markets because of imperfections that exist in intermediate products markets. For example, when a major food processor invests abroad in a plantation, it is internalizing a part of the product channel. This allows the firm to control what is grown and when and where it is grown. This internalization of the intermediate market reduces uncertainties and risks. Indeed, Buckley and Casson feel that internalization explains all international operations.[8] Rugman states that the MNC invests abroad to internalize markets because internalization is the only way for the firm to gain full value from the knowledge it creates.[9] In other words, firms invest abroad to internalize segments of the product channel to collect the profits of those segments. In a sense, Rugman's definition of international internalization is similar to vertical integration on a global scale.

Hymer suggests that MNCs invest abroad as part of their normal multiplant strategy to generate economies in sales, promotion, advertising, administration, and research.[10] A result of this multiplant approach is that the MNC gains control over markets, prevents competition, and maximizes corporate returns on unique skills and abilities. The multiplant operations explanation for foreign direct investment indicates that the firm is following its "normal" expansion path when it enters the international arena.

MNFs as High Technology Firms

Multinational corporations invest abroad when the firm-specific know-how and other intangible assets constitute a barrier to the entry of others. This gives temporary monopoly power to the owners of that specific know-how.[11] Hirsch found that foreign direct investments are more likely by firms in industries in which it is important to use firm-specific know-how to create differentiated products. Past investments in such areas as research and development, advertising, and managerial know-how create firm-specific know-how. Firms that have little uniquely specific know-how tend to utilize greater levels of trade and lesser levels of investment.[12]

The monopolistic/oligopolistic advantage theory states that firms invest abroad to exploit market imperfections and to gain a competitive advantage because of a unique skill or asset.

International Product Life Cycle Theory

The international product life cycle (PLC) theory states that MNCs invest abroad as part of an international life cycle of products or processes.[13] New product innovations tend to occur in the advanced industrialized nations and are initially marketed there.

As was explained previously, the life cycle of a new product progresses through five stages: introduction, rapid growth, competitive turbulence, maturity, and decline. During the introduction stage, the product or process that was designed to meet the needs of the home market is produced domestically. Costs are high because the scale of production is quite small. At this point there are usually no international activities or at most, minimal exports to similar markets.

During the rapid growth and competitive turbulence stages, exports to other developed nations expand rapidly. At this point, firms from the inventor's home nation and in other industrialized countries attempt to break the monopolistic position of the innovator firm. In the home market and in other industrialzied countries, competition and supply capacity increase, resulting in a dramatic decline in market prices. This decline in prices and the resulting profit squeeze invariably result in more efficient methods of production and declining production costs. Firms that cannot achieve these efficiencies are forced to merge, are acquired, or go out of business—which is why these stages of the product cycle are often termed the "wash-out" phases.

Early in the mature stage of the home market, continuing growth depends upon the development of foreign markets. Exports to industrialized countries are usually short-lived, as firms in those countries begin the production of similar products. The replacement of imports with local production is often accelerated by import barriers imposed by the host government, which lead to licensing agreements or joint ventures with firms in the foreign country (host country), or to wholly owned investments.

As the home country market continues to mature, production methods become standardized and process improvements are made, resulting in reduced production costs. Mature industries are generally dominated by a few large firms that have the economic and managerial capacity for continued major investments abroad. The result is manufacturing investments in low-wage-rate developing nations. The results of low-cost production in the industrialized countries and even lower production costs in LDCs is an even wider market for the products. Imports begin to enter the home country and other industrialized countries, and exports begin to disappear. Major multinational firms compete for market share in the industrialized nations with products produced in the LDCs.

During the final (decline) stage of the product life cycle, producers in the developed countries can no longer meet the competition provided by imports. Home country production begins to disappear. Electronic calculators provide an excellent example of the international product life cycle. American firms were once major producers and exporters, but with the spread of technology, they were unable to compete in foreign markets by means of exports. To retain their global and domestic market share, they set up plants in low-labor-cost areas such as the Far East. The United States is now a net importer of such goods.

The international PLC theory explains foreign direct investment as necessary for retaining market share in home and foreign markets, and as a natural consequence of the free flow of products, capital, and technology.

Risk Reduction

This theory states that multinational corporations make foreign direct investments to minimize earnings risks. Risk minimization is important because the value of the firm is a combination of profit maximization and risk minimization. Lloyd, investigating the return on assets across several different countries, concluded that nondiversifiable (i.e., country-specific) risks can be greatly reduced by international diversification of investment, especially if the investments were in countries from several different regions.[14]

Rugman argues that MNCs are at an advantage compared with local firms because of higher absolute level of profits and greater stability of profits. This greater stability of profits is a result of international investments in foreign economies that are imperfectly correlated with the U.S. economy.[15]

Aggarwal states that the relevant risk of a specific foreign direct investment is the net effect of that investment on overall corporate risk and on the expected income streams of the firm. Therefore, before investing the MNC should

By setting up operations in different countries, MNEs can minimize their economic risks because the leads and lags in the business cycles among countries result in greater stability of earnings.

1. consider both the cash flows and risks of the investment,

2. determine the investment's impact on the stability of the corporate earnings, and

3. analyze the correlation between that country's business cycles and the business cycles of the corporation's home country.[16]

Market Potential

Another factor of importance in explaining foreign direct investments is the future potential of the market. This theory is perhaps the most straightforward of all. It states that MNCs invest abroad because there is great potential for the sale of the firm's products or services, which in turn means the potential to earn profits.[17]

Miscellaneous Reasons for Foreign Investments

One of the principal reasons for foreign direct investments can be traced to a firm's attempt to get underneath trade barriers that are adopted by a number of countries. A firm might be forced to go abroad if domestic costs prevent it from competing effectively. In the manufacture of labor-intensive products, foreign labor might be available at a fraction of the domestic wage rates. The assembly of electronic products by American firms in Taiwan, South Korea, Singapore, Central America, and other Third World countries is largely due to the high cost of domestic labor.

Raw materials might be available in a particular country. If a country feels that it has a monopoly of such resources, it will levy a tax on the export of the raw material to generate revenues and to discourage exporting. This will stimulate local processing of the raw material. Savings in transportation charges might determine whether a firm can compete effectively by means of exporting or needs to invest abroad. Bulky or perishable commodities can usually be processed most efficiently near their source. Manufactures can be transported disassembled to an assembly plant near the market. North American meat-packing plants process corned beef in Argentina, Paraguay, or Uruguay and transport the finished product to the United States. Firms may also invest to control a critical raw material source and to improve the chances of uninterrupted availability.

Many firms find it more efficient to manufacture products abroad when adaptation to local market conditions is essential. Without a complete understanding of the local customs, cultural conditions, and other factors influencing demand, exports to such markets might be unpredictable. Some firms establish joint venture relationships with an existing operation that is familiar with the market conditions.

If a nation adopts a domestic content law, a firm has no alternative but to invest or to give up the market. There is no doubt that the threat of Congress adopting a domestic content law has encouraged Japanese auto parts manufacturers to establish manufacturing plants in the United States.

One might decide to produce in the host country because of consumer nationalism. The government might reinforce this desire by requiring the complete manufacture of certain goods domestically. If the major competitor

There are a variety of explanations for firms' investing outside of their home nation because no single theory provides a complete explanation of all investments.

of a firm is located in a particular market, the firm might for defensive reasons establish foreign operations.

SUMMARY

The classical theories explained international trade in terms of absolute, comparative, and equal advantages. These explanations were generally accepted, with slight modifications, until well into the twentieth century. In 1933, Hecksher and Ohlin introduced the factor endowments or proportions theory of international trade, which states that countries will produce and export those goods that make use of an abundant and low-cost resource. Nevertheless, there are real-life situations wherein resource-deficient countries are major exporters. Such situations do not contradict the Hecksher-Ohlin theory; they merely extend this theory to include acquired as well as natural advantages that enable the countries to produce certain goods efficiently. These acquired advantages are generally related to the accumulation of capital, the development of a nation's infrastructure, the learning of certain skills, and the development of technological superiority.

According to the product life cycle theory, innovations will be marketed first in the country of development. The initial foreign demand will be satisfied by exports and later demand by production in other industrialized countries. With continued growth in the domestic market, standardization becomes possible, reducing per unit costs. Mechanization decreases the need for skilled labor, leading to production in the less developed countries for both domestic and foreign markets. The innovator nation first loses its export markets and later becomes a net importer of the product.

Foreign investments might be either indirect or direct. Indirect investments are generally made by individuals or corporations, usually on the basis of exchange rates, interest rates, and returns on equity investments.

There are numerous foreign direct investment theories, and no single theory can explain all investments. Market imperfections and the possession of unique assets enable a firm to benefit from monopolistic or oligopolistic advantages. Foreign investments minimize overall corporate risks, thereby increasing the value of the firm. By internalizing the international product and supply channels, the firm can reduce risks and participate in the profits that accrue at each stage of that channel. Market potential and the need to adapt to market conditions also provide a rationale for investments abroad. The PLC theory of direct investments presents foreign investments as a natural and necessary condition of business. Overall, there are numerous and interrelated reasons that firms invest abroad but they all involve increasing profits, reducing risks, and increasing the wealth of the shareholder.   □

KEY TERMS AND CONCEPTS

Absolute advantage	Comparative advantage
Acquired advantage	Direct investment
Barter economy	Equal advantage

Factor proportions or endowments
theory
Foreign direct investments
Foreign exchange
Import tariffs
Indirect or portfolio investments
Intangible capital
Interest rate differential theory
Internalization

Investment climate
Leontief Paradox
Market potential
Monopolistic-oligopolistic advantage
Natural or native advantage
Product life cycle theory
Rate of exchange
Tariffs

REVIEW QUESTIONS

1. How do natural advantages enable producers in a country to produce goods at lower costs?

2. Is it possible for countries that are not well endowed with natural resources to produce goods at lower costs than nations that are resource rich?

3. Explain the factor proportions theory. What is the Leontief Paradox?

4. Is trade profitable in a barter economy under a condition of absolute advantage? Comparative advantage? Equal advantage?

5. Explain why a condition of comparative advantage changes to one of absolute advantage when money is introduced into a barter economy.

6. Why is the interest rate differential theory considered less applicable in explaining foreign direct investments than indirect investments?

7. Explain how market imperfections can result in a monopolistic or oligopolistic situation that will benefit a multinational corporation.

8. Explain why and how international investments reduce overall corporate risks.

NOTES

1. Adapted from Paul V. Horn and Henry Gomez, *International Trade Principles and Practices* (Englewood Cliffs, N.J.: Prentice-Hall, 1961).

2. H. Igor Ansoff, *Corporate Strategy: An Analytic Approach to Business Polocy for Growth and Expansion* (New York: McGraw-Hill, 1965).

3. Carl Iverson, *Aspects of the Theory of International Capital Movements* (London: Oxford University Press, 1953).

4. Richard E. Caves, "Causes of Direct Investment: Foreign Firms' Shares in Canadian and U.K. Manufacturing Industries," *Review of Economics and Statistics* 56 (August 1975), 279–293.

5. Ibid., p. 280.

6. Ibid., p. 281.

7. Ibid., p. 280.

8. Peter J. Buckley and Mark Casson, *The Future of the Multinational Enterprise* (London: Macmillan, 1976).

9. Ibid., p. 103.

10. Stephen H. Hymer, *The International Operations of National Firms: A Study of Direct Investment* (Cambridge, Mass.: MIT Press, 1976).

11. Alan M. Rugman, "A New Theory of the Multinational Enterprise: Internationalization versus Internalization," *Columbia Journal of World Business* 16 (Spring 1980), 23–29.

12. Seev Hirsch, "An International Trade and Investment Theory of the Firm," *Oxford Economic Press* 2 (July 1976), 258–270.

13. Raymond Vernon, "An International Investment and International Trade in the Product Cycle," *Quarterly Journal of Economics* 80 (May 1966), 190–207; Louis T. Wells, Jr. (ed.) , *The Product Life Cycle and International Trade* (Boston: School of Business Administration, Harvard University, 1972).

14. William P. Lloyd, "International Portfolio Diversification of Real Assets: An Inquiry," *Journal of Business Research* 3 (April 1975), 113–120.

15. Alan M. Rugman, "Motives for Foreign Investment: The Market Imperfections and Risk Diversification Hypothesis," *Journal of World Trade Law* 9 (Sept.–Oct. 1975), 567–573.

16. Raj Aggarwal, "Theories of Foreign Direct Investment: A Summary of Recent Research and a Proposed Unifying Paradigm," *Economic Affairs* 22 (Jan.–Feb. 1977), 31–45.

17. Robert T. Green and William H. Cunningham, "The Determinants of U.S. Foreign Investment: An Empirical Examination," *Management International Review* 15 (1975/2–3), 113–120.

REFERENCES AND SELECTED READINGS

Aggarwal, Raj. "Theories of Foreign Direct Investment: A Summary of Recent Research and a Proposed Unifying Paradigm." *Economic Affairs* 22 (Jan.–Feb. 1977).

Agodo, Oriye. "The Determinants of U.S. Private Manufacturing Investments in Africa." *The Journal of International Business Studies* 9:3 (Winter 1978).

Ansoff, H. Igor. *Corporate Strategy: An Analytic Approach to Business Policy for Growth and Expansion.* New York: McGraw-Hill, 1965.

Buckley, Peter J., and Mark Casson. *The Future of the Multinational Enterprise.* London: MacMillan, 1976.

Contractor, Farok J. "Choosing Between Direct Investment and Licensing: Theoretical Considerations and Empirical Test." *The Journal of International Business Studies* 15:3 (Winter 1984).

Calvet, A. Louis. "A Synthesis of Foreign Direct Investment Theories and Theories of the Multinational Firm." *The Journal of International Business Studies* 12:1 (Spring/Summer 1981).

Caves, Richard E. "Causes of Direct Investment: Foreign Firms' Shares in Canadian and U.K. Manufacturing Industries." *Review of Economics and Statistics* 56 (August 1975).

Davidson, William H. "The Location of Foreign Direct Investment Activity: Country Characteristics and Experience Effects." *The Journal of International Business Studies* 11:2 (Fall 1980).

Farmer, Richard N. (ed.). *Advances in International Comparative Management*, Vol. 1. Greenwich, Conn.: AI Press, Inc., 1984.

Franko, Lawrence G. "Foreign Direct Investment in Less Developed Countries: Impact on Home Countries." *The Journal of International Business Studies* 9:3 (Winter 1978).

Green, Robert T., and William H. Cunningham. "The Determinants of U.S. Foreign Investment: An Empirical Examination." *Management International Review* 15 (1975/2–3).

Grosse, Robert. "An Imperfect Competition Theory of the MNE's." *The Journal of International Business Studies* 16:1 (Spring 1985).

Hennart, Jean-François. "Internalization in Practice: Early Foreign Direct Investment in Malaysian Tin Mining." *The Journal of International Business Studies* 17:2 (Summer 1986).

Hirsch, Seev. "An International Trade and Investment Theory of the Firm." *Oxford Economic Press* (July 1976).

Horn, Paul V., and Henry Gomez. *International Trade Principles and Practices.* Englewood Cliffs, N.J.: Prentice-Hall, 1961.

Hymer, Stephen H. *The International Operations of National Firms: A Study of Direct Investment*. Cambridge, Mass.: MIT Press, 1976.

Iverson, Carl. *Aspects of the Theory of International Capital Movements.* London: Oxford University Press, 1953.

Lutz, James M., and Robert T. Green. "The Product Life Cycle and the Export Position of the United States." *The Journal of International Business Studies* 14:3 (Winter 1983).

Mullor-Sebastian, Alicia. "The Product-Cycle Theory: Empirical Evidence." *The Journal of International Business Studies* 14:3 (Winter 1983).

Rugman, Alan M. "Motives for Foreign Investment: The Market Imperfections and Risk Diversification Hypothesis." *Journal of World Trade Law* 9 (Sept.–Oct. 1975).

Rugman, Alan M. "A New Theory of the Multinational Enterprise: Internationalization versus Internalization." *Columbia Journal of World Business* 16 (Spring 1980).

Sleuwaegen, Leo. "Monopolistic Advantages and the International Operations of Firms: Disaggregated Evidence from U.S.-Based Multinationals." *The Journal of International Business Studies* 16:3 (Fall 1985).

Vernon, Raymond. "An International Investment and International Trade in the Product Cycle." *Quarterly Journal of Economics* 80 (May 1966).

Wells, Louis T. Jr. (ed.). *The Product Life Cycle and International Trade*. Boston: School of Business Administration, Harvard University, 1972.

*P*art Two is composed of four chapters explaining the organizations and activities among nations that facilitate or discourage international trade and investments.

Chapter 3, "International Agreements to Minimize Conflicts," discusses various forms of intergovernmental agreements designed to end conflicts that have developed or to prevent future conflicts. Included among these are informal agreements, cartels, commodity agreements, and non-trade-related agreements such as those for the protection of intangible assets. In addition, this chapter explains both bilateral and multilateral trade agreements. As the most important of the various multilateral agreements, the General Agreement on Tariffs and Trade (GATT) is discussed at length. Finally, this chapter addresses two other significant issues: the Law of the Sea, and Immigration.

International business would be nearly impossible if it were not possible to sell one currency for another; thus, foreign exchange is an extremely important component of the international environment of business. This issue is addressed in Chapter 4, "Foreign Exchange." Chapter 4 discusses rates of exchange under both fixed and floating conditions, and also explains the role of central banks and governmental actions in maintaining stability of exchange rates. Finally, Chapter 4 describes the function of foreign exchange markets, the various types of foreign exchange transactions (speculation, arbitrage, currency, and credit swaps), and the significance of international money markets.

Chapter 5 presents an analysis of international monetary relations among nations and an explanation of a nation's balance of payments. Included in the presentation of international monetary relations is a detailed discussion of the organization and activities of the International Monetary Fund (IMF). The section on balance of payments deals not only with the components and nature of recording a country's international transactions but also with the causes for disequilibrium and measures to restore equilibrium.

The final chapter in this part of the text is Chapter 6, "International Business and the Role of Financial Institutions." This chapter first presents an analysis of the role and function of private institutions: commercial banks, investment companies, insurance companies, securities markets, and foreign factors and finance companies. Second, this chapter discusses the activities of U.S. government agencies: the Export-Import Bank, Agency for International Development (AID), and Commodity Credit Corporation and Cooley Amendment Funds. Finally this chapter explains the international financial activities of international agencies: the IMF, International Bank for Reconstruction and Development (IBRD) and its affiliates, and International Development Association (IDA).

The International Environment for International Business

CHAPTER

3

International Agreements to Minimize Conflicts

LEARNING OBJECTIVES

- Understand why conflicts arise among nations

- Analyze critically the measures nations adopt to minimize conflicts

- Be able to differentiate among different types of agreements and their purposes

- Learn the nontrade issues dealing with the ownership and exploitation of the minerals on the ocean floor

- Become familiar with the problems of immigration and emigration and the issues dealing with illegal aliens

INTRODUCTION

Conflict among nations generally arises because of their having different goals. Even within a country, measures adopted to achieve one objective often interfere with the achievement of others. For example, nations attempt simultaneously to achieve full employment, stable prices, maximum growth, and equilibrium in the balance of payments. These are desirable goals, and government policies should be directed toward their achievement. However, the monetary or fiscal policies that facilitate one objective may negatively impact the others. To take one possible strategy, increasing the supply of money might lower interest rates, stimulate borrowing for investment purposes, and increase employment; however, it might also increase price levels and result in inflation. These increases in domestic prices would discourage exports and encourage imports, adversely affecting the trade balance and reducing the hard currency reserves of the country.

Given that a national policy can conflict with the achievement of some of the nation's own objectives, there is no doubt that some of the policies adopted by nations to achieve their respective goals will lead to international conflicts. To minimize these conflicts, nations use persuasion, compromise, and cooperation to conclude intergovernmental agreements. The purpose of this chapter is to provide some examples of how agreements that have been reached through negotiations minimize conflicts among nations.

INTERGOVERNMENTAL AGREEMENTS

Informal Agreements to Minimize Conflicts

A slowdown in economic activities or a decrease in demand for goods is often the cause for conflicts among nations. As long as domestic industries can dominate the market or as long as the market is large enough to accommodate both domestic and imported goods, there is little opposition to imports. However, when the domestic industry loses its market share to foreign competition, international conflicts arise. Both producers and labor unions demand the adoption of barriers to limit the import of competitive goods.

The U.S. auto industry in the 1980s illustrates such a situation. Historically, U.S. automobile manufacturers did not worry about foreign competition. In fact, some of the leading executives of the auto industry were strong supporters of the policy of free trade. Not only did the auto industry dominate the domestic market, but automobiles were among the leading U.S. exports. Foreign car imports were generally luxury or specialty cars that did not compete with Detroit's major lines. The average American was perfectly content with cars that were large and comfortable, and that were especially suitable for driving great distances without regard to the fuel costs. Labor was not concerned about imports because layoffs in the automotive industry had always resulted from slowdown in the domestic economy rather than competition from imports. This lack of concern regarding imports has changed dramatically.

In the 1950s, some foreign automobile producers saw the potential for cars that would compete in the U.S. used-car market. This led to the introduction of the German Volkswagen "beetle." There was little objection by American producers to these imports because they did not compete with new domestic cars. They lacked the comfort of American cars, but were purchased because of their low initial cost and economical operating costs.

Germany's entry into the U.S. market was followed by Japan. In the early 1950s, Toyota sent representatives to study the buying habits of American consumers. These representatives provided the information necessary to tailor their product to meet the needs of the U.S. market. The oil embargo of 1973 and the following rapid increase in the price of gasoline from about 30 cents per gallon to more than $1.00 per gallon resulted in an increased demand by the American automobile buyers for more fuel-efficient cars. American manufacturers were ill-prepared to meet this change in demand. The result was the loss of market share to imports.

As the economical imports began to cut into the domestic market, conflicts began to arise. Producers and labor unions put pressure on the government to restrict imports, especially from Japan. The results of the negotiations between the governments of the United States and Japan regarding automobiles provide an excellent example of the effectiveness of informal agreements in defusing conflicts. In 1980, the Japanese Ministry of Trade and Industry (MITI) agreed to adopt five years of voluntary quotas on the export of automobiles to the United States This enabled the U.S. automobile manufacturers to regain their general competitive position and was largely reponsible for the unprecedented profits of the industry during 1983–1984.

With the expiration of the voluntary quotas in 1985, the U.S. government decided against pressuring Japan, hoping that the country would retain the quotas. Early in 1985, however, Prime Minister Nakasone announced that the export quota would be increased by 25 percent. Immediately, a cry went up from labor and the automobile manufacturers that the increase would have dire effects upon the industry. It was also pointed out that increased imports would further add to the U.S. trade deficit. MITI responded by increasing the quota by less than the 25 percent that was announced. The automobile industry was not seriously affected by the increase in imports, but the increase did add to the deficit in the U.S. trade balance with Japan.

A similar situation existed in many other industries. The lack of modernization of the U.S. steel industry and the installation of modern equipment abroad permitted Japan, Brazil, South Korea, and other countries to produce and export steel to the United States at prices below the U.S. costs of production. The Voluntary Restraint Agreement of 1984 was an attempt to limit the imports of steel to 20 percent of the U.S. market. U.S. manufacturers of textiles, flatware, and shoes experienced a similar situation. The impact was immediate. Organized labor and manufacturers sought relief from imports. The sentiment in Congress was overwhelmingly in favor of restricting the import of these products. The Reagan Administration, however, attempted to mollify the situation, fearing trade retaliation if congressional action were taken. The alternative was to conduct negotiations with the major suppliers of these products to voluntarily restrict their exports to the United States. These negotiations resulted in the establishment of voluntary quotas on the export of these products to the United States without the passage of legislation or the signing of a commercial treaty.

In addition to Japanese exports to the United States, the commercial conflict between the United States and Japan related to the comparative inability of American producers to export to Japan, even those goods produced more efficiently in the United States. Quotas and nontariff barriers on the import of agricultural products such as citrus fruits, tobacco, rice, and beef are examples. Bilateral negotiations were conducted between the two countries resulting in the promise on the part of the Japanese government to remove some of the nontariff barriers and to increase its purchases of American products. In fact, Prime Minister Nakasone went so far as to appeal on Japanese television in 1986 for consumers to increase their purchases of American products. This was followed by the promise in October 1986 to remove the duty on the import of American cigarettes. In 1988,

Informal trade agreements among nations usually take the form of voluntary quotas or agreements to purchase; these can be effective in reducing political friction.

the newly elected Prime Minister Takeshita announced that the quotas on the import of citrus fruits and beef would be increased annually for the next five years. These bilateral agreements are informal in nature, since no treaty or convention was signed and there is no assurance that they will be implemented. However, noncompliance would probably result in the adoption of retaliatory measures by the U.S. government.

Cartels

A cartel is a production or marketing agreement between opposing interests or rival producers. It is generally formed to replace competition and conflict with cooperation and joint action. The effectiveness of a production and marketing cartel requires strict adherence to the assigned quotas.

Although international cartels are not uncommon (for aluminum, shoes and boots, iron and steel scrap, dyestuffs, and other products), the most recent and important cartel is that of the oil-producing and -exporting countries, the Organization of Petroleum Exporting Countries (OPEC). Since oil was first discovered in Titusville, Pennsylvania, in 1859, the price of the commodity has been determined primarily by supply and demand. The price of crude petroleum remained below $2.00 per barrel until the early 1970s. Countries that were primarily dependent upon the production of crude petroleum were at the mercy of the market forces and of those companies that controlled production and distribution. In 1960, the major producers of petroleum attempted to better their economic position through the formation of OPEC. Their efforts at that time were largely in vain: Cooperation within the cartel was lacking as members exceeded their production quotas. A glut in the world markets kept prices from rising.

World market prices for crude oil remained at a low level during the decade of the 1960s and early 1970s. However, worldwide demand continued to increase rapidly, and the importance of the 13 OPEC countries continued to increase. By 1971 OPEC was producing nearly 53 percent of the world's output. Realizing their oligopolistic position as a supplier, the OPEC cartel began to work cooperatively. A politically motivated oil embargo was instituted in 1973. This was followed with a massive increase in the price for crude oil, from less than $2.00 per barrel in 1971 to $10.38 by January 1974. Because OPEC not only increased prices but also cut production, many importers found that they could not buy OPEC oil even at the higher prices and had to purchase oil on the spot markets at prices of three and four times the listed OPEC price.

The success of OPEC in the 1970s, as with any international cartel, was due to a number of factors:

1. A limited number of supplier countries
2. A commonality of needs and values among the cartel nations

3. A willingness on the part of member states to accept production limits and pricing controls even if these adversely affect economic or political strategies

For most of the 1970s OPEC met these conditions. The nations within the organization were trying to maximize their oil revenues within the context of their long-term needs, and realized that to maintain the optimal revenue maximizing price, supply had to be limited. Each nation was willing to limit production to its allocated quota. When the shortage of petroleum occurred in mid-1978 because of the political crisis in Iran, other OPEC nations needing additional revenues were permitted to produce at full capacity. When Iran began producing again and reached its prerevolutionary level after months of inactivity, Saudi Arabia voluntarily absorbed the cutback to limit production.

Although cartels have substantial economic power, especially in the short run, the importing nations are not without means for dealing with this oligopolistic exploitation. To overcome the dependence on OPEC oil, importing nations adopted various measures to reduce oil consumption and sought alternative sources of energy such as coal, natural gas, and nuclear power. These have been relatively successful, as indicated by the decrease in demand for oil since 1979. In spite of the restricted output of Iran and Iraq because of their war, prices have remained low. This is a result of lower worldwide demand and excess supply of oil on world markets. This excess reflects not only overproduction by OPEC nations but also the development of Great Britain and Norway (non-OPEC members) as major producers of crude oil. The USSR, Mexico, and the People's Republic of China, also non-OPEC members, are adding to the world supply.

During the decade of the 1980s, the effectiveness of the OPEC cartel weakened. The world market demands for crude oil from OPEC nations decreased, while the revenue needs of the OPEC countries increased. To prevent a further decline in world market prices, OPEC held periodic meetings to prevent violations of production quotas and set a floor on prices. Monitoring production and maintaining a floor on the price of crude oil proved very difficult and resulted in conflicts. Many OPEC members attempted to meet their projected financial needs by producing more than their allocation or selling below the agreed price. During the latter part of 1987 and during much of 1988, the price of crude petroleum fluctuated around $15 per barrel, far below the benchmark price of $18 per barrel. As Sarah Miller wrote in the March 28, 1988, issue of *Business Week*, "OPEC, in effect is no longer a formal price-setting cartel."[1] Although the price of crude oil increased somewhat in 1989 (to around $18 per barrel), the OPEC cartel has lost much of its power to dictate world prices.

With most cartels, actions to minimize conflicts give rise to further conflicts. In the case of OPEC, the instigation of production and export quotas caused some member nations to feel that they had been treated

International cartels succeed only if member nations abide by production limits and consumer nations cannot find alternative supplies, or reduce their demand.

unfairly. Further deterioration of cartels occurs as consumers seek alternative sources, substitute products, and methods of conservation. This is exactly what happened with OPEC. Consumer nations increased oil explorations, resulting in the discovery of petroleum in non-OPEC countries. The major reserves of Mexico and the North Sea are prime examples. Furthermore, the automobile industry, which is the major consumer of petroleum, developed more efficient engines, thus decreasing the overall demand for petroleum. Efforts to reduce dependence upon petroleum are also being made as nations seek to harness the energy of the sun, winds, and tides as well as to make better use of nuclear energy, coal, and natural gas.

Commodity Agreements

Intergovernmental commodity agreements are generally attempts by major producing countries or producing and consuming countries to stabilize the prices by controlling supply. Commodity agreements can be made among private producers as well as among governments. It is important to differentiate between commodity agreements and cartels: The former are basically protective, while the latter are fundamentally exploitative. Commodity agreements attempt to protect the interests of a large number of small producers or consumers who singly are unable to influence the market supply or price. Cartels, on the other hand, are agreements among a limited number of dominant producers to maximize their gain by controlling the market.

Intergovernmental commodity agreements are adopted for two reasons. The first is to place a floor on prices of primary goods by regulating global production and worldwide marketing. Such agreements are necessary because low and unstable prices have been a major problem for less developed countries, making it difficult for them to earn the necessary foreign exchange to pay for essential imports and to service debt obligations. The second reason for commodity agreements is socioeconomic or political. Agreements have been formed to protect the health and morals of the population, to deny strategic materials to unfriendly nations, or to conserve international resources such as those dealing with the whaling and fur seal industries.

Commodity agreements often determine the mechanisms for controlling world market prices by utilizing buffer stocks, initiating production controls, and setting export quotas. Buffer stocks are quantities of the commodity held by the international agencies which are sold on or purchased from world markets to control price levels. All three dimensions of intergovernmental commodity agreements seek to stabilize world market prices but have differing time horizons, as shown in Figure 3.1.

Commodity agreements have not completely eliminated conflicts among nations. Producing countries desire to stabilize prices at a high level, whereas consuming countries strive to achieve stabilization at a low level.

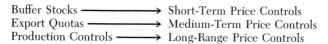

Buffer Stocks ⟶ Short-Term Price Controls
Export Quotas ⟶ Medium-Term Price Controls
Production Controls ⟶ Long-Range Price Controls

Figure 3.1   Dimensions of Intergovernmental Commodity Agreements

The level at which prices are stabilized has a direct impact on production levels. When the intervention price is set too low, it tends to discourage investment. This is usually followed by an increase in prices, since supply cannot keep pace with demand. On the other hand, if the intervention prices are set too high, overproduction occurs, resulting in a drop in prices.

Another obstacle to the successful operation of commodity agreements is that not all major consumers or producers are participants in the agreements. Such is the case with the Cocoa Agreement, in which the Ivory Coast and the United States are not participants. Other factors affecting the overall effectiveness of commodity agreements are political events, monetary and economic conditions (see Global Insight), and the availability of substitutable products.

Despite the difficulties associated with stabilizing the prices for primary products, this remains an issue of major concern for countries that are economically dependent upon the sale of these products. In fact, the United Nations Committee on Trade and Development (UNCTAD) has as a continuing priority the creation of a buffer stock system for products not covered by agreements.

The three basic forms of commodity agreement serve primarily to stabilize world market prices for those commodities.

Buffer Stocks in Commodity Agreements

An important aspect of commodity agreements is the buffer stock system, which helps control world market supplies and prices. Under this system, sales are made from the buffer stock when prices go above a maximum; conversely, purchases of commodities for addition to the buffer stock occur when prices fall below a minimum. Thus, the buffer stock system controls fluctuations in world market prices of commodities by controlling the supply on world markets. The result is that world market prices are permitted to fluctuate within a stated price band.

The success of the buffer stock system depends upon setting the price band at realistic levels, having the market be large and inclusive of many buyers and sellers, and maintaining sufficient funds for stocking the commodity. Products such as cocoa, coffee, sugar, rubber, and tin fulfill these criteria and represent the only commodity agreements in effect at this time. The stockpiling of some products is precluded due to high costs and of others because the products are highly perishable.[2]

Export Quotas and Production Controls in Commodity Agreements

In addition to the role of buffer stocks in maintaining stability in the world market prices of commodities, there are export quotas and production

The Imminent Collapse of the International Coffee Agreement

A selling war among coffee-growing countries is likely since the collapse of price stabilization mechanisms. World coffee prices have fallen sharply. For Latin American producers who rely on coffee exports for a large share of foreign exchange earnings, this new free market will further damage their already struggling economies. Countries of Central America as well as Colombia and Brazil will be hardest hit.

The 74 importing and exporting signatories of the International Coffee Agreement (ICA) could not reach an agreement over country quotas and discounting practices, and have dismantled the 27-year-old accord. The ICA had generally been effective in meeting its objective of keeping coffee prices in the $1.20–$1.40 per pound range. Without this commodity agreement prices plunged almost immediately to $1.00, and later to $0.85 per pound.

In the face of dramatically lower prices, the 50-odd producing nations will have to try to expand their exports to generate projected levels of foreign exchange. In the short run this will mean using coffee stocks to supplement harvests. In the longer term, the producing nations will need to grow and export more coffee and will thus require more labor, higher investments, improved marketing, and more shipping.

Industry analysts predict low prices for at least the next two years, due to an oversupply of coffee coupled with stable demand. They further believe that exporters will undercut each other in a rush to grab market share.

The collapse of the ICA and the failure to reach a new accord can be traced to three primary causes. One, many countries of Central America felt that due to nature of the market and the size of their coffee harvest they could export as much as they produced. The current market saturation is proving this position wrong. Two, there developed in Eastern Europe a parallel market. Firms in these countries had been allowed to purchase excess world supplies at discounted prices for resale in those countries; however, recently these firms began transshipping this coffee into the markets of ICA member countries and underselling the exporter, who had to pay regular prices. Three, the attitudes of both the U.S. Congress and the presidency during the 1980s largely supported "free markets" and did not provide support for a new price stabilization pact.

Source: adapted from Lynn B. Morrissey, "Coffee Argeement [sic] Collapse Could Have Severe Impact On LA's Top Producers," *Business Latin America*, July 31, 1989, pp. 238–239.

controls. Export and production quotas are often signed along with the buffer stock agreements and serve to limit the amount of a particular commodity that each signatory nation may export or produce.

When export quotas or production controls are adopted, commodity agreements often lead to friction among producers. Established producers desire to maintain their share of world markets, whereas newcomers desire to expand their shares. This has been especially true in the coffee agreement. Further dissension may arise because consuming nations oppose the stabilization programs, which maintain higher prices despite production surpluses.

Import Quotas and Commodity Agreements

Import quotas can be unilateral, bilateral, or multilateral agreements between producing and consuming nations. These generally specify the amount of the commodity the consuming nation will import from each producing nation. The purpose of these import quotas is often more political than economic in character. The United States provides an excellent example since it often will agree to greater purchases from political allies than from other producers. For example, the United States cut its sugar purchases from Honduras by some 90 percent for purely political reasons.

Other Nontrade Agreements

Protection of Intangible Assets

Although there are international treaties and conventions regarding the protection of intangible assets, losses from piracy amount to billions of dollars annually.[3] This reflects the fact that not all nations are signatories to the agreements that attempt to protect intangible assets; thus, firms must go through the expensive and time-consuming process of separately registering assets in each country. Some nations that are signatories of international treaties do not make a sincere effort to enforce the agreements. For nations that are signatories to the appropriate treaties and conventions, the registering of a patent, copyright, or trademark in one country assures that protection will be provided not only in that country but also in other signatory countries.

The first universal attempt to provide protection for intangible property was through the Paris Convention of 1883. This resulted in the establishment of the International Bureau for the Protection of Industrial Property, to which the United States and 95 other countries belong. The pact provides protection for patents, trademarks, and other properties of the signatory nations. The Patent Cooperation Treaty provides for reciprocal recognition of patent applications among member nations. Likewise, the European Patent Convention and the EEC Patent Convention recognize patent applications and the issuance of patents. Similar agreements and provisions in the General Agreement on Tariffs and Trade provide some guidelines regarding the protection of intangible property rights, but there is no body to enforce violations of the agreements. Various other agreements regarding the protection of intangible assets exist on a bilateral or regionally multilateral basis.

Agreements for the protection of intangible assets are essential if piracy and counterfeiting are to be avoided. Products such as computer software, textbooks, recordings, pharmaceuticals, and spare parts are subject to counterfeiting. Relatedly, patents are often pirated. This is not a minor problem. The millions of dollars that firms spend building up the reputation of the product can be ruined by trade name violations. For example, shoddy Gucci or Levi replicas with these well-known labels can be purchased at a fraction of the cost of the original, legitimate product.

Other Agreements

Related forms of nontrade agreements include the International Air Transport Association (IATA), which sets fares and rates that prevent ruinous competition among common air carriers. Because of the IATA, regardless of the airline on which reservations are made, travel rates will vary only according to the differences in the services provided. Steamship conferences determine shipping procedures, freight charges, sailings schedules, routes, and other matters that are of benefit to conference members.

This topic cannot be dismissed without mentioning other cooperative efforts that tend to reduce tension among nations—especially between the communist countries and the free world. Industrial cooperation agreements exist between the free market economies of Western Europe, the United States, or Japan and the planned economies of Eastern Europe and the Soviet Union. Interfirm agreements in the spheres of industrial development, production, marketing, and research indicate efforts to minimize future conflicts and are increasingly important to international business.[4]

TRADE AGREEMENTS

Although trade agreements are a form of intergovernmental agreement, they are of such enormous importance to international business that they are handled in a separate section of this chapter.

Bilateral Agreements

Specific problems between two nations are often solved through negotiations that result in bilateral agreements. Such agreements, whether they pertain to disputes, commercial relations, or other problems, provide the basis for long-term relations between those nations. In spite of the increasing importance of multinational trade agreements, bilateral trade agreements continue to be an important dimension of every national and international commercial activity.

The United States-Canadian Automobile Agreement of 1965 provides an example of how conflicts have been minimized through a bilateral agreement. During the 1950s, Canada was faced with a large deficit in its balance of trade, due primarily to the import of automobiles, accessories, and parts from the United States. Although the major American automobile manufacturers had subsidiaries located in Canada, there was little incentive for them to produce or purchase component parts in that country when these could be imported at lower cost from the United States. Such imports, however, had an adverse effect upon the trade balance of Canada. To correct the situation, the Canadian government decided to provide aid to its struggling automotive suppliers.

Subsidies were provided to the Canadian subsidiaries of American companies to encourage them to use Canadian-made parts and even to export parts to the United States. Independent producers of accessories and parts in the United States complained that subsidized parts were being imported from Canada and sold below domestic prices. The U.S. government threatened to levy a countervailing duty on imports to offset the effect of these subsidies.

Before the adoption of any retaliatory measure, however, the two countries turned to negotiations to settle the dispute. These resulted in the bilateral agreement of January 16, 1965: the United States-Canadian Automobile Agreement that provided for the duty-free movement of automobiles and original accessories and parts between the two countries. The rapid growth in the trade of automotive products between the United States and Canada could not have occurred without this bilateral agreement. This important, although limited, agreement actually provided the foundation for the comprehensive Canada-United States Free Trade Agreement of 1988.[5]

Another example of a conflict that led to a bilateral agreement was Japan's refusal to permit the free import of American agricultural products. Economically, there was no justification for this policy. Japan was a high-cost producer. Farmers were subsidized and the market prices of products were often three and four times the world market price. Through negotiations, the United States convinced Japan to permit an increase in imports of products such as beef, citrus fruits, tobacco, and rice. The major problem to be overcome in these negotiations and in the implementation of the agreement was the political power of the Japanese agricultural interests, which opposed opening up their markets to more efficient producers from abroad. Various other bilateral agreements have been made with Japan regarding fishing rights, banking services, restricted businesses, and so forth. Agreements in these areas of conflict have not fully eliminated the problems between these two nations, which are straining political relations.

Bilateral trade agreements between nations often result from negotiations necessitated by a specific problem that resulted in conflict.

Multilateral Agreements: General Agreement on Tariffs and Trade (GATT)

Since multilateral agreements involve more than two nations, their effect on international relations is generally of greater significance than bilateral agreements. The most important trade-related multilateral agreement is the General Agreement on Tariffs and Trade (GATT). The development of GATT has replaced many of the U.S. bilateral agreements.

The history of the post–World War II economic boom is a testimony to the success of multilateral agreements, including the Atlantic Charter, the Lend-Lease Agreement, the International Monetary Fund, and the International Bank for Reconstruction and Development. In fact, many of these multilateral agreements, which have fundamentally influenced the international business climate for much of the last 50 years, are linked to one another. For example, while the Charter of the International Trade Organization (ITO) was being worked out, the governments involved began negotiations for the reduction of customs duties and other barriers to trade. The outcome was the General Agreement on Tariffs and Trade (GATT). GATT was intended to serve only as a stop-gap measure until the ratification of the ITO, but when the U.S. Congress, in December 1950, refused to ratify the Charter of the ITO, further attempts to establish it as a specialized agency of the United Nations were abandoned and GATT became the permanent instrument for laying down codes of conduct for international trade.

The General Agreement on Tariffs and Trade defines the rights and obligations of the signatory nations. It is characterized by four major principles, which are summarized as follows:[6]

1. *Nondiscrimination in trade relations* among the contracting parties. This means that all GATT signatories must be treated in the same way with regard to import and export duties and charges. This is often called the "unconditional most favored nation clause"; however, the most favored nation clause may be waived where tariff preferences already exist, as in the EEC, where internal trade barriers have been abolished.

2. *Prohibition in the use of quantitative restrictions* requires that nations protect domestic industries through the use of customs duties rather than through the use of other nontariff measures; however, import quotas may be used for balance of payments reasons. Even in these cases, quotas must comply with the conditions laid down to minimize damage to the trade of other countries.

3. *Consultation to avoid damage* to the trading interests of contracting parties is inherent throughout the Agreement.

4. *A framework for negotiations* within which negotiations can be held for the reduction of tariffs and other barriers; a structure for embodying the results of such negotiations in a legal instrument is included.

GATT is a multilateral commercial agreement which seeks to reduce the use of tariffs and other nontariff barriers to trade.

GATT Conferences (Rounds)

Since the organizational meeting that established GATT, seven meetings have been held and completed. The eighth and most recent round of GATT negotiations got underway in Punta del Este, Uruguay, on September 21, 1986, and is scheduled to be concluded in 1990. There is no doubt that each of these meetings has contributed greatly toward liberalizing world trade. After the Tokyo Round, the seventh meeting of GATT, Oliver Long, Director General of GATT, described the results as "an important boost to international trade in the coming years and a check on protectionism," the integration of developing countries into the world trading system, and the first legal and permanent basis for trade preferences for and among developing countries. He described the consequences of the Tokyo Round as creating a "multilateral trading system that will be more free and more fair than it has been up to now."[7]

Tariff Cuts and Tariff Harmonization

In the Tokyo Round as in the previous rounds of the GATT negotiations, the reduction of duties was an important item on the agenda. The participants agreed that the highest duties would be reduced the most. As a result Japan, Canada, and the United States granted the most concessions. This round of negotiations also resulted in an average reduction of 41 percent on agricultural products. The industrial countries accepted tariff cuts averaging 33 percent on industrial goods; however, only 14 percent of world trade qualifies for these cuts. Furthermore, previous cuts in duties had reduced the levels to a point where the effect of these cuts was not as significant as it seems. This was also true for the cuts that were made on the import of raw materials because trade of those products had already been liberalized. These cuts in raw material duties seem to have reflected a desire on the part of the industrial countries to assure the supply of low-cost raw materials since the duty treatment of goods was based upon the degree of processing involved: 0.4 percent on raw materials, 4.1 percent on semimanufactures, and 6.9 percent on manufactures.[8]

Nontariff Barriers

It was during the Tokyo Round that GATT first considered the problems of nontariff trade barriers. The existence of low import duties is often misleading because some nations use nontariff barriers that are just as protective as high duties in restricting imports. The participants reached a consensus on five codes regarding nontariff barriers.

Customs Values   Variations in customs valuation among different countries affect the amount of duties payable, and thus protection. This is especially true in the case of the United States, where a complex system of nine different methods of valuation have been used. Such differences in valuation methods permit arbitrary action and cause uncertainty as to what the duties should be. GATT participants agreed that the invoice value (the price actually paid for the goods) would be used as the customs value, but they also allowed for four alternative methods in the event of questions or problems.

Government Procurement   Central governments are major purchasers, but most of these purchases are reserved for domestic suppliers through various regulations or rules that effectively shut out foreign bidders. The Tokyo Round set up procedures regarding notification of anticipated government purchases to enable outsiders to participate on contracts exceeding $195,000. To ensure compliance, surveillance is provided by a committee composed of representatives of signatory nations.

Subsidies and Countervailing Duties   Subsidies are a part of the domestic economic policies of nations that enable high-cost producers to compete more effectively in foreign markets. By receiving subsidies, manufacturers are able to set prices that are not completely dependent upon the cost of production. The affected country generally retaliates by levying a countervailing duty to offset the advantage of the subsidy. To eliminate this vicious cycle of subsidies followed by countervailing duties, the participants agreed to prohibit the use of subsidies on industrial goods and minerals. Regulations affecting aid to primary industries (agriculture, forestry, and fisheries) through restrictions in the use of subsidies are less stringent unless it can be proved that such assistance causes substantial harm to certain branches of industry in the importing country. In these cases, countervailing duties may be employed.

Technical Barriers to Trade   Nations often adopt measures to protect the environment and consumers from the adverse effects of imported products. These standards vary among countries and often create unnecessary obstacles to trade. Some nations impose technical or environmental standards that have no real connection with health or safety but merely serve to keep out foreign goods. For example, European countries have set "health" standards regarding chemicals in meats that effectively exclude U.S. beef. The U.S. beef industry claims that these standards are protectionist and not intended for the maintenance of the public health. The participating GATT nations agreed that all countries should adopt standards as close to existing international standards as possible and should provide for the freer international exchange of information regarding technical standards.

Import Licenses   Some nations use import licenses as a statistical tool to keep track of the amount of imports while others use them as a means of controlling imports. To avoid arbitrary actions in the granting of licenses, agreement was reached to simplify the procedures for obtaining licenses and to grant them in a neutral way.

The Tokyo Round agreements, it is hoped, will reduce tariff and nontariff barriers.

Position of Developing Nations

The original signatory nations of GATT considered the position of the developing nations; however, promoting the trade of the less developed countries proved to be more difficult than anticipated. The fact that trade in manufactured goods from less developed countries would mean increased competition for goods from the developed countries has undoubtably resulted in less than equal treatment of LDCs. This is reflected in the reduction of duties on imports of industrial products from the LDCs by 26 percent between 1980 and 1987 as compared to the average reduction of 33 percent for products from the industrial countries.

The needs of the less developed countries were more favorably considered in nontariff barriers. For example, if industrial countries adopt barriers because of balance of payments problems, these barriers will not be applicable to LDCs. Furthermore, the less developed countries may impose trade restrictions for broad developmental purposes and, in certain cases, without prior consultation. In spite of these concessions, most LDCs felt they did not receive favorable treatment. This was indicated by the fact that of the 60 LDCs attending, only Argentina initialled the final agreement of the Tokyo Round.

There is some evidence to support the claims of LDCs that industrialized countries receive preferential treatment in GATT decisions.

THE LAW OF THE SEA

In some areas of international relations, agreements have not been concluded, resulting in uncertainty as to the rights of specific nations. One of these has to do with the degree of control a nation has over the seas adjacent to its coastline, including fishing and mineral resources.

In anticipation of the increasing conflicts that are likely to arise without some sort of agreement, conferences have been held to establish legal rights and boundaries. Most of the discussions to date have dealt with the extent of a nation's jurisdiction over the various areas of the ocean floor. Even pertaining to those issues wherein some form of agreement among nations generally exists, there is still a great deal to be done. For example, jurisdiction over the continental shelf (the underwater extension of the land mass adjacent to the coast of a nation) is recognized by most nations. However, the area that a nation owns and who owns the area beyond that limit are still to be decided.

In 1945, President Harry Truman proclaimed that the United States reserves jurisdiction over the resources of the continental shelf contiguous to the nation's coast.[9] This concept was adopted in 1958 by the United Nation's Conference on the Law of the Sea. This continental shelf doctrine provides that a coastal state has exclusive rights to exploit minerals under the continental shelf adjacent to its land mass. In support of the doctrine, the United Nation's Conference on Law of the Sea III drafted a document known as the Informal Composite Negotiating Text. While this text is not law, it represents a first step. To become law the text must be signed by all members of the Law of the Sea Conference and ratified by each government. With some 150 nations participating, the agreement created by the conference would represent the body of international law of the sea, and the sovereign right of the coastal state over the continental shelf for exploration and exploitation of its natural resources would be recognized. Consent of the coastal state would be necessary before mining activities could be undertaken by any other state.

Even if agreement is reached on the idea of jurisdiction over a contiguous continental shelf, one still must determine who has jurisdiction when the shelf is contiguous to two or more nations. Such a dispute arose in the North Sea among West Germany, Denmark, and the Netherlands. Article 6 of the Geneva Continental Shelf Convention states that in the absence of agreement, and unless another boundary line is justified by "special circumstances," the boundary line is the line every point of which is equidistant from the coast of each adjacent or opposite state. This dispute was resolved in 1969 when the International Court of Justice took up the case and made use of the "special circumstance" language of the law. A similar dispute involves the United States and Canada. The United States is claiming that the concave coastline of the Georges Bank (lying off the coast of Cape Cod), represents a "special circumstance." Canada claims that the general rule of equidistance should apply. The interpretation is important because this area of the continental shelf is rich in both oil reserves and fishing. If the International Court of Justice rules as it did in the North Sea continental shelf case, the result would be favorable to the United States.

A second existing source of conflict among nations regards the extent or limit of the continental shelf. According to Article 1 of the 1958 Geneva Convention on the Continental Shelf, the continental shelf consists of the "seabed and subsoil of the submarine areas adjacent to the coast but outside of the area of the territorial sea, to a depth of 200 metres or, beyond that limit, to where the depth of the superadjacent waters admits of the exploitation of the natural resources of the said area."[10] Unfortunately, this definition fails to set a clear limit on the continental shelf. The United Nations Conference on Law of the Sea III has proposed a 200-mile exclusive economic zone within which a coastal state will have exclusive jurisdiction over the natural resources of the ocean seabed. If the continental shelf extends beyond 200 miles from the coast, should jurisdiction of the coastal state go beyond the 200-mile zone? Since there is no agreement as to the exclusive legal right, conflict might well be anticipated until an agreement has been reached and a treaty on the Law of the Sea is concluded.

A third potential area of conflict relates to mineral resources that straddle and extend to both sides of a boundary line. Norway and the United Kingdom agreed on joint ownership of the oil field as opposed to national ownership. This eliminated the jurisdictional conflict, but there is no assurance that similar problems in the future will be settled in such a friendly manner. The desirability of joint ownership is emphasized by one authority who states, "In contrast to the inability of the world generally to agree on matters of seabed exploitation elsewhere, the North Sea nations supply an encouraging model consisting of a matrix of treaties, agreements, and administrative rules."[11]

A U.N. Conference on the Law of the Sea is underway to determine jurisdiction over continental shelf and seabed resources.

IMMIGRATION AND EMIGRATION

Nations are free to adopt measures to control the movement of goods, services, capital, and people across their national boundaries. The adoption of such measures, however, might result in conflict with the desires of other countries. Immigration laws that classify entrants as legal or illegal are of this nature.

The increasing global demand for crude oil following World War II and the rapid increase in oil prices after 1973 have led to off-shore drilling and the development of technologies for the development of undersea reserves.

Prior to the latter part of the nineteenth century, few countries had laws restricting immigration and emigration. Since then, most countries have adopted measures to control illegal entries by passing laws or by making agreements with other countries. A brief review of the U.S. immigration laws illustrates the nature of these laws.

In the United States, the first immigration law was passed in 1862, prohibiting the entry of prostitutes and alien convicts. In 1885 and 1887, Congress enacted the contract labor laws to prohibit the immigration of cheap foreign labor to work on such projects as the railroads. These were directed primarily against the Chinese.

Before World War I, there were no general limits; only specific exclusions were placed on those eligible to immigrate into the United States. In 1907, the United States concluded an agreement with Japan to limit the entry of laborers into the country. During the same year, a commission was established to study the immigration problem. Its report in 1911 led to the passage of the Immigration Act of 1917, which added Indians and other Asians to the inadmissable list. In 1921, a temporary quota law was enacted, and in 1924 a permanent quota law was passed on the basis of national origin of the population as it stood in 1920. Aliens were divided into three categories: (1) Those racially ineligible for citizenship (Asians) were barred from permanent admission; (2) those born in the Western Hemisphere were not held to any quota (providing they were not Asians); and (3) all others were assigned quotas on the basis of their country of birth.[12]

The use of these categories meant that those from certain parts of the world were prohibited from immigrating into the United States. This policy remained in effect until after World War II. When China entered the war as an ally of the United States, immigration laws were changed to exempt Chinese from the section prohibiting Asians from entering the United States. In 1946, immigrants from the Philippines (after it became independent) and the East Indies were made eligible for permanent admission and U.S. citizenship. In 1952, the Immigration Act of 1917 was replaced by the Immigration and Nationality Act (McCarran-Walter Act). The new act retained the provision for national quotas. Race was eliminated as a barrier to immigration and citizenship, except that Asians, no matter where they were born, could enter the United States only on the basis of racial quotas rather than the country of birth.

The inequality of the law in the treatment of Asians, the national origin system, and the unlimited immigration from the Western Hemisphere came under increasing attack. In 1965 these laws were amended and as of 1968,

The influx of emigrants, like these from Europe in 1906, provided the labor for the growth of the U.S. economy.

annual maximums of 170,000 from the Eastern Hemisphere and 120,000 from the Western Hemisphere were established. The effect of the new formula was to reduce immigration from Canada and Europe, while increasing it from Mexico and Asia. Rather than adhering to a quota based on national origin, immigration from each country was limited to 20,000, and allocated on the basis of family relationships (74 percent), needed talent (20 percent), and refugees (6 percent).

After several years of debate, the Immigration Reform and Control Act was signed into law on November 6, 1986.[13] The law has three major parts: legalization, employer sanctions, and temporary agricultural provisions. The legalization provision established a method by which aliens who had been in the United States illegally before January 1, 1982, could gain legal status as temporary residents and after 18 months could apply for permanent resident status. Aliens who had been employed in agriculture for a minimum of 90 days between May 1985 and May 1986 could also apply for temporary residence, and became eligible to transfer to permanent residence status beginning in December 1989.

The employer sanctions portion of the legislation subjects to civil and criminal prosecution employers who knowingly hire, recruit, or refer aliens who are not authorized to work in the United States. These sanctions began on September 1, 1987. The temporary agricultural worker provisions divide workers into two categories: temporary workers for agricultural labor or services, and all other temporary workers. These provisions became effective on June 1, 1987. The act authorized employers to file a petition with the Department of Labor indicating that there are insufficient workers to perform the labor and that there will be no adverse effect on wages or working conditions of workers similarly employed.

In addition to these major restrictions, there are many other provisions affecting the immigration of various categories of immigrants, such as non-preference immigrants who were adversely affected by the amendments to the Immigration and Nationality Act in 1965, and the immigration of refugees (Refugee Act of 1980) who are of special humanitarian concern to the United States. A further discussion of these provisions is beyond the scope of this chapter.

All nations regulate the entry of aliens for permanent residence.

SUMMARY

Conflicts often arise among different nations because each has certain objectives it wishes to achieve. Some nations consider exports as the primary economic objective; others consider industrialization as the primary objective and adopt unilateral measures to stimulate the growth of industries.

To minimize these conflicts, nations often conduct informal negotiations that result in cooperation and compromise; these are not legally binding, however. When nations adopt binding measures in their relations with other countries, such measures take the form of bilateral or multilateral treaties, agreements, and conventions.

Commodity agreements are made among producers or between producers and consumers of basic commodities for the purpose of stabilizing prices. Noncommodity agreements such as copyright, patent, and trademark laws are attempts to protect intangible assets. Air transport agreements and steamship conferences aim to standardize rates and fares among carriers of different nations to prevent cutthroat competition.

In recent years efforts have been made to reduce or eliminate the overall barriers to trade. Nations have participated in conferences dealing with trade. The General Agreement on Tariffs and Trade (GATT) was the outcome of one such conference. The result of these negotiations was a commercial agreement among most of the free-world countries to adopt measures that would encourage freer trade among the members. Despite the fact that cartels such as OPEC still exist, the world seems to be moving away from resource cartels and toward information-based cartels or cooperative agreements.

Two nontrade issues that have trade implications were covered in this chapter. The United Nations Conference on the Law of the Sea is an attempt to anticipate and handle problems that are sure to arise regarding the ownership and exploitation of mineral resources in the seas adjacent to a nation's coastline. The second issue is the movement of people across the national boundaries. The large-scale illegal immigration of foreign citizens into the United States has resulted in conflict between the U.S. government and the home governments of the illegal aliens, especially Mexico.   □

KEY TERMS AND CONCEPTS

Bilateral agreement	Immigration
Buffer stock	Most favored nation clause
Cartel	Multilateral agreement
Commodity agreement	Noncommodity agreement
Continental shelf	Price band
Countervailing duty	Organization of Petroleum Exporting Countries (OPEC)
Customs value	
Emigration	Reference price
General Agreement on Tariffs and Trade (GATT)	Subsidy
	Tokyo Round
Illegal aliens	Voluntary agreement

REVIEW QUESTIONS

1. What are commodity agreements? Who participates in these agreements and why?

2. What is meant by a buffer stock? What conditions are necessary for the successful operation of a buffer stock system?

3. Why is OPEC considered to be a cartel? What are the long-range prospects for the successful continuation of OPEC?

4. What are the major reasons for entering into agreements dealing with intangible assets?

5. Describe the differences between bilateral and multilateral commercial agreements. Explain the rationale for bilateral agreements as opposed to multilateral agreements. Use the U.S.-Canadian Automobile Pact as an example.

6. What are the major reasons for the establishment of GATT? Explain the four major principles under which GATT operates.

7. Describe the relationship between subsidies and countervailing duties.

8. Give some examples of technical barriers that prevent the free movement of goods among nations.

9. What is meant by voluntary agreements? How effective are voluntary agreements in minimizing conflicts among nations?

10. Why is it important that nations reach an agreement regarding the jurisdiction of the waters and the ocean floor adjacent to their own coastline?

11. Why do nations adopt laws pertaining to immigration and emigration?

DISCUSSION CASE

The International Protection of Intellectual Property

There is strong corporate support at the Uruguay Round of GATT for a possible agreement on intellectual property (IP) protection. In light of the increasing unilateral actions by governments, such a multilateral accord would seem likely. Trade sanctions have been used by the United States and the EEC to get the home countries of IP violators to take corrective actions.

In fact the United States, the EEC, and Japan have recently joined forces to confront piracy, counterfeiting, and the buying of illegal IP. This cooperation included UICE (Union of European Industry Confederations), the U.S. Intellectual Property Committee, and Keiandren (Japan's Federation of Economic Organizations). The group developed guidelines to ensure minimum protection for each IP category as well as proposed enforcement

Source: adapted from Chris Matthews, "NICs Make Progress but Do Not Make Grade on Intellectual Property," *Business International*, May 23, 1988, p. 155.

procedures. This is the first time that industries from the three blocs have worked together and agreed on a proposal to submit to their governments. Despite this pressure, any proposals discussed at the GATT meeting are sure to meet resistance from developing countries, especially those who are the chief IP offenders.

An International Trade Commission (ITC) survey on foreign protection of the IP rights of U.S. companies found that for the responding firms (431), the 1986 losses totaled $24 billion. Obviously, the total for all U.S. firms is significantly larger. Of the 431 responding firms, 269 reported that IP was "of more than nominal importance" to their businesses. In addition to the dollar value, pirating and counterfeiting can damage a company's reputation.

According to the survey, the top five violators (in number of reported stated offenses) were Brazil, Mexico, Korea, Taiwan, and India. Although Korea has strengthened IP protection, the display and sale of counterfeit and other infringing goods still abound. In monetary value of losses, Taiwan ranked first, followed by Mexico, Korea, Brazil, and China.

The countries that present the greatest problem for firms are the Pacific Rim countries and India because of the size of their markets and their ability to pirate and export high-tech goods. In other words, excepting certain audio and video piracy, the production of most infringed goods is concentrated in countries that can produce a variety of products—in other words, the newly industrialized countries. African, Middle Eastern, and Central American countries are primarily the markets for piracy, not source. Nevertheless, the United States plans to take an aggressive negotiating stance in countries where the Asians sell their counterfeit products.

There are some positive developments to report, particularly governmental attitudes toward stricter IP protection. In the past few years many countries have enacted IP protection laws; enforcement remains the problem. Hong Kong has made the most progress on this front, setting up the world's only unit that specializes in the fight against counterfeiting.

In March 1988, the Asia-Pacific Council of American Chambers of Commerce cited Thailand as the region's worst abuser of IP rights. The United States threatened retaliatory actions if no progress was shown. Just when it appeared that a new, acceptable copyright bill would be enacted, Thailand's Prime Minister Prem Tinsulanonda dissolved the lower house of the legislature, scuttling the bill and ensuring continued poor IP protection. Relatedly, the EEC has already taken action against Korea, and two U.S. pharmaceutical firms have filed a Section 301 suit against Seoul for patent abuse. It appears that Korea and many of the other violator nations will enforce stronger IP legislation only under the threat of sanctions.

NOTES

1. *Business Week*, March 28, 1988, p. 26.

2. One major difficulty with a buffer stock system is the lack of funds, which limits the stockpiling and the ability to control prices.

3. "U.S. Says Counterfeits Cost Concerns Billions of Dollars in Lost Sales," *Wall Street Journal*, April 27, 1984, p. 35.

4. Carl H. McMillan, "Trends in East-West Industrial Cooperation," *The Journal of International Business Studies* 12:2 (Fall 1981), 53–62.

5. Ministère du Commerce Extérieur et du Développement Technologique, *The Canada-United States Free Trade Agreement* (Quebec 1988).

6. *GATT* (Geneva, Switzerland: GATT Secretariat, 1966), p. 5.

7. Kredietbank, *Weekly Bulletin* (Brussels: No. 3, 18 January 1980).

8. Ibid.

9. D. J. Harris, *Cases and Materials on International Law* (London: Sweet and Maxwell, 1979), pp. 380–381.

10. William T. Onorato, "Apportionment of an International Common Petroleum Deposit," *International Comparative Law Quarterly* 26 (April 1977), 724.

11. Ibid.

12. When China entered the war as an ally of the United States, it was excluded from this provision.

13. U.S. Immigration Law, *World Almanac 1989* (New York: Newspaper Enterprise Association, 1988), p. 740.

REFERENCES AND SELECTED READINGS

Business Week. March 28, 1988.

GATT. Geneva, Switzerland: GATT Secretariat, 1966.

Harris, D. J. *Cases and Materials on International Law*. London: Sweet and Maxwell, 1979.

International Monetary Fund. *IMF Survey* 8:9 (May 21, 1979).

Kredietbank. *Weekly Bulletin* (Brussels: No. 3, 18 January 1980).

Kredietbank. *Weekly Bulletin* (Brussels: No. 38, 23 October 1987).

McMillan, Carl H. "Trends in East-West Industrial Cooperation." *The Journal of International Business Studies* 12:2 (Fall 1981).

Onorato, William T. "Apportionment of an International Common Petroleum Deposit." *International Comparative Law Quarterly* 26 (April 1977).

Tung, Rosalie L. "U.S.-China Trade Negotiations: Practices, Procedures, and Outcomes." *The Journal of International Business Studies* 13:2 (Fall 1982).

CHAPTER

4

Foreign Exchange

- Understand how fluctuating exchange rates result in financial risks
- Learn the differences between spot and forward rates of exchange
- Become aware of factors that affect exchange rate fluctuations
- Learn the methods used to transfer funds among countries
- Learn how central banks control exchange rate fluctuations
- Understand the development and functioning of international money markets
- Differentiate among exchange hedging, speculation, and arbitrage
- Understand currency and credit swaps

INTRODUCTION

When a sale is made between individuals or businesses of a country, payment will be made in the currency of that country; therefore, there is no need to be concerned about the value of a foreign currency. Since international transactions involving buyers and sellers originate in different nations, the relative values of the various national currencies must be considered and the problem of foreign exchange arises.

Foreign exchange can be defined as the money and short-term credit instruments of one country circulating in another country. In London, American dollars are referred to as dollar exchange and Japanese yen are called yen exchange. The dollar exchange might be in the form of dollars, short-term drafts, or other documents representing the dollars that could then be used to make payment to an American creditor. Similarly, in the United States, the pound sterling is referred to as sterling exchange and may be used to settle an obligation in the United Kingdom or in any country that accepts pound sterling.

RATES OF EXCHANGE

The *exchange rate* is merely the price of one country's currency in terms of a second country's currency. For example, the exchange rate between the U.S. dollar and the Japanese yen is nothing more complicated than the price in dollars that would have to be paid to purchase one yen. As with any product, the price of the foreign currency will change with changes in the supply and the demand for those two currencies. Because of the variability in the exchange rate, international transactions have an added risk over purely domestic transactions. The exchange rate might change so that the goods purchased become more expensive than expected or the receipts from the sale of goods might be less than expected. The risk of loss arising from the fluctuations in exchange rates will fall on the party who accepts responsibility for exchanging one currency for the other. It is for this reason that many firms prefer to quote their prices in terms of their home currency and insist on receiving payment in that currency. However, the availability of competitive goods often makes these demands unrealistic.

Fluctuations in Rates of Exchange

When there are no restrictions to the exchange of currencies, the mechanics of exchange are rather straightforward and easily understood. The process is analogous to a continuing auction. The uncertainties associated with exchanging currencies come from their fluctuating value rather than the transactional process itself. Exchange rate fluctuations are important for international business because of their significance for sales agreements and for loan agreements.

Supply and Demand

At the most elementary level, changes in the rates of exchange can be explained in terms of changes in the supply or demand for the currencies involved. If one recognizes that the currency of a country is merely a commodity to be purchased or sold as is wheat, rice, or crude oil, then understanding the fluctuations in its value is easier. For example, the price of wheat on the world market is determined largely by supply and demand. A bumper crop of wheat will create a surplus in world markets, causing the price of wheat to fall and, conversely, if a drought results in a decrease in world wheat production, the price of wheat will rise. On the demand side, if the demand for wheat increases faster than supply, the price of the grain will rise. Conversely, if demand falls (or rises more slowly than supply), the price of wheat will fall. Similarly, the market price of a particular currency (the exchange rate) will fluctuate because of changes in supply and demand (see Figure 4.1). An exchange rate will remain constant only so long as supply and demand remain constant or change in exactly the same proportions (supply-demand equilibrium). This phenomenon is obviously unlikely; therefore, exchange rates change almost continuously. Exchange rate figures as given in the *Wall Street Journal* for two consecutive days show slight but nonetheless real variations (see page 86). Although exchange rate changes from hour to hour or day to day are often relatively minor, the exchange rate fluctuations over longer periods of time are often substantial.

It is important to note that the exchange rate offered by one bank will

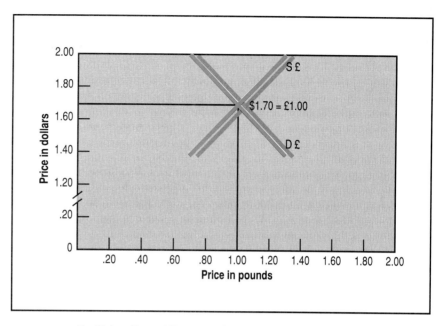

Figure 4.1   Equilibrium Rate of Exchange. Comment: The equilibrium rate of exchange is the point at which the supply of pound sterling is equal to the demand for pound sterling. The point of equilibrium is the point at which it takes $1.70 to obtain £1.00. It will take fewer (more) dollars to purchase £1.00 if the supply of pounds increases (decreases), demand remaining the same.

probably be slightly different from that of another, even if the banks are located in the same country. For example, £1 may be equal to $1.7210 at Citibank in New York but $1.7215 at the Bank of America in San Francisco. The reason for this is not only differences in demand at the various banks but also differing policies of the banks themselves. These slight differences may not be important for an exporter selling $10,000 worth of equipment to a buyer in the United Kingdom but it could be of major consequence to one selling $100,000,000 worth of equipment.

Factors Affecting Changes in the Supply and Demand for Currencies

Since both supply and demand are important for understanding exchange rates, it is important to isolate those factors that affect the levels of both supply and demand.

First, consider the effects of a trade imbalance between two nations—for example, the United States and Japan. If Japan has exports in excess of imports with the United States, there will be both a supply and a demand effect. If Japan accepts payment in dollars for its exports to the United States, it will experience an inflow of dollars, thus increasing Japan's supply of the dollar. As Japanese banks try to exchange (sell) these dollars for yen there will result a downward pressure on the dollar relative to the yen. The

EXCHANGE RATES

Tuesday, October 9, 1990

The New York foreign exchange selling rates below apply to trading among banks in amounts of $1 million and more, as quoted at 3 p.m. Eastern time by Bankers Trust Co. Retail transactions provide fewer units of foreign currency per dollar.

Country	U.S. $ equiv. Tues.	Fri.	Currency per U.S. $ Tues.	Fri.
Argentina (Austral) ...	.0001701	.0001708	5880.28	5855.14
Australia (Dollar)	.8335	.8335	1.1998	1.1998
Austria (Schilling)	.09307	.09194	10.75	10.88
Bahrain (Dinar)	2.6532	2.6532	.3769	.3769
Belgium (Franc)				
Commercial rate	.03182	.03140	31.43	31.85
Brazil (Cruzeiro)	.01115	.01220	89.70	81.97
Britain (Pound)	1.9660	1.9630	.5086	.5094
30-Day Forward	1.9561	1.9524	.5112	.5122
90-Day Forward	1.9400	1.9320	.5155	.5176
180-Day Forward	1.9178	1.9055	.5214	.5248
Canada (Dollar)	.8690	.8669	1.1507	1.1535
30-Day Forward	.8656	.8637	1.1553	1.1578
90-Day Forward	.8598	.8576	1.1630	1.1660
180-Day Forward	.8520	.8502	1.1737	1.1762
Chile (Official rate) ...	.003072	c.003072	325.54	c325.54
China (Renmimbi)	.211864	.211864	4.7200	4.7200
Colombia (Peso)	.001912	.001908	523.00	524.00
Denmark (Krone)	.1716	.1693	5.8275	5.9064
Ecuador (Sucre)				
Floating rate	.001168	.001168	856.00	856.00
Finland (Markka)	.27655	.27367	3.6160	3.6540
France (Franc)	.19552	.19298	5.1145	5.1820
30-Day Forward	.19524	.19267	5.1220	5.1902
90-Day Forward	.19467	.19197	5.1370	5.2092
180-Day Forward	.19368	.19083	5.1632	5.2402
Germany (Mark)	.6547	.6466	1.5275	1.5465
30-Day Forward	.6545	.6465	1.5278	1.5467
90-Day Forward	.6539	.6460	1.5293	1.5481
180-Day Forward	.6522	.6446	1.5332	1.5514
Greece (Drachma)	.006562	.006494	152.40	154.00
Hong Kong (Dollar) ...	.12896	.12889	7.7545	7.7585
India (Rupee)	.05556	.05571	18.00	17.95
Indonesia (Rupiah)	.0005365	.0005479	1864.00	1825.02
Ireland (Punt)	1.7560	1.7325	.5695	.5772
Israel (Shekel)	.4943	.4990	2.0229	2.0040
Italy (Lira)	.0008730	.0008621	1145.50	1160.01
Japan (Yen)	.007648	.007561	130.75	132.25
30-Day Forward	.007651	.007563	130.71	132.22
90-Day Forward	.007649	.007561	130.74	132.26
180-Day Forward	.007642	.007551	130.86	132.43
Jordan (Dinar)	1.5485	1.5485	.6458	.6458
Kuwait (Dinar)	z	z	z	z
Lebanon (Pound)	.000952	.000909	1050.00	1100.00
Malaysia (Ringgit)	.3707	.3706	2.6975	2.6980
Malta (Lira)	3.3557	3.2787	.2980	.3050
Mexico (Peso)				
Floating rate	.0003478	.0003448	2875.00	2900.00
Netherland (Guilder) .	.5807	.5734	1.7220	1.7440
New Zealand (Dollar) .	.6205	.6180	1.6116	1.6181
Norway (Krone)	.1692	.1676	5.9100	5.9650
Pakistan (Rupee)	.0462	.0463	21.65	21.61
Peru (Inti)	.00000230	.0000032	435540.07	431592.58
Philippines (Peso)	.04032	.04032	24.80	24.80
Portugal (Escudo)	.007454	.007312	134.15	136.77
Saudi Arabia (Riyal) ..	.26734	.26738	3.7406	3.7400
Singapore (Dollar)	.5784	.5722	1.7290	1.7475
South Africa (Rand)				
Commercial rate	.3941	.3919	2.5374	2.5518
Financial rate	.2667	.2635	3.7495	3.7950
South Korea (Won) ...	.0013986	.0013986	715.00	715.00
Spain (Peseta)	.010409	.010293	96.07	97.15
Sweden (Krona)	.1773	.1757	5.6410	5.6920
Switzerland (Franc) ..	.7834	.7722	1.2765	1.2950
30-Day Forward	.7836	.7726	1.2761	1.2943
90-Day Forward	.7837	.7727	1.2760	1.2941
180-Day Forward	.7831	.7721	1.2770	1.2952
Taiwan (Dollar)	.036657	.037341	27.28	26.78
Thailand (Baht)	.04011	.03957	24.93	25.27
Turkey (Lira)	.0003701	.0003702	2702.00	2701.24
United Arab (Dirham) .	.2723	.2723	3.6725	3.6725
Uruguay (New Peso)				
Financial	.000740	.000746	1352.00	1340.00
Venezuela (Bolivar)				
Floating rate	.02123	.02056	47.10	48.63
— — —				
SDR	1.42886	1.41574	.69986	.70634
ECU	1.35212	1.34275	....	....

Special Drawing Rights (SDR) are based on exchange rates for the U.S., German, British, French and Japanese currencies. Source: International Monetary Fund.

European Currency Unit (ECU) is based on a basket of community currencies. Source: European Community Commission.

z-Not quoted. c-corrected.

EXCHANGE RATES

Wednesday, October 10, 1990

The New York foreign exchange selling rates below apply to trading among banks in amounts of $1 million and more, as quoted at 3 p.m. Eastern time by Bankers Trust Co. Retail transactions provide fewer units of foreign currency per dollar.

Country	U.S. $ equiv. Wed.	Tues.	Currency per U.S. $ Wed.	Tues.
Argentina (Austral) ...	.0001757	.0001701	5693.14	5880.28
Australia (Dollar)	.8273	.8335	1.2088	1.1998
Austria (Schilling)	.09298	.09307	10.75	10.75
Bahrain (Dinar)	2.6532	2.6532	.3769	.3769
Belgium (Franc)				
Commercial rate	.03176	.03182	31.48	31.43
Brazil (Cruzeiro)	.01152	.01115	86.82	89.70
Britain (Pound)	1.9670	1.9660	.5084	.5086
30-Day Forward	1.9575	1.9561	.5109	.5112
90-Day Forward	1.9410	1.9400	.5152	.5155
180-Day Forward	1.9196	1.9178	.5209	.5214
Canada (Dollar)	.8703	.8690	1.1490	1.1507
30-Day Forward	.8669	.8656	1.1536	1.1553
90-Day Forward	.8611	.8598	1.1613	1.1630
180-Day Forward	.8532	.8520	1.1720	1.1737
Chile (Official rate) ...	.003072	.003072	325.54	325.54
China (Renmimbi)	.211864	.211864	4.7200	4.7200
Colombia (Peso)	.001912	.001912	523.00	523.00
Denmark (Krone)	.1717	.1716	5.8250	5.8275
Ecuador (Sucre)				
Floating rate	.001168	.001168	856.00	856.00
Finland (Markka)	.27670	.27655	3.6140	3.6160
France (Franc)	.19550	.19552	5.1150	5.1145
30-Day Forward	.19522	.19524	5.1225	5.1220
90-Day Forward	.19465	.19467	5.1375	5.1370
180-Day Forward	.19366	.19368	5.1637	5.1632
Germany (Mark)	.6545	.6547	1.5280	1.5275
30-Day Forward	.6544	.6545	1.5281	1.5278
90-Day Forward	.6539	.6539	1.5293	1.5293
180-Day Forward	.6528	.6522	1.5319	1.5332
Greece (Drachma)	.006536	.006562	153.00	152.40
Hong Kong (Dollar) ...	.12895	.12896	7.7550	7.7545
India (Rupee)	.05556	.05556	18.00	18.00
Indonesia (Rupiah)	.0005365	.0005365	1864.00	1864.00
Ireland (Punt)	1.7555	1.7560	.5696	.5695
Israel (Shekel)	.4943	.4943	2.0229	2.0229
Italy (Lira)	.0008726	.0008730	1146.00	1145.50
Japan (Yen)	.007713	.007648	129.65	130.75
30-Day Forward	.007715	.007651	129.61	130.71
90-Day Forward	.007712	.007649	129.66	130.74
180-Day Forward	.007708	.007642	129.74	130.86
Jordan (Dinar)	1.5485	1.5485	.6458	.6458
Kuwait (Dinar)	z	z	z	z
Lebanon (Pound)	.000952	.000952	1050.00	1050.00
Malaysia (Ringgit)	.3707	.3707	2.6975	2.6975
Malta (Lira)	3.3557	3.3557	.2980	.2980
Mexico (Peso)				
Floating rate	.0003478	.0003478	2875.00	2875.00
Netherland (Guilder) .	.5802	.5807	1.7235	1.7220
New Zealand (Dollar) .	.6175	.6205	1.6194	1.6116
Norway (Krone)	.1691	.1692	5.9145	5.9100
Pakistan (Rupee)	.0462	.0462	21.65	21.65
Peru (Inti)	.00000230	.00000230	435540.07	435540.07
Philippines (Peso)	.04032	.04032	24.80	24.80
Portugal (Escudo)	.007454	.007454	134.15	134.15
Saudi Arabia (Riyal) ..	.26734	.26734	3.7406	3.7406
Singapore (Dollar)	.5777	.5784	1.7310	1.7290
South Africa (Rand)				
Commercial rate	z	.3941	z	2.5374
Financial rate	z	.2667	z	3.7495
South Korea (Won) ...	.0013986	.0013986	715.00	715.00
Spain (Peseta)	.010395	.010409	96.20	96.07
Sweden (Krona)	.1775	.1773	5.6350	5.6410
Switzerland (Franc) ..	.7794	.7834	1.2830	1.2765
30-Day Forward	.7797	.7836	1.2826	1.2761
90-Day Forward	.7797	.7837	1.2825	1.2760
180-Day Forward	.7791	.7831	1.2835	1.2770
Taiwan (Dollar)	.037341	.036657	26.78	27.28
Thailand (Baht)	.04011	.04011	24.93	24.93
Turkey (Lira)	.0003712	.0003701	2693.97	2702.00
United Arab (Dirham) .	.2723	.2723	3.6725	3.6725
Uruguay (New Peso)				
Financial	.000740	.000740	1352.00	1352.00
Venezuela (Bolivar)				
Floating rate	.02123	.02123	47.10	47.10
— — —				
SDR	1.42794	1.42886	.70031	.69986
ECU	1.35105	1.35212	....	....

Special Drawing Rights (SDR) are based on exchange rates for the U.S., German, British, French and Japanese currencies. Source: International Monetary Fund.

European Currency Unit (ECU) is based on a basket of community currencies. Source: European Community Commission.

z-Not quoted.

Shown here are the rates of exchange for two successive days as shown in the October 10 and October 11 issues of *The Wall Street Journal*.

exchange rate stated in dollars per yen will decline. The dollar will depreciate. If the Japanese exporters had demanded payment in yen, the result would have been an increased demand for yen on the U.S. foreign exchange markets. This increased demand would drive up the dollar price of yen. The yen would appreciate. It should be obvious that the effect on the exchange rate is the same in both cases: The dollar depreciates relative to the yen.

Second, if major firms, including banks, believe that a currency is about to depreciate they may dump their foreign exchange holdings of that currency. The result will be an increase in the supply of that currency and a decrease in demand for that currency on foreign exchange markets.

Third, when a currency is devalued, there is often an increased demand for it on world foreign exchange markets as firms seek to exploit the lower prices of commodities, securities, and other assets.

Fourth, the needs of many Third World nations to service dollar-denominated debt and other obligations lead to an increased demand for dollars in those countries and, therefore, the depreciation of that currency in terms of U.S. dollars. A good example of this was the unusually large demand for U.S. dollars in Mexico, Brazil, and Argentina in 1984 as these countries attempted to keep current their interest payments to American banks.

One of the most significant factors that influences exchange rates (especially in the short run) is differences in the rate of interest among countries. Individuals or firms from countries with lower interest rates will try to exchange their currency for that of the nation with the higher interest rate so that they can make investments in the high-interest-rate nation; thus, demand for the currency of the high-interest-rate nation will increase. Relatedly, firms from the high-interest-rate nation will borrow off-shore and then exchange those funds for their home country's currency, thus creating still greater demand. This is exactly what occurred during the early years of the Reagan administration, in 1980–1982. Higher U.S. interest rates created a very strong dollar.

Indeed, it can be demonstrated that exchange rates will change in response to differing national interest rates such that differences in national interest rates will be eliminated. This is called the *international Fisher effect*.

Another major, albeit long-term factor influencing exchange rates is relative inflation rates of the two nations. In the long term, exchange rates will change to maintain equal purchasing power among the nations. For example, if a market basket of goods sells for $10 in the United States, and the same basket of goods would sell for 20 francs in Switzerland, then the exchange rate should be $1 = 2 SF. As inflation in each country changes the cost of that market basket of goods, the exchange rate should change to maintain a parity of purchasing power. For example, if inflation in the United States were 11 percent but in Switzerland only 1 percent, then the exchange rate should change proportionately. This is generally called the *purchasing power parity* theory.

$$
\begin{aligned}
\$10 \times 1.11 &= 20 \, \text{SF} \times 1.01 \\
\$11.10 &= 20.2 \, \text{SF} \\
\$1.00 &= 20.2 \, \text{SF}/11.10 \\
\$1.00 &= 1.82 \, \text{SF}
\end{aligned}
$$

There are numerous other factors that have an influence on exchange rates. Political instability often leads to the flight of capital from a country as citizens of that country convert their domestic currency into that of another country for safety reasons. This generally results in downward pressure on the domestic currency relative to major currencies. Similarly, the various economic indicators that are published by governments can have an impact on the value of a currency. If the news is favorable, the currency will appreciate in value, and conversely, it will depreciate if the news is unfavorable. An increase in the amount of money in circulation will generally cause a fall in the value of the currency in the expectation of inflationary pressure. Thus, those with liquid assets seek to convert their holdings into those of a more stable currency. Speculators might add to the demand for a particular currency in the expectation that its value will increase in the future.

Foreign exchange rates fluctuate daily depending upon supply and demand, which in turn are affected by economic and noneconomic factors.

Rates Under a Free Gold Standard

Wide fluctuations in rates of exchange are commonplace in spite of governmental efforts to stabilize them. Such was not the case when nations were on a free gold standard or a gold exchange standard (currency backed by the currency of a country that is on the gold standard). When nations were on the free gold standard, the exchange rate between currencies was determined by each currency's gold value (par of exchange). Thus the purchasing power of each currency was known. Any fluctuations in exchange rates were limited to the operation of *gold points*.

Gold points were the upper and lower limits within which exchange rates might fluctuate before it became cheaper to make payment in gold rather than foreign exchange. That is, under a free gold standard, a currency that was backed by gold could be freely converted into gold at the rate determined by the government. To make payment for imports, a buyer could either go to the open market and purchase foreign exchange (including a draft or commercial bill of exchange) whose value was determined by supply and demand, or go to the central bank and obtain gold at the established price. If one were to ship gold, it would be necessary to pay for its packing, transportation, and insurance; therefore, if the cost for the foreign exchange was greater than the price of gold plus the costs associated with its shipment, the purchaser would make payment in gold. Under these

Gold certificates like this one illustrate the significance of precious metals for providing the foundation value of currency and other financial instruments.

conditions, the price of foreign exchange could not fluctuate by more than the cost of shipping the gold. If it was more favorable to make payment in foreign exchange, the increase in demand would cause the price to rise. If the demand for foreign exchange fell off, its price would decrease, but not by more than the limits of the gold points.

Under a free gold standard, exchange rate fluctuations are limited because of the operation of the gold points.

Government Intervention

Role of Central Banks

Nations now operate on a *managed paper standard*. Authorities within a country determine the amount of money in circulation. The amount of currency that may be printed is not limited, as was the case under a gold or silver standard. In most countries, determining the amount of money in circulation is the function of the nation's central bank. In the United States, the role of the central bank is performed by the Federal Reserve System (FRS).

The members of the Board of Governors of the Federal Reserve System are appointed by the President of the United States and are theoretically independent of politics. It is the function of the board to determine and to control the amount of money in circulation. Four major methods are used by the FRS and other central banks to control the supply of money and exchange rates. Of these, three are economic in character (see Figure 4.2).

Expand   Buy ⟵————————————Securities——————————→ Sell   Contract
Money   Reduce ⟵——————————Discount Rate ——————————→Increase   Money
Supply   Lower⟵————————Reserve Requirement——————————→Raise   Supply

Figure 4.2   Methods Used by the U.S. Federal Reserve to Control the Money Supply

First, through the operation of the Open Market Committee, the Board of Governors goes into the market and buys government securities (i.e., treasury bills) if it feels there is a need to increase the money supply. Such payments end up in commercial banks that use them to make loans, which increase the supply of money. If the board feels there is a surplus of money in circulation, it will attempt to decrease the amount by selling securities in the market to absorb some of the money supply. This reduces the loan-making capabilities of commerical banks. The FRS may also buy or sell foreign exchange to influence the value of the U.S. dollar.

Second, the Board of Governors can change the discount rates—that is, the interest rate charged to commercial banks that are members of the Federal Reserve System. An increase in the discount rate will discourage commercial bank borrowing. This in turn will tend to reduce the amount of money loaned to individuals and corporations, increase the interest rate charged to individuals and corporations, and increase the interest rate paid to individuals on demand deposits. This is done to influence the amount of money in circulation (checkbook money). Conversely, if discount rates are reduced, banks are encouraged to borrow from the Federal Reserve System to make loans to their customers, thus increasing the amount of money in circulation.[1]

Third, the Board of Governors can control the amount of loans commercial banks may make by changing the reserve requirement. The reserve requirement is the percentage of a bank's assets that must be held in a liquid form, thus reducing by that percentage the funds available to be loaned. A lower reserve requirement enables banks to make more loans, thus increasing the amount of money in circulation.[2]

A fourth method that the Board of Governors may use to influence the amount of money in circulation is moral suasion. The board does not take any official action but pressures commercial banks to tighten loan standards, thus cutting down on the amount of checkbook money being created.

The number of dollars in circulation and their value are of direct concern to many countries because most of the world's trade is conducted in dollars and because many smaller countries have pegged their currencies to the U.S. dollar—in other words, the values of their currencies fluctuate with the value of the dollar. Singapore is an example of a nation whose currency is pegged to the U.S. dollar. The result of such linkages is that the actions of the U.S. monetary authorities have little if any effect on the exchange rate between the dollar and these currencies. This combined with dollar reserves held outside of the United States, the Eurodollar market, and the

Through central banks, governments attempt to prevent wide fluctuations in exchange rates by controlling the amount of money in circulation.

Asian-dollar markets has resulted in a lack of control over the value of the dollar. The dollar, in addition to being a national currency, is in fact a world currency.

Exchange Controls

With the exception of prohibitions against carrying large sums of U.S. currency out of the country or special currency provisions for travel to countries with which the United States does not have diplomatic relations, the United States has very few exchange controls. The same is not true for many other countries. Although exchange controls are most common in developing nations, even many advanced industrialized nations have rather stringent controls. In the case of developing nations, exchange controls are often established to conserve a limited supply of "hard currencies" (dollars, yen, Swiss francs, German marks, and so forth) for the import of essential commodities. However, exchange controls may also be adopted as a tool of commercial policy and to prevent foreign manipulation of the value of the nation's currency.

Regardless of the purpose, the mechanics of exchange control are similar. Usually, a nation will designate some agency such as the central bank to be responsible for exchange control. It is the function of this agency to determine the allocation of foreign exchange to those demanding the foreign currency. The first step for those requesting foreign exchange is to apply for a permit or license for foreign currency. Applicants must indicate the proposed use for the exchange. If the application is approved and the license is issued authorizing the purchase of foreign exchange, the applicant must deposit with the agency an amount of domestic currency necessary to cover the purchase of foreign currency. This foreign exchange will usually be given in the form of a draft that the importer may use to make payment abroad.

Since the rate of exchange is determined by the government, foreign currency is usually sold to the buyer at a cost that is greater than the official rate (the rate at which the government will buy foreign exchange). The difference between the buying rate and the selling rate, the *spread*, provides the government with a profit to cover administrative costs. It is also common for governments to use sliding scale or multiple rates of exchange. Under a multiple exchange rate system, the rate charged to an importer is dependent upon the type of goods being imported. For the import of commodities that the government deems essential, a more favorable rate will be granted. The rate for less essential commodities will be less favorable, and for luxury items, least favorable. For example, if Great Britain were using exchange controls, the Bank of England would function as the control agency. If the official rate between the pound sterling and the U.S. dollar were £1 = $1.70 U.S., and Britain were using a multiple exchange rate system, the Bank might give the exporter only $1.65 for every pound sterling for the import of essential commodities, $1.60 for the import of less essential goods, and $1.55 for the import of luxury items. This would discourage the import of these nonessential items.

When exchange controls are adopted, nations often commandeer all foreign exchange that is earned from exports; all foreign exchange must be turned over to the government. Thus, an exporter who earns foreign exchange may not use it to import from abroad but must sell it back to the government and then go through the process of applying for the foreign exchange like any other importer. As might be expected, the adoption of exchange controls creates uncertainty in international transactions. A firm exporting to a buyer in an exchange control nation does not know whether the importer will be able to obtain the necessary foreign exchange to complete the transaction. Because of these uncertainties many firms attempt to circumvent the costly, time-consuming, and often highly politicized process of applying for foreign exchange. This topic is discussed in Chapter 15, "Exporting, Importing, and Financing International Trade."

Clearing Agreements

Exchange controls often result in agreements between countries to settle the trade transactions of their residents without the transfer of foreign exchange. The importer in one country will pay domestic currency to the government's clearing account. The exporting firm in the second country receives payment from its own government's clearing account. In reality, this is a form of exchange restriction since the respective governments are handling the financing of the trade transactions that are taking place between the two countries, and the agreements regulate the flow of exchange between the parties.

Exchange controls and clearing agreements influence the supply and demand for foreign exchange.

Mechanisms to Promote Exchange Stability

Immediately after World War II, a number of countries had an inadequate supply of dollars to purchase necessary commodities from the United States. To ensure the import of essential commodities, some of these countries formed *currency blocs*, or agreements to use a common currency for all transactions among themselves.

Great Britain and the Commonwealth countries formed what was referred to as the Sterling Bloc, since they agreed to use the pound sterling in all transactions among the members. Any Commonwealth country that earned dollars was required to exchange these for pound sterling at the Bank of England, and when dollars were required, application had to be made to the Bank of England. Pounds sterling had to be deposited with the central bank in exchange for the dollars received. As should be apparent, a currency bloc functions in a manner similar to exchange controls, only on a multinational basis.

The member countries pegged their currencies to the pound sterling. Thus, the currencies of Commonwealth countries moved in accord with the British pound sterling. They kept their sterling balances and other liquid assets in London. The pound sterling served as the principal reserve for the currencies of the member countries. In the Far East, the Japanese yen played a similar role in international transactions.

International efforts to promote exchange stability occurred in 1944 when the *International Monetary Fund* was established. The IMF adopted a fixed but adjustable exchange system wherein fluctuations were not to exceed 1 percent of the par value of the currency. This was changed to 2.25 percent in 1971, and was abandoned in favor of the floating exchange rates in 1973. (See Chapter 6 on the operation of the IMF.)

Most central banks enter the foreign exchange markets to prevent wide fluctuations in the rates of exchange. This is especially true when the U.S. dollar gets out of line with a particular domestic currency. The Bank of Japan uses its reserves of dollars to prevent the dollar from appreciating too much in terms of the yen, by selling dollars on the open market or buying dollars when they decrease in value relative to the yen. The central banks of other countries operate in a similar manner, buying or selling U.S. dollars to stabilize the exchange relationship.

When none of these actions by central banks is effective in creating a balance between worldwide supply and demand for a nation's currency, a floating currency increases (appreciates) or decreases (depreciates) in value. If the currency is not one that floats on foreign exchange markets, the nation will come under increasing pressure to change its official exchange rate. (See Global Insight.) The usual situation is one in which supply of nation's currency exceeds demands, and a devaluation is called for.

Nations have moved from fixed exchange rates to floating rates, with central banks attempting to stabilize the value of their currencies relative to the U.S. dollar.

MONEY MARKETS

Sales of goods or services among firms of different nations are facilitated by the existence of the foreign exchange markets. In the absence of such markets, sellers of goods would have to accumulate foreign exchange that they could not spend in their home nation, or they would have to barter for goods that could be resold in their home nation. If these markets were not fair and efficient, international transactions would be extremely risky, costly, and difficult. Fortunately, foreign exchange markets and other institutions involved in international financial transactions have been developed and maintained for centuries.

Foreign Exchange Markets

The foreign exchange markets are the "financial system for the exchange of currencies."[3] Transactions take place in large financial centers where commercial banks, brokers, and dealers in foreign exchange conduct their businesses. The most important of these markets are located in New York City, London, Frankfort, Paris, Zurich, Amsterdam, Milan, Tokyo, Toronto, and

Brazil's New Cruzado Increasingly Overvalued

The gap between the official New Cruzado (NCz) to U.S. dollar exchange rate and the so-called parallel (free market) rate has reached new heights. The official rate remains 1.03 NCz per dollar, while the parallel rate has topped 2.40—a 132 percent differential. This gap is partly due to the overvaluation of the official rate but mostly reflects capital flight from Brazil, distrust of local currency money markets due to the continuing deterioration of Brazil's economic situation, and apprehensions concerning the forthcoming elections. The high demand for U.S. dollars in Argentina is reducing their supply in international money markets, thus adding to the rise of the parallel market rate in Brazil.

Source: Adapted from "Management Alert," *Business Latin America*, May 8, 1989, p.143.

Hong Kong. As a group, they constitute a single world market because they are closely linked together by telecommunications networks. This makes possible transactions among the large commercial banks that have international departments or divisions located in these centers.

Functions of Commercial Banks

Commercial banks perform a variety of foreign exchange functions. They engage in lending by discounting drafts or bills of exchange. By participating in hedging contracts, they enable buyers and sellers to minimize the risks that arise from the fluctuations in the rates of exchange. When they buy and sell foreign exchange for individual customers, they are actually converting the currency of one country to that of another. They constitute the major vehicle for making payments and are directly involved in the transfer of funds from one country to another. The rate at which funds are transferred is based on the existing rate of exchange. However, the cost varies with the method of transfer that is used.

The most common methods of transfer are by cable or telegraphic transfer, sight drafts, and time bills of exchange. An international cable transfer is accomplished when a local bank telegraphs funds to a correspondent bank (agent) in a foreign country. This is very much like the domestic telegraphic transfer of funds. Sight drafts are used by an importer (purchaser) to make payment for an international purchase. The draft is made out to the exporter (seller) in the seller's currency and is payable upon presentation to the importer's correspondent bank in the seller's country. Since receipt is not instantaneous, the payee (exporter) will receive an amount slightly less than the face value of the draft due to interest charges. Time drafts are those that are drawn by the exporter on the importer calling for payment at a future date: 30-, 60-, 90-, or 180-day drafts are most common. Exporters often sell these time drafts to banks as a means of receiving their funds sooner. When a bank buys a draft, it is actually lending money to the exporter on the basis of the promise of an importer to honor the draft at maturity. Since payment of the draft is deferred, a bank will pay the drawer (exporter) the face value of the draft less an interest charge. Note: Some banks may assess a service change in addition to the interest. (See Chapter 15 for a more detailed description of financing international transactions.)

> Commercial banks function as lending agencies, participate in hedging contracts, convert currencies, and transfer funds.

Exchange Hedging

Hedging is the utilization of counterbalancing transactions to protect oneself from possible loss. The simplest example of a hedge might be explained in terms of betting. If one bets $10 that team A will beat team B and team A wins, one will win $10. However, if team A loses to team B, there will be a loss of $10. If, for some reason, one decides that team A is unlikely to win, that person may hedge and place a second bet that team B will win. Ignoring the possibility of a tie score, the loss of one bet will be counterbalanced with a win in the other bet. Regardless of the outcome, no money will be lost from the bets.

Foreign exchange hedging is a method of transferring the risk of possible loss from the fluctuation in exchange rates to a third party. This is done by making a contract with a bank to buy or sell foreign exchange at a future date. If the exporter makes a £10,000 sale to an importer, payable in the importer's currency 30 days from today, there is no assurance that the rate of exchange will be the same as it is today (e.g., £1.00 = $1.50). If the rate changes to £1.00 = $1.40, the exporter will still receive £10,000, but when converted into dollars it will amount to $14,000 rather than the $15,000 the exporter expected. There will be an exchange loss of $1,000. On the other hand, if the rate of exchange changes to £1.00 = $1.60, the £10,000 will convert into $16,000, or provide the exporter with a windfall profit of $1,000. Although this may sound wonderful, most exporters would prefer to make a profit from the sale of the product and minimize the chance of a foreign exchange loss rather than to try to speculate on foreign exchange gains.

To eliminate the possibility of a foreign exchange loss, the exporter can make a forward hedging contract with a bank to sell £10,000, 30 days hence at a fixed exchange rate, the *forward rate*.[4] This forward rate is either given outright (i.e., £1 = $1.485) or in terms of a premium or discount on the current spot rate (1 percent below the current spot rate). If the currency is considered "hard," the bank will make such a contract; however, if the currency is "soft" or unstable, it may refuse. Thus, there is no possibility of loss or gain from the fluctuation in the rate of exchange except the costs associated with the contract to sell pounds sterling forward: *selling forward*. The exporter might end up with the situation shown in Figure 4.3.

In a seller's market, an exporter may attempt to transfer the risks due to the fluctuations in the rates of exchange to the buyer. This is done by

Contract Exchange Rate:	£1.00 = $1.50
Contract fee:	1%
Receipt from customer	£10,000
Dollar value of receipt	$15,000
Fee:	−150
Net receipt from sale	$14,850

Figure 4.3   The Effect of Selling Forward on the Revenue from an International Sale

quoting prices in the exporter's currency. In this situation it will probably be in the buyer's best interest to hedge. Note that the buyer (importer) can hedge in the same manner as described above for the seller (exporter), *buying forward*. It is not unusual for the exporter and importer to share the cost of the forward contract.

Transferring the risk to the bank does not mean that the bank subjects itself to exchange risks. For every contract to buy pound sterling, the bank will make an offsetting contract to sell pound sterling; the bank will *hedge*. Thus, exchange fluctuation effects cancel themselves out and the bank profits from the charges for the hedging contract.

Exchange Transactions

Speculation

Hedging must not be confused with speculation. If an exporter or an importer decides not to make a hedging contract, the effect is speculation in foreign exchange. The risk is deliberately taken in the attempt to profit from exchange rate changes.

A contract to buy currency that is made in expectation that the foreign currency will rise in value is called a *long transaction*. Selling foreign currency in the expectation that it will depreciate in value is called a *short transaction*. Individuals and firms may execute these transactions through the foreign exchange departments of commercial banks or in futures markets, such as the international money markets. Futures markets enable speculators to operate on margin—that is, they are required to deposit only a percentage of the value of the transaction.

Speculation is an attempt to make a profit from fluctuations in the exchange rate.

The following is an example of speculation in foreign exchange (see Figure 4.4). An agreement to sell £10,000 in 30 days for $15,000 will be profitable only if the rate of exchange is less than £1.00 = $1.50. Thus, if the rate of exchange 30 days from today is £1.00 = $1.40, the speculator will purchase £10,000 for $14,000 in the spot market, deliver the £10,000 for the $15,000 as per the contract, and make a profit of $1,000 on the transaction.

Contract on April 1 to deliver

£10,000 on April 30 for	$15,000
Cost of £10,000 on April 30	−$14,000
Profit from the transaction	$1,000

(cost $14,000; collect $15,000)

Figure 4.4   An Example of Profit from Speculation

Arbitrage

Arbitrage is a type of transaction wherein a profit arises because of the simultaneous differences in the prices of commodities, including foreign exchange, in different markets. Arbitrage transactions are not speculative because they are the simultaneous sales and purchases of foreign exchange in two different markets. A hypothetical example of such a transaction will help explain its operation. Suppose today's rate of exchange between the pound sterling and the U.S. dollar is £1 = $1.68 in New York and £1 = $1.70 in London. One can readily see that a profit can be made by purchasing pounds sterling in New York City and then selling the pounds in London for dollars. For every pound sterling exchanged, there will be a profit of 2 cents.

Certain other conditions must exist before arbitrage transactions can be profitable. Exchange controls cannot exist for the currencies used in such a transaction. In other words, such transactions would not be possible in countries that prohibit the conversion of currencies or that require delays in the purchase or sale of foreign exchange. The participants must be well financed because profits might amount to only a fraction of a cent for every dollar exchanged. Instant communication is essential if one is to take advantage of the fluctuations in currencies in different markets at any given instant. Given these conditions, such transactions tend to eliminate differences in exchange rates among different financial markets.

Arbitrage transactions might be classified as simple or compound. In *simple arbitrage*, only two currencies and two countries are involved, as in the above example. In *compound arbitrage*, the transactions become more complicated because several currencies and several countries are involved in the transactions. Only the arbitrage departments of large commercial banks or financial institutions become involved in compound arbitrage.

Arbitrage is a type of transaction wherein a profit arises from the simultaneous purchase and sale of foreign exchange in different markets.

Currency and Credit Swaps

A *currency swap* is a method of raising capital in a foreign market without paying a currency premium. For example, a company in the United States might have a financing requirement in London. At the same time, a company in London might have a financing requirement in the United States. What these firms can do is to provide each other with cash. The U.S.

company will provide the British company with cash in the United States, while the British company will provide cash in Great Britain to the U.S. company. They enter into an agreement to reverse the transaction at some future date. These transactions are usually carried out by subsidiaries of major multinational firms. The interest rates and the date for future reverse exchanges are usually agreed upon at the outset.

A swap is a hedge against possible loss due to the fluctuation in the rate of exchange because the foreign currency liability is matched by a foreign currency asset. The loan does not require government approval and the cost of the funds is usually less than borrowing from other sources.

A *credit swap* is an exchange of currencies between a company and a bank, usually the central bank, when local credit is not available and where there is no forward exchange market. An American company will deposit dollars with the foreign central bank and will receive a foreign currency loan at the current rate. Even if the foreign currency drops in value, the firm will repay only the original amount. After repayment, the central bank will repay the United States company in dollars. This type of transaction provides the central bank with dollars free of charge for the period of the swap and provides the firm with both local currency and the original amount of dollars regardless of the rate of exchange. Credit swaps minimize the risks and costs in a weak-currency country.

> Currency and credit swaps are hedges through the exchange of currency or credit against possible loss due to fluctuations in the exchange rate.

International Money Markets

The principal foreign exchange markets are also international money markets. These are centers dealing in currencies that have a forward exchange market (bought and sold for delivery in the future), are freely convertible, and are available in sufficient quantitites to be used for making loans. These markets provide funds to large corporations, national governments, and international institutions whose opportunities for long-term borrowing are restricted in local national markets. International money markets provide capital to banks and commercial customers who need funds for financing international trade and investments. Many Third World countries turn to these markets to avoid borrowing from agencies such as the International Monetary Fund because of IMF restrictions. (Loan policies of the IMF are discussed in Chapter 6.)

Eurocurrency Market

Since most commodities entering international trade are priced in U.S. dollars, and dollars are most generally acceptable as a means of payment, it is not surprising that the U.S. dollar is the dominant currency in the international money markets.

The most important international money markets are located in western Europe, although other important ones are located in New York, Tokyo, Hong Kong, Singapore, and other major financial centers. London is unique in that its banks have been accepting currencies of foreign denomination for deposit since the 1920s. Since the 1950s, the dollar portion of the Eurocurrency deposits constitutes between 75 and 80 percent of the total currencies of foreign origin. Its importance is due primarily to the dollar having replaced the British pound sterling as the international reserve currency.

The dollars that are deposited in foreign banks or in branches of U.S. banks in western Europe are referred to as Eurodollars. Similarly, other national currencies that are deposited in banks outside of the country of origin are referred to as Eurosterling, Euromarks, Eurofrancs, Euroyen, and so forth.

The sources of dollars in the Eurocurrency market can be traced to the initial dollar deposits that were made by the USSR. Because of their desire to retain their dollar reserves for purchase of goods from the West, yet unwilling to keep these dollars in the United States, the Soviets sought to deposit these funds in western Europe. When the banks in London accepted these funds for deposit, large amounts of dollars were made available for loan purposes. Soon other sources added to the supply of dollar deposits. Knowing that these funds are completely liquid while drawing the best short-term interest, multinational corporations deposited their surplus cash with these banks. Governments and businesses, including other European banks desiring to hold dollars outside of the United States, deposited their funds in the Eurocurrency market. Further encouraging the flow of funds to the Eurocurrency market was the passage of Regulation Q in 1958 by the Board of Governors of the Federal Reserve System, placing a ceiling on the interest rates U.S. banks were allowed to pay on deposits. Depositers are able to earn higher returns through Eurodollar deposits than at home, without having to exchange their dollars for some other currency. Thus, central banks and other financial institutions deposited their dollar reserves in the Eurocurrency market rather than investing them in the U.S. money market, adding to the supply of Eurodollars. In recent years, the OPEC countries have been the major suppliers of dollar funds to the Eurocurrency market. Adding to these dollars were the proceeds of Eurobonds (discussed later in the next section). The Eurocurrency banks also sell their own certificates of deposits to large investors. Well-established secondary markets exist for these securities, providing maximum liquidity. Eurocurrency banks have numerous advantages over U.S. commercial banks, explaining their rapid growth:

1. No regulations regarding minimum reserve requirements
2. No payment of insurance premiums on deposit accounts
3. Higher interest rates on deposits due to no regulations
4. Interest rates on loans lower than those of other financial institutions because there is little danger of default

5. Low per-dollar processing costs because of the large size of the loans, and because most borrowers are governments, central banks, international financial institutions, or large multinational corporations

6. No reporting and disclosure requirements

Borrowers turn to these markets because terms are more attractive than those available domestically. International corporations are able to borrow large amounts that are generally unavailable from domestic banks at favorable rates. If the amount desired is too large for a single bank, syndicates or consortiums of banks will be formed to oblige the borrower. The rate that is charged is slightly higher than the London Interbank Offer Rate (LIBOR). The rate charged is generally between one-fourth of 1 percent to 2 percent above the LIBOR rate depending upon the credit standing of the borrower, the time period, and other factors; nevertheless, this rate is still lower than those charged by most other sources.

One might question the effect of the Eurocurrency market on the monetary policy of countries such as the United States, which has such a large amount of its currency in circulation beyond its borders. There is no doubt that currency deposits outside of the country of origin mean that a country will have little control over those deposits and will thus have less influence over the value of the nation's currency since the country's monetary policies are in part being circumvented. A good example of this occurred when the U.S. government adopted an Interest Equalization Tax in 1963 to restrict the outflow of dollars from the country. To evade these restrictions, borrowers turned to the Eurocurrency market, which provided an alternative source of capital for borrowers who sought dollar exchange. American corporations also deposited their earnings from overseas operations abroad rather than repatriating them to the United States. This made capital available for their overseas operations when needed without their having to worry about regulations limiting the outflow of capital. At the same time, the earnings on their deposits were greater than elsewhere, while the payment of some taxes was postponed since the earnings had not been repatriated to the United States.

Excluding interbank deposits, the Eurocurrency market is estimated to be in the hundreds of billions of dollars, and growing. In 1982 the Eurocurrency market was estimated at $915 billion U.S.[5] By 1984, it had increased to $2,257 billion.[6]

Eurobonds

Eurobonds came into being because of the high cost of borrowing in the United States with the passage of the Interest Equalization Tax in 1963. The popularity of the Eurobonds arose during the 1960s and 1970s because of capital controls and other restrictions on borrowings in the United States. American corporations found it advantageous to seek funds in Europe rather than in the United States. Eurobonds are denominated in a currency other than that of the country in which the bonds are sold. Thus, a dollar bond may be sold in London, yen bond in Hong Kong, pound sterling bond in Paris, and so forth.

The issuing firms are large international corporations that are in need of large amounts of capital, usually denominated in U.S. dollars. Exxon, Texaco, IBM, Proctor & Gamble, and other large international corporations have raised funds abroad through the flotation of Eurobonds. National governments and international agencies such as the World Bank also raise capital through Eurobonds. As with Eurocurrency, the reason for the popularity of Eurobonds is that such issuances are not subject to the regulatory constraints that exist in the home country, such as the United States. There is no registration or disclosure requirement, and the income is untaxed. Since they are issued to the bearer, they provide anonymity to the investor. These bonds are often convertible into common stock and may even be denominated in ECUs (European Currency Units), which represent a basket of currencies of the European Community. There is greater flexibility in the issuance of the bonds. The international character of the bonds means that they can be issued in several countries simultaneously. The issuer can select the currency in which the bond will be floated.

These bonds are generally of long-term maturity, often between 6 and 15 years. According to one estimate, 60 to 85 percent of the borrowers are large industrial and financial corporations.[7] Other borrowers are national governments and international financial institutions such as the International Bank for Reconstruction and Development.

International money markets are exchanges for currencies that have a forward market, are fully convertible, and are available in large quantities.

SUMMARY

When a sale is made in domestic trade, there is no need to worry about a possible loss due to the fluctuation in the rate of exchange because the whole country is on the same currency standard. However, as soon as the political boundaries among nations are crossed, one must become familiar with a different type of currency and the relationship of its value to the domestic currency. This problem arises because the value of currency is no longer precisely determined by its gold conversion value. There is no longer the alternative of making payment in gold (except in rare cases). Foreign exchange markets provide a system of exchanging currencies. Foreign exchange rates fluctuate according to supply and demand just as the prices of commodities fluctuate. There are also nonmarket forces that affect supply and demand, such as government intervention or political instability.

Through their central banks, governments attempt to prevent wide fluctuations in the rate of exchange. This is accomplished through buying and selling certain currencies in the open market. Such transactions might be undertaken in an attempt to influence the value of a particular currency, which will affect exports and imports, or for political or other reasons.

To protect itself from possible losses arising from the fluctuations in the rates of exchange, business firms make hedging contracts. They transfer the risks to a third party, just as one might take out risk insurance. Such forward contracts protect the firm from possible losses resulting from wide fluctuations in the rates of exchange, but they do require the payment of a fee.

If a firm does not hedge under conditions of uncertain future rates of exchange, it is speculating that exchange rates will not fluctuate or that it will make a profit from the spread between the spot rate and the future rate of exchange. This transaction must not be confused with arbitrage, which takes advantage of simultaneous differences in exchange rates among different markets.

KEY TERMS AND CONCEPTS

Arbitrage

Cable rates

Commercial bills of exchange

Credit and currency swaps

Demand or sight rates

Discount drafts

Eurocurrency market

Exchange controls

Exchange hedging

Foreign exchange

Foreign exchange markets

Forward rate

Free gold standard

Gold exchange standard

Gold points

Hard and soft currencies

Hedging contracts

Long transaction

Margin

Moral suasion

Open market operations

Rate of exchange

Required reserves

Short transaction

Sliding scale foreign exchange rate

Speculation

Spot rate

Spread

REVIEW QUESTIONS

1. What are the major functions of the commercial banks in the foreign exchange markets?

2. Explain the differences between transferring funds by cable and by a bill of exchange.

3. What is meant by a forward exchange market? Why do these rates differ from the spot rates?

4. What are Eurodollars?

5. Explain why international currency markets exist.

6. Why do rates of exchange fluctuate?

7. Explain why exchange rates tended to fluctuate less under a free gold standard than under the current system of a managed paper standard.

8. Explain how the Federal Reserve System of the United States attempts to control the amount of money in circulation and the dollar exchange rate.

9. Explain the relationship between the U.S. money supply and the dollar exchange rate.

10. Explain how multiple exchange rates might be used and why a nation would adopt such controls.

11. What is meant by exchange hedging? When might it be advantageous for an exporter to hedge? An importer?

12. What is meant by speculation? How does speculation differ from exchange arbitrage?

DISCUSSION CASE

Multinational Firms Hedge Their Bets In Brazil

The overvaluation of the cruzado and the prospect for erratic movement of the exchange rate has left MNFs seeking cover under the dollar. The uncertainties resulting from Brazilian policies have caused MNFs to seek methods for hedging potential exchange losses.

Critics of the new policy of tying devaluation to changes in general price index (IGP) rather than to the consumer price index (IPC) argue that the IGP seriously underestimates the actual level of inflation. Theoretically, the IGP should be a better gauge of inflation because it includes both wholesale and retail prices, including construction costs. Unfortunately, the IGP lagged the IPC by 15.5 percent in 1989.

This has created difficulties in determining the amount of devaluation necessary to maintain export competitiveness. As a result the cruzado has remained overvalued and the nation's exports adversely affected. Exports have also been hurt by a wave of strikes, resulting in higher wages and government cuts in export subsidies. It is expected that the government will adopt an aggressive devaluation policy to regain its competitiveness.

In the meantime, multinational firms are faced with uncertainties regarding exchange rates.

Hedging Practices of MNFs in Brazil

To protect themselves against the possibility of minidevaluations or a single maxidevaluation, firms are utilizing various forms of hedging.

Adapted from Axel de Tristan, "MNCs Step Up Hedging As Devaluation Pressures Intensify in Brazil," *Business Latin America*, May 22, 1989, pp. 158–159.

1. *Dollar-indexed deposits.* This is the most common hedge. Deposits are made in dollar-dominated accounts with subsidiaries of large international banks or locally owned establishments. Although these accounts are not legally enforceable in Brazil, they are generally honored due to side agreements made between the foreign parents of the company and bank.

2. *Export exchange contract.* Managers move funds temporarily offshore by purchasing the export exchange contract of a firm before it matures. This is done by offering a better discount rate than a bank to get the paper.

3. *Indexed intercompany loans.* Intercompany loans indexed to the cruzado-dollar exchange rate are becoming increasingly popular as a means of short-term financing. Intercompany loans are transacted through an investment bank as an intermediary and are secured by the parent company or a bank letter of credit.

4. *Investing in gold.* This is a difficult hedge to manage and is very risky because it is subject to wide and prolonged fluctuations on the world commodity market.

Questions

1. Why might some critics say that Brazil's unannounced minidevaluation policy is one of "too little too late?"

2. Are the hedging activities followed by firms a protection of their assets against minidevaluations and maxidevaluations? Why?

3. What should the Brazilian government do?

NOTES

1. On May 8, 1981, the rate of interest (discount rate) for all Federal Reserve Banks and the Federal Reserve Bank of New York was 14 percent. On February 27, 1989, it was set at 7 percent (*Federal Reserve Bulletin*, May 1986, p. A7).

2. The reserve requirement of depository institutions with transactions between $0 and $41.5 million was set at 3 percent. The required reserves for transactions in excess of $41.5 million was set at 12 percent (*Federal Reserve Bulletin*, May, 1986, p. A8).

3. Christopher M. Korth, *International Business Environment and Management*, 2nd ed. (Englewood Cliffs, N.J.: Prentice-Hall, 1985), p. 141.

4. If the forward quote is selling at more than the spot rate, the currency is selling at a premium. If the forward rate is selling at less than the spot rate, the currency is selling at a discount.

5. *Wall Street Journal*, March 26, 1982, p. 9.

6. "International Economic Condition," *The Federal Reserve Bulletin of St. Louis*, October 1984, p. 8 and August 1985, p. 8.

7. William H. Baughn and Donald R. Mandich (eds.), *The International Banking Handbook* (Homewood, Ill.: Dow-Jones-Irwin, 1983), pp. 207–210.

REFERENCES AND SELECTED READINGS

Baughn, William H., and Donald Mandich (eds.). *The International Banking Handbook*. Homewood, Ill.: Dow Jones-Irwin, 1983.

Board of Governors of the Federal Reserve System. *Federal Reserve Bulletin.* Washington, D.C.: Publications Service. Monthly.

Calderon-Rossell, Jorge, R., and Moshe Beh-Horim. "The Behavior of Foreign Exchange Rates." *The Journal of International Business Studies* 13:2 (Fall 1982).

Chrystal, K. Alec. "A Guide to Foreign Exchange Markets." *Federal Reserve Bulletin of St. Louis,* March, 1984.

Cornell, W. Bradford. "Determinants of the Bid-Ask Spread on Forward Foreign Exchange Contracts." *The Journal of International Business Studies* 9:2 (Fall 1978).

Cosset, Jean-Claude, and Bruno Doutriaux de la Rianderie. "Political Risk and Foreign Exchange Rates: An Efficient-Markets Approach." *The Journal of International Business Studies* 16:3 (Fall 1985).

Editorial Staff, IMF and IBRD, "The Institutional Evolution of the IMF." *Finance and Development*. Washington, D.C.: World Bank Publications, September 1984.

Everett, Robert M., Abraham M. George, and Aryeh Blumbert. "Appraising Currency Strengths and Weaknesses: An Operational Model for Calculating Parity Exchange Rates." *The Journal of International Business Studies* 11:2 (Fall 1980).

Folks, W. R., and R. Aggarwal. *International Dimensions of Financial Management*. Boston: Kent Publishing Company, 1986.

IMF. *Annual Report on Exchange Arrangements and Exchange Restrictions.* Washington, D.C.: IMF, 1984.

Korth, Christopher M. *International Business Environment and Management*, 2nd ed. Englewood Cliffs, N.J.: Prentice-Hall, 1985.

Somanath, V. S. "Exchange Rate Expectations and the Current Exchange Rate: A Test of the Monetarist Approach." *The Journal of International Business Studies* 15:1 (Spring/Summer 1984).

Vinso, Joseph D., and Richard J. Rogalski. "Empirical Properties of Foreign Exchange Rates." *The Journal of International Business Studies* 9:2 (Fall 1978).

Wall Street Journal, March 26, 1982.

5 The International Monetary System and the Balance of Payments

- Understand the international monetary system as it exists today

- Learn why the abandonment of the gold standard resulted in instability in exchange rates

- Become familiar with the role of the U.S. dollar as a reserve currency in the international monetary system

- Understand why the U.S. balance of payments deficit led to the dollar's devaluation and its decreased role as a reserve currency

- Learn the major components of a balance of payments statement

- Be able to explain the causes of balance of payments disequilibrium and the measures nations adopt to restore equilibrium

INTRODUCTION

This chapter explains the role of the International Monetary Fund in attempting to bring about stability in exchange rates once nations went off the gold standard, and shows the relationship between the existing monetary system and the balance of payments of nations. Special emphasis is given to nations with balance of payments disequilibria.

MONOMETALLIC STANDARD OF CURRENCY VALUE

Gold Standard

As discussed in Chapter 1, trade among primitive societies was carried on under a system of barter. But with the growth of nations and the development of trade, the inconvenience of barter led to the use of a medium of exchange, generally gold or silver.

When Great Britain in 1821 officially adopted the gold standard, nations began to think in terms of standards of currency values. In 1879, Germany, France, and the United States adopted gold as the monetary standard. Countries that were major producers of silver or had close ties with major silver producers adopted the silver standard.

When a nation was on a gold or silver standard, there were no restrictions on free coinage, conversion, and movement of the metal. The country's currency was linked to the metal at a fixed parity; that is, the currency's value was defined in terms of its metallic content. If paper money was issued with gold backing, that paper currency would circulate side by side with gold coins as legal tender because it was freely convertible at a fixed price.

The relationship between currencies using the same standard was determined by the amount of the metal of a given quality that backed the respective currency. If two currencies were both backed by gold of the same quality but of differing amounts, the exchange rates would be essentially fixed. For example, if 1 dollar equaled 1 ounce of gold and 2 pesos equaled 1 ounce of gold, then $1 = 1 oz. gold = P2. Thus, the rate of exchange was definite, $1.00 = P2.00. Fluctuations in the values of these currencies were held within narrow limits because of the operation of the "gold points": the upper and lower limits within which exchange rates might fluctuate before it becomes cheaper to make payment in gold rather than foreign exchange (see Chapter 4, "Foreign Exchange").

Until World War I, the monetary standard in existence among most countries was the free gold standard. The relationships between currencies on the same standard can be illustrated by comparing the British pound sterling (£) with the United States dollar ($) prior to 1914. The British pound sterling contained 113.066 grains of fine (pure) gold. The United States dollar contained 23.22 grains of fine gold. Thus, the gold content of the British pound sterling was 4.866 times greater than the gold content of the U.S. dollar. The rate of exchange between the pound and the dollar was quoted as £1 = $4.866. Since gold served as a common denominator, the values of other national currencies on the gold standard could be determined similarly.

Abandonment of Gold as an International Standard

The limited supply and uneven distribution of gold prevented its widespread use in international transactions while serving as reserves for a nation's monetary system, and led to the abandonment of the free gold standard in 1914.

Following World War I efforts were made to reestablish the gold standard. This was accomplished in 1928 but the effects of the Great Depression made its collapse imminent. In 1931, Great Britain abandoned the gold standard, and the pound sterling was permitted to depreciate in terms of other currencies still on gold. In 1933, the United States abandoned the free gold standard and prohibited the circulation of gold coins and gold certificates; all gold coins, bullion, and gold certificates had to be turned over to the government. In 1934, the dollar was devalued, decreasing its gold content from $20.67 per ounce to $35 per ounce. The nation was now on a gold bullion standard for international transactions, permitting government-to-government transfers at the new price.

Despite these actions by the United States and Britain, a group of countries in continental Europe, led by France, attempted to maintain convertibility at the old price, but to no avail. These countries were forced to abandon the gold standard. By 1937 not a single country was on the free gold standard. The complete collapse reflected the fact that countries that attempted to maintain their currencies in terms of gold could not compete internationally against goods that were priced in terms of the depreciated British pound sterling and the American dollar.

The financial chaos following World War I, especially the Great Depression, caused nations to abandon the free gold standard.

RESTRUCTURING THE INTERNATIONAL MONETARY SYSTEM

Bretton Woods Agreement and the IMF

As World War II drew to a close, the free world countries saw the need to restructure the international monetary system to prevent a recurrence of the financial chaos that had followed World War I. In 1944, 44 nations met at Bretton Woods, New Hampshire, to establish an institution that would promote the stability of exchange rates. As a result the International Monetary Fund (IMF) was established.

The members of the IMF agreed to adopt a gold exchange standard using a fixed exchange rate system. They agreed to fix the values of their currencies in terms of gold without being obligated to convert them into gold. (Only the U.S. dollar was convertible into gold, at $35 per ounce.) They agreed not to permit their currencies to fluctuate by more than 1 percent from these fixed rates (parity rates). Fluctuations were to be controlled by central banks through the buying or selling of foreign exchange or gold.

The following example describes the operation. Suppose the Belgian franc had declined in value relative to the U.S. dollar. This would mean that the demand for Belgian francs had decreased or the supply of Belgian francs had increased, or both. The government of Belgium would be called upon to enter the foreign exchange market and buy back its own currency with other currencies or gold. By its action, the supply of Belgian francs would be decreased and the value of the currency would increase.

This system did not address the reasons for the decreased demand or increase in supply; it simply required that nations utilize the dynamics of supply and demand to maintain exchange parity. Furthermore, nations were required to remedy fundamental balance of payments disequilibria. To achieve this objective, they were permitted to devalue their currencies up to 10 percent without approval of the IMF; any devaluation in excess of 10

The Bretton Woods Agreement of 1944 established the IMF with the objective of stabilizing exchange rates.

percent required prior IMF approval. In other words, the agreement had provisions for altering the parity level of a currency without regard to its real worth, despite the fact that frequent devaluations would result in wide variations in prices and disruptions of international business transactions. This system of maintaining an orderly exchange arrangement among the IMF members remained in effect for almost 20 years.

U.S. Dollar as a Reserve Currency

Because the United States held most of the world's gold supply and the dollar was freely convertible into gold, the dollar served as a reserve currency.

The U.S. dollar was accepted as an international reserve currency because of its strength and stability and because it was freely convertible into gold. Since the gold content of the U.S. dollar could not be changed without IMF action, nations tended to value their currencies in terms of dollars. Even the 25 percent of a nation's IMF subscription fees that could not be paid in local currencies could be submitted in dollars as well as gold.

Deficit Policy of the United States

The eventual breakdown of the international monetary system can be traced in part to the post–World War II political and economic policies of the United States. Because the United States ran a trade surplus against most other countries, it accumulated a large part of the world's gold supply ($24 billion in 1948). Something had to be done to alleviate the developing world economic problems, so the U.S. government adopted a deficit balance of payments policy. The United States provided foreign aid for the reconstruction and rehabilitation of the war-devastated areas and for the development of less developed countries. U.S. firms were encouraged to invest abroad. The total cost for stationing American troops abroad was borne by the United States. These and other measures were adopted to create claims against the United States and an outflow of dollars to offset the U.S. trade surplus.

Deficits in the U.S. balance of payments provided the much-needed reserves for the international monetary system. Since the IMF did not have the authority or the financial means to meet the needs of its own programs, the international monetary system became dependent upon the United States to provide the reserves. As long as the United States continued its deficit policy and as long as nations had confidence in the dollar, the system worked well. But sooner or later nations were bound to question the value of a currency that was issued without adequate backing.

Realizing that a continuation of the deficit policy of the 1950s would have an undesirable effect on the value of the dollar, the U.S. government in the 1960s attempted to reverse its course. Measures were taken to stem the outflow of dollars. The European countries and Japan, having largely recovered from the effects of the war, were asked to participate in the foreign aid program. Offshore procurement of U.S. military needs abroad was discontinued. American firms were discouraged from making direct investments abroad, and restrictions were placed on U.S. bank loans to European businesses. Americans were discouraged from traveling abroad, and the amount of duty free imports was reduced. Loans granted by the U.S. government to foreign nations were altered to include tying clauses specifying that these funds must be spent in the United States. Medium-term treasury certificates that were floated abroad called for redemption in foreign currencies. Export trade promotion programs were instituted by the Department of Commerce, while imports were discouraged. In 1965 Congress removed the 25 percent gold reserve requirement for all domestic currency (except notes), thus making gold available for foreign transactions. An interest equalization tax was adopted to discourage Americans from investing in European securities that paid higher rates of interest.

But these unilateral measures were not enough to solve the deficit problem. A part of the blame can be placed on external factors over which the United States had no control. The undervaluation of the West German mark and the Japanese yen made exports from these nations to the United States inexpensive, enabling them to accumulate huge trade surpluses. The overvalued dollar encouraged U.S. firms to make foreign direct investments and made U.S. exports extremely expensive abroad, thus worsening the situation.

Devaluation of the U.S. dollar appeared to be a likely solution, but this could not be done without serious international financial repercussions reflecting the pivotal role played by the dollar in the IMF system. Increasing the price of gold would result in the devaluation of the dollar, but since many other currencies were pegged to the dollar, the value of the dollar in terms of these currencies would remain unchanged. The world was on a dollar standard and there was little the U.S. could do about it. The most plausible solution lay in the revaluation of the currencies of those countries with the surpluses.

The suggestion that West Germany revalue its currency was met with opposition. Germany feared inflation and German exporters did not want to lose their competitive advantage in the world markets. German farmers also opposed revaluation because of the possible increase in imports of agricultural products. Both political pressure from special interest groups and national self-interest discouraged change.

Pressure was also placed on Japan to revalue the yen as the country built up huge trade surpluses with the United States. Like West Germany, Japan resisted because of its past experience with inflation and the fear of losing its overseas markets. The dollar reserves accumulated by Japan and the industrialized nations of Europe were in excess of U.S. gold reserves, thus leading to further erosion of confidence in the dollar. For reasons that extended well beyond economics, France demanded that its dollar holdings be converted into gold. Other nations holding dollars also began to demand gold. The gold stocks of the United States plummeted from $24 billion in 1948 to $15 billion in 1964. Realizing that its gold reserves were inadequate

The deficit policy of the United States and the issuance of currency beyond gold holdings caused nations to lose confidence in the dollar.

to convert all the dollars outstanding, the United States in 1968 suspended the exchange of dollars for gold, except for official purposes. The policy of having gold define the value of a currency but not allowing the currency to be converted into gold is called the "inherent contradiction of the gold exchange standard."

THE DECREASING ROLE OF GOLD IN THE INTERNATIONAL MONETARY SYSTEM

Two-Tier System

To reduce the role of gold in the international monetary system, a two-tiered gold-pricing system was adopted in 1968 by the world's major central banks. Accordingly, the prices of gold in official and in private transactions were divorced from one another. For public dealings the price was fixed, while for private transactions gold was treated as a commodity, permitting supply and demand conditions in world markets to determine its price. To relieve the pressure on the dollar and to increase international reserves, the International Monetary Fund in 1969 introduced Special Drawing Rights (SDRs).[1] The value of one SDR was set at one U.S. dollar. SDRs totalling $10 billion were created and allocated to member nations over the three-year period, 1970 to 1972. These allocations were made according to the subscription quota of each nation, resulting in the greatest number of SDRs being allocated to the nations with the largest quotas.[2] Despite these steps, confidence in the dollar continued to erode.

Devaluation and Revaluation

The dollar holdings of other nations remained greatly in excess of the gold reserves of the United States. It was obvious that the United States could not possibly exchange gold for these outstanding dollars. On August 15, 1971, President Nixon prohibited the conversion of U.S. dollars into gold and placed a 10 percent surtax on imports to limit the outflow of dollars.

The United States abandoned the gold bullion standard. The dollar was permitted to float freely and, at the Smithsonian Agreement in December 1971, the dollar was officially devalued when its gold content was reduced 8.57 percent. In effect, the dollar price of gold was increased from $35 per ounce to $38 per ounce. Japan revalued its currency when it lowered its yen price of gold by 8.5 percent, and Germany lowered its mark price of gold by 5 percent. The combined effects of these changes meant that the yen was revalued 17.07 percent in relation to the dollar and the West German mark was revalued 13.57 percent. The British pound sterling and the French franc retained their relationship to the U.S. dollar through the devaluation of each by 8.57 percent.[3] The values of other European currencies were changed by varying amounts in terms of the dollar. The Special

Drawing Rights of the International Monetary Fund, initially equal in value to the U.S. dollar, now appreciated relative to the dollar. In essence, SDRs became a currency whose value changed in relation to national currencies.

International financial turmoil characterized this period. The British pound sterling came under attack because of the country's high rates of inflation, high unemployment, and recurrent labor unrest. Britain was forced to abandon its policy of pegging its currency to the U.S. dollar and gold. Immediately, the pound sterling began to depreciate. This caused a steady outflow of capital from Great Britain to Japan and Switzerland. The Italian lira also came under speculative attack, forcing the government, in 1973, to adopt a two-tier system like those of France and Belgium, with an officially fixed rate of exchange for commercial transactions and a floating rate for capital transactions.[4]

When the published statistics showed a further deterioration in the balance of payment of the United States, the dollar came under further attack. The devaluation of the dollar and the revaluation of some of the other major currencies did not have a sufficient effect on the deficit problem of the United States. The massive flight of capital from U.S. dollars to West German marks continued. The German central bank was forced to accumulate unwanted dollars to prevent the inflationary effect that an influx of dollars would have on the economy. To prevent the further inflow of dollars, it adopted controls on the import of capital by foreigners and on borrowing abroad by West German firms.

The U.S. Federal Reserve System sold $319 million worth of German marks and $20 million in Dutch guilders for U.S. dollars in an attempt to support the dollar. The U.S. government was decreasing the supply of dollars and increasing the supply of marks and guilders in the market. But the downward pressure on the dollar continued and on February 12, 1973, the dollar was devalued another 10 percent, thus increasing the price of gold from $38 per ounce to $42.20 per ounce.

The Japanese yen, which was permitted to float, settled at 260 yen per dollar. Other currencies that were permitted to float were the British pound sterling, the Canadian dollar, the Swiss franc, and the Italian lira.

The calm that prevailed on foreign exchange markets was short-lived. The supply of dollars in West Germany and other European countries increased as holders of short-term dollar assets began to dispose of their holdings to minimize transaction exposure risks. (See Chapter 17, "International Financial Management," for a discussion of transaction exposure risks.) In an attempt to prevent a further depreciation of the dollar that would disrupt European exports, the foreign exchange markets were closed for a two-week period while the European Economic Community sought a solution through a partial float.[5] The currencies of France, West Germany, Denmark, and the Benelux countries were pegged to each other and were permitted to float jointly against the dollar but with a spread of no more than 2.25 percent between the strongest and weakest currencies. Prior to the pegging, the German mark was revalued an additional 3 percent. Sweden and Norway, nonmembers of the EEC, also agreed to adhere to this joint float. The British pound sterling, the Irish pound, the Italian lira, and the Swiss franc were permitted to float freely rather than to join the joint float. Japan and Canada also permitted their currencies to float freely. The existence of the floating currencies spelled the end to the fixed rate system that had been established under the Bretton Woods Agreement.

Expecting a further decrease in value, private foreign banks continued to dispose of their huge supply of dollars. This accelerated a further decline in the value of the dollar. The dollar was becoming an undervalued currency. This was reflected in an increase in exports, a decrease in imports, and an inflow of foreign investment capital into the United States. By the second and third quarters of 1973, the United States experienced the first surplus in its balance of payments position since 1969. (See Figures 5.1 and 5.2.)

Since the overvalued dollar was the major reason for the United States B/P deficit, the dollar was devalued and the German mark and Japanese yen revalued.

IMF and the Managed Float System

In 1974, the IMF officially severed the linkages among the SDR, gold, and the U.S. dollar. The daily market exchange rates of 16 major currencies were used as the basis for determining the value of the SDR.[6] In April 1976, with the approval of the Board of Governors of the IMF, the international monetary system formally moved to a *managed float* system. The daily rates of exchange were determined by market forces and not by government decisions. Currencies of most smaller nations were not permitted to float independently but were linked to the SDR or pegged to the currency of their major trading partners. The currencies of South Korea, Singapore, and Taiwan retained their relationship to the U.S. dollar, so the devaluation of the dollar did not affect the exchange rates with the currencies of these nations or their export sales to the United States. In fact, the pegging of their currency to the dollar gave these nations the opportunity to increase their exports to the United States because their goods became comparatively less expensive than yen- or mark-denominated products. There is no doubt that the continued trade deficit with these and some other trading partners is partially because their currencies are pegged to the U.S. dollar.

Eight members of the European Economic Community formed the European Monetary System (EMS) in 1979. The rates of their currencies were fixed in relation to each other, and their currencies were permitted to float as a bloc with respect to the currencies of the rest of the world. The U.S. dollar, the Japanese yen, the British pound sterling, the Swiss franc, and the Canadian dollar were not pegged to any other currency and were free to float. Excessive fluctuations were to be prevented by intervention of the central bank of each country. This resulted in a so-called *dirty float* as contrasted to a free float. The currencies of the communist countries remained outside of the managed float system and continued to be inconvertible.

The IMF attempted to decrease the role of gold and dollars as reserves by creating SDRs.

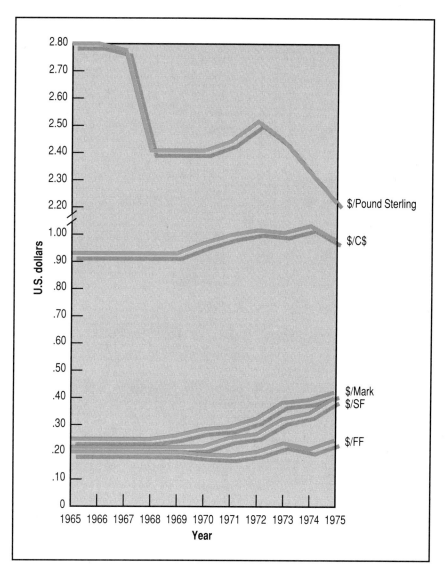

Figure 5.1   Exchange Rates Between U.S. Dollar and Selected World Currencies (1965–1975)
Source: International Monetary Fund, *International Financial Statistics Yearbook,* 1989.

The Value of the SDR

In 1981, the IMF changed the basis for determining the value of the SDR to the weighted average of the daily values of five currencies: the U.S. dollar, the British pound sterling, the French franc, the West German mark, and the Japanese yen. The current weight assigned to each of these five

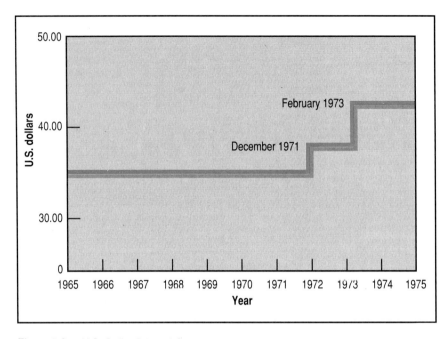

Figure 5.2   U.S. Dollar Price of Gold (1965–1975)
Source: International Monetary Fund, *International Financial Statistics Yearbook,* 1989.

currencies is the U.S. dollar, 42%; the West German mark, 19%; the Japanese yen, 15%; the French franc, 12%; and the British pound sterling, 12%.

The value of the SDR was and is important because it serves as an alternative to gold or dollars as a standard of value for the currencies of member countries. However, the U.S. dollar remains the dominant international currency and is the medium most widely used for reserves and for international transactions.

When the SDR was first introduced, $1.00 was equal to 1.00 SDR and that ratio endured through 1971. Since then, the dollar in relation to the SDR has fluctuated widely, as shown in Figure 5.3. The dollar continued to depreciate in value until 1980, then appreciated through 1985. This resulted in a conscious effort to unofficially depreciate the value of the dollar to reduce the trade deficit.[7] The success of this effort is reflected in a decrease in the dollar's value in relation to the SDR from an average of $1.17 in 1986 to $1.29 in 1987, and to $1.34 on June 20, 1988.[8]

Meanwhile, currencies of other nations have also fluctuated widely in relation to the dollar. The British pound sterling closed on January 14, 1985, at only $1.1125 = £1.00, and then depreciated still further to a record low of only $1.05 in March 1985.[9] Since then, the pound has gained strength. Table 5.1 (p. 118) lists the values of selected world currencies, showing the changes in their values in relation to the U.S. dollar between 1980 and 1989.

The SDR's value is based upon the market values of 5 major currencies rather than the 16 currencies previously used.

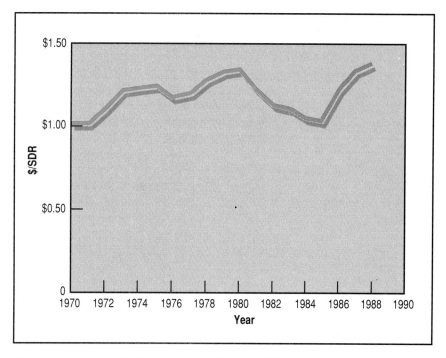

Figure 5.3   Relationship Between U.S. Dollar and SDR (1970–1990)
Source: International Monetary Fund, *International Financial Statistics Yearbook*, 1989, pp. 716–717;
IMF Survey, August 7, 1989, p. 254.

The Future of the International Monetary System

At the twenty-fifth Per Jacobsson Lecture in Basel, Switzerland, on June
12, 1988, three participants in the symposium envisioned the future of the
international monetary system. Sir Kit McMahon, Chairman and Group
Chief Executive of Midland Bank, stated: "We will never have one dominant
currency or country; we will have an oligopolistic situation forever."[10] To-
maso Padoa-Schioppa, Deputy Director-General of the Banca d'Italia, stated
that the international monetary system "will have to adapt to a complex
world that resembles a galaxy rather than the solar system of Bretton
Woods."[11] The third, C. Fred Bergsten, Director of the Institute for International Economics in Washington, D.C., believed that the most feasible
and promising solution lay in the evolution of the international monetary
system into one that is based on equilibrium exchange target zones rather
than on dollar and yen blocs.[12]

　　The conclusion to be drawn from these three very different projections
of the future of the international monetary system is that no one is quite
sure what the future holds. Will the future be an oligopolistic system
dominated by the advanced industrialized nations, will it be a yen- and

Table 5.1   **Values of Selected World Currencies (Units of Foreign Currency per U.S. Dollar)**

	1980	*1985*	*1986*	*1987*	*9/15/89*
British pound	0.4298	0.7714	0.6817	0.6101	0.6441
Canadian dollar	1.1947	1.3655	1.3895	1.3260	1.1848
French franc	4.2256	8.9852	6.9261	6.0107	6.6285
Japanese yen	226.74	238.54	168.52	144.64	146.43
Swiss franc	1.6757	2.4571	1.7989	1.4912	1.6966
West German mark	1.8177	2.9440	2.1715	1.7974	1.9660

Source: IMF, *International Financial Statistics Yearbook*, 1989; *Wall Street Journal*, September 15, 1989, p. C10.

dollar-dominated system, or will it be a system dominated by a galaxy of influences from the many nations of the world? Only time will tell.

BALANCE OF PAYMENTS

The balance of payments (B/P) statement itemizes and categorizes the commercial and financial transactions between the residents of one country and the residents of all other countries during a stated period of time.

Exchange Rates and the Balance of Payments

The rates of exchange among currencies affect trade and investment flows and are accounted for in a nation's balance of payments statement. Relatedly, changes in exchange rates generally result in changes in the level of a nation's trade balance (exports minus imports) and investment flows.

Exchange Rates and the Trade Balance

If the currency of a nation depreciates or is devalued in terms of the currencies of other countries, its products will become relatively less expensive compared to products from other countries; thus, exports will be stimulated and imports discouraged. Conversely, if a nation's currency appreciates in terms of other currencies, its products become more expensive in terms of foreign currencies; exports will be discouraged and imports encouraged (see Figure 5.4 and Global Insight). These trade transactions

Figure 5.4   Effects of Exchange Rate Changes on Trade Flows

X up $\longrightarrow$ XP down,   MP up,   and TB down
X down $\longrightarrow$ XP up,   MP down,   and TB up

X = Exchange Rate; XP = Exports; MP = Imports; TB = Trade Balance.

are recorded in the *Current Account* portion of a nation's balance of payments statement.

There are two major exceptions to this relationship between exchange rates and trade balance. First, if a nation's imports are essential goods (crude oil, food, and so forth), the volume of imports may not diminish sufficiently to offset the higher unit cost. For example, assume that a nation imports 100M barrels of crude oil at $18.00 per barrel before devaluing its currency by 10 percent. After the devaluation, the oil would cost $19.80 per barrel. If the nation's imports of oil drop to 95M barrels, the total cost of imported crude oil would actually increase.

$$\text{Before devaluation} \quad 100\text{M barrels @} \quad \$18.00 \quad = \$1.80\text{B}$$
$$\text{After devaluation} \quad 95\text{M barrels @} \quad \$19.80 \quad = \$1.88\text{B}$$

Second, a devaluation will not affect the trade balance with nations whose currency values are pegged to that of the depreciating nation because the values of the currencies will move jointly.

Exchange Rates and Investment Flows

Similarly, the value of a country's currency will affect foreign investment flows. The devaluing of a nation's currency (depreciating exchange rate) might make it more difficult for foreign firms to export to a country but it will also become less expensive for those foreign firms to invest in the host nation. Thus, a nation may devalue its currency to assist local firms only to find that after the devaluation, those local firms encounter increased competition from foreign investors or are even acquired by a foreign investor. Conversely, a depreciating exchange rate will make it more expensive for firms of the devaluing country to make investments outside of their country. Exactly the opposite situation occurs in a nation with an appreciating currency (see Figure 5.5).

The international flow of funds associated with foreign investments are recorded in the *Capital Account* of a nation's balance of payments.

X up $\longrightarrow$ OF up; IF down

X down $\longrightarrow$ OF down; IF up

X = Exchange Rate; OF = Outflows–Investments abroad by firms or individuals of the host country; IF = Inflows–Investments in the country by firms or individuals from abroad.

Figure 5.5 The Effects of Exchange Rate Changes on Investments.

Balance of Payments Accounting

The balance of payments statement is like standard corporate accounting in that it utilizes normal double entry bookkeeping; for every debit entry there is credit entry of equal value. *Credit items* contain all of the claims of a country against foreigners that give rise to payments into a country (receipts). *Debit items* include all foreign claims against a country that result in outpayments. Thus, any transactions that give rise to claims against foreigners are recorded in the credit column, and those that give rise to claims against the home country are recorded in the debit column of the balance of payments statement. Due to the similarity with corporate accounting, the record-keeping behind the balance of payments is often called *national income accounting*.

Balance of payments statements list the credit and debit items under three major categories: Current Accounts (including unrequited transfers), Capital Accounts, and Net Errors and Omissions. The Current Account may be thought of as a record of the value of the flows of goods and services into and out of a country. For example, exports are the sending of goods to the importing country and the creation of claims against the importing country that ultimately result in receipts for the exporting country. The export of Honda Accords from Marysville, Ohio, to Japan creates claims against Japan and later the receipt of funds from Japan. These claims and the later receipts are credit items on the U.S. balance of payments. Conversely the automobiles received by Japan represent a debt on the Japanese balance of payments. Figure 5.6 presents the U.S. and Japanese balance of payments if this were the only transaction of each nation and if we assume

Figure 5.6 A One-Transaction Balance of Payments for the United States and Japan

	U.S.		Japan	
	Inflow (Credit)	Outflow (Debit)	Inflow (Credit)	Outflow (Debit)
Current Account				
Products				
Cars		10 $\longrightarrow$	10	
Money or Claims	$100,000 $\longleftarrow$			$100,000

that 10 cars were sold to Japan for $100,000. In this situation, the United States would have a trade surplus of $100,000.

Another interesting aspect of this highly simplified example is that these exports to Japan and the trade surplus reflected above would not have occurred had it not been for the fixed investments that Honda made in the United States for the production of automobiles. Such foreign direct investments (stocks) are listed as claims against Japan in the Capital Account section of the balance of payments since they were the result of a flow of funds from Japan to the United States. Thus, capital inflows are analogous to exports in the Current Account. Similarly, if U.S. corporations make direct investments in a foreign country, these create claims against the United States, are analogous to imports, and would be recorded as a debit in the Capital Account of the U.S. balance of payments statement.

Like an accounting balance sheet, each credit item in the balance of payments statement must have an offsetting debit item, and total credits must equal total debits. By contrast with corporate accounting, it is not always possible to identify the offsetting items in the balance of payments statement since they lose their identities in the foreign exchange. By further contrast with corporate accounting, the figures are often mere approximations. It is therefore necessary to include a balancing entry. This entry in the balance of payments statement is referred to as Errors and Omissions, or Discrepancies. Without this entry, the total debits will not equal total credits and the statement will not balance. Thus, in analyzing a balance of payments statement of a given country, one must bear in mind that errors, omissions, and unrecorded transactions could result in differences between the total debit and total credit items amounting to millions or even billions of dollars for large nations like the United States. These terms will be clarified and explained more completely in the following sections.

A nation's international financial transactions are shown on the B/P statement. As with an accounting balance sheet, the credit and debit items must be equal.

Major Components of the Balance of Payments

A nation's balance of payments statement consists of three major categories: Current Accounts, Capital Accounts, and Net Errors and Omissions. Table 5.2 shows the major components of each. Depending upon the claims created or the direction of the flow of capital, the transaction can be either a credit item or debit item.

Unlike the simplified example presented in Figure 5.6, which showed debit and credit items as positive numerals but in separate columns, a "real" balance of payments statement lists debit items (outflows) as negative and credit items (inflows) as positive. For example, exports are denoted as positive numbers and imports as negative numbers.

Current Account

The Current Account of a nation's balance of payments is comparable to the revenues and expenses of a corporation's accounting statement. Any

Table 5.2 Aggregate Presentation of the Balance of Payments

Current Account (excluding exceptional financing)
  Merchandise exports f.o.b. . . . . Credit
  Merchandise imports f.o.b. . . . . Debit
  Other goods, services, and income . . . . Credit . . or . . Debit
  Private unrequited transfers . . . . Credit . . or . . Debit
  Official unrequited transfers . . . . Credit . . or . . Debit

Capital Account
  Long-term capital
    Direct investment . . . . Credit . . or . . Debit
    Portfolio investment . . . . Credit . . or . . Debit
    Other long-term capital . . . . Credit . . or . . Debit
  Short-term capital
    Resident official sector . . . . Credit . . or . . Debit
    Deposit money banks . . . . Credit . . or . . Debit
    Other sectors . . . . Credit . . or . . Debit

Net Errors and Omissions . . . . Credit . . or . . Debit

Reserves and Liabilities
  Monetary gold
  SDR holdings
  Reserve position in the fund
  Foreign exchange
  Other claims and use of fund credit

Source: IMF, *Balance of Payments Statistics*, vol. 36, Yearbook, Part I, 1985.

transaction resulting in an inflow of funds to a country (claim against another country) is a credit, while any transaction resulting in an outflow of money from a country (claim by another country) is a debit in the balance of payments statement. The most important credit- and debit- creating items in the Current Account are exports and imports of tangible items of trade.

When products are exported from one country to another, a claim is created against the foreign country for the amount of the export. This is recorded as a credit item in the exporting nation's balance of payments statement because the sale has resulted in or will result in an inflow of income (revenues) into the exporting country. On the other hand, importing a product from another country results in a claim by the other country and the necessity for making payment, thus an outflow of funds (expenses) from the importing country. Therefore, imports are recorded as a debit item in the balance of payments statement. In 1988, merchandise exports from the United States totaled $322.225 billion (excluding military exports) and merchandise imports totaled $440.940 billion, resulting in a negative trade balance (a trade deficit) of $118.715 billion.[13]

The second major component of the Current Account is service or intangible items of trade that include the transfer of cash or credit. In this category are payments made for such services as transportation and freight charges, tourist expenditures, consulting fees, accounting and legal services, and so forth. If these services are purchased from foreigners, they create a claim against the purchaser country and result in an outflow of funds (expenses), so they are recorded as debit items in the balance of payments. On the other hand, if these services are provided to foreigners, they result in claims against foreigners and result in an inflow of funds (revenues), so they are recorded as credit items in the balance of payments.

Income earned from foreign investments results in an inflow of funds (a credit) while an outflow of funds from such investments results in a debit. In addition to investment income this category includes interest income, labor income, property income, and other goods and services income.

The third major component of the Current Account is unrequited or unilateral transfers. These include noncommercial transactions of both private and governmental origin in which there is no repayment. Private transfers of this type include gifts to relatives abroad, pensions, or donations to charitable and religious organizations. Unrequited government transfers include aid in the form of money, goods, and services to other governments where nothing is required in return. These transfers, even though goods and services are sent abroad instead of money, can not be viewed as exports and must be shown as an outflow of money (a debit) on the balance of payments statement. Thus, both a $50 birthday present to a friend in Rome and government funds sent for disaster relief in Africa would be considered debit items in the U.S. balance of payments statement.

Since World War II, government aid for the reconstruction of war-devastated areas, military assistance, grants to Third World countries, and contributions to the budgets of international organizations have increased the importance of unrequited transfers in the U.S. balance of payments. Israel, the Philippines, South Korea, and India have consistently received large amounts of military or economic aid from the United States.

A cursory review of the Current Account of the U.S. balance of payments statement will show that merchandise imports have exceeded merchandise exports for most years during the last two decades. This was of little concern until quite recently, because income from other sources offset the negative trade balance. The major sources of cash inflows included repatriation of profits by corporations or loan repayments by foreign entities. This was true in 1976, 1979, 1980, 1981, and even in 1982, when the current account deficit was only $8.64 billion.[14] This is no longer true.[15] (See Table 5.3.) The Current Account deficit reached a record $152 billion in 1987. Only with a concerted effort has the United States been able to reduce the deficit to $134.72 billion in 1988.[16]

Capital Account

The most important item in the current account of a B/P statement is merchandise trade.

The capital account shows short-term and long-term capital transactions of both the private and public sectors. Short-term capital transactions are of

Table 5.3 **The U.S. Current Account Balance Since 1982**

Year	Current Account Deficit
1982	$8.64B
1983	$46.29B
1984	$107.14B
1985	$115.16B
1986	$138.84B
1987	$152.47B
1988	$134.72B

Source: IMF, *International Financial Statistics Yearbook*, 1989, p. 725.

less than one year's duration, while long-term capital transactions are those of more than one year's duration.

Whether public or private, long-term capital transactions where the ownership interest is greater than 10 percent are categorized as direct investments. These may represent new investments or reinvestment of earnings in such activities as mines, factories, forests, agricultural land, and so forth. The direction in which money flows determines whether the transaction is a debit or credit item in the Capital Account of the balance of payments statement.

When such investments are made by U.S. investors, money flows out of the country or claims are created against the United States; thus, the transaction is a debit in the long-term Capital Account. Interest, dividends, and profits from these foreign direct investments result in the inflow of funds, which are recorded as credits in the short-term capital account. Similarly, when foreign capital is invested in the United States, a claim is created against the foreign country, resulting in a credit in the Capital Account of the U.S. balance of payments statement; the outflow of funds (interest and dividends) from these investments are debits.

Long-term portfolio investments are treated in a manner similar to fixed asset (direct) investments but are recorded in the Portfolio Investment Account in the balance of payments statement. When an individual or institution purchases stock in a foreign corporation and holds less than a 10 percent ownership position, a debit is recorded in the Portfolio Investment section of the capital account of the purchasing nation's balance of payments. Interest or dividends that flow to the holders of the securities are treated as credits in the short-term capital account.

If foreigners make investments in the United States whether they are direct or portfolio, claims are created against the home country of those investors; thus, the investments are recorded as a credit item in the U.S. balance of payments statement. The outflow of funds (interest and dividend) from portfolio investments result in a debit to the short-term capital account to show the transfer of funds. Bank deposits, short-term bonds, and certificates are considered short-term capital transfers and are listed in the short-term capital account.

Short-term capital transfers occur because of the differential in interest rates, speculation in foreign exchange, temporary flight of capital due to political or economic instability, and the like. Many short-term capital flows occur independently of the nation's balance of payments. These are called *autonomous transactions* because they are not carried out to compensate for disequilibrium in the balance of payments; thus, credits are not expected to equal debits. The resulting disequilibrium must be settled, either through the transfer of some asset such as gold or foreign exchange, or through official debt that increases the country's liabilities. These transactions are referred to as *compensatory* or *balancing items* to finance any imbalance in the autonomous items.

The capital account is made up of long-term and short-term capital transactions.

Assume the following: U.S. individuals or corporations invest $100 million abroad—$70 million in production facilities and $30 million in long-term corporate bonds. In the same year these investors receive $3 million in interest income and $5 million in dividend income. Foreign investors purchase a U.S. firm for $115 million and invest $40 million in short-term U.S. notes. Table 5.4 summarizes the balance of payments effects of these foreign capital transactions.

In this situation the United States would have a positive balance in its capital account and a negative balance in its portfolio account.

Errors and Omissions

The final section of the balance of payments statement is Errors and Omissions. This is the balancing entry in the statement. For example, the amount of discrepancy for the United States in 1988 was a net credit of $16.548 billion.[17] Because of errors, omissions, and approximations, credit items do not balance with the debit items in the balance of payments statement.

Reserves and Liabilities

The total reserves determine the liquidity position of a country. They are assets owned by the government and result from purchases and sales by the official monetary authorities such as the central bank. These are composed of foreign exchange holdings that are freely convertible on the international money markets such as the U.S. dollar, British pound sterling, and German mark. A country's own currency is not considered a part of a nation's reserves. Monetary gold is considered a reserve because it is freely convertible into other currencies. Special Drawing Rights are reserves because they are freely convertible and may be used to settle international accounts.

The official liabilities reflect the amount of domestic currency held by foreign monetary authorities as a part of their reserves. For example, the

Table 5.4 **Foreign Investment Effects on the U.S. Balance of Payments**

	Credit	*Debit*
Portfolio investments account		
Bond investment		− $30M
Capital account—long-term		
Production investment		− $70M
Company purchase	+ $115M	
Capital account—short-term		
Dividend income	+ $5M	
Interest income	+ $3M	
Purchase of U.S. notes	+ $40M	

dollar holdings of the Bank of England are a liability of the United States and are so indicated on the nation's balance of payments statement, but they serve as reserves of the Bank of England. An increase in dollar holdings by foreign monetary authorities will increase the liabilities of the United States, and a decrease of such holdings will decrease the U.S. liabilities. Thus, the reserves of the country are somewhat comparable to a firm's current assets, while the countries' liabilities are analogous to a firm's current liabilities.

Value of a Balance of Payments Statement

The balance of payments statement of a particular country provides a summary position of a nation's economic performance and its financial position during any given year. The visible items of trade, together with the invisible items and unrequited transfers, indicate the current account position of a country. A surplus will indicate the country's ability to meet its foreign obligations or to import goods and services it might require. A deficit, on the other hand, might mean that the nation will have difficulty in meeting its financial obligations.

The Capital Account shows, among other things, the inflow and outflow of long-term capital. It also provides some indication of the future inflow of capital. The Capital Account together with the Current Account will show the basic balance of payments position of a country for the year. A comparison with past balance of payments statements will indicate a nation's financial health and its future economic outlook.

Disequilibrium in the Balance of Payments

Disequilibrium can be either a surplus or a deficit in the balance of payments. These may exist when the current claims against a country are not equal to the current claims of that country against all other countries. If the claims by country A against other countries are greater than all claims against country A, the situation is referred to as a surplus disequilibrium. If the claims of other countries against country A are greater than country A's claims against others, this is called deficit disequilibrium. The ideal situation exists when a nation's balance of payments position is in equilibrium, but that is rare (see Figure 5.7).

Reasons for Disequilibrium

Disequilibrium in the balance of payments might occur for a number of reasons, but the most important source can be traced to a nation's trade relations with other countries. The United States provides one of the best examples of a country whose balance of payments position changed because of a shift from a positive to a negative balance of trade.

Historically, the United States has been an exporting nation. From the

$$\begin{bmatrix} \text{Exports of} \\ \text{Goods \&} \\ \text{Services} \end{bmatrix} - \begin{bmatrix} \text{Imports of} \\ \text{Goods \&} \\ \text{Services} \end{bmatrix} + \begin{bmatrix} \text{Capital} \\ \text{Inflows} \end{bmatrix} - \begin{bmatrix} \text{Capital} \\ \text{Outflows} \end{bmatrix} + \begin{bmatrix} \text{Changes in} \\ \text{Reserves} \end{bmatrix} = \text{B/P}$$

Source: David K. Eitemann and Arthur J. Stonehill, *Multinational Business Finance* (New York: Addison-Wesley Publishing Co., 1989), p. 70.

Figure 5.7   Formula of Credit and Debit Items in a B/P Statement

1890s to the mid-1950s, the United States was the supplier of both manufactured goods and agricultural products to the world markets. Year after year, exports exceeded imports by a considerable amount, leading to a shortage of dollars to pay for the imports. This resulted in what the world referred to as a dollar gap. Between 1914 and 1956, United States exports of goods and services exceeded imports by some $126 billion. The huge export surplus was paid for by U.S. government grants and loans. Private long-term investments, gifts, and the central bank foreign exchange reserves of most nations were still inadequate to meet the needs.

With the restoration of the economies of western Europe and Japan, the United States experienced the reverse situation. These countries found a ready market for their products. Claims against the United States began to mount as the growth in imports outpaced the growth in exports. U.S. investments abroad added to the outflow of capital. By 1985, the United States had an unprecedented negative balance of trade due in part to the deficit balance with Japan, which alone reached $30 billion.

This unfavorable trade position can be attributed to a number of factors. The aftermath of U.S. military activities in Vietnam combined with domestic government spending created pressure on domestic prices, resulting in double digit inflation. But even after inflation was reduced to reasonable levels in the early 1980s, the value of imports continued to rise faster than exports. The exhaustion of domestic raw materials meant increased costs of production for many industries. The tenfold increase in oil prices in the early 1970s and the depletion of domestic oil reserves were also contributing factors. Industries depending upon oil for fuel or raw materials experienced a rapid increase in costs, which discouraged exports and encouraged the import of alternative products.

The demand for U.S. automobiles, one of the major exports since the inception of the industry, fell as the price of fuel increased worldwide. Economy rather than comfort dictated the purchase of automobiles in most countries. U.S. automobiles were less competitive with the fuel-efficient automobiles from western Europe and Japan. The United States was faced with increasing competition in other industries as well. Lower foreign production costs, especially in the Third World countries, resulted from the implementation of more modern and efficient productive facilities, which, coupled with lower wage rates, have made it difficult for American industry to compete in the production of steel, electrical and electronic products, transportation equipment, textiles, garments, flatware, and many other products.

The increase in the value of the American dollar in the first half of the 1980s in relation to the currencies of western Europe and Japan also had a dramatic effect on the trade position of the United States. The overvalued dollar meant a decrease in the prices of foreign goods, encouraged imports from abroad, and made it difficult to bring about equilibrium in the current account. The balance of payments position was further worsened because of the billions of dollars in economic and military assistance given to many foreign countries.

A nation's B/P is in disequilibrium if the claims and counterclaims do not balance.

Need for Adjustment

Disequilibrium in the balance of payments, whether a surplus or a deficit, cannot continue indefinitely. If a country continues to experience a deficit, its gold and foreign exchange reserves will ultimately be depleted. Furthermore, it cannot expect unilateral transfers to meet these deficits. It must adopt measures to restore equilibrium. On the other hand, a country with a surplus disequilibrium can maintain its surplus only as long as there are countries that continue to run a deficit. Thus, a surplus country should also adopt measures to restore equilibrium among the deficit countries before the latter countries adopt measures that are discriminatory. Since the trade balance is usually the most important component of a balance of payments disequilibrium, most countries seek a solution by adopting barriers to restrict imports.

Measures to Restore Equilibrium and Their Effectiveness

There are four basic measures that a nation may adopt to restore equilibrium in its balance of payments:

1. Policies of internal deflation
2. Controls to restrict the outflow of capital
3. Policies to increase the inflow of foreign capital
4. Devaluation of currency

Policies of Internal Deflation   Under a free gold standard, deflation was not uncommon because the supply of money was determined by the amount of gold reserves. Only an increase in the supply of gold could increase the supply of money; even then limits could be placed on the increase in reserves by "sterilizing" gold—that is, earmarking it as nonreserve gold. However, nations are no longer on the free gold standard. Some government agency or institution such as the central bank determines the amount of money in circulation. In the United States, as mentioned earlier, the Federal Reserve System serves as the central bank. (See Chapter 4 for a discussion of the operations of the U.S. Federal Reserve System.)

If a deflationary policy is adopted, the Board of Governors may decrease the amount of money and credit in circulation, or keep the money and credit supply constant while the economy continues to expand. The amount of money will be insufficient to pay for the goods and services at the current price levels because a smaller amount of money must serve a greater number of transactions. Although a deflationary policy might be the most effective method to achieve equilibrium in the current account of the balance of payments, a deliberate attempt to decrease wages, costs, and prices will usually be resisted vigorously by both labor and management.

Controls to Restrict the Outflow of Capital   Barriers on imports generally take the form of import duties (tariffs) or quantitative restrictions (quotas). If the duties are considered too low to discourage imports, the government may take emergency action and adopt a surtax on imports. An example is the 150-day, 10 percent import surtax that President Nixon imposed on August 15, 1971, to restrict the outflow of dollars from the United States. To supplement import tariffs, many nations make use of quantitative restrictions. (For a more detailed discussion of tariffs and quotas see Chapter 7.) Quotas are generally used to protect domestic industries, but may also be used to restrict imports when a nation has a negative balance of trade. Since they are absolute and inflexible, quotas tend to be more effective than tariffs. Even voluntary quotas are quite effective, such as those used to restrict the import of automobiles, steel products, textiles, flatware, and the like.

Many governments make use of exchange controls during national emergencies to limit imports from abroad. A system of licensing or permits is used to allocate the foreign exchange. Although exchange controls are used primarily by countries to ensure the imports of only the most essential commodities, they may also be used when a nation has a negative balance of trade.

To prevent the outflow of both short-term and long-term capital, a country may adopt various restrictive measures:

1. Limit the amount of loans a financial institution may make to foreign firms
2. Restrict the purchase of foreign stocks and bonds
3. Tax interest or dividend income from foreign securities
4. Restrict private foreign direct investments by U.S. firms
5. Limit the amount of money that may be taken out of the country
6. Decrease the dollar value of goods that can enter the country tax free
7. Require the use of domestic carriers to transport goods between domestic ports or between domestic and foreign ports

Policies to Increase the Inflow of Foreign Capital   A nation may adopt various measures to increase the inflow of funds by stimulating exports. Both direct and indirect subsidies are frequently used to give the domestic producer an advantage in foreign markets. The nonapplicability of value added taxes on exports, tax deferral on income earned abroad, and lower transportation rates on shipments destined for foreign markets are among the measures used to stimulate exports.

When measures are adopted to limit imports while encouraging exports, the assumption is that foreign countries will continue to make purchases at the same level. However, nations do not have unlimited supplies of gold or foreign exchange; they must earn the foreign exchange through sales. Without the foreign exchange, a country will not be able to import. Thus, imports are dependent upon exports. But nations often retaliate against a country that adopts protective measures. Thus, the adoption of duties, quotas, and subsidies may result in a trade war and make matters worse. For example, in 1986 when the United States placed a 15 percent duty on the import of Canadian lumber products, Canada immediately adopted measures to retaliate against the import of U.S. products.

Devaluation of Currency   By decreasing the value of its currency, a nation is actually reducing the prices of its commodities on a national scale, hoping to encourage the export of its products. At the same time, a decrease in the value of its currency will make purchasing goods from abroad more expensive, thus discouraging imports. If exports are encouraged and imports are discouraged, the impact on the balance of trade could help to restore equilibrium in a nation's balance of payments.

It is important to note that devaluation may actually worsen the B/P situation. If the domestic demand for imports is inelastic, the quantity of imports might not decrease sufficiently to offset the higher unit prices. Relatedly, the foreign demand for a nation's exports may not increase sufficiently to counter the higher costs of imports. Thus, the overall effect can be the opposite of what is desired. This is exactly what happened when the United States, with the cooperation of other industrial countries, informally depreciated the dollar early in 1986. The value of imports increased, and exports did not increase substantially. In addition to demand elasticities, one must also consider the effects of corporate strategies. When Japanese auto manufacturers were faced with a devalued U.S. dollar, they did not increase the dollar prices of automobiles sold in the United States to reflect the new exchange rate; they merely opted for a smaller profit margin. Finally, if exports do increase following devaluation, a large inflow of money could increase the domestic money supply, adding to the increasing pressure on prices (inflation) and again discourage exports.

Quotas can also "backfire." Despite voluntary quotas, the actual value of Japanese cars exported to the United States increased. Although Japanese auto manufacturers technically adhered to the voluntary quotas, they shifted exports from lower-priced models to higher-priced ones.

Even when devaluing the currency has the desired effect on the trade balance, the effects are not long-lasting since nothing has been done to remove the underlying causes of the imbalance. If devaluation results in retaliation, foreign markets will be closed to exports. Even if they are not, countries that devalue their currencies are faced with immediate cost problems. If they are dependent on the import of raw materials, devaluation will increase raw material costs, which will translate into higher production costs. Furthermore, if the nation must import foodstuffs and other necessities, the increased pressure on the cost of living is going to cause labor to demand higher wages. Higher wages, like raw material costs, lead to higher costs of production and higher prices, therefore discouraging exports.

Generally, devaluation will at best have a short-term positive effect on exports. How long the effects last will depend largely on how rapidly domestic prices rise, the reaction of other countries to the devaluation, and the elasticity in demand for a nation's products.

The only real long-term solution for a trade imbalance is to increase the diversity and quality of goods produced by the nation, while simultaneously increasing the productivity of the nation's manufacturing capacity, which would result in the following situation:

1. Greater variety of goods
2. Better-quality goods
3. Lower prices for goods sold on world markets

Many methods used to address B/P problems do not remove the major cause of disequilibrium: poor national productivity.

Since these lasting changes take a great deal of time to implement, the foregoing policies need to be used as temporary measures.

SUMMARY

With the growth of nations and the rapid development of trade, a medium of exchange acceptable to all parties was of utmost importance. This need was met when Great Britain adopted the gold standard in 1821, which served its purpose admirably until the early decades of the present century. The metal provided for the first time a common denominator, enabling the relationship among different currencies to be clearly established. But with the tremendous growth in foreign trade and other international transactions, the supply of gold proved inadequate. The U.S. dollar supplemented gold for many years after World War II because it was freely convertible into gold. With the growing deficit in the U.S. balance of payments in the 1950s and the 1960s, confidence in the dollar as a substitute for gold eroded. The United States no longer had a sufficient supply of gold to convert outstanding dollars. In 1965 the United States had to suspend the 25 percent reserve requirement so that it could issue more currency. But without the gold backing, some countries anticipated a further fall in the value of the dollar. They decided to convert their dollar holdings into gold. The result was a run on the U.S. gold reserves and a further loss in confidence in the value of the dollar.

Continued U.S. balance of payments deficits caused nations to question the value of the dollar. To restore this confidence, the United States made every effort to bring about equilibrium in its balance of payments. Its efforts failed. Unable to restore equilibrium in its balance of payments, the country was forced to devalue its currency, first in December 1971, then again in February 1973. To minimize the continuing downward pressure on the value of the dollar, Germany and Japan were asked to revalue their currencies upward. They reluctantly complied, and the value of the dollar continued to be linked to gold but with a lower gold content ($38 per ounce in 1971 and $42.20 in 1973).

One can readily see the relationship between the value of a country's currency and the balance of payments. Overvaluation discourages exports, leading to a negative balance of trade. Since trade is the most important component of a nation's balance of payments, a negative balance of trade usually results in an overall deficit in a nation's balance of payments position. Nations with a deficit disequilibrium make every effort to bring about equilibrium since their supplies of gold and foreign exchange are limited. This becomes especially serious when a country such as the United States, whose dollar is used as a reserve currency, must increase its money supply to clear its deficit account.

To restore equilibrium in their balance of payments, nations adopt different measures. The most common are those to restrict imports while stimulating exports. However, these often result in retaliation and do not achieve their purposes. As an alternative, countries often devalue their currencies, hoping to encourage exports and discourage imports. Short-term success is often achieved, but in the long run such measures are not effective because they do not remove the basic causes for the negative balance of trade. In the long run, nations must make goods of sufficient quality and price to be competitive on world markets, or their disequilibrium will return. □

KEY TERMS AND CONCEPTS

Autonomous items

Balance of payments

Capital Account

Compensatory items

Credit and debit items

Deflation

Depreciation

Devaluation

Dirty float

Disequilibrium

Dollar gap

Errors and omissions

European Monetary System

Free float

International Monetary Fund

Managed float

Pegging operation

Revaluation

Smithsonian Agreement

Special Drawing Rights (SDRs)

Sterilizing gold

Subscription quotas

Surtax

Unrequited transfers

REVIEW QUESTIONS

1. Explain the significance of the gold exchange standard as adopted at the Bretton Woods Agreement in 1944.

2. What caused the breakdown of the international monetary system in the 1970s?

3. What was the Smithsonian Agreement of 1971?

4. Why were Japan and West Germany reluctant to adopt a policy of revaluation as suggested by the United States?

5. Explain the "two-tier" system of pricing gold.

6. What is the difference between a free float and a dirty float?

7. What is the Special Drawing Right? How is its value determined at the present time?

8. Distinguish between the debit items and the credit items in the balance of payments statement.

9. Describe those items that make up the Currenct Account in the balance of payments statement.

10. What are the differences between short-term and long-term Capital Accounts?

11. What is meant by disequilibrium in the balance of payments of a nation? What are the major reasons for disequilibrium? What measures may a nation use in an attempt to bring about equilibrium in its balance of payments?

12. Explain why a surplus disequilibrium or a deficit disequilibrium cannot continue indefinitely.

DISCUSSION CASE

Venezuela Takes Major Action to Prevent a Balance of Payments Crisis

As is true with many Latin American countries, Venezuela has encountered difficulties in meeting its foreign debt obligations. However, it is the only country that has restructured its debt and has been making principal payments in the last few years. In 1988, principal repayments totaled $1.9 billion and in 1989, $1.5 billion. Unfortunately, the price of making these payments has been the Central Bank's reserve position: foreign exchange

Adapted from Peter Kennedy and Douglas Ford, "Venezuela Moves on Debt to Ward Off BOP Crisis," *Business Latin America*, January 9, 1989, pp. 1, 2, and 7.

reserves plummeted by $2 billion to $7 billion (1989). Because of this, Venezuela decided to suspend its principal payments on the bulk of its $26 billion foreign bank debts contracted before 1984, saving the nation about $340 million quarterly.

Venezuela has requested foreign creditors to accept a rescheduling of its maturities and a seven-year grace period on principal repayments. To support the request for the suspension of the principal repayments, it has decided to adopt an austerity program to control imports and correct a deteriorating balance of payments. Creditor banks are expected to agree to the nation's requests, which are similar to terms received by Argentina, Brazil, and Mexico in their recent debt deals.

Venezuela is demonstrating to foreign banks and official creditors its willingness to shoulder its share of the adjustment burden by devaluing its currency by 40 to 50 percent and by adopting major cuts in imports.

This will be accomplished in three ways. First, the private sector import budget will be cut by 40 percent, to $4.2 billion. This has caused a furor in the industrial sector. Second, the nation has introduced a new 60 percent surcharge on top of existing ad valorem duties for 500 finished products. Among the goods affected are fish, fruit, household appliances, photocopiers, calculators, typewriters, and most liquor. It is not yet clear whether this move is being taken in place of the government's earlier plan to subject luxury goods to the free market exchange rate. Third, the government has decreed a technical change in establishing the effective exchange rate on financed imports. It has declared that goods paid for in cash or letters of credit of less than 180 days will receive the rate in effect at the time of purchase, but those financed under longer terms will be subject to the exchange rate in effect at the time the merchandise arrives in Venezuela.

Questions

1. What effect will these measures have on the price levels within the country? Why?
2. How will they affect domestic producers?
3. What effect will they have on the nation's balance of payments?

NOTES

1. SDRs were the artificial deposits created by the IMF for use by the members.
2. Subscription quota was the amount of capital each IMF member was required to pay to the IMF, based upon the wealth of each country.
3. Mordechai E. Kreinin, *International Economics: A Policy Approach* (New York: Harcourt Brace Jovanovich, 1975), p. 178.
4. Ibid., p. 184.
5. Ibid., p. 186.
6. The 16 national currencies that were used to determine the value of the SDRs

prior to 1981 were the Australian dollar, Austrian schilling, Belgian franc, Canadian dollar, Danish krone, Deutsche mark, French franc, Italian lira, Japanese yen, Netherlands guilder, Norwegian krone, British pound sterling, South African rand, Spanish peseta, Swedish krone, and the U.S. dollar.

7. IMF, *International Financial Statistics Yearbook*, 1984, pp. 110–111; IMF, *IMF Financial Statistics*, vol. 39, no. 1, January 1986. The increasing value of the dollar was due to extremely high interest rates, the reduced inflation rate, and the strength of the U.S. economy.

8. IMF, *IMF Survey*, July 11, 1988, p. 239.

9. IMF, *International Financial Statistics Yearbook*, 1989.

10. IMF, *IMF Survey*, vol. 17, no. 14, July 11, 1988, pp. 225, 235–236.

11. Ibid.

12. Ibid.

13. Board of Governors, *Federal Reserve Bulletin*, April 1989, p. A56.

14. IMF, *International Financial Statistics Yearbook*, 1989, p. 725.

15. Board of Governors, *Federal Reserve Bulletin*, April 1989, p. A55.

16. IMF, *International Financial Statistics Yearbook*, 1989, p. 725.

17. Board of Governors, p. A55.

REFERENCES AND SELECTED READINGS

Board of Governors of the Federal Reserve System. *Federal Reserve Bulletin*. Washington, D.C.: Publications Service, Monthly.

Eiteman, David K., and Arthur I. Stonehill. *Multinational Business Finance*, 5th ed. Reading, Mass.: Addison-Wesley Publishing Co., 1989.

Hansen, Alvin H. *The Dollar and the International Monetary System*. New York: McGraw-Hill, 1965.

IMF. *Annual Report on Exchange Arrangements & Exchange Restrictions*. Washington, D.C.: IMF, 1983, 1984.

IMF. *Balance of Payments Statistics*, 1986. Washington, D.C.: IMF, 1987.

IMF. *Balance of Payments Statistics*, vol. 36, Yearbook, Part 2, 1985. Washington, D.C.: IMF, 1986.

IMF. *International Financial Statistics Yearbook*. Washington, D.C., 1989.

IMF. *IMF Survey*, vol. 17, no. 14, July 11, 1988.

Moore, Geoffrey H. "Will The 'Real' Trade Balance Please Stand Up." *The Journal of International Business Studies* 14:1 (Spring/Summer 1983).

Park, Yoon S., and Jack Zwick. *International Banking in Theory and Practice*. Reading, Mass.: Addison-Wesley Publishing Company, 1985.

Shapiro, Alan C. *Multinational Financial Management*. Boston, Mass.: Allyn and Bacon, 1982.

CHAPTER

6 International Business and the Role of Financial Institutions

- Identify and describe the principal financial institutions and agencies that are instrumental in financing international business

- Become familiar with those U.S. government agencies that are responsible for developing the nation's commerce

- Become familiar with the international agencies that attempt to bring about international financial stability and aid the economic development of the less developed nations

- Understand how these institutions and agencies are financed

- Become familiar with the plans and programs that various financial institutions offer to business firms, governments, and government agencies

  Learn the impact of these institutions on international business

INTRODUCTION

During the course of operations, most international business firms must turn to financial institutions for loans or advances to finance their overseas transactions. Different types of financial institutions, both private and public, exist to provide general or specialized services to business firms. Commercial banks play a major role in promoting international trade. In most nations, government agencies complement the functioning of commercial banks by providing funds where greater risk is involved. In addition, there are a number of international agencies that are of primary importance in financing various types of projects in less developed countries.

This chapter focuses on these institutions and provides the framework within which international trade is conducted; explains the role of private, governmental, and international institutions; and describes the types of loans provided, including those for economic and infrastructure development in less developed countries.

PRIVATE FINANCIAL INSTITUTIONS

Commercial Banks

Commercial banks are a major source of capital. Their importance as lending agencies is reflected by U.S. bank claims against all foreigners totaling $489,749 million at the end of December 1988. These claims were distributed as follows: Europe $116,696 million; Latin America and the Caribbean $213,172 million; Asia $130,178 million; Africa $5,720 million; Canada $18,965 million; other countries $2,720 million; and $2,272 to nonmonetary international and regional organizations.[1]

Because the Federal Reserve Act prohibits member banks from accepting commercial drafts or bills with a maturity date exceeding six months, and drafts and notes exceeding six months may not be rediscounted at a Federal Reserve Bank, the activities of the commercial banks are concentrated primarily in short-term financing. These involve the selling of banker's acceptances, discounting bills of exchange, and providing direct loans. Furthermore, U.S. laws and regulations that promote sound banking practices limit the commercial bank activities in providing medium- or long-term venture capital.

When commercial banks are forced to reject applications from firms for medium-term financing, they generally try to find ways to accommodate their capital-seeking clients. One method is to seek Export-Import Bank participation or guarantees on funds used to purchase capital equipment that is to be exported. Banks may also involve the Private Export Funding Corporation (PEFCO) described below, or provide funds through an Edge Act corporation owned by a commercial bank that is authorized to engage in both equity and long-term debt financing.[2]

Private Export Funding Corporation

The Private Export Funding Corporation was established by the American Bankers Association for Foreign Trade to expand the export business of the United States. The principal stockholders are the major U.S. commercial banks and corporations. PEFCO will co-lend with commercial banks or the Export-Import Bank (Eximbank), or will handle the loan by itself. Its major activity is to hold medium- and long-term obligations from foreign buyers of U.S. products. Its capital is raised through the sale of its own securities to investors, either private or governmental.

PEFCO does not grant a loan until the Eximbank has also approved that loan. Once approval has been received, the loan made by PEFCO is guaranteed against default by the Eximbank. A fee of $\frac{1}{2}$ to 1 percent is charged for this guarantee. This aids the sale of the securities of PEFCO.

Investment Companies

There are a number of private investment companies that specialize in providing equity financing for foreign ventures. One of the largest of the American investment companies is the International Basic Economy Corporation (IBEC), founded by Nelson Rockefeller shortly after World War II. It does not grant loans, reserving this role to its affiliate, Transoceanic AOFC Ltd. IBEC will buy stock in joint ventures with U.S. firms and/or firms in a host country, and strives to secure control of the foreign venture either alone or jointly with the U.S. investor.[3] IBEC seeks between 20 percent and 100 percent equity in its foreign operations. It engages only in projects that not only aid the development of the economy of the host country but also are profitable investments.

Insurance Companies

Although insurance companies, union pension funds, and similar sources of capital are frequently used for domestic investments, they seldom participate in investments abroad because of federal regulations or because of the policies under which they operate.

Securities Markets

Well-established investment banks, underwriting houses, and brokerage firms of the United States do not play an important role in providing venture capital to firms abroad. Their primary interest lies in floating new issues of stocks or bonds for domestic operations. Rarely do U.S. firms issue the stock of their foreign subsidiaries in the United States. The Securities and Exchange Commission regulations, low demand, and high issuance costs generally make it unprofitable to float such issues.

Foreign Factors and Commercial Finance Companies

Commercial banks are the primary source for short-term financing; Eximbank, Edge Act corporations, or PEFCOs for medium-term financing; and investment companies for equity capital.

Exporters in need of funds can shorten the period between the shipment of goods and the receipt of payment by selling their accounts receivable to a factor. Factors generally serve the exporter who is unable to obtain funds from commercial banks or the Eximbank. The major disadvantage in using a factor is the high cost. Factors pay only a percentage of the face value of accounts receivable, and the older the account, the lower the percentage.

U.S. GOVERNMENT AGENCIES

A number of U.S. government agencies aid firms involved in international trade and investment. Three such agencies that supplement private sources of capital to increase the trade of the United States and to aid in the development of the less developed countries are the Export-Import Bank, (Eximbank), the Agency for International Development (AID), and the Commodity Credit Corporation (CCC). Most industrialized countries have similar agencies that support the foreign trade and investment activities of the home country.

Securities exchanges the world over provide the physical arena for the dynamics of the market to set the value of negotiable instruments and saleable commodities.

Export-Import Bank

The first Eximbank was established in February 1934 with $10,000,000 of initial capital to provide credit for developing trade with the Soviet Union. In the same year, a second Export-Import Bank was established to aid Cuba in paying for coins minted in Philadelphia. In May 1936, the two institutions were merged into a single bank. Its first loan operation involved the financing of sales to European countries just before the outbreak of World War II. This was followed by aid to Brazil for the construction of a steel mill, and a loan to the Universal Trading Company, an agent of the Chinese government, for the construction of the famous Burma Road during World War II. However, the bank was not established to carry out extensive operations.

Anticipating the world's postwar financial requirements and the U.S. responsibility to take a leadership role, Congress in 1945 passed the Export-Import Bank Act, formally organizing the Bank as we know it today. With expanded resources, it was able to serve as the major lending agency of the U.S. government to assist in the reconstruction of war-devastated areas of Europe. The launching of the Marshall Plan in 1948 enabled the Bank to give more attention to countries in Asia, Africa, and the Middle East.

Because of the rapid European economic recovery in the 1950s and Europe's increasing ability to compete in the world markets, the Export-

Import Bank began helping American producers to compete with foreign exporters. It initiated numerous trade-financing programs to overcome the subsidies that were being provided to many foreign producers by their governments.

Management and Sources of Capital

The management of the bank is in the hands of a board composed of a President, Vice-President, and three Directors, and appointed by the President of the United States with the advice and consent of the Senate, as shown in Figure 6.1.

In 1958, the Export-Import Bank was capitalized at $1 billion, with the capital stock subscribed to by the U.S. Treasury. Additional credits of $6 billion were made available from the Treasury, which increased the total lending authority of the bank to a maximum of $7 billion. Its capital stock and accumulated reserves provided it with the bulk of its capital requirements and were sufficient to meet its needs during the early years of its operation. However, as demand increased beyond its resources, additional funds were raised from debentures, short-term discount notes, and certificates of participation. The Eximbank is also authorized to seek additional funds from the U.S. Treasury and the capital markets, but it may not borrow in the open market.

The Export-Import Bank Act of 1945 established the Eximbank as the primary source of direct credit and financial guarantees for U.S. exporters.

Programs of the Export-Import Bank

The Export-Import Bank offers various services in financing international transactions. These are described below.

Direct Credit and Financial Guarantees   Many foreign countries and enterprises in need of development loans to purchase capital equipment for major renovations, construction of rail lines, or other projects that entail large expenditures are aided by medium- and long-term Eximbank loans. The Eximbank also aids firms of any country that cannot obtain private-sector financing because of political risks, the size of the loan, or other such reasons. For example, the Eximbank may extend the maturity date of loans if economic conditions weaken or may charge rates below those of the public sector.

The Eximbank offers exporter credits that are created on sales of capital goods. It offers financial guarantees to U.S. lenders who might otherwise refuse to make a loan so as to encourage U.S. banks to become more active

Figure 6.1   Management of Export-Import Bank

Board of Directors ⟵——————————— Appointed by U.S. President

President
Vice-President
Three Directors

Advice and consent of the Senate

in export lending and to decrease the lending functions of the Eximbank. The Bank also extends commodity loans to finance the sale of surplus agricultural products from the United States.

Preliminary Commitment and Letters of Interest   To aid exporters who are unsure of the financial arrangements that might be available, the Eximbank provides certain services at no charge. It will analyze the portfolio of the importer desiring aid and then issue a *letter of commitment* that describes all the terms under which the Eximbank will grant the loan: the amount it will loan, interest rate, terms, conditions of guarantees, expiration date, and so forth. It also indicates what aid it will give to a U.S. bank or agency. This information enables the parties to anticipate the aid the Eximbank will provide, freeing the buyer and seller to negotiate other matters.

The *letters of interest*, although similar to letters of commitment, are nothing more than information letters that are provided to the exporter by the Eximbank. They do not assure the exporter of Eximbank support.

Export Credits, Guarantees, and Insurance   On May 23, 1960, the Export-Import Bank began offering export guarantees covering noncommercial and political risks on short-term transactions.[4] These enable American exporters to obtain political risk insurance from U.S. commercial banks and export credit insurance companies without direct contact with the Eximbank. Commercial banks are authorized to act as agents of the Eximbank. American insurance companies that offer export credit insurance are also designated to act in behalf of the Eximbank in the issuance of political risk guarantees. Included in the noncommercial category are inconvertibility of currencies, adoption of new laws or regulations, cancellation of import licenses, wars, hostilities and civil commotion, expropriation of goods by foreign authorities, and similar risks. Other than for the inconvertibility of currencies, the Eximbank will pay to the exporter 90 percent of losses incurred.

In contracting for an Eximbank short-term political risk guarantee through a commercial bank, the exporter must agree to declare and pay fees on all exports for a period of one year. To initiate the agreement, the exporter must estimate the total dollar volume of short-term export business for the year, and deposit a fee that varies with the time period of the credit. Each eligible shipment made by the exporter will be protected against political risks provided monthly declarations and payments are made for the coverage of individual shipments.

Protection from possible loss on medium-term (180 days to 5 years) transactions is also provided the exporter.[5] On these transactions the importer is required to make a down payment of 20 percent of the invoice value of the export at the time of delivery of the goods. The participation of the Eximbank is limited to the balance of the financed portion of the transaction. A fee of $\frac{3}{4}$ of one percent is charged for the medium-term political risk guarantees.

Exporters may arrange for comprehensive guarantees that cover both credit risks and political risks on 85 percent of the financed portion of the export. The fee is about $1\frac{1}{2}$ percent per year on the declining balance. When an exporter anticipates making repeat sales to an importer with an established credit standing, the Eximbank may grant the exporter a credit ceiling against which the exporter may carry out a series of transactions without contacting the Eximbank in each instance.

To encourage private participation in financing medium-term transactions, the Eximbank will, under certain circumstances, participate solely on the basis of the credit judgment of the commercial bank. In these cases the foreign buyer must pay at least 20 percent of the invoice value by the time of delivery.

To facilitate requests from individual exporters or their bankers in connection with medium- and short-term transactions, the Eximbank has established within its Loan Division an Export Credit and Guarantee Section.

In 1962, the Eximbank helped establish the Foreign Credit Insurance Association (FCIA), made up of casualty, maritime, and property insurance companies. This association provides protection against political and commercial risks that might be encountered by those who extend credit. It deals in both short-term (up to 180 days) and medium-term (181 days to 5 years) obligations. For short-term loans, 100 percent coverage is provided against commercial and political risks.[6] Although not directly related to the Eximbank, the Overseas Private Investment Corporation (OPIC) provides additional political risk insurance to firms that invest in less developed countries. This was established in 1969 under the Foreign Assistance Act of 1961.

The Cooperative Financing Facility was set up to aid foreign banks in making loans to importers. The importer pays 10 percent of the purchase price in cash, and the foreign bank and the Eximbank share equally in the balance of the loan. Each assumes the risk for the amount it loaned. This encourages banks outside the exporter's country (generally in the importing nation) to participate in making loans. Such loans are often of lower cost to the importer. Furthermore, this risk-sharing with a foreign bank usually generates goodwill among the countries and firms involved.

Commercial Bank Guarantees   Two major plans were offered to meet the individual needs of specific commercial banks in financing foreign trade. The first plan is designed so that in the early stages of the loan (first half of the loan period up to 18 months), the commercial bank is responsible for commercial credit losses. For the second half of the loan period, the Export-Import Bank will absorb any commercial credit losses. Losses from political risks are covered from the first day by the Eximbank.

Under the second plan, the Eximbank provides for 90 percent coverage of commercial losses and 10 percent coverage for political losses during the early part of the loan period. During the second half of the loan period, the

Eximbank may provide 100 percent coverage for both if it feels conditions support this. For the commercial bank, the plan it selects will depend on whether it feels one or the other danger is greater. Many other variations are available, such as political risks only, special public buyers of goods risks, commercial risks only, and so forth.

Discount Loans   Even though the risks are not great, some banks might hesitate in making loans to finance export transactions. For banks that find themselves short of cash, the Eximbank offers discount loans sufficient to help U.S. exporters. It will provide funds to such a bank at a cost of $\frac{1}{2}$ percent less than the yield on the loan it has extended to the exporter. These discount loans can be used to extend short-term or medium-term credit to exporters or nations as long as they aid U.S. exporters. If a bank feels it would have to obtain a loan to finance a transaction, it should forewarn the Eximbank that it will not make a certain export loan unless it is able to get a discount loan. Furthermore, the bank must show that the importer is dependent upon the loan to make the purchase.

Small Business Programs

In 1976, the Export-Import Bank adopted measures to encourage small firms to engage in the export business. Under the direction of the Eximbank, the Small Business Administration, the Department of Commerce and the Overseas Private Investment Corporation established a program to create various aids, information, and services to aid small business firms. Every effort was made to ensure the wide dissemination of information regarding the availability of these services.

The Export-Import Bank encourages commercial banks to finance export transactions by providing guarantees and discount loans.

Short- and Medium-Term Insurance and Guarantees for Small Business
Because small businesses are more vulnerable to the effects of losses from defaults, the Eximbank felt that an insurance plan was essential to protect these newcomers in international trade. The Eximbank and FCIA provide 95 percent protection against commercial risks and 100 percent coverage against political risks for firms whose exports have not exceeded $350,000 in the last two years. The policy relieves small exporters from worries on short-term and medium-term transactions.

Small Business Advisory Service   The Export-Import Bank greatly expanded its small business advisory service. It provides complete information regarding credit insurance and guarantees, and it even supplies information regarding potential export markets.

Engineering, Planning, and Feasibility Studies   The Export-Import Bank is involved in projects that might indirectly increase exports by U.S. firms. One such example is the loan or grant it extends to firms to conduct feasibility studies for foreign countries. Since there is no guarantee that a country will accept the recommendations of a study, or that a U.S. firm will receive the business once the study is completed, the role of the Eximbank becomes quite important. It will finance the costs involved in having the studies conducted by U.S. firms if the possibility exists that this will result in additional outlets for U.S. goods or services. To obtain such assistance, a firm must provide a statement indicating the purpose of the loan and how it will help the U.S. exports. After the study is completed and the firm makes export sales, the Eximbank will give the firm a year's grace before the start of repayment.

Use of Export-Import Bank Facilities

Each year, the Export-Import Bank provides billions of dollars of assistance to many countries, some of which are used to finance U.S. exports, but most of which are concentrated in projects that would aid a country in its economic development. For example, Mexico, Algeria, and Brazil have used Eximbank loans for the expansion of oil and natural gas research. South Korea used its funds for the purchase of two nuclear power plants, Trinidad for fertilizer plants, Argentina for petrochemical plants, and Mexico for tire and tube production. Large amounts are also provided for insurance guarantees. The various projects that the Export-Import Bank has helped finance have resulted in direct sales abroad by U.S. firms and have opened up additional markets for U.S. exporters.

In addition to the insurance and guarantees, the Eximbank provides business firms with advisory services as well as engineering, planning, and market feasibility studies.

Agency for International Development

The U.S. State Department's Agency for International Development (AID) was created by the Foreign Assistance Act of 1961 to consolidate under one agency the functions of the International Cooperation Administration and the Development Loan Fund. It is one of the agencies most familiar to the American public because of its various foreign aid activities, such as the Peace Corps. The only restriction imposed on AID is that it may not provide assistance to countries nationalizing, expropriating, or seizing control of properties of U.S. citizens or nullifying contracts and agreements with U.S. citizens.[7]

Development Loans

AID makes development loans to less developed countries. The major purpose is to assist such countries in making long-range plans or programs for developing resources or increasing productive capabilities. The recipients of the loans are the governments and qualifying private enterprises.

One of the conditions for loan approval is that AID must have a reasonable chance of repayment. Other factors—such as the availability of funds at reasonable terms from other free world countries, the debt-bearing capacity of the borrowing country or enterprise, and other requirements of sound development lending—are considered before loans are made. In such loan agreements, *tying clauses* are used requiring the proceeds of such loans to be spent in the United States.

The terms of the loan are dependent upon the stage of economic development of the country and the nature of the enterprise involved. Loans to governments may be amortized over 40 years. The rate of interest for the first 10 years is 2 percent per year, and 3 percent thereafter. Terms of the loans to private enterprises are negotiated on a case-by-case basis with a minimum rate of 6 percent. An enterprise may repay such loans to the host country in local currency, but the foreign government is obligated to repay AID in dollars at the government's loan rates and terms.

Investment Guarantees

The Agency for International Development provides investment guarantees. These are (1) specific risk guarantees, (2) extended risk guarantees, and (3) extended risk guarantees for housing. Specific risk guarantees protect eligible U.S. investors in developing countries against inconvertibility, expropriation or confiscation, and war, revolution, or insurrection. Eligible investors are U.S. citizens, corporations substantially or beneficially owned (more than 50 percent) by U.S. citizens, or wholly owned subsidiaries of U.S. corporations. Guarantees for equity investments are for a maximum period of 20 years.[8] Host government approval of projects is necessary for investment guarantees.

The extended risk guarantees cover up to 75 percent of an investment against losses arising from all risks except fraud or misconduct of the investor. These guarantees serve primarily to assist in the development of small business enterprises and for economic development projects that aid social progress.

The extended risk guarantees for housing provide 100 percent coverage on housing project loans in which the private investor participates. Additional guarantees on investments in housing projects in Latin America were specifically provided for under the Foreign Assistance Act of 1966. U.S. investors are guaranteed against loss for the following types of Latin American housing investments:

1. Loans made to credit institutions financing home mortgages
2. Housing projects for lower-income families
3. Housing projects that further the aims of the Alliance for Progress
4. Housing projects where at least 25 percent of the mortgage financing is from Latin American sources

Thus, guarantees by AID help to further the objectives of adequate shelter for lower-income families under the Alliance for Progress.

Investment Opportunity Surveys

AID provides long-term assistance and loans to developing countries as well as guarantees for investors against most risks, except fraud or misconduct.

If, after the survey has been completed, the private enterprise decides against investing in a project, AID will repay half of the cost of investment surveys done in less developed friendly countries.

Commodity Credit Corporation

The Commodity Credit Corporation (CCC) is an agency of the U.S. Department of Agriculture that is engaged in promoting the sales of surplus agricultural products. The program is open to exporters and covers commodities in the CCC inventory, under loan to the agency, or private stocks of certain agricultural commodities. The credit that is extended (up to three years) is limited to the value of the products in the United States (FOB vessel, named port of export) and may not include the cost of marine insurance, ocean freight, or letter of credit charges. Shipments are restricted to "friendly countries." U.S. bank confirmation of at least 10 percent of the amount of each advised credit is necessary before the CCC will deliver the commodities or issue its certificates for the value of the private stock shipped.[9]

Cooley Amendment Funds

Under Public Law 480 (the Cooley Amendment to Title I of the Agricultural Trade Development and Assistance Act), foreign currencies (Cooley Funds) received in payment for export sales of agricultural products may be allocated to AID, which may lend such funds to U.S. companies and their branches, subsidiaries, or affiliates for trade expansion or business development. Foreign countries may also borrow these funds to expand the market for U.S. agricultural products. The rates of interest on the loans are those prevailing in the foreign country. The final decision for the use of PL 480 funds is made by the U.S. Secretary of Agriculture.

The CCC credits and Cooley Funds promote the sales of U.S. surplus agricultural products by extending credit for their purchase.

INTERNATIONAL AGENCIES

The Bretton Woods Agreement of 1944 resulted in the establishment of the International Monetary Fund (IMF) and the International Bank for Reconstruction and Development (IBRD), or World Bank. These institutions were assigned different but complementary tasks. Close and regular consultations take place between these two institutions to coordinate their activities and to avoid contradictory advice to member states. The IBRD is the specialist in the development of the LDCs, while the IMF is the specialist in balance of payments disequilibria. Thus, both institutions play a major role in countries facing financial difficulties.

International Monetary Fund

The Articles of Agreement of the IMF provide for a Board of Governors, an Executive Board, a Managing Director, an international staff, and a Council (see Figure 6.2). The highest authority of the Fund is the Board of Governors, which consists of a Governor and an Alternate appointed by each of the member countries.

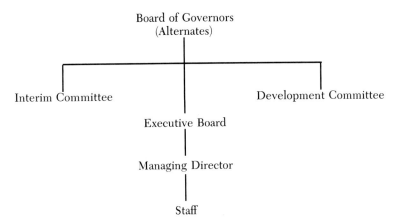

Figure 6.2   Organizational Structure of IMF
Source: IMF *Survey* (Supplement on the Fund), August 1989.

Member countries appoint the Governors, who are usually high-ranking financial officials such as the Minister of Finance, the governor of a central bank, or someone of comparable rank. There are 22 Executive Directors. The People's Republic of China, France, Germany, Japan, Saudi Arabia, the United Kingdom, and the United States each appoint one director. The remaining 15 are elected from the remaining 144 members. In 1978, the Articles of Agreement were amended to authorize the Board of Governors to establish a Council as a decision-making body "to supervise the management and adaptation of the international monetary system and consider any proposals to amend the Articles of Agreement."[10] To date the Board has opted to operate with an Interim Committee as an advisory body with a composition and scope comparable to that of the Council. The Ministerial Committee on the Transfer of Real Resources to Developing Countries (Development Committee), which was established at the same time, is involved in development issues.

Loan Objectives

The IMF was established to bring order to the international monetary system.[11] It is not directly involved in international business except to create an environment for the balanced growth of international trade by eliminating exchange and payments restrictions. Its primary function is to provide short- and medium-term credits to member countries to help them "bridge their balance of payments difficulties" until a permanent solution can be worked out. It normally does this by providing the countries with foreign currencies in exchange for deposits of the members' own currencies or stand-by credits.

Sources of Capital

The major source of capital for the IMF is from subscription quotas assigned to each of the 151 (in 1989) member countries, borrowing in the world capital markets, and from net earnings. The amount that each country contributes is determined by the wealth of the country based on economic and financial factors. Thus, the quota of the United States of SDR 17,913.3 million (about $23,082 million = 19.91 percent) is larger than that of any other country.[12] These quotas are reviewed every five years since the voting power, the line of credit, and the share in the allocation of SDRs are determined by the member's quota subscription in the Fund. Each member is required to pay the first 25 percent of its quota in SDRs or currencies of other members selected by the Fund with their concurrence. This is called the member's *reserve tranche*. The remainder is paid in the member's own currency (see Figure 6.3). The total value of the quota subscriptions amounted to SDR 89,987.55 million (about U.S. $113,762 million) in October 1989.[13]

Because member nations resist the periodic increases in quotas, the IMF must turn to official financial institutions for funds. This was made possible through the General Arrangements to Borrow (1962), which provided the IMF with a line of credit with the central banks of the Group of Ten.[14] Arrangements were made in 1976 to borrow from 17 member nations, including some oil-producing countries, to aid oil-importing countries in balance of payments difficulties,

To provide the IMF with additional funds, "supplementary financing" and the "enlarged access facilities" were created in 1979 and 1981, respectively. These are lines of credit with central banks of the major industrial countries, the Bank for International Settlements, and the Saudi Arabian authorities. The Board of Governors was discussing the possibility of doubling each nation's quota by the end of 1989 to reduce their dependence on external sources, but no decision had been made and discussions are expected to continue well into the 1990s.

Terms and Conditions for Loans

A member nation has unconditional drawing rights in convertible currencies for an amount equal to its *reserve tranche*. The first 25 percent it borrows is not considered IMF credit, so interest is not charged on this amount. However, drawing on the resources of the IMF beyond the *reserve tranche* is conditional—that is, certain criteria of financial stability and credit worthiness must be met.

The IMF adopted new conditions to enable member countries to meet their needs because of changes in the international financial environment. The amount members may borrow was increased and the terms extended.

Figure 6.3   Quota Subscription for IMF Members

First 25% ⟵————— Special Drawing Rights or
(reserve tranche)   currencies of other members

Remaining 75% ⟵——— Member country's currency

This was accomplished in September 1974 through the Extended Facility, which authorized members to borrow up to 140 percent of their quota. The maximum credit that a nation may obtain has been fixed at 600 percent of the quota, and under certain conditions even the upper limit may be exceeded.

A Compensatory Financing Facility was introduced in 1963 to permit member nations to turn to the IMF for loans when their export earnings dropped temporarily due to circumstances beyond their control. A Food Facility was established in 1981 as a part of the Compensatory Financing Facility to supply funds for the import of food. Members may draw up to 100 percent of their quota separately and 125 percent of their quota cumulatively under the Food Compensatory Facility.

Since 1969, members having difficulties financing buffer stocks under the international commodity agreements have had access to the Buffer Stock Financing Facility, up to a maximum of 50 percent of their quota. Since all of these facilities exist to help members solve their balance of payments problems, members are expected to make a "reasonable" effort to achieve their goals.

Loans generally take one of three forms: (1) Standby credits are usually for 1 year; (2) drawings by members are generally for a period between 3 and 5 years; and (3) extended credit facilities are for a period between $4\frac{1}{2}$ and 10 years (see Figure 6.4).

The rate of interest on SDR credits is between the foreign aid rate and the commercial loan rate. Other loans by the IMF carry a higher floating rate of interest. To aid poorer countries, an interest subsidy fund was established in 1980. The conditions for loans are defined in the standby agreements.

As a general policy, the IMF loans are extended to countries whose balance of payments deficits are larger than what they might reasonably be expected to eliminate within a reasonable time. The loans made to bridge this gap are subject to policy corrections based upon IMF recommendations.

The country that is applying for a loan must first submit a letter of intent describing the economic policy it will pursue. Second, it must provide technical details concerning the desired amounts of credit and the date when it is required.

The IMF makes recommendations regarding the exchange rate adjustments, interest rates, income and price policy, and the gradual elimination of trade and payments restrictions. It monitors the economic performance of the country (test criteria), and if certain standards are not met, the country

Figure 6.4   Forms of Credits Granted to IMF Members

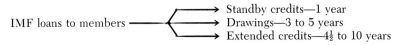

IMF loans to members — Standby credits—1 year / Drawings—3 to 5 years / Extended credits—$4\frac{1}{2}$ to 10 years

The short- and medium-term loan activities of the IMF supplement its other activities to bring order into the international monetary system.

is not permitted to draw on its credit tranches. The standards deal with such things as the increase in domestic credit, national budget, volume of foreign debt, and the net foreign exchange position of the country. The policies recommended by the IMF have been successful in restoring equilibrium in the balance of payments position of many borrowers. It is interesting to note that the IMF has operated at a profit since its inception.

International Bank for Reconstruction and Development (World Bank)

The International Bank for Reconstruction and Development (IBRD), or World Bank, is an institution that was established to assist in the reconstruction of the war-devastated areas and to aid in the development of the resources of the less developed countries of the world. It is owned by member nations that have subscribed to its capital stock according to the economic capability of each nation. It complements the International Monetary Fund in that it grants long-term credit for economic development, primarily to Third World countries. The World Bank has two subsidiaries that supplement its activities. These are the International Development Association (IDA) and the International Finance Corporation (IFC).

Administrative Organization

The administration of the IBRD is composed of a Board of Governors, Executive Directors, President, Vice-President, and staff. The powers of the Bank are vested in the Board of Governors, to which each member nation appoints a single representative. The five largest stockholders appoint five of the Executive Directors, and the remaining are elected by the Governors of the remaining member nations. Each member country is entitled to 250 votes plus 1 vote for each share of stock held. The Executive Directors select the President of the Bank, who serves as the Chief Executive Officer and as the ex officio Chairman of the Executive Directors. The President is responsible for the operation of the Bank and the organization of the staff (see Figure 6.5).

Figure 6.5   Administrative Organization of the IBRD

Board of Governors

|

Executive Directors

|

(President—ex officio Chairman of Executive Directors)

|

Vice-President

|

IBRD Staff

Objectives

Since 1948, the IBRD has been aiding the development needs of the less developed countries. Its objectives may be summarized as follows:[15]

1. To grant credit for development purposes
2. To render technical assistance by training officials in matters of development
3. To coordinate international development aid
4. To study the economic conditions of member states

Sources of Funds

Funds for the IBRD are derived from capital subscriptions of the member nations, loans obtained in international capital markets, repayments of principal and interest, and earnings on investments. When the bank was established, its authorized capital was $10 billion. The continued high demand for capital for development purposes has resulted in several increases of its authorized capital. The increase agreed upon in January 1980 will result in a total subscription of $83 billion when fully subscribed. The total subscribed capital (paid-in and callable) through fiscal year 1984 was $56 billion.[16]

Loan Policies and Credit Terms

The Articles of Association prevent the IBRD from making loans in excess of its own capital and reserves, but there are no constraints on the rates or terms the Bank may offer. Loans to national governments or to private institutions (if there are governmental guarantees) are below market rates. Credits are extended for periods of 15 to 30 years, including a grace period of up to 5 years. Most loans or credits mature in 20 to 25 years. Interest charges are computed quarterly on the basis of the weighted average costs of IBRD borrowings, with a front end fee of $\frac{1}{4}$ of 1 percent.

Loans are made to governments, government agencies, and private enterprises of member countries for well-defined projects usually related to infrastructure development. Only a part of the total cost of these loans is borne by the World Bank. The rest is covered by local sources or other international organizations such as the International Finance Corporation.

For the member nations, the World Bank is a bank of last resort, making loans when private capital is not available at reasonable terms. It provides loans for the purchase of imported goods and services, and disburses these funds over the period of the project, upon evidence that the funds are being used for the agreed purposes. The Bank demands that purchases be made on the basis of competitive bidding in any member country or in Switzerland, a nonmember that has special arrangements with the Bank.

If the borrower is not a government, the Bank requires the guarantee of the member government. The loans are amortized over a given number of years, depending on the project. Payment of the loan does not begin until the project has been completed and is in operation. The Bank enlists the direct participation of private investors such as commercial financial institutions.

One of the major criteria for granting credit is the per capita income of the borrowing nation. Loans are extended to countries with a per capita income of less than $2650 (1980 prices). Once this figure is reached, the credit to the country is gradually reduced to zero over the next five years. Other criteria are the credit worthiness, access to commercial capital markets, economic performance, and the population of the country.[17]

Initially, the primary concern of the IBRD was the development of electric power, transport systems, agriculture, industry, and education (infrastructure) of the less developed nations. In the mid-1950s, priority was given to project loans to stimulate economic growth in the Third World countries. It was believed that developing the infrastructure of the country would result in a fast and spontaneous growth of the country. However, this policy resulted in the neglect of agriculture to the detriment of the poorest population group, so greater emphasis was placed on the growth of those areas that would decrease poverty. Since the end of 1960, the World Bank has directed its efforts toward the development of education, housing, public health, water supply, and agriculture. It has also increased aid to national development banks that finance smaller projects. Energy loans have been increased since 1979 to exploit the oil, gas, and coal reserves of the less developed oil-importing countries.

In 1980, Structural Adjustment Loans were introduced to enable those in balance of payments difficulties to bring their Current Account deficits within reasonable limits. Program aid was instituted to solve the immediate difficulties rather than to solve the structural problems that cause the difficulties. The Structural Adjustment Loans, therefore, supplement the aid granted by the IMF for nations with balance of payments problems. Because of the limited amount of working capital, Structural Adjustment Loans tend to reduce World Bank loans available for project purposes.

In recent years, the World Bank has been attempting to stimulate private capital flows to the less developed countries. In addition to its own credits, third parties have been involved in granting credit through cofinancing. To make cofinancing more attractive, the Bank developed new techniques. First, the World Bank supplements its direct loans by participating up to 15 to 20 percent in commercial bank credits. The credit terms can thus be extended. Commercial banks are repaid before the World Bank is paid. Second, a syndicate of banks can finance the whole loan. Such situations work as follows. Since commercial loans carry a floating rate, the debt-servicing requirement (interest payments and principal repayment) would normally increase if world market interest rates were to increase; however, World Bank involvement assures that the debt service remains fixed. If the interest rates go higher, the term of the loan is merely extended, and the loan is not redeemed completely by the end of the term. The World

Bank takes over any outstanding balance at the end of the normal redemption period. Third, the World Bank does not participate directly in commercial loans, but grants credit guarantees for the last repayments.

The World Bank has introduced a consulting program to help developing countries tide over their cash difficulties. The program includes both financial and policy measures. It provides guidance in evaluating projects, attempts to provide more efficient economic policies, and encourages better institutions in the borrowing countries.

The IBRD was established with the primary purpose of providing long-term credit to aid the development of the less developed countries.

IBRD Affiliates

International Development Association

The International Development Association (IDA) was established in September 1960 as a subsidiary of the IBRD. The stated purpose of the IDA is to meet the needs of the poorest of the developing nations. Countries with a per capita income of less than $730 (1980 dollars) qualify for IDA loans. Territories and dependencies of member states also qualify. Assistance by the IDA to member nations may take the form of agency drafts, which are essentially IBRD loans guaranteed by the IDA, or credits extended by the IDA itself.

The projects that are financed by IDA are similar to those financed by the IBRD, except that the IDA views the credit conditions and the state of development of the borrowing countries more liberally. The two institutions have similar rules regarding competitive bidding, procurement, disbursement, and regulations regarding the countries in which the funds have to be spent. Since its inception, IDA activities have been focused on financing the development of electric power, harbor dredging, inland port development, irrigation, drainage and flood control, water supply construction, and school building.

The resources of the IDA are entirely separate from those of the IBRD. Whereas the IBRD uses borrowed funds to extend long-term credits, the IDA gets its funds entirely from periodic payments of member nations, the redemption of loans, and the annual appropriations of IBRD profits. These periodic payments are made by 33 donor countries, including 9 developing countries. Of the IDA's total resources, 6 percent have come from the profits of the IBRD.[18]

The terms extended by the IDA are extremely favorable. It grants interest-free loans repayable in 50 years. Amortization begins after a grace period of 10 years, then 1 percent of the principal is repayable in each of the next 10 years, and 3 percent per year in the last 30 years. A service fee of $\frac{3}{4}$ percent of the total loan value is charged each year to cover administrative costs and an additional $\frac{1}{2}$ percent fee on undisbursed balances.[19] The latter represents a profit margin for the IDA.

An interesting note is that these institutions, established to aid the LDCs, have proven profitable. According to the Operations Evaluation

Department, most of the projects financed by both the World Bank and the IDA have resulted in a profit. Average yield on World Bank loans is 17 percent. IDA projects yield 18 percent; however, returns from projects vary from country to country. The 40 IDA projects in South Asia had average returns of 22 percent, while 88 projects in Africa had an average return of only 14 percent. This difference is due largely to the lower development level and the political instability of the African nations.[20]

The IDA, an affiliate of the IBRD, was established to meet the needs of the poorest countries for development projects.

International Finance Corporation

The International Finance Corporation (IFC) was established by the IBRD in July 1956 to stimulate the growth of the private sector in the less developed member nations by extending credit to private enterprises. It purchases the stocks of those firms and borrows needed funds directly from the IBRD. Membership is open to World Bank members.

The IFC participates in projects with nationals of countries in which the projects are located, with private foreign investors or both. It may not accept government guarantees or repayments, and it may not invest in government-owned or -operated undertakings. If a project is initiated with public funds and later privatized, however, the IFC may participate. Loans have been used for such projects as road construction, electric power, port improvement, water supply, sewage projects, export of capital goods among member nations, and direct loans to private enterprises. Procurement anywhere in the free world is permitted.

The ordinary capital resources of the IFC are provided by member countries whose quotas are paid half in gold or dollars, and half in the currency of the member nation. Its capitalization was established at $100 million, with the U.S. share set at $35,168,000. Additional capital is provided from loan repayments, interest and commitment charges, and profits from equity investments. Terms of IFC loans are usually from 7 to 12 years at rates of interest between 6 and 7 percent, and are repayable in the currency in which the loan was made.

The IFC aids private enterprises in Third World countries by making loans or investing in the stock.

Fund for Special Operations

The Fund for Special Operations is used for special projects. The terms and conditions are adapted to the special circumstances in specific countries. The funds have been used to provide loans to development institutions for relending to private enterprises and to make direct loans to private enterprises and government entities for projects involving electric power, transportation, water supply, sewage projects, improved land use, agricultural credits for low-income farmers, housing for low-income groups, and education.

Other International Agencies

The Inter-American Development Bank (IDB; see Global Insight) is a Western Hemispheric version of the World Bank.[21] It was established in 1959 by the United States and 19 Latin American republics. Through its Social Progress Trust Fund it provides loans for land settlement and improved land use, the construction of low-income group housing, the development of water supply and sewage facilities, and advanced education and training. U.S. dollar funds that are made available under the Social Progress Trust Fund must be spent in the United States, or for goods and services of local origin in the country of the borrower. Funds may be spent elsewhere if the Inter-American Development Bank authorizes procurement in other member countries. Since 1964, the Bank has also administered funds provided by Canada and the United Kingdom. The Canadian funds are used to finance economic, technical, and educational assistance projects in Latin America. Funds from the United Kingdom are loaned out for procurement only in the United Kingdom.

The Asian Development Bank promotes economic development and cooperation in developing countries in Asia through loans, technical assistance, and investment promotion. The African Development Bank promotes the economic and social progress of regional members, individually and jointly, and promotes the economic development of least developed member countries by offering credits on concessionary terms.[22]

Various World Bank Group institutions have been assigned specific tasks for aiding in the development of Third World countries.

SUMMARY

The major private source of capital for financing international transactions are the commercial banks. However, their operations are primarily limited to short-term financing. Other private financial institutions are less important because of their specialized roles or because government regulations limit the type of operation in which they may engage.

In the long-term financing of international transactions, government agencies play the most important role. The most important government agency for American firms engaged in international business is the Export-Import Bank. This institution was established to promote the trade of the United States through its various agencies and affiliates by extending direct credits and financial guarantees to enable American exporters to compete in the world markets with non-U.S. business firms. Many countries turn to the Eximbank to finance the purchase of capital goods for the construction of manufacturing facilities or for infrastructure development. Since these purchases must be made from U.S. firms, they increase U.S. sales abroad.

The Agency for International Development provides long-term assistance to develop the resources and to increase the productive capacities of the less developed countries. The Commodity Credit Corporation was established specifically to promote the sale of surplus U.S. agricultural products.

The International Monetary Fund and the International Bank for Reconstruction and Development have tremendous influence in the world financial environment. The two institutions were assigned different but complementary tasks. The major function of the IMF is to promote the

Multilateral Banks and Friendly Creditors Aid Bolivian Economy

At the end of 1988, the Inter-American Development Bank approved $40 million of additional credits for Bolivia. These are specifically for the development of industry and tourism. This brings total IDB credits for Bolivia in 1988 to $119 million. In addition to these IDB funds, the Japanese government has granted to Bolivia credits worth over $55 million to be used to finance imports of equipment and parts for the state-owned oil, railroad, and electricity companies. It has also been reported that negotiations are underway for another Japanese loan of about $70 million. A U.S. short-term Treasury loan of $100 million was granted to Bolivia in 1989 to help pay for imports.

Source: Adapted from: *Business Latin America*, January 9, 1989, p. 7; August 14, 1989, p. 255.

balanced growth of international trade by bringing about stability in the international monetary system. It provides funds to member nations to bridge their current balance of payments difficulties. The IBRD, on the other hand, was established primarily to aid Third World countries in developing their economies by granting them long-term credit at very favorable rates. The IDA, a subsidiary of the World Bank, was established to meet the needs of the poorest nations. The IFC, another subsidiary of the IBRD, participates in projects with nationals of the countries where the projects are located. Other World Bank affiliates and international agencies provide various types of aid to the Third World countries. □

KEY TERMS AND CONCEPTS

Accumulated reserves

Agency for International Development (AID)

Alliance for Progress

Capital subscriptions

Commercial risk

Commitment letter

Commodity Credit Corporation (CCC)

Cooley Amendment Funds

Credit tranche

Edge Act Corporation

Equity financing

Export Import Bank (Eximbank)

Factor

Foreign Credit Insurance Association (FCIA)

Inter-American Development Bank

International Bank for Reconstruction and Development (IBRD)

International Development Association (IDA)

International Finance Corporation (IFC)

International Monetary Fund (IMF)

Letter of interest

Public Law 480

Reserve tranche

Special Drawing Rights

REVIEW QUESTIONS

1. What private sources of capital are available to those engaged in international business to finance their transactions?

2. What are the advantages and disadvantage of turning to foreign factors and finance companies to finance an export shipment?

3. What were the major purposes for the establishment of the Export-Import Bank?

4. What types of services are provided to exporters by the Eximbank? How does the Eximbank attempt to encourage small business to enter the export markets?

5. What is the FCIA? Briefly describe its purposes.

6. Briefly explain how the Eximbank provides bank guarantees to commercial banks.

7. Describe the various operations of the Agency for International Development.

8. How does the Commodity Credit Corporation help the U.S. government get rid of its surplus agricultural products?

9. What are the major objectives of the International Monetary Fund?

10. How does the operation of the International Bank for Reconstruction and Development differ from the operation of the IMF?

11. Why was the International Development Association established?

12. What is the Social Progress Trust Fund?

DISCUSSION CASE

External Funds Prop up Trinidad While Reforms Are Planned

Prime Minister Robinson is struggling to bring Trinidad back from the brink of economic disaster. In the closing weeks of 1988 Trinidad secured multiple new foreign loans, which should help stop the economy's decline. Foreign firms should not expect the local market to pick up in 1989 but they may witness a long-overdue reform of investment policies.

Trinidad's condition became critical in July 1988. Since petroleum still accounts for over 85 percent of the nation's foreign earnings, declining oil revenues caused Trinidad's international reserves to fall below zero. In response, Robinson devalued the local dollar by 18 percent to TT

Adapted from John Babb and Peter Kennedy, "New Funds Prop up Trinidad While Reforms Are Planned to Pave Way for Recovery," *Business Latin America*, January 9, 1989, pp. 6–7.

$4.251:U.S. $1 and increased talks with foreign lenders. In November, the IMF granted the country a U.S. $111 million loan (under its Compensatory Finance Facility) to offset lost oil revenues. The Inter-American Development Bank supplied modest sums for technical cooperation funding, and the government then sold off aircraft owned by the state airline. Trinidad & Tobago obtained private credit of U.S. $120 million from Nissho Iwai Corp. of Japan in 1989.

Robinson, who is also Finance Minister, is now negotiating another IMF loan, U.S. $75 million. The country is hoping for a structural adjustment loan from the World Bank. The next step will be a rescheduling of at least part of its U.S. $1.2 billion foreign commercial bank debt.

New Policies Aimed at Recovery

Any additional foreign funds will probably demand economic reforms, which until now, Trinidad has refused. Although the move will be politically unpopular, Robinson will have to cut the pay of civil servants and reduce subsidies. Fortunately for him national elections do not have to be called for another three years. As for business conditions, the key policy moves ahead are the following:

1. *Foreign exchange allocation.* It is unlikely that there will be any significant improvement in the foreign exchange position in the near future. Import budgets will remain extremely tight. However, companies whose exports meet or exceed 80 percent of their import needs—"net exporters"—will receive preferential treatment in the allocation of foreign exchange. Furthermore, some exporters will be eligible to hold foreign exchange in officially monitored accounts in local banks. To avoid shortages, an allocation of 110 percent of last year's level is being assigned for the import of basic foods, drugs, and spare parts.

2. *Devaluation.* Additional currency devaluations in the near term have not been ruled out.

3. *Fiscal reforms.* Trinidad is undertaking a two-year tax reform aimed at simplifying the system and reducing marginal rates for direct taxes. To prevent a revenue shortfall, indirect taxes will be increased in 1990. A value added tax will be introduced, and excise charges, import duties, and other fees raised. Beginning in 1989, the four separate corporate taxes currently used will be consolidated into a single tax of 45 percent.

4. *Foreign investment rules.* Trinidad's foreign investment policy and especially the Aliens Landholding Act is targeted for reform. Although nothing is definite, it is expected that policies will be changed to allow foreign investors to acquire 100 percent ownership in privately held local companies and to hold full control of any project they initiate. In companies whose shares are traded publicly, foreign investors would be able to purchase up to 49 percent equity, subject to approval of the Stock Exchange Board. Purchase of shares exceeding 49 percent would require the approval of the Aliens Landholding Committee.

Questions

1. Describe the role of the International Monetary Fund and the International Bank for Reconstruction and Development in propping up the financial position of Trinidad.

2. What measures must be adopted to restore economic vitality to the country? Do you believe these measures will be sufficient? If so, why? If not, why not?

NOTES

1. Board of Governors of the Federal Reserve System, *Federal Reserve Bulletin*, May 1989, p. A62.

2. Two types of corporations may be established under the Edge Act. First are the banking corporations that may engage in commercial banking, accept foreign or domestic deposits that are incidental to foreign business transaction, accept drafts or bills of exchange, and make loans to foreign businesses; however, they may not make equity investments abroad, except in stocks of other corporations engaged in foreign banking activities. The second type are the financing corporations that may not engage in commercial banking operations. They are permitted to engage in equity financing and to make investments in foreign enterprises not engaged in commercial banking. This type of corporation is allowed to participate only in domestic activities that are incidental to its foreign activities. These financing corporations are an important source of capital for financing the foreign operations of U.S. companies. All transactions are medium term, with an average time period between 5 and 7 years, although they may be extended to 10 years.

3. "Financing Foreign Operations," *Business International*, 1961, p. 1.

4. Export-Import Bank of Washington, News Release, May 10, 1960.

5. Ibid.

6. Export-Import Bank, *Export-Import Bank Programs*, vol. 2, 1973, pp. 12–16.

7. Bankers Trust Co., "Washington Agencies That Help Finance Foreign Trade," 5th ed. (New York: Bankers Trust Co., 1967), p. 6.

8. Ibid., p. 7.

9. Ibid., p. 10.

10. IMF, *Survey* (Supplement on the Fund), August 1989, p. 3.

11. Kredietbank, *Weekly Bulletin*, no. 22, 3 June 1983.

12. IMF, *Survey*, p. 5.

13. Ibid.,

14. United States, Great Britain, West Germany, France, Italy, Japan, Canada, Netherlands, Belgium, and Sweden.

15. Kredietbank, p. 3.

16. Kredietbank, *Weekly Bulletin*, No. 23, 10 June 1983, p. 1.

17. Ibid., p. 2.

18. Ibid.,
19. Ibid.,
20. Ibid, p. 4.
21. *Business America*, April 15, 1985, p. 17.
22. Ibid., pp. 18–19.

REFERENCES AND SELECTED READINGS

Bankers Trust Co. "Washington Agencies that Help Finance Foreign Trade," 5th ed. New York: Bankers Trust Co., 1967.

Bhattacharya, Anindya K. "Offshore Banking in the Caribbean by U.S. Commercial Banks: Implications for Government-Business Interaction." *The Journal of International Business Studies* 11:3 (Winter 1980).

Board of Governors of the Federal Reserve System. *Federal Reserve Bulletin*. Washington, D.C.: FRB Publications Services, Monthly.

Export-Import Bank. "Export-Import Bank Programs," vol. 2. Washington, D. C.: Export-Import Bank, 1973.

Kredietbank, *Weekly Bulletin*, no. 22 (3 June 1983) and no. 23 (10 June 1983).

Nigh, Douglas, Kang Rae Cho, and Suresh Krishnan. "The Role of Location-Related Factors in U.S. Banking Involvement Abroad: An Empirical Investigation." *The Journal of International Business Studies* 17:3 (Fall 1986).

U.S. Dept. of Commerce, *Business America*, April 15, 1985.

The Intranational Environment of International Business

Part Three consists of five chapters that explain the most important aspects of the internal environments of nations. Chapter 7, "Commercial Policies and Instruments for Protection," discusses the history of governmental policies, the nature of the policies most commonly used today, and the impacts of these policies. Most governmental policies are rooted in either free trade or protectionism. Indeed, when examined over time, nations are found to vacillate between these two attitudes. Chapter 7 also discusses the primary instruments used to restrict trade: tariffs (including import and export duties), quantitative controls (quotas, embargoes, and boycotts), exchange controls, and nontariff barriers. Furthermore this chapter addresses the policies of nations to mitigate the effects of duties: drawbacks, bonded warehouses, and foreign trade or free zones. Finally, Chapter 7 deals with the effects of trade restrictions.

Chapter 8 explains the effect of a nation's geographic environment on international business and deals with three major considerations: climate, the influence of environment on the location of manufacturing, and the significance of the oceans.

Chapter 9 presents an analysis of the political and legal environments of nations in three major sections. The first is the interactions among political, legal, and economic systems. The second is a discussion of the differences among legal systems and their significance for arbitration, resolution of disputes, and the protection of intellectual property. The third section deals with the political environment and political risks: the nature and sources of political risks, methods for assessing political environments, and strategies for coping with political risks.

Chapter 10, "Economic Environment," discusses the most salient features of the economic environment of a nation and focuses on industrialized countries (the European Economic Community, Japan, North America, and Australia and New Zealand), newly industrialized countries (South Korea, Taiwan, Singapore, Hong Kong, Brazil, and Mexico), and less developed countries. In discussing the EEC, the chapter also deals with the topic of economic integration.

Chapter 11 explains the importance of the human and cultural environment of a country for international business. This chapter is composed of four major sections: understanding culture and cultural differences, preparing for success in a different culture, adapting business systems, and cultural change. Culture here includes national culture, organizational culture, and cultural consciousness in dimensions such as time, the future, wealth, material possessions, rewards, decision-making, bribery, value exchanges, language, religion, interpersonal relations, authority, individuality, competitiveness, extended family, personal criticisms, social structure, and so forth. For creating success in foreign cultures, Chapter 11 addresses several key issues: selecting expatriate managers, training expatriates, and facilitating and supporting expatriate activities. Additionally, this section deals with the key barriers to performance: ethnocentrism, and a lack of cultural empathy and adaptability.

CHAPTER

Commercial Policies and Instruments for Protection

LEARNING OBJECTIVES

- Understand the types of commercial policies used by nations through various periods of history: Mercantilism, free trade, and protectionism

- Know the reasons for the adoption of the various types of policies and the validity of each

- Become familiar with the various measures and instruments nations may adopt to restrict the movement of goods and services

- Analyze the effectiveness of these measures in restricting imports

- Understand the effects of trade restrictions on the nation imposing them, including the effects on differing sectors of the economy

INTRODUCTION

Commerce is defined as the "exchange or buying and selling of commodities on a large scale involving transportation from place to place."[1] It follows that the term *international commercial policies* refers to those policies that a country adopts regarding the export and import or exchange of goods and services with other countries.

Laws, institutions, and executive decisions determine the commercial policies of nations. Generally, the policies are directed toward increasing trade among nations, but this is not always the case. Many laws or regulations, such as those dealing with tariffs and quotas, have the objective of discouraging trade. Although most commercial policies are economically motivated, others are adopted for reasons of politics, national security, or revenue generation. Some are even instituted to protect the health, welfare, or morals of the people.

Often a nation will unilaterally adopt a particular type of commercial policy, but these are usually modified through negotiations with trading partners. Japan, for example, had a number of regulations that limited the import of certain agricultural products. Many of these have been relaxed through direct negotiations with the United States. If a nation refuses to modify its commercial policy, its trading partners usually retaliate. The failure of Japanese automobile producers to limit voluntarily the number of automobiles exported to France resulted in policies that restrict the unloading of automobiles to a single, inland port that is incapable of handling a large volume of cars at any given time.

The objective of this chapter is to provide a brief historical review of commercial policies since ancient times and to familiarize the student with the principal instruments of commercial policy that are used by nations. Major emphasis is placed upon the direct role of tariffs and quotas as instruments to control the movement of goods. Exchange controls and other nontariff barriers are less obvious in their effect on trade. The chapter concludes with a brief evaluation of the major arguments used in support of protectionist policies, and the effects of trade restrictions on various sectors of a nation's economy.

HISTORY OF COMMERCIAL POLICIES

Ancient Period: Local and Municipal Policies

During the period of antiquity, international commercial policies as we know them today did not exist. What few policies existed were local or municipal in character. The Arabs, who were the great land merchants of antiquity, organized caravans and were under no form of government. Their only regulations were those they imposed on themselves.

The commercial policies of the Phoenicians merely emphasized their distribution monopoly of certain goods. Greek commercial policies were largely a continuation of those of the Phoenicians. The Romans had essentially no commercial policy except as it related to conquering and exploiting colonies, and establishing and administering laws.

Middle Ages: Policies of Restrictionism

After the fall of the Roman Empire and the growth of feudalism, the only centralizing force was the church, which had essentially no commercial policy except for the monopolization of commerce. Ironically, the Crusades, which resulted in contact with the more advanced Byzantine and Arabic cultures, led to the breakdown of feudalism and the decline of the church's commercial activities. The Crusades also gave impetus to commerce and made commercial policies a necessity. Demand for food and spices, clothing, and other products from the Arab cultures led to the development of new commercial centers. Cities in Italy and later leagues of cities in northern Europe grew, became quasi-political in character, and laid the groundwork for the modern nation. The most important of these was the Hanseatic League.

The Hanseatic League was established in the thirteenth century when Hamburg and Lubeck joined together to protect their trade against pirates. As others joined, this league grew to almost 100 cities. From a purely protective association, it soon assumed important political prerogatives. This confederacy enacted regulations for both domestic and foreign trade, just as the European Community is doing in preparation for 1992. The movement of trading vessels was highly monitored as regards such things as time of departure, routes, objective of the trip, route for the return voyage, and armaments. Municipal regulations restricted the dealings of foreigners with the native population as well as limiting the number of visits and the length of their stay. Laws regulating prices, weights, measures, and quality were also common. The city of Lubeck even tried to prevent the Dutch from engaging in trade with the Baltic region.

The Hanseatic League possessed a powerful fleet and an army that it used to protect its trading interests and to dominate the commercial activities of northern Europe. The security the league gave to commerce and industry did much to increase the wealth and standard of living of its members and to prepare them for the principles of orderly government, thus paving the way for a constitutional system of government.

Policies during the ancient period were primarily municipal; however, with the growth of city-states, both domestic and foreign trade were minutely regulated.

Modern Period

Mercantilism

With the growth of national governments in the fifteenth and sixteenth centuries, city leagues were no longer necessary. Central governments gradually took over. Spain, France, and England became nations in the modern sense.

The closure of the overland route following the fall of Constantinople to the Turks in 1453 necessitated seeking a water route to the Orient. Explorations during this period resulted in discoveries that have had far-reaching effects on commercial activities. Columbus "discovered" America, Vasco da Gama discovered an all-water route to India via the Cape of Good Hope, and Magellan's crew circumnavigated the globe. These discoveries meant the shifting of the commercial centers of Europe from the Mediterranean to the Atlantic.

The use of water routes greatly reduced the costs of transportation and for the first time made possible the trade of goods other than luxury goods, giving new impetus to commerce and resulting in increased competition among the leading nations of the period. The attempt to achieve a strong state through economic means gave rise to the movement that is referred to as *Mercantilism*. This policy emphasized the accumulation of money and precious metals, and resulted in the beginning of national commercial policies.

In retrospect, the policy of Mercantilism is readily understandable. During the preceding centuries, purchases of products from the East had resulted in the rapid depletion of precious metals. At the same time, the demand for money to support a large standing army and high-salaried officials had risen. Nations had to either find a means to meet these payments or lose sovereignty. Since none of the countries of western Europe had important gold or silver mines, the only alternative was to obtain these precious metals through trade. Because exports provided the only source of precious metals, foreign commerce was considered productive, while domestic commerce and agriculture were considered sterile.

Once a nation obtained the precious metals, it had to find some means of preventing their outflow. This led governments to adopt various measures to keep money in the country. Corsa, the Italian economist, wrote of three phases of Mercantilism.[2]

The first phase was to prevent the actual outflow of precious metals by debasing coinage and using exchange controls.

The second phase, known as the "Balance of Bargains," attempted to conserve precious metals through the detailed regulation of dealings with foreign traders. This scheme prohibited the export of precious metals. In England it required merchants who sold at staple towns, such as Antwerp and Calais, to bring back a fixed proportion of what they received from their sales. Furthermore, the "statutes of employment" required that foreign traders selling in England spend their money for British goods.

The third phase of Mercantilism emphasized a favorable balance of trade that would result in the inflow of money. To make sure that an unfavorable balance did not occur, domestic and foreign products were required to be carried in domestic vessels using native sailors. Domestic manufactures were favored and the import of competitive goods was discouraged or even prohibited. Raw material exports were discouraged and their imports were facilitated.

Mercantilism embraced several principles that were to have a significant impact for centuries to come. Manufacturing and trade were more highly valued than other economic activities. Trade was viewed as being one-sided—that is, exporting was good, importing was bad, and the larger the trade surplus the better. Colonies were exploited so that the mother country would have a favorable balance of trade.

Mercantilism is subject to many criticisms. Mercantilists looked upon trade as a means to achieve a particular end rather than considering the ensuing mutual benefits. They ignored the fact that a large proportion of trade payments were made in merchandise and that selling could not continue without buying. They failed to realize that exports without imports would result in domestic shortages and that the inflow of money combined with decreased supply would lead to inflation. Because of these beliefs, high tariffs were adopted, often resulting in retaliation by other countries.

Using the terms *favorable* and *unfavorable* to describe a positive and negative balance of trade, still common today, is a carryover from the Mercantilist period. In fact, many people still believe that only a positive balance of trade is desirable and fail to understand that many of the gains from trade are intangible and cannot be measured in terms of the net accumulation of precious metals or currencies.

Mercantilism sought to foster a strong government by maintaining a positive balance of trade and a continuing inflow of precious metals.

Policies of the Physiocrats and Free Trade

As nations grew, centralized regulations tended to retard commercial and industrial development. Political and economic reactions to the constraints of Mercantilism gradually began to develop. In France, this reaction was led by the Physiocrats (Quesnay, Turgot, and Gournay), while in England, this movement was led by the free traders (Adam Smith).

Whereas the Mercantilists had emphasized the importance of commerce and manufacturing for the welfare of a nation, the Physiocrats believed that wealth was land-based. They contended that agriculture and the extractive industries were the only productive economic activities because they alone added to the net product of a nation. Manufacturing merely changed the form or location of the product.

The Physiocrats believed in the natural order of society, so they opposed the regulation of trade as being contrary to natural law. This is the doctrine of "laissez-faire, laissez-passer." This doctrine did not gain popularity even in France, although many of its tenets were incorporated in the writings of Adam Smith and his followers in England.

The reaction to Mercantilism took a somewhat different form in the free trade movement in England. Adam Smith agreed with the free trade and laissez-faire principles of the Physiocrats, but did not agree that productivity was limited to agriculture and other land-based activities. He stressed the importance of commerce and industry, and refuted the Mercantilist idea that the benefits of trade were one-sided. Hume and Smith argued for specialization and trade, recommending that each country should produce those goods that it could produce at least cost, and should exchange them for those goods it could produce less efficiently, thus benefiting society as a whole. Smith further agreed with the Physiocrats that if individuals were left to do what would benefit themselves, the greatest good would accrue to the greatest number.

The publication of Adam Smith's *Wealth of Nations* in 1776 had a great influence on the free trade movement. From tariff reforms to the commercial treaty with France in 1786, the movement toward laissez-faire and free trade was evident in England's colonial policies. The industrial revolution and the development of liberal commercial policies enabled England to become the dominant industrial nation in the world.

The manufacturing interests looked with favor on the importation of low-cost foodstuffs for the workers, and raw materials that could be converted into manufactured goods for export. The case for lower import duties was further strengthened because England had become a net importer of grain. Yet, to protect the interests of the landlords, the Corn Law was passed in 1815 that levied prohibitory duties on the import of grain. Immediately, the free traders began to work toward the repeal of this newly passed law, but it was not until 1846 that the Corn Law was repealed. In

1849, the Navigation Laws that provided British shipping interests advantageous privileges were repealed, and in 1854 the Coastwise Navigation Law that restricted coastal trade to British bottoms met the same fate. Free trade characterized the commercial policy of England and was evidenced by the commercial treaty that was negotiated with France in 1860.

Until the Civil War, the dominant commercial policy of the United States was that of relatively free trade and laissez-faire. What few duties existed were for revenue purposes, and protectionist policies were limited to the New England shipping interests.

In continental Europe, the doctrine of free trade was not generally accepted. By the end of the Napoleonic Wars, many of the industries that had been newly established under the restricted "Continental System" of Napoleon found themselves facing ruinous competition. The immediate response was the adoption of customs duties to protect these industries. However, the Industrial Revolution and the lowering of duties on raw material imports in England resulted in support for free trade by the agrarian population of continental Europe. They did not want to accept restrictions on the sale of their agricultural products or to pay higher prices for British manufactures. The official and academic classes espoused the principles of free trade, and with the support of the agricultural population and those industrialists who did not fear British competition, the policy of free trade gained support. This change in attitude resulted in the signing of a number of commercial treaties. Regrettably, within ten years, reaction against free trade began to reappear.

Reaction against the Mercantilist policies resulted in support for free trade in England and the United States and protectionism in continental Europe.

Recent Period

Vacillation Between Free Trade and Protectionism

Even within Great Britain and the United States, where government policies supported free trade, there were some who voiced support for a protective policy. Alexander Hamilton, in 1791, published his "Report on Manufactures," favoring a policy of protection to aid in the development of domestic industries. In a very real sense, this was the first time the "infant industry" argument was effectively used to support a protective policy. In Germany, economist Frederick List furthered the protective principles of Hamilton in his "National System of Political Economy." Henry C. Carey and his son, H. C. Carey, Jr., made further contributions to the protectionist doctrine. These writings were influential in swaying many toward protectionism during the second half of the nineteenth century.

This drift toward protectionism was brought about by the growth of nationalism and the costs that typify all wars. The nationalistic fervor of war usually makes it easy to raise taxes, especially those on imports. Once the conflict is over, it is difficult to get those taxes reduced. The American Civil War and the Franco-Prussian War support this thesis.

Another factor leading toward greater protectionism was the increased competition resulting from the rapid industrial development of western Europe and the United States, and the growth of extensive agriculture in the United States and other parts of the world. Cheap manufactures from western Europe deluged the less developed countries, adversely affecting their economic development. At the same time, European farmers resented the inflow of agricultural products from the less developed countries.

While free trade was still in its infancy, the drift toward protectionist policies was already growing in both the United States and continental Europe.

Policy of Protectionism

By the end of the nineteenth century, commercial agreements and reciprocity treaties alleviated some of the barriers to trade, but the outbreak of World War I voided most of these agreements. The post–World War I period was again characterized by a feeling of extreme nationalism. The costs of the war resulted in huge indebtedness and economic stringency, which led to the passage of high protective tariffs. Even Great Britain adopted high duties to encourage the development of key industries, to protect domestic manufacturing and agriculture, and to use as a bargaining tool.

Following the economic recovery from the post–World War I recession and the boom conditions of the late 1920s, American agriculture and manufacturing expanded rapidly. The domestic market was largely reserved for domestic industries under the protection of the Fordney-McCumber Tariff Act of 1922. Following the stock market crash in 1929 and the ensuing depression, cheap foreign manufactures began to flood the U.S. market. Furthermore, increased competition by agricultural imports from Canada, Cuba, Mexico, and other countries caused American farmers to clamor for protection. In response, Congress passed the Hawley-Smoot Tariff Act in 1930. The already high duties of the 1922 Tariff Act were increased, and many other products were added to the dutiable list.

Foreign reaction to the passage of the Hawley-Smoot Tariff Act was almost immediate. Within a year, some 45 nations retaliated by raising duties on imports from the United States. Furthermore, nations adopted other measures to favor their domestic industries. Quotas, exchange controls, currency manipulation, licenses, subsidies, preferential systems, and nationalistic legislation were passed. These measures curtailed U.S. exports. The result of these protectionist policies was a decrease in trade of all countries (see Chapter 1).

In an effort to reverse the protectionist trend that characterized the period of the Great Depression, the United States took the leadership toward reducing the barriers to trade. It passed the Reciprocal Trade Agreements Act in 1934, an amendment to the Tariff Act of 1930, which authorized the President of the United States to enter into bilateral trade agreements with other countries and to grant concessions in exchange for concessions. These bilateral agreements reduced duties to only a fraction of what they had been under the 1930 Act. Furthermore, the most favored nation (MFN) policy meant that the bilateral treaties had the effect of multilateral agree-

The post–World War I recession followed by the Depression was largely responsible for the growth of the worldwide protectionist sentiment.

ments, as concessions granted to one country were granted to other countries with which similar agreements had been concluded. The Act also authorized the President of the United States to participate in multilateral negotiations such as GATT to modify existing duties and restrictions.

Trade Tensions of the Post–World War II Period

The post–World War II period is largely characterized by international efforts to reduce the barriers to trade through multilateral agreements despite continued pressure from the protectionists. When the GATT called a preliminary meeting in Geneva in 1973 in preparation for the forthcoming Tokyo Round, the U.S. President found himself without the authority to participate. The Trade Expansion Act of 1962 (the twelfth renewal of the Reciprocal Trade Agreements Act) was permitted to expire in 1967 because of the widespread protectionist sentiment. In 1973 Congress finally passed the Tariff Reform Act authorizing the President to participate in the 1974 Tokyo Round of the GATT negotiations.

International commercial policies have been influenced greatly by the General Agreements on Tariffs and Trade. During the four decades of its existence, much has been done to reduce the barriers to trade. The average duties on products of the industrial countries have been reduced greatly, resulting in a twentyfold increase in the volume of trade in manufactures. However, the reduction in duties has not eliminated the protectionist trend among nations. Nontariff measures to restrict the free movement of goods have replaced tariffs as a barrier to trade. The adoption of these protective measures has resulted in increased tension among nations. The GATT negotiations that got under way in September 1986 in Punta del Este, Uruguay, have not been able to defuse the conflict between the European Community and the United States on the problem of agricultural subsidies and import barriers. Problems remain to be solved relating to trade in natural resource-based products that have been affected by various support programs, such as metals and minerals, and forest and fishery products. Market access for textiles and clothing, important products of the less developed countries, has met with resistance from the industrialized countries. The protection of intellectual property rights, a major cause of trade tensions in recent years, is another major issue that remains to be solved before the meetings are concluded in 1990.

One of the most serious economic conflicts that has resulted in international tensions is the accumulation of trade surpluses among some countries at the expense of deficits in others. The United States, for example, has used various measures in an attempt to reduce its trade deficit with Japan. The depreciation in the dollar has cut the deficit with Europe but has had little effect on trade with Japan. The supposedly open door in Japan on supercomputers and telecommunications has increased U.S. market share in Japan to only 2.4 percent in five years. The concessions the United States won pertaining to the export of beef and citrus fruits have had only marginal results, and the voluntary curbs in the import of automobile and steel have had little effect. However, the 1986 bilateral semiconductor accord forced Japanese suppliers to abide by the established quotas and to stop dumping its products in the United States. These problems have caused many both inside and outside of government to suggest that the Administration adopt a "results-oriented" trade program. Japan has been warned to adopt measures to reduce its trade surplus with the United States, or face possible unilateral action by the United States.

Trade tensions among nations have resulted in bilateralism and the adoption of various nontariff barriers to trade.

Evaluation of Arguments for Protection

Although many arguments are advanced to justify protectionism, most of them lack economic validity. The strategic industries and national economic independence arguments support protectionism more on political than economic grounds. Proponents state that during a national emergency, nations cannot depend upon others to provide them with their needs. For example, during World War II, U.S. rubber supplies were cut off from the Far East, so the U.S. government aided the synthetic rubber industry to preclude future reliance on foreign sources. This argument has been used to justify protection of many industries.

As noted above, the infant industry argument has long been used to justify protectionism. In the United States, the industries established during the War of 1812 were protected by the Tariff Act of 1816 and by later tariffs on the grounds that they needed temporary government support against imports. This same argument is used today by the South Korean automobile industry, the Brazilian computer industry, and, surprisingly, the Japanese pharmaceutical industry. The argument's weakness is that even after such industries mature, they often require continued protection because of inefficiency.

The third major argument favoring protectionism is that domestic markets can best be developed by domestic firms. This argument dates back to Henry Clay, who first used it to foster the development of the Northern and Eastern markets for Western agricultural products. The home market argument emphasizes the importance of the domestic market and is especially common in a country such as the United States, where the domestic market is much larger than most foreign markets. The United States uses this argument to protect the dairy industry and the agricultural interests who object to the import of fresh fruits and vegetables during the harvesting season. The weakness of *this* argument lies in the fact that restricting imports will add to domestic prices and deter exports, and may result in retaliation by other countries.

Fourth, the difference in wages argument was used as early as the Civil War. According to this argument, because U.S. wages are higher than those of other countries, protection is necessary. There is no doubt that this argument is equally attractive today. Industries argue that because of higher wages, domestic production costs are higher than those abroad, and thus it is necessary to protect domestic goods from foreign competition. Labor argues that domestic wages will be pulled down to foreign levels, lowering the standard of living. Furthermore, there is the fear that if protection is not forthcoming, firms that are unable to compete will transfer their operations to low-wage countries, resulting in a loss of jobs.

As an extension of this argument, union leaders assert that imports take away jobs from domestic workers. If a firm is unable to compete with imports because of high production costs, the result will be a loss of jobs for domestic workers. It is difficult to criticize this argument if one is employed in such an industry, yet a better solution to import competition lies in increasing efficiency. Protection of such industries fosters inefficiency. Furthermore, using protective measures to keep out foreign products can result in the loss of jobs for persons who are employed in industries handling imports. If other nations retaliate, it will also cost jobs in the export industries.

Fifth, using protectionism to maintain a positive balance of trade is a remnant of Mercantilism. Even today, many argue that the United States must maintain a favorable balance of trade. Those who use this argument ignore the contribution of the intangible items to the overall balance of payments position of the country. A negative trade balance might be more than offset by the inflow of capital from abroad in the form of dividends, interests, profits, and so forth. Wide fluctuations in the merchandise trade balance might occur with individual countries or from year to year, yet the overall trade balance might be in equilibrium. One of the major fears is that a negative balance of trade will result in the outflow of money from the country, reducing the available investment capital and leading to higher rates of interest. Closely related to this argument is the belief that the accumulation of wealth is dependent upon a favorable balance of trade. This goes back to the old Mercantilist idea that money constitutes wealth. It is difficult to accept the fact that it is not the amount of money within a country that determines its wealth and well-being, but rather the availability of various commodities that determines the standard of living of a country. Actually, the use of protective measures will keep out many desirable products.

Sixth, it is often argued that tariffs should be adopted to equalize the costs of production at home and abroad. If this argument were valid, the United States would be justified in levying a protective tariff equal to the difference between the cost of producing coffee in the United States under artificial conditions and the cost of producing coffee in Brazil. Obviously this would be absurd. The result would be coffee that costs $5.00 per cup. The simple fact is that many countries, including the United States, have natural advantages that enable them to produce some goods more efficiently than their competitors, and that trade allows all parties to benefit from those production advantages.

Finally, it should be mentioned that there are some who support a policy of protection to be used as a cudgel for bargaining. It seems inappropriate for nations to use threats, yet it is relatively common practice to threaten to impose sanctions if a particular measure is adopted. When the European Community threatened to prohibit the import of fresh beef from the United States because of the use of certain hormones that were considered harmful to the health of individuals, the United States immediately threatened to retaliate.

Most arguments used to justify protectionism are economically unsound.

INSTRUMENTS FOR PROTECTION

When a nation decides to adopt a protective type of commercial policy to achieve its national economic or political objectives, it must decide which of the various instruments of control it will adopt to prevent the free flow of goods and services across its national boundaries. Some are less restrictive, while others completely prohibit targeted imports. The available instruments are tariffs or customs duties, quantitative controls, exchange controls, and other nontariff barriers. Although tariffs might be more familiar because of their historical use, nontariff barriers are probably more restrictive as obstacles to the free movement of goods. Japan, for example, has one of the lowest tariff rates among the industrial countries, yet it is extremely difficult to compete in that market because of the use of nontariff barriers.

Tariffs as Barriers to Trade

Import Duties

A tariff or customs duty is a tax that is levied on imports or exports. Import tariffs are those duties that are levied on commodities entering a country. These serve two major purposes—revenue and protection. If the duties are for revenue purposes, they must of necessity be relatively low. If the duties are too high, they will discourage the import of such items, thus limiting the amount of revenue that can be collected. If they are too low, the amounts that are collected might be insignificant. Countries that have used revenue tariffs generally have found them to be most effective when they are about 5 percent ad valorem (5 percent of the value of the goods).

Import duties are often an important source of revenue for the less developed countries, especially if the country is dependent upon imports for its major necessities. For the more highly developed countries, national revenues from duties on imports generally provide a relatively small percentage of the total revenues. In fiscal year 1988, customs duties provided $16,198 million (1.8 percent) of the total federal receipts of the United States.[3] Unless competition prevents them from doing so, importers who pay these duties generally pass them on to the end users in the form of an increase in prices, so this "tax" is ultimately paid by the consumers of the importing nations.

If duties are levied on imports for protective purposes, they must be high enough to be effective. Nations often levy duties with the intention of offsetting the competitive advantage of foreign producers. Complete exclusion of foreign products can be achieved by levying unrealistically high duties. Examples of such duties occurred immediately after World War II when some countries, notably Chile and the Philippines, levied duties as high as 1500 percent on the import of luxury items to discourage the outflow of foreign exchange. Unlike an embargo, such duties do not prohibit imports, but are just as effective.

The height of the tariff will determine its effectiveness for revenue or protective purposes.

Export Duties

Export duties on goods leaving a country are generally levied for three major purposes: to provide revenue, conserve domestic resources, or stimulate the growth of domestic industries. The United States is prohibited by the Constitution from levying export duties, but many other countries, especially the less developed nations, are frequent users of export duties for revenue purposes. They are most effective when a nation has a monopoly in the production of minerals or other resources. However, there is the danger of losing both the market and a major source of revenue if importers can find alternative sources of supply.

A classic example of the potential negative effects of export duties occurred in Chile when that country was the principal producer of crude sodium nitrate (caliche), which is used in the production of fertilizer and explosives. The $12 per ton duty that was levied on the export of the ore provided that country with as much as 80 percent of its national revenues between 1880 and 1930.[4] The high cost of the Chilean nitrates caused the major consuming nations to seek alternative sources of nitrogen. This led to the development of low-cost processes for producing synthetic nitrogen as a by-product of coal and atmospheric nitrogen. In 1885, Chile was the source of about 85 percent of the world's nitrogen; today, the figure is less than 10 percent.

Export taxes may be used to restrict the outflow of certain resources that are limited in supply. Levying such taxes increases the cost to the buyers, thus discouraging the purchase of such products. An alternative would be to control the quantity of such goods that could be exported. In the United States the shortage of copper during World War II was handled through the use of licenses and permits, while an embargo was imposed during the grain shortage in the 1970s.

Export duties may be used to stimulate the development of domestic industries or to provide domestic manufacturers with a competitive advantage. Many less developed countries that were formerly principal exporters of raw materials and crude foodstuffs have, through the use of export taxes or incentives, encouraged investments in manufacturing. If, for example, a nation is a major exporter of raw materials for the production of paper, the government may use export taxes as a means of giving its own manufacturers

If a nation has a monopoly in a product, export duties can be a major revenue producer; otherwise, they can cause lost markets and revenues.

a cost advantage in markets abroad. Clearly, the competitive advantage will be proportional to the height of the export tax on the raw material.

Single- and Multiple-Column Tariffs

A single-column or unilinear tariff refers to one rate of duty that is applicable to any given article, regardless of the country of origin. If the same rate of duty is levied on sugar imports from Taiwan, the Philippines, and Brazil, the duty is a unilinear tariff. In contrast, a multiple-column tariff employs two or more schedules of duties on any article. These may take the form of a maximum-minimum tariff where the rates are determined by statute. The maximum or general rate will be applicable to all countries and it may be modified by negotiations and commercial agreements, but may not be reduced below the minimum rate. The general- conventional tariff is similar except that no minimum is specified.

Penalty Duties

Nations may adopt one or more schedules for duties on imports. They may adopt penalty duties for the violation of their customs regulations.

Penalty duties are levied on imports for the violation of some customs rule or regulation of the importing country. Because different countries have different rules and regulations, something that is perfectly legal in one country might be a violation in another country. Therefore, it is important that an exporter be familiar with all customs rules and regulations. Discrepancies in weights and measures, typographic errors in documents, or any other violation of the customs regulations might result in penalty duties or fines, confiscation, and even prison terms.

Antidumping Duties

Dumping occurs when a product is imported at prices below the established export price or below the cost of the product in the country of export. A firm might resort to dumping for different reasons, but it is generally practiced to destroy competition (predatory dumping), to dispose of a surplus, or to maintain production in times of domestic or world depression.

In the United States, the Treasury Department, upon the recommendation of the Tariff Commission, is authorized to levy antidumping duties on goods that are sold below the fair market value or below the cost of production in the country of export.

Retaliatory and Preferential Duties

A retaliatory duty is one that a country may levy on imports from a country in retaliation for the nation's discriminatory treatment of its products. However, such duties are generally levied only after negotiations have failed.

Nations use many different types of duties: penalty, antidumping, retaliatory, and preferential duties.

Preferential duties are often granted for the purpose of maintaining close ties with certain countries for political or economic reasons. Former colonies that have gained their independence are often granted preferential treatment by the mother country, as is the case with England and the British Commonwealth.

Methods for Levying Duties

Ad Valorem Duties

When a customs duty is levied as a percentage of the value of the commodity being imported, it is referred to as an *ad valorem duty*. The amount of the duty changes with the price of the imported commodity. Thus, a duty of 5 percent ad valorem on an item valued at $100 will be $5.00, and on a $200 item, $10.

There are a number of disadvantages of ad valorem duties. They are difficult and expensive to administer because of the temptation on the part of importers to undervalue their goods to minimize the duties payable. Valuation for duty purposes varies greatly from country to country. For example, a 5 percent ad valorem duty that is based on the price at the factory of the exporter (FOB) will be quite different from the amount of duty based on a cost, insurance, and freight (CIF) price at the port of debarkation. The amount of duty is more difficult to calculate when the product being imported is unique or unfamiliar. The customs appraisers must decide whether the customs declaration and commercial invoice accurately reflect the value of the product. If the product does not fit some category in the tariff schedule, the appraiser must determine its classification and value for duty purposes.

Ad valorem duties often provide most protection when it is needed least, and least protection when it is needed most. A 20 percent duty on a $100 item of import will be $20, increasing the price to $120. If the domestic product is selling for $110, this means that the protection is more than adequate since the imported product is priced well above the domestic goods. However, if the foreign product is priced at $90, the 20 percent duty will still be applicable under the tariff schedule. The duty will amount to $18. The product will sell for $108, or below the price of the domestic product. Thus, the ad valorem duty does not provide the necessary protection.

Specific Duties

A specific duty is a fixed amount of import tax levied on the basis of some unit of measurement: quantity, weight, or volume. Thus, the specific duty on the import of wool might be 50 cents per pound. Textiles may be dutiable on the basis of yards, steel ingots on the basis of tons, crude petroleum on the basis of barrels, and so forth.

Specific duties facilitate the work of customs officials. Once the rate is established, the problem of determining the value of an import is eliminated. These duties are simple and cheap to administer. The major disadvantage of the specific duty is the fact that without a detailed classification in the tariff schedule, the effectiveness of the duty will vary. For example, suppose a duty of $1.00 per yard were imposed on all imports of cloth. On woolen serge cloth worth $20 per yard the $1.00 duty might be quite low, but a duty of $1.00 per yard on cheap synthetic cloth worth only 50 cents per yard would be extremely high.

Compound Duties

To make duties more equitable and to gain the advantages of both the ad valorem and specific duties, nations usually adopt a compound duty. The combination of the two might provide for a 40 percent ad valorem duty plus a specific duty of 50 cents per piece on the import of a particular product such as chinaware. Theoretically, a compound duty will retain the advantages and minimize the disadvantages of each. Two types of compound duties are often used by countries: a countervailing duty, and a compensatory duty.

A *countervailing duty* is one that is levied to offset an advantage granted by a country to its exporters by means of bounties, subsidies, or grants. In the United States, the Secretary of the Treasury will estimate the amount of such grants that are being paid by a foreign government and will then order a countervailing duty to be levied on the import of such products equal in amount to the subsidy.

A second method that might be used by an exporting country to provide an advantage to its producers is to levy a tax on its raw material exports. If this country is the major source of supply for a manufacturer in the raw-material-importing country, its raw material costs will be higher by the amount of the tax. The foreign producer who has to import these materials will be at a competitive disadvantage with producers who do not pay the export tax. That would be the case if a U.S. manufacturer used imported pulp wood from a country that levied an export tax. The manufacturer who does not pay the export tax will be able to market paper in the United States at a lower cost than the U.S. producer. To offset this advantage, which was largely due to the export tax, the U.S. government will levy a countervailing duty on the import of paper equal in amount to the export tax that the U.S. producer had to pay on the raw materials used to manufacture a given amount of paper.

A *compensatory duty* is one that is levied on the import of a manufactured item equal in amount to the duty that was paid on imported raw materials used in the manufacture of the product. Unlike the countervailing duty, however, the duty is not in response to something a foreign country did but rather to offset something the home government did. If a duty is levied to protect a domestic raw material producer from foreign competition, it might adversely affect the imported raw material cost of a domestic manufacturer of a particular product. For example, U.S. wool producers are protected from foreign competition by a specific duty that is levied on the import of raw wool from Argentina, Chile, Uruguay, Australia, and other countries. However, the production of raw wool in the United States is inadequate to meet the domestic demand of textile manufacturers; therefore, they must use imported wool. This means that the textile manufacturers' raw material costs are higher than they might be by the amount of duty placed on the import of raw wool, making it difficult for these manufacturers to compete with imported woolen textiles from a country that permits raw wool to be imported duty free. To compensate these manufacturers for the higher costs of the raw materials, a compensatory duty is levied equal in amount to the duty that was paid on the raw material used in the manufacture of the product. In addition to this duty, an additional duty in the nature of an ad valorem tax may be levied on the import of the woolen textile.

Duties may be levied on the basis of value, some unit of measurement, or a combination. Duties may be adopted to protect domestic goods.

Mitigating the Effects of Tariffs

Tariffs, as instruments of commercial policy, can be effective in protecting domestic industries from foreign competition. However, they often place a burden on many firms that further process imported goods for export. To mitigate the effects of such tariffs, the United States and many other governments provide firms with schemes to improve their competitive positions abroad.

Drawbacks

The U.S. government provides for a drawback. This is a refund of 99 percent of the duties paid on imports and on the internal tax paid on alcohol if the goods are processed and exported. Theoretically, the drawback should do much to increase the competitive position of American exporters; however, in actual practice, the red tape involved in applying for the refunds is such that few companies apply. Drawback agents have attempted to fill this gap by providing the service for a commission.

Bonded Warehouses

Bonded warehouses can alleviate the effects of a tariff since duties are not payable until imported goods leave the warehouse. Importers may take advantage of quantity discounts offered by foreign suppliers and store the inventory in a bonded warehouse. If the goods are reexported, the duties need not be paid at all. In the United States, bonded warehouses are limited primarily to storage, whereas in some countries firms may store, repack, repair, remark, manipulate, and even process materials in bonded warehouses.

Foreign Trade Zones, or Free Zones

As with a bonded warehouse, goods entering a foreign trade zone (FTZ) theoretically have not entered the country. Goods entering an FTZ do not have to go through customs, so no duty is levied at this time. Storing, marking, mixing, repairing, manufacturing, and other functions may be conducted in a foreign trade zone. Storage time is not limited. Goods may be marked to meet customs requirements. Damaged goods may be repaired before delivery to customers or returned to the supplier. An example of strategic and extensive use of an FTZ is the Honda assembly plant in Marysville, Ohio, which is actually a subzone of the Cincinnati FTZ.

The rapid growth of such facilities in recent years is an indication of the advantages offered by the foreign trade zone. In 1937, Staten Island in New York City was the only foreign trade zone in the United States. Between this date and 1960 numerous FTZs were established: New Orleans (1947), San Francisco (1948), Los Angeles and Seattle (1949), San Antonio, Texas (1950), and Toledo, Ohio (1960). At the end of 1985, there were more than 118 foreign trade zones in the United States and Puerto Rico.[5]

Many foreign nations are also using the concept of a free trade zone as a means of attracting foreign direct investment without throwing their entire nation open to any and all foreign investors. Uruguay is one country that is trying to use FTZs along with a history of political and economic tranquillity to attract firms that would otherwise invest in its giant neighbors, Argentina and Brazil (see Global Insight).

Perhaps the most obvious example of a free zone and the one with which many people are familiar is the duty free shop in an airport. Although such shops are far more limited in their scope than FTZs, they are very similar in legal and economic concept.

Quantitative Controls

Types of Quotas

Quantitative controls or quotas are often used to supplement tariffs as instruments of commercial policy. Various types of quotas are used to restrict the import or export of goods and services.

Import quotas are used to restrict the quantity of imports of a particular article from one or more countries. These are more effective than tariffs in protecting industries because they prohibit imports beyond the limit established by the government (e.g., they are inflexible). Tariffs and quotas also differ in another important way. Although they both increase the price of goods, with tariffs the revenues are collected by the government, whereas with quotas, the higher prices result in higher profits for producers. Thus, importers generally prefer quotas to tariffs. Quotas are suitable for quick action because they can be imposed by the President under his emergency powers and can be used as a tool for bargaining or retaliation. They are simple and easy to administer, and can be used in conjunction with import licenses and permits.

Import quotas may be used to protect domestic industry from foreign competition or to foster infant industries. They are effective in promoting the diversification of domestic industries. Nations in balance of payments difficulties find quotas to be more effective than import duties in correcting disequilibria. However, like tariffs, quotas result in a misallocation of resources.

To improve the competitive position of domestic manufacturers, nations often adopt measures to mitigate the effects of duties.

Free Trade Zones with Special Incentives Attract Foreign Firms to Uruguay

Uruguay's new FTZ rules offer investors attractive incentives. In addition to the existing FTZs, new FTZs can be established anywhere in the country. Even an individual firm can be considered an FTZ. FTZs can be owned and operated by private firms. All types of industrial, commercial, and service activities, including banking, are permitted in FTZs. Within FTZs there are no restrictions on the inflow or outflow of bills, local and foreign currency, precious metals, or other monetary instruments.

In addition to these liberalizing rules there are specific incentives that should translate into improved profits:

1. Exports into an FTZ are duty-free.
2. Imports from Uruguay's non-FTZ territory into an FTZ are considered exports; thus, a non-FTZ firm is eligible for export incentives.
3. Goods and services exported from FTZs are free of any charges or duties.
4. Free-trade-zone users are exempt from all local taxes, except payroll taxes.
5. Non-Uruguayan employees can be exempted from social security taxes.
6. FTZ users are also exempt from the Industry and Commerce Income Tax, but profits and dividend remittances are levied when such taxes are normal in the country of origin and when credits are granted for taxes paid in Uruguay.

Source: adapted from Jorge Rebella, "Uruguay's FTZs: The New Rules," *Business Latin America*, July 3, 1989, p. 203.

There are different types of import quotas. *Individual quotas* may allocate the amount, volume, or value that may be imported from each country, usually on the basis of past imports. The total constitutes the *global quota* for all countries. *Tariff quotas* limit the amount that may be imported at any one rate of duty. Anything in excess of this amount is usually dutiable at a higher rate.

Export quotas place a limit on the quantity of raw materials, manufactures, and so forth leaving the country. As with import quotas, strict limits are placed on the exports of the products, and licenses or permits may be used to supplement the regulations. Export quotas may be adopted to conserve domestic resources or to limit the outflow of goods in short supply. The United States, for example, used export quotas in the late 1970s to limit the shipment of grain when weather conditions damaged the grain harvest, causing a shortage and an increase in prices. Nations may limit the export of commodities in an attempt to maintain high prices abroad.

Export quotas may be used to stimulate domestic industries. If a nation is a major supplier of raw materials, it could restrict the export of those raw materials to encourage domestic use of the product. This might also result in foreign investments, aiding the economic development of less developed raw-material-exporting countries.

Voluntary quotas are usually adopted when pressure is exerted by domestic producers or labor, and are agreed to by the exporting country in an effort to prevent countries from adopting more stringent measures to

This airport duty-free shop in Glasgow, Scotland, is in some ways a simplified example of the concept behind a free port or even a free trade zone.

restrict the import of certain products. One of the best examples of this was the voluntary quota adopted by the Japanese government in 1981 to limit the number of automobiles exported to the United States to 1.68 million units per year for five years, then subsequently increased voluntarily to more than 2 million units. Japan also agreed to limit exports of cars to France to 3 percent of the domestic market and to Britain to 11 percent of the domestic market.

When negotiations do not result in voluntary limits, the importing country may take unilateral action. For example, on January 15, 1983, the United States imposed a limit on textile imports from the People's Republic of China. In retaliation, China announced it would stop buying cotton, synthetic fibers, and soybeans from the United States.

Because quantitative controls are absolute and inflexible, they are generally more effective than duties in restricting imports.

The actual administration of the quota and the allocation to individual firms are the responsibility of the government or of some trade organization in the exporting country.

Embargoes and Boycotts

An *embargo* is an official act on the part of the government to prohibit the import or export of a product. This term may also be used with reference to ships that are detained in a port or excluded from a port. Embargoes may be imposed for a variety of reasons: during a war, for military objectives; to prevent the landing of undesirable cargoes such as cattle from a country with the hoof-and-mouth disease; or to protect the health and morals of the people, as with the import of mislabeled food products or pornographic material. An embargo may also be placed on the export of military supplies or other goods of national security interest, or on the shipment of goods to countries with which a nation does not have diplomatic relations. Such "political" embargoes might result in conflict within the government if the State Department for national security reasons prohibits the export of goods while the Commerce Department might feel that the only effect of the prohibitions is to penalize U.S. exporters since foreign importers will not be deprived of the product: They will just turn to other sources.

A *boycott* is an unofficial act on the part of a country to discourage commercial relations with any person, firm, or country. Prior to the outbreak of the war with Japan in 1941, there was a boycott on the shipment of scrap iron and aviation fuel to that country. More recently, certain Arab nations have boycotted firms that conducted trade with Israel. Because of the unofficial nature of boycotts, they are less effective than other methods in restricting trade.

Exchange Controls

The third major instrument of commercial policy to restrict imports is the use of exchange controls. Exchange controls were adopted by the belligerent nations during World War I as a means of assuring essential imports. Since then, exchange controls have been used for other purposes, such as to prevent the flight of capital, to conserve gold, to facilitate national planning, to achieve full employment, to assure essential imports, and to bring about equilibrium in the balance of payments.

Governments attempt to achieve the desired objectives by restricting the allocation of foreign exchange from those purposes that it feels are undesirable. By controlling the amount of foreign exchange that gets into the hands of importers, the government is able to limit the import of those commodities that do not fit into its plans. Foreign exchange that the government has accumulated is then released to importers to be used for payment of those commodities the government considers essential. Furthermore, the rate charged for that foreign exchange will vary with the significance of the imports to the national welfare. For imports of essential commodities, the most favorable rate will be provided. For goods that are less essential, the rate will be less favorable. For the import of luxuries and nonessentials, the rate will be least favorable. This sliding scale or multiple exchange rate is common practice when exchange controls are adopted.

Exchange controls are rarely used among industrial countries during peacetime, but are a common practice among the less developed countries that have a shortage of hard currency for the import of necessities.

Whenever exchange controls are adopted, attempts are made to circumvent the regulations. This might be in the form of *black market* operations in the foreign currency, or overvaluation of the products being imported to provide the importer with a credit account in the foreign country

When a government adopts exchange controls, it limits the availability of foreign currency to pay for imports.

(in the form of a bank deposit or credit with the exporting firm). Another possible effect of exchange controls is the conclusion of bilateral payment agreements among the countries, eliminating the need for foreign exchange to carry on trade. Naturally, this type of agreement will eliminate multilateral trade among nations.

Other Nontariff Barriers

In addition to the three major instruments of commercial policy discussed above, nations make use of other measures to control trade. Some are adopted for reasons other than to restrict trade but have become effective nontariff barriers; others are adopted specifically to restrict foreign competition in the domestic market.

France requires customs and import documents to be written in French "to protect the French language and culture." Cheese imported into France from Switzerland must pass through customs in remote cities, and Japanese videocassette recorders may be imported only through the tiny customs port at Poitiers, causing long delays. Japan does not accept tests conducted abroad on cosmetic and pharmaceutical products, requiring lengthy tests within the country before these may be imported. Britain has restrictions on foreign insurance companies, banks, and law firms. Some countries even restrict foreign retail operations.

In the United States, the various departments of the federal government have their own regulations. Among the most common are the licenses issued by the State Department for exports of goods that are restricted for national security or military reasons. Certain shipments must first have Congressional approval—such as the stinger missiles that were requested by Saudi Arabia and Bahrein in the spring of 1984. (Some missiles were shipped to Saudi Arabia under the emergency powers of the President, but further shipments called for Congressional approval. Shipments to Bahrein were deferred.)

The Department of Agriculture has control over the import of plants and animals to prevent the possible spread of insects and diseases. The sanitary embargo, for example, prohibits the import of fresh beef from countries where the hoof-and-mouth disease exists. The Food and Drug Administration (FDA) regulates the import of drugs and foodstuffs that might be harmful to the health of the people. Drugs must have prior approval of this agency and foodstuffs must meet minimum standards as to contents and labeling before they may be imported. Regulations prohibit pornographic material and other goods that might be harmful to the morals and health of the population. Technical regulations of the Environmental Protection Agency (EPA) control the import of motorized vehicles that might be harmful to the environment. The Department of Commerce, the Department of the Interior, the Naturalization and Immigration Services, and other federal agencies have regulations that each enforces.

Firms that set up manufacturing plants in other countries often find that domestic content laws prevent their importing certain parts from the home country. They must manufacture these parts locally or use parts manufactured in the host country. In the United States, the labor unions have put pressure on Congress to pass a domestic content law requiring foreign automobile manufacturers to use a stated percentage of U.S. rather than imported parts. Only products made in the United States may be used in the construction of bridges and highways that are financed by the gasoline tax. Such constraints weaken the advantages of specialization and lead to the misallocation of resources.

Internal commodity taxes, government purchasing preferences, excessive valuation of imports subject to duties, and blacklists often make it difficult for goods to cross the boundaries among nations. Trademark and copyright laws, marks of origin, credit limits, the operation of cartels and monopolies, and subsidies to domestic producers act as impediments to trade. Bilateral trade agreements, clearing and payments agreements, and barter arrangements channel trade into controlled markets.

Nontariff barriers are becoming increasingly important as a method to restrict imports, as duties on imports are reduced. A 1989 study by the IMF showed that nations are turning increasingly to nontariff barriers and that these are offsetting some of the gains that have resulted from the reduction of duties through multilateral negotiations.[6] If experience is any indication, the uniformity in tariffs within the European Community after 1992 will certainly result in the adoption of various nontariff barriers as each country attempts to provide its own producers with an advantage.

State trading (where the government is actually involved) has resulted in a distortion in trade and in the misallocation of resources in recent years. It has tended to limit the free flow of international products. An example is the "Buy America" policy that requires the government to purchase from domestic producers unless domestic prices are more than 6 percent above the prices bid by foreign producers. In certain special cases, the price differential is set at 12 percent, and for items used for defense, the level is set at about 50 percent. Such legislation strongly favors domestic producers and eliminates most of the foreign competition. Many countries have similar legislation.

Nationalized companies have grown steadily since World War II and are not limited to the communist nations. They have spread rapidly in the West and in Third World countries. The world's oil industry is largely government-owned, as are the airlines. In western Europe, the steel industry is mostly government-owned. Since the 1970s, state enterprises have gained a significant share of the market in such industries as aerospace, steel, aluminum, shipbuilding, and auto manufacturing. State-owned enterprises have gone into the manufacture of pharmaceuticals, petrochemicals, electronics, computers, telecommunications, and office equipment. Not only do state companies act as a barrier to free trade, but they have also entered various markets and have underbid private firms. As Duignan and Gannin in the *Wall Street Journal* of May 24, 1984, stated, "A state owned corporation does not have to be efficient; it can afford to accumulate losses because it can sell its products below cost, at taxpayers' expense." These writers concluded that "widespread state ownership inhibits the free market and free international trade; it is a threat not only to free trade but also to U.S. capitalism."[7]

Various nontariff barriers to trade are adopted by nations for national security, health, morals, political, or other reasons.

These and other regulations control the movement of goods and services across national boundaries. Many of them are perfectly justifiable for non-economic reasons and serve a very important purpose. Some, however, deprive the nation of many of the benefits of specialization and trade, and are not justifiable for economic or other reasons. Those that benefit only the special interest groups at the cost to the general public should be abolished, yet the likelihood of this occurring is rather remote.

EFFECTS OF TRADE RESTRICTIONS

Nations often adopt trade regulations in their attempts to achieve stated objectives, but these generally have undesirable effects upon the different sectors of the economy. Retaliation is almost immediate when a barrier is adopted against imports from a country or group of countries. The United States, for example, is prepared to target for retaliation countries that maintain barriers against U.S. exports under the Omnibus Trade and Competitiveness Act of April 1988. History abounds with examples of measures resulting in countermeasures.

Perhaps one of the most interesting occurred a couple of decades ago when the European Common Market placed barriers on the import of frozen chickens from the United States at prices that were ridiculously low. The United States threatened to retaliate if the barriers were not removed. Some five years ago, Hong Kong watchmakers decided to boycott French brandy to get back at France for setting quotas on watches made in Hong Kong. Australia has imposed tariffs on Japanese outboard motors, alleging that Japan is flooding the market. Currently, negotiations are being conducted between Thailand and the United States regarding the import and distribution of American cigarettes in that market.

Experience during the Depression of the 1930s should have taught us that restricting imports does not necessarily increase domestic economic activity. Trade is a two-way street, and the limiting of purchases from abroad adversely affects exports. Nations do not have an unlimited supply of gold or foreign exchange, so they must depend upon their sales abroad to provide them with the necessary means to pay for what they import.

When nations stop buying from others, domestic production is adversely affected. The decrease in production is accompanied by a further decrease in employment—just what the barriers were supposed to prevent. Decreasing imports will do away with many jobs that arise from the handling, transportation, and distribution of these products and the ancillary activities associated with importing and exporting.

Restrictions on imports have an adverse effect upon domestic price levels. As long as goods are permitted to enter a country, they prevent domestic prices from rising too rapidly, but if competitive goods are kept out, domestic manufacturers need to worry only about their domestic competitors. In the automobile industry, manufacturers adopt comparable price increases to retain their share of the market, but these increases are limited because of the possible competition from abroad. If it were not for imported automobiles, there is great likelihood that domestic automobile prices would be much higher than they are at the present time. Recently, the import of Korean Hyundai cars at prices below $6000 has encouraged other automobile manufacturers to come out with less expensive automobiles.

Trade restrictions tend to foster inefficiency. This is especially true if import quotas or tariffs to equalize the costs of production are adopted. There is little incentive for a manufacturer to invest in modern capital equipment if it does not have to worry about possible competition from more efficient foreign producers. The steel industry of the United States has been slow to make capital investments because the foreign steel producers are limited to a percentage of the domestic market. There is no doubt that the industry is less efficient than those of other countries, including newly industrialized countries such as Brazil and South Korea, because of the lack of modern methods of production. On the other hand, imports of automobiles have forced American automobile manufacturers to adopt revolutionary changes, including robots and new management methods.

The adoption of restrictive measures deprives consumers of many products and of a broader choice of products. Thus, their standard of living is affected. Products such as tea, coffee, chocolate, and many tropical fruits that add to our enjoyment cannot be produced in the temperate regions of the world where most of the world's population is located.

This is only a partial list of the possible impacts of restrictive measures on a country that adopts barriers to trade. Yet in spite of these effects, trade restrictions are increasing. As indicated in Chapter 3, "International Agreements to Minimize Conflicts," GATT has been effective in reducing tariff rates; unfortunately, nations have enacted other measures to restrict free trade. Additionally, more nations are using tariffs. In essence, despite cuts in tariff rates, their frequency of usage has increased and other forms of protectionism have been adopted. According to GATT estimates, in 1980 half of the world's trade was restricted by quotas and tariffs, as compared to 40 percent in the mid-1950s.

Trade restrictions adversely affect many sectors of the nation's economy; usually consumers are hurt the most.

SUMMARY

During the ancient period, commercial policies were only local or municipal in nature. Commercial policies of nations as we know them today came into being only with the establishment of nations.

Under the policy of Mercantilism, governments adopted policies that would lead to an accumulation of precious metals—a means to foster the development of a strong state. Their commercial policies placed emphasis on a "favorable" balance of trade. There were many who did not believe that this policy benefited most of the people.

The reaction against Mercantilism in France was led by the Physiocrats, who believed that manufacturing and commerce were contrary to the "natural" order, so their emphasis was on agriculture and the extractive industries. Their doctrine of "laissez-faire, laissez passer" was adopted in part by the free traders, who believed that mutual benefits would arise through specialization and trade.

Although free trade dominated the commercial policies of most nations during the latter part of the eighteenth and early nineteenth centuries, countries in the early stages of industrial development felt that they could not compete with manufactured imports from the highly developed countries, and began to set up import barriers. Various arguments were advanced to justify the policy of protectionism, but most of these are economically invalid.

There are three basic instruments for restricting imports: customs duties, quantitative restrictions, and exchange controls. Other nontariff barriers may also be adopted. The adoption of any restrictive measure will have an impact upon the countries involved. Measures for protecting domestic industries from foreign competition often result in retaliation that might affect adversely other sectors of the economy and generally foster inefficiency. Unfortunately, short-term benefits generally seem to be favored over the solution of the long-term problems.   □

KEY TERMS AND CONCEPTS

Ad valorem duty

Antidumping duty

Bonded warehouse

Boycott

Compensatory duty

Compound duty

Dumping

Embargo

Exchange controls

Export duty

Foreign trade or free trade zone (FTZ)

Free trade

General-conventional tariff

Global quota

Import duty

International commerce

Maximum-minimum tariff

Mercantilism

Multiple-column tariff

Multiple exchange rates

Preferential duties

Protectionism

Quotas

Retaliatory duty

Single-column or unilinear tariff

Specific duty

Tariff quota

REVIEW QUESTIONS

1. Describe the commercial policies of the Middle Ages.

2. What is meant by the policy of Mercantilism? Why did the Mercantilists feel that commerce was the only productive activity?

3. Who were the Physiocrats and what policy did they support? Why?

4. What were the reasons for the support of the free trade policy in England during the eighteenth and nineteenth centuries?

5. Compare the protectionist sentiment of the 1980s with that during the Depression of the 1930s. What impact would a policy of protectionism have on the economies of the United States and its trading partners?

6. Should the President of the United States be given the authority to negotiate and put into effect commercial agreements with foreign countries without Senate ratification? If so, why? If not, why not?

7. Should measures such as the most favored nations clause be used to achieve political objectives? If so, why? If not, why not?

8. List the major purposes of import duties, and of export duties.

9. When might a nation be justified in levying a countervailing duty? How does this differ from a compensatory duty?

10. How might a nation mitigate the effects of import duties?

11. Why are quotas considered to be more effective than tariffs?

12. List the various reasons why nations might adopt export quotas.

13. Are voluntary quotas effective? Why?

14. How are exchange controls used to achieve commercial policy?

15. Explain briefly what effects restrictive trade measures might have on different sectors of a nation's economy.

DISCUSSION CASE

Overhauling European Commercial Policies for 1992: A Formidable Task

Making Europe's single market work will require a major remodeling of the Community's existing external policies and the creation of new commercial policies where none exist, says a top Brussels official. These efforts have

Adapted from Elizabeth de Bony and Chris Matthews, "The Single Market: Fertile Ground for Protectionist Bloc?" *Business International*, June 27, 1988, pp. 197–198.

just begun, but it is clear that the task will be nearly as formidable as establishing the single market. Remodeling of commercial policies is so problematical because it flies directly in the face of the economic nationalism that is the heart of the self-identity of most European republics. In theory, the European Commission has had jurisdiction over Community trade policy for 20 years but in reality trade has continued to be controlled by an abundance of national restrictions "from quotas on autos and textiles to national licensing rules on strategic exports."

Since the new commercial policies will also affect services, the Commission will have to address such complex issues as public sector procurement, single banking licenses for the entire Community, and EC-wide insurance services. These new policies will clearly result in major new benefits as well as fierce competition for EC and foreign firms. Many people believe the Commission's internal market crusade has left no time for reflection on how competitive the European market will be after 1992, and how this competition may adversely affect European companies.

Danger Signals

U.S. Ambassador Alfred Kingon spoke for many when he said that we fear protectionism is "on the rise in Europe." Based on current European attitudes, this anxiety may not be unfounded. Some EC governments, especially Italy's, are moving slowly to pass the more than three hundred pieces of national legislation needed to create the single market. Governments fear negative effects on local industry and labor markets, and want to ensure that the benefits of a single market do not bypass them.

Several industrial sectors, particularly automakers and financial services, are concerned about intense Japanese and U.S. competition when national protections are abolished, and want to preserve or institute new restrictions on non-EC competitors, at least for a transition period. Clearly, "transitory" protectionist measures could lead to a trade war.

Antidumping actions taken recently against Japanese exporters—covering electronic printers, typewriters, scales, photocopiers, and ball bearings—serve as a portent of future external trade policy when European industries are threatened. The Japanese are stepping up the rate of direct investment and seem to believe that the threat of exclusion from the single market is real.

Reciprocity or Else

Willy De Clercq's repeated calls for reciprocity have Washington and the Pacific capitals concerned. Many EC watchers believe that political realities will require the Community to introduce EC-wide protection if it is to convince national governments to relinquish their current protection of national firms and sectors. EC President Jacques Delors labels as "absurd" the concerns that the Community's single-market plans will be accompanied by protectionist measures leading to the creation of "fortress Europe." He points out that the EC is one of the world's most open markets and will remain so. He says it is "extraordinary" that Japan, with the world's most closed market, is worrying about the external impact of 1992. But Delors makes clear that in those areas governed by GATT ruling, Europe will honor its commitments but in other areas it will follow the principle of reciprocity. This means that in order for third-country companies to benefit from EC policies, their governments will have to grant similar advantages to European companies.

Reciprocity will be a key factor for service industry firms. Harmonization of banking regulations and licensing procedures could enable U.S. and Japanese banks to go where they have never been before, especially in the highly regulated Southern European countries. In response, the EC has already, in the proposed second banking directive, made a formal call for reciprocity. Under the proposed directive a single banking license would be valid throughout the EC; however, for third-country banks to benefit, EC banks would have to be given similar rules in that third country. While this call is a direct aim at the closed Japanese financial-services market, it sets a precedent for other areas.

The Uruguay Factor

It is fortuitous for third countries that the EC's 1992 efforts coincide with the GATT Uruguay Round talks. This will not only keep the EC in line with its international obligations, but will also provide a forum to negotiate any needed changes or compensation. The EC has already announced that its rollback commitment (whereby any existing barriers to free trade will be abolished on a quid pro quo basis) will be fulfilled by the elimination of many of Europe's remaining 736 quantitative trade restrictions (QRs). Community negotiators are playing down Article 115, which permits member states to maintain controls on intramember state trade. The article essentially means that the remaining QRs will be unenforceable, since a member state will have no power to prevent non-EC exporters from routing restricted goods through a second member state. Hence, the EC is giving nothing away.

A common EC import policy is particularly necessary to prevent member states from introducing quasi-illegal measures to protect sectors. As one official explains, eliminating existing QRs does not eliminate the need for these QRs. In order to prevent a backlash or even disintegration of the Community, major new funding for the less developed regions and sectors will be required. Without this funding, the single market may be a medicine so strong that it kills the patient. If Greece were to suddenly allow the free import of textile, the Greek domestic industry would die.

Because it is unlikely that the member states will suddenly agree to these major new funds, the Commission will be forced to increase protectionism aimed at third countries. With luck, the Uruguay Round will prevent the protectionism from getting out of hand; however, without some protection, member states will never give their consent to the single market.

Questions

1. What effect will the desire on the part of some members to retain current restrictions on foreign or non-EC competitors have on the adoption of a common external trade policy?

2. Do you agree with the statement of U.S. Ambassador Alfred Kingon that protectionism is on the rise in Europe? Discuss.

3. EC Trade Commissioner Willy De Clercq has repeatedly called for reciprocity in treatment by those non-EC countries to which certain trade privileges are granted. Is this a reasonable demand on the part of the EC members? If so, why? If not, why not?

4. What effect will the adoption of quasi-illegal measures by member states to protect certain sectors after the elimination of quantitative restrictions have on a common external trade policy?

5. Describe the possible role of GATT in preventing protectionism by the EC as a single market. Discuss the possible impact if the EC adopts a protectionist stance against non-EC countries.

NOTES

1. *Webster's New Collegiate Dictionary* (Springfield, Mass.: Merriam, 1973), p. 226.

2. George Mygatt Fisk and Paul Skeels Peirce, *International Commercial Policies* (New York: Macmillan, 1925), pp. 15–26.

3. Board of Governors of the Federal Reserve System, *Federal Reserve Bulletin* 75:4 (April 1989), p. A29.

4. J. Russell Smith, M. Ogden Phillips, and Thomas R. Smith, *Industrial and Commercial Geography* (New York: Henry Holt and Co., 1955).

5. Don R. Beeman and Sharon L. Magill, "The Role of Foreign Trade Zones in Business Strategy," *Mid-American Journal of Business* 3:1 (Spring 1988), p. 14.

6. Sam Laird and Alexander Yeats, "Nontariff Barriers of Developed Countries, 1966–86," in IMF and IBRD, *Finance and Development*, March 1989, pp. 12–13.

7. *Wall Street Journal*, May 24, 1984.

REFERENCES AND SELECTED READINGS

Beeman, Don R., and Sharon L. Magill. "The Role of Foreign Trade Zones in Business Strategy." *Mid-American Journal of Business* 3:1 (Spring 1988).

Board of Governors of the Federal Reserve System. *Federal Reserve Bulletin* 75:4 (April 1989).

Fisk, George Mygatt, and Paul Skeels Peirce. *International Commerce Policies.* New York: Macmillan, 1925.

Globerman, Steven R. "The Consistency of Canada's Foreign Investment Review Process: A Temporal Analysis." *The Journal of International Business Studies* 15:1 (Spring 1984).

Grosse, Robert. "The Andean Foreign Investment Code's Impact on Multinational Enterprises." *The Journal of International Business Studies* 14:3 (Winter 1983).

Fagre, Nathan, and Louis T. Wells, Jr. "Bargaining Power of Multinationals and Host Governments." *The Journal of International Business Studies* 13:2 (Fall 1982).

IMF. *Finance and Development* 26:1 (March 1989).

Root, Franklin R., and Ahmed A. Ahmed. "The Influence of Policy Instruments on Manufacturing Direct Foreign Investment in Developing Countries." *The Journal of International Business Studies* 19:3 (Winter 1978).

Smith, J. Russell, M. Ogden Phillips, and Thomas R. Smith. *Industrial and Commercial Geography.* New York: Henry Holt and Co., 1955.

CHAPTER

8

Geographic Environment

- Understand the impact of geography on the economic activities of countries and regions

- Learn how geography influences international trade

- Analyze the different regions of the earth in terms of their economic uses and potentialities

- Understand the different climatic types and their relationship to the production of primary goods

- Become familiar with the major products that enter commerce from the different climatic zones

- Understand how geographic as well as nongeographic factors influence the location of manufacturing industries

- Learn the current and potential economic importance of the oceans

OUTLINE OF TOPICS

INTRODUCTION

The study of international business would be incomplete without consideration of geographic and climatic factors. The purpose of this chapter is to describe the influence of these factors on the nature and location of economic activities and industries, as well as to facilitate an understanding of world commerce and geography.

The types of occupation people pursue are affected by the geographic environment in which they reside. In some regions, the type of activity is limited, whereas other areas offer a choice of many occupations. Some countries, because of limited resources or climatic impediments, depend upon the world community to provide them with the necessities for economic survival. Others, more favorably endowed by nature, are able to follow virtually an independent course.

The continents of the world constitute only 29 percent of the earth's surface, of which one third consists of inland seas, rivers, swamps, and ponds. It is on the remaining 20 percent that most people live and most economic activities take place. These activities are strongly influenced by the climatic conditions, distribution of resources, physical features of the land, size and distribution of the population, and other environmental and nonenvironmental factors.

The starting point for any analysis of the influence of the geographic environment on international business is climate because it strongly influences the geographic distribution of people, animals, and crops and directly affects economic activities. Closely related to climate is the influence of natural vegetation, soil types, the flow of rivers, erosion, and even the presence of minerals.

THE RELATIONSHIP OF CLIMATE TO PRODUCTS ENTERING COMMERCE

Climates can be classified as tropical, subtropical, intermediate, and polar or arctic. These climatic zones are presented on the World Climate Zones map found in the color insert section.

Tropical Climates

The tropical climates lie between $23\frac{1}{2}$ degrees north and $23\frac{1}{2}$ degrees south latitudes. Regardless of the time of year, there is little change in temperature; this zone is continuously warm or hot. The heat of tropical climates tends to restrict both mental and physical activities. There are, however, tropical areas that, due to elevation, are not hot the year round. Mount Kilimanjaro in Africa, at an elevation of 19,000 feet (5,895 meters) above sea level, is located within 5 degrees of the equator, yet it is often snow-covered. Similarly, the Andes mountains of Ecuador and Peru are near the equator and yet are often snow-covered.

Within the tropical climatic zone are the humid tropical climates that are characterized by rainfall throughout the year. On either side of these tropical rainforests are the tropical savannas, with a long rainy season and a short dry season. Farther from the equator come the low-latitude steppes, with a short rainy season and a long dry season. Farthest from the equator but still within the tropics are the low-latitude deserts, which are generally very dry with an almost nonexistent rainy season.

Humid Tropical Climates

The humid tropical climate is found near the equator in the doldrums (an equatorial belt of variable winds and calms) and farther from the equator in the belts of the trade winds. Humid tropical climates can be described as having a rainy season and a less rainy season; there is no dry season. Rainfall averages between 60 to 100 inches per year. The Amazon Basin in South America and the Congo Basin in Africa provide good examples of this type of climate. An example of humid tropical climate in an area of trade winds is the Hawaiian Islands, as well as numerous other areas of the world including Southeast Asia, the Philippines, and Central America.

The temperatures in tropical rainforests are not excessively high, but the heat and humidity results in an enervating type of climate. During the hottest part of the day, the temperature might reach 90°F (32.2°C), then fall to 70° (21.1°C) just before dawn, with an annual average of about 80°F (26.7°C).

The canopy of green, as viewed from an airplane, does not indicate fertile soils. The fertility is only the result of the continuous rotting of fallen vegetation on the forest floor, which is rapidly washed away, resulting in soil erosion. Thus, these areas are generally unsuitable for commercial

This rainforest seems to suggest extremely rich soil. In reality, the lush growth is because of the decaying vegetation on the forest floor. The soil below that mat of vegetation has few minerals or nutrients because of the leaching effects of the nearly continuous rainfall.

agriculture. This together with the unfavorable climatic conditions have acted as a barrier to development.

The most common type of economic activity in the more sparsely settled areas of this climatic zone is a subsistence economy of gathering, hunting, and fishing. A nomadic type of agriculture is conducted by natives who make a clearing in the forests by girdling and felling the trees, burning them, and spreading the ashes over the ground for fertilizer. Crops such as beans, cassava, yams, and melons are grown in the clearing. After a few years, the soil becomes depleted of nutrients. The natives move to another area to repeat the practice and the jungle takes over again. Primitive as these methods sound, they are the most ecologically responsible method of using this land. Unfortunately the press of population growth is causing increasing areas of these tropical rainforests to be cut for plantation agriculture. This generally results in little agricultural production but massive ecological damage. Indeed, there is growing global concern about the ecological damage being done by the clearing of massive areas of tropical rainforests.

Where there is an abundant supply of cheap labor, plantation agriculture is conducted. One of the first crops to be grown in the rainy tropics was rubber. The industry got its start when the seeds of the rubber tree were smuggled out of Brazil in 1875 by Sir Henry Wickham, planted in the Kew Gardens in London, and from there transplanted to plantations in the British possessions in Southeast Asia, where the heat, humidity, and soil conditions were ideal for the growth of the trees. Unlike the Amazon Basin, Southeast Asia provided an ample supply of cheap labor and excellent transportation both within the plantation areas and to the coast, for the shipping of natural rubber latex to the great rubber port of Singapore. These factors accounted for the early dominance of Malaya and Sumatra in plantation rubber, although Java, Borneo, Thailand, and parts of the coastal area of Southeast Asia also became major producers of rubber.

The natural rubber industry is no longer as important as it was 50 years ago. This decline is due to the development of synthetic latex, which occurred when the Japanese cut the supply routes to the United States during World War II.

Another commodity that depends on a humid tropical climate is bananas. The banana is a basic source of food for the peoples of the tropics. It is grown in native gardens and as a plantation crop in Asia, South America, Central America, and Africa. Because the fruit is perishable, the availability of transportation or access to a major market is a principal factor influencing the location of the plantations. The U.S. market is supplied mostly from plantations in the Western Hemisphere.

Cacao, used for chocolate, is native to northern South America, but most of the world's commercial production now takes place in the rainy tropics of the Guinea Coast of Africa (Ghana, Nigeria, Togo, Dahomey, Sierra Leone, and the Ivory Coast). There are, however, producers in the Western Hemisphere: the state of Bahia in Brazil as well as the Caribbean and Central America. Cacao is produced primarily for export to the temperate regions of the world.

Palm oil, produced from palm nuts, is one of the most important commercial crops of the Guiana Coast of Africa. In tropical Asia, the islands of the East Indies and Sumatra are the leading commercial producers. Other crops of the rainy tropics that are exported to the temperate regions of the world are coconuts, jute, abaca fiber (commonly referred to as Manila hemp), spices, quinine, kapok (whose fiber is used for mattress fillings and for life-saving equipment because of its buoyancy), and tapioca made from the root of the manioc.

Commercial plantations of the rainy tropics supply numerous products to the more highly developed countries including rubber, coconuts, palm oil, bananas, cacao, and spices.

Tropical Savanna

On either side of the rainy tropics are areas known as tropical savannas. These areas have a long rainy season and a short dry season. The climate is not nearly so monotonous as that in the rainy tropics and is more stimulating for both mental and physical activity. The major areas with this type of climate are the Campos of Brazil and the Llanos of the Orinoco Basin in Venezuela, southern Mexico and the Yucatan, Central America, the southern Sudan of Africa, parts of India and Thailand, and northern Australia.

The soils here are more fertile than those in the tropical rainforests, so commercial agriculture is an important economic activity. Sugarcane is a major commercial crop within this climatic zone. Cuba, with its ideal geographic conditions, cheap land, and sparse population, is a major producer and exporter of sugarcane. Other major commercial producers of sugarcane in the Western Hemisphere are the Hawaiian Islands, Puerto Rico, the Dominican Republic, Peru, Brazil, and Argentina. Important commercial producers of sugarcane in the Eastern Hemisphere are the Philippines, Formosa, Queensland, Natal, Mauritius, and Réunion. India and Java produce primarily for domestic consumption.

In the more humid portions of the tropical savannas, especially in regions of dense population, lowland rice is the leading crop. This is the staple grain crop in India, southeast Asia, the southern two thirds of China, Korea, and Japan. In the drier areas of Southeast Asia millet, sorghum, and wheat are important crops.

The tropical savannas have distinct rainy and dry seasons, making them suitable for rice and sugarcane production.

Cattle grazing has developed in the Brazilian Campos, the Guiana Highlands, and the Orinoco River Valley in Venezuela. Cattle here are raised primarily for their hides rather than for beef.

Tropical Highland

The tropical highlands have a temperate climate because their nearness to the equator is offset by elevation. On the average, temperature decreases 3 degrees for every 1000 feet in elevation. There is no great variation during the year except for a dry season and a wet season.

The tropical highland type of climate is found primarily in Africa, southward and westward from Lake Victoria across the headwaters of the Congo and Zambezi rivers. Parts of Ethiopia, southern Africa, Madagascar, southern Arabia, southern Brazil, and southern Mexico also have this type of climate.

Agriculture is an important economic activity in the tropical highlands because of moderate temperatures and sufficient rainfall. The most important commercial crop is coffee. The leading producers and exporters are located in the highlands of eastern Brazil, Colombia, Venezuela, Central America, southern Mexico, and the higher slopes of Jamaica, Puerto Rico, and Haiti. These areas have rich, well-drained soils of volcanic origin that are ideal for the production of coffee. Other areas of coffee production are Indonesia, the Ivory Coast, Angola, Madagascar, the Congo, Kenya, Uganda, and Tanganyika. Small quantities are produced in Yemen, Abyssinia, and India. The only other crops that are produced for export are cotton and tea. Many of these areas have deposits of various minerals that are in demand in the industrialized countries, indicating that the future prospects for development are good.

Coffee is the most important commercial crop of the tropical highlands; Brazil is the leading producer and exporter of the product.

Dry Tropical Climates

In the low latitudes close to the equator are areas that are extremely dry. These are referred to as the dry tropical climates, including the tropical steppes and the low-latitude deserts.

Tropical Steppes The semiarid tropical steppes in this climatic zone have a short rainy season and a long dry season. Rainfall averages about 35 inches annually but the evaporation rate is so great that the effective rainfall is minimal. High daytime temperatures, cloudless skies, and dry parching winds characterize the weather of the tropical steppes. The vegetation reflects these climatic conditions. Soils are generally rich in chemicals because there is little leaching, but they are deficient in humus because of the lack of vegetation.

The irregularity of rainfall discourages the development of commercial grain production without irrigation. Thus, nomadic herding is the dominant economic activity, especially the grazing of goats and sheep that are not dependent on a reliable supply of rainfall.

The major areas with the dry tropical climates are in Tunisia, Algeria, and Morocco in north Africa, and the Kalahari steppes in southern Africa. The Sudan steppes extend east and west from Senegambia to Somaliland. In Australia, the semiarid steppes border the arid interior. In South America, the Brazilian states of Ceara, Pernambuco, and Bahia fall within this climatic zone. Northern Argentina and southern Bolivia are also located in the dry subtropics. Other areas include parts of lower California and the Plateau of Mexico.

Low-Latitude Deserts The driest areas of the dry tropical climates are the low-latitude deserts. The descending warm air causes rapid evaporation and discourages rainfall. The area is subject to great diurnal ranges in temperature, often varying by 50 Fahrenheit degrees (10 Celsius degrees) from dawn to midday. Moisture from showers sinks into the ground immediately, providing the source of water for the wells and oases.

There is little vegetation in these deserts. The lack of water precludes the development of agriculture, except in the oases, where vegetables, dates, and grains are produced. In the large oases of Egypt, Iraq, and northern India, rivers fed by mountain streams provide water for the commercial production of dates, cotton, wheat, and vegetables. The Atacama Desert in northern Chile, one of the driest deserts in the world, is the principal natural source of sodium nitrate, salt, and borax.

Agricultural production in the low-latitude deserts is limited to the oases and to areas that can be irrigated.

The major areas of the low-latitude deserts are the Sahara, Arabian, Thar, Australian, Kalahari, Atacama, and Sonora deserts. The interior of Iran and western Argentina also have the low-latitude desert climate.

Subtropical Climates

North and south of the tropic zone lies the subtropical climate zone. This climatic zone is composed of three types of climate: the dry subtropics located in the interior portions of this climatic zone, the Mediterranean type of climate, and the humid subtropics.

Dry Subtropics

The interior of the subtropics is dry. The area receives a small amount of rainfall, which falls during the cool winter months. The summers are hot and dry, and temperatures usually rise above 90°F (32.2°C). Seven major areas fall within this climatic zone:

1. Interior southwestern United States and northern Mexico
2. Northwestern Argentina
3. Interior South Africa
4. The Atlas Upland of North Africa
5. The Spanish Plateau
6. The plateaus of Turkey and Iran
7. The Murray-Darling river basin in the southeastern interior of Australia

These climatic conditions influence the types of economic activities in these areas. The grazing of sheep and goats is the most important activity, although cattle and other livestock are also raised in the more favorable areas. The Anatolia plateau of Turkey and the interior of South Africa are especially important for the commercial production of mohair and goatskins. Less important for the grazing of goats are northwestern Argentina and central Spain. The southwestern portion of the United States is a producer of mohair. South Africa, Algeria, and Morocco raise goats for their wool. In all of these areas, where forage is better, sheep are raised. Cattle are raised in the most favorable areas, as in the southwestern United States. Ostriches, donkeys, mules, and dairy goats are other animals that are also raised for commercial purposes in the dry subtropics. Hides, skins, wool, mohair, and some beef and mutton are exported to the world markets.

In the more humid edges of the climatic zone, dry farming is practiced, using two years' rainfall for one year's crop. Millet and sorghum, the most drought-resistant of the grains, are grown for either forage or for grain in areas that are too dry for corn or rice and too hot for wheat. Where water is available, irrigation farming is practiced for the production of peaches, apricots, grapes, figs, citrus fruits, vegetables, and long-staple cotton.

The agricultural importance of the dry subtropics is largely a function of the availability of water for irrigation.

Mediterranean Type of Climate

The Mediterranean type of climate is located between 30 and 40 degrees north and south latitudes, mostly on western coasts. The Mediterranean climate is almost ideal for human habitation. The seasonal range in temperature is small. The summer temperatures average about 70°F (21.1°C), with little humidity. Winter temperatures range between 40° and 50°F (4.4° to 10°C). Killing frosts are rare, resulting in a 12-month growing season.

Large-scale irrigation like that pictured above allows semi-arid regions to become major producers of fruits and vegetables.

The rainfall, which averages less than 30 inches per year, occurs during the cool season, so it is most effective.

There are five major areas with this type of climate:

1. Areas bordering the Mediterranean and Black seas
2. Central and southern California
3. Southwest Africa, Capetown, and Port Elizabeth
4. The southern parts of Australia
5. Central Chile

Commercial agriculture is the most important economic activity within this climatic zone. The products are fruits and vegetables that are produced for both domestic and international markets.

The Mediterranean Basin is the major source of the world's olive production. Most of the world's grapes are produced in the areas with the Mediterranean climate. Southern Europe, the coastlands of Greece, the Izmir district in Turkey, and the Algiers district in north Africa are especially important for the production of grapes for wine. In the United States, grape production for raisins is centered around Fresno, California, while other producing areas grow grapes primarily for wine. In the Southern Hemi-

One of the most important commercial agricultural regions in the world is located in the areas with the Mediterranean type of climate.

sphere, central Chile, Capetown in South Africa, New South Wales, Victoria, and South Australia are important grape producers.

Humid Subtropics

Heat and humidity best describe the humid subtropical type of climate. The summers are oppressive and resemble the climate of the tropical zone. Occasional thundershowers from the tropical air masses and the cold fronts bring temporary relief. With the exception of the short, cold winter, when the cold air masses might bring killing frosts, the remainder of the year is hot and humid. In the Northern Hemisphere, the average temperature in the winter months range between 45° and 55°F. (7.2° to 12.8°C), although in parts of China the winters are frequently more severe. Precipitation in the form of snow is rare in these areas.

In the Northern Hemisphere, the humid subtropical type of climate is found in the southeastern United States, southeastern China, southern Japan, and southern Korea. In the Southern Hemisphere, the Rio de la Plata area of Argentina and Uruguay, southeastern Africa, and eastern Australia are located in this climatic zone.

In the Orient, rice is the major crop produced in this climate zone. Vegetables, wheat, and barley are planted after the rice has been harvested. Tea, mulberries for silk worms, and citrus fruits are produced. In the United States, cotton, corn, and hogs dominate, but these give way to the grazing of cattle and the production of wheat and cotton in the westward margins as in Texas. In southwestern Louisiana, southeastern Texas, and eastern Arkansas, rice is the leading crop. Many of these areas are rich in mineral resources (petroleum, coal, iron ore, or bauxite), which provides for a more diversified economy.

The humid subtropical regions of Argentina and Uruguay are major producers of wheat, cattle, and sheep. Corn production in the Pampas of Argentina ranks second only to that in the United States. Cotton has been introduced to the drier margins. In southeastern Brazil, the land is used for potatoes and other vegetable crops as well as the grazing of cattle. In Australia, cattle and sheep are raised in the drier interior, while wheat is produced in the more humid portions. In the north, some sugarcane is produced, while the hills and lowlands in the eastern part are devoted to grazing and mixed farming. In southeastern Africa, sugarcane has been introduced as a commercial crop.

Rice is the major crop in the humid subtropics of the Orient and in the southern states of the United States.

Intermediate Climates

Marine West Coast

Along the west coast of continents between 35 and 60 degrees north and south latitudes are the areas where the prevailing westerlies blow onto land throughout the year. These areas are said to have the marine west coast type of climate. These regions are cloudy and cool throughout most of the year. The summers are damp, often foggy, while most of the precipitation occurs during the mild fall and winter months. Where the influence of the westerlies is felt farther inland, the summers are warmer and sunnier, winter months are colder, and the rainfall is more evenly distributed throughout the year, as in Western Europe.

In the United States, this zone extends from San Francisco to the Aleutian Islands, but the influence of the westerlies does not go far inland because of the coastal mountain ranges. In Europe, where there are no high coastal mountains, except in the Scandinavian countries, this climatic zone stretches from the British Isles into northwestern Europe. Southeastern Africa, southeastern Australia, New Zealand, and Tasmania are located in this climatic zone. In South America, the Andes mountains prevent the influence of the westerlies beyond the narrow strip along the southern coast of Chile.

The weather conditions and the acidic soils are ideal for the growth of coniferous forests, as in the Pacific northwest of the United States and Canada, and in southern Chile, making lumbering an important economic activity. This climate is also suitable for the production of crops such as potatoes, turnips, and grasses. In areas such as northern Germany and Scotland, where the weather is too cool for the production of corn and too humid for wheat, oats are the important crop. The only important agricultural exports from these regions are cured meats, dairy products, and fish. Grains and fruits must be imported. In New Zealand, the grazing of sheep for mutton and the raising of dairy cows for butter and cheese for export are of major importance.

Coniferous forests dominate the marine west coast type of climate. Forestry, agriculture, and the grazing of sheep or dairy cows are important commercial activities.

Humid Continental with Long Summers

There are four major areas in the world with the humid continental type of climate:

1. The midwestern and North Atlantic states in the United States
2. The humid Pampas of Argentina, extending into Uruguay
3. The plains of north China and Manchuria
4. Southeastern Europe, centering in the Po and Danube valleys, the Ukraine, and the north Caucasus of the USSR

Climatically, this zone has four distinct seasons with great seasonal and diurnal ranges in temperature. The southeasterly winds bring warmth, clouds, and moisture, while the northwesterly winds bring cooler weather. The more rapid heating and the faster cooling of the land masses affect weather conditions. The area, located between 35 and 65 degrees north and south latitudes, has a changeable type of weather during both summer and winter. The summers might become extremely hot and the winters severely cold. The last killing frost in the spring and the first in the fall determine the length of the growing season. Between 35 and 43 degrees latitudes, the frost-free growing season is from five to six months. Precipitation occurs as rain in the summer and snow in the winter, thus generally providing ample moisture for the production of crops.

The fertile soils and the hot humid growing season are especially ideal for the production of corn. The Corn Belt of the United States, extending from central Ohio to central Nebraska, is the world's premier corn-producing area. Corn provides feed for animals, resulting in the development of a "corn-hog" economy wherein corn is marketed in concentrated form through the animals that consume it. Although the Pampas of Argentina has conditions somewhat comparable to those of the United States, it does not cover the territorial extent of the Corn Belt.

Corn is also an important product in Hungary, Yugoslavia, Rumania, and the Ukraine. In Asia, the Yangtze Valley and the plains of Manchuria have become extremely important producers of corn both for human and animal consumption. Truck crops and deciduous fruits such as apples, peaches, and pears can be successfully produced in commercial quantities in this climatic zone.

The U.S. Corn Belt is located in the humid continental climate. Such areas are very important in producing various commercial crops.

East Coast Continental

The east coast continental climate in Eurasia extends from central Germany, southern Sweden, and Finland to the Amur River Basin north of Manchuria. In North America, it stretches from the central portion of North Dakota to Minnesota, Wisconsin, Michigan, New York, and into northern New England. In Canada, it extends from the base of the Rocky Mountains in Alberta to the Gulf of St. Lawrence and the maritime provinces of New Brunswick, Nova Scotia, and Prince Edward Island.

This climatic zone's growing season is too short for the production of corn and too cold for the production of winter wheat. However, the climate is ideal for producing spring wheat and potatoes. In the United States, wheat production prevails in western Minnesota, North Dakota, northeastern South Dakota, and northeastern Montana. The wheat belt reaches into the Canadian provinces of Manitoba, Saskatchewan, and Alberta. In the Soviet Union, the spring wheat belt extends north of the Black Sea and the Sea of Azov for about 400 miles, and stretches east and west about 1500 to 1800 miles. In Asia, northern Manchuria is important in the production of spring wheat.

Spring wheat is the principal commercial crop of the humid continental climate because of the short summers and long cold winters.

Potato production is important in Germany, Poland, southern Sweden, southern Finland, and the Baltic republics of the USSR. Rye is also an important commercial crop in this area. Hay and pastures are excellent, so there is an important dairying industry in both the United States and Canada.

Middle-Latitude Steppes and Deserts

Located inland from the humid continental type of climate are the middle-latitude steppes and deserts. These areas are arid because they are located on the leeward side of the mountain ranges. Annual precipitation occurs mostly in summer, averaging less than 20 inches in the steppes and 10 inches in the deserts. The seasonal range in temperature is great in the Northern Hemisphere, often exceeding 100°F (38°C) during the summer and below zero Fahrenheit (−18°C) in the winter. In the Southern Hemisphere, the range in temperature is much less because the land masses are located within 300 miles of the sea.

Typical of the vegetation are the short grasses in the steppes of the western part of the United States and Central Asia. These areas are important for grazing beef cattle before they are shipped to better grasslands and grain-producing areas for fattening. Sheep, goats, and camels are also raised for their wool, hair, and hides. The amount of moisture affecting plant growth is the major factor that determines the population density of animals that can be grazed on such land.

The rains are insufficient to wash away the plant nutrients, so the soils are very productive if water for irrigation is available. The irrigated lands in the middle-latitude steppes and deserts are important producers of sugar beets, cantaloupes, and potatoes—crops that can stand the high cost of transportation to distant markets. Agriculture is, however, not without its hazards. Drought conditions such as those in the 1930s and again in 1988 resulted in the soils being blown away and creating "dust bowls" as in Oklahoma and Kansas.

The type of agriculture and importance of agri-business are determined by the amount and reliability of rainfall.

Subarctic

The subarctic climate zone is located north of the humid continental type of climate. The regions characterized as being subarctic are areas of intense, dry, cold winters. Temperatures range from 66°F (18.9°C) in July to −46°F (−43.3°C) in January, with temperatures as low as −90°F (−68°C) being recorded. One such zone extends from Alaska to Labrador and Newfoundland; the other stretches across Europe and Asia from northern Sweden to eastern Siberia.

The vegetation is mostly coniferous such as spruce, fir, pine, and larch. Hardy deciduous trees such as birch, poplar, and willow make up about a fourth of the forests. Poleward, the forests become sparse. With the area's great range in temperature, short summers, and long winters, economic activity is limited. Forestry and the production of short-season crops in the southern fringes of Sweden, Finland, and European Russia are the most important economic activities. Trapping is carried on in the forests. Mineral production, especially iron ore, and crude oil drilling are becoming increasingly important as other sources become exhausted.

Economic activities in the subarctic region are generally limited to forestry and mining or oil drilling.

ENVIRONMENTAL FACTORS AND THE LOCATION OF MANUFACTURING

Climatic conditions and geographic considerations not only influence the distribution of the world's population and the nature of agricultural production, they also have much to do with other primary economic activities such as lumbering, grazing, and fishing. However, these primary activities do not completely explain the nature and dispersion of the economic activities of the modern world.

Given the suitable climate and physical features, industries will locate their manufacturing plants in areas that will provide the greatest advantages in the assembly, production, and distribution of the final product. Thus, consideration must be given to the availability of raw materials, skilled but inexpensive labor, capital for investment purposes, sources of energy, and transportation facilities. Other important considerations are the perishability of the product, value relative to weight, weight loss in processing, available services, the location of competitors and complementary producers, and industrial inertia. Even the cultural, political, and historical factors play a role in the location of manufacturing. The U.S. Department of Commerce's analyses of manufacturing provide a brief survey of the influence of geographic and other factors in the location of specific industries.

Machinery Manufacturing

The manufacture of machinery requires creative and skilled labor, energy for processing of specific raw materials, an economy that is in need of such products, and the means for distributing the finished goods. Thus the large farms of the United States and Canada resulted in the invention and manufacture of equipment for the practice of extensive agriculture.

Some machinery is manufactured close to the markets because of its bulk, while machine tools are produced near the markets because of the necessity for servicing. This in part explains why the Ohio and Michigan areas are not only a center for the automotive industry but also the machine tool industry.

Electronic Products

Electronic products require skilled labor, electricity for power, a well-established machinery industry, and sufficient capital for investments. These requirements are found in the countries of western Europe, the United States, Canada, and Japan, but the industry is rapidly spreading to other areas that formerly lacked these requirements.

One of the most rapidly growing industries is the manufacture of computer hardware. The location of the industry in the "Silicon Valley" of northern California is due largely to the initial research and development conducted in the laboratories of universities and corporations in the San

Francisco Bay area. Similarly, the northeastern Ohio area is a center of polymer research and development because of the research of that area's rubber companies.

Transportation Industry

The ideal location for a transportation industry is in a country that has a developed steel industry and a large home market. The United States, Germany, and France meet these requirements. All have been very important in the manufacture of railroad equipment and the development of associated industries.

The automobile industry was ideally suited for development in the United States because of the great distances to be traversed and the lack of a dense network of railroads. Initially, the industry was concentrated in the state of Michigan, which was important for the manufacture of wagons and buggies and because it provided access to hardwoods, iron and steel, coal, skilled labor, and end-user markets. Recently, assembly plants have been established near major population centers because of the high cost of shipping the finished product.

The increase in fuel costs since the oil crisis in 1973 has spurred the manufacturers of western Europe and Japan to become major producers of automobiles for export to the United States. The slowness of the American auto industry to retool for the manufacture of economical cars allowed other nations to capture part of the American market. More recently, the major Japanese firms have been establishing manufacturing plants abroad because of the protectionist measures adopted by many countries. Specific locations in the United States have been determined by both the investment incentives provided by state governments and the labor climate in a particular area.

Aircraft

Although most industrialized nations manufacture airplanes, the United States is the major supplier to world markets. The industry is widely dispersed because the cost of delivering the finished product is minimal relative to the total cost of the product. Los Angeles, Fort Worth, Tulsa, Kansas City, Omaha, Seattle, Wichita, St. Louis, and other cities participate in the manufacture of various components that are finally assembled into a completed airplane. Another factor that has influenced the varying geographic locations of the industry in the United States is the linkage between aircraft technology and national defense considerations. Wide dispersion in plant location prevents the industry from becoming vulnerable to enemy attack.

Shipbuilding

The shipbuilding industry has special requirements. The industry must be located adjacent to deep, quiet waters. Skilled labor must be available. Raw materials, especially steel, must be manufactured nearby. These conditions were present on the northeast coast of England, centering around Newcastle-on-Tyne, Sunderland, and the Clyde estuary below Glasgow in Scotland. Great Britain was the leading shipbuilding nation prior to World War II. Since then, many other countries with the necessary prerequisites have become major shipbuilding nations. Even Japan, one of the leading shipbuilding nations since World War II, is unable to compete with low-wage countries such as South Korea in the construction of ocean-going vessels. Countries with high-cost structures such as the United States must depend on government subsidies to keep their shipbuilding industry afloat.

Textiles

The cotton textile industry was most successfully developed in Lancashire, England, because its damp climate was most suitable for cotton manufacturing. Coal as a source of power and cheap water transportation to import raw cotton and export the finished product were available. British dominance in the industry declined with the development of technology for temperature and humidity control, and the growth of other textile centers in the United States and, more recently, in low-wage countries.

The woolen and worsted goods industry obtains its raw material primarily from the Southern Hemisphere, although the major manufacturing centers are located in the United States, Western Europe, and the Far East. These countries all possess cheap power, skilled labor, established plants, and extensive marketing systems. The wearing apparel industry is located in the major cities of the world, where communication between the designers and manufacturers is facilitated.

Silk is indigenous to countries with both a climate suitable for the production of mulberry trees and an abundance of cheap labor. Today, the industry is still centered in China and Japan despite the fact that Japan no longer has cheap labor. This continuance in part reflects industrial inertia.

Rayon, an artificial fiber produced from spruce and cotton as the raw materials, was first developed in France. Its production rapidly spread to other countries with established textile industries. The United States, France, Czechoslovakia, Italy, Belgium, the Netherlands, the United Kingdom, Germany, and Japan are major producers. Nylon, using coal as its basic raw material, was developed in the United States. Currently nylon has many uses, from cord in automobile tires to parachutes. It has almost completely replaced rayon and silk for hosiery.

Chemicals

The chemical industry, which is basic to many other industries, obtains its raw materials directly or indirectly from such minerals as sulphur, sodium nitrate, coal tar, sulphur, pyrite, potash salts, phosphates, and crude oil.

The availability of raw materials has enabled the United States, Italy, Spain, Japan, Germany, the United Kingdom, and France to develop important chemical industries. Acids, alkalies, bleaching compounds, dyestuffs, paints and varnishes, explosives, plastics, and synthethic fibers are important products of the industry. Drugs and medicines of various types are produced in countries with a highly developed chemical industry.

Rubber

The manufacture of rubber products began as an industry totally dependent upon the sap derived from the rubber trees grown in Malaysia, Indonesia, and the Amazon Basin in Brazil. The latex was then exported to major rubber production centers, such as Akron, Ohio. Now, however, the raw material source for rubber is petroleum and alcohol, and is a product of the industrialized countries. With the increased use of synthetic rubber and its superiority in many respects to natural rubber, the use of the latter has declined in importance. The industry is still concentrated in Ohio because of industrial inertia and proximity to the market.

Food Processing

Food processing is heavily dependent upon geographic factors. The industry develops in areas with the available raw materials. The canning industry is located near fruit and vegetable producers because of the perishability of the products and the cost of transporting them unprocessed. Wineries are located in areas of grape production because the finished products can withstand the cost of transportation to the markets. The location of other food-processing industries can be explained in terms of transportation costs and the nature of the product.

Leather

The leading producers of leather goods are not the leading producers of the raw material. The hides from cattle and horses and skins from smaller animals such as calves, sheep, goats, pigs, alligators, snakes, and other reptiles are generally imported from South America or Africa. They are processed into leather either by use of natural tannin extracts or by the use of chromium compounds produced by the chemical industries of more highly developed countries. The major markets for leather products include the United States, Germany, France, and the United Kingdom.

The location of many industries is influenced by the geographic environment and other factors peculiar to each industry.

THE IMPORTANCE OF OCEANS AND THEIR PRODUCTS

A survey of the geographic environment would be incomplete without a cursory discussion of the role of the seas. The seas are of major importance in facilitating trade; they serve as free highways. There is no upkeep involved as for motor highways and railroads, although the terminals must be developed to provide port facilities for loading and unloading goods. The seas are also the source of many products that are exploited by people.

Most of the world's important ocean fisheries are concentrated on the submerged edges of continents, known as continental shelves. Most countries that are located on coasts are dependent upon the fishing industry. Thus, as the scarcity of fish in a particular area develops because of overfishing or pollution, the fishing fleets must go farther and farther from their home base. Many fishing vessels travel thousands of miles to other fishing grounds. The catch is processed (either canned or frozen) on board the vessel, which enables the vessels to remain in the fishing grounds for months at a time. The products are then transported back for domestic consumption or for export.

Potentially more important than fishing is the existence of various mineral deposits. The ocean water itself is an important source of sodium chloride—salt that is derived from the evaporation of seawater. Seaweed is an important source of iodine and potash, and has been one of the basic sources of food in China, Japan, Korea, and other countries of the Far East. The oceans are an important source of magnesium and bromine, nitrates and sulphates. More recently, the large petroleum reserves found on the continental shelves of North America and the North Sea have reduced dependence on Middle East reserves.

The seas provide the world population not only with fish but also with mineral resources.

SUMMARY

The geographic environment influences the types of economic activity conducted in a particular area. This is especially true in the production of primary products, where the climatic and soil conditions largely determine the type of crop that is produced.

The analysis of the geographic environment began with describing the climatic regions near the equator. These are the tropical climatic zones that are less suitable for human habitation, generally resulting in a lower density of population. Economic activities amenable to the humid tropical climates were introduced to these regions. These were plantations for the production of crops that are unavailable in the temporate regions of the world. Natural rubber, bananas, coconuts, cacao, cane sugar, and coffee are such products. Within this climatic zone are other areas of varying rainfall and humidity that are important in the production of other agricultural products, such as rice and cane sugar in the lowland areas and coffee in the tropical highlands.

On either side of the tropical climates is the subtropical climatic zone. Within this climatic zone are regions with the Mediterranean type of climate. These areas are the world's premier producers and suppliers of vegetables and deciduous fruits. Furthermore, they are considered to be ideal climatically for human habitation.

The native vegetation of the drier portion of this zone consists of grasslands that have resulted in the development of commercial grazing of sheep and goats, with cattle in the more favorable areas, especially in Austrialia. The more humid portions of the subtropics are important in the commercial production of crops such as rice, especially in the Orient, and cotton, wheat, corn, and livestock in North and South America.

Poleward from the subtropics are the intermediate climates. The most extensive and the most important commercial agricultural regions of the world are located in the intermediate climatic zone. Along the west coast of the zone is the marine west coast type of climate, which is cloudy and cool throughout the year. The weather conditions and acidic soils are ideal for the growth of coniferous forests. Thus, lumbering is the principal economic activity of the region, although agriculture is an important occupation in the areas that have been cleared of forest.

The humid continental climate of the intermediate climatic zone has created the Corn Belt of the United States. Its hot and humid summers and cold winters are ideal for the production of corn, resulting in its growth for the commercial fattening of livestock and the corn-hog economy. North and east of this humid continental climatic zone is the east coast continental climate, whose growing season is too short for the production of corn and too cold for the production of winter wheat. This is the spring wheat belt, which covers parts of the great plains of the United States, Canada, and the Soviet Union.

Inland from the humid continental climates are the middle-latitude steppes and deserts. Only short grasses and shrubs can be supported by the low and unreliable precipitation, limiting the economic activities to the grazing of livestock.

Farthest from the equator are the subarctic and polar regions. At present these areas are relatively limited in their economic activities to forestry and mineral or oil production.

The climate and the resultant distribution of population explain to a great extent the primary activities of man, but they in themselves do not explain the dispersion of other types of economic activities. These are also influenced by nongeographic factors, as evidenced by the location of specific manufacturing industries.

The industries described in this chapter provide a general idea of the influence of the various environmental factors in location of the manufacturing industries. Analyses show that some industries develop in particular locales because of the existence of or accessibility to raw materials and energy. The location of other industries is influenced by the availability of those factors that are essential in the processing of the raw materials or the semifinished product, such as capital, management, and skilled labor. Finally, the distribution of the finished product is an important factor in influencing the location of industries. Products that are bulky, perishable, or of low unit value might be uneconomical to ship great distances, so the industry generally moves closer to the source. On the other hand, service and repair facilities are best located near to the market.

KEY TERMS AND CONCEPTS

Continental shelf

Diurnal range in temperature

Doldrums

Dry farming

East coast continental climate

Enervating climate

Humid continental climate

Leaching

Low-latitude steppes

Low-latitude desert

Marine west coast climate

Middle-latitude steppes and deserts

Subarctic climate

Subtropical climate

Tropical climate

Tropical highlands

Tropical rainforests

Tropical savanna

Tropical steppes

REVIEW QUESTIONS

1. What countries in the humid tropics are the major commercial producers of plantation crops? What are those crops?

2. Describe the general location of the areas with the tropical savanna type of climate. What are its major commercial products?

3. What are the major economic activities in the area with the tropical highland type of climate? How do the products of this area affect the daily consumption pattern of the people in the temperate areas?

4. Describe the major products of the low-latitude deserts. Why are the types of products of this climatic zone limited?

5. List those areas with the Mediterranean type of climate. What are the area's major products that enter world trade?

6. What are the three major categories of the intermediate climate? List those states within the United States that fit the description of each of these climatic types. Describe the commercial products of each of these areas.

7. What are the basic factors that determine the location of manufacturing industries?

8. Select a particular manufacturing industry and explain those factors that influenced its location.

9. Discuss briefly the future economic potential of the oceans.

DISCUSSION CASE

Gold in the Ground Is Worth Debt in the Hand

According to a recent report, Bishimetal Corporation, Ltd., a subsidiary of the Mitsubishi conglomerate, has offered to take over the entire Brazilian foreign debt in exchange for full rights to the gold fields in the Amazon Basin. The respected Rio de Janeiro daily *O Globo* estimates that the gold fields are worth $260 billion, while Brazil's foreign debt totals some $115 billion. The proposal was presented to President José Sarney for study in 1989. The proposal will be presented again to the new administration of President-elect Fernando Collor de Mello after he takes office in March 1990.

In the past, Brazilian officials have rejected those proposals by foreign interests to cancel or swap the nation's debt that the government perceived would damage or destroy the Amazon rainforest. In fact, the officials have called such schemes an impingement on the nation's sovereignty. According to *O Globo*, the proposals by the Japanese would not preserve the rainforest, but rather would exploit its vast mineral resources.

Ecologists have often cited gold mining as one of the main causes for the destruction of the rainforest because gold miners use mercury to separate gold from the worthless ores, resulting in the poisoning of rivers and the soil.

Questions

1. Should Brazilian officials pursue the proposal submitted by the Japanese firm?

2. What possible effect will mining of the gold have on the future of the tropical rainforest of the Amazon Basin?

3. Would the economic development of the Amazon Basin justify the destruction of the tropical rainforest? Why?

Adapted from "Japanese Offer Brazil Debt-for-Gold Deal," *The Blade*, February 5, 1990, p. 1 (Toledo, Ohio).

REFERENCES AND SELECTED READINGS

Alexander, J. W., and L. J. Gibson. *Economic Geography*, 2nd ed. Englewood Cliffs, N.J.: Prentice Hall, 1979.

Butler, Joseph H. *Economic Geography—Spatial and Environmental Aspects of Economic Activity*. New York: Wiley, 1980.

Conkling, E. C., and M. Yeates. *Man's Economic Environment*. New York: McGraw-Hill, 1976.

Coyle, John J., and Edward J. Bardi. *The Management of Business Logistics*. New York: West Publishing Co., 1976.

De Souza, Anthony R., and J. Brady Foust. *World Space-Economy.* Columbus, Ohio: Charles E. Merrill, 1979.

Miller, E. Willard. *Manufacturing: A Study of Industrial Locations.* University Park: Pennsylvania State University Press, 1977.

Smith, D. M. *Industrial Location.* New York: Wiley, 1971.

Wheeler, James O., and Peter O. Muller. *Economic Geography*, 2nd ed. New York: Wiley, 1981.

Zimmerman, Erich W. *World Resources and Industries*, 3rd ed. New York: Harper & Row, 1972.

CHAPTER

9

Political and Legal Considerations in International Business

- Learn the relationships among the legal, political, and economic environments

- Understand the foundations of different legal systems

- Provide examples of how a country's legal system influences international trade

- Describe the use of arbitration in business disputes

- Learn how legal systems influence the resolution of commercial disputes

- Understand the sources of political risks

- Learn how firms assess the amount of political risk associated with a foreign investment

- Be able to describe the risk reduction strategies used by firms in their international operations

INTRODUCTION

The political, legal, and economic systems of a nation generally reflect societal values and philosophies. They determine how decisions will be made and the nature of economic activities within the nation, including whether foreign firms will be allowed to operate within that country and, if so, in which industries. It is critically important that the practitioner of international business understand the variety of world political, legal, and economic systems. These systems influence a firm's decision regarding whether to do business in a particular country.[1] Indeed, no factors present more serious problems of adjustment for foreign investors than the varieties of legal and political environments encountered abroad. Furthermore, these political and legal environments are dynamic, thus requiring continuous monitoring, evaluation, and adjustment.

THE INTERRELATIONSHIPS BETWEEN POLITICAL SYSTEMS AND ECONOMIC SYSTEMS

Political Systems

The political system of a nation essentially determines who makes the decisions of governance and how those decisions are made. In a somewhat simplistic model, one can view political systems as existing between two extremes: *autocracy,* wherein one person makes all the decisions, and *democracy,* wherein all adult persons share equally in the making of all decisions. The situation in which political control is held by a small group is called an *oligarchy.* White minority control in the Union of South Africa, military control in Chile, or Communist Party control in the People's Re-

The political system of a nation determines who makes the decisions of governance and how those decisions are made.

public of China are examples of oligarchies. Table 9.1 summarizes these systems.

Economic Systems

The economic system of a nation determines who owns and/or controls wealth-producing assets. As with political systems, one can develop a simple one-dimensional model that defines the two theoretical extremes: *capitalism*, wherein individuals are allowed to possess, own, and control wealth-producing assets; and *communism*, wherein private property is abolished and the people collectively own and control all wealth-producing assets. It is important to differentiate between communism in theory and communism in practice, as well as between communism and socialism. In theory, communism advocates common ownership of the means of production; in practice, communism is government ownership and control of the means of production. *Socialism* in theory is a system in which those who produce goods own or control the means of production and distribution. Stated more simply, socialism advocates worker ownership, while communism means governmental ownership.

Capitalistic economies are often called open, free, or market economies since anyone who wishes can purchase, own, and operate wealth-producing assests. Socialistic economies in politically free countries are often termed *indicatively planned economies*, since the government will often develop plans to indicate the way it would like the economy to grow. Socialistic or communistic economies in politically repressive countries also develop plans but these are generally called *imperative plans*, since the operators of the productive assets are required to comply with these plans. Another term used for imperatively planned economies is *command economies*. Table 9.2 summarizes these systems.

The economic system of a nation determines who owns and who controls wealth-producing assets.

Changing Economic and Political Systems in Communist Countries

From 1917 through 1987, communist nations argued that they were merely in a custodial stage of socialism that required governmental control until such time as the people were ready to control things themselves. Most free societies rejected this argument as an excuse for government domination since this custodial care period in the USSR continued for more than 70 years.

The recent signs of a lessening of economic control in the form of

Table 9.1   **Spectrum of Political Systems**

	Democracy	*Oligarchy*	*Autocracy*
Political decision-maker	All persons	A small group	One person

Table 9.2 **Spectrum of Economic Systems**

	Capitalism	*Socialism*	*Communism*
Economic decision-maker	Private individuals	Workers	Government
Nature of the economy	Market	Planned, indicative, or imperative	Planned, imperative

Gorbachev's policies of *Glasnost* and *Perestroika* are welcomed by most Western nations. Although these appear to result from economic and political pressures from within the USSR as well as the personal philosophy of Gorbachev, it is not clear what would happen if the General Secretary were to be replaced by a more hard-line party member.

Since economic control within communist nations and by the Soviet Union with the nations of Eastern Europe was used as a means of political control, one has to wonder what effects the recent movements toward

Democracy is on the rise almost everywhere in the world. These thousands of students in Tiananmen Square who paraded their version of the Statue of Liberty left no doubt as to their desires for freedom.

greater economic and political independence in Eastern Europe will have on the continuance of these policies. Of even greater concern to Western governments are the increasing demands for political independence among states within the USSR. As the Baltic republics and others demand self-determination, the survival of Gorbachev and his policies of *Glasnost* and *Perestroika* seem increasingly problematical. Perhaps the Soviet Union's February 1990 decision to become a multiparty country will hold the union together without military force. Only time holds the answer to these and other critical questions. This much is certain: If Eastern Europe and the USSR become social democracies with market-driven and open economies, world commerce will experience another period of explosive growth as it did during the 20 years following World War II.

Legal Systems

The legal system of a nation is actually an extension of its political and economic systems since it is a means of operational control of these systems.

A nation's legal system operationalizes its political and economic systems.

It is within these diverse political and economic environments that the international business enterprise must operate.

The Interrelationships Between Political and Economic Systems

Each nation presents a unique combination of political and economic systems. These can be represented on a two-dimensional model. Nations may have common economic systems but very different political systems (see Figure 9.1). Two countries may have capitalistic economic systems but dramatically different political systems. One capitalistic country might be a repressive dictatorship, controlled by one or a few persons as in Chile (quadrant IV), while the other nation might be a free and open representative democracy, such as the United States (quadrant I). A socialistic nation might be a politically repressive oligarchy such as Albania (III) or a free and democratic nation such as Sweden (II).

By focusing on common political systems, we can see substantial differences in the economic systems employed. Democratic political systems can have capitalistic economic systems, as does the United States, or indicatively planned socialistic systems, as do France and Sweden. In theory, a nation could have a democratic form of government and an imperatively planned economy; however, we know of no instance where such a system has remained stable. There seems to be a fundamental incongruity between being politically free and economically repressed. Oligarchical political systems can have capitalistic economies, as does the Union of South Africa, or imperatively planned economies, as does Yugoslavia. There are few true autocracies among the major nations of the world.

The model presented in Figure 9.1 is also useful in representing na-

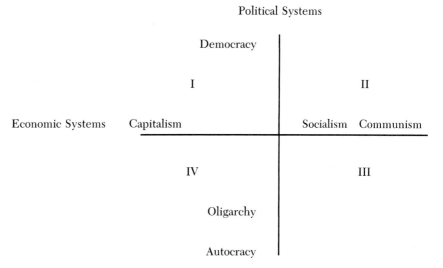

Figure 9.1   Two-Dimensional Model of Economic and Political Systems

tional changes in political or economic policies. The decade of the 1980s saw a shift by many of the Western democracies toward more capitalistic economic policies. Reaganomics in the United States and the policies of Margaret Thatcher are prime examples. Even New Zealand, which had some of the most socialistic economic policies, has made fundamental changes toward greater capitalism and more reliance on the role of the market. In Figure 9.1 this would be represented by a shift from quadrant II to I. The new Soviet policies of *Glasnost* and *Perestroika* as well as the dramatic political and economic reforms within Poland can also be represented on Figure 9.1. These would be a movement from quadrant III toward I. Only time will tell whether this movement is a temporary aberration or whether the countries of Eastern Europe will ultimately become indicatively planned, social democracies on the model of France and Sweden.

Figure 9.1 can also be used to conceptualize the changes taking place in the PRC. That country's leaders wanted the economic invigoration of Western capital and technology. To get this, they needed to allow some elements of economic independence, capitalism, and market economics. What they got along with the economic invigoration were demands for more political independence and democracy. In other words, the government wanted to move slightly from III to IV, but what the students wanted was a radical shift from III to I. The results horrified the world, as students and workers were killed in the streets and the Chinese news media played out an Orwellian nightmare of doublespeak.

Even the shift of Latin American republics from military dictatorships to constitutional democracies over the last two decades could be represented on Figure 9.1. This generally could be viewed as a shift from quadrant IV to I (see the Global Insight).

This two-dimensional model works quite well in capturing the essentials of the political and economic systems of world societies, with some notable exceptions. *Theocracies*—that is, countries where the head of the state is also the head of the religion—are usually difficult to position. The situation in Iran under the Ayatollah Khomeini was an example of a theocracy. If one were to position Iran, it would be in quadrant III since politically it is autocratic, but economically it is imperatively planned—that is, dominated by governmental ownership and control. It is interesting to note that Iran and the USSR would be positioned at almost the same spot. The death of the Ayatollah Khomeini has changed this situation only slightly, since the linkage between state leadership and religious authority remains strong. Saudi Arabia (also a theocracy) would be in quadrant IV since politically it is between an autocracy and an oligarchy but economically more capitalistic.

One final comment on global political systems is in order. Democracy is on the rise. There has been no time in this century when such a large percentage of people have lived under a democracy, and no time in recent memory when so many persons in communist nations could believe that political freedom and democracy were possible.

The interrelationship between political and economic systems differ among nations and determine the nature of life in each society.

LEGAL SYSTEMS

A nation's legal system operates within the political framework of that country and serves to operationalize the nation's political and economic

When the East German authorities allowed free visitation to West Berlin, crossing points like Checkpoint Charlie were nearly gridlocked with visitors. Only a few weeks later these same East Berliners were using sledgehammers to knock chunks off the Berlin Wall to show their contempt for the Communist regime.

systems. Nevertheless, even nations with similar political and economic systems can have different laws. Among the nations with very different political and economic systems, the legal differences are immense. Because of these differences, it is essential that the international manager has a working knowledge of the legal systems in which the firm operates. To minimize potential problems, the international manager should obtain legal services in the corporation's home country and host country.

When a firm operates in a foreign country, it must abide by the laws and regulations of that country and must conduct its business within the framework of those laws and regulations. There is no single uniform international law governing international business transactions, nor is there much commonality of laws among countries.

Bases of Legal Systems

The laws of most countries can be classified into one of two basic types: common law and codified law. *Common law* is based on past court decisions, usage, and customs as well as on legal statutes. Even if there is no legal precedent or statute, common law requires the court to make a decision. This legal system evolved from English law and is the basis for the legal systems of England, the United States, Canada, and other countries that were influenced by the British.

Codified law (also called Roman law) is organized by subject matter into specific codes: commercial, civil, administrative, and criminal. It is thought to be less flexible and adaptable than common law. Codified law is less subject to interpretations because it does not rely on a precedent. It evolved from the legal system of ancient Rome and is the basis for the legal system of most countries that have been influenced by the legal system of Rome—for example, France, Italy, Spain, and Portugal.

Roman law countries usually have substantially more statutes within each code than do common law countries. If one were to look at book shelves lined with the bound volumes of the statutes of a nation's laws, a few shelves would easily hold the statutes of a common law nation; however, it might take the remainder of the library to hold the books on cases that form the precedents for decision-making. On the other hand, in countries where the legal system is based on Roman law, the volumes containing the statutes may themselves nearly fill the library since the lawmakers of that country would have written statutes to cover nearly every conceivable legal situation.

Many non-Western nations have legal systems that are substantially different from those in traditional common law and codified law countries. In many Islamic states, the statutes are often strongly influenced by the religious commandments of the Koran. Communistic states often have codified laws in which the statutes are applied differently by a tribunal of state-appointed judges or military leaders depending on the current political interests of the government. Many totalitarian states have legal systems more in name than in substance.

Legal systems of Western countries are generally based on either Common or Codified Law; the legal systems of non-Western countries may be linked to religion, a Theocracy.

Home Country Legal System

International business firms must be familiar with the relevant laws of their home country as well as those of the foreign countries in which they operate. Home country laws often affect both where and how a firm can do business. For example, the laws of the United States affect the movement of certain goods across its national boundary. Many products of a technical nature and products considered essential to national security may not be shipped, directly or indirectly, to communist countries; however, there are differences regarding what can be sold to which of the communist countries. For example, general trade with Cuba is prohibited, while many technical products are now being exported to the People's Republic of China. To ensure strict control over designated exports and their destinations, general and validated licenses are issued to exporters by the Department of Commerce. Without the appropriate license, goods cannot be sold and in fact carriers are not allowed to transport the goods.

The U.S. government, under Section 486 of the Internal Revenue

Code, has control over the prices that an American firm may charge to its subsidiaries (transfer pricing). This is to prevent the accumulation of profits in low-tax countries in order to minimize the payments to the United States government. In spite of these IRS regulations, many firms still make extensive use of foreign tax havens (low-tax countries where profits can be accumulated to reduce the overall corporate tax burden). (See Chapter 20, "International Accounting and Taxation of Foreign Source Income," for a discussion of tax havens.)

The United States also has legal jurisdiction over the business practices of U.S. foreign subsidiaries. For example, the foreign subsidiaries of U.S. firms must obey U.S. antitrust laws. If a U.S. corporation's operations abroad adversely affect domestic competition through the acquisition of established firms, joint ventures, or marketing agreements, it becomes a concern of the Department of Justice. This is generally referred to as the "Extraterritorial Reach." Foreign subsidiaries of American firms may not carry on trade with countries unfriendly to the United States even when the host country does not have such restrictions. These issues of extraterritoriality raise serious questions of violating the host nation's sovereignty.

The legal departments of multinational firms generally have a high degree of expertise with these home country laws and regulations; however, when a firm goes abroad, it must conduct business under a different legal system and abide by its extraterritorial restrictions and requirements. Thus, foreign activities substantially increase legal complexities and problems.

Arbitrating Disputes

There is no doubt that disputes are bound to arise when a firm does business abroad. Thus, every effort should be made to minimize the possibility of disagreements, but if disputes arise with the host firm or government, every effort should be made to settle the dispute amicably. If agreement cannot be reached, most corporations will seek arbitration before taking legal action. Since arbitration is seldom legally binding (i.e., the parties to the arbitration do not have to abide by the arbitrator's decision), most contracts will have an arbitration clause stipulating that the parties must (1) agree to arbitrate in case of a dispute according to the rules and procedures of an arbitration tribunal, and (2) agree to abide by the decision of the arbitration tribunal.

International arbitration tribunals exist for just such situations. The Inter-American Commercial Arbitration Commission conducts arbitrations in disputes among the American Republics, including the United States. The Canadian-American Commercial Arbitration Commission arbitrates disputes between the United States and Canadian firms. The London Court of Arbitration restricts its operations to those cases that can be legally arbitrated in England. The American Arbitration Association arbitrates disputes on a worldwide basis, as does the International Chamber of Commerce.

Most of these organizations handle disputes in a similar manner. For example, the International Chamber of Commerce first attempts to reconcile the differences. If these fail, the process of arbitration begins. The plaintiff and the defendant each select an arbitrator, and the International Chamber of Commerce appoints a third member from a distinguished list of lawyers, jurists, and professors. At a meeting of the body, each side presents its case. When this group arrives at a decision, the acceptance of the decision would settle the dispute.

The settlement of a dispute amicably through arbitration is preferable to litigation.

Legal Resolution of Disputes

Since litigation will be costly and there is no assurance that the outcome will be favorable to the firm, especially if the legal action is taken in a foreign country, lawsuits should be avoided. Of greater importance is the adverse public relations effect of a disagreement and lawsuit.

Methods of settling disputes vary with the legal system of the country. Under common law, commercial disputes may be subject to either civil or commercial law. Under codified law, commercial disputes are handled under the commercial code, which is specifically designed to handle business problems.

Compliance to a contract will vary with the legal system. In some code law countries, agreements may not be enforceable unless properly notarized and registered, whereas in a common law country this same agreement will be binding as long as proof of the agreement can be established. Both common law and code law will probably absolve a firm from noncompliance of a contract if an act of God prevented the fulfillment; however, substantial differences can exist regarding what constitutes an act of God. For example, a fire caused by lightning that destroys goods in a warehouse would be considered an act of God under both legal systems. If, however, the goods were damaged because of the bursting of a water pipe due to freezing, the code law country will probably consider that an act of God, whereas the common law country may reject this interpretation, reasoning that if the warehouse is located in an area where freezing is a common occurrence, then the owner/manager should have taken steps to prevent such a problem. In fact, differences in the interpretation of laws are often due to differences in legal systems.

Jurisdiction in disputes is an area of concern to business enterprises. Therefore, to provide some measure of protection, contracts often include a clause indicating that the jurisdiction lies in the country where the contract was signed or where the provisions of the contract were performed. In the event of a conflict, such clauses will alleviate the uncertainty over jurisdiction. Although the foreign corporation would prefer to have disputes settled

Business should draw up a contract that defines the court in which the disputes will be litigated.

in its home country courts, clauses that place legal jurisdiction in the host country are now commonplace. These are generally called Calvo Clauses.

Legal Protection of Intellectual Property

Although the protection of all property owned abroad is of concern, the protection of intellectual properties is particularly troublesome for firms operating in different legal environments. The failure to protect trademarks, patents, processes, and copyrights could result in losses of these rights in potentially profitable markets. In some countries, a local firm might knowingly use an established trademark, hoping to deceive the consumers as to the origin of the product. The owner of the trademark might not have any legal recourse if the country is not a member of an international convention or treaty.

In the United States, ownership of intellectual property rights is established by prior use—that is, whoever can establish first use is the rightful owner. This interpretation is true in other common law countries; however, in code law countries, ownership is established by registration. These variations in laws of different countries have led to international conventions designed to recognize and protect intellectual properties.

Most industrialized countries are signatories to one or more of the three principal international conventions. The Paris Union recognizes the rights of the signatory nations in the protection of patents, trademarks, and so forth. Registration in one member country provides protection in all member countries. The Inter-American Convention includes most of the Latin American nations and provides protection similar to the Paris Union. The Madrid Convention established the Bureau of International Registration of Trademarks and serves as an information source as well as providing protection similar to that described above.

In addition to concerns regarding arbitration and home versus host country legal jurisdiction for disputes pertaining to intellectual property, the nonprotection of intellectual property has become a common policy used by nations to promote their own economic expansion and self-interests. In fact, in some nations nonprotection could more correctly be called obstruction of property rights. The consequence of this situation is the frequent "pirating" of computer software, videotapes, audiotapes, and other proprietary products and the resultant loss of substantial profits. This problem of pirating is quite common in Brazil and numerous Asian nations. For the nation, these activities not only advance economic goals but also serve as a protectionist measure since firms are unwilling to enter a market where they have reason to believe that intellectual property rights will not be safeguarded. Arbitration between Fujitsu and IBM concerning encroachment of copyright-protected IBM software provides an excellent example of the merging of different legal statutes regarding this issue. The function-

Variations in the laws of the different countries have resulted in agreements among many countries to protect intellectual property against use without the consent of the owners.

ing of the arbitration board that monitors copyright compliance represents a merger of traditional arbitration activities with the basic precepts of common law.

THE POLITICAL ENVIRONMENT AND POLITICAL RISKS

Doing business is always fraught with risk, especially when a firm leaves its home country. Some products that are sold successfully at home simply do not sell abroad. Sometimes the market becomes so competitive that prices drop to the point of eliminating profits. There are problems of strikes, unavailability of raw materials, high interest rates, and economic recessions. All of these are business risks because they are a fundamental part of the business system of a nation and are faced by all firms operating in that environment.

Political risks are not inherently related to the nation's business or economic system, but are a direct result of decisions made by political authorities. Because political risks are so difficult to forecast and so potentially damaging, they are among the primary concerns of international firms. The fact that some countries provide incentives to attract foreign investments while others denounce the intrusion and influence of multinational enterprises means that firms must carefully evaluate the political environment of a nation before beginning operations. The geographic dispersion of the investments of most multinational corporations has added to these uncertainties since the firm must deal with many different political environments in which it has operations as well as evaluating sites for future operations. Since operating in one nation can have political implications for operations in a second, understanding the political relationships among nations is also of substantial importance. For example, having operations in Israel might heighten the political risks in some Arab states.

The Nature of Political Risks

Broadly defined, *political risks* are any governmental actions or politically motivated events that adversely affect the long-run profitability or value of the firm.[2] These actions can be divided into two categories: *macro political risk* events, which affect all foreign firms, and *micro political risk* events, which affect only one firm or a small number of firms.[3] Macro political risk includes such events as a governmental overthrow installing a regime that is against all foreign ownership of wealth-producing assets, or the deterioration of the political relations between the firm's home government and the host government resulting in discriminatory treatment of the firm. During the period of 1950 through 1965, macro political risks were the most important form of political risk.

In recent years, micro political risks and more subtle governmental actions against foreign investments have become far more common. These new and increasingly important forms of political risk can be called *creeping expropriation*. This term is particularly appropriate and insightful since it defines the basic governmental intention behind these actions (expropriation, or taking the firm's assets) and the mode of execution (creeping incrementalism). Risk types 2 through 7 listed below represent the basic nature of political risk events today.

1. Expropriation of corporate assets without prompt and adequate compensation
2. Forced sale of equity to host country nationals, usually at or below depreciated book value
3. Discriminatory treatment in the application of regulations or laws
4. Barriers to repatriation of funds (profits or equity)
5. Loss of technology or other intellectual property (patents, trade marks, trade names, etc.)
6. Interference in managerial decision-making
7. Dishonesty by government officials, including canceling or altering contractual agreements, extortion demands, and so forth.[4]

Sources of Political Risk

U.S. executives tend to overestimate the level of political risk, especially in developing nations, because they tend to focus on the impact of political risk events without seeing their rarity or understanding the causes. This overestimation is also due to the fact that the political instability and level of host government involvement in economic activities faced by U.S. firms abroad are so radically different from the economic and political stability and the *laissez-faire* policies enjoyed in the United States. Just because a political system is different from the U.S. system does not mean that it is necessarily more risky. Furthermore, greater political instability does not necessarily equate with greater political risk. Several studies have found that political instability and risk are essentially different phenomena.[5] Relatedly, not all political changes within a country produce greater risk. Unless host country political changes negatively affect the relevant business environment of a particular firm, they do not result in greater political risk. For example, Italy has had numerous governments since World War II; however, that does not mean that the country represents a high political risk. Iran has had only one change in government in the last two decades and yet politically it is one of the most risky countries in the world.

Micro political risks result from the interaction of the host country government with a specific corporate investment. Thus, it is the characteristics of the nation and the investment that jointly determine the level of micro political risk.[6] Therefore, micro political risks generally vary among countries, industries, and firms. It is not unusual for the second- or third-largest foreign firm in an industry to be expropriated while the other firms remain untouched. It is also common for firms that sell locally or those with old technologies to be expropriated while other firms in the same industry are left alone.

Political risks, particularly micro risks, are generally less important in advanced industrialized countries. Political risks that occur in developed nations are generally macro political risks that do not single out any one firm or one nationality of firm for discrimination. Nevertheless, there are examples of political changes in developed nations that result in substantially altered economic environments, thus making business more difficult. For example, the election of Mitterand in France ushered in a wave of socialism resulting in the nationalization of certain industries and increased governmental involvement at all levels of the economy. These changes affected the overall business climate for all firms but did not represent macro political risk because they did not affect foreign firms differently from French firms.

In developing nations, political risk levels vary dramatically; however, the presumption that all developing nations are typified by high levels of political risk is simply not true. One aspect of the political environment of developing nations that differs markedly from that of developed nations is the likelihood that a governmental change will bring to power individuals who are radically opposed to the entire concept of capitalism and free enterprise. Such radical changes in governmental economic philosophy often result in substantial increases in the frequency and magnitude of macro political risk events: expropriations, contract cancellations, changes in foreign ownership limits, and so forth. Examples of these situations abound: Cuba under Castro, Chile under Allende, and Iran under the Ayatollah Khomeini. These types of political risks were extremely common in Africa and Latin America during the 1950s and 1960s.

Most situations that result in increased political risks are not nearly so dramatic. More often increases in the political riskiness of a country result from relatively subtle changes in the social, political, economic, or cultural environment of the country. However, environmental changes may result in decreases as well as increases in political risk. Even when environmental changes do result in increased political risks, they may be micro in character, thus affecting only one multinational or a particular class of multinationals in a particular industry or from a particular country. The effect could also differ with the type of operation (i.e., marketing versus manufacturing), the capital structure of the firm, or the type of technology employed. It is quite possible for a particular political action to be disastrous for some multinationals, have little effect on others, and be beneficial to others. Changes might have little effect on the multinational in the short run but present serious long-term problems. The changes could have a different impact on

Political risks are generally the result of the interaction of a firm's operation and the specific policies or attitudes of the host government.

multinationals depending on whether their objective is to enter a market, continue operations in a country, or discontinue operations.

Conflicts Regarding Control and Political Risk Levels

The question that remains is why do host governments take discriminatory actions that increase the risks for a foreign investor when such actions are likely to result in a loss of jobs, technology, capital, availability of foreign markets, and managerial know-how? The answer is that governments, especially those in smaller developing nations, fear domination from outsiders.

The Nation's Perspective on Control   To many foreign governments, multinational corporations have appeared to be more interested in achieving the objectives of the parent company and of the home country than those of the host country. This combined with the immense size and enormous power of MNCs has led some governments to fear that these firms will dominate their national economies and exercise undue influence on economic and political decision-making.[7]

This fear of economic domination by the multinational enterprises centers on four basic concerns. First, the investments of the multinational might be concentrated in certain key sectors of the economy, thus resulting in greater overall influence than the actual volume of investments might suggest. Since basic industries such as steel, energy, or communications are considered crucial for economic well-being, many countries have restrictions on foreign investments in these industries.

Second, firms from less developed countries generally have small operations that have difficulty competing with the large modern plants of multinational firms. MNCs not only produce at lower per-unit costs but also attract the best workers by paying higher wages and providing greater benefits. To survive, the small domestic firms need protection. Indeed, some multinational firms are so large that their global sales often exceed the total national income of the small nations in which they have operations. Third, multinationals might exert their dominance through the use of modern technology. Although the less developed country might benefit from the technology, it could also become dependent on the multinational for continuing technological advances. Finally, the multinational enterprises can have a profound political, economic, and social impact upon the host country through their personnel practices. For example, a simple activity such as the hiring of women could have tremendous social, familial, or religious impact in countries where women are not customarily a part of the workforce.

The Firm's Perspective on Control   From the perspective of the multinational firm, control is often viewed as an essential precondition for investment and successful operations abroad. Most multinational firms are generally unwilling to put all aspects of management control and decisions within the host nation. One of the most common reasons given by international executives for not seeking local participation in foreign operation is their fear of loss of control. In fact, it could be said that control is the primary operating motive of multinational corporations.

The Firm-Nation Control Conflict   The struggle between the foreign firm and the host government for control of economic decision-making results in several areas of tension and might be a major cause of discriminatory actions by host governments (micro political risk). Areas of tension include the distribution of benefits, conformity of subsidiary activities to national development plans, fear of foreign economic domination, and employment or promotion practices.[8]

The definition of control used here is simply who has the final word on fundamental management decisions:

1. The nature and magnitude of production
2. The distribution and sale of the goods produced, including issues of where the goods will be sold and at what price
3. The rate of expansion or contraction of host country operations
4. The distribution or repatriation of profits and equity
5. The determination of employee policies and the selection of the management team
6. Other significant managerial decisions

Control is not necessarily the same as ownership. Even when 100 percent or majority ownership is not possible, control can often be maintained by means of various types of contractual agreements.

Figure 9.2 depicts the relationships between MNC and host government desires for control of subsidiary operations as well as the resultant level of political risk. It should be pointed out that this model does not consider all of the many complex factors that result in political risks or even the rationale for a firm or a host nation having a low, medium, or high desire for control. Rather this model provides the student with a framework for discussing political risk situations in both real and hypothetical ways. Furthermore, it provides a platform for developing an awareness of the rational bases of the needs and desires of both firms and nations.

This matrix can best be understood by considering several examples. First is the case of a vertically integrated firm whose raw material is extracted abroad. This firm must view the extractive subsidiary operation with a desire for a high level of control. As long as the nation's desire for control of economic decision-making is low, the political risk of the investment is relatively low. The operations of major oil firms in Saudi Arabia during the 1960s would have been in cell 31 of the Figure 9.2 matrix. This cell represents a situation in which the firm held a high desire for economic control while the nation had a low desire for economic control. When the

		Host Government Desire for Control of Economic Decision-Making		
		Low	Medium	High
Firm desire for Control of Economic Decision-Making	Low	very low political risk (11)	low political risk (12)	medium political risk (13)
	Medium	low political risk (21)	medium political risk (22)	high political risk (23)
	High	medium political risk (31)	high political risk (32)	very high political risk (33)

Figure 9.2   Political Risk Source Matrix

country's desire for economic control increased (as with the formation of OPEC), the political risk of these subsidiaries increased.

This model also accommodates the differences among OPEC nations. Saudi Arabia has generally supported OPEC positions regarding ownership, price, and production quantity levels but has been willing to leave a large amount of economic decision-making in the hands of the oil firms by means of management contracts, while Libya has sought much greater levels of governmental control. Thus, with the formation of the OPEC, Saudi Arabia may have shifted from cell 31 to 32 while Libya would have shifted from cell 31 to 33.

Second, this model can be used to explain some apparently incomprehensible situations. For example, why would the political risk of an investment in Peru be considered relatively high, while a coproduction agreement in a communist nation such as Yugoslavia is viewed as relatively low-risk? The coproduction agreement in Yugoslavia would preclude the firm from having any level of ownership and would be accompanied by an extensive contract defining in great detail all aspects of decision-making. For the investment in Peru, comparable issues would be covered with substantially less contractual specificity and left for arbitration or court resolution in the event of a disagreement. Thus, it is not the political system of the nation nor the governmental position regarding foreign equity that results in political risk but the investment-specific details regarding control of economic decision-making.

It must be emphasized that micro political risks are investment-specific. The host government might desire control of an extraction operation but not an assembly plant. It might desire control of a firm that sells locally but not one that exports the bulk of its production. It might desire control of capital-intensive operations but not labor-intensive industries.

This model (Figure 9.2) also handles those situations wherein the firm's desire for control is low. Although firms generally want explicit control to ensure the preservation of assets or earning streams within the host nation, or earning streams from outside of the host nation that are strongly influenced by operations in the host nation, there are ways that a firm can reduce its need to exercise explicit control over activities within the host nation.

A low level of desire for explicit management control by the firm could result if the investment is of minimal current or future importance or if the firm has a lesser level of asset exposure. An example of the latter situation might be a firm whose involvement in the host country is limited to licensing, franchising, management contracts, or turnkey operations. (These are discussed in depth in Chapter 13.) There is also less desire for explicit control if the firm's initial investment had been repaid many times over or the market (or raw material source) has substantially diminished. A firm might also have less desire for control if it has had a long and successful relationship with the host government and is confident that its interests and the government's are in accord.

In this conflict for maintaining control of subsidiary decision-making, there are many steps that can be taken. These are discussed later in the section entitled "Strategies for Dealing with Political Risks."

Assessing Political Environments

Before management can develop political risk reduction strategies, it must have processes in place to collect environmental information, analyze that information, and develop contingency plans or take appropriate actions. These processes comprise the activity of political environmental assessment.

Unstructured Assessment

Among firms using an unstructured assessment of the political climate, certain common patterns emerge. First, the process is centered at the top management level; responsibility resides with the chief executive officer or someone reporting directly to top management. Unstructured assessments tend to be sporadic and often are made only in reaction to a specific event. If a problem arises, there is a flurry of activity that subsides with the passage of the event. There is no ongoing evaluation, and the information tends to be fragmented and impressionistic. In-depth analysis is seldom carried out. Companies using the unstructured system do not feel that close monitoring is necessary despite having investments in areas that are politically volatile.

The key to a successful unstructured assessment system is the foreign subsidiary general manager. With little or no headquarters staff devoted to the analysis of political risks, the local general manager is responsible for evaluating the political scene in addition to managing the foreign operation. Expatriate general managers are generally at a distinct disadvantage since both the overall environment and the political structure of the host country are to a greater or lesser extent foreign to them. Local national general managers will be familiar with local customs, language, and politics; however, cultural factors or identification with the country's goals and needs could compromise objectivity. The tendency with both types of general manager is to minimize the importance of any political conditions and to report what it appears the superior wants to hear.

Unstructured assessment depends on the ability, objectivity, and effort of subsidiary general managers; it generally yields weak and inconsistent results.

In spite of the numerous disadvantages of unstructured assessment, most firms use this method, place little emphasis on political risks, and do not closely monitor the political climates of foreign operations. They plan their operations within the existing political system and seldom have alternative courses of action mapped out in the event of changes in the political climate. They take this "arm's length" approach to avoid any suspicion of their being connected with the CIA and not to give the impression that the firm is attempting to influence political changes. Unfortunately this is not the best procedure.

Structured Assessment

For a firm to plan for political or governmental contingencies, a more reliable flow of information is essential. To obtain this ongoing flow of reliable information, firms turn to a structured approach to political assessment.

Structured assessment begins with the establishment of a political affairs or business-governmental relations unit. These units are often located in the treasurer's office because of the possible monetary impact of political risks. In some rare occasions, a separate department is created for political analysis, headed by a highly knowledgeable official who reports directly to the chief executive officer. This method is usually adopted when a multinational enterprise has experienced large losses because of political events abroad.

The use of political affairs specialists is not necessarily free from problems nor is it a guarantee against future losses. Much of the information that is collected is based on hearsay or half-complete information that might be difficult or impossible to measure or verify. The unreliable quality and the enormous quantity of data make it difficult to sort out what is really significant. Information is often contradictory. An ideological bent might dominate and color the data. As might be expected, the conclusions drawn by such departments are not always completely dependable.

Once the data have been analyzed, the public affairs specialist often has difficulty getting the attention of corporate executives. Like most people, top managers are often swayed more by what they see or hear in the news media than by what has been found from research and analysis. Even

Structured assessment is successful when the analysts rationalize the incomplete and conflicting information, and convince top management to consider it in decision-making.

with formal risk analysis departments, corporations are often slow to act. By the time the headquarters is ready to take action, it might be too late.

Implementing Structured Assessment

Numerous methods are employed for the structured assessment process: simply trying to stay informed, developing scenarios of possible political futures of the country, and complex computer simulations. Trying to stay informed can range from fielding unsolicited feedback from international personnel to hiring political experts from other corporations, the U.S. State Department, or international intelligence organizations such as the CIA. The most common staying-informed method is often called the "grand tour," wherein executives tour countries of current operations and countries that the firm is contemplating entering.

Perhaps the best approach for implementing structure assessment is the scenarios approach. The scenarios approach involves determining possible futures and assessing their probability. This can be depicted as a tree diagram of possible events, to each of which a probability is assigned. The scenario that would have to develop for this event to occur is written up, and a variety of possible corporate responses are developed. For example, the possible governmental events in the face of an upcoming election may be

1. Same party wins election and stays in power
2. Socialist party wins election
3. Communist party wins election
4. Military *coup* cancels elections and rules by a *junta*

For each of these the firm would have to assess probabilities, write an occurrence scenario, and develop contingency plans.

The breakdown in both structured and unstructured assessment systems often lies with the U.S. manager. Whether one is dealing with an expatriate manager of some foreign operation or a home office manager receiving and analyzing the data, many Americans simply lack the international experience and cultural sensitivity to really understand the underlying issues. This problem is compounded by the fact that U.S. attitudes and beliefs are somewhat rare among the world's peoples. Americans tend to believe in the individual more than the group, that exploitation of resources helps to develop the economy, that youth is desired, that equality is a shared goal, that mobility is acceptable or even desired, that time can be managed and the future planned, and that success is measured by material gain. These pillars of U.S. culture are not widely shared abroad and can impede the political assessment. (For a more detailed discussion of this issue see Chapter 11, "The Human and Cultural Environment of Business.")

American managers also have unique attitudes regarding governments and political systems that tend to make overseas political analyses difficult. There is a widespread belief that the less governmental involvement in business, the better. Furthermore, American business leaders use standards for decision-making and evaluation that are alien or unacceptable to many foreign nations and government officials, such as profit maximization, efficiency, and the "invisible hand" of competition. These concepts and others are regarded at best as amoral and in many nations totally immoral. Although still present to some degree, this rejection of market economics and the profit motive is being slowly eroded by the increasing global interdependence of economies.

If the political assessment is dependent upon information from U.S. expatriate managers the problems become multiple. New expatriate managers often cling to home country values even more strongly than when at home, and then later become more like local nationals in attitudes than the locals themselves. Furthermore, U.S. corporations tend to select managers for foreign assignment on the basis of their technical expertise and past domestic performance. The result is that the social attitudes, educational experiences, cultural sensitivity, political background, and personal temperament of a great many managers are particularly ill-suited for assessing foreign political environments.

Because U.S. culture is so different from that of many other countries, U.S. managers often have great difficulty accurately evaluating the political risk information.

Strategies for Dealing with Political Risks

MNCs not only need to develop better understanding of the sources of political risks and methods for assessing the level of risks but also must develop strategies for dealing with them. As a first step in the development of these strategies, the multinational firm must accurately determine the chances of these political risk events (likelihood) and how they might affect the firm if they were to occur (impact). Management must not overreact to political events that will not alter the relevant business environment of their operations; instead, corporations must manage their political risk situations.

First, management must not equate all political instability with macro political risk. Second, management must focus its attention on those factors that relate directly to micro political risks: the management style of the firm, management's desire for control of subsidiary decision-making, the firm's contributions to the host society (jobs, new technology, tax revenues, foreign exchange generation, and so forth), and the nation's desire for control of economic decision-making. By proactively managing these variables rather than merely reacting to political events, the firm can actually reduce the political risks below those faced by competitors. Relatedly, they must also guard against the tendencies of expatriate U.S. managers and host national managers to underestimate these risks.

Third, management needs to focus on the changing nature of political risks. The information and data collected must reflect the newer, more subtle forms of political risk. Only with relevant information and accurate assessment can the corporation formulate and implement the appropriate proactive strategies. Reactive corporate strategies will do little more than facilitate damage control; they will not actually serve to reduce the likelihood or the impact of political risks. The reality of strategic political-risk management is that firms must simultaneously adopt proactive strategies for risk reduction and reactive strategies for damage control.

Nature and Content of Proactive Risk Reduction Strategies

There are four basic approaches for managing political risks: avoidance, dependency, adaptation, and hedging.[9,10] Table 9.3 presents a paradigm explaining the mode of operation of each.

The strategy of *avoidance* involves making no investment, making no further investments, or divestment. *Adaptation* is composed of four substrategies:

1. Equity sharing includes the initiation or acceptance of joint ventures with local nationals (individuals, firms, labor unions, or government) for the purpose of reducing political risks.

2. Participative management requires that the firm actively solicit the involvement of host nationals, including labor or government in subsidiary management.

3. Localization of the operation includes a modification of name, management style, and so forth. Localization seeks to transform the subsidiary from appearing as a foreign firm to appearing as a local national firm.

4. Development assistance includes the firm's active involvement in infrastructure development, foreign exchange generation, local sourcing, management training, technology transfer, securing external debt, and so forth.

Dependency includes four substrategies.

1. Input control involves management's maintaining control over key factor inputs such as raw materials, components, technology, and know-how.

2. Market control requires that management keep within its grasp the

TABLE 9.3   **Mode of Operation of Risk Reduction Strategies**

Strategy	*Risk Likelihood*	*Risk Impact*
Avoidance	Reduced to zero	Reduced to zero
Adaptation	Reduced	Not affected
Dependency	Reduced through increased bargaining power	Reduced in global markets
Hedging	Not affected or could increase	Reduced through insuring losses

   means of distribution (i.e., manufacturing components to be used only by the parent firm, or legally blocking sales outside of the host country).

3. Position control involves keeping certain key subsidiary positions in the hands of expatriate or home office managers.

4. Staged contributions strategies require that the firm plan its activities such that in each successive year, subsidiary contributions to the host nation increase (i.e., tax revenues, jobs, infrastructural development, hard currency generation, and so forth). The staged contributions strategies also require that the firm make sure that the host nation is aware of these projected contributions.

   Hedging is the fourth major strategy. Hedging is composed of two substrategies: (1) investment insurance and (2) local debt financing.

Mode of Operation for Risk Reduction Strategies

Corporations need to formulate and implement strategies to minimize the occurrence of detrimental political risks and to make these events less damaging if they do occur.[11] The effects of adopting a particular strategy are shown in Table 9.3.

   Avoidance strategies address both dimensions to the maximum. They reduce risks to zero. Unfortunately, they also reduce profits and cash flows to zero. Adaptation strategies reduce the likelihood of risks but do nothing to affect the impact of those events if they were to occur. The reduction of likelihood is presumed to occur because the nation gets what it wants without direct control; governmental actions that result in increased political risks would be unnecessary. By equity sharing, participative management, localization, and development assistance, the firm is actually trading profits for reduced political risks.

   Dependency strategies are essentially aimed at keeping the subsidiary and the host nation dependent upon the parent corporation. The effect of this strategy is that if the host nation were to take over the operation, it would have difficulty running the business because it would not control and could not gain control over the essential ingredients of effective and efficient operations.

   By following dependency strategies, the corporation has substantially more bargaining power in its dealings with the host government. Thus, dependency strategies aim primarily at reducing the likelihood of political risk events, and secondarily at mitigating the negative impacts of occurrence. The reduction of impact can assume either of two forms. By lacking certain inputs (e.g., technological advances or essential components) the foreign subsidiary would not be able to compete effectively in global markets and in some cases could not even create a saleable product for the host market. Actually in today's intensely competitive global market place, the foreign subsidiary could probably find suppliers of almost any needed hardware or technical expertise; however, all of these things would have a cost.

Finally, U.S. firms can and do employ hedging strategies in the form of investment insurance and local debt financing. These strategies have little or no effect on the likelihood of political risk events; however, they do substantially negate the impact of political risk events. Investment insurance can cover some or all of a corporation's potential asset losses. Private companies such as Lloyds or government agencies such as the Overseas Private Investment Corporation (OPIC) supply insurance for everything from currency inconvertibility to war damages and direct expropriation. (OPIC insurance is not available for all nations.)

Local debt financing reduces the impact of political risk events only when the corporation is forced completely out of operation and is not adequately compensated. In this case the parent corporation would argue that since the compensation was not adequate it will not honor any local debt. It should be noted here that domestic debt capital is often a very scarce resource in developing nations. The use of large amounts of host country debt by a foreign investor (which is often not allowed) could be viewed as depleting a scarce resource and therefore could actually heighten political risks. In addition, using locally denominated debt can heighten translation risks (see Chapter 15 on international financial management).

Strategies for dealing with political risks may take the form of avoidance, adaptation, dependency, or hedging.

SUMMARY

The political and legal systems faced by U.S. corporations in their operations abroad present numerous new and different challanges since these systems reflect the varying value systems and philosophies of each nation. The nations of the world present a variety not only of political systems but also of economic systems. Political systems can be viewed on a continuum from democracy to autocracy, while economic systems can be viewed on a continuum from capitalism to communism. When these are combined, one can create a two-dimensional model for positioning world political and economic systems.

Most of the legal systems of the world evolved from one of two common bases: common law (British) or codified law (Roman). Common law leans more heavily on the precedent of prior court decisions, while codified law is built on extensive and detailed statutes. Most of the nations whose legal systems are not based on either of the forms are theocratic states where religious law is also the law of the nation.

In international business as in domestic business, arbitration is often necessary to settle disputes. International arbitration tribunals exist for just such situations. Since substantial legal differences exist among nations, contracts usually define whose courts have jurisdiction.

In international business, the protection of intellectual as well as real property is of great concern. For this reason numerous conventions exist among nations regarding international rights for patents, trademarks, trade names, and so forth.

Multinational corporations face substantial and changing politically induced risks in their operations abroad. These political risks are not characteristics of countries but rather result from a particular investment interfacing with a particular government. The basic source of the political risks is the underlying conflict for control of economic decision-making. Each party's desire for control may be predicated upon economic or political motivations. Whatever the rationale, this control conflict is a major source of political risks.

Political risks are simply another form of environmental threat, and as with any threat, corporations seek to reduce both the likelihood and the impact. To reduce these political risks, corporations develop both reactive and proactive strategies. These strategic responses fall into four categories: avoidance, adaptation, dependency, and hedging. Corporations do not have to select from among those four but may use several at a time, and may move from one to another over time. Furthermore, these strategies may come about almost accidentally or serendipitously as by-products of more traditional economic strategies. For example, economies of scale might dictate that engines be produced in country A, axles in country B, and electronic components in country C; this logic would not only reduce total system costs but also reduce political risks in A, B, and C by means of the dependency substrategy of critical input control.

Whether the development of political risk reduction strategies accompanies the development of economic strategies or follows the formulation of economic strategies is not nearly as important as the fact that they are developed and utilized. Although risk reduction may result from pleasant serendipity, one should not allow hope to replace planning. Political risk strategies must be systematically developed and specifically focused on protecting in-country assets, earnings streams, and cash flows from the effects of political risks. ☐

KEY TERMS AND CONCEPTS

Adaptation strategies

Arbitration

Autocracy

Avoidance strategies

Codified law (Roman law)

Common law

Communism

Creeping expropriation

Democracy

Dependency strategies

Expropriation

Hedging strategies

Intellectual property

Oligarchy

Participative management

Political risk

Risk

Socialism

Structured assessment

Tax haven

Theocracy

Transfer pricing

Unstructured assessment

REVIEW QUESTIONS

1. Discuss the political impact of U.S. foreign investments on local societies, both positive and negative.

2. How do common law and codified law systems differ?

3. What is meant by the statement that a nation's legal system operationalizes its political and economic system?

4. Why is host country litigation of disputes generally bad for the MNC?

5. How do the legal issues of trade with communist nations differ from those of trade with noncommunist nations?

6. Define intellectual property. Why is it of legal concern for U.S. firms operating abroad?

7. What is meant by political risk? Describe some of the most common risks.

8. What are the basic sources of political risks?

9. Does it always follow that political instability will lead to political risks? Why or why not?

10. How might top management assess political risks? Explain the strengths and weaknesses of each method.

11. What measures or strategies might a firm adopt to reduce political risks? Describe strategies a firm might use to reduce (1) the impact of political risk events, and (2) the likelihood of a political risk.

DISCUSSION CASE

Should the United States Impose Sanctions on the PRC?

Pressure has been mounting on the Bush Administration to take stronger measures against the communist regime in Beijing following the Tiananmen Square crackdown on the democracy movement. This has resulted in uncertainty regarding future United States-China trade. Both the House and the Senate of the U.S. Congress have supported measures that call for sanctions against China. Some members of Congress have even suggested that the most favored nation status that had been granted to China be revoked. This would result in higher duties on imports from the PRC. In 1988 imports of toys and textiles alone came to $3.5 billion. China would

Adapted from Pam Yatsko, "Update on US Sanctions Against China," *Business International*, August 7, 1989, p. 240.

obviously retaliate by raising tariffs on U.S. goods such as grain. Grain sales to China in 1988 came to some $721 million.

The Bush Administration does not favor such severe measures. However, it is in favor of suspending all weapons exports and sales, freezing World Bank and other types of development loans, banning high-level United States-China exchanges, and extending visas for PRC nationals in the United States.

Since June 4, 1989, the Department of Commerce has discontinued approval for export of riot-control equipment and fingerprinting machines. The trade pact that eased the procedures of high tech firms trading with China has also been suspended. The Bush Administration has argued that tougher sanctions would merely isolate China and complicate dealing with the rapidly changing situation.

To support the Administration's position, government sources indicate that only a small portion of sales to China would be affected. It is estimated that total losses from suspension of trade with the PRC would amount to less than $2 billion.

Americans who viewed the Beijing massacre are urging Congress to take stronger measures. One Administration official said, "If the situation in China calms down, maybe Congress will do the same—but if the repression continues . . . the pressure will be on to escalate the U.S. response."

Questions

1. Discuss the relationship between the political considerations and the commercial implications of this case.

2. Would the people of China be better or worse off if the United States were to impose more severe sanctions?

3. Should a country apply the economics of cost-benefit relationships when addressing issues such as human rights violations?

4. Is it acceptable to tolerate major repression and human rights violations in order to try creating greater long-term good?

NOTES

1. M. W. Kelly and G. C. Philappatos, "Comparative Analysis of the Foreign Investment Evaluation Practices by U.S.-Based Manufacturing Multinational Companies," *The Journal of International Business Studies* 13:3 (Winter 1982), pp. 19–42.

2. Stefan H. Robock and Kenneth Simmonds, *International Business and Multinational Enterprises*, 4th ed. (Homewood, Ill.: Richard D. Irwin, 1989), p. 378.

3. Ibid., pp. 380–381.

4. Don R. Beeman, *An Empirical Analysis of the Beliefs Held by the International Executives of United States Firms Regarding Political Risks and Risk Reduction*

Methods in Developing Nations, unpublished doctoral dissertation, Indiana University Graduate School of Business, 1978, pp. 36–41.

5. Stephen J. Kobrin, "The Environmental Determinants of Foreign Direct Manufacturing Investments: An Ex-Post Empirical Analysis," *Journal of International Business Studies*, vol. 8, no. 2 (Fall-Winter, 1976). See also many others, including Green and Cunningham, 1975; Nigh, 1985; Thunell, 1977.

6. J. Frederick Truitt, *Expropriation of Private Foreign Investment*, International Business Research Series–Number 3 (Bloomington, Indiana: Division of Research, Indiana University, Graduate School of Business, 1974), pp. 133–134.

7. Raymond Vernon, *The Economic and Political Consequences of Multinational Enterprises: An Anthology* (Boston: Division of Research, Graduate School of Business Administration, Harvard University, 1975), p. 143.

8. L. Gordon, "The Investor's Point of View," in Don Wallace, Jr. (ed.), *International Control of Investment, The Dusseldorf Conference on Multinational Corporations* (New York: Praeger Publishers, 1974), p. 82.

9. Franklin R. Root, "International Business Enterprise and Host Governments," *Business Viewpoints* (Washington University), May, 1969, p. 93.

10. David B. Zenoff, *International Business Management: Text and Cases* (New York: Macmillan, 1971), p. 165.

11. Beeman, pp. 46–56.

REFERENCES AND SELECTED READINGS

Argus Research Corporation. *A Primer on Country Risk* (Argus Capital Market Report). New York: Argus Research Corporation, 1975.

Beeman, Don R. *An Empirical Analysis of the Beliefs Held by the International Executives of United States Firms Regarding Political Risks and Risk Reduction Methods in Developing Nations*. Unpublished doctoral dissertation. Indiana University Graduate School of Business, 1978.

Duerr, Michail G. *The Problems Facing International Management*. New York: The Conference Board, 1974.

Green, Robert T. *Political Instability as a Determinant of U.S. Foreign Investments*. Austin: Bureau of Business Research, Graduate School of Business, University of Texas at Austin, 1972.

Green, Robert T., and William H. Cunningham. "The Determinants of U.S. Foreign Investments: An Empirical Examination." *Management International Review* 15 (February 3, 1975).

Haendel, Dan H., Gerald T. West, and Robert G. Meadow, *Overseas Investment and Political Risk*. Philadelphia Foreign Policy Research Institute, 1975.

Jones, Randall J. "Empirical Models of Political Risks in U.S. Oil Production Operations in Venezuela." *The Journal of International Business Studies* 15:1 (Spring/Summer 1984).

Kelly, M. W., and G. C. Philappatos. "Comparative Analysis of the Foreign Investment Evaluation Practices by U.S.-Based Manufacturing Multinational Companies." *The Journal of International Business Studies* 13:3 (Winter 1982).

Kobrin, Stephen J. "The Environmental Determinants of Foreign Direct Manufacturing Investments: An Ex-Post Empirical Analysis." *The Journal of International Business Studies*. Vol. 8, no. 2 (Fall-Winter, 1976).

Kobrin, Stephen J. "Political Risk: A Review and Reconsideration." *The Journal of International Business Studies* 10:1 (Spring/Summer 1979).

Kobrin, Stephen J., John Basek, Stephen Blank, and Joseph La Polombara. "The Assessment and Evaluation of Noneconomic Environments by American Firms: A Preliminary Report." *The Journal of International Business Studies* 11:1 (Spring/Summer 1980).

Mascarenhas, Briance, and Ole Christian Sand. "Country-Risk Assessment Systems in Banks: Patterns and Performance." *The Journal of International Business Studies* 16:1 (Spring 1985).

Nigh, Douglas. "The Effect of Political Events on U.S. Direct Foreign Investments: A Pooled Time-Series Cross-Sectional Analysis." *The Journal of International Business Studies,* Vol. 16, No. 1, Spring 1985, pp. 1–17.

Robock, Stefan H., and Kenneth Simmonds. *International Business and Multinational Enterprises,* 4th ed. Homewood, Ill.: Richard D. Irwin, 1989.

Robock, Stefan H. "Political Risk: Identification and Assessment." *Columbia Journal of World Business* (July-August, 1971).

Root, Franklin R. "International Business Enterprise and Host Governments." *Business Viewpoints* (Washington University), May 1969.

Simon, Jeffrey D. "A Theoretical Perspective on Political Risk." *The Journal of International Business Studies* 15:3 (Winter 1984).

Stobough, Robert B. Jr. "How to Analyze Foreign Investment Climates." *Harvard Business Review* (September-October, 1969).

Stoever, William A. "A Business Analysis of the Partial Nationalization of Zambia's Copper Industry." *The Journal of International Business Studies* 16:1 (Spring 1985).

Thunell, Lars H. *Political Risks in International Business.* New York: Praeger Publishers, 1977.

Truitt, Frederick J. *Expropriation of Private Foreign Investments.* International Business Research Series, no. 3. Bloomington: Division of Research, Indiana University Graduate School of Business, 1974.

Zenoff, David B. *International Business Management: Text and Cases.* New York: Macmillan, 1971.

CHAPTER

10

Economic Environment

LEARNING OBJECTIVES

- Compare and contrast the economic environments of industrialized countries (the EEC, Japan, the United States, Canada, Australia, New Zealand, and the newly industrialized countries) with those of less developed countries

- Learn the advantages and disadvantages of economic integration

- Review the provisions and objectives of the Treaty of Rome establishing the EEC, and understand how these affect the operations of multinational enterprises

- Anticipate some of the problems that firms might expect after 1992 when the Single Europe Act goes into effect

- Understand the reasons for the rapid economic development of the NICs

- Become familiar with the economic environment of the less developed countries and the problems foreign firms might expect

- Understand the major obstacles to economic development in less developed countries and the role multinational enterprises could play

OUTLINE OF TOPICS

INTRODUCTION

A nation's economic environment is influenced greatly by the political system of the country. The business environment in democratic societies permits private enterprises relatively free rein to produce and distribute their products without undue government restraint or interference. In the nondemocratic societies, firms are faced with many restrictions in the conduct of their business activities. In the less developed countries (LDCs), business enterprises are confronted with uncertainties that are due largely to the instability of both political and economic systems. Thus, multinational corporations generally look for investment opportunities in politically stable, procapitalistic, democratic countries where there are fewer risks.

The purpose of this chapter is to acquaint the student with the fact that economic environments among different countries vary greatly. In spite of these differences, it is often advantageous to group nations according to their stage of economic development because of similarities in economic characteristics. Thus, countries may be classified as advanced industrialized or more developed countries (AICs or MDCs), newly industrialized countries (NICs), and less developed countries (LDCs).

SALIENT FEATURES OF THE ECONOMIC ENVIRONMENT

Differences in the stage of economic development generally account for the great variations in the economic environment among nations. Clearly visible are the differences in wages and salaries that are translated into per capita income. Equally clear are differences in levels of unemployment and underemployment. The degree of development of the infrastructure and the availability of services vary from country to country. Countries differ as to the degree of economic diversification and dependence upon the production and export of primary goods. Rapid inflation is common in some countries, while others show great economic stability. Financial institutions and service facilities are abundant in some countries and lacking in others. Some countries have highly developed capital markets, while these markets are still in their infancy in other countries.

In addition to these economic aspects of environment, other factors that have an influence on economic environment are the rates of population growth and the illiteracy rates. Even the political, legal, and cultural environments leave traces of their influence on the economic environment.

Comparing these and other features constitutes the starting point for analyzing the economic environments of nations.

Firms encounter different types of risks and business opportunities due to the stage of economic development of the host nations.

THE ECONOMIC ENVIRONMENT OF INDUSTRIALIZED COUNTRIES

Industrial countries are generally politically and economically stable. Most firms prefer stability for overall safety and peace of mind even though it often results in lower earnings. As indicated in earlier chapters, most world trade and investments occur among those nations that are highly industrialized.

The United States, Canada, countries of the European Economic Community, Japan, Australia, and New Zealand are among the most advanced industrialized nations in the world. In all of these areas, the economies are highly diversified. The types of manufacturing are many and varied, the service sector is highly developed and growing, capital markets are well developed and deep, and educational and health care services are extensive.

Among the AICs of the world, western Europe is somewhat unusual in being an economically integrated unit. Indeed, after 1992 this unification will be even more complete. Discussing Europe not only illustrates the nature of advanced industrialized countries but also illustrates the nature of *economic integration*; therefore, Europe will be discussed first.

European Economic Community (EEC or EC)

The economic environment of the European Economic Community (see Map 4 in color insert section) is strongly influenced by the provisions of the treaty under which it was established. These provisions describe the various aspects in the operation of the European Community and the privileges, obligations, and responsibilities of the member nations. Furthermore, these provisions directly influence the operation of business. As a result of the formation of the EEC, doing business in member states is somewhat akin to doing business in a single country.

Treaty of Rome and the EEC

The Treaty of Rome of 1957 established the European Economic Community. The 248 articles set forth specific goals to be achieved. These were to "promote . . . the harmonious development of economic activities, continuous and balanced expansion, increased stability, a more rapid improvement in the standard of living and closer relations between its Member States."[1] The ultimate objective was to form an economic union that went beyond the formation of a customs union.[2]

The original goal was to achieve common market status in 12 years, but if necessary, to extend the time period for an additional 3 years. Customs duties among member states were to be reduced in three stages, and at the end of the third stage (12 years), all protective duties were to be eliminated. Common external tariffs were to be adopted. The rates would be the arithmetic average, with certain exceptions, of the duties of the four customs areas composed of the Benelux countries (Belgium, the Netherlands, and Luxembourg), France, Italy, and West Germany. Quantitative restrictions among member states would be removed by the end of the transition period. The only exceptions would be those that protect the public morals and health, national security, and other such traditional purposes.

The trade in agricultural products was treated separately, but these regulations were also to be in full effect by the end of the transition period. Agricultural regulations called for joint coordination of agricultural markets, the elimination of import quotas among member states, the implementation of a minimum import price system, and a common external tariff. The common agricultural policy was to "increase agricultural productivity, assure an equitable standard of living to the agricultural population, stabilize markets, guarantee supplies, and assure reasonable consumer prices."[3]

The Treaty provided for the elimination of all barriers to permit the free movement of workers through the Community by the end of the transition period. Nationality discrimination in employment, wages, and working conditions were also to be eliminated. The Treaty provided as well for the free movement of services and capital and the establishment of a common transportation policy.

The Treaty dealt with the rules governing competition, dumping, and state aid. Differential taxes and tax rebates were not to be used as protective devices or to distort competition. The Treaty also dealt with coordinating legislation and regulations of the member countries that affect the operation of the common market. Economic policies regarding stabilization and the balance of payments were also covered. Commercial policies were to be coordinated during the transition period, which was to be followed by a common commercial policy.

Collaboration in the social field was also specified. The European Social Fund was established to increase employment possibilities and to improve the geographic and occupational mobility of labor. Members contribute to the Fund on the basis of their economic importance.

The treaty called for the establishment of a European Investment Bank with the objective "to contribute to the balances and smooth development of the Common Market in the interests of the Community through recourse to the capital markets and its own resources."[4] The bank was to operate on a nonprofit basis, making loans and guarantees to facilitate the financing of projects in all sectors of the economy. Included among the designated projects are the following:

1. Projects for developing underdeveloped regions
2. Projects for modernizing that by their size or nature cannot be covered by the existing financing methods of the member states
3. Projects of common interest to several member states that by their size or nature cannot be covered by existing financing methods of the member states[5]

The Treaty deals with the Community's association with overseas countries and territories. It provides for the establishment of a Development Fund for social and economic development of the territories, and for the absorption of the territories into the tariff system of the European Economic Community.

The EEC, established under the Treaty of Rome, began operations in January 1958.

Evaluation of the EEC

After more than 30 years of operation, sufficient time has elapsed to evaluate the European Economic Community. Does a common market actually exist? Have the basic objectives been achieved? Is the environment conducive to the operation of multinational enterprises?[6]

Today the European Economic Community is composed of 12 nations, each with its own language and culture. Loyalty toward the EEC is often secondary to nationalism, but on the whole the members have been cooperative. The establishment of a customs union as the first step toward economic and monetary union is largely complete. Customs duties and quotas on individual products have been eliminated. Most barriers to the free movement of services and productive factors have been abolished, and external trade relations of member nations have been unified. However, many of the goals necessary for complete economic integration have not been achieved. There remain differences in wages, taxes, and prices. Differences in the monetary policies of member nations have resulted in substantial differences in the magnitude and direction of exchange rate movement, and have caused other related problems for intra-EEC trade. Integration of institutions such as a single central bank or the acceptance of a common currency remains problematical.

There is still a lack of coordination among social security systems, and many professional services have not been recognized on a mutual basis. The absence of a common policy in agriculture has been one of the major stumbling blocks toward complete harmonization. Complete agreement has not been reached on customs procedures, forms, and regulations. The value added tax (VAT) is not the same among the member nations, and must be paid on imported goods but not on exports.[7] National import formalities such as applications for licenses, permits, certificates of conformity, registration forms, statistical documents, and so forth create excessive red tape and inflexibility. Such technical barriers to intracommunity trade as standards, regulations, and procedures still remain. Individual countries maintain their own standardization regulations regarding product or packaging characteristics: shape, dimensions, quality, and the like.

Particularly detrimental to foreign producers are national production standards regarding safety and environmental protection. Costly adaptations are often necessary to meet these standards and regulations, resulting in an increase in prices to consumers. These costs often make foreign goods more expensive than those of the inefficient domestic producers. Each member nation has its own regulation regarding trademark protection, again penalizing firms that wish to export into a country. Price ceilings that are placed on individual imports often make it difficult for outsiders to market their products at a profit, thus favoring domestic producers.

Statutory preference in favor of national enterprises has been prohibited in public purchases since 1969, but past performances show that public bids are less important than other means for awarding contracts. The technical specifications of the invitations to tender are often "made to measure" for domestic enterprises, effectively shutting out foreign bidders. Even deadlines are often impossible for outsiders to meet because ample time is not provided. These types of action diminish the advantages of large-scale production and make it difficult for many European producers to compete in third markets with producers from the United States and Japan.

Intracommunity trade is far from being similar to domestic trade; in fact, national standardization institutes and national trade policies are not compatible with the existence of the common market. A true common market requires more than the elimination of customs duties and quotas. It requires the complete freedom in the movement of services and productive factors, the elimination of customs formalities, the adoption of European standards and regulations, and the complete harmonization of indirect taxes.[8]

To what extent the shortcomings of the European Community can be overcome prior to 1992 remains to be seen. Some of the problems dealing with marketing in the European Community are covered in the following section.

Nationalism still stands in the way of true economic integration, and the conduct of intra-EEC trade is still not like domestic trade.

The European Community as a Market After 1992

The organizers of the European Community were well aware of the advantages of economic integration, even though it meant waiving the traditional sovereignty of the individual nations. The formation of the EEC has made the countries of western Europe a major economic force, comparable to the United States and Japan. The six original nations had a population of 170 million at the time of inception. With the addition of six nations since 1957, its current population of 324 million is considerably larger than that of the United States (246 million).

As a group, the nations making up the EEC are the world's most important importers of raw materials and foodstuffs. Their production of goods and services is growing more rapidly than that of the United States, and their combined purchasing power is comparable to that of the United States. All indications are that after December 31, 1992, when complete integration of the European Community into a market "without borders" is completed, the Community will become an even more important factor in international trade.

Complete integration in 1992 will permit the free flow of goods among the member nations, while barriers will continue to be imposed on imports from outside of the EEC. Producers will be able to take advantage of a large home market that will permit them to improve their mass production techniques, leading to greater efficiency and lower costs, and improving their competitive position. Exporters of manufactures to the Community will be faced with increasing competition from domestic producers.

To meet the challenge, firms will have to establish factories and subsidiaries within the Community, or be shut out from that huge market. Many multinational firms, especially U.S., Japanese, and non-EEC European countries, have been making direct investments in the EEC at record pace since 1984 to ensure that they will not be excluded from the potential gigantic market (see Figure 10.1). For example, Nestlé made a hostile takeover of Rowntree, a British candymaker, at a cost of $4.2 billion.[9]

Once plants have been established within the EEC, there is no assurance that competition will be easy. Competitors will include large European companies that have been formed through acquisitions and hostile takeovers. Even smaller companies will no longer be faced with the customs delays and red tape encountered at border crossings within the EEC that have added much to their costs of doing business.

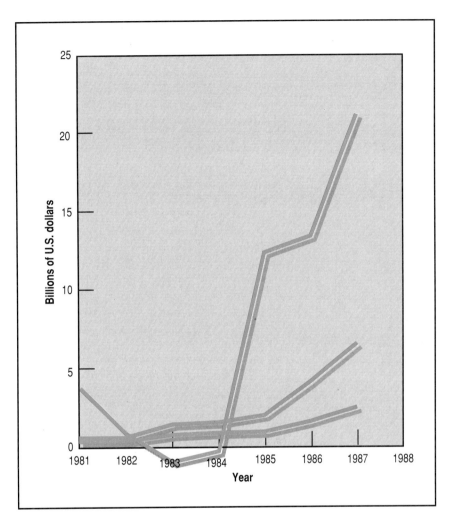

Figure 10.1   Foreign Direct Investments in the EEC
Source: Richard I. Kirkland, Jr., "Outsider's Guide to Europe in 1992," *Fortune,* October 24, 1988, p. 126.

Furthermore, Willy de Clercq, the EEC's top trade official, implies that direct investments will be no guarantee of access to the market in 1992 for "cross-border sales of services and information—insurance, mutual funds, mortgages, TV programs—and access to heretofore protected industries, such as telecommunications."[10] Access to the market may depend upon assurance of similar market availability in the home country of the foreign investor.

There is no assurance that 1992 will be devoid of problems for the member states. For example, unanimity is lacking regarding the details of the economic relations with nonmember countries. Some seem to favor insulating the EEC market from external competition by adopting the measures of the most protectionist state—regarding quotas, local content requirements, and other nontariff barriers. For example, will France, which has a quota on the import of Japanese automobiles to 3 percent of the domestic market, be willing to accede to free traders such as Ireland, Denmark, and the Netherlands? Will the EEC go along with the French limitations in order to protect Renault and Peugeot?

There are many other areas of conflict that need to be solved before 1992. The local content law of France is 80 percent, prohibiting the export of automobiles from Britain to France because of the differences in content laws. Differences in the value added taxes range from 6 to 20 percent in Britain for nonfood items, 14 percent in Germany, and 22 percent in Denmark. The lack of a single distribution system within the EEC and the differences in infrastructure must be overcome to transform the EEC into a truly common market. The 10 different national languages are bound to create problems of communications.

The economic environment of most industrial countries is quite similar to that in the European Community. However, the economic environment in the EEC is influenced by 12 sovereign nations acting as an entity. Otherwise, most are politically and economically stable, eliminating many of the risks that are common in less developed countries. Most firms prefer the overall safety and peace of mind of the more highly developed countries, even though it often results in lower earnings, to the uncertainty that characterize the less familiar environments of the developing countries and the communist bloc nations.

The EEC is a market that is comparable to the United States in purchasing power, but with a considerably larger population.

Japan

As in other advanced developed nations, the population of Japan is highly educated and skilled. Out of the total labor force of 60.6 million, 55 million are employed in nonagricultural activities. A recent study of the Ministry of Labor indicates that employment in the service sector is expected to rise to more than 60 percent of total employment by 1990. The service industries are not nearly so highly developed as in the United States, although some of the financial institutions are among the largest in the world. Another large segment of the population is still in the export-oriented manufacturing industries and in the protected agricultural activities.

Although the nation's unemployment rate generally ranges between 2.5 and 3.0 percent, wages have been increasing at only about 4.2 percent per year. This together with the increase in labor productivity of 12.5 percent and lower yen-denominated import prices resulted in an increase of the consumer price index of only 0.6 percent in 1988. This inflation rate would probably have been even lower were it not for the complicated distribution system that exists in Japan and the fact that barriers to imports of certain agricultural products have not been completely removed. For example, the price of beef is three to four times that in the United States and the price of rice about five times as much.

Unlike most industrialized nations, Japan is not endowed with the basic resources necessary for industrialization. Because it is deficient in coal, iron ore, and petroleum, it is almost totally dependent upon international trade. In spite of these shortcomings, the Japanese economy today is one of the most dynamic in the world. But this was not true immediately after World War II. The economic and commercial structure of the country had collapsed completely upon its surrender in 1945. Trade was conducted under the auspices of the Supreme Command of the Allied Powers (SCAP) until August 1947, when it reverted to private enterprise. With grants and credits from the United States, the nation recovered and again became a major factor in trade by 1951. The achievement of this position was not accidental.

Cateora states that although Japan is accused of unfair trade practices, "the truth is Japan's success is more the result of good competitive business than unfair trade tactics. The Japanese plan their efforts carefully, and once they decide there is a market, they pursue it effectively and efficiently."[11] To this end, the government, through the Ministry of International Trade and Industry (MITI), and banks participate with industry in developing markets abroad. This has been true in the case of optics and cameras in the 1950s, automobiles in the 1970s, and computers in the 1980s. New products are designed specifically for each market. This contrasts with the practices of the firms from other nations that often try to market domestic goods in the foreign market.

The function of determining what markets to enter, where to obtain raw materials, and where to invest belongs largely to the Ministry of International Trade and Industry. MITI spends billions of yen in research in conjunction with industries to establish Japan as a leader in specific areas of endeavor. It cooperates with industry to carry out national economic policy. It often permits firms to take part in cartels for the survival of the industry. It influences the direction of investments through its system of review and licensing to further the position of Japanese industries. For example, Japanese investments in the Asian NICs in recent years were increased largely at the urging of MITI because of the huge trade surplus with these areas. In fact, MITI has almost complete control over investments and the reinvestment of earnings.

MITI plays a major role in attempting to reduce trade tension with other countries. The Trade and Tariff Act of 1984, which ended the dumping of microchips by Japanese manufacturers, was negotiated between the Minister of MITI and a U.S. Trade Representative.

The Bank of Japan complements the work of MITI. The Bank plays a major role in the nation's foreign trade by attempting to stabilize the value of the yen. For example, it followed a stimulative monetary policy to get the country out of the economic slump when the yen began to appreciate in 1985. Like other central banks, it steps into the money market and carries out open market operations to increase or decrease the amount of a particular currency in circulation, especially if it influences the value of the yen. In addition, it controls the amount of money in circulation by changing the discount rates and by changing the reserve requirements of commercial banks.

In recent years, the dramatic increase in the value of the yen relative to the dollar has had several effects. It has had an influence on the economic structure of the country. Foreign substitutes have become much cheaper, encouraging the import of parts and semimanufactures from abroad. There has been an increase in manufactured imports from the NICs of the Pacific Rim. Because of pressure from trading partners with whom it has had a surplus trade balance, Japan is being transformed from a country that is totally dependent upon the export of manufactured goods to one that is more dependent upon domestic demand. This is indicated by the fact that the decline in net exports in 1987 was offset by an increase in domestic demand by 5.1 percent, resulting in a growth of 5.0 percent in the nation's GNP.[12]

Although the appreciation of the yen in relation to the dollar has opened up the market for some products such as beef, fish and shellfish, fruits and vegetables, wood products, gasoline, and so forth, the United States is meeting stiff competition from the NICs of the Pacific Rim and the European Community in the sale of manufactured goods to Japan. The rates of increase in manufactured imports from the NICs of the Pacific Rim and the EEC in 1987 were larger than Japan's manufactured imports from the United States.

The appreciation of the yen has resulted in the rapid increase in Japanese investments abroad, especially in the United States and the NICs. During 1988, foreign direct investments totaled $34.71 billion, almost double the $18.33 billion of the previous year, resulting in a rapid growth in net investment income.[13] For example, investment income increased to $16.7 billion in 1987, almost 10 times greater than the $1.7 billion in 1983. Japan's net external asset position reached $240.7 billion in 1987, the largest net foreign investment position in the world. Foreign direct investments in the United States alone totaled $14.7 billion in 1987, with $4.8 billion in the manufacturing industries.[14] Investments in the nonmanufacturing industries have been in real estate, banking, and insurance.

The rapid changes in the Japanese economic environment have far-reaching implications, especially for the United States. Two-way trade between the United States and Japan in 1987 totaled $115 billion, more than double the $55 billion two-way trade with all of the EEC countries combined. The economic dependency of Japan on the United States is indicated by the fact that the United States was the destination of 36.5 percent of Japan's exports in 1987, and the source of 34.5 percent of that nation's imports.[15]

Automobile exports dominate Japan's trade figures, with some $25 to

$30 billion of its sales going to the United States. To help solve the deficit in the trade balance with the United States, pressure was put on Japan to adopt voluntary limits on its exports of automobiles to the United States and to open its domestic markets to U.S. exporters. The continued seriousness of the problem resulted in the passage of the Omnibus Trade Bill of 1988, permitting the United States to adopt retaliatory measures against any country that does not take steps to reduce its surplus trade balance with the United States.

Japan's success in exporting has resulted in a surplus in both its current account and its merchandise trade balance, in spite of the appreciation of the yen from $2.40 per yen in 1977 to an average of $1.28 per yen in 1988. At the end of 1988, Japan's share of world exports was 9.8 percent and of world imports, 6.7 percent.[16] Japan's rise to the forefront in international trade has encouraged many NICs, especially the Pacific Rim countries, to emulate Japan's export-oriented development strategies.

Although Japan was a manufacturing nation prior to World War II, its position as an advanced developed nation did not occur until after World War II.

United States and Canada

The continent of North America is made up of many countries but the United States and Canada dominate its economic activities. Because this section deals with industrialized countries, the discussion will be limited to

The highly developed infrastructure of the United States aids all forms of economic activities but also can create nightmares of human stress and environmental pollution as depicted in this photograph of a major freeway at rush hour.

the United States and Canada. Mexico, a newly industrialized country, and the other less developed countries that are a part of the North American continent, are not discussed here.

The United States is the most highly industrialized country in the world. It has an abundance of essential raw material and energy sources, the availability of capital, a well-trained populace, an enormous agribusiness base, and a well-developed infrastructure.

It has a population of 246 million with an annual per capita income of $17,598 in 1988 (1985 prices) and a gross national product of $4,433 billion (1985 prices). It is the world's most important trading nation, selling about 11 percent of the world's exports and purchasing about 16.5 percent of the world's imports.[17] The United States is open to trade and foreign direct investments with the minor exception of those industrial or service sectors that involve national security.

Using 1985 as the base year equal to 100, in 1988 consumer prices were at 109.9, wages 106.7, and industrial production 110.2. Nonagricultural employment was at 108.6. More significant, perhaps, is the fact that the economic, commercial, financial, and political policies of the United States have tremendous influence over economic conditions worldwide.[18]

Like the United States, Canada is highly developed economically and has a very important agricultural base. It has the basic resources necessary for industrialization. Its population totals only 25.95 million, with a per capita income of $16,013 and a total GNP of $520.59 billion in 1985 prices. Consumer prices have increased to 113.1 in 1988, again using 1985 as the base year. Industrial production was 111.8 and wages were 110.7.[19] Canada's labor movement is more powerful than that in the United States, often resulting in escalating demand for increases in wages when corporate profits rise. Canada is the most important trading partner of the United States, as evidenced by the United States' taking 75 percent of Canadian exports and providing 70 percent of that nation's imports. The passage of the U.S.-Canada Free Trade Agreement in January 1989 means the removal of barriers to trade and investment between the two countries for most industrial, agricultural, and service sectors. Tariffs will be rolled back and various restrictions on the operation of U.S. financial institutions in Canada will be removed. A new settlement mechanism for trade-related disagreements has been established. Discrimination according to nationality has also been removed.[20]

The Canadian government liberalized its foreign investment requirements by abolishing the Foreign Investment Review Agency (FIRA) and replacing it with Investment Canada, which promotes Canadian investments rather than making it difficult to get approval for foreign investments as practiced by the FIRA. However, provisions have been made for the review of investments in certain activities related to Canada's cultural heritage or identity such as publications, distribution and sales of books, magazines, video, films, and radio and television broadcasting, and the energy industries. The federal government runs a deficit that is considerably larger, as a percentage of national income, than that of the United States.

Australia and New Zealand

Australia and New Zealand are not discussed as a part of the Pacific Rim countries because their economic environments are substantially different from those of the newly industrialized countries of South Korea, Taiwan, Singapore, and Hong Kong.

Australia has an area of almost 3 million square miles, slightly smaller than that of the continental United States. It has a population of only 16.5 million that is highly urbanized, with 70 percent living in cities of over 100,000.[21] Unlike its neighbor to the west, New Zealand is a small country, with an area of less than 104,000 square miles and a population of 3.37 million. The populations of both countries are highly educated, with a per capita income comparable to that of other industrialized countries.[22] In U.S. dollars, Australia's per capita income was $12,070 (1988) and New Zealand's was $10,449 (1987).[23]

The economies of both of these countries are largely dependent upon the production and export of agricultural and pastoral products. Thus, domestic economic conditions are subject to wide fluctuations due to changes in weather conditions and world market prices. More than 50 percent of the exports of Australia originate from the land. The principal exports are wool, beef, and wheat. The export of iron ore and coal depends largely upon the demand of the Japanese steel industry.

Manufactures constitute the major imports of Australia, with about 25 percent of the nation's imports from the United States. About 12 percent of the nation's exports are to the United States, resulting in a negative balance of trade with that country.

The labor force of Australia totals about 8.2 million, with an unemployment rate of 6.3 percent in 1988.[24] Between 1985 and 1988, wages increased by 21.2 percent while productivity rose only 5 percent. These combined to cause substantial inflationary pressures; wholesale prices increased by 27 percent. The roots of this problem can be traced to a lack of capital investment and the militant Australian labor unions.

Current economic policies seek reforms at sector and industry levels to boost productivity, efficiency, and output. The government is also attempting to stimulate domestic investments through various incentives. A policy of lower interest rates, accelerated depreciation of new plant and equipment, tax write-offs, drawbacks, and other concessions are provided by the government to encourage development.[25]

Australia is an attractive outlet for foreign direct investments. The country is stable politically. New regulations are quite liberal and do not unduly restrict foreign investments. The Foreign Investment Review Board (FIRB), established in 1972, has not impeded foreign investments that do not affect national security. Since July 1986, FIRB has functioned as advisor to the Treasurer, who makes the final decision on foreign investments for restricted industries such as finance, insurance, media, and civil aviation. In April 1987, additional regulations were passed liberalizing the insurance, stockbrokering, and resource-processing sectors. The government is also encouraging technology transfer and export-oriented investments through the Corporate Partnership Program.

Unlike the economies of most industrialized countries, that of New Zealand has been highly regulated. Only in recent years has the government introduced reforms to transform the nation from one that is dependent upon subsidization and protection to one that is market oriented. It has taken action to selectively apply free market principles to the business and financial sectors of the economy.

In 1983, New Zealand and Australia signed the Closer Economic Relations Agreement, an area free trade agreement to progressively eliminate trade barriers on a wide range of products and to provide for reciprocal access to each other's market. The agreement encourages the two countries to harmonize laws on standards, trading practices, and industry safeguards. This agreement makes New Zealand attractive for foreign firms wishing to serve both Australian and New Zealand markets, thus effectively increasing market size.

Tariffs on a wide range of consumer products were abolished in December 1985. In July 1986, the government further reduced normal and preferential tariffs. To increase efficiency, import licenses were eliminated at the end of 1988. Barriers to protect the less competitive industries are gradually being phased out to persuade local industries to become more efficient and better able to compete with imports. However, special conditions were imposed to protect local automobile, footwear, plastics, rubber, and electronics industries.

These major changes in the economy of New Zealand were necessary because of continuing economic problems. Decreasing domestic demand, high interest rates, and decreasing corporate profits have all contributed to depressed investment levels. The unemployment rate rose from 4.1 percent in 1987 to 5.0 percent in 1988 and 6.0 percent in 1989. The causes of the massive increase in unemployment are the relatively static domestic demand, the decrease in public employment, and the phaseout of the subsidized employment schemes. The only areas of employment increases have been in finance, insurance, and real estate. Real disposable income has also been falling due to declining agricultural income.

Although the per capita income rose to $10,449 in 1987, New Zealand's economic growth rate was only 1.8 percent, and in constant dollars was −0.3 percent in 1989. However, the 18.3 percent inflation rate for 1987 was reduced to 9.0 percent in 1988 and was only 4.7 percent in 1989. The nation expects to reduce its foreign debt, which totaled $11,968 billion in 1988, with the expected surplus in its balance of trade.[26]

New Zealand's main sources of export earnings are beef, wool, lamb, fruit, fish, and cheese. The most important markets for New Zealand are Japan followed by the United States. New Zealand is a technologically sophisticated society, so it is one of the most attractive small markets in the Pacific for high technology products. Imports are mostly office machines, fertilizers, and engines. Markets exist for such products as computers, software, telecommunications equipment, and sporting goods. The major sources for the nation's imports are Australia, Japan, and the United States.

The New Zealand government is actively encouraging all forms of private foreign investments and it has established an Investment Unit within the Department of Trade and Industry to help investors. Especially welcome are those that provide new technology or managerial skills. Investments are encouraged in tourism and in forestry or manufacturing where growth will replace imports, expand exports, or create jobs. The repatriation of capital and profits is assured. The deregulation of the financial sector has opened opportunities for financial institutions to compete with domestic banks.

Although investment proposals involving 25 percent or more foreign ownership require approval by the Overseas Investment Commission, approval is granted in almost all cases. In many areas, it is even possible to have 100 percent overseas ownership. However, in energy, majority New Zealand ownership is required. Investments by overseas companies or individuals are also restricted in farming and natural resource development.

Both Australia and New Zealand are classified as industrial nations, but their economies are land based, and both depend upon international trade.

THE ECONOMIC ENVIRONMENT OF NEWLY INDUSTRIALIZED COUNTRIES

Pacific Rim Countries

Unlike the advanced industrialized countries (AIC), which gained their industrial status before and immediately following World War II, the newly industrialized countries (NICs) are those whose industrial development has occurred primarily during the last two decades. These countries of the Pacific Rim are at the stage of economic development that Japan reached in the 1960s and the early 1970s. South Korea, Taiwan, Hong Kong, and Singapore, often referred to as the "Four Dragons," are the countries that make up this group (see Figure 10.2). Table 10.1 provides a statistical summary of the economies of these countries.

Although not discussed here, Indonesia, Malaysia, and Thailand are just beginning to develop their industrial base and will probably become NICs in another 15 to 25 years.

The total population of the "Four Dragons" at the end of 1987 was about 70 million, ranging from 42.0 million in South Korea to 2.6 million in Singapore. Thus, these countries possess a substantial and formidable

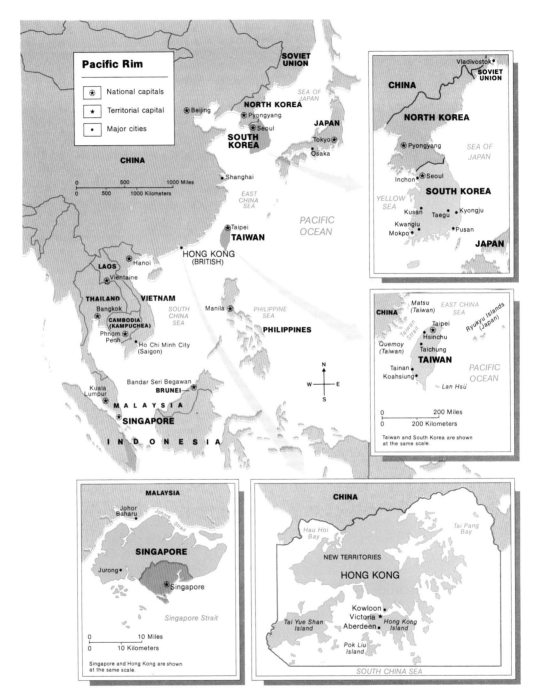

Figure 10.2   Newly Industrialized Countries of the Pacific Rim

Table 10.1   **Economic Statistics of the Pacific Rim NICs (1987/1988)**

	South Korea	*Taiwan*	*Singapore*	*Hong Kong*
Population	42.0 M	19.6 M	2.6M	5.7 M
Labor force	17.3 M	8.4 M	1.2M	2.9 M
GNP growth rate	12.6%	7.0%	8.8%	8.5%
Unemployment	2.5%	2.0%	4.3%	1.7%
Per capita GNP	$4,040	$6,045	$7,300	$9,300
Inflation rate	7.1%	1.4%	1.3%	8.0%
Exports	$60.7 billion	$60.6 billion	$56.7 billion	$25.0 billion
Imports	$51.8 billion	$46.8 billion	$57.2 billion	$25.0 billion
Trade balance	$8.9 billion	$13.8 billion	($9.5 billion)	$0.472 billion

Source: U.S. Dept. of Commerce, *Foreign Economic Trends*, 1989; IMF, *International Financial Statistics Yearbook*, 1989.

labor force. In comparison to the LDCs, the NICs' populations are well educated, highly skilled, and well disciplined. The unemployment rates in the NICs are substantially below those of most other industrialized nations. Taiwan has unemployment of 2.0 percent, Hong Kong 1.7 percent, Singapore 4.3 percent, and South Korea 2.5 percent. The generally tight labor market has resulted in pressure on wages. Where labor is highly unionized, as in South Korea, the workers are militant and assertive, so strikes are more common than in the other three countries. Nevertheless, wage rates are still relatively low by Western standards.

Although the GNPs remain lower than those of North America, Europe, and Japan, the overall economic growth rates are striking, ranging from 7.0 percent in Taiwan to 12.6 percent in South Korea. The continuous growth has resulted in the development of strong domestic markets.

All of these countries have excellent infrastructure, facilitating the development of a national market. They have excellent transportation to the coastal ports, enabling them to take advantage of cheap water transportation to reach foreign markets. The business climate is generally excellent. The inflationary pressure is tolerable. All four of these NICs are dependent upon the import of foodstuffs to feed their populations and raw materials to supply their factories. The nations concentrate manufacturing efforts on goods for export. South Korea and Taiwan are running a trade surplus, while Hong Kong and Singapore are currently experiencing a trade deficit.

Unlike most less developed countries, these NICs do not experience a shortage of investment capital. Foreign direct investments continue to pour in because of the favorable investment climate. These countries are economically and politically stable, with the exception of South Korea. Governmental policies facilitate foreign investments. In Singapore, foreign investments in manufacturing are expected to exceed $580 million in 1988, with about 38 percent from the United States. Investments in Taiwan from 1952 to 1988 have totaled $8.5 billion, with 31.4 percent from the United States.

Investments in Hong Kong exceeded $2.7 billion in 1987, with $986 million (36.5 percent) coming from the United States. Foreign investments approved by the South Korean government during the first 10 months of 1987 totaled $830 million as compared to $350 million for all of 1986, indicating confidence in the future of the country.[27]

South Korea   Although these Pacific Rim countries are discussed as a group under NICs, each has a different basis for its rapid growth. South Korea is the most dynamic of these countries. Not even Japan has come so far and grown as fast in so short a period of time. The driving force behind its industrialization has been the government-subsidized conglomerates. These have been supplemented with foreign capital as evidenced by the approval of foreign equity investments of some $1,283 million in 1988, a 21 percent increase over 1987.[28] As in previous years, the leading foreign investors are Japanese, followed by U.S. and European sources. Tax incentives are provided for projects involving the production of advanced electronics, defense products, aircraft, chemicals, new materials, and biotechnology. The government eliminated tax incentives (tax holidays and special depreciation allowances) for foreign-invested firms that export over 50 percent of their production.

The service sector has been liberalized and is being opened up to foreigners. The insurance sector permits U.S. companies to establish joint ventures with Korean firms or wholly owned subsidiaries in addition to the previous authorization of branch offices. The government has implemented a partial liberalization of the advertising market and has agreed to allow U.S. carriers to establish branch offices and to establish minority joint ventures with Korean maritime freight forwarding agencies.

From having had a per capita income of only $595 just 30 years ago, the economic strides of Korea are amazing. Today Korea exports Samsung computers, Hyundai cars, and other products totaling more than $44 billion (40 percent to the United States) and prides itself on having one of the largest middle classes in Asia, with a per capita income of more than $2900 and an annual growth rate of 12.5 percent.[29] The most important exports from Korea are electrical products, textiles, automobiles, footwear, nonelectrical machinery, iron and steel, toys, luggage and handbags, tires, and tubes. Imports are nonelectrical machinery, electronic products, chemicals, and raw materials.

Taiwan   In the Pacific Rim, Taiwan is second only to South Korea in economic importance. Its industrial strength is derived from family-based firms rather than the large conglomerates of Korea. It is a primary producer and exporter of light manufactures such as electronic and electrical products, chemicals, food, wine and cigarettes, machinery, soybeans, and corn products. The success of Taiwan as an exporter has gained for it the unenviable position of being targeted with Japan, under the Omnibus Trade Bill of 1988, for retaliation unless it adopts some measures to reduce its surplus trade balance with the United States. It is an importer of electronic and electrical goods, textiles and apparel, machinery, and footwear. Taiwan is also experiencing rapid growth in domestic demand.

The current trend is for the labor-intensive light industries to be replaced by capital-intensive heavy industries. Since 1986, Taiwan has initiated liberalization and internationalization policies. Most restrictions on foreign investments in the manufacturing industries have been lifted. Foreign banking, mutual funds, and insurance companies have been placed under less restrictive conditions. However, the nation's changing economic and social structures have fostered new impediments to foreign investments. The rising value of the currency, rising labor activism, and environmental disputes have caused some firms to move their operations to lower-labor-cost areas in Thailand, Indonesia, Malaysia, and mainland China. In fact, even some domestic capital is flowing out of the country for investments abroad.

Singapore   Singapore is the regional center for trade, sales, servicing, and warehousing. It maintains a free and open market policy. It is the financial center for most of Asia. Although its initial function was to service trade, it now provides full banking services. Its central geographic location, business orientation, good labor relations, high credit standing, and excellent communication facilities make it an ideal base for penetrating the Asian markets. It places major emphasis on education and training programs to upgrade the productivity and skill levels of the work force. It has a free and open economy with few restrictions on the import or export of goods or the flow of capital. It has a deficit in its trade balance, but its short-term capital inflows from the intangible items of trade provide it with an overall surplus in its balance of payments.

In an attempt to influence the pattern of investment and industrial activity, the government makes use of incentives. It makes no distinction between foreign and domestic investments. Those desiring to invest in manufacturing negotiate their incentives with the Economic Development Board (EDB), which operates under the Ministry of Trade and Industry. A premium is placed on maximizing the capital/labor ratio and the value added per worker in any manufacturing proposal. The firms that propose the use of the most advanced technology are favored. The most common form of incentive is the tax concession. In addition, there are special incentives for foreign investors; however, labor-intensive assembly operations are not offered incentives. There are some restrictions in certain service industries such as insurance, banking, and related finance.

Hong Kong   The economy of Hong Kong, like those of the other Pacific Rim NICs, is upbeat. The growth rate was 16.0 percent in 1987 and increased another 6.0 percent in 1988.[30] This condition is due largely to the strong overseas demand for its products because of the depreciation of the currency, which is linked to the U.S. dollar. The strong domestic performance can be traced to the increase in wages and salaries, low interest rates, and the availability of personal loans. Adding to the stimulus are such factors as increased tourism and increased investments in plants, machinery, building, and construction. These boom conditions have adversely affected prices. Inflation increased from 2.8 percent in 1986 to 5.5 percent in 1987, 7.5 percent in 1988, and 9.5 percent in 1989 due to the inadequacy of supply relative to demand. The unemployment was 1.4 percent in 1989 and underemployment was only 1.0 percent.[31]

Hong Kong is primarily an export and reexport center to mainland China and other Asian markets. Most products are light industrial products of which 90 percent are exported, such as textiles and apparel, electronics, plastics, electrical appliances, watches, and clocks. That wages have not increased more rapidly with the shortage of labor reflects the fact that many firms are shifting their labor-intensive operations from Hong Kong to mainland China. The increase in money and credit, the low interest rates, the depreciation of the Hong Kong dollar, and the increase in the price of goods from China have added to the inflationary pressure. Contributing to the pressure were tourists, who spent $3.3 billion in Hong Kong in 1988. The future status of Hong Kong remains uncertain when it reverts back to China.

The Pacific Rim NICs have become very influential in international trade and have caused the dominant area of trade to shift from the Atlantic to the Pacific.

Latin America

Brazil is the largest republic in South America, occupying 48 percent of the total land area of the continent. It is larger than the continental United States, excluding Alaska, and has a population of 145 million. It has an abundance of natural resources, but much remains as yet unexploited. It is the most highly industrialized country of Latin America and has the ninth-largest economy in the world. Its gross domestic product of $385 billion is derived 54 percent from services, 35 percent from industry, and 11 percent from agriculture. The United States is its most important trading partner, taking 28 percent of the nation's exports in 1987 and 26 percent in 1988. The United States supplied Brazil with 21 percent of its imports in 1987 and 22 percent in 1988.[32]

Given the size and the seemingly dynamic nature of the nation's economy, questions arise as to the reasons for the debt crisis. The country borrowed in the world markets in anticipation of income to be derived from continued economic expansion and the expected economic growth rate of 6 percent per year. It did not foresee the difficulties that arose with the rapidly rising price of petroleum and the slowdown in economic activity. But other factors were also involved. Immediately following World War II, the government placed major emphasis on the consumer goods sector as the key to industrial growth. Barriers were adopted to protect such industries as food processing and textile manufacturing, but emphasis was gradually shifted to the manufacture of light capital and consumer durable goods.

More recently, the emphasis has shifted to the more sophisticated technological products. The government supported research and development programs and provided incentives for exports. Profits from exports were exempted from taxes, while specific markets were reserved for domestic firms. To meet the ever-increasing need for capital, the government resorted to deficit financing. Thus, it borrowed heavily abroad, resulting in an outstanding debt of $114.9 billion in 1988.[33]

The trade policy of the nation is characterized by various tariff and non-tariff barriers to foster indigenous technological growth and to service the nation's debt. It follows a policy of import substitution by restricting imports and encouraging production and exports through various incentives. This trade policy resulted in a trade surplus of $11 billion in 1987 and $19 billion in 1988, but these surpluses were insufficient to meet the nation's capital requirements.[34]

In order to service its foreign obligations and to maintain the per capita income of its growing population ($2\frac{1}{2}$ percent per year), a 6 percent annual growth rate was necessary. Instead, real growth rate decreased to -0.3 percent in 1988, down from 3.6 percent in 1987. The slowdown in economic growth was partly due to the inability of the government to come to grips with the new constitution that was promulgated on October 5, 1988. Many of the nationalistic policies of the past are reiterated in this new document, including controls over corporate structure, foreign investments, taxation, foreign joint venture operations, and the extent to which foreign businesses are permitted to develop industries in Brazil. Furthermore, the nation seems unable to control its runaway inflation. Starting from a base of 100 in 1985, wholesale prices in 1988 were 6325. Furthermore, there is great concern over a possible recession.[35] Thus, it has been necessary for the nation to negotiate agreements to reschedule its debt interest and principal repayments with multinational financial institutions.

The situation of Mexico has been somewhat similar to that in Brazil. Mexico is a newly industrialized country located in the Latin American portion of North America. Its population totaled 82.7 million in 1988, with a GDP of $175 billion ($2096 per capita). Total labor force in 1988 was 26.1 million, with unemployment equal to 18.0 percent of the workforce. Its annual growth rate was only 1.4 percent in 1987 and 0.5 percent in 1988.[36] Like other countries of Latin America, it is plagued by inflation. Using 1985 as the base year equal to 100, the consumer price index reached 924.6 in 1988.[37]

The trade policy of Mexico is determined largely by GATT. As a member, it has agreed not to increase tariffs on 373 products. It also agreed to open import quotas on consumer and intermediate goods. It has adopted a policy of import liberalization and has eliminated most import licensing requirements. It has reduced items subject to export taxes and controls, and has increased government programs and incentives for exports.

Mexico is very dependent upon the production and export of petroleum. Its annual output makes it the world's fifth-largest producer of petroleum.

About half of the daily production of 2.52 million barrels is exported and the remainder is refined and consumed domestically. On the basis of continued increases in anticipated revenues from petroleum exports, the nation borrowed heavily from foreign financial institutions to carry out its plan for economic development. The nation soon realized that it had overextended its various development programs as the demand and price for petroleum softened.

Foreign investments in Mexico have taken the form of the disbursement of funds based on debt/equity swap transactions. These totaled some $2 to $2.5 billion in 1988. Such transactions permit foreign investors to purchase Mexican public sector debt at a discount, sometimes as much as 50 percent, and give it to the government in return for its face value in pesos. Investors use these funds to make new investments, increase equity in an existing firm, or retire the debt of an existing company.[38] Leading the investors is the United States, with 64.3 percent of the total. Others include West Germany, Japan, Switzerland, Great Britain, and Canada.

The foreign investments laws of Mexico generally reserve for the government and Mexican nationals certain economic activities and limit foreign ownership to 49 percent. Exceptions must be approved by the National Foreign Investment Commission. The principles governing trade and investment between the United States and Mexico were agreed to with the signing of the Bilateral Trade and Investment Framework Understanding, in November 1987.

THE ECONOMIC ENVIRONMENT OF LESS DEVELOPED COUNTRIES

Although the definition of a less developed country varies, one might think of it as a country that is in the early stages of economic development, has relatively low standards of living, and does not make most efficient use of its resources. The economic environments of LDCs contrast sharply with those of industrialized countries and even the newly industrialized countries.

Two-thirds of the countries in the world are less developed and are the home for nearly three fourths of the world's population, many in extreme poverty. Although most LDCs are located in Africa, Asia, and Latin America, the communist countries of Eastern Europe, the USSR, and the PRC can be considered less developed. In the case of Eastern Europe and the USSR, this lack of development stems largely from the inherent shortcomings of Marxian economics, mismanagement of these economies, and the short-sightedness of the central planning. With the dramatic movements toward democracy and market economies of these nations during 1989, one might expect rapid economic development. This can be anticipated because it was not population growth, lack of economic diversification, or any of the normal problems that had caused the economic stagnation of the communist bloc. There will, however, be a period of major structural adjustment (see Global Insight). These nations will also have to implement changes that enhance productivity and develop a consumer-driven internal economy to experience substantial economic development.

Unlike Eastern Europe or the USSR, most developing countries (including the PRC) experience grave economic and social conditions that have existed for centuries. It is only in recent years that attention has been given to the plight of these countries' citizens. Global mass communications have brought the horrors of impoverishment, disease, and starvation into all of our homes.

Even those few LDCs with an abundance of natural resources usually have not exploited these to their fullest. Land suitable for agriculture is often improperly utilized, and mineral resources remain unexploited. Even the cheap and abundant labor, one of the primary resources, is not utilized to its potential. The contrast between most LDCs and the highly successful NICs of the Pacific Rim is readily noticeable.

Characteristics of the Less Developed Countries

Most developing countries, regardless of geographic location, share some characteristics that help explain the lack of economic development.

Low Per Capita Income

One of the distinctive features of a developing country is the low per capita income. In the United States a family of four with an annual income of less than $12,000 is considered below the poverty line. More than two thirds of the population of the world have an average annual income of less than $1,000. India's population of more than 800 million has a per capita income of less than $300 per year. In 1987, the per capita income in the PRC, with a population of more than one billion, was only about $230.[39] Yet, there are great variations of income within most less developed countries. Scattered among the poor are very wealthy individuals. Many measure their land-holdings in terms of thousands of acres. In the oil-producing countries of the Middle East, the national income is very high. For example, Kuwait had a per capita income of about $19,400 in 1987.[40] However, this does not mean that every individual has that income. Since oil production is usually a government monopoly, most individuals make substantially less than the average.

Dependence on Primary Goods

Dependence on the production and export of primary goods for the basic source of income is common among many less developed countries. Eco-

GLOBAL INSIGHT
Understanding Eastern European Economies in the 1990s

The adjustments of Eastern European (EE) economies to open market principles present both opportunities and challenges. Western firms need to understand what is coming as well as what is probably coming. The economies of EE are segmented not only across countries but also within countries. This segmentation consists of more than mere problems of transportation; it also includes cultural stereotyping and ethnic prejudices to the extent that an agent from one region may not be acceptable in another.

Rigid five-year planning is dead. The economies of EE will now be trying to solve urgent problems of consumer goods, inflation, job creation, and so forth in a far more realistic and flexible manner. This will demand that Western firms, banks, and governments be ready to supply credits. Relatedly, EE countries seem to have made the establishment of joint ventures one of the cornerstones for development. Thus, they will be looking for joint venture partners who can supply capital, technology, and marketing channels. It is expected that most countries of EE will be following Hungary's model of selling ownership shares in state-owned enterprises and allowing wholly owned subsidiaries.

The EE economic interrelations organization, COMECON, must not be viewed as an eastern version of the EEC. It has never been that and probably will not become a unit of economic integration for the foreseeable future. There is no free exchange of goods across borders. Firms must plan country by country.

Although EE countries say that they accept the profit motive, the term *profit* may have a very different meaning there than in the West. Flexibility is the watchword for Western firms. Furthermore, even though these markets are becoming "open," that does not mean there is no risk or even necessarily a good economic reason to invest. On the other hand, firms that invest now and ride out the tough times of structural adjustments could profit handsomely if the EE and the USSR develop as Gorbachev and most Western governments hope.

Source: Adapted from "Guidelines for Success in Eastern Europe in the 1990s," *Business International*, March 27, 1989, p. 96.

---

nomic activities that depend upon the benevolence of nature make it extremely difficult to develop a stable economic society. During periods of drought, sufficient crops cannot be produced to feed the population, let alone to export. If conditions are ideal, resulting in bumper crops, the surplus supplied in the international markets results in low prices, again adversely affecting the income of these countries. Furthermore, many of the industrialized countries that were once markets for the products of the less developed countries are no longer major importers due to the development of substitute products or alternative sources. The replacement of natural rubber by synthetic rubber, or of jute for carpet backing by polypropylene fiber are examples.

Producers of mineral products encounter similar cycles of booms and busts. One of the best examples is that of crude petroleum. By limiting output in the early 1970s, OPEC was able to increase prices several-fold within a very short period of time.[41] But when importing nations discovered alternative sources of crude petroleum and supplemented their energy requirements with natural gas, coal, nuclear, and solar energy, the OPEC cartel was no longer able to control market prices. The impact of the decrease in demand on the price of petroleum was rapid and significant.[42] OPEC countries that had embarked on ambitious programs of development based on the anticipated oil revenues encountered financial problems. They even had difficulty servicing their financial obligations, while creditors were faced with the possibility of wholesale defaults.

Lack of Economic Diversification

A related problem of the less developed countries is the lack of diversification in economic activities. This makes a country's revenues uncertain and amplifies the effects of business cycles, particularly regarding employment. Costa Rica, for example, is largely dependent upon the production and export of coffee and bananas. If the prices for these products fell or if the crops were damaged by frost, the loss of revenues would make it difficult for the country to import essential goods or meet its foreign financial obligations. A similar situation exists for sugar and other agricultural or extractive products that are adversely affected by external factors over which producers have little control. A partial solution for the less developed countries lies in economic diversification.

High Illiteracy Rates

The illiteracy rates in the less developed countries often run as high as 80 percent. The lack of literacy can be attributed largely to the lack of educational facilities sufficient to meet the needs of the large population. Establishing schools without the necessary financial resources while trying to develop different sectors of the economy is a major undertaking. Financial support for education is generally inadequate even though education is high among the priorities for development. Furthermore, even where schools are available, many students drop out after a few years because of economic necessity and end up seeking jobs on farms and in factories.

Population Explosion

The population explosion is a severe problem with substantial economic implications for most less developed countries. The high rate of population growth puts tremendous pressure on the food supply. Domestic production is generally insufficient to meet their needs, so they must depend upon imports. But imports must be paid for with foreign currencies, of which the LDCs have an inadequate supply; therefore, borrowing abroad is necessary. Thus, the population growth consumes resources that could have been invested to solve basic economic problems. This forces many of these countries to postpone projects that are essential for economic development, creating a repetitive cycle.

Although the rate of economic growth is rapid in many less developed countries, they face difficulty keeping pace with the population explosion. The introduction of modern technology in agriculture decreases the need for farm workers, encouraging many to migrate to the urban areas to seek employment. The limited number of factories cannot absorb the additional workers, resulting in permanent rather than cyclical unemployment. Further adding to the problems of the migrants is the lack of housing, sanitation, water, power, and police and other social services. The result is the growth of many temporary shelters where the people seek refuge. A visit to Calcutta, Caracas, Mexico City, and many other cities experiencing a rapid influx of population, provides ample evidence of the effects of mass migration to urban areas. Such conditions contribute to the high mortality rate among the population. Only during the Great Depression of 1929–1933 has the United States had any experience with these types of problems, which are common in many Third World countries.

The solution to the population explosion lies in birth control; however, the dissemination of information is not effective because of the low level of literacy. One-to-one contact is the only effective method that can be used, but this means that only a small percentage of the population can be reached. Adding to these difficulties are the religious and cultural beliefs that encourage large families. Whatever the reason, the large and dense populations have had an adverse effect upon the economic development and the standard of living in the LDCs.

Rapid growth in population, high illiteracy, dependence on primary products, and a lack of economic diversity generally characterize LDCs.

Obstacles to Economic Development

The objective of every less developed country is to reduce its dependence on the export of primary products through industrialization. Some countries have made great progress toward industrialization: South Korea, Taiwan, Hong Kong, Singapore, Mexico, and Brazil. Others have not been nearly so successful. The lack of an educated population, business managers, government administrators, infrastructure, and technology act as barriers to economic development. But above all industrialization cannot be achieved without sufficient capital for investment purposes.

Lack of Internal Sources of Capital

Most countries would like to depend upon domestically generated capital for investment purposes. Savings are the most important internal source of capital; however, savings by individuals in the LDCs are insufficient to meet investment needs. With a per capita income of less than $1000, savings are all but impossible.

The low savings rate in the less developed countries results from the low income. Low income is due to the low productivity. Productivity is low because investments in modern machinery and equipment are low. Investments are low because savings are low. Savings are low because income is low. Thus, the less developed countries are faced with the vicious cycle of low income, low savings, low investment, low productivity, and back to low income (see Figure 10.3).

Undistributed profits of business firms are an important source of capital in the more highly developed countries. This is generally not true in the less developed countries, where business operations are usually small and earnings are relatively limited. The alternative to using undistributed profits is using credit, but since individual savings are inadequate, domestic financial institutions have only limited financial resources for loan purposes.

The lack of productivity improvements also creates another problem that is all too common in developing countries—extremely high rates of inflation. During the late 1970s the United States inflation rate exceeded 15 percent and the results were dramatic. Fixed rate savings accounts rapidly eroded in value, the buying power of pensions deteriorated, and investors sought inflation hedge investments rather than solid growth investments. Consider the fact that many nations have not had an inflation rate that low in decades. Indeed, countries like Argentina have had annual inflation rates over 1500 percent. In fact, in many countries 25 to 50 percent inflation rates would be considered low. Figure 10.4 shows the aggregate inflation rates for developing countries, industrialized countries, and the world as a whole.

The availability of indigenous capital for investment purposes is generally lacking in the less developed countries. Not only is there a shortage of such capital, but most of it is in the form of *commercial capital* that is not available for investment in debt or equity of firms. Wealthy individuals who make up a small percentage of the population prefer to hold such capital in liquid form. This is invested in such tangible items as precious metals, foreign currencies, or other short-term securities that have a great deal of liquidity. Thus, at the slightest sign of political upheaval or financial crisis, there is a flight of capital to safer havens abroad.

Those wealthy individuals who prefer not to keep their capital abroad usually invest in real estate or other tangible assets that are less affected by

Figure 10.3   The Saving and Investment Cycle in LDCs

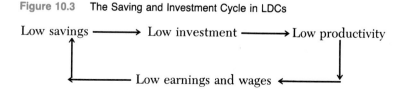

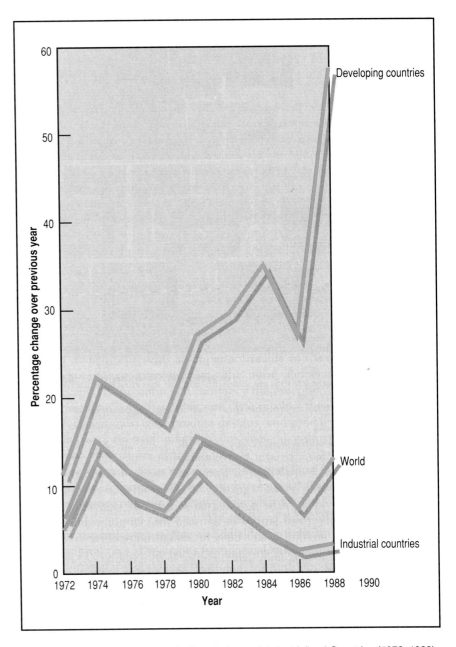

Figure 10.4 Consumer Prices for Developing and Industrialized Countries (1972–1988)
Source: International Monetary Fund, *International Financial Statistics Yearbook,* 1989, pp. 116–117.

the fluctuations in the economy and thus serve as a hedge against the massive inflation characteristic of many LDCs. Lack of confidence in the domestic economy precludes their investing in debt or equity of local industries. Thus, indigenous capital is not available for investment in the machinery, equipment, and plants that are so sorely needed for development. The lack of indigenous capital for industrialization will probably continue as long as individuals have the alternative for safer and more profitable outlets abroad.

Developing countries are often overly dependent upon export earnings as a source of capital for investment purposes. But export earnings are very unreliable because of the fluctuations in demand for the LDCs' products, or because of the wide fluctuations in their market prices. For example, Mexico and other oil-exporting countries that had borrowed on the basis of anticipated earnings from the exports have had to postpone or abandon many of their projects because of the collapse in the price for crude petroleum. Recent events show that even the economies of the highly developed countries such as Great Britain can be affected adversely when the demand and price of a major export product such as oil softens. The problem of using export earnings to fund economic development is further intensified because the foreign exchange that these countries earn must also be used to purchase foodstuffs and other necessities.

The LDCs' efforts to industrialize face many obstacles. One of the most serious is their inability to generate sufficient investment capital from internal sources.

External Sources of Capital

Since the internal sources of capital are generally inadequate to meet the minimum requirements for investment purposes, the less developed countries turn to external sources, both private and public. The outstanding obligations in 1986 to commercial banks and other financial institutions in industrialized countries are shown in Table 10.2. This table shows the extent to which some countries have sought capital from abroad. Many of these countries have even found it impossible to meet their external obligations without additional outside assistance. Some have attempted to renegotiate agreements with creditors to prevent default, while others have sought aid

Table 10.2 **External Debt of Developing Countries: 1986**

Country	Million U.S. Dollars	Country	Million U.S. Dollars
Argentina	49,908.2	Brazil	110,675.1
Mexico	101,721.9	Morocco	15,148.0
Nigeria	21,876.3	Philippines	28,172.5
Venezuela	33,891.2	Yugoslavia	21,363.6

Source: U.S. Dept. of Commerce, "Improving U.S. Competitiveness: Swapping Debt for Education," Washington, D.C.: International Trade Administration, August 1988.

from international financial institutions such as the IMF. A few have stated that they have no alternative but to default on their obligations. Thus, they find themselves in another vicious cycle (see Figure 10.5) not unlike the savings and investment cycle.

Private Sources of Funds   Loans from private financial institutions to meet the capital needs of the LDCs will no doubt continue in the future; however, because of the delays in repayment and the possibility of default, many lenders will probably be more selective, especially where repayment is based upon expected revenues from the export of primary products.

An indirect source of funds for development purposes is multinational corporations. Some less developed countries have encouraged multinational firms to make direct investments by offering various types of incentives and guarantees. The establishment of factories, often managed by expatriates until nationals can be trained to take over, has speeded up economic development. Continued growth is assured because the firms provide the expertise, technology, processes, components, and market contacts. They even provide an additional source of foreign exchange for the less developed country when products are imported for processing and are re-exported.

Public Sources of Funds   Government-to-government assistance is also provided to the less developed country by industrialized countries. Many agencies of the U.S. government have been specifically set up to aid the less developed countries. Other countries, especially those of western Europe and Japan, have various institutions comparable to those of the United States. The Soviet Union is also active in granting financial assistance to the less developed countries, although at a substantially lower level than that of the United States or the western European countries.

International Agencies   The most important of the international agencies that provide aid to the less developed countries belong to the World Bank group, as discussed in an earlier chapter. The International Bank for Reconstruction and Development was set up specifically to provide assistance for the development of infrastructure. Terms are generally very favorable when loans are granted. If this source refuses assistance, a less developed country may turn to the International Development Association, whose

Figure 10.5   The Foreign Debt Servicing Cycle

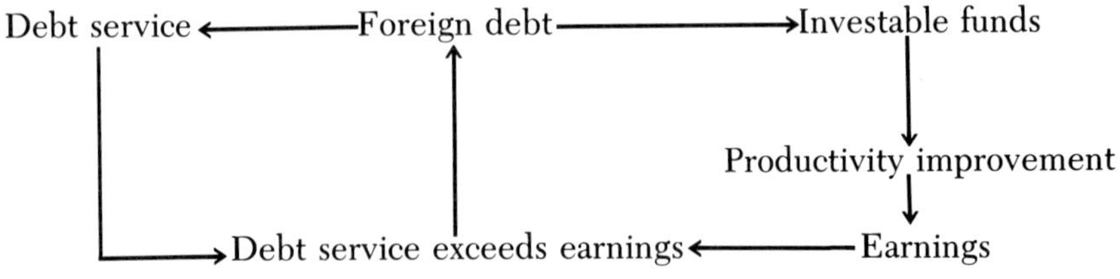

Debt service ⟵————Foreign debt————⟶Investable funds

Productivity improvement

Debt service exceeds earnings⟵————Earnings

Most LDCs attempt to supplement their capital needs from external sources such as commercial financial institutions, governments, and international agencies.

standards are less rigid and whose terms are even more favorable. Another source is the International Finance Corporation, which was set up to grant loans to private firms in the developing countries. In addition to the World Bank group, the United Nations and its agencies continue to provide developing nations with support in a variety of forms.

Inadequate Infrastructure

The infrastructure of most LDCs is inadequate for the development of the economy. There are few roads and railroads to the interior of the country, making it extremely costly to move products from the interior to the coastal ports for exporting, or to move products from the coast to the interior. Africa, South America, and continental Asia provide good examples of such inadequacies being commonplace. The result is that major centers of population are located along the coast or in the interior along navigable rivers. The map of the continent of South America clearly illustrates this concentration of population centers along the coastal areas (see Figure 10.6).

Power facilities are lacking in most of the LDCs; it is only in recent years that electricity has been made available in the urban areas of many of these countries. There is a need for warehouses for the storage of agricultural products. Bridges and highways are largely lacking. Until the basic framework of these countries is developed, little can be done to develop the interior except along natural waterways or along existing roads and railroads. It will be difficult to stimulate economic growth since infrastructure is a precondition to development of national markets.

Import Substitution

Many less developed countries attempt to manufacture domestically what is normally imported by adopting a policy of import substitution. Very often, obsolete equipment or complete factories are purchased from abroad in the belief that it will conserve the limited supply of foreign exchange while speeding up industrialization. Priority is given to local producers. However, the lack of expertise, technology, processes, components, and market contacts all tend to deter efficient operations.

The limited demand prevents scale operations, resulting in high unit cost production. The industry cannot compete with imports, necessitating the adoption of barriers to protect this infant industry. Consumers are forced to purchase domestically produced goods of lower quality and higher prices. The adoption of protective measures tends to foster inefficiency, as it becomes difficult to discard protection even after the industry becomes mature. Thus, import substitution does little to aid in the development of a particular industry, regardless of the stage of economic development.

One of the countries that has adopted import substitution as an economic policy is South Korea. That nation is currently requiring the domestic production of more than 400 goods that are normally imported. The stated

Figure 10.6   Major Urban Areas of South America

purpose is to trim the nation's huge trade deficit, especially with Japan. The result has been an increase in local prices and decrease in quality. Another country that has adopted import substitution is the People's Republic of China. In 1987, that nation adopted import substitution to protect the home industries against foreign competition. Here again, the policy has not aided in the development of the economy because of the misallocation of resources. This is especially true when several small firms are permitted to manufacture a particular product for which demand is limited, resulting in overall inefficient operations and the retardation of industrialization.

Other Obstacles

Experienced managers trained in modern methods of business are largely lacking in developing countries. Thus, business is conducted by those who rely on experience gained in small business operations or agricultural production, and this background is often inadequate to deal with the economic and financial problems of modern industry.

In many countries, the lack of managers is in part due to the limited opportunities for local nationals during the colonial period. Many colonial powers looked upon the colonies as sources of raw materials and markets for their finished goods rather than training grounds for future managers and engineers. Educational facilities for training business leaders are also lacking in many LDCs. A similar situation exists for government administrators. Most LDCs do not have sufficient skilled personnel or training programs for government administrators. Incompetent leadership has often resulted in opposition to those in power, resulting in the overthrow of elected government officials and the introduction of dictatorship under the guise of democracy.

Inadequate infrastructure and a shortage of business managers and qualified government administrators are among the most intractable obstacles to economic development.

SUMMARY

The economic environment of nations is influenced by the geographic, human, cultural, political, and legal environmnents. Thus, in describing the economic environment, one cannot ignore the noneconomic environmental conditions that exist. Furthermore, there is no sharp demarkation in the economic environment of countries in the different stages of economic development since the categories are largely arbitrary.

The United States, Canada, the European Economic Community, Japan, Australia, and New Zealand were used as examples of industrialized countries. The Pacific Rim countries along with Mexico and Brazil represent the newly industrialized countries. The LDCs are discussed as a group of nations with common characteristics.

The EEC serves to illustrate not only the economic conditions of advanced industrialized societies but also economic integration. In many ways the EEC reflects the general economic conditions that multinational firms encounter in any industrialized country, with one important difference.

Unlike most industrial countries, many of the specific objectives the Community hopes to achieve, the measures to be adopted, and the timetable for the achievement are specifically defined by the Treaty of Rome. A Community without borders in 1992 has been set as the goal. Thus, multinational firms know in advance the economic environment within which they will be operating.

Japan is an advanced industrialized country. With the aid and support of the government, the nation became an economic superpower. It has fully developed capital and service markets, and its infrastructure is equal to that found in any industrialized country. It is highly developed technologically and many of its exports are sophisticated goods. Yet, in spite of these characteristics, the country is unique in that market penetration is somewhat more difficult than in countries of the West. This is due in part to cultural and linguistic unfamiliarity and in part to the complexity of the Japanese distribution system.

Australia and New Zealand, located in the South Pacific, are unlike the NICs of the Pacific Rim. Although both countries are considered advanced developed nations, their economic activities are largely land-based. The population is sparse compared with that in other regions of the world. Thus, the potential for the economic importance of these two countries cannot be overlooked.

The economic environment of the NICS of the Pacific Rim—specifically South Korea, Singapore, Hong Kong, and Taiwan—present a very different picture from that of western Europe or North America. These economies are fairly exploding. Unemployment is very low and inflation is under control. Rapid economic growth and increasing importance in manufacturing and world trade characterize these countries. The result is that the economic center of the world has shifted from the Atlantic to the Pacific.

Two Latin American countries that may be considered newly industrialized are Brazil and Mexico. The economic environments of both of these countries are quite different from those in the Pacific Rim. Both of these nations have serious problems with inflation and the servicing of foreign debt. Attempts to control the rapid inflation have acted as a detriment to the more rapid development. Meeting the debt payments will require tremendous resources that will, most likely, affect future economic development.

Generally, multinational corporations are less familiar with the economic environments of the less developed countries that are scattered throughout Africa, Asia, and South America. Yet these countries should be of primary interest to international business firms because they have as their major objective economic development, primarily through the development of modern manufacturing industries. Multinational enterprises will probably play an increasing role in the more rapid economic development of the LDCs. They will probably serve as investors and as trainers of business leaders. However, conducting business in the less developed countries will require that these firms learn to deal with dramatically different environmental conditions from those of the more highly industrialized and democratic countries.   ☐

KEY TERMS AND CONCEPTS

Economic diversification

European Economic Community (EEC or EC)

Expatriates

External source of capital

Infrastrucure

Internal source of capital

Less developed or Third World country (LDC)

OPEC

Population explosion

Primary good

Value added tax

REVIEW QUESTIONS

1. What areas of economic activity have created the greatest problems for the EEC in achieving economic union? Why?

2. How does the EEC compare to the United States as a market for products?

3. Why must multinational enterprises establish branches and subsidiaries in the EEC if they wish to compete with domestic producers?

4. Briefly describe the economic characteristics of nations at the different stages of economic development.

5. What are the reasons for the rapid development of the Pacific Rim countries?

6. Explain why most LDCs have difficulty generating sufficient capital from internal sources for development purposes.

7. What are the major external sources of capital for the LDCs? Describe those that are especially helpful to these countries.

8. Explain fully why most less developed countries have difficulty in meeting their foreign debt obligations.

9. Compare the infrastructure of the less developed countries with that of your own country.

10. In addition to the obstacles described in this chapter, list others that might be equally important.

11. Select one less developed country and analyze the various positive and negative factors that would influence its economic development.

12. Select and justify one country as an outlet for investment by a multinational corporation.

13. The inability to meet their debt obligations is one of the major problems facing the LDCs. How can these countries meet the problem?

DISCUSSION CASE

The European Community Becomes a Single Market

The EC Commission's emphasis on achieving an Internal Market [IM] by 1992 is essentially a stratagem. Companies should view 1992 as not so much a date, but as a shorthand for Europe's institutional response to changes in the global economy. After European economies began reviving in the early 1980s, it quickly became apparent that Europe did not have the competitive environment to sustain the revival. The 1992 program is a shock tactic intended to create that business environment: It is already clear that the program is the most significant development in European commercial policy since 1945.

Dismantling Core Barriers

The ultimate goal of the EC is to restructure European economies into a single market of 320 million people that is equipped to handle increased global competition from the United States, Japan, and the NICs. To achieve this aim, the EC member states (France, West Germany, Italy, the UK, Belgium, the Netherlands, Denmark, Spain, Portugal, Greece, Luxembourg, and Ireland) are to have in place a common legislative framework in all areas affecting commercial practice by 1992. This will be no small task considering the diverse nationalities involved and the plethora of member state legislation that will need to be eliminated or amended.

The IM calls for the creation of free EC trade, with the elimination of both nontariff trade barriers and customs duties. The three core barriers that the EC is hoping to dismantle by 1992 are the following:

1. *Physical*, i.e., the dismantling of border controls within the Community and the abolition of internal customs duties, together with a corresponding strengthening of the control of external borders;
2. *Product and workplace standardization*, with a unification of regulations on products standards and health and safety in the workplace; and
3. *Fiscal*, where the harmonization of indirect tax rates is already under way and the harmonization of direct tax rates is still to be tackled by the Commission.

Source: Richard Walker, "The European Community Comes of Age with Its Single Market," *Business International*, January 27, 1988, pp. 193–194. Reprinted by permission.

Key Issues to Be Resolved

In addition to the dismantling of the above barriers, the Commission's Internal Market brief implies the creation of a wider range of new commercial policies. Many of these are extremely controversial. They involve the deregulation of sectors long accustomed to protection against competition, including the following:

Capital markets and financial services. Many EC member states have already dismantled their exchange control regime, while several others have not, notably Italy and France among the "big five" economies. The IM requires a free capital market by 1992 that will end direct state control of interest rates and lending quotas. A related issue is the European market for financial services, where member states that have already pursued deregulation (like the UK) are well placed to take insurance and investment business away from those member states that have not (like France).

Public procurement. Most member states have not yet fully grasped that the use of public procurement to sustain domestic industries will end with the IM's introduction in 1992. The Commission's requirements for the progressive introduction of "transparent" public procurement practices, under which cases of national favoritism can be overturned in the European Court, is a potent tool for the deregulation of key markets like telecommunications and construction.

Antitrust. The Competition Directorate of the EC Commission is increasingly active in monitoring and managing the level of business concentration in Europe and in policing member states' attempts to subsidize their domestic industries. In 1987, the Commission ruled that ECU 747 million ($1.18:ECU) of illegal state subsidies to industry had to be returned. (The European Currency Unit is the basket of currencies of the members of the EC against which individual member currencies may be stated to show the relationship among the currencies of the members.) The Commission is fighting and gradually winning a battle to establish that the Community institutions, rather than the member states, are the final court on issues raised by European mergers and trade practices.

Intellectual property rights. The Internal Market program has coincided with the global crisis in the field of protection of intellectual property rights. The Commission has been struggling to create a European policy to deal with the case with which recorded material may be illegally copied. This has been an uphill fight, however, in the absence of a clear mandate from industry. As a result, many of the Community's member states are beginning to jump the gun with their own revised versions of intellectual property legislation.

Questions

1. How will the restructuring of the 12 European Community member nations into a unified Internal Market change the economic environment of companies located within and outside of the EC?

2. What are some of the problems that might be foreseen for the development of a truly common market?

3. How will the elimination of so-called core barriers to trade affect subsidiaries of multinational firms operating in this market? How will the deregulation of certain sectors of the economy affect the operations of multinational firms?

NOTES

1. Committee for Economic Development, *The European Economic Community and Its Meaning to the United States.* (New York: CED, 1959), p. 92.

2. Ibid.

3. Ibid.

4. Ibid., p. 95.

5. Ibid., p. 105.

6. Kredietbank (Belgium), *Weekly Bulletin*, March 6, 1981.

7. Tourists from the EEC, for example, will pay the VAT in the country of purchase, and if they import products into their own country, they are again charged a value added tax. Thus, they pay the tax twice unless they make purchases in a tax free store.

8. Political institutions have been set up to enforce the treaty and ensure that European interests prevail over strictly national interests.

9. Richard I. Kirkland, Jr., "Outsider's Guide to Europe in 1992," *Fortune* (October 24, 1988), p. 121.

10. Ibid.

11. Philip R. Cateora, *International Marketing* (Homewood, Ill: Richard D. Irwin, 1983), p. 39.

12. U.S. Department of Commerce, *Foreign Economic Trends* (88-101), *Japan*, October 1988.

13. Ibid.

14. Ibid.

15. Ibid.

16. Ibid.

17. IMF, *International Financial Statistics Yearbook*, 1989.

18. Ibid.

19. Ibid.

20. U.S. Department of Commerce, *Marketing in Canada* (OBR 88-1), May 1988.

21. U.S. Department of Commerce, *Marketing in Australia* (OBR 89-06), May 1989.

22. U.S. Department of Commerce, *Foreign Economic Trends* (89-08), *New Zealand*, January 1989.

23. IMF, *International Financial Statistics Yearbook,* 1989.

24. U.S. Department of Commerce, *Foreign Economic Trends* (89-94), *Australia*, September 1989.

25. U.S. Department of Commerce, *Marketing in Australia* (OBR 89-06), May 1989.

26. U.S. Department of Commerce, *Foreign Economic Trends* (89-08), *New Zealand*, January 1989.

27. U.S. Department of Commerce, *Foreign Economic Trends* (for individual countries in 1989).

28. U.S. Department of Commerce, *Foreign Economic Trends* (89-67), *Korea*, June 1989.

29. Ibid.

30. U.S. Department of Commerce, *Foreign Economic Trends* (90), *Hong Kong*, February 1990.

31. Ibid.

32. U.S. Department of Commerce, *Marketing in Brazil* (OBR 81-33), August 1989.

33. U.S. Department of Commerce, *Foreign Economic Trends* (89-06), *Brazil*, July 1989.

34. Ibid.

35. IMF, *International Financial Statistics Yearbook*, 1989.

36. U.S. Department of Commerce, *Foreign Economic Trends* (89-16), *Mexico*, February 1989.

37. IMF, *International Financial Statistics Yearbook*, 1989.

38. U.S. Department of Commerce, *Foreign Economic Trends* (89-16), *Mexico*, February 1989.

39. IMF, *International Financial Statistics Yearbook*, 1989.

40. Ibid.

41. The established per barrel price of Saudi Arabian crude petroleum increased from $1.90 in 1972 to $2.70 in 1973, $9.76 in 1974, and $33.47 in 1982.

42. Per barrel prices slid to $29.31 in 1983, $28.47 in 1984, $20.00 in 1986, and below $12.00 in October 1988, but by October 1989 they had recovered to about $20 per barrel.

REFERENCES AND SELECTED READINGS

Cateora, Philip R. *International Marketing*, 5th ed. Homewood, Ill.: Richard D. Irwin, 1983.

Committee for Economic Development. *The European Economic Community and Its Meaning to the United States.* New York: CED, 1959.

Czinkota, Michael R., and Martin J. Kohn. *Improving U.S. Competitiveness: Swapping Debt for Education.* Washington, D.C.: U.S. Department of Commerce, August 1988.

De la Torre, José. "Foreign Investment and Economic Development: Conflict and Negotiation." *The Journal of International Business Studies* 12:2 (Fall 1981).

International Monetary Fund. *International Financial Statistics Yearbook*, 1989.

IMF. *International Financial Statistics Yearbook*, 1985.

Kirkland, Jr., Richard I. "Outsider's Guide to Europe in 1992." *Fortune Magazine* (October 24, 1988).

Kredietbank (Belgium). *Weekly Bulletin* (March 6, 1981).

Mazzolini, Renato. "European Government-Controlled Enterprises: An Organizational Politics View." *The Journal of International Business Studies* 11:1 (Spring/Summer 1980).

Owen, Richard, and Michael Dynes. *The Times Guide to 1992: Britain in a Europe Without Frontiers*. London: The Times Book, Ltd., 1989.

Poynter, Thomas A. "Government Intervention in Less Developed Countries: The Experience of Multinational Companies." *The Journal of International Business Studies* 13:1 (Spring/Summer 1982).

Sullivan, Scott. "Who's Afraid of 1992?" *Newsweek* (October 31, 1988).

UNESCO. *Statistical Yearbook*, 1985. Louvain, Belgium.

CHAPTER

11

The Human and Cultural Environment of International Business

LEARNING OBJECTIVES

- Understand the meaning of culture, including national and organizational culture

- Understand the cultural differences among countries

- Learn the criteria for selecting an expatriate manager

- Learn the essentials of predeparture and transition expatriate training

- Understand the role of the multinational firm in facilitating and supporting the expatriate during foreign assignment

- Know how the multinational corporation might adapt its business system to a foreign culture

- Understand the dynamics of cultural change

- Know why there is built-in resistance to change

INTRODUCTION

Cultural diversity typifies the countries of the world. Although no individual can be familiar with the cultural environments of all countries, it is essential that expatriates of multinational enterprises become familiar with the culture of the country to which they are assigned. It is equally important for corporate executives to be familiar with the cultures of countries in which their firms operate. Cultural understanding, empathy, and competence are necessary for handling the various problems that are sure to arise.

This chapter analyzes the components and dimensions of culture and the nature of the cultural differences among countries. Furthermore, it explores the cultural differences that exist within as well as among countries. For example, not all residents of the Netherlands, Argentina, Japan, Egypt, or the United States share a common culture. Even relatively homogeneous societies often have numerous and different subcultures. The chapter illustrates how cultural differences that might seem insignificant can be of vital concern for understanding and cooperation. Cultural misunderstandings often result in problems that have significant implications in business relationships among and within firms. Such problems can be avoided with a minimum effort from both home and host country personnel if they become more familiar with the human and cultural environments of the other. Finally, the chapter emphasizes the cultural aspects in the selection and training of expatriate managers to improve their likelihood of success during foreign assignments.

UNDERSTANDING CULTURE AND CULTURAL DIFFERENCES

Differences in culture are the most distinguishing features among countries; therefore, understanding the essence of culture is essential.

Culture can be defined as learned patterns of behavior or guidelines for behavior. This learning is called acculturation. Culture manifests itself in traditions, values, beliefs, morals, and laws. Cultural differences are most observable through the everyday behavior of peoples, their standards for beauty and success, and their definition of what is good, proper, and acceptable. To a lesser extent, culture is reflected in the laws, customs, art, and other expressions of material things.

Behavior as well as attitudes, beliefs, and norms develop into distinct patterns that are passed down through generations. These generally undergo modifications and adjustments, but maintain elements distinguishing that culture from others.

National Culture

A national culture is a set of beliefs, values, and norms shared by a majority of the inhabitants of a country. These become embodied in the laws and regulations of that society as well as in the generally accepted norms of the social system of that country. Although most nations have a dominant culture, even the most homogeneous nation will have subcultures with unique characteristics. In other words, each nation is actually composed of groups with differing behavior patterns, beliefs, values, and attitudes. These variations are due to the tremendous differences in history, family structure, social values, education, religion, and language of individuals in a nation. For example, great subcultural differences exist within the United States, yet there exists a national culture. Although Americans[1] may not see that common culture, it is readily apparent to foreign visitors. The cultures of the various subgroups within any society may mix in a complementary way or may be in a state of conflict.

Organizational Culture

Given the tremendous importance of formal organizations in the modern world, one must recognize the existence of culture in these organizations.

Corporations, like nations, develop common and acceptable patterns of behavior, standards of success, and definitions of what is good, proper, and acceptable. Larger organizations even develop their own laws, customs, rewards, jargon, definitions of truth, and other dimensions of culture. Organizational culture influences worker assumptions, attitudes, beliefs, and aspirations. In other words, organizations also acculturate their members.

The organizational culture of a multinational enterprise will influence and be influenced by the national cultures in which it operates. Since multinational firms operate in numerous cultures, they may develop organizational cultures that differ from the culture of any one nation. The strongest influence on the corporate culture is usually the home country. This is true because the corporation has operated there for the longest time and because it is usually the home nation of most of the firm's executives. Furthermore, most of the firm's stockholders come from the home country. This home country cultural bias can result in serious conflict between the firm and the host nation. Many of the cultural problems of international firms occur because the expatriates who go on foreign assignment take along their home culture and are ill prepared to make the necessary cultural adjustments to be successful at their new tasks.

> Culture is a pattern of behavior or a set of guidelines for behavior. Multiple subcultures are evident even in homogeneous countries.

The Importance of History in Understanding Different Cultures

The first and perhaps most important step in understanding a different culture is to gain an insight into the country's history and to recognize that that country might be very different from one's own. To a great extent, it is the common history of a people that shapes cultural values. The United States can be used to illustrate how history helps shape culture and to indicate why U.S. culture differs from that of other nations.

The presence of a frontier, together with economic and political concepts emphasizing the importance of the individual, has created a gospel of individualism among most Americans. This commitment to the importance of the individual over the group represents a significant difference between the American culture and that of most other countries in the world. Many foreigners believe that the concept of individualism has been carried to such an extreme in the United States that Americans ignore or neglect others. This national attitude stands in sharp contrast to that in a country like Japan, whose dominant culture puts the good of the group ahead of that of the individual.

The Atlantic and Pacific oceans, separating the United States from Europe and Asia and separating it also from the battlefields of two world wars, have created a tendency toward isolationism, a distrust of alliances, and a general lack of concern for issues of foreign policy. It took the Vietnam war to sensitize the average American citizen to issues of foreign affairs. This contrasts dramatically with national awareness in countries like the

Since all countries in which multi-national firms operate have their own unique history and culture, one can improve cultural understanding by studying history.

Netherlands, which is located only a few hundred miles from many culturally diverse nations. As a result, the Dutch tend to have far more internationalized attitudes.

Cultural Dimensions of Business

The multinational firm and its expatriate employees must become familiar with the cultural dimensions of business in the host country. Substantial differences exist among cultures regarding the nature of society and the role of the individual. These cultural differences can cause misunderstanding or disagreement, and can affect the success or failure of the firm's operations in that culture.

Time and the Future

Cross-cultural misunderstandings can occur because of differences in the concept of time. In many countries, workers are not accustomed to precise scheduling and routinizing of work around a timetable. Time might be conceptualized in terms of seasons rather than in hours or minutes. Furthermore, to Americans time is a commodity to be controlled for financial gain, giving rise to the common American expression "time is money." In many cultures this concept is considered crass, vulgar, and even offensive. Time concerns such as punctuality vary greatly among cultures. Being late for an appointment in northern Europe might be considered so disrespectful as to sever future business ties, whereas in various areas of the Middle East, Africa, or South America, being late for such a meeting may be acceptable and normal. Similarly, there are differing attitudes toward punctuality at social events. If one is invited to the home of a Swedish executive at 7:00 P.M., it would be a social blunder to arrive at 7:15; in Argentina the same invitation would mean that guests are expected to arrive between 8:30 and 9:00, and dinner may be served at 10.30 P.M.

Closely related to the concept of time is the cultural view of the future. A major assumption in U.S. business is that people can influence and even control future events. In many other countries, especially in Latin American or Moslem nations, the viewpoint is much more fatalistic. In Moslem countries, it is religous heresy to think that people could control the future since "only God can control the future." In other fatalistic cultures, it is not God but the blind hand of fate that determines the future. In such cultures, workers may feel that events will occur regardless of personal behavior and that they can do nothing to shape or control future events. Long-range planning is generally ineffective in these countries.

Wealth, Material Possessions, and Workplace Rewards

In most countries, wealth and material possessions are viewed as desirable and a motivator in the workplace. However, in some cultures individuals work only long enough to earn a little money and then miss work until those funds have been exhausted. These persons work merely to live.[2] In more affluent countries such as the United States, people often live to work, and thus are more interested in job security, workplace participation, and self-actualization than in traditional monetary rewards. These different perceptions of job compensation suggest that the multinational firm must identify the types of reward that are considered important to employees in each foreign culture.

Decision-Making

Effective decision-making in the United States is presumed to be based on objective analysis, often using statistical data to support the decision. This is not the practice in many societies. Factors such as personal judgment of senior executives are regarded as superior. While U.S. corporations often force management to justify individual decision-making, similar demands made in other countries might be considered insulting and interpreted as a lack of confidence in management. In such cultures, it might also be inappropriate for top managers to consult subordinates in decision-making situations since the executive is expected to maintain a posture of being knowledgeable on all matters. In such situations, it would be very difficult to implement a participative management system. The multinational manager must be aware of local attitudes regarding decision-making and must combine traditional decision-making techniques with modern scientific methods.

Bribery and Value Exchange

In international business, the term *bribery* has two meanings. The first type of bribery encountered in international business is the use of large sums of money to distort political or economic decision-making to gain an unfair advantage. This is culturally frowned upon, if not actually illegal, in most cultures. Although this type of bribery does occur in both developed and developing countries, the instances when payments are demanded by government officials far outweigh the times bribes are offered by international firms. From the Netherlands to Nigeria, extortion demands are a real and unpleasant aspect of international business. Few firms honor these demands for massive payments or kickbacks.

The second definition of bribery is the payment of relatively small, if not trivial, amounts of money to low-level public officials. It is common knowledge that in many underdeveloped countries, civil servants perform certain services in exchange for "reasonable" payments. These are often necessary for the civil servant to make a livable wage. Without this small "bribe," a package that should clear customs in a matter of hours or days might lie around for weeks or even months. These payments are not seen as harmful or even illegal, as they are in the United States. Local nationals and firms in such cultures consider these payments to be normal value exchanges and essentially similar to hiring a person; therefore, such payments are merely a cost of doing business. These petty bribes are often called tips, gifts, exchanges, or lubrication. These are comparable, in U.S. culture, to the tips one gives to a waiter or waitress in restaurants.

Such customs can create problems for the expatriate trying to operate abroad. Following the local custom is necessary for effective operation but could result in violation of U.S. laws. In theory, such lubrication bribes violate the U.S. Foreign Corrupt Practices Act; however, in practice officials look the other way as long as adequate accounting of such expenses is maintained. Most corporations will publicly disapprove of such practices but will privately tell their expatriate managers to do what is customary in each culture.

Language

Languages present continuing problems for international businesses. The need exists not only to be able to translate documents, advertising messages, and the like, but also to deal with multiple languages within a country. For example, Canada and Belgium have two official languages; thus, firms must label every product in both languages and be prepared to deal with employees, customers, suppliers, and others in either or both languages. Even where there is only one official language, it is not uncommon for some people to speak other than that language. In Peru, Bolivia, Chile, Ecuador, and other South American countries, many individuals speak only one of the Indian languages and do not understand Spanish. In addition to verbal communication, it is important for the firm to understand the forms of nonverbal communications that are generally unique to each culture.

Examples in the misuse of a language are legendary in international business. The authors are personally familiar with a situation involving an American manufacturer of greeting cards who merely translated the cards into French. The result was a card in the shape of a "B" that, when translated into French, read "Congratulations on the birth of your boy." Ignored was the fact that the French word for boy begins with a "G." As one might guess, the card for congratulations on your baby girl was in the shape of a "G"; the French word for girl begins with an "F." Unfortunately, the cultural mistakes were not limited to the language. The "boy" card contained pictures of an American football and a New York Yankees baseball cap, which have little significance to French children.

Religion and Superstitions

Peoples in many countries have religious beliefs or superstitions that affect the operation of the multinational enterprise. For business purposes, superstitions must be respected and not ignored. For example, colors in advertising, sales promotion, and affiliations should be used with great care. Certain colors are considered lucky in some countries: red in China and yellow in Thailand. On the other hand, certain other colors or combination of colors are considered unlucky. White carnations, which are often worn

In the Islamic world, prayer is not something that is done only privately and at a "convenient" time. Whether in the workplace or in a Mosque like this, prayer schedules are strictly observed.

to weddings or formal events in the United States, are a symbol of death in some countries of the Far East. Often an elaborate advertising campaign turns out to be a complete failure because market researchers did not explore beyond the conventional data on religion or superstition. Sometimes a large country is composed of so many religions that careful diversification of advertising is needed to appeal to all segments of the population.

Success in international business is often based upon the firm's ability to understand and adapt its operations to the host nation's cultural dimensions.

Religion also plays an important role in the management of local national employees. Rose Knotts emphatically states that "successful foreign businesses operating in cultures where religion governs business and social practices are those who respect and deal with their hosts' customs, such as prayer requirements and dietary restrictions."[3]

Interpersonal Relations

Authority, Individuality, and Competitiveness

Views toward authority among different societies might range from an autocratic perspective to a democratic-participative perspective. If the nationals see strong authority as being a right and obligation of formal leaders (such as management), then the multinational firm may want to utilize a

The cultural and religious customs of countries can be highly visible, as with the mourners at the "Wailing Wall" in Jerusalem, or very subtle and easily missed by a foreigner.

higher degree of centralization and less delegation. On the other hand, if local workers view authority in a more democratic light, decentralization should be the standard operating procedure.

Individuality and competitiveness are valued by most Americans and are perceived by Americans as natural conditions of human beings. In some firms these characteristics are even preconditions for promotion to the managerial rank. Only when these traits are so extreme as to damage the firm do they lose their desirability. In many other cultures, the aggressive and independent behaviors that stem from individuality and competitiveness are actively discouraged. From the Netherlands to Japan, team spirit and consensus development are the valued traits. The aggressiveness so valued by American management is often interpreted as a lack of concern for one's associates. Relatedly, in most Asian cultures, modesty and patience are valued, and the "American way" is purely unacceptable.

Extended Family

In many countries the concept of the extended family still exists. Near and distant relatives make up the interdependent unit, with family leaders being the key decision-makers on various issues. This concept often extends to the workplace. Managerial and other key positions are often held by family members (*nepotism*). Business goals may be oriented toward family needs and interests, with decision-making being based on these goals.

There are advantages and disadvantages to having such family relationships in the workplace. It can promote loyalty and strong commitment, giving workers another reason for not seeking other employment. At the same time, it might limit personal incentives since nepotism rather than personal competence might be the basis for hiring and promotions.

Marketing as well as management decisions within the foreign firm will be affected by the cultural perspective of the extended family. The marketing manager must understand the decision-making power of the family and particularly the head of the family. In many developed societies, the husband and wife share the decision-making process with some input provided by the children; however, in most extended families, the family patriarch (or matriarch) makes most of the decisions. Thus, the sales effort must focus on that key decision-maker.

Personal Criticisms

There are great variations in the tolerance of criticism among countries. Some cultures value frankness while others value subtlety and vagueness. In some Far Eastern cultures, politeness is valued over truthfulness. Japanese business persons often find it difficult to tell Americans that their product or service is unsuitable, or that they do not want to continue the business relationship. Instead, they will agree to "think it over" to avoid being unpleasant. They have actually said "no" but the American thinks that the final decision is yet to be made. In Latin American countries, there is a likelihood that constructive criticisms will be interpreted as a personal insult. In matters of managerial decisions, subordinates are expected to support the manager even if they disagree.

Views toward authority, family responsibility, and personal criticism vary across cultures and must be respected by the expatriate manager.

The international manager must be aware of these cultural norms and behaviors in order to perceive business acquaintances accurately, and to understand their intentions and desires.

Social Structure

Social structure includes cultural variables such as interclass mobility and status symbols that can influence the quality of workers available to the multinational corporation.

Interclass Mobility

A rigid social structure that ranks individuals according to ethnic, racial, economic, or educational backgrounds might prevent certain individuals from moving into managerial positions. Prejudices and class consciousness are readily apparent in many societies, as evidenced by the position of Indians in Latin America, the "Scheduled Class" in India, Algerians in France, the Irish in Britain, and so forth. In the United States, a country that likes to consider itself "classless," many barriers have been erected to such groups as Jews, Orientals, Blacks, Hispanics, and women. Such barriers deprive corporations of valuable human resources and may also lose them consumer support.

Occupational Status

A related problem occurs when society places a relatively low occupational status on business or engineering and a higher status on positions associated with land ownership, government work, law, or academic pursuits. When the status associated with business positions is low, it is often difficult to attract adequate numbers of top-quality young people into those careers. This is particularly true in many South American countries. In Argentina, for example, law and architecture are much more prestigious than business and engineering.

A rigid social structure inhibits economic development by locking out of management large sections of the population, resulting in a loss of talent.

PREPARING FOR SUCCESS IN A DIFFERENT CULTURE

The most practical reason for studying culture is to help those who must live and work in a different culture to do so successfully. This does not mean merely to accomplish one's job objectives, however important. Other goals need to be considered also:

1. Psychological success—being happy and feeling good about oneself, one's job, and one's family
2. Sociological success—having meaningful social relationships with members of that culture
3. Task success—accomplishing task objectives

In actuality it is difficult to separate the three. Although there are instances of individuals who have "succeeded" abroad by hiding in the company compound and working 100-hour weeks, the more common result of this detached and narrow approach is minimal success on the job and a very unhappy employee (or family) who demands to be repatriated under the threat of resignation. A far better approach for both the individual and the corporation is to understand the nature of the culture in which the expatriate has to work, select an individual who is likely to succeed, train the individual and family, design the task to enhance the expatriate's chances of success, and facilitate the achievement of that success. This broad and comprehensive approach to expatriate management is presented briefly here and addressed in detail in Chapter 19, "Human Resource Management."

Selecting the Expatriate Manager: Attitudes, Traits, and Skills

Several factors need to be considered in selecting an individual for foreign assignment. Attempts should be made to select an individual who has a minimum of prejudices and who has a record of nondiscrimination on the basis of race, gender, or ethnic background. The manager should be receptive to new ideas and be able to tolerate differences. Strength of personality is also of critical importance. The frustrations and uncertainty of foreign assignments will certainly test even the strongest personality. The manager must have a good self-image without being egotistical and will need to interact effectively with many different individuals. Intelligence is another key personality trait. No domestic assignment requires so much learning in so short a period of time. Since many individuals on foreign assignment feel lost and forgotten, it is critically important that the person be self-motivated and self-sustaining in the quest for success at the task.

Six types of skill are important in selecting an individual for success in a foreign assignment.

1. Knowledge of the job
2. Specific task performance abilities
3. Working knowledge of the language
4. Communication competencies
5. Interest in the job and foreign assignment
6. Opportunism

The expatriate employee must have a broad general knowledge base that is related to the assignment, as well as proven and task-specific abilities (experience and expertise). In other words, the individual must have already demonstrated that he or she can do that job well. Skills 3 and 4 above are communicative in character. A manager needs to speak the language and feel comfortable communicating with others. The last two of the desired skills are intangible. The good expatriate has demonstrated an ability to capitalize on the opportunity embodied in new job situations and looks forward to the foreign assignment.

Training the Expatriate

Training represents one of the most important determinants of the expatriate's success. This training should be provided not only for the employee who is going abroad but also for the entire family. In fact, training the spouse might be more important than training the employee. The employee will be going to a job that is in some ways similar to previous assignments, whereas the spouse will be immersed almost totally in the new culture. Such activities as interacting at the children's school, shopping, social interactions with neighbors, dealing with the telephone or postal system, and selecting and supervising domestic help often fall almost entirely on the spouse. It is, therefore, not surprising that one of the major reasons why expatriate managers request repatriation is the unhappiness of spouse and family.

Effective training programs usually consist of two phases: predeparture training and transition training after arrival in the host country. Predeparture training should focus on language, history, and culture for both the employee and family as well as job-specific training for the employee. Transition training should begin with an adaptation period followed by continuous training for several months after arrival. This adaptation period should provide at least two weeks to become accustomed to the new life. This enables both the employee and spouse to jointly learn about schools, hospitals and doctors, shopping, and the myriad of mundane things that one takes for granted at home. After this initial period, transition training should include continued language and culture training along with periodic support group meetings. These are often disguised as social get-togethers with other foreign nationals and local residents who have visited the expatriate's homeland.

The ideal is the development of complete cultural competency. This involves being able to function effectively in almost every social or professional situation. Unfortunately, many expatriates and their families never approach cultural competence. Being barely able to cope with the alien culture, they retreat into a form of psychological withdrawal. For example, a few years ago one of the authors visited an American professor on temporary assignment in Europe. The following account of the conversation will illustrate the problem of coping and the psychological withdrawal.

"Would you like a cup of coffee? We have some *real* American coffee."

"Yes, thank you. I thought that you were going to be housed elsewhere. How long have you been in this house?"

"Forever! No, actually only 3 months. It just seems like forever. But we get to go home in 6 months, 2 weeks, and 3 days."

"The university has really made some nice improvements in the house since we left."

"Perhaps, but the floors are cold and it is not even winter yet."

"You're lucky to be living here because you have great neighbors. They are some of the nicest people I've ever met."

"I guess we've been too busy. I haven't had a chance to meet them yet."

Facilitating and Supporting the Expatriate

There are many things the organization can do to help the expatriate achieve success. If the previous holder of that position created problems or a bad image, this fact should not be covered up. The local nationals will have a negative stereotype that could present problems for the expatriate. The details of organizational operations should be made to work for rather than against the expatriate. For example, issues of money, housing, deadlines, reporting relationships, and so forth should be taken care of before the expatriate begins working. Relatedly, the expatriate employee should be fully aware of the status symbols of that culture and the political dynamics of the foreign organization. Most managers are clever enough to determine who has power and who has influence in their own culture; however, that does not mean that they will be able to discern the same thing in the unfamiliar culture.

The multinational firm should be sensitive to the fact that the expatriate manager should get out of the host culture on a regular basis, perhaps once or twice a year. This will offset some of the more common problems experienced by both expatriate and home office management, especially the home-field dilemma. The individuals in the foreign culture begin to believe that those in the home office have forgotten them, do not care what happens "in the field," and do not understand what it is really like "out here." Additionally, it helps to have people from the home office visit foreign subsidiaries. It is not only good training for the domestic staff but also provides the expatriate with peer group contact. Expatriates often, and correctly, feel that they have no peers and no constituency. They are viewed not only as foreigners, but also as the representative of the foreign corporate headquarters.

Another aspect of the home-field dilemma is that expatriate managers often become convinced that they would be further ahead had they remained at home. Because they do not hear about job advancement opportunities, they become convinced that they are being passed by. The nature of foreign assignments, especially in less developed country operations, is that successes tend to be minimized at the home office because they are of minor significance from the perspective of the entire corporation. This creates a condition of invisible success and visible failure. Those from the home office who deal with the expatriate must be sufficiently knowledgeable about the subsidiary to truly understand the nature of successes and failures.

Finally, home office management must keep abreast of any sign of "burnout." The heightened levels of uncertainty, value conflict, job demands, and culture dissonance can translate into enormous stress and resultant early burnout.

Expatriates must be selected on the bases of attitude, personality traits, and job skills. Multinational enterprises then provide training and support for expatriates and their families.

Barriers to Performance in the Host Culture

Perhaps the greatest barriers to expatriate success are an ethnocentric attitude and a lack of cultural empathy. Believing that one's culture is always right or better, and being unable to internalize the new culture will impede many aspects of cross-cultural success.

Ethnocentrism

The expatriate working in a foreign country brings along cultural patterns of values, beliefs, and behaviors from his or her home culture. These are deeply rooted in the expatriate's successful past behavior and self-perception. It is easy to conclude that the new culture is bad, stupid, or ineffective merely because it is different. This form of evaluation is at the heart of ethnocentrism. Instead of looking at the new way of life in a receptive manner, the expatriate tries to impose this perspective on the ways of the local society and attempts to maintain familiar behavior patterns.

Relatedly, the ethnocentric person fails to understand that individuals from the new culture might interpret actions very differently from the way they would be interpreted in the home culture. For example, Americans see questioning and offering opinions as a sign of being open and friendly; in a different culture these might be viewed as being meddlesome and domineering. On the other hand, it is not uncommon for host nationals to refuse to accept changes that might be very beneficial. Ethnocentrism occurs on both sides and, when practiced indiscriminately, is always self-defeating.

A Lack of Cultural Empathy

Individuals develop a frame of reference from which they evaluate and interpret actions and events in the environment. When the environment is culturally consistent with the individual's conditioning, it provides a basis for accurate decision-making and individual behavior. However, when the cultural environment is new and different, the past reference system is no longer appropriate. Continuing to apply these standards, and not recognizing the necessity of a different set of standards and points of reference will normally result in misunderstanding, poor decisions, and inappropriate behaviors. One can never completely eliminate the dependence on one's past reference system, but every effort should be made to monitor and reassess the basis for one's actions. When this is continually done, the expatriate usually develops the ability to view things from the perspective of the host culture. This is called cultural empathy.

Insufficient Cultural Adaptability

Cultural adaptability is the ability to translate cultural empathy into new behaviors—that is, to think and behave in a manner consistent with the new culture. It involves acquiring a new set of habits and responses. Cultural adaptability is similar to learning a second language.

A good international businessperson develops a cultural sense of what is appropriate behavior and a tolerance that stems from the realization that all persons have biases and faults: No people are better or worse than others, just different. Furthermore, the good international manager finds the differences between cultures to be a challenge rather than a barrier. This ideal manager is also someone who has learned to keep stereotyping, prejudice, and discrimination out of the workplace and to approach each assignment with an open mind. In other words, a good international manager is culturally empathic and adaptable.

An expatriate assigned to another country must be sensitive, empathic, and adaptable to the new cultural environment.

ADAPTING BUSINESS SYSTEMS

Modifying Subsidiary Management to Fit the Culture

Key elements within the host cultural environment will directly and indirectly affect the international firm's local operations. These cultural variables must be analyzed and used as the basis for modifying the way a subsidiary is managed.

One of the best approaches to assessing which cultural components need to be utilized in adapting business systems is that developed by Farmer and Richman:[4]

Educational-Cultural Variables

Literacy level

Vocational/technical training and secondary education

Higher education

Management development programs

Attitudes toward education

Match between education and societal needs

Sociological-Cultural Variables

Attitudes toward management and managers

View of authority and subordinates

Interorganizational cooperation

Attitudes toward work and achievement

Class structure and individual mobility

Attitudes toward wealth and material gain

Attitudes toward the scientific method

Attitudes toward risk taking

Attitudes toward change

This model identifies a number of cultural elements (environmental constraints) that relate to the effectiveness of managerial processes. Farmer and Richman's educational and sociological variables represent key cultural elements that influence the basic functions of management: planning and innovation, controlling, organizing, staffing, directing, leadership and motivation, and policymaking for operations. They point out that as the cultural variables of an environment change, the systems of management must also be modified or adjusted. In other words, to be effective, management styles and methods must be viewed as contingent on the culture and must be regularly reassessed in light of cultural change. No one pattern or managerial policy can fit all situations.

Indeed, every aspect of management needs to be reconsidered in light of the particular culture within which the firm is operating. The Global Insight illustrates the degree to which American management is culture-bound and the nature of modifications that could be implemented. The traditional American way of rewarding an employee is for the manager to call that employee into a private office, tell the employee the nature of the reward, and remind the employee to keep it a secret. In a culture where social and peer recognition are more important than money, such a procedure would be ineffective and perhaps even offensive. Clearly in such a culture monetary rewards, promotions, and like matters should be handled publicly and perhaps even with an awards ceremony.

Consider the other extreme, the reprimand. In the United States it is not uncommon for that reprimand to be given publicly. Although this approach is not considered good management, it is common practice and seldom results in anything more significant than anger or profanities from the employee who was disciplined. In a culture where avoiding confrontation and saving face are very important, a public reprimand could result in the employee resigning or even committing suicide.

Consider a situation when a boss asks subordinates for their opinions. In the United States most subordinates will give their opinions, some publicly and others privately. However, there is no assurance of complete agreement. In many cultures where position-based power and authority are very strong and where respect for authority is almost complete, there might be complete agreement even if the employee feels the position is totally wrong.

Modifying Products, Services, and Messages

The modification of products, services, and packaging or advertising messages to fit the host environment is as important as modifying managerial methods. In the modification or redesign of products for cultural reasons, the two key issues that have to be addressed are form and function. Cultural perceptions and culturally determined usages will have an impact on both aspects. Although this topic is addressed in more detail in Chapter 14, "International Marketing Strategy," a brief discussion will serve to illustrate the importance of culture for marketing and product design.

First, consider the issue of perception. Quality, durability, and other characteristics are often impossible for a consumer to determine; nevertheless, the consumer must make a judgment. This judgment is often based on totally irrelevant matters of design or on culturally ingrained attitudes. For example, for many years European-manufactured consumer goods sold poorly in the United States because the products were made of plastic; comparable U.S. products were made of metal. In the United States, plastic

Culture Counts at Avon

Avon Products sees its global competitiveness riding on its ability to nurture diversity in its work force. To accomplish this, Avon has radically transformed its corporate culture.

This change has shifted Avon away from the traditional "melting pot" philosophy emphasizing conformity and homogeneity and toward a "mosaic" conceptualization. Marcia Worthing, Vice-President of Human Resources, describes the new Avon culture as akin to a flower bed.

In a flower bed different flowers require differing amounts of light, water, soil, fertilizer, and so forth. Avon wants to cultivate cultural differences so that differing points of view will be developed and then utilized in a synergistic way.

Source: Adapted from Pamela J. Sparr, "Avon Sees Cultural Diversity as Key to Its Competitiveness," *Business International*, June 6, 1988, pp. 169–171.

had the connotation of being cheap, breakable, and inferior. People were described as "plastic" if they were phoney and not dependable. As the American culture changed to accept plastics, these European products became acceptable. Similarly, the nationality of a product can have cultural connotations. In the late 1950s, the term "made in Japan" was interpreted by Americans as meaning poor quality. Comedians referred to a microphone that was not working with the phrase "must have been made in Japan." Today the opposite cultural connotation exists.

Since products encounter different uses or different problems in different cultures, the manufacturer might have to modify or completely redesign products. Traditional American cereal bowls do not sell well in France because French bowls have handles. This is because children are expected to pick up the bowl and drink whatever milk is left. These bowls are also used for *café au lait*, so the handles are necessary. American washcloths would not sell well in the Netherlands because a washcloth there is more like a mitt into which one's hand is inserted. This is purely a culturally based factor. American toasters would be impractical because few Europeans toast bread. Toy Santas would not sell well in most countries because the American Santa Claus does not look like the European version.

Related to these cultural issues are technological differences among countries and climatic differences. When combined with these, marketing and product design becomes significantly dependent upon factors of the host country.

The significance of culture is perhaps the dominant concern in advertising and packaging. Care must be taken not to offend while sending the intended connotative message. To use a female model wearing very bright makeup to sell cosmetics might be appropriate in Spain or Argentina, but would be counterproductive in Sweden or Switzerland. In these countries, that level and style of makeup would not create an image of beauty, but rather of prostitution. In the United States, dishwashers are sold with messages of saving labor and keeping one's hands out of hot water; in Switzerland these same dishwashers are sold emphasizing the sanitary nature of the wash cycle, which kills more germs. In the Swiss culture, cleanliness is more important than decreasing the time spent on household chores.

Culture often determines the method of packaging. The individual packages of food products for children's lunch boxes are in less demand in the Netherlands because nearly 80 percent of all mothers with school-age children do not work, so their children return home for lunch. Products like shaving cream and tomato paste are sold in relatively large quantities and packaged in cans in the United States, but are more often sold abroad in smaller quantities and packaged in tubes like those for toothpaste. Packages of individual portions of frozen foods are culturally inappropriate in societies where families are large and where they eat together as a family unit. Tamper-proof packaging was culturally irrelevant before terrorists and lunatics found that they could induce terror in a whole society by putting poisons into products.

If an MNC is to succeed abroad, it must often modify its managerial methods, its products, and advertising message to fit the culture.

UNDERSTANDING CULTURAL CHANGE

Cultural change represents an important reality in the modern world. Two hundred years ago, constancy was the norm and change the exception. Today, change is the norm and constancy the exception. The modern world is changing at an ever-increasing rate. The result is that management methods, advertising messages, product designs, and product packaging need to be constantly reassessed in light of the changing culture. The international manager must be aware of these changes.

Cultural change takes place by the alternation of the three basic forms of cultural rules: formal, informal, and technical.[5] Formal elements determine the essence of culture. They define what is right and wrong, and rules are rigidly taught and enforced. These formal rules often take the form of laws. For example, respecting an individual's right to privacy might be a formal cultural rule. Deviations from formal rules result in strict penalties. Informal rules are not taught but are learned through observation and imitation of the acts of others. There are no real penalties for the violation of informal rules. Bathing and using deodorant are informal cultural rules in the United States; if an individual violates this informal rule, there will be no real punishments but people will "keep their distance" literally as well as figuratively until that norm is adopted. Individuals within a culture must also be aware of technical rules. Technical rules are the basis for binding agreements between parties. In the United States, these agreements generally take the form of written contracts, usually following negotiations. In other cultures, negotiations may follow the signing of a contract. In some societies, agreements are made orally. Insistence on written contracts may be interpreted as a reflection on the honor of the individual.

Resistance to change varies in each of these three categories. Formal rules are held onto very strongly and are resistant to forces of change. Informal rules are more easily changed. The key to cultural change is at the informal level. Here, imitation of behaviors and attitudes may be tried and rejected until those that best suit the environment are adopted and developed into technical rules.

Social Dynamics of Change

Besides identifying the cultural elements that resist change, the international manager must also identify the roles that individuals play in the process of cultural change. In any culture some individuals lead the way in accepting cultural change. It is important that the manager be able to identify and to utilize these groups when introducing both new products and new business methods.

Innovators	First 5 percent
Early adopters	Next 20 percent
Early majority	Next 50 percent
Late majority	Next 20 percent
Laggards	Last 5 percent

Innovators regard themselves as deviants from their cultures. They have generally seen more of other cultures and usually have international backgrounds. Early adopters rate high as opinion leaders, and often have influence on later adopters. They also have a higher position in the social hierarchy than innovators. The early majority seems to deliberate more than the other groups. They do not adopt change until other respected groups, such as early adopters, have done so. The late majority are highly skeptical of change and wait until opinion is definitely in favor of the change before they will sanction it. Laggards are very traditional and suspicious of change. They tend to be older and use the past as a point of reference.

There is also a five-stage process that an individual goes through, from first hearing of change to adoption:

1. Awareness
2. Interest
3. Evaluation
4. Trial
5. Adoption

Nonlocal, impersonal sources of information are more important in the earlier process stages, while local, more personal sources are dominant in the later stages. All of this has a great bearing on the international business firm that is introducing a new product within the cultural environment. It must be aware of the most effective time to push the product during the adoption process, and which adoption groups will be most likely to receive it.

Promoting Cultural Change

In selecting a management system for a foreign subsidiary, the international firm adapts to the local culture but generally does not fully adopt that culture's way of doing things. In fact, a great deal of time, effort, and money are expended to promote cultural change among the host national managers and other employees for the implementation of the corporation's way of running its business. If this cultural change is successful, the result is an effective and efficient hybrid of the parent corporate culture and the host national culture. If the union does not go as planned, the result is continuing problems and poor performance.

Certain guidelines and steps can be taken to pave the way for smoother cultural transition:

1. Make sure that the changes do not openly conflict with traditional values or practices; instead, try to build upon them.
2. Take advantage of effective timing by introducing change when there is a need for it.
3. Offer incentives that increase individual motivation and reward behavioral changes.
4. Protect employees from possible economic or status loss from those changes.
5. Increase the flow of communications between those of differing cultural environments.

Cultural change is a very slow process because beliefs, attitudes, knowledge, morals, and other matters have been well established over time.

SUMMARY

Differences in culture are observable in the behavior of different peoples and are reflected in their laws, customs, arts, and other expressive or materialistic things. These develop into distinct patterns as they are passed from generation to generation, and differ from those of other countries. If they are shared by the majority of the inhabitants in a country and become norms of that society, they are referred to as national culture. However, even within a country that is relatively homogeneous, there often exist subcultures with their own unique characteristics.

The large number of organizations in modern society have given rise to organizational culture, with its common pattern of behavior, customs, laws, beliefs, and other characteristics. The organizational culture of a multinational enterprise will influence and be influenced by the cultures in which the firm operates. The greatest influence is generally that of the home country. Cultural differences can result in conflict between the organization and the host country.

Cultural problems that are encountered in the foreign operations of a multinational corporation usually arise because the expatriate manager is thoroughly ingrained with the home cultural values and is unwilling or unable to make the necessary cultural adjustments.

Understanding the history of a country provides insight into the development of a nation's culture. The economic and political concept of the importance of the individual in the United States has created a culture that stresses individualism over the good of the group. Furthermore, the relative geographic isolation of the United States has created an indifference to other countries and an attitude of isolationism in international affairs.

Cultural differences are evident among different countries regarding the concept of time, the individual's influence over future events, attitude toward wealth and rewards, decision-making, bribery, language, and religion and superstitions.

Great differences are evident in interpersonal relations among different cultures. A successful operation requires the expatriate to be familiar with differences among countries regarding the role of the family, decision-making, views toward authority, and personal criticism.

The social structure varies from country to country. The lack of interclass mobility and differing status of groups present substantial ethical as well as managerial problems for expatriate managers, and to a great extent inhibit economic development for the nation itself.

Chances of success for both the expatriate and the multinational firm will be greater if the corporation selects an individual who is understanding, empathic, and adaptable to the foreign culture. Other desirable qualities are minimum prejudices, self-confidence, intelligence, and the necessary job skills. Once the individual has been selected, training is an important aspect of foreign assignment. This should include predeparture training in the language, history, and culture of the country for both the expatriate and the family. This should be followed by transition training in the host country to facilitate the acculturation of both the individual and the family. The firm should also make every effort to support the expatriate to prevent the home-field dilemma. However, there are obstacles to successful performance in the host country, perhaps the most serious of which is the ethnocentrism found in every individual.

KEY TERMS AND CONCEPTS

Acculturation

Culture

Empathy

Ethnocentrism

Expatriate

Fatalism

National culture

Nepotism

Norms

Organizational culture

Patriarch

Subculture

REVIEW QUESTIONS

1. What is meant by national culture? How does it differ from organizational culture?

2. Why are cultural sensitivity and empathy so important for an expatriate employee of a multinational corporation?

3. Explain the meaning of ethnocentrism as it applies to the culture of different countries.

4. What is meant by behavioral adaptability?

5. Are you aware of any cultural differences between yourself and a foreign friend who is studying in your country? Have these created any problems?

6. Why might long-range planning be ineffective in some countries? Explain.

7. How should expatriates handle conflict resulting from a cultural difference if it is contrary to their own beliefs?

8. What are the advantages and disadvantages of nepotism in the workplace?

9. Are there any barriers to interclass mobility in employment in the Western world? Explain.

10. What factors should be considered in assessing the cultural environment for the benefit of the multinational corporation?

11. Is it accurate to state that the cultural environments of countries change little over time? Why?

12. Should an expatriate employee of a multinational corporation recommend changes in the hiring practices or in adapting an inefficient method of employment? Explain.

DISCUSSION CASE

Is Cultural Competitiveness the Key to Success at Avon?

The Hudson Institute states that the United States is in the midst of a profound shift in its labor force. In 1985, 47 percent of the work force consisted of white males; they will constitute only 15 percent of the new entrants between 1985 and 2000. Firms must deal with the changing gender, racial, and ethnic mix of employees at all levels. This may be especially

Source: Adapted from Pamela J. Sparr, "Avon Sees Cultural Diversity as Key to Its Competitiveness," *Business International*, June 6, 1988, pp. 169–171.

hard for non-U.S. investors unused to managing a heterogeneous pool of workers and executives.

In 1983, Avon had one eye on these statistics and the other on its affirmative action problems. At that point, Avon executives began to alter their corporate culture. This began with the Beauty Group, which is responsible for about 90 percent of Avon's $2.5 billion earnings. The group had been successful at hiring women and minorities in the United States (73 percent of U.S. employees are female and more than 15 percent are minority), yet it had problems retaining and promoting them into upper management. Avon suffered from high turnover and "plateauing"—employees reaching their level of maximum competency. As a result, employee and management frustrations were developing. These were diagnosed as a "cultural blockage." Stated simply, either management was not recognizing the managerial potential of women and minorities because of cultural differences, or the organization was not structured and managed in a manner conducive to developing women and minorities to their ultimate potential.

Dr. Roosevelt Thomas, executive director of the American Institute for Managing Diversity and an Avon consultant, explained that Avon and most firms take an affirmative-action viewpoint. This begins with the premise that some group has a condition that gets in its way for particpating in the organization. The assumption is that the group has to be "fixed." This focus puts the burden on people who are different, and ignores such issues as culture and organizational structure. Furthermore, this approach tends to view cultural diversity as a problem rather than an opportunity, and is driven by legal, moral, or social responsibility concerns. Thomas got Avon to stop thinking that individuals or groups needed to be "fixed" and to see the strategic need for changing Avon's corporate culture. He convinced them that synergistic gain could come from the firm's pluralistic work force. Interestingly, this got Avon's executives to stop thinking in moral and ethical terms and back to viewing economic gains from cultural diversity, says Marcia Worthing, VP of Human Resources. Avon's ability to relate to women and minorities as workers, managers, and consumers is viewed as vital to its success. As a company that has women selling women's products to other women, it needed to view the women within its organization as a great strategic asset.

Avon's Approach

Worthing stated that companies in the United States traditionally have been melting pots that stressed employee conformity and homogeneity; Avon now is building a "mosaic" culture wherein staff "look for and value differences." She says Avon is moving from an "equal opportunity" approach to one of "equitable opportunity." Avon is moving toward being less of a melting pot and more of a "flower bed," where differences are cultivated and where the individuality of each part creates the wonder of the whole. Avon wants to foster different points of view, to have employees go beyond tolerance to placing equal value on different cultural backgrounds and creating a synergy of differences.

In the developing Avon culture the good manager is also a sociologist, says Daisy Chin-Lor, former director of the Multicultural Planning and Design Department, and now an international area director. "You need to be curious about the diversity you are faced with, but you don't have to be an expert. You will get work done if you know the people. . . . It may take longer in the planning and the process, but in the end, expectations are clearer, there is more diversity, . . . a broader range of solutions, answers to problems."

Avon implemented this new culture with several educational efforts and structural reforms:

1. A new department (Multicultural Planning and Design) was created and given responsibility for education and the coordination of the cultural change. Ideally, it will soon become obsolete.

2. Multiculturalism became an element in Avon's strategic plan, making it a business rather than human-resource issue. This may have been the most important change. Multiculturalism also became a leadership requirement. Strategic planners and managers in each department must develop multicultural objectives, which cover how they are going to lead the effort, specific development plans for employees, recruitment, and training issues. Accountability is built into the system, and every executive's compensation is tied to the ability to manage diversity.

3. Multicultural councils were formed at each corporate layer, and each meets monthly to discuss issues and make recommendations to senior management.

4. Strong, management-sanctioned employee "networks" were created for black, Hispanic, and Asian employees to bring issues to management, serve as a support system, and practice leadership skills.

5. Avon's existing and prospective leaders undergo awareness training. Executives from the president of the Beauty Group on down participate in workshops designed to reexamine and change negative attitudes about people they see as different. Avon is seeking to change not only behaviors but attitudes, or at least learn how to manage them. Teams of managers are sent once a year to a special three-week "managing diversity" program at Morehouse College in Atlanta.

Efforts to foster multiculturalism are beginning to have an impact. So far, the new approach has altered how Avon's meetings are conducted. For example, through their network, Asian employees raised questions about Avon's cultural norms, which value strong presentation skills and employees speaking at meetings. Worthing says that this works against Asians, who sometimes hold back in public situations. "Now, managers are conscious of this and conduct meetings appropriately." There has also been an effect on Avon's advertising. People in marketing now choose diverse models for a brochure in order to be more reflective of Avon's customers.

Multiculturalism Goes Global

Avon feels it can be a better global competitor by leveraging its international experience back into its operations and transferring its U.S. multicultural learning abroad. Avon's experiment with multiculturalism in the United States recognizes that diversity extends beyond issues of race and gender. In global operations Avon has focused on moving women into overseas management positions. Avon probably has the largest number of women executives of any firm in Japan.

Questions

1. Do you see any weakness in Avon's plan to nurture diversity? What are its strengths?

2. What are the prospects of this system being adopted by other firms? Why?

3. Would this system work in the Middle East, where women are often excluded from the workplace?

4. Discuss the various conditions that might facilitate implementation of the Avon plan.

NOTES

1. Following custom, the term *American* is used throughout to designate people from the United States.

2. Rose Knotts, "Cross-Cultural Management: Transformations and Adaptations," *Business Horizons*, January-February, 1989, p. 31.

3. Ibid., p. 32.

4. Richard N. Farmer and Barry M. Richman, *Comparative Management and Economic Progress* (Homewood, Ill.: Richard D. Irwin, 1965), p. 29.

5. Edward T. Hall, *The Silent Language* (Greenwich, Conn.: Fawcett, 1959).

REFERENCES AND SELECTED READINGS

Adler, Nancy J. "A Typology of Management Studies Involving Culture." *The Journal of International Business Studies* 14:2 (Fall 1983).

Brooke, Michael Z., and H. L. Remmers. *International Management and Business Policy*. Boston: Houghton Mifflin Company, 1978.

England, George W., and Itzhak Harpaz. "Some Methodological and Analytic Considerations in Cross-National Comparative Research." *The Journal of International Business Studies* 14:2 (Fall 1983).

Farmer, Richard N., and Barry M. Richman. *Comparative Management and Economic Progress*. Homewood, Ill.: Richard D. Irwin, 1965.

Farmer, Richard N., and Barry M. Richman. *International Business*. Homewood, Ill.: Richard D. Irwin, 1984.

Gladwin, Thomas N., and I. Walter. *Multinationals Under Fire*. New York: Wiley, 1980.

Graham, John L. "The Influence of Culture on Business Negotiations." *The Journal of International Business Studies* 16:1 (Spring 1985).

Hall, Edward T. *The Silent Language.* Greenwich, Conn.: Fawcett, 1959.

Haner, F. T. *Global Business Strategies for the 80's.* New York: Praeger Special Studies, 1980.

Hofstede, Geert. "The Cultural Relativity of Organizational Practices and Theories." *The Journal of International Business Studies* 14:2 (Fall 1983).

Knotts, Rose. "Cross-Cultural Management: Transformations and Adaptations." *Business Horizons,* January-February, 1989.

Phatek, Arvind V. *International Dimensions of Management.* Belmont, Calif.: Wadsworth, 1983.

Radebaugh, Lee H., and Janice C. Shields. "A Note on Foreign Language Training and International Business Education in U.S. Colleges and Universities." *The Journal of International Business Studies* 15:3 (Winter 1984).

Ronen, Simcha. *Comparative and Multinational Management.* New York: Wiley, 1986.

Schiffman, Leon G., William R. Billon, and Festus E. Ngumah. "The Influence of Subcultural and Personality Factors on Consumer Acculturation." *The Journal of International Business Studies* 12:2 (Fall 1981).

Sekaran, Uma. "Methodological and Theoretical Issues and Advancements in Cross-Cultural Research." *The Journal of International Business Studies* 14:2 (Fall 1983).

PART FOUR

Functions of International and Multinational Firms

Some firms become involved in international business as a part of a strategically planned entry. Other firms merely pursue what appear to be domestic sales opportunities and evolve almost unintentionally into international firms. Regardless of the path to internationalization, the firm will eventually have to adapt to the demands of the international business environment by developing new strategies and new organizational structures to facilitate these strategies. Chapter 12, "Strategies and Structures of International Firms," deals with the strategies of international firms and the various organizational structures to assist in implementing these strategies.

Once these new strategies and structures have been implemented, the firm has to initiate operations and develop functional strategies: "Modes of Entry and Forms of Involvement for Exploiting International Business Opportunities" (Chapter 13), "International Marketing Strategy" (Chapter 14), "Exporting, Importing, and Financing International Trade" (Chapter 15), "Transportation and Logistics Management" (Chapter 16), "International Financial Management" (Chapter 17), "International Supply Strategies: Production and Sourcing" (Chapter 18), "Human Resource Management" (Chapter 19), and "International Accounting and Taxation of Foreign Source Income" (Chapter 20).

12 Strategies and Structures of International Firms

LEARNING OBJECTIVES

- Learn the meaning of strategy and the stages of strategy formulation

- Become familiar with the various levels of strategies within international firms and their subsidiaries

- Understand the models or constructs that are available for assessing the strategic situation of a firm and for formulating strategies

- Understand the types of strategy a firm may adopt for its international operations and the rationale for each

- Become familiar with the major international business structures: international division, international headquarters company, and world company (functional, regional, product, and matrix)

INTRODUCTION

This chapter addresses the strategies used by international firms and focuses on corporate-level as well as division- or subsidiary-level strategies.

International strategy formulation requires that the firm deal not only with the traditional strategic considerations of market, technology, and competition but also with the realities of national sovereignty and international political relations. Indeed, no other corporate activity is so fraught with the potential for conflict between the firm and the nation. Firms want to develop strategies and allocate resources in a globally rational way to maximize long-term corporate profits, while nations want a maximal contribution to their development and prosperity. The result can be win-win cooperation or intense conflict. To minimize conflicts that could threaten successful operations, international firms must develop strategies that are flexible enough to adapt to diverse country environments.

In international as in domestic business, the appropriate strategy for a firm is largely determined by the environment in which the firm must compete. The appropriate structure for the firm is determined by the strategy the firm adopts. If a firm's structure is inappropriate, the firm will be less successful in implementing its strategy. In fact, in highly competitive industries the difference between success and failure may be the fit between strategy and structure.

$$\text{Environment} \longrightarrow \text{Strategy} \longrightarrow \text{Structure}$$

In the broadest sense, the selection of a structure is a choice between centralized control and foreign operations' responsiveness. Decentralized structures enhance the firm's ability to recognize and adapt to changes in the local environments but make coordination and control among foreign operations by the home office much more difficult. Centralized structures minimize control and coordination problems but constrain the ability of local operations to react quickly to market factors.

Despite the complexities and uncertainties associated with selecting an international structure, there are still general guidelines that a firm can follow for determining the appropriateness of its current structure and for making the needed changes or developing hybrid forms of organizational structure.

STRATEGIES FOR INTERNATIONAL FIRMS

Strategy in international firms involves two phases: (1) the formulation and implementation of a strategic plan and (2) the allocation of capital necessary to execute the selected strategy.

Strategic planning defines objectives, resource availability, and policies and specific actions toward meeting those objectives. It is critically important that the strategies of the international firm be sufficiently flexible to allow for differences among national environments and to ensure responsiveness to competitor actions. It is also important that management seek to develop employee commitment to these strategies by involving all affected levels of the organization in the development of their respective plans.[1]

The second major activity of corporate strategy is the allocation of investment capital. This process is also driven by corporate goals and objectives. Once capital is allocated, strategic plans often have to be revised. Divisions or subsidiaries generally develop their strategic plans on the basis of a presumed level of capital support. These preliminary plans are usually based on the capital requested or some percentage of that amount determined from historical differences between the amount of capital requested and that actually allocated. After capital is officially allocated, operating units have to revise their preliminary plans and performance forecasts to reflect the actual capital available. Thus, the process of arriving at a final strategic plan is iterative.

It is essentially impossible to separate strategic planning from international capital budgeting and capital allocation. Figure 12.1 illustrates the interactive and interdependent nature of these two important activities. A

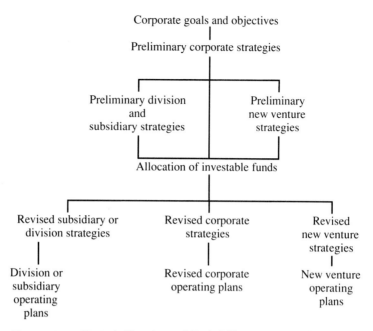

Figure 12.1   Strategic Planning and Capital Allocation in the International Firm
Source: Adapted from William A. Dymsza, *Multinational Business Strategy* (New York: McGraw-Hill, 1972), p. 190.

further discussion of capital budgeting and capital allocation processes is presented in Chapter 17, "International Financial Management."

Stages of Strategy Formulation

At the level of the parent corporation or a diversified subsidiary, strategy begins by determining the markets in which the firm will compete. This process starts with a detailed assessment of the firm's current strategic situation.

Strategic Assessment and Situational Analysis

Strategic assessment involves analyzing a firm's strengths and weaknesses, environmental threats and opportunities, position relative to key competitors, and product position in current markets.

Strengths and Weaknesses Analysis   A firm can assess its strengths and weaknesses in either an informal or formal manner. Whichever method is used, it is critically important that management be candid with themselves and avoid the tendency of some managers to "shoot" the person who brings the bad news.

A common formalized method is the development of an internal factor evaluation matrix (IFE). This tool summarizes and evaluates the major strengths and weaknesses of the firm in key functional areas, assigns a weight to each based on its relative importance for success, and then rates the firm on each. A weighted score of under 2.5 indicates that weaknesses exceed strengths.[2] See Table 12.1.

For the multinational firm this type of analysis may be necessary at both the total corporation level and the subsidiary or division level.

Threats and Opportunities Analysis   Threats and opportunities analysis is similar to strengths and weaknesses analysis in that the firm's assessment can be either informal or formal, and must avoid self-deception.

One common formalized method is the external factor evaluation matrix (EFE). This tool summarizes and evaluates the threats and opportunities of the firm in key functional areas, assigns a success weight to each, and then rates the firm on each. A weighted score under 2.5 indicates that threats exceed opportunities.[3] See Table 12.2.

As with strength and weakness analyses, it is important that the multinational firm conduct these analyses on both the total corporation and the subsidiary or division levels.

Competitor Analysis   Accurately knowing one's competition may be the most important component of the firm's situational analysis. Firms that underestimate their competitors usually pay a very high price. For example, in the late 1960s and early 1970s the American auto industry clearly underestimated foreign competition, and it is still paying for that mistake.

An analysis of the firm's situation is also critically dependent on a valid comparison with its most important competitors. This, too, can be done in a formalized or informalized manner. One method for analyzing competition is the Competitive Profile Matrix.[4]

Table 12.3 represents a situation in which the sample company is

Table 12.1   **Internal Factor Evaluation Matrix—Example for European Subsidiary**

Key internal factor	Weight	Rating*	Weighted score
R&D productivity—low	0.15	1	0.15
Customer service—good	0.20	3	0.60
Production cost control—excellent	0.10	3	0.30
Product quality—variable	0.30	1	0.30
Distribution system—poor	0.10	1	0.10
Financial condition—strong	0.15	4	0.60
Total	1.00		2.05

*Rating: 1 = major weakness, 2 = minor weakness, 3 = minor strength, 4 = major strength

Source: Adapted from Fred R. David, *Strategic Management*, 2nd ed. (Columbus, Ohio: Merrill Publishing Company, 1989), p. 150.

Table 12.2   **External Factor Evaluation Matrix—Example for European Subsidiary**

Key external factor	Weight	Rating*	Weighted score
Major competitors lack production inside the EEC	0.35	4	1.40
Economic reform in Eastern Europe	0.20	3	0.60
Increasing mobility of labor within EEC	0.10	3	0.30
Expected barriers to exports to North America	0.15	1	0.15
Technological changes	0.10	2	0.20
Increased Japanese investment	0.10	1	0.10
Total	1.00		2.75

*Rating: 1 = major threat, 2 = minor threat, 3 = minor opportunity, 4 = major opportunity

Source: Adapted from Fred R. David, *Strategic Management*, 2nd ed. (Columbus, Ohio: Merrill Publishing Company, 1989), p. 150.

approximately equal to Competitor 2 although they have different strengths and weaknesses, but at a substantial disadvantage to Competitor 1.

To the extent that a firm's competitive position varies across industries or countries (markets) such comparisons will need to be conducted many times.

Product-Market Position Analysis   Various models can be used to aid in this assessment. Perhaps the best known of these is the Boston Consulting Group (BCG) Business Portfolio Matrix. This matrix allows the firm to position its existing businesses in terms of the firm's competitive position and the growth rate of each market. Figure 12.2 presents a modified version of the BCG matrix.[5]

Table 12.3   **Competitive Profile Matrix—Example for European Subsidiary**

Key success factor	Weight	Sample Company		Competitor 1		Competitor 2	
		Rating*	Weighted score	Rating*	Weighted score	Rating*	Weighted score
Market share	0.25	1	0.25	4	1.00	2	0.50
Price competitiveness	0.20	2	0.40	4	0.80	3	0.60
Brand recognition	0.10	3	0.30	3	0.30	2	0.20
Product quality	0.20	4	0.80	1	0.20	4	0.80
Distribution system	0.10	1	0.10	4	0.40	2	0.20
Financial condition	0.15	4	0.60	3	0.45	1	0.15
Total	1.00		2.45		3.15		2.45

*Rating: 1 = major weakness, 2 = minor weakness, 3 = minor strength, 4 = major strength

Source: Adapted from Fred R. David, *Strategic Management*, 2nd ed. (Columbus, Ohio: Merrill Publishing Company, 1989), p. 150.

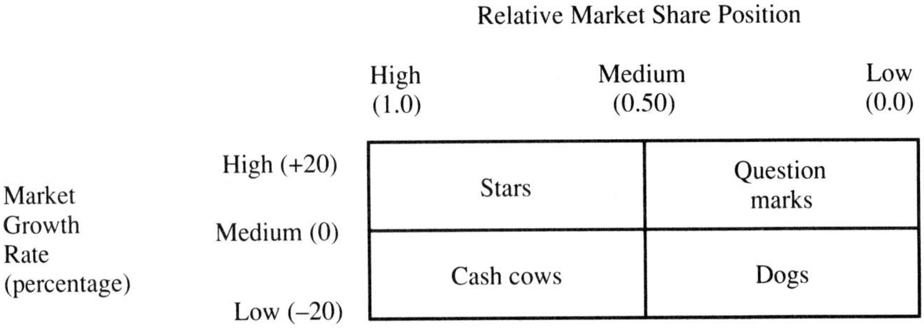

Relative Market Share Position

		High (1.0)	Medium (0.50)	Low (0.0)
Market Growth Rate (percentage)	High (+20)	Stars		Question marks
	Medium (0)			
		Cash cows		Dogs
	Low (−20)			

Figure 12.2   BCG Business Portfolio Matrix

This matrix shows the rate of growth of markets within which the firm competes and the firm's market share in comparison to that of the dominant firm. For example, 0.50 on the horizontal axis means that the firm's market share is half (50 percent) that of the market leader.

As with the preceding assessment methods, a multinational firm generally has to evaluate product-market positions for each industry and market in which it has operations. Consider, for example, the relatively simple products produced by the glass container division of Owens-Illinois. The division produces glass packaging including such common products as bottles for beer, wine, and soft drinks; jars for food products; and so forth. While the market growth rates for such products may be slow in the United States or the EEC, it may be increasing rapidly in a newly industrialized or developing country. Similarly, Owens-Illinois's position may be very different from one country or market to another. Thus, Owens-Illinois's BCG position may be that of a cash cow in the United States but a dog in the EEC. Similarly, the BCG position could be that of a star in Brazil and a question mark in Korea.

The first step of strategy formulation is an in-depth analysis of the firm itself, its markets, and its competitors.

Models for Determining Strategic Thrust

Once the strategic situation of the firm at all levels has been analyzed, management must turn its attention to the process of formulating a strategic direction for the medium and long term, usually three to seven years. This definition of strategic direction is the planned development of a match between corporate competencies and the environmental situation. This matching and the corresponding corporate strategic direction are determined by four key decisions.

Product or Service—What product(s) or service(s) will the firm sell?

Market—What market (usage or geographic) will the firm serve?

Customers—What specific group of customers within that market will the firm serve?

Technology—Is the technology employed in the proposed activity related to the technology with which the firm is familiar?

This strategic direction or thrust can take any one of three basic directions: growth, no-growth, or contraction.

Growth Strategies   The growth strategies of a firm seek to expand the firm's operations in sales, profits, and assets. The variety of growth strategies is determined by the firm's decisions on the four aforementioned variables. These are presented in Figures 12.3 and 12.4.[6]

No-Growth And Contraction Strategies   There are two related forms of no-growth strategy: redeployment, and redeployment with concentration. *Redeployment* involves selling existing assets while purchasing and deploying assets in a different area such that the total assets of the firm remains essentially constant. The strategy of *redeployment with concentration* also involves redeploying existing assets but in a manner that makes one existing business unit a greater percentage of total corporate assets without increasing the total assets of the firm.

There are three contraction strategies: retrenchment, divestiture, and liquidation. *Retrenchment* involves reducing the existing asset base and regrouping operations to reduce costs and reverse a sales or profit decline. A firm can retrench but keep the same breadth of operations, or retrench to service fewer product market segments (*retrenchment to a niche*).

Divestiture is similar to retrenchment except whole sections of the organization (divisions or subsidiaries) are sold instead of individual assets. *Liquidation* consists of selling all of the company's assets for the market value and ceasing to be a going concern.[7]

A few examples may make these strategies of no-growth and contraction clearer. Consider a firm with three product divisions: consumer electronics, publishing, and commercial real estate development. If that firm decides to sell its real estate development division and purchase a chain of nursing homes, it would be practicing redeployment but not concentration. If the firm sells the real estate development division and uses the funds to expand either its publishing or consumer electronics divisions, then the firm would be practicing redeployment with concentration. If the firm sells assets from

Figure 12.3   Growth Strategies: Expansion and Diversification
Source: Adapted from H. Ausoff, *Corporate Strategy: An Analytic Approach to Business Policy for Growth and Expansion* (New York: McGraw-Hill, 1965), p. 132.

Products or Services

Markets Served	Same	Different
Same	Market penetration	Product development
Different (usage or geographic)	Market development	Diversification

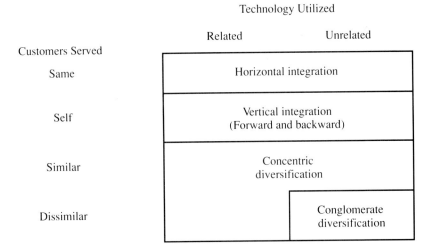

Figure 12.4   Diversification Growth Strategies
Source: Adapted from H. Ausoff, *Corporate Strategy: An Analytic Approach to Business Policy for Growth and Expansion* (New York: McGraw-Hill, 1965), p. 132.

its publishing division in an effort to reduce its losses but continues as a full-line publisher, it would be practicing retrenchment. If, however, the firm sells assets from its publishing division, focuses all future publishing activities on the textbook market, and gets out of the self-help trade book market, it would be practicing retrenchment to a niche. If the firm sells the real estate development division and uses the cash to retire debt, buy back its own stock, or simply increase its liquidity, it would be practicing a strategy of divestiture. Finally, if the firm were to sell all three of its divisions and cease operations, this would be the strategy of liquidation.

Firms can adopt three basic types of strategies: growth, no-growth, and contraction.

Portfolio Logic   The BCG matrix presented earlier can be used prescriptively. Many firms believe that they should manage their business as they do components of a portfolio, and that they should have businesses in all quadrants of the BCG matrix. This means balancing cash cows and dogs, which supply the funds to keep stars growing with their markets, and allowing question marks to grow faster than their markets so that they can become stars. As star product markets mature into slower growth, the previous stars become cash cows and the firm's dogs can be phased out.

At risk of being overly simplistic, here is the rather solid logic behind this portfolio thinking. Cash cows and dogs have better cash throw-off characteristics than either stars or question marks. Thus, they provide excellent internal sources of funds that are not substantially affected by market interest rates. Although stars and question marks tend to have weaker cash flow characteristics, they generally have higher profitability rates (return on equity, return on assets, or return on sales). A firm with all cash cows and dogs would have plenty of cash but poor profitability figures, while a firm with all stars and question marks would have great profitability but poor cash flow characteristics. Positioning all of the firm's businesses on a BCG matrix provides strategic direction for the corporation.

The BCG matrix is particularly useful for the international firm since an industry with slow growth in the United States could show rapid growth in Brazil. Stated somewhat differently, a product market that may be mature in the United States or any other developed country might be in a growth stage in a less developed country. Making an investment abroad in the area of a firm's greatest expertise could create a star to offset a domestic cash cow. This would provide the firm with the same leveling of cash streams as would domestic diversification. Thus, using the Owens-Illinois example previously cited, to level business cycle-induced variations in cash flows, the firm would have to select between developing a new domestic product market (diversification) or taking its primary product line abroad (international market development). There might actually be less total risk for the firm by investing abroad because the international investment would involve known technologies, an existing product, and brand identification.

Since countries have very different levels of market development and growth rates, a firm could actually develop a balance of stars, question marks, cash cows, and dogs by merely taking its existing product line into a variety of different countries.

Some firms that utilize portfolio logic for the management of international product markets use the Product Life Cycle (PLC) instead of the BCG matrix. The logic is essentially the same. The PLC was presented in detail in Chapter 2.[8]

Generic Strategies

A combination of the alternatives presented previously created a catalog of generic strategies (see Table 12.4).

Levels of Strategy

All but the smallest firms have various levels and types of strategies. Even purely domestic firms, except those supplying only one product to one market, have corporate- and business-level strategies. Multidivisional firms usually have both corporate- and business-level strategies (see Figure 12.5).

Domestic Multidivisional Firms

Corporate-level strategies define the businesses (industries) in which the firm will participate. Business-level strategy answers the question of how to compete more effectively in an industry. However, as the number and diversity of industries in which a firm competes increases, it becomes increasingly difficult to maintain control and coordination. In this situation similar businesses are grouped into strategic business units (SBUs) and strategies are developed for each.

Table 12.4   **Generic Corporate Strategies**

Types of strategy	Definition
Expansion strategies	
Market penetration	Increasing market share for current products (services) in existing markets
Market development	Introducing existing products or services into new geographic or new usage markets
Product development	Introducing new or modified products (services) into existing markets
Diversification strategies	
Horizontal	Supplying existing customers with new products (services) that put the firm in a new market
Vertical (forward)	Gaining ownership or control over elements of the distribution channel
Vertical (backward)	Gaining ownership or control over elements of the supply chain
Concentric	Entering into businesses that involve not only supplying new products (services) to new markets but also new technologies and/or new customers
Conglomerate	Entering into businesses that involve supplying new products (services) in new markets utilizing new technologies and new customers
No-growth or contraction strategies	
Redeployment	Selling existing assets while deploying new assets in a different area such that the total assets of the firm remain essentially constant
Concentration	Redeploying existing assets but in a manner that makes one existing business unit a greater percentage of total corporate assets
Retrenchment	Reducing existing asset bases and regrouping operations to reduce costs and to reverse declining sales and profits
Divestiture	Selling whole pieces of the organization such as divisions or subsidiaries
Liquidation	Selling all of the company's assets for the market value and ceasing to be a going concern

Source: Adapted from Fred R. David, *Strategic Management*, 2nd ed. (Columbus, Ohio: Merrill Publishing Company, 1989), p. 66.

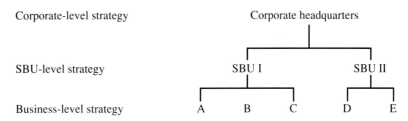

Figure 12.5   Levels of Strategy in a Domestic Firm

Domestic Firms with International Divisions

Internationally oriented corporations have related but somewhat more complex tasks in formulating strategy. Indeed, several different layers of strategy need to be developed. A firm that is predominantly domestic in focus but still has substantial international business activity will probably use an international division structure and will develop the following levels of strategy: (1) corporate; (2) domestic SBU; (3) domestic business level; (4) international division and, if appropriate, international SBU; and (5) international subsidiary business (see Figure 12.6).

Multinational Firms: Multidomestic and Global Industries

For multinational firms there are also several levels of strategy to be formulated and implemented; however, these vary with the nature of the industry within which the firm competes:

1. Corporate-level strategies
2. Global industry- or regional-level strategies
3. Subsidiary-level corporate strategies
4. Subsidiary business-level strategies

First, the firm decides which goods or services it wishes to supply and the nature of these industries: global or multidomestic. Global industries

Figure 12.6   Levels of Strategy in a Domestic Firm with International Operations

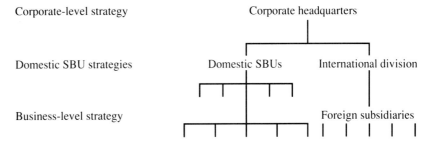

require developing global industry strategies; multidomestic industries require choosing countries of operation and developing regional as well as subsidiary (country) strategies. At the subsidiary level, there are two types of strategy: those that determine the local businesses in which the firm will be involved, and standard business-level strategies that define how the subsidiary will achieve competitiveness in each business.

Multidomestic Industries   In some industries, competitive success or failure is determined on a country-by-country basis. Firms in these types of industries are called *multidomestics* because they follow strategies that allow subsidiaries to function as quasi-independent, market-oriented profit centers. Each subsidiary is given considerable autonomy from the parent corporation to produce products that are customized to meet local preferences. As a result, multinational firms in these industries compete on a market-by-market basis. These firms may experience a one-time competitive advantage from the transfer of know-how but they do not gain continuing advantage from operations in other countries. This strategy means that subsidiaries are often high-cost producers with low levels of scale economies and are, therefore, vulnerable to price competition from firms that use a more standardized approach to world markets. Retailing, distribution, and insurance represent multidomestic industries.[9]

As a result of the emphasis on regionalization by multidomestic firms, strategic plans tend to stress subsidiary and regional plans. The corporate plans are more of an aggregation of these with rationalization of the financial aspects of the strategy (see Figure 12.7).

Global Industries   In *global industries*, firms compete on a worldwide basis. The strategy of the global firm is to maintain centralized management and control, and to pit its worldwide resources against competitors everywhere in the world. The global firm rationalizes its interdependencies, maximizes economies of scale in all aspects of its operation, and subsidizes parts of the corporation to enhance its worldwide competitive position. While a multidomestic corporation may set standard financial objectives for its subsidiaries, the global firm will use objectives that more directly reflect compet-

Figure 12.7   Levels of Strategy in a Multidomestic Multinational Firm

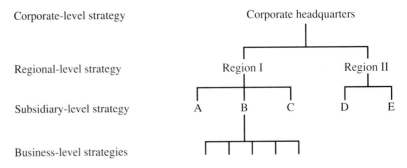

itive success—that is, market share, market share increase, market share as a percentage of the market leader, and so forth.[10] Commercial aircraft, television sets, semiconductors, and automobiles are examples of global industries.

As a result of the emphasis on global standardization and rationalization by global firms, the corporate-level strategic plans that are industry-driven tend to dominate those of subsidiaries (see Figure 12.8).

Strategy Formulation in Multinational Firms

This is the highest level of analysis; it is usually conducted at the corporate headquarters and involves the executive policy committee of the firm. This level of strategy determines the worldwide mix of businesses for the corporation. The central questions that need to be addressed in formulating corporate level strategy concern (1) the nature of the worldwide industries in which the firm will participate (multidomestic or global), (2) the countries in which the firm will have operations, and (3) other factors, including strategic alliances among firms or production platform considerations. A production platform strategy is the utilization of an operation in the target country exclusively for servicing other markets.

Corporate Strategies—Industry Considerations

For most firms the first of these questions is partially predetermined by the firm's prior activities.

Global Industries   Firms that have a significant standing in truly global industries need to develop global strategies for those industries. Key issues such as market position must be viewed worldwide. If the firm views its operations in various countries as if they were stocks in a portfolio, it will actually undermine its own possibility of achieving competitive advantage. As Porter states, "In a global industry, a firm must in some way integrate its activities on a worldwide basis to capture the linkages among countries. This includes, but requires more than, tranferring intangible assets among countries."[11] Developing a global industry strategy is the only reasonably sure way to gain an edge over global competitors. For example, a firm may

Figure 12.8   Levels of Strategy in a Global Multinational Firm

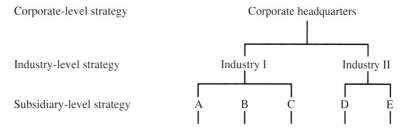

make an investment in a saturated market despite weak profit potential because that investment will hurt a competitor, thus weakening the competitor and making it less able to compete effectively in third countries.

Multidomestic Industries   When the industry is multidomestic, regional strategies need to be formed to maintain efficiency and coordination among the operations of quasi-independent subsidiaries. International regional strategies are similar to domestic SBU strategies.

Regional strategies are developed by firms primarily for those industries that have been described as multidomestic; however, the presence of regional offices in the firm's overall organizational structure does not necessarily mean that regional strategies have been developed. Such offices serve a legitimate function of facilitating information flows and exercising financial control over subsidiaries even in the absence of unifying regional strategies.

It is important to note that even in global industries there may be some need for slight product differentiation. This is particularly true in industries that are in transition from being more multidomestic to being global in character. The automobile industry is an example of an industry in transition (see the Global Insight). In the 1950s the automobiles of the United States, Japan, and Europe were dramatically different. Today many of those differences have vanished.

Corporate Strategy—Country Considerations

The selection of countries for operation is generally based upon three factors:

1. Market attractiveness (current market size, future market potential, level of competition, and so forth)
2. Risks
3. Other factors, including incentives and disincentives

Market Attractiveness   An assessment of market attractiveness may be made on the basis of direct or company-specific information and data (previous company sales to the country, competitor sales in the market and so forth) or indirect data (per capita income, per capita income growth rate, cultural preferences or values, etc.). These indirect data can serve as the basis for forecasts of company sales or of production costs; however, one must be careful in the use of indirect data. A country may appear to meet the criteria for a large market when none exists. For example, India has more than 50 million people who are nearly as wealthy as the average citizen in the United States and yet there is essentially no demand for products such as electronic dishwashers. This reflects the presence of more than 650 million people who are poor and who represent an abundant supply of low-cost domestic labor. The impact of cultural or religious factors should not be underestimated in assessing market attractiveness. (See Chapter 11 on the human cultural environment of business and Chapter 14 on international marketing strategy.) Consider the low demand for alcoholic beverages in

VW in the United States: Great Expectations Turn to Naught

In 1978 Volkswagen (VW) became the first foreign automaker to establish a production operation in the United States. The market was favorable and the investment climate ideal. In fact from the time the 200,000-car-capacity plant opened, VW had plans for a second facility. Business progressed as planned for the first four years and VW began building that second facility. In 1988, VW closed its U.S. operations. How did this happen? Was it bad luck or strategic failure?

In early 1981 the VW plant was producing 1,100 cars per day, an all-time high, but then the bottom fell out. A recession hit in the second half of 1981 and production was cut to 856 cars per day. By 1982 production problems brought that total down to 652 per day. In 1983 an entire work shift was eliminated and the plans for the second plant were scrapped even though it was 80 percent complete. From that point on it was all downhill for VW.

As the energy crisis abated, Americans turned back to their first love, larger and more stylish cars. The Big Three in Detroit began successfully down-sizing cars. The Japanese began to up-scale their cars to try to satisfy the Americans' first love. Furthermore, VW's most direct competitors, the Japanese, were receiving better quality ratings and delivering new cars much faster. The original advantage of being located in an FTZ was copied by other manufacturers.

Perhaps most surprising is that VW seemed to leave in Germany much of what had made them successful, embracing those aspects of the American way that hurt their competitiveness. They welcomed the UAW and followed Big Three wage scales. Nevertheless, the UAW called a strike early in VW's first year of operations. VW utilized Big Three production techniques and suppliers rather than the ones with which they were most familiar. They seemed to totally ignore their own key strategic success factors. Thus strategic nearsightedness and the inability to react to market needs killed the VW venture.

Source: Adapted from "VW's US Pullout: Great Expectations Turn to Naught," *Business International*, October 24, 1988.

high per capita income Islamic states or the relatively low demand for cosmetics in the very affluent Scandinavian countries.

Risks   Risk analyses usually focus on four types of risks:

1. Ordinary business risks in that country
2. Financial and foreign exchange risks
3. Political risks
4. Corporate system risks

Business risks include the level of competition and barriers to the entry for future competitors, price levels, and the nature of markets. Financial or foreign exchange risks have to do with obstacles to the repatriation of profits or equity, effects of currency devaluations, and the local costs of capital. (See Chapter 17, "International Financial Management.") Political risk involves both the likelihood and the impact of government actions that discriminate against some or all foreign firms; these include expropriation and the various forms of creeping expropriation. (See Chapter 9, "Political and Legal Considerations in International Business.")

The executive team will also need to consider the effects of doing business in a particular country on the overall risks of the firm. Because the business cycles of countries usually differ from one another in length, intensity, and timing, investments in various countries serve to reduce overall system risks through diversification of earnings and cash flow streams. When sales in country A are declining, they may be just beginning to level out in country B and continuing to grow in country C. These lags are particularly apparent in industries with a rapidly changing technology, such as microcomputers. The net effect of investing in numerous countries is the smoothing of sales fluctuations and the leveling of earnings streams—hence the reduction in total system risks.

Investment Incentives, Disincentives, and Other Factors   Incentives such as tax holidays, accelerated depreciation, rent-free land and buildings, low-interest loans, loan guarantee programs, and subsidized energy or transportation are becoming commonplace in less developed countries that try to attract foreign businesses.[12] While playing the incentives game to attract foreign investments, many of these same countries are adopting regulations to get the most out of the current investments through job creation quotas, maximum market share levels, export minimums, obligatory local ownership participation, or limits on import purchases. These regulations often serve as disincentives to investment. The result is that these issues are increasingly difficult to factor into a firm's long-range strategic plans.

Although numerous other factors affect country selection, market attractiveness and risk are still of major importance (see Table 12.5).

Corporate Strategies—Other Factors

Although the nature of the industry and the selection of country are two of the most important considerations in corporate-level strategies of multinational firms, there are other factors of significance.

Strategic Alliances   Strategic alliances are interrelationships among corporations such that they become loose confederations of corporations whose economic objectives have become interdependent. Strategic alliances often form around a major international company. Strategic alliances also generally include suppliers, commercial banks, investment bankers, distributors, other major companies whose products are used in concert, and service organizations such as CPA firms, advertising agencies, and so forth.

NHK Spring, Japan's largest manufacturer of all types of springs for the automobile industry, has an ownership structure that reflects the interconnections of strategic alliances (see Table 12.6).

Strategic alliances are further solidified by each company having retired

Table 12–5   **Strategic Responses to Market Attractiveness and Country Risk Factors**

	Level of Country Risk		
	Low	*Medium*	*High*
Market attractiveness			
High	Maximum commitment of human and financial resources Seek wholly owned affiliate	Limit financial exposure Seek majority ownership	Minimize financial exposure Seek minority ownership with licensing agreement
Medium	Maintain high resource commitment Seek joint venture	Limit resource commitment Seek joint venture	Zero financial exposure No equity involvement
Low	Token resource commitment Seek independent distributor	No resource commitment Use export agent or license	No interest Export to orders only

Source: Adapted from James C. Baker John K. Ryans, Jr., and Donald G. Howard, eds., *International Business Classics* (Lexington, Mass.: Lexington Books, 1988).

executives from the others sitting on its board of directors or being hired as consultants. It is becoming increasingly common for strategic alliances to develop among competitive firms. The existence of such alliances can most easily be seen by tracing equity and supplier relationships among "competitive" firms. For example, if one studies the international automobile industry, many interesting relationships can be seen. (The list below presents a very cursory summary of these.)

Strategic alliances among Japanese firms are more complex and more

Table 12.6   **The Ownership Structure of NHK Spring**

Major Shareholders	*Percentage*
Daido Steel	14.8
Nissho Iwai (trading company)	9.3
Kobe Steel	6.5
Nomura Securities (Japan's largest securities firm)	3.9
DKB	2.9
All non-Japanese owners	3.5
Bank of Yokohama	3.6
Nomura International (major Japanese trading company)	1.8
Sogo Taxi (a part of a major Japanese retail conglomerate)	1.5

Source: *Japanese Industrial Directory.*

common than among U.S. firms, because the activities of quasi-governmental organizations such as MITI facilitate the formation of these alliances. The strategic alliances of major Japanese firms also differ from those of other nations in that they include Japanese trading companies with their diverse and far-reaching organizations. Furthermore, in the strategic alliances of Japanese firms, the larger members of each alliance or "family" are generally major stockholders in each other and in the smaller members of the family. As a result, smaller firms in these tightly linked supplier chains are often instructed to invest abroad after an investment by larger members of the alliance. Despite these close linkages, smaller firms that are part of a major firm's supplier chain may supply products to the major competitors of that major firm. For example, Toyoda Gosei, which is owned by Toyota, supplies brake hoses to Daihatsu Motors, Hino Motors, Fuji Heavy Industries, Honda, Mazda, Mitsubishi, Isuzu, and Suzuki.[13]

General Motors

GM owns 5.0 percent of Suzuki and 34.2 percent of Isuzu
  Suzuki supplies cars and Isuzu small truck parts to GM
  Suzuki owns 1.3 percent of Isuzu and Isuzu owns 3.5 percent of Suzuki

GM has a joint venture with Toyota
  Toyota has a technology licensing agreement with Lotus
  Toyota owns 14.6 percent of Daihatsu and 10.4 percent of Hino
    Daihatsu sells engines and transmissions to Innocenti

Chrysler

Chrysler owns 15 percent of Mitsubishi
  Mitsubishi supplies cars and engines to Chrysler, technology to Porsche, and diesel engines to Ford

Chrysler owns 14 percent of Peugeot
  Peugeot is $\frac{1}{3}$ owner in FSM along with Renault and Volvo
    Renault is 15 percent owner of Volvo cars

Chrysler buys diesel engines from Nissan Diesel, 45.6 percent owned by Nissan
  Nissan is 36 percent owner of Motor Iberica and is a 50/50 partner with Alfa Romeo in a joint venture (ARNA)
  Nissan builds the VW Santana
    VW is 99 % owner of Audi NSU
    VW has contractual agreement with Fiat and Renault

Production Platforms   Establishing a production platform can also result in investments that seem contrary to market attractiveness and risk factors. Numerous U.S. firms have established operations in Mexico, Central America, or the Caribbean, despite small markets and high risks, to serve as a production platform from which to service the North American market. The primary strategic concerns regarding the establishment of production platforms are labor productivity, production costs, production quality, transportation costs and convenience, and host country environmental factors. For example, baseballs are made in Haiti despite the fact that the market is small and sufficiently poor that very few citizens can afford to purchase a baseball. This production platform is primarily for servicing the U.S. market. There is, however, a downside to the economic logic of platform production. Many firms that have considered only production cost factors have found that the geographic and cultural distance from customers has created problems that more than offset the economic advantages.

Subsidiary Strategies

Strategies at the subsidiary level are similar to those of purely domestic firms in the United States. The subsidiary needs to decide what products or services it wishes to sell in which local markets. However, the process for foreign subsidiaries differs in that the parent company will play a major role; thus, subsidiary-level strategies are more like those of a domestic division. The strategies of foreign subsidiaries, as with domestic divisions, need to fit with those of other divisions or subsidiaries to form an integrated and complete corporate strategy. If a subsidiary is involved in more than one industry, the subsidiary should develop a unique business-level strategy for each.

In formulating strategies for existing subsidiaries, parent-company management tends to respond in one or more of five ways:

1. Continuously reviewing strategic options
2. Using host government laws and regulations to its own benefit
3. Creating future bargaining chips
4. Anticipating governmental policy changes
5. Listening to local managers

Considering strategic options almost always means reviewing such possibilities as leaving the country or initiating defensive strategies. Using the law involves doing what the government wants in exchange for concessions or favorable treatment. Creating bargaining chips includes doing things the nation needs (exporting, creating jobs, and so forth) as well as doing things that keep the nation dependent on the firm (developing a monopolistic position, keeping key elements of the production process outside of the host nation, utilizing the company's global marketing network, etc.).[14]

Subsidiary business-level strategies focus on how to compete effectively in each of the selected product markets. This involves the development of strategies for each business function: sales and marketing, production and

Multinational firms develop strategies on multiple levels: corporate, global industry or regional, subsidiary, and subsidiary business.

operations, finance, research and development, human resources, and so forth. Differences such as language, currency, laws, cultures, and economic systems make subsidiary business-level strategy formulation extremely difficult.

STRUCTURES FOR INTERNATIONAL FIRMS

Despite the complexity of international business strategies, firms exploit international business opportunities in one or more of three basic ways: through exporting, contractual agreements with foreign entities, or direct investment. The first two of these approaches require little if any modification of the corporation's structure.

Structures to Facilitate a Strategy of Exporting

A firm following a strategy of exporting must initially decide whether it wishes to handle all of the details associated with finding customers abroad, delivering the products to them, and getting paid by them. If the firm is willing to handle all of these details, then it will follow a strategy of direct exporting. If, however, the firm is willing to accept a somewhat lower level of profit in order to be able to have someone else handle these details, it will follow a strategy of indirect exporting. For both direct and indirect exporting there are numerous organizational structures and legal forms that the firm can employ. Although these are covered in depth in Chapter 15 ("Exporting, Importing, and Financing International Trade"), the basic concepts of operation are introduced below.

The organizational forms that can be used to implement a strategy of direct exporting are the built-in export department, the separate export department, and export sales subsidiaries. The simplest form is the *built-in export department*. Support for the export department will have to be supplied by the domestic functions groups: advertising, accounting, finance, traffic, and shipping. As export sales and profits develop, the firm may want to expand to a *separate export department or division*. This type of unit will generally include all of the functional areas found in domestic sales departments or divisions. These units may be organized geographically or by product. The firm may opt for one of the various forms of *export sales subsidiaries* instead of a sales division. These may have headquarters either in the United States or abroad. Such subsidiaries are usually independently incorporated, wholly owned subsidiaries of the parent corporation. The president of the export sales subsidiary is generally a corporate vice-president. Under the president there is usually a group of geographic or product vice-presidents or directors. The distinctive difference between sales subsidiaries and traditional international subsidiaries is that the former are not involved in manufacturing. They merely buy products from the parent company or from other sources for export. Indirect exporting usually does not require the alteration of the corporation's organizational structure beyond the establishment of an export department since the details are handled by others. Chapter 15 explores the structural forms for direct exporting, the various concerns of export channel selection and management, and the types and functions of indirect export intermediaries.

Direct exporting demands an internal organization to conduct all details of exporting. Indirect exporting requires little alteration of a firm's structure.

Structures to Facilitate Foreign Operations

Whenever a firm makes a foreign direct investment establishing a subsidiary or branch, it is putting assets and future earning streams at risk. This necessitates altering the firm's corporate structure to effectively and efficiently control and coordinate these operations and to aid the successful implementation of its international strategies.

Similarly, exploiting foreign business opportunities through contractual agreements such as licensing, franchising, technology sharing, or sales agreements generally requires substantial alteration of the corporation's structure.

International Division

One of the most significant changes in the structure of international firms during the post–World War II period was replacement of export sales divisions with international operations divisions. The seemingly minor change actually represented a fundamental philosophical change and strategic shift. Foreign countries were no longer to be seen only as markets for U.S. exports but as locations for an expanding business presence. Sales, service, warehousing, manufacturing, product design, and research would all be conducted abroad if management felt that that would enhance the firm's competitive position and would be economically justified. Whether the form of involvement was primarily through contractual agreements such as licensing, franchising, or turnkey operations, or through the establishment of businesses in which the parent company held an ownership position, the international division was appropriate. Indeed, the international division is still the common organizational structure for international business operations (see Figure 12.9).

As international operations became more extensive and international strategies more complex, the international division replaced the export sales divisions.

International Headquarters Company (IHC)

As the export sales division structure gave way to the international division, so was the export subsidiary frequently being replaced by the international headquarters company form of structure. Implementing an IHC structure finally and completely ended the pretense of international business being merely an offshoot of sales and marketing. Indeed, when a firm establishes an IHC structure, it is saying that international business will be handled as an operationally independent and autonomous enterprise having its own

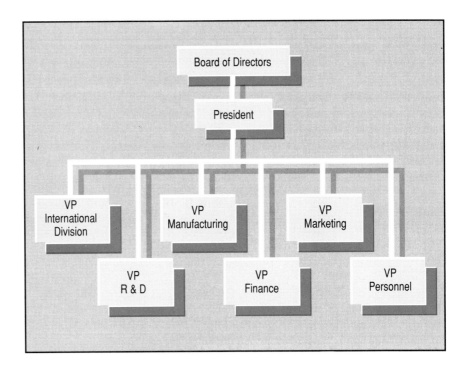

Figure 12.9   International Division Structure

factories, warehouses, sales offices, and employees scattered among many different countries.

Establishing an IHC represents the completion of the journey from being purely domestic to becoming truly international. The IHC signifies that international business has grown to be a near-equal partner with the firm's domestic activities. Indeed, the organization chart of an IHC is often a mirror image of the parent corporation with all of the same business functions including its own board of directors, board chairman, and president. There are several significant connections beween the parent and the IHC. The president of the parent company is generally the chairman of the board of the IHC, and the vice-president for international operations of the parent company is usually the president of the IHC (see Figure 12.10).[15]

The IHC form of structure establishes unique line and staff activities allocated specifically to the firm's international strategies.

Numerous firms that adopted the IHC structure discovered that these companies, generally located in the home country, were not effective in coordinating or controlling foreign operations because of the geographic, communicative, and cultural distance. IHC management had to deal with everything from foreign labor problems in Italian production plants or Guatemalan banana plantations to competitive pricing in Egypt or advertising problems in Sweden. The IHC management simply did not have enough information or the cultural closeness to deal promptly and effectively with the myriad of decisions required. As a result, many firms moved their entire

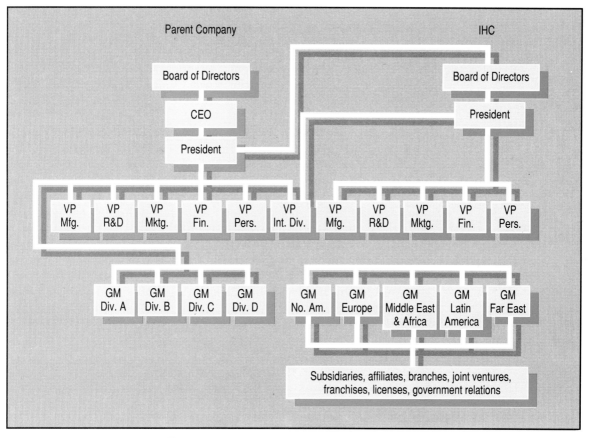

Figure 12.10   International Headquarters Company Structure
Source: Adapted from Endel J. Kolde, *International Business Enterprise,* 2nd ed. (Englewood Cliffs, N.J.: Prentice-Hall, 1973), p. 180.

IHC abroad. These are often called foreign base companies (FBCs). Firms with widely dispersed foreign operations often established multiple FBCs, each controlling and coordinating the operations in a geographic region. These were the precursors of regionally structured world companies.

World Company (WC)

As the internationalization of a firm continues, it will ultimately reach the point where the differentiation between domestic and foreign has little meaning. This usually occurs when domestic sales, potential sales, profits, or assets deployed are approximately equal to those of other countries or regions. The world company, at least in theory, abandons the domestic versus foreign dichotomy and treats home country activities in the same mannner as it would any other country. Indeed, the organization chart of a world company is similar to that of a large domestic firm utilizing a functional, product, or regional (geographic) structure.

Functional Structure   The functional structure organizes divisions along business function lines: production, marketing, finance, and so forth. The structure tends to be more common among European than U.S. firms. Each division head has worldwide line and staff responsibilities for that functional activity.

The structure has the advantage of concentrating management's attention on business issues rather than product, technical, or regional ones. The functional structure seems to work best when the firm manufactures and sells a limited product line, has only minor levels of competition, and has a nonexpanding market. Unfortunately, the disadvantages seem to outweigh the advantages. Each function group tends to develop its own goals and objectives, often in a manner that it is less than optimal for the firm as a whole. Subsidiary or branch management ends up reporting to several people. There tends to be tremendous duplication of geographic expertise across the divisions. Finally, and perhaps most importantly, the functional structure has great difficulties dealing with multiple product lines.[16] See Figure 12.11.

Figure 12.11   International Functional Structure
Source: Adapted from Stefan H. Robock and Kenneth Simmonds, *International Business and Multinational Enterprises* (Homewood, Ill.: Richard D. Irwin, 1983), p. 380.

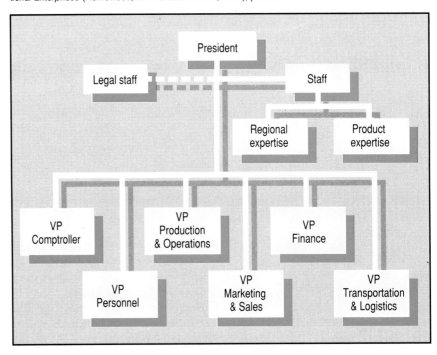

Product Structure   A product structure is perhaps the most common form for world companies. Each division has responsibility for a line of related products, while corporate staff support for the various business functions and area specialists remain at the corporate headquarters. Each product division plans and controls worldwide activities in its product line whether those activities are conducted through distributors, licensees, branches, or subsidiaries.

A product structure seems to function best when the firm needs to adapt to rapid technological changes and when end-user markets or product lines are highly diversified. This type of organization facilitates coordination and control among foreign production plants and in markets where product knowledge is highly important. In essence, a product structure works best when similar products are sold worldwide, as in global industries (see Figure 12.12).

A product structure faces three basic problems. Division managers frequently have excellent product knowledge but limited understanding of or experience in the local environments in which the division operates. As a result of the product and technical orientation of divisional management, expatriate assignments are often based almost exclusively on these considerations. Foreign operations that produce or market multiple products often have problems of coordination and control. Subsidiary management finds itself reporting to two or more divisions, each of which has different objec-

Figure 12.12   International Product Structure
Source: Adapted from Stefan H. Robock and Kenneth Simmonds, *International Business and Multinational Enterprises* (Homewood, Ill.: Richard D. Irwin, 1983), p. 384.

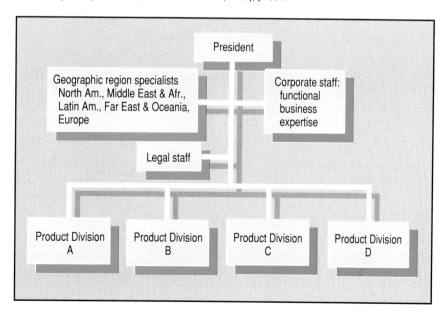

tives for that market. It might also be difficult to allocate costs or production capacity among various divisions' products. Fortunately, many of the problems are offset by the presence of a group of area specialists at the corporate headquarters.[17]

Regional Structure   The regional structure places primary responsibilities for all activities in a region with the vice-president or general manager. Each region has its own head of marketing, production, finance, and so forth. Each of these functional heads receives support from staff specialists housed at the corporate headquarters (see Figure 12.13).

This type of structure gives greater independence and autonomy to regional and subsidiary management. It is not uncommon for subsidiaries to be independent profit centers. As a result, products, advertising messages, and production processes can more easily be modified to better fit local needs and conditions. Although this structure does not allow for global economies-of-scale operations, it does facilitate regional economies. Furthermore, a regional structure facilitates prompt and informed response to matters of regional importance. In essence, the structure is appropriate for multidomestic industries.

Figure 12.13   International Regional Structure
Source: Adapted from Stefan H. Robock and Kenneth Simmonds, *International Business and Multinational Enterprises* (Homewood, Ill.: Richard D. Irwin, 1983), p. 382.

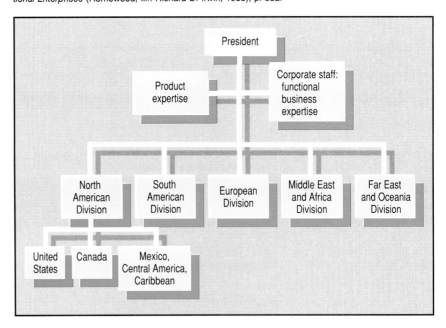

Unfortunately, a regional structure has difficulty with a highly diverse product line or rapidly changing product lines. A rapidly changing production technology is also problematical. If each region were to maintain a staff of technical experts in all of the products and processes, the costs would be prohibitive and much effort would be duplicated. Furthermore, the trend toward global convergence of product preferences is increasingly placing firms with a regional structure at a competitive disadvantage.[18]

Matrix Structure   Since all of the structures discussed previously have disadvantages, firms generally establish hybrid forms that capture the advantages of more than one of the basic structural forms. These almost endless varieties of "real world" structures are generally referred to as matrix structures since they can be represented by a grid or matrix of interconnecting responsibilities. For example, a firm may have an export subsidiary for some product lines; an international division to service branches, licensees, and franchisees; a regional structure for products in multidomestic industries; and a product structure for products whose industry is globally competitive.

If the matrix structure creates the desired advantages and avoids the disadvantages of the basic forms, it will be highly successful; however, firms must be careful that the reverse does not occur. The major problems of matrix structures stem from their inherent complexity. Coordination and communications can suffer. At times it is difficult to tell who is in control and who is supposed to make which decisions. As a result, managers often ignore the structure and its requirements. When this occurs informal communications become the norm and chaos occurs.

A completely internationalized firm resembles a large domestic firm with a functional, product, or regional structure that operates worldwide.

SUMMARY

In spite of uncertainties, business opportunities exist in many foreign countries. A key question for firms is what strategies to employ for the firm as a whole and for the specific countries. The process of determining strategy for the various levels and businesses of the firm involves assessing the firm's current situation, determining an overall thrust, developing specific strategies for each level, and then allocating sufficient capital to execute these strategies.

When the industries involved are globally competitive and operations in one country result in competitive advantages in other countries, it is not sufficient to have corporate and subsidiary strategies. The firm must also develop global industry strategies. When the industry is multidomestic, the firm must develop regional strategies to facilitate control and coordination among the various subsidiaries and their strategies.

Once a firm has selected a strategy, it must then determine a structure for implementing that strategy. Aternatives range from simple exporting to an international division, international headquarters company, or one of the various world company forms. The world company forms might use a function structure, product structure, regional structure, or some hybrid or matrix form. The most common structures used by international firms today are the international division, the world product structure, and a matrix structure.

In the more than forty years since the end of World War II, the trend has clearly been toward greater diversity of strategies and structures for international businesses. Given the increasingly competitive nature of world markets, one can only expect that both strategy and structures will themselves become more complex and more important. □

KEY TERMS AND CONCEPTS

BCG matrix

Capital allocations

Direct export

Functional structure

Global industry

Growth strategies

Indirect export

International division

International headquarters company

Multidomestic industry

No-growth strategies

Product structure

Regional structure

Strategic business units

REVIEW QUESTIONS

1. Compare and contrast global industries and multidomestic industries.

2. Explain how a firm could diversify its corporate cash flows by investing abroad in its primary product line.

3. Besides market attractiveness and risk, what factors can affect a firm's decision to invest abroad?

4. Explain how the BCG matrix can be used by a firm to guide its international strategy.

5. Explain the stages of strategy formulation and the levels of strategy in a multinational firm.

6. Explain the differences between an international division and an international headquarters company.

7. Compare and contrast a functional structure, regional structure, and product structure.

8. How does the nature of competition in an industry affect the selection of an appropriate structure?

9. Explain the differences between an international division and an export sales division.

Luxury in France: The Rise of Bernard Arnault

Bernard Arnault, at the tender age of 40, has built an empire of luxury goods. He brought a bankrupt textile company back to life and then used it as a foundation for his diversified empire, which now includes Möet & Chandon and Dom Perignon champagne, Christian Dior and Givenchy clothing and perfume, Hennessy cognac, and Louis Vuitton luggage. Furthermore, he has done all this without losing equity control.

Although Arnault once dreamed of being a concert pianist and can still play Chopin from memory, reads nineteenth-century Romantic novels for fun, and was educated at one of France's best schools, the Ecole Polytechnique, don't get the wrong idea. Despite the fact that Arnault does not come from the school of hard knocks, did not work his way up from the bottom, and does not smell like the shop floor, he is still a tough-minded executive. When asked how he stays on top of this growing empire, Arnault responded, "I always control the stock—and I always have the last word."

Furthermore, Arnault is a capitalist through and through. After graduating from the Ecole Polytechnique, he was highly successful at building luxury homes on the French Riviera, but when the socialists took control in 1981, Arnault took his real estate development talents to the United States. From 1981 until 1984, he developed luxury condominiums in the United States.

In 1984, Arnault returned to France to take over a bankrupt textile firm. After making this business profitable, he sold the textile manufacturing group to devote more attention to the couturier Christian Dior. In the summer of 1988 the remainder of Arnault's luxury empire fell into place. In 1987 Möet-Hennessy and Louis Vuitton had merged but still found that they were targets for takeover attempts. The divided management resulting from the merger could not agree on a method for fending off takeovers. The Möet group wanted to sell a part of the business to Guinness, while the Vuitton family resisted without a clear alternative. Arnault became the "White Knight" for the Vuitton group, although he knew that his business could not withstand a fight with Guinness. To get control of Möet-Hennessy Louis Vuitton (MHLV), Arnault made a deal with Guinness to form a holding company that would own 38 percent of MHLV. Arnault owns 60 percent of the holding company.

Arnault sums up his strategy for his luxury empire as follows: "Deluxe brands command big margins because they're so hard to compete with."

Case written by Don R. Beeman (1989) based upon "An Elegant Strategy Based on Classy Brands," *Fortune*, December 19, 1988, p. 166.
This case was developed for class discussion purposes and should not be viewed as representative of good or bad management practices or decision-making.

Questions

1. Is Arnault's luxury empire operating in global or multidomestic industries?

2. What type of a corporate-level strategy would be appropriate? Justify your answer.

3. Would the worldwide strategy be different if Arnault dealt in low-priced items?

4. How would you structure Arnault's empire? Justify your answer.

NOTES

1. William A. Dymsza, *Multinational Business Strategy* (New York: McGraw-Hill, 1972), p. 190.

2. Fred R. David, *Strategic Management*, 2nd ed. (Columbus, Ohio: Merrill Publishing Company, 1989), pp. 193–196.

3. Ibid., pp. 149–151.

4. Ibid., pp. 147–149.

5. Ibid., pp. 217–220.

6. H. Igor Ansoff, *Corporate Strategy: An Analytic Approach to Business Policy for Growth and Expansion* (New York: McGraw Hill, 1965), p. 132.

7. David, op. cit., p. 66.

8. Charles W. Hofer and Dan Schendel, *Strategy Formulation: Analytical Concepts* (St. Paul, Minn.: West Publishing Company, 1978), p. 32–34.

9. Michael E. Porter, "Changing Patterns of International Competition," in David J. Teece, ed., *The Competitive Challenge*, (Cambridge, Mass.: Ballinger Publishing Company, 1987), pp. 29–30.

10. Thomas Hout, Michael E. Porter, and Eileen Rudden, "How Global Companies Win Out," *Harvard Business Review* 60: 5 (September-October, 1982), 98–108.

11. Porter, op. cit., p. 30.

12. Dennis J. Encarnationa and Sushil Vachani, "Foreign Ownership: When Hosts Change the Rules," *Harvard Business Review* 63:5 (September-October, 1985), 152–160.

13. *Ward's Automotive International*, Researched and Published Documents—Special Issue Chart (researched by assistant editor, Linda Knight and intern, Laure Utley), October 1986.

14. Encarnationa and Vachani, op. cit., p. 160.

15. Endel J. Kolde, *International Business Enterprise*, 2nd ed. (Englewood Cliffs, N.J.: Prentice-Hall, 1973), pp. 246–249.

16. Stefan H. Robock and Kenneth Simmonds, *International Business and Multinational Enterprises*, 4th ed. (Homewood, Ill.: Richard D. Irwin, 1989), pp. 262–263.

17. Ibid., pp. 264–266.

18. Ibid., pp. 263–264.

REFERENCES AND SELECTED READINGS

Ansoff, H. Igor. *Corporate Strategy: An Analytic Approach to Business Policy for Growth and Expansion.* New York: McGraw Hill, 1965.

Baker, James C., John K. Ryans, Jr., and Donald G. Howard. *International Business Classics.* Lexington, Mass.: Lexington Books, 1988.

Boddewyn, Jean J. "Foreign and Domestic Divestment and Investment Decisions: Like or Unlike?" *The Journal of International Business Studies* 14:3 (Winter 1983).

Caves, Richard E., and Karen B. Hisey. "Diversification Strategy and Choice of Country: Diversifying Acquisitions Abroad by U.S. Multinationals, 1978–1980." *The Journal of International Business Studies* 16:2 (Summer 1985).

Channon, Derek F., and Michael Jalland. *Multinational Strategic Planning.* New York: AMACOM, (a division of American Management Association), 1978.

Chase, C. D., C. H. Walther, and J. L. Kuhle. "The Relevance of Political Risk in Foreign Direct Investment." *Management International Review* vol. 28 (1988).

Cray, David. "Control and Coordination in Multinational Corporations." *The Journal of International Business Studies* 15:2 (Summer 1984).

David, Fred R. *Strategic Management,* 2nd ed. Columbus, Ohio: Merrill Publishing Company, 1989.

De la Torre, José, Jeffrey S. Arpan, Michael Jay Jedel, Ernest W. Ogram, Jr., and Brian Toyne. "Corporate Adjustments and Import Competition in the U.S. Apparel Industry." *The Journal of International Business Studies* 8:1 (Spring/Summer 1977).

Doz, Yves, and C. K. Prahalad. "Patterns of Strategic Control Within Multinational Corporations." *The Journal of International Business Studies* 15:2 (Summer 1984).

Dymsza, William A. *Multinational Business Strategy.* New York: McGraw-Hill, 1972.

Dymsza, William A. "Global Strategic Planning: A Model and Recent Developments." *The Journal of International Business Studies* 15:2 (Summer 1984).

Encarnationa, Dennis J., and Sushil Vachani. "Foreign Ownership: When Hosts Change the Rules." *Harvard Business Review* 63:5 (September-October, 1985).

Farmer, Richard N. *International Business: An Operational Theory,* 4th ed. Bloomington, Ind.: Cedarwood Press, 1984.

Frame, J. D. *International Business and Global Technology.* Lexington, Mass.: Lexington Books, 1983.

Fry, E. H. *The Politics of International Investment.* New York: McGraw-Hill, 1983.

Garland, John, and Richard N. Farmer. *International Dimensions of Business Policy and Strategy.* Boston, Mass.: Kent Publishing Co., 1986.

Gates, Stephen R., and William G. Egelhoff. "Centralization in Headquarters-Subsidiary Relationships." *The Journal of International Business Studies* 17:2 (Summer 1986).

Grosse, R. E. *Foreign Investment Codes and the Location of Direct Investment*. New York: Praeger Publishing, 1980.

Hall, R. Duane. *Overseas Acquisitions and Mergers*. New York: Praeger Publishing, 1986.

Hofer, Charles W., and Dan Schendel. *Strategy Formulation: Analytical Concepts*. St. Paul, Minn.: West Publishing Company, 1978.

Kennedy, Charles R., Jr. "The External Environment-Strategic Planning Interface: U.S. Multinational Corporate Practices in the 1980s." *The Journal of International Business Studies* 15:2 (Summer 1984).

Kojima, K. *Direct Foreign Investment*. New York: Praeger Publishing, 1978.

Kolde, Endel J. *International Business Enterprise*, 2nd ed. Englewood Cliffs, N.J.: Prentice-Hall, 1973.

Kredietbank (Brussels, Belgium). *Weekly Bulletin*, no. 1. 6 Jan. 1984.

Mascarenhas, Briance. "International Strategies of Non-Dominant Firms." *The Journal of International Business Studies* 17:1 (Spring 1986).

Porter, Michael E. "Changing Patterns of International Competition." In David J. Teece, ed., *The Competitive Challenge*. Cambridge, Mass.: Ballinger Publishing Company, 1987.

Robock, Stefan H., and Kenneth Simmonds. *International Business and Multinational Enterprises*, 4th ed. Homewood, Ill.: Richard D. Irwin, 1989.

Terpstra, Vern. *International Marketing*, 2nd ed. Hinesdale, Ill.: Dryden Press, 1978.

Toyne, Brian, Jeffrey S. Arpan, Andy H. Barnett, David A. Ricks, and Terence A. Shimp. "The International Competitiveness of the U.S. Textile Mill Products Industry: Corporate Strategies for the Future." *The Journal of International Business Studies* 15:3 (Fall 1984).

Walter, Ingo, and Tracy Murray. *Handbook of International Management*. New York: Wiley, 1988.

Ward's Automotive International, Researched and Published Documents—Special Issue Chart (researched by assistant editor, Linda Knight and intern, Laure Utley), October 1986.

Weigand, Robert. "International Investment: Weighing the Incentives." *Harvard Business Review* (July-August, 1983).

Wilson, Brent D. "The Propensity of Multinational Companies to Expand Through Acquisitions." *The Journal of International Business Studies* 11:1 (Spring/Summer 1980).

Zif, Jehiel. "Explanatory Concepts of Managerial Strategic Behavior in State-Owned Enterprises: A Multinational Study." *The Journal of International Business Studies* 14:1 (Spring/Summer 1983).

13

Modes of Entry and Forms of Involvement for Exploiting International Business Opportunities

LEARNING OBJECTIVES

- Learn the forms of international involvement that firms use to implement their international strategies, including exporting, nonequity ventures, and equity investments

- Gain an understanding of nonequity investments, including licensing, franchising, management contracts, turnkey operations, turnkey plus operations, buy-back agreements, and tie-in buying and selling agreements

- Understand equity investment strategies that may be adopted by an international firm, including joint ventures and wholly owned operations

INTRODUCTION

To avoid conflict and to promote cooperation with host nations in the implementation of their strategic plans, firms make use of different forms of international involvement. Many of these do not require an investment of capital, such as exporting either directly or indirectly, licensing, franchising, management contracts, and turnkey operations. Others do require partial or complete corporate ownership.

There are essentially three forms of involvement available to the international firm for implementing the strategies that have been adopted: (1) exporting, (2) foreign involvement without equity commitment, and (3) foreign involvement with equity commitment (see Figure 13.1). Most firms utilize a combination of all three types.

EXPORTING AS A CORPORATE STRATEGY FOR INTERNATIONAL INVOLVEMENT

The simplest and least risky method of participating in international business is to maintain all economic activities within the home country and to export goods to other countries. Unfortunately, this strategy is generally the least profitable. An export strategy also makes the firm extremely vulnerable to trade barriers, local content legislation, and other governmental policies that may be adopted to protect local firms or to encourage foreign investment. Why, then, do firms adopt this strategy?

The reasons for engaging in exporting vary from firm to firm. Some firms might unknowingly become involved in exporting if products are shipped abroad by a domestic buyer. Others might decide to sell their surplus output abroad rather than to saturate the domestic market. Some

Figure 13.1   Primary Forms of Involvement for Implementing International Strategies

produce a particular product for both the domestic and foreign markets, while others go a step further by producing specific products for foreign markets. Regardless of the reasons for engaging in exporting, the firm's goods must reach the foreign market. This can be achieved by either direct exporting or indirect exporting.

As stated in Chapter 12, if a firm selects direct exporting, it must handle most of the details of getting the goods to the foreign market. If it decides in favor of indirect export, most of the details are handled by one or more intermediaries located in the country of export. To make the proper choice between these alternative approaches, the firm should be familiar with each.

With indirect exporting, the firm wishing to export its goods subcontracts with other firms to perform all of the necessary activities involved in getting the goods to a foreign market. It is therefore extremely important that the indirect exporter learn the role and function of each type of intermediary and then evaluate each of these to select the appropriate one with whom to work. There are several types of indirect export intermediary firms: those representing the seller (export management companies, export agents, export trade associations, and partners in trade), those representing the buyer (resident agents, export commission houses, and export brokers), those acting on their own behalf (export merchants, export trading companies, and export jobbers and wholesalers), and those performing specialized functions (freight forwarders). Analyses of both direct and indirect exporting, including the functions performed by each of the aforementioned indirect export intermediaries, are discussed in greater detail in Chapter 15, "Exporting, Importing, and Financing International Trade."

NO-EQUITY (CONTRACTUAL) FOREIGN INVOLVEMENTS

These types of activity replace the control provided by holding an ownership position with that of a contractual agreement. Since World War II, the number of multinational enterprises entering foreign markets through the use of contractual agreements has been steadily increasing. The opportunity to participate in the profits of international business without committing valuable resources is probably the major reason. The types of international contractual agreement vary greatly and are predicated on many factors. Two of the most important considerations are the host country's regulations regarding the products or services involved and the financial strength of the international company.

Most contractual relationships deal with the control and utilization of intellectual property such as patents, trademarks, copyrights, or proprietary processes, although firms do use no-equity types of involvement to generate additional profits from nonproprietary, firm-specific technical and managerial know-how. These contractual agreements include

Licensing and franchise agreements

Management contracts

Turnkeys and turnkey plus operations

Buy-back agreements

Tie-in buying and selling agreements

Licensing Agreements

Licensing agreements are by far the most common form of no-equity involvement. In a licensing agreement, a firm in one country authorizes a firm in another country to use its intellectual property (patents, trademarks, trade names, copyrights, or know-how) in exchange for certain considerations, usually royalty payments. Licenses may be granted to subsidiaries of the parent multinational firm, to a totally independent firm, to a local government agency, or to an individual.

A licensing agreement may be made because the owner of the intellectual property desires to profit from a foreign market without making a financial investment in that country; however, there are numerous other reasons for entering into a licensing agreement. The license owner may lack the capital to establish production facilities abroad. The government of the foreign country may prohibit foreign investments or restrict the importation of certain goods. Licensing may be selected even when there are no such governmental or economic obstacles because it provides the firm with a foothold in a market without a capital expenditure. Furthermore, a firm may enter into a licensing agreement to recoup part of the R&D costs associated with the process, product, or know-how, or to generate additional profits from such assets once development costs have been covered.

Before a company grants a license to a foreign firm, there must be a clear understanding between the licensor and the licensee concerning the responsibilities and obligations of each. Only then will the agreement prove to be of lasting and mutual benefit. Licensing agreements should be highly detailed and specific and should include pertinent matters to eliminate possible conflicts. The length of the agreement and the conditions for renewal or termination must be made clear. The jurisdiction for dispute resolution must be included. The licensee should be given exclusive rights to a given territory. The rights to or limitations on exports from that foreign country or region should also be specifically defined. Terms of payment should be made clear: down payments, fee schedules, the basis for determining fees, and the conditions for any penalties. Although royalty payments are usually based on total sales with guaranteed minimum payments when sales drop below a base level, they may be defined as a fixed amount. Variable fees are usually preferred because this minimizes the licensee's risk.

From the point of view of the licensor, there are a number of advantages to introducing its products in a market through licensing agreements: minimum capital outlay, greater acceptability of products produced in the host country, protection of the patent or trademark through local production (prior usage) and through the efforts of the licensee, inexpensive testing of local market demand, and avoidance of traditional marketing barriers such as language and cultural differences.

There are also a number of drawbacks to international licensing. The licensor has less control over production quality, quantity, channels for distribution, and advertising. Royalties, generally 4 percent, may not adequately cover R&D costs or provide an acceptable level of profit. Some countries levy higher taxes on royalty income or have exchange controls that make it difficult to repatriate royalty earnings. Conflicts can arise if a licensee produces a substitutable product. Licensing arrangements may result in a loss of unpatented know-how. After the agreement ends, the licensee might dominate the market, making it difficult for the licensor to compete. Even after the termination of the agreement the licensee might continue to exploit the asset.

Licensing agreements are contracts exchanging limited rights to intellectual property for royalty payments or other compensation.

Franchise Agreements

A contractual agreement that is quite common in the United States and is becoming increasingly common as a means of capitalizing on potential in foreign markets is franchising. In this type of agreement the franchisor sells to the franchisee the right to use a specialized sales or service formula, and provides the support and service assistance for a fee. The franchisee operates at its own risk and for its own account; however, the title to the sales or service system remains with the franchisor.

The franchisee pays an up-front fee for the right to use the specific brand name, emblem, process, or system. Additionally, the franchisee is charged a royalty fee based on the amount of sales. This may be specifically paid or included in the cost of the goods that the franchisee is required to purchase from the franchisor. Periodically, the franchisee will also be charged consulting fees to cover the continuous training and guidance or advertising fees to cover a portion of the cost.

Franchising began in the United States in 1892 but did not experience

The economic opening of the U.S.S.R. to Western capitalism is no more dramatically represented than in this photograph of McDonald's in Moscow. It is perhaps symbolic of things to come that in the McDonald's logo on the wall, the "Golden Arches" are large and appear to be rising, while the hammer and sickle are small and almost appear to be sinking.

rapid growth until the 1960s. Since then, it has expanded to cover most fields of economic activity—from fast foods (McDonald's) to motels (Holiday Inn) or transmission repairs (AAMCO). It is estimated that franchises account for about 5.5 percent of the total retail trade of the United States. Franchising has also grown in attractiveness as a strategy for exploiting business opportunities abroad. In 1982, there were 1,200 franchisors in Europe with 78,800 franchises accounting for 4 percent of total retail trade (excluding motor vehicles, petrol, and soft drinks).[1]

The rapid growth of franchising is explained in part by the fact that franchise operations tend to fare better in periods of economic down-turn. For example, the average failure rate for U.S. franchises after the first year is only 6 percent as compared to 35 percent for other new businesses.[2] In part this reflects that franchisees are carefully selected and the product is of proven reliability and established reputation. Furthermore, the franchisor provides continuous guidance and support, and assumes a number of tasks (e.g., market research, new product testing, updating the product, securing adequate sources of supply, and conducting nationwide advertising campaigns). The franchisee also benefits from economies of scale in the purchase of equipment, materials, or services.

One of the major advantages of a franchise is that the market share can be increased without making large investments. Furthermore, the franchisee takes over all or part of the financing, bears the cost of facility acquisition, finances initial stock, and recruits and remunerates employees. However, a franchise agreement will mean a loss of control and a decrease in profits. The franchisor must also collaborate with independent partners over whom it has less authority than over employees.

From the perspective of economic development, franchising leads to more efficient use of the factors of production since it unites entrepreneurs who have commitment and capital with firms that have managerial know-how and technical expertise. Furthermore, the franchisee stimulates the franchisor to keep the system up to date and continuously improving.

Franchising provides the international firm with the opportunity to expand faster and with less risk than its capital budget might otherwise allow.

Management Contracts

Management contracts generally involve the sales of technical assistance, management expertise, or both. The use of technical assistance contracts involves the sale of technical expertise to a foreign firm or government for a predetermined fee. This fee may be a fixed amount, percentage of sales, or portion of cost savings. Technical assistance agreements may be used when they are the only method available for the foreign firm to enter a market, although these agreements are often initiated to generate additional profits from one's expertise or as a means of learning about local markets.

The second form of management contract involves the sale of managerial expertise and talent. Such contracts are usually made between firms when one firm hires a second to manage all or part of its operation for a fixed period of time. When only managerial skills are part of the contract, the foreign firm is usually seeking access to world markets and tends to seek out firms that have an extensive global distribution system.

Contracts that include both technical and managerial expertise are usually made when the management of the foreign firm encounters difficulties in many different aspects of a production operation. Although such agreements may last up to 10 years, the hiring firm often stipulates in the contract that one of the responsibilities of the firm being hired is to train local nationals so that they will be able to run the business or facility independently by the time the contract expires.

International firms enter into a management contract when the foreign country is reluctant to permit direct investment in the production or distribution of a particular good or service. Management contracts are a low-risk, high-profit technique for exploiting market potential. If a firm is nationalized, the government might make a contract with the nationalized firm or one of its competitors to provide the necessary managerial or technical personnel to continue operations until native personnel can be trained. The expropriated firm might participate in such a management contract to facilitate future export possibilities, maintain access to raw materials, or recover some of its expected future earnings. A management contract might be made when a foreign firm undertakes a new venture without sufficient qualified personnel.

The type of management contract varies greatly from industry to industry and from country to country. For example, USS Engineers and Consultants, Inc., entered into a contract with Brazil to train government employees in management activities such as product planning, quality control, cost accounting, marketing, personnel relations, and accident protection. Kaiser Trading Company offers a full range of management services including financial, transportation, documentation, insurance, and other forms of technical assistance.[3]

Management contracts are not popular with most American firms. One of the major objections is that these contracts are usually less profitable than standard direct investments. Another objection is that they make it difficult to compete in those markets after local managers have been trained. Conflicts might also arise with the host government because of differences regarding the operation of a venture. Conversely, some major international firms, such as Bechtel Corporation, prefer management contracts because they keep risks to a minimum and allow growth that is not constrained by the amount of capital available for investments.

Management contracts allow a firm to buy the managerial or technical expertise of a multinational firm in exchange for monetary rewards and future business opportunities.

Management contracts will probably increase in the future as many host governments attempt to develop their economies without relying on foreign direct investments. Many governments practice a policy called *unbundling* that entails hiring one firm to build a facility, a second to manage the facility, and a third to market the output. Thus the nation gets the best of all three firms while giving up little control.

Turnkey Operations

Turnkey contracts are usually made between multinational corporations and a firm or the government of a less developed country. For a fee the MNC makes a commitment to construct an entire facility (e.g., hotel, hospital, dock, or factory) and provide the supplies, equipment, and technical or engineering skills to deliver it in working order. Often, as a part of the agreement, local managers are trained to operate the plant. Because of the time necessary to complete such projects and the large sums of money involved, provisions are usually made for possible changes in cost that might result from fluctuations in exchange rates or inflation. Usually, a down payment is made when the project gets under way, another payment during some phase of construction, and the final payment when the project has been completed. The plant is transferred to the owner when it is in satisfactory operational order. It is of the utmost importance that the term *satisfactory* be clearly defined in the contract.

Many turnkey projects have been located in communist countries where foreign investments have been restricted and foreign ownership prohibited.

Due to the substantial economic and political reforms taking place in Eastern Europe, one has to wonder whether direct foreign investment will be replacing turnkey operations in these countries. Nevertheless, turnkey operations tend to be of great benefit to all involved parties. Foreign firms are generally very highly paid for their role in such projects, while host countries get the latest technology without surrendering control to foreign interests. The financing of such projects is usually provided by credits from international financial institutions or financial agencies within the recipient country; however, to increase business, the nation of the supplying firm may also grant credits.

Turnkey contracts provide state of the art facilities with no loss of control.

Turnkey Plus Contracts

A turnkey plus operation essentially combines a turnkey project and a management contract. The original contract defines the complete construction and set-up of the facility, and then operates the venture for a period of time during which host country nationals are trained in all of the managerial and technical aspects of operating the facility. Furthermore, the management contract portion of the turnkey plus assures the continuing influx of process and product developments from the foreign firm. Under turnkey plus contracts, the firm from the developed country receives design, construction, and management fees, while the firm from the less developed country benefits from the management training and the continuous technical development as well as the building of a new production facility.

Turnkey plus agreements are turnkey operations combined with a management contract.

Buy-back Agreements

The types of operation described above are often tied to buy-back agreements wherein the firm agrees to take all or part of its turnkey and management contract fees in the form of products from the new facility. These products may be supplied free of charge or at a reduced price, but must be exported out of the host country. This ensures that production quality will be kept up to world market standards. Furthermore, these agreements ensure that the operator will continue to upgrade the products to keep them consistent with home country customer demands.

Tie-in Buying and Selling Agreements

Tie-in buying and selling agreements are contractual arrangements wherein assets held by a firm are exchanged for the raw materials of a foreign country. For example, a company may receive permission to extract oil in exchange for shares of stock in a firm incorporated specifically for the extraction, or stock in the parent firm. These assets could also include the rights to proprietary technology. In essence, these agreements allow for the exchange of raw material for technology or partial ownership.

These strategies (licensing, franchising, technical or managerial assistance contracts, turnkey operations, turnkey plus operations, buy-back agreements, and tie-in contracts) have one thing in common: The firm benefits from foreign business opportunities and has a high degree of management control but does not have to commit corporate funds. These strategies are often chosen over exporting because they minimize the effects of trade barriers and allow for increased control with only minimal increases in risk and no asset exposure.

Tie-in buying and selling contracts exchange raw materials for technology or partial ownership in the parent corporation.

EQUITY FOREIGN INVOLVEMENT

When a firm buys an existing foreign company (acquisition) or commits capital to start a new operation in a foreign country (new establishment), it has embarked on one of the highest potential profit and highest-risk forms of international involvement. Although ownership generally carries with it control and profit potential, it also results in the greatest risk of loss. When a firm makes an equity investment abroad it has fully embraced both the business and nonbusiness risks of that country.

Equity involvements in international business take two forms: joint ventures and wholly owned operations. Joint ventures are operations in which there is joint ownership of the foreign business; in wholly owned operations, the foreign investor is the sole and complete owner.

Joint Ventures

The term *joint venture* in international business is used two ways. First, it can define a contractual agreement involving two or more parties. Second, it can describe a jointly owned and independently incorporated business operating abroad. In actuality, there is little practical difference between these situations.

The participants in a joint venture can be individuals, firms, or governments. They may come from the country in which the investment is to be made (the host country), the foreign investor's country (the home country), or another country (third country). The joint venture can be one in which the foreign investor holds a majority ownership position, a 50 percent ownership position, or a minority ownership position. Usually joint ventures include at least one party from the country in which the investment is made.

In manufacturing, a joint venture is often similar to a licensing agreement in that the investing firm usually provides the technical skills and the intellectual property or know-how, while the host country firm supplies the marketing and environmental expertise. By contrast with a licensing agreement, however, the investing firm has greater participation in management decision-making because of its equity in the venture. In some countries, because of government regulations, the equity level of the foreign firm in the joint venture must be less than 50 percent, enabling the domestic partner to retain a controlling interest. These regulations, often called *indigenizational laws*, usually allow greater than 50 percent foreign ownership at the beginning of an operation but require that local ownership be increased to greater than 50 percent within a fixed period of time. The Global Insight describes a recent development in Mexico.

Although the most common form of joint venture is still the type wherein each partner contributes differently to the business, there are increasing instances of joint ventures in which each partner contributes throughout the value chain. This is typically a joint venture between competitive firms to exploit a business opportunity. The General Motors and Toyota joint venture in Fremont, California (discussed below), could be viewed as such an arrangement.

Joint ventures may take any form of business organization such as a general partnership, limited partnership, corporation, or other form of resource pooling that is permitted in the country of operation. As with licensing and franchise agreements, there has been a steady growth in the number and importance of joint ventures since the end of World War II and especially since 1960. One reason is the increasing governmental restrictions on foreign trade. Regional economic integration has also made joint ventures more attractive because of larger foreign markets and increased trade restrictions.

For the international firm, joint ventures have numerous advantages:

1. The local national firm usually makes it much easier to enter the market.
2. The profits are generally greater than in no-equity ventures.
3. The local partner provides knowledge of local markets and influence with local governments and institutions.
4. If the local partner has a production facility, some of the problems of starting a new operation can be eliminated.
5. Greater control can be exercised than under licensing.
6. Local capital may be more easily generated.
7. Risks can be shared jointly among the partners.
8. The danger of nationalization or expropriation might be reduced.
9. It is easier to meet host country investment regulations.
10. Greater opportunities exist for smaller firms with limited capital.

Many firms find that through joint ventures, they are able to compete successfully in markets that might otherwise have been closed. An example is that of the General Motors joint venture with the Daewoo Group of South Korea. Manufacturing and service expertise are provided by General Motors to build automobiles, buses, and trucks for the South Korean market. South

Mexico Now Permits 100 Percent Ownership for Foreign Investments

In a further modernization step, Mexican President Carlos Salinas de Gortari has announced major revisions of foreign investment regulations and reversed the nationalistic practices of restricting foreign capital. Combined with opening the country to more imports, tax reforms, financial deregulation, and anticipated changes in intellectual property rules, these revisions have fundamentally altered the investment climate of Mexico.

Foreign ownership limits have been increased from 49 percent to 100 percent in nearly two thirds of the economy, including such important industries as glass, cement, iron and steel, and cellulose. Investors have only to meet six conditions:

1. The investment may not exceed $100 million.

2. The funds must come entirely from abroad.

3. The project may not be in the industry zones of the Federal District, Guadalajara, and Monterrey.

4. Imports and exports must be in balance for the first three years.

5. The investment must create permanent jobs and provide the workers with training, education, and personal development programs.

6. The technology used must comply with existing environment regulations.

Although some sectors of the economy still have limits on foreign participation, the new openness to foreign investment is a major step forward for global integration of the Mexican economy.

In a step toward facilitating foreign ownership, the new rules state that when all six of the conditions for 100 percent ownership are met, no prior authorization is necessary. The investment project must merely be registered with the authorities.

The reaction of MNFs has been positive, with the exception of those from certain industries. Pharmaceutical executives say that they will wait until the promised intellectual property rules are announced. Representatives of banking and telecommunications feel that it is unfortunate that these industries are still state-controlled. Although some firms feel that these changes make Mexico highly competitive for attracting foreign direct investment now, most project a "wait, see, and study" reaction in the short term and increased investment in the medium term.

Source: Adapted from Alan Robinson, "Mexico Revamps Rules for Foreign Investment to Permit 100% Ownership," *Business Latin America*, May 22, 1989, pp. 154, 155, 159.

Korea provides skilled, inexpensive labor and access to the market. No doubt the South Korean government prefers this arrangement to that of complete foreign ownership or an attempt to produce domestically a product in which it lacks expertise.

In countries where the culture, language, customs, and other conditions differ markedly from those of the foreign investor, joint ventures eliminate many of the obstacles or problems that these cultural differences could create in the production and distribution of products.

Joint ventures are also becoming popular for foreign firms wanting to do business in the United States. One of the most highly publicized of these partnership arrangements is that between General Motors and Toyota in Fremont, California. This cooperative operation partly reflects the voluntary import quota on Japanese automobiles entering the United States. Opposition to such a partnership was voiced by Chrysler because of the possibility that this joint venture could result in GM-Toyota domination of the small-car market in the United States. In spite of the opposition, the U.S. government approved the venture. Toyota got around the quota without a massive capital outlay and General Motors got Japanese engineering and production technologies.

There are, however, several major disadvantages associated with joint ventures. Neither partner has complete control over operations. Joint ventures create the risk of losing capital assets or intellectual property as a result of the actions of the joint venture partner. There is the possibility of conflicts among the partners on any one of several significant points:

1. Reinvestment or distribution of the profits
2. Product line or marketing decisions
3. Product design, quality, and standardization
4. Transfer pricing (the price charged by the foreign firm to the joint venture)
5. Labor relations and personnel matters

Joint ventures require less capital, provide both parties with some degree of managerial control, and result in a sharing of resources, expertise, and knowledge.

Once a company enters into a joint venture it is usually a long-term commitment; however, there is no assurance of success. The TRW agreement with Fujitsu in the manufacture of computer hardware and software, and Honeywell's experience with the French firm Sesa in the manufacture of data transmission devices are only two examples attesting to the fact that failure is possible. Problems not anticipated when the joint venture was formed often result in final dissolution. A joint venture is like an economic marriage: It can be beautifully complementary when both parties benefit, or a source of continuing frustration and tension.

Wholly Owned Subsidiaries

Wholly owned foreign operations still represent the preferred way of doing business abroad by most U.S. firms, especially manufacturers. Despite the increased costs and risks, wholly owned operations provide the highest possible levels of control and 100 percent of all profits generated. Furthermore, there are no partners who may object to key managerial or financial decisions. In fact, it is fair to say that were it not for indigenization laws, many firms would not take on local partners. Even if investable funds were deficient, most firms would opt for long-term debt or a local stock issuance.

Even local stockholders attending stockholder meetings would be preferable to a local partner being involved in day-to-day operations.

This preference for wholly owned operations results in large part from the desire for the control over subsidiary operations that allows for rationalization of decision-making on a global corporate basis. This control is essential for attainment of worldwide strategies, especially in what were previously defined as global industries. It can be very difficult to transfer funds from one joint venture subsidiary to another even if the economics call for such a move. For example, to remove funds from a joint venture, both partners would have to agree to a dividend pay-out; for funds to be added to a joint venture as equity both partners would have to contribute funds, or else the percentages of ownership would change. This latter problem could be eliminated by adding the new funds as debt; however, in some countries debt supplied by the foreign partner in a joint venture is considered equity. The former problem is not nearly so easily solved. The local partner may want the subsidiary's profits invested in that country, while the foreign investor may have better investment alternatives elsewhere. Furthermore, the local partner may not want any more dividends since these may be taxed at a very high rate.

Clearly this situation would be substantially easier if the subsidiaries were wholly owned. The subsidiary could simply declare a dividend to be paid to the parent corporation, which is the sole owner. If taxes make this action prohibitively expensive, the parent corporation could increase the costs for support services or materials: administrative cross charges, research and development expenses, technical and engineering assistance, component parts, and so forth. Thus, profits in the host country would be reduced and profits elsewhere increased. If this were not possible the parent corporation could authorize a loan from one subsidiary to another. Overall, wholly owned subsidiaries create the maximum of control and return but also the maximum of risk and exposure.

Taking an ownership position in foreign business, whether joint venture or 100 percent ownership, is still the preferred way to do business abroad.

Both joint ventures and wholly owned operations provide the firm with greater profit potential and greater control at the expense of increased risks than contractual agreements. Joint ventures create a condition of risk sharing but result in lesser profits and substantially diminished control over the foreign operation. This loss of control is the major reason that most firms prefer wholly owned operations. Unfortunately, many foreign governments, especially those in less developed countries, are as concerned as multinational firms with subsidiary control and have enacted laws to prohibit wholly owned operations.

SUMMARY

In spite of uncertainties, business opportunities exist for business in many foreign countries. An important decision for executives of firms with international business opportunities is which form of involvement is appropriate for each business opportunity. Firms generally make use of all three modes of operation: exporting, no-equity (contractual agreements), and equity investments.

In many large American firms, exporting is treated as merely an extension of international marketing and often viewed as having secondary importance or being an intermediate step to establishing a foreign operation in a country. This is clearly not the case with many of the larger firms of Japan and numerous other companies. Indeed, exporting, either directly or indirectly, needs to be viewed strategically as a viable long-term mode of involvement in a particular foreign market.

Smaller firms in the United States often dismiss foreign markets because of a lack of familiarity or understanding of the profit potentials. In these instances, the use of indirect exporting intermediaries can be of critical importance in unlocking this potential.

For firms that want a greater involvement in foreign business situations than exporting but for some reason do not want to put equity at risk, there are several no-equity or contractual methods available. Licensing one's technology, know-how, or intellectual property (intangible assets) is the most common method. Licensing basically allows the firm to collect an up-front fee and a percentage of revenues in return for exclusive rights to use the valuable "asset." Franchising is similar to licensing in that the firm collects an up-front fee and a percentage of revenues. The differences are that the franchisor may also collect funds for advertising, may require that the franchisee purchase equipment or raw materials from the franchisor, and so forth. Each of these contributes to the franchisor's overall profits. Franchising is also different from licensing in that it usually involves the marketing of consumer goods.

Management contracts provide another no-equity method for exploiting foreign market potentials. Under a management contract the firm sells its expertise in the operation of a business for a fixed or variable fee. For example, a firm may contract to manage a hydroelectric plant for a period of 10 years, performing all of the details of operation, maintenance, equipment modification, and so forth. Most management contracts also require that during the life of the contract, the foreign contractor must train local nationals in all of the skills of operation so that at the end of the contract period, the operation will continue to run effectively and efficiently without the involvement of the contractor.

Turnkey and turnkey plus operations are closely related, as the names suggest. Turnkey operations involve a firm's selling its expertise, for example, in building a facility, selecting and installing all of the equipment, and taking the facility through all of the difficult decisions and modifications of start-up. Turnkey operations also involve preliminary training of personnel. This is done in return for a fixed fee, which is usually paid in installments over the period of the contract. Turnkey plus operations are identical except that when start-up has been completed the contractor stays on as operator of the facility and trainer for the local nationals who will ultimately operate the facility. In other words, a turnkey plus operation is really a turnkey contract combined with a management contract.

For firms that wish to exploit a foreign business opportunity in a manner that provides them all or part of the profits of that venture, and that is not afraid to put equity capital at risk, there are two choices: joint ventures and wholly owned operations. In the case of joint ventures a part of the ownership and therefore a part of the profits are shared. Joint ventures occur for two primary reasons: Local laws prohibit 100 percent foreign ownership, or the partner supplies something important for the success of the venture. These necessary additions can be capital, technology, market information, political contacts and influence, and so forth. There are numerous forms of joint venture. The joint venture may involve two or more parties, the partner(s) can be from the host country or some third country, one of the partners can be the host government, and the foreign firm can be a majority, equal, or minority partner. Despite the significant advantages that joint ventures may offer, they result in a loss of some degree of ownership control. It is for this reason that most U.S. firms opt for wholly owned operations when it is possible.

KEY TERMS AND CONCEPTS

Buy-back agreements	Majority ownership—joint venture
Contractual agreement	Management contract
Direct export	Minority ownership—joint venture
Equity foreign investments	No-equity foreign investment
Factors of production	Patent
Franchise agreement	Royalty
Indigenization laws	Technical assistance
Indirect export	Tie-in buying and selling
Intellectual property	Turnkey operation
Joint venture	Turnkey plus contracts
Licensing agreement	Wholly owned operations
Local content legislation	

REVIEW QUESTIONS

1. Define and explain the no-equity forms of international involvement.

2. Why might a firm opt to continue exporting to a market when there are few barriers to establishing a manufacturing operation? Which of your reasons adequately explains the slowness of Japanese automobile manufacturers' establishing assembly plants in the United States?

3. Discuss the advantages and disadvantages of joint venturing with a foreign government.

4. Explain the potential problem areas of international franchising.

5. Explain why many persons believe that foreign investment and international licensing are exporting U.S. jobs.

6. Explain the operation of a turnkey plus operation with a buy-back agreement.

DISCUSSION CASE

PepsiCo India—Joint Venture

The opportunity for PepsiCo to consider a joint venture in India in 1988 was actually a result of the fact that Coca-Cola pulled out of India in 1978 after a vigorous and highly publicized dispute with the Indian government. The Indian government demanded that Coke turn over the secret formula for its soft drink to an Indian company, transfer other technical know-how to local management, and reduce its ownership position in India to 40 percent or less. This government position was tantamount to demanding that Coke give up ownership as well as management and technical control of its Indian operations. Coke rejected these demands and pulled out of India. Ten years later PepsiCo decided to move to fill the void left by Coke.

On March 28, 1988, Simon Anderson, director of marketing research for PepsiCo, received a memo from his boss, Jim Dawn, Vice-President for Marketing.

> Simon,
> Attached you will find a proposal that was put together by the folks in our international operations group. This calls for us to establish a joint venture in India. We could really scoop Coke on this one or end up looking like fools.
>
> This is going to be discussed next Friday at the executive policy meeting, so get on it right now. I don't want only a marketing analysis. I want a thorough review of not only this joint venture proposal but also your ideas for the other ways we ought to consider for exploiting the potential of the Indian market.
>
> If you need any help just reassign one of your people. I really need a first-class analysis. This is either a great possibility or a time bomb.

By Don R. Beeman, 1989.

This case is based on numerous *Wall Street Journal* articles during September 1988 regarding the PepsiCo joint venture in India as well as information from *Moody's Industrial Manual*. The authors have taken some literary license with the facts by hypothesizing memos, characters, and decision situations to create a case suitable for classroom discussion, but have tried to stay consistent with the facts. This case should not be viewed as either an historic or a journalistic account of the actual situation at PepsiCo.

Furthermore, this case is not intended to represent good or bad management practices or decision-making.

Simon, the "Big Guy" is strongly behind our entry into the Indian market so *it is going to happen*; however, I have my doubts as to whether this proposal is the best way to go about it. I'm counting on your group to help me decide whether this is the right approach and if not, what we should be doing.

Jim

P.S. Rumor has it that Coke is trying to reenter India.

Background

PepsiCo, Inc., was incorporated in North Carolina on December 4, 1986, as a successor to the original company, incorporated in Delaware in 1919 as Loft, Inc. PepsiCo is engaged through its various divisions and subsidiaries in soft drinks, snack foods, and restaurants both in the United States and abroad, but its principal business is the manufacture and sale of soft drinks. PepsiCo International sells and distributes soft drink products outside the United States under various trade names: Pepsi-Cola, Diet Pepsi, Mirinda, and others. This is done through company-owned bottlers, joint ventures, and independent bottlers. PepsiCo products are available in nearly 150 countries and U.S. territories. The principal foreign markets include Argentina, Brazil, Canada, Egypt, Japan, Mexico, the Philippines, Saudi Arabia, the United Kingdom, and Venezuela. PepsiCo International operates 65 plants throughout the world in which the proprietary syrups and concentrates for the soft drinks are made or in which carbonated beverages are bottled.

Proposal for a Joint Venture in India

Coke's leaving India in 1978 presents us with an excellent opportunity to dramatically increase our worldwide sales volume and global market share by moving into that market. However, the only way we can effectively exploit the market potential of that 730,000,000-person market is by forming a joint venture.

Our research and analysis has developed the following facts that are fundamental to this venture.

1. Our initial investment will be about $17 million for a facility to produce soft drink concentrate, along with fruit juice concentrates and snack foods.
2. We will use local foodstuffs in the production of these products.
3. The best site for such an operation is in the state of Punjab.
4. We will use franchised bottler contract distributors for the entirety of India.
5. The government of India has indicated that it will allow us to import what we need provided that we have exports from the venture exceed the value of those imports by a factor of five (5).
6. If this ratio of exports to imports is not met, we will not be able to repatriate profits or royalties.

This venture would be a three-way jointly owned operation: 39.9 percent PepsiCo, 36.1 percent the Indian central government, and 24 percent Tata. Tata is India's largest industrial corporation. Although these terms are harsh, even in comparison to those we have signed with the USSR and the PRC, we believe that there are numerous good reasons for accepting them. In the words of our president and chief executive officer Robert H. Beeby, "We are willing to make sure we get an early entry while the market is developing. The Indian middle class is beginning to emerge, and we see that as a big growth market." His position is supported by the following market demographics. Indians consume about 2.4 million bottles of name-brand soft drinks each year. Although this is quite small when viewed on a per capita basis, we think that this is more than offset by the size of the market (population) and the consumption growth rate (20 percent per year).

This $17 million plant will allow us to produce enough concentrate for 1.2 billion bottles of Pepsi each year. This is much more than we will need in India for many years to come; however, we anticipate making this plant an exporting platform for numerous other Asian markets. We also feel that it is important to move quickly and successfully into the Indian market because we believe that we will not have to face major competition in India. Although we have no formal assurances from the Indian government, none of us anticipates India's welcoming Coke back with open arms. Furthermore, we are experiencing major price competition in both the USSR and the PRC. If this competition erodes profit margins for those two operations, India could be a major financial strength in the increasingly competitive global marketplace. The aggressive proactive nature of this proposal is also consistent with the international mission that Mr. Beeby has articulated on numerous occasions, stating that it is better to enter a market with or ahead of Coca-Cola. "Viewing them [Coca-Cola] as our leading competitor, if we get into a big market ahead of them we are that much better off." We want to move fast so that we don't have to fight it out in the stores as we are probably going to have to do for the diet cola market in Brazil.

To ensure that we can meet the export targets for this operation we will take several additional steps. First, we will build modern food-processing plants for locally grown tomatoes, pears, apples, mangoes, and other fruits which will be used to make fruit juice concentrates. Beverages made from fruit juices will be not only a major source of sales in India but also the most important source of exports. In India, unlike the United States, fruit juices and nonfruit beverages are basically in competition with each other. Relatedly, Asian people are much more health conscious than they were 15 years ago. This is especially true in Southeast Asia. The large capacity of the proposed plant will give us the opportunity to move aggressively into the fruit juice markets of this entire region. Second, we will establish an agricultural research center to develop high-yield crops and disease-resistant seeds.

In addition to the technology transfer and Indian ownership aspects of this venture, it will also create 1,000 jobs and give work to about 15,000 farmers.

Questions:

1. Should Pepsi go forth with the joint venture as outlined in this case?
2. Is India a good place from which to supply the Southeast Asian market?
3. What do you think are the chances of Coke getting back into India?
4. If Pepsi goes forth with the joint venture and if you were the officers of Coke, what would be your competitive response?

NOTES

1. Kredietbank, Weekly Bulletin no. 1, 6 Jan. 1984 (Brussels, Belgium), p. 2.
2. Ibid., p. 2.
3. Vern Terpstra, *International Marketing*, 2nd ed. (Hinesdale, Ill.: Dryden Press, 1978), pp. 330–332.

REFERENCES AND
SELECTED READINGS

Anderson, Erin, and Hubert Gatignon. "Modes of Foreign Entry: A Transaction Cost Analysis and Propositions." *The Journal of International Business Studies* 17:3 (Fall 1986).

Boddewyn, Jean J. "Foreign and Domestic Divestment and Investment Decisions: Like or Unlike?" *The Journal of International Business Studies* 14:3 (Winter 1983).

Chase, C. D. and J. L. and Walther Kuhle. "The Relevance of Political Risk in Foreign Direct Investment." *Management International Review* 25, 1988.

Contractor, Farok J. "Choosing Between Direct Investment and Licensing: Theoretical Considerations and Empirical Tests." *The Journal of International Business Studies* 15:3 (Winter 1984).

Contractor, Farok J. "The 'Profitability' of Technology Licensing by U.S. Multinationals: A Framework for Analysis and an Empirical Study." *The Journal of International Business Studies* 11:2 (Fall 1980).

Encarnationa, Dennis J., and Sushil Vachani. "Foreign Ownership: When Host Countries Change the Rules." *Harvard Business Review*, Sept.-Oct. 1985.

Fry, E. H. *The Politics of International Investment*. New York: McGraw-Hill, 1983.

Hall, R. Duane. *Overseas Acquisitions and Mergers*. New York: Praeger Publishing, 1986.

Kojima, K. *Direct Foreign Investment*. New York: Praeger Publishing, 1978.

Kredietbank. Brussels, Belgium. Weekly Bulletin no. 1, 6 Jan. 1984.

Oman, Charles. *New Form of International Investment in Developing Countries*. OECD, 1984.

Terpstra, Vern. *International Marketing*, 2nd ed. Hinesdale, Ill.: Dryden Press, 1978.

Walter, Ingo, and Tracy Murray. *Handbook of International Management*. John Wiley and Sons, 1988.

Weigand, Robert. "International Investment: Weighing the Incentives." *Harvard Business Review*, July-August 1983.

Wilson, Brent D. "The Propensity of Multinational Companies to Expand Through Acquisitions." *The Journal of International Business Studies* 11:1 (Spring/Summer 1980).

CHAPTER

14 International Marketing Strategy

INTRODUCTION

International marketing today is more than merely the selling of goods or services to a second country, or a firm's market involvement in another country. The complexity of contemporary international marketing is such that most internationally active firms develop equally complex international marketing plans and strategies. The serendipity of becoming an international marketer by following unsolicited orders or by unsystematic investigation is largely a thing of the past. It now requires thorough research of the market or country, as well as the possible problems that might be encountered in promoting the product in that market, and a determination of those factors that might affect the future needs of the market.[1]

From a total corporation perspective, international marketing strategy includes the determination of worldwide as well as country-specific strategies. These strategies must define the locus of decision-making between headquarters and subsidiary management. The marketing strategies must operationally define how regional and global control and coordination will be maintained. They must decide which markets the firm wishes to exploit and how it will exploit those markets, including entry into new markets and the maintenance or growth of existing markets. The strategies must also determine a particular culture's perception and reception of the product.

STRATEGIES FOR INTERNATIONAL MARKETING

Dimensions of International Marketing Strategy

The successful international marketer must first develop worldwide marketing strategies. These include plans to compete either in global industries where the world is considered a single market rather than a collection of national markets, or in multidomestic industries where subsidiaries compete independently in different markets. This involves setting long-range objectives and specific plans for meeting those objectives. The decision will be based upon a number of factors, including the willingness of the firm to commit its resources for a long term before the success of the strategy might be realized.[2]

Developing strategies involves setting objectives and specific plans for meeting those objectives. Depending on the size of the firm, the nature of the product, the markets in which it operates, and the aspirations of top management, the strategies call for careful evaluation of several issues. In which foreign markets and global industries does the firm wish to compete? How does management want to service those markets: indirect exporting, direct exporting, or company sales operations? Will it have standard products for all markets or will it adapt the product for each market? Will the firm follow one basic pricing approach worldwide or adapt prices to local conditions? Will it have one promotional message worldwide or will it adapt its message to each individual country?

The product and message decisions result in nine basic corporate-level international marketing strategies, as presented in Table 14.1. As a firm moves from 1 to 9, it loses synergies and economies of scale. This requires more staff or contract agents to develop a unique product, and a unique advertising and promotional message for each market it serves. It is also obvious that designing a unique product for each market improves the chances of effectively satisfying the needs of that market.

Developing a new advertising and promotional message for each market enhances the likelihood of effectively communicating the benefits of the firm's product. Although some firms make corporate decisions on products

Table 14.1   **International Marketing Strategies**

Message	Product		
	Same	*Adapted*	*New*
Same	1	2	3
Adapted	4	5	6
New	7	8	9

and messages that are applicable to all markets, it is far more common for firms to decide independently on the product and message for each market.

The achievement of the objectives of the marketing strategy might well depend on where the final decision is made. Traditionally, international marketing strategy placed the bulk of marketing responsibility in the hands of local subsidiary management. Today, firms are increasingly placing responsibility in the hands of marketing executives at the corporate headquarters. This change largely reflects the development of multinational firms and the increasing number of global industries. In addition to deciding between centralized versus decentralized decision-making, international marketing strategies must operationally define how control and coordination will be maintained among the various subsidiaries. This control and coordination will need to be maintained on both a regional and global basis.

Marketing Strategy Activities

International marketing strategy includes three basic activities that are essential for the successful development of individual markets:

1. Selecting markets to be exploited

2. Determining strategies for exploiting each market (the four Ps)
   a. Selecting, adapting, or developing products (*Product*)
   b. Determining an appropriate pricing strategy (*Price*)
   c. Developing an advertising and promotion plan (*Promotion*)
   d. Deciding on the channels for distribution and the outlets to be used (*Place*)

3. Developing strategies for maintaining or increasing one's involvement in each market

These three dimensions of international marketing strategy can be portrayed as a flow chart (see Figure 14.1).

Coordination of International Marketing Strategies

An appropriate organizational structure will facilitate coordinating the marketing strategies. Four alternative structures are commonly used to achieve coordination. First, the firm may establish an international marketing division to separate international from domestic marketing activities. This structure places greater focus on the international strategies.[3] With growth in the international activities of the firm, modifications may be necessary. A second type of organizational form is the geographic structure, with each group having its own functional support staff. Europe, for example, may be divided into northern Europe, southern Europe, and the eastern bloc countries. The major advantage of this form of structure is that each group

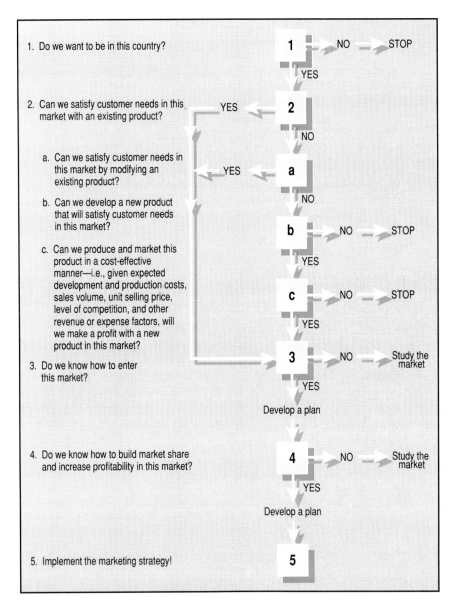

1. Do we want to be in this country? — **1** → NO → STOP
   YES ↓

2. Can we satisfy customer needs in this market with an existing product? ← YES ← **2**
   NO ↓

   a. Can we satisfy customer needs in this market by modifying an existing product? ← YES ← **a**
      NO ↓

   b. Can we develop a new product that will satisfy customer needs in this market? — **b** → NO → STOP
      YES ↓

   c. Can we produce and market this product in a cost-effective manner—i.e., given expected development and production costs, sales volume, unit selling price, level of competition, and other revenue or expense factors, will we make a profit with a new product in this market? — **c** → NO → STOP
      YES ↓

3. Do we know how to enter this market? — **3** → NO → Study the market
   YES ↓

   Develop a plan ↓

4. Do we know how to build market share and increase profitability in this market? — **4** → NO → Study the market
   YES ↓

   Develop a plan ↓

5. Implement the marketing strategy! — **5**

Figure 14.1 The International Marketing Strategy Process

develops expertise in the diverse product lines. This facilitates product adaptations and communications, and shortens distribution lines.[4] Third, the organization may be structured along product lines. Separate divisions will be established for each product line with an appropriate support staff. The major weakness here is that each product line will tend to develop independently.[5] Although technical or product expertise is maximized, there can be redundancy in marketing efforts and an absence of technological cross-fertilization. The fourth variation in marketing structures is the matrix approach. This approach seeks to combine product management with a market orientation to achieve the best of both worlds.[6] Unfortunately, the matrix organization structure also has problems. Power struggles often develop and interdepartmental communications might be weakened.[7]

The three essential elements of organizational coordination are communication, authority-line definition, and human factors. Effective coordination requires that management be able to receive and transmit information quickly and accurately. One important variable of this is language. Structuring a firm along lines that ignore language differences is apt to be ineffective.[8] Organizational patterns with ambiguous lines of authority are self-defeating. Confusion as to who is responsible to whom for what results can weaken coordination and lead to ineffective operations. This is especially true in matrix structures where dual chains of command exist. Coordination of foreign marketing efforts is actually the coordination of the efforts of all of the firm's employees; therefore, the human dimension of any management system must be considered. It is important to examine these wishes, expectations, and ambitions of the people involved and the effect of these on working relationships.[9]

Controlling International Marketing Strategies

The control of international marketing strategy can be accomplished through performance measurement—that is, establishing and evaluating performance standards. Standards against which performance is measured should reflect the overall goal of the parent company. Performance standards include return on investment, contribution to profit, and cash flow. Nonfinancial standards include degree of market penetration, evaluation of promotional effort, and distribution and service evaluation.[10]

Once marketing performance standards are established, a monitoring system must be set up to evaluate performance against these standards. Thus, the key component in the monitoring system is feedback. The only way subsidiaries will be able to improve performance is through continual feedback as to performance deficiencies.[11]

Overall, an international marketing control system should meet several basic requirements in order to ensure effective monitoring and evaluation of the performance of subsidiaries:[12]

1. Subsidiary management should
   a. Understand and accept the controls
   b. Have an active role in formulating controls
   c. Actively participate in the appraisal process
   d. Be evaluated only on activities it directly controls

2. Subsidiary objectives should be realistic considering the internal and external environment

3. Evaluations should include nonfinancial as well as financial data

4. Control systems should promptly detect deviations from plans

5. Control techniques should be tailored for each subsidiary

6. Control systems should be revised and improved as required by changes in the subsidiary's environment

7. Top management must tie compensation to results achieved, and outstanding performance must be tangibly rewarded

The international marketer must develop a market strategy regarding products, pricing, and promotion. Coordination and control of these are essential for success.

SELECTING INTERNATIONAL MARKETS

Although most firms rigorously plan their international market selection strategies, some firms discover a foreign market opportunity almost by accident. Stories regularly appear in the business press about market opportunities that someone uncovered while on vacation, hosting a foreign exchange student, visiting a son or daughter who was studying abroad, traveling with a church missionary group, or engaging in a variety of other international activities. Indeed, this type of unsystematic discovery can still be an important source of information on foreign market opportunities for small or medium-sized firms. For example, a small firm from south central Indiana that manufactures jacks for light trucks discovered a market in Scandinavia during the owner's trip to Denmark. This initially resulted in exporting and later in Danish production to service markets throughout western Europe. Nevertheless, with the increasing number of sophisticated multinational firms, the role of the unplanned market identification is of decreasing importance.

Over the past three decades international firms have systematically selected foreign markets in one or more of four basic ways:

1. Preferential consideration

2. Surplus sell-off opportunities

3. Similarity

4. Researched potential[13]

Preferential Consideration Markets

In the days before GATT, bilateral treaties were used to counter the damaging effects of protectionism. These bilateral treaties often extended political and economic relations that had begun during the period of European colonization. Despite the reductions in bilateral treaties and protectionism as a result of the various GATT negotiations, there remains a tendency for firms to look first to markets in countries with a common heritage or previous colonial ties. British firms still tend to look for markets in nations that were members of the Commonwealth, and Dutch firms have more economic contacts with Indonesia than would seem reasonable had it not been a Dutch colony. The quasi-colonial involvement of the United States in Latin America helps explain the early and frequent ventures of U.S. firms in the Caribbean, Central America, and South America. Despite these remaining linkages with the past, preferential consideration is becoming less important as a means of selecting foreign markets.

Surplus Sell-off Markets

Surplus sell-off markets are those that will, for various reasons, generally purchase a firm's excess production. In the days when U.S. firms were recognized world leaders in the manufacture of most goods, it was not difficult to find such markets. Today surplus sell-off markets are generally limited to less developed countries, which have a shortage of hard currency reserves. As a result, these markets often require extremely generous payment terms or even credits from U.S. government foreign aid programs. Surplus sell-off strategies are today limited to basic commodity items that are largely indistinguishable from one company to another, such as PVC (plastic) resin or agricultural products.

Similarity Markets

Seeking markets that were similar in customer needs, patterns of product usage, and distribution characteristics was the way many U.S. firms planned their first forays into international markets during the post–World War II period. The logic was faultless for a seller in a seller's market. The more similar a market was to the firm's domestic market, the fewer the adaptations required. As a result, American firms went first to Canada and then to the United Kingdom. From this beginning, firms learned how to attack other markets of western Europe.

This method, too, is increasingly of limited value in selecting foreign markets, although it is still employed by many smaller firms. The competition today is so fearsome in most countries that a company that does not modify its products, packaging, advertising and promotional messages, or distribution strategies to reflect seemingly insignificant market differences might just as well stay home or let an exporter handle the adaptations.

Researched Potential Markets

Today international marketing begins by identifying potential foreign markets on the basis of market size and market structure. Market structure includes the stage of development, the number of competitors and their market shares, and the channels through which the market is to be reached.

With the rapidly increasing competitiveness of most national and global markets, it is no longer sufficient merely to identify good market opportunities; the firm must move rapidly to satisfy the needs of those markets. Many large firms have learned the hard lesson of missing the take-off of a foreign market. Because of the complexity of researching potential foreign markets, many small or medium-sized firms as well as a substantial number of large firms have adopted a "follow the leader" strategy. They let the industry leader spend substantial sums on international market research, then merely invest wherever the leader invests.

In addition to identifying foreign market opportunities, the firm must decide whether to concentrate initially in only the best markets or to enter all markets simultaneously. If the firm competes in a "global industry" where activities in one country influence competitiveness in a second, then the firm may want to enter multiple markets simultaneously. If, however, the firm's industry is multidomestic in character, then the firm is largely free to decide whether its objectives could be better met by intensively exploiting one market rather than by initiating a lesser involvement in several markets.

Various methods may be used by a firm in selecting markets for its products.

Whatever foreign market is selected, the firm must decide what to sell and at what price, what outlets or channels to use, and how it is going to promote sales. The 4 Ps (product, price, place, and promotion) are the operational foundations of any marketing strategy for any country.

STRATEGIES FOR EXPLOITING FOREIGN MARKETS

Product Strategies

A firm that makes a long-term commitment to a foreign market must develop a product strategy. This means that it must decide whether to market the same product that it is selling in the domestic market, adapt a product for the foreign market, or develop a new product specifically for that market.[14] (See Figure 14.2.)

The final decision on standardization, product adaptation, or new product development should be made only after careful evaluation of the prod-

Figure 14.2   International Product Strategies

Product strategy

Standard product   Adapted product   New product

uct's market acceptance and an analysis of those factors affecting costs and revenues.

Standardization Versus Adaptation

An important consideration in determining an international product strategy is understanding the advantages and disadvantages of standardization and adaptation. Selling standard products in both foreign and domestic markets often results in increased production levels and possible economies of scale in purchasing, manufacturing, research and development, and administrative or overhead expenses. Using standard packaging, trademarks, and promotional material could result in further economies. Global product standardization can also result in more effective planning and control and better use of management time and talent.[15] An added advantage might be the creation of greater consumer loyalty due to increased product and brand familiarity. Offsetting these advantages is the fact that marketing standard products can result in loss of sales due to incomplete satisfaction of buyer needs and wants, or a poor cultural fit. Fear of such losses may account for the relatively low number of "global brands" today (see the Global Insight). Worldwide sales would be difficult without the standardization of products such as electric light bulbs, spark plugs, automobile tires, and computer disks, or where standards are established for weights and measures.

Through adaptation, the needs and tastes of a particular market can be more completely met. For example, British automobiles are exported to the United States with a left-hand drive. U.S. electrical appliances manufactured for export are adapted to meet the different voltage requirements of most countries. Clothing items exported from the West to Asia are adapted to meet the smaller stature of the average population, books are translated to meet the language requirements of foreign nations, certain ingredients in food items are omitted to meet religious or cultural requirements, and trademarks are often modified to prevent their offending some people for religious reasons. Even superstitions toward certain colors must be taken into consideration, as discussed in Chapter 11.

Of primary concern to a firm will be the cost-benefit trade-offs of the adaptation. The firm must determine whether the market is large enough to be worth the cost of modifying the product. Will adaptation be necessary to retain or increase its market share? On the other hand, a number of factors beyond the control of the firm might force adaptation.

The physical or climatic conditions, or mechanical and technical differences might necessitate adaptations. Government regulations often require product adaptation. Some products may not be imported unless they meet certain minimum standards, or changes must be made before they can be distributed in that country. For example, many European countries have less stringent automobile emission requirements than those in the United States, so cars imported into the United States have to be modified to meet minimum standards.

Importers may have a say in adaptations. One of the major complaints voiced by the Japanese is that American automobiles are not adapted for sale in their market. Many cars are exported to that country with a left-hand drive, forcing the Japanese to convert them to right hand drive at considerable expense. Additional costs must be incurred to reposition the outside mirrors because they protrude from the side of the car by more than the legal maximum. Numerous other examples may be drawn from different countries where government regulations, market differences in weights and measurements, differences in quality and tolerance of products, labeling, and so forth make it necessary for adaptations before products may be marketed.

The cultural and physical environments may require product adaptations if a firm expects to garner a larger share of the overseas market.[16] Such adaptations tend to minimize conflicts that may arise due to the various differences among nations. Some of these cultural considerations were discussed in depth earlier, in Chapter 11, dealing with the human and cultural environment of business.

New Products

The development of new products for overseas markets involves the same processes as domestic product development: learning customer needs (both form and function), generating product ideas, screening those prototype products, making preliminary estimates of production costs, test marketing prototype products that are most likely to generate market acceptance, selecting the product(s) to be marketed, making final modifications, and finally going to full-scale production and marketing. The firm should also investigate how this new product will fit in with its organizational objectives and policies.

The details of the product should be worked out during the development stage because the firm cannot constantly modify a product once it is in production. These details include the major features of the product, brands, packaging, and physical appearance as well as the functional performance of the product. Testing should be conducted by introducing the product to a representative area of the market. This should uncover any problems that call for changes before full-scale production gets under way.

Understanding "New Product" Acceptance   When a "new product" is introduced into a market, the initial reaction is generally negative. This reflects the perceived newness of the product and the psychological resistance of most individuals to change. As a result, marketing management needs to design its new products or the modifications of existing products to minimize those factors that will impede market acceptance. Five basic factors determine the degree and the rapidity of market acceptance of a new product:

1. The relative advantages of the new product
2. The cultural compatibility of the product
3. The relative ease of product use
4. The opportunity to try out the product before purchase
5. The ease of observing product advantages[17]

Additionally, most individuals utilize some form of perceived cost-benefit consideration in their decision to adopt a new product. The marketing manager must understand that individuals will be more likely to purchase the product if they perceive greater utility relative to price than in the product they are currently using. Finally, the international marketing manager needs to be keenly aware of the possible negative consequences of introducing a new product in a market.[18]

Even when a product has a number of benefits, management must be aware of the possible negative effects. Insecticides have saved crops from insects and helped nations feed rapidly expanding populations; however, these have also caused substantial and long-term harm to the environment. The excessive use of DDT, before it was finally banned, is a classic example of ignoring the negative consequences. The introduction of fast foods also represents an example of both positive and negative effects. The increase in high-fat diets has been paralleled by the spread of coronary diseases. Nestlé's promotion of baby formula as the "modern" and "scientific" way to feed infants did far more than merely replace breast feeding. In some less

Firms must weigh the possible loss of sales from marketing a standardized product against the costs of product adaptation or new product development.

developed countries, the consumers lacked the sophistication to use these products properly, and the dilution of the liquid formula or mixed dry formula with contaminated water led to the spread of diseases and the death of thousands of children. Consumer groups have accused Nestlé of false advertising that prompted mothers in the LDCs to use the infant formula instead of breast feeding. Nestlé withdrew its advertising in the LDCs while other companies have changed their marketing practices of milk products in these countries.

Marketing Differences Between Consumer and Industrial Goods

There are some fundamental differences between marketing consumer and industrial goods. These differences reflect both buying decision criteria and processes, and the importance of cultural factors. For example, industrial goods are generally sold on the basis of performance relative to price, whereas consumer goods are sold based on culture and a myriad of other factors. This is especially true of nondurable consumer goods, which require more adaptation than durable consumer goods because they appeal to the customs, habits, and tastes of the consumer. Industrial goods, therefore, require less adaptation than do consumer goods.

Marketing Consumer Goods   Consumer goods are more sensitive to cultural factors and taste preferences than are industrial goods. However, the international marketing of consumer goods all too often falls into one of two categories: adapting domestic products to meet the needs of foreign consumers, or introducing products abroad that have completed their life cycle in a more highly developed country. This is particularly true for consumer products that are introduced for the first time in less developed markets.[19]

Marketing Industrial Goods   The buyers of industrial goods are usually firms or governments that are engaged in productive activities. The level of economic development of the country will generally determine the type of industrial goods it demands.[20] Less developed countries will place major emphasis on machines that are inexpensive, simple to operate, durable, and easy to maintain. They are the markets for industrial goods that are used for the production of basic consumer goods or equipment to carry out some simple economic activities. For example, small electric motors have been imported into Indonesia and some of the other countries in Southeast Asia to replace human "treadwheels" for irrigation purposes.

Countries that are somewhat further advanced generally want industrial machinery for processing primary products. The Philippines have imported equipment for the manufacture of plywood, which has resulted in the growth of the plywood industry, enabling that country to export mahogany plywood rather than mahogany logs. Countries that are even further advanced, such as Costa Rica, import industrial equipment for the manufacture of simple consumer goods such as transistor radios, camera cases, and flashlights.

During this stage, obsolete equipment from the more highly developed countries will often meet the needs of these countries. Nations more highly developed economically import industrial equipment for the manufacture of both capital goods and consumer goods. Finally, a nation will reach the stage of complete industrialization when it is capable of producing most equipment for the production of both producer and consumer goods. These are countries such as the United States, Japan, West Germany, and other countries of western Europe. However, even these nations consider it advantageous to import specialized capital goods from other highly industrialized countries.

Competition is keen in the marketing of industrial products. The newly industrialized countries of the Pacific Rim, Brazil, and Mexico are major competitors of the well-established industrialized countries.

Since the needs of each market differ, the producer who adapts the product to the market and meets the conditions unique to each country has a major advantage. Prompt delivery, uniform standards, service, and the availability of replacement parts provide further advantages. Furthermore, liberal credit terms are more important than the price of the goods to some buyers. (See Chapter 15 on exporting, importing, and trade financing.)

The strategy adopted for marketing consumer goods will differ from that used in marketing industrial goods.

Pricing Strategies

The international marketing manager plays a major role in determining the prices for a firm's products in overseas markets. In developing a pricing strategy, the marketing manager must operate within the parameters of the market, the nature of the competition, and government regulations. For example, trade associations and cartels determine prices for their members. International commodity agreements attempt to control prices of coffee, sugar, and cocoa, or cartels such as OPEC establish the base price for crude petroleum, to which members are expected to adhere. The number, size, and degree of competition and what the leaders in the industry charge tend to influence prices, as in the automobile industry. The government may determine the margin of profit or establish price floors and ceilings for certain products. Under those circumstances, the marketing manager will have little control over prices. In other cases, governments may compete directly with private enterprise, or establish government monopolies that make sales by private firms impossible at any price. Even the sensitivity of consumers to changes in prices and their perception of prices may influence prices.

However, where the marketing manager is in a position to establish prices, they will be determined in accord with the strategy of the firm to help it meet its objectives. A predetermined return on investments or sales, taking into consideration the cost of production, may be an influential factor in price determination.

Pricing Strategies to Maximize Profits

Usually the price of goods or services is established to maximize profits or market share in the target market. Sometimes, however, products are sold outside of the firm's domestic market merely to prevent saturating that market. In such cases, prices are often set at or below the market level merely to dispose of the surplus (dumping). In a sense, a strategy of maximizing market share is actually profit maximization, but over a longer planning horizon. In both profit maximization and market share maximization strategies, the actual price charged for goods is determined by the firm's strategy and the average price for comparable goods in that market. To implement the strategy of profit maximization, the firm must decide whether to price its goods above, equal to, or below the price charged for similar goods in that market.

Pricing Above the Market Price (Skim Pricing)   Pricing above the average local market level is called skim pricing. A firm may skim if it has limited production or inventory capacity and does not want to jeopardize future sales by having prospective customers find the retailers always "stocked out" or by subjecting customers to long waits for delivery. Second, above-market pricing may be used as part of a strategy that seeks to create the brand image of a high-quality, status, or prestige product. Third, a firm may price its products above the average market price if its products possess some unique feature(s) that provide(s) the firm with a monopolistic position in the market. These features could include quality or performance, product differentiation, loyalty, style, brand identification and trademark, patent, or copyright protection.

Numerous external factors can raise the price charged to the ultimate purchaser; however, these are the result of economic circumstances, not corporate pricing strategy. The use of special equipment to load goods on the vessel, marine insurance premiums, ocean transportation charges, costs of documentation, fluctuations in the rates of exchange, inflation, import duties, and various other fees and charges as well as the intermediary's mark-up are some of the costs that are encountered and ultimately end up being added to the final price of the goods. A firm may also find its goods priced above the average foreign market price if exports to that market require the use of export or import intermediaries. In such situations, the firm will not have full control over the price of those goods in the foreign market.

Pricing Equal to Foreign Market Prices (Average Market Pricing)   A firm will price at the average for a market when it wants to create sales on the basis of product features without any assistance or deterrence for price differences. For example, if a firm believes that its products are superior in satisfying the buyer's needs on quality, performance, service, style, or some other feature, it may follow a strategy of average market pricing in the expectation of creating very high levels of sales and substantial market share development. Although the firm's per unit profit margin might be smaller than with skim pricing, total profits can be increased through increased sale of the product. Second, a firm may use average market pricing because it has production capacity that it wishes to utilize fully, thereby lowering the per unit cost of production. Third, despite having a superior product a firm may use average pricing to drive competition out of a market and to prevent other competitors from entering a market. Fourth, it may price its goods equal to those of the competitors if it is unable to pass additonal costs on to the importers without losing its share of the market. In such a situation, the exporter may have to absorb the additional costs whether they be transportation, marine insurance, documentation, import duties, or other costs involved in marketing the product abroad.

Pricing Below the Market Average (Penetration Pricing)   A firm will price below the market average when it wants to build up market share at the expense of unit profit margins. The economic logic of penetration pricing is twofold. First, a larger volume of sales usually results in economies of scale not only in production and purchasing but also in marketing and distribution activities. Second, a firm may pursue a strategy of penetration pricing if it is willing to forgo current profits in the expectation of greater future profits. This approach can be effective if below-market pricing drives competitors out of the market and generates for the firm a larger share of the market (often referred to as predatory dumping). Once those two situations occur, the firm not only experiences economies of scale but will have so few competitors that it can largely determine the market price.

Some firms may use penetration pricing to enter markets where there is no clear demand if the firm believes that exposure to the product will result in future demand. This is often the case with consumer goods where consumer tastes or style consciousness must be developed.

Pricing Strategies to Maximize Market Share

For a market share maximization strategy, the firm will usually price its goods equal to or below the market price in the target market. The pricing strategies of Japanese firms in the United States present an excellent example of market share maximization pricing. From automobiles to cameras to sporting goods, most Japanese firms enter the low-price end of the market with a product that is of better quality and has more desirable features. When dominance has been achieved in the low-price market, they move up to the medium-price market with the same strategy: medium price, higher quality, and more product features. In contrast, the more typical American approach of maximizing profits in the short run is through skim pricing.

Market share maximization pricing policy is in many ways similar to traditional penetration pricing since the ultimate goal is to build market share and drive competitors out of the market. The firm will thus achieve its objective of economy of scale and minimum competition.

Cost-Plus Pricing

The concept of cost-plus pricing—wherein the firm sets a price that is determined by its total delivered cost plus a profit margin—is generally inappropriate in most competitive markets and especially international marketing. Cost-plus pricing is effective only when the firm has a monopoly by virtue of (1) being the only supplier of certain goods, (2) having goods that are clearly superior to all others in that market, or (3) having brand name identification that allows the firm to price as if it were the only supplier in the market.

A firm will adopt a pricing strategy that enables it to gain a larger share of the market and maximize its profits.

Pricing to Subsidiaries

When a firm is exporting to its overseas subsidiaries, various factors must be considered in the determination of prices. Under normal circumstances, a parent corporation will use arms-length pricing, which is the price it would quote to unrelated entities or to independent foreign buyers. However, it might be advantageous to deviate from the arms-length pricing policy in sales to its subsidiaries.

If the parent company charges below arms-length prices, it will result in a greater margin of profit for the subsidiary. Thus, by the firm's accumulating its earnings in subsidiaries located in low-tax countries, that country can serve as a tax haven if such profits are not subject to corporate taxes until they are repatriated in the form of dividends. Furthermore, with a lower valuation, tariffs payable on goods dutiable on an ad valorem basis will be lower, enabling the subsidiary to gain a competitive edge in the market. However, charging the subsidiary lower prices might be against the import regulations of the country. Customs appraisers may confiscate the goods or levy penalty duties on such imports if they feel the products are being undervalued to minimize tax payments.

In the United States, the Internal Revenue Service will revoke the deferral principle if it believes the firm is adopting low prices to accumulate profits in tax havens to minimize tax payments to the U.S. government. (See Chapter 20 on accounting and taxation for a detailed discussion of transfer pricing.)

A firm may charge above arms-length prices to its subsidiaries if the corporate taxes in countries where the subsidiaries are located are above those of the home country. In this way, it will limit profits in such countries and minimize tax payments to that country, but this might be offset by the payment of additional customs duties. Limiting subsidiary profits would also be advisable if such countries adopt exchange controls to restrict the repatriation of profits because of the inadequate supply of foreign exchange.[21]

Pricing Policies of Subsidiaries

Subsidiaries operating abroad must also adopt a pricing strategy that conforms with the overall objectives of the multinational corporation. If the goal is long-term development of the market, an appropriate pricing policy must be adopted to develop and retain that market. If, on the other hand, there is little future in the market, the subsidiary will probably adopt a policy to maximize income in the short run without regard to the future.

Lower prices for products of the subsidiaries might result in the least-cost combination of the factors of production. Labor, raw material, energy, and other costs might be lower there than in the home country. Adding to these advantages will be the elimination of the marine transportation and other charges, leaving only the domestic distribution costs to be added to the price of the goods. Domestically produced goods need not pay import duties. Lower service charges and cost of replacement parts could result in further savings. The fact that the product is produced in local factories in the host country using local labor might stimulate demand for the product, requiring an increase in output and greater economy of scale. Finally, the competitive situation in the host market might prevent an increase in prices.

A policy of higher prices may be adopted if there is a rapid rate of inflation in the country, as is often the case in many less developed countries. The upward pressure on prices would justify an increase in prices, but increases above the prescribed limit may be prohibited by government. The addition of sales taxes, high corporate taxes, and the distribution costs affect the prices that are charged.

Pricing between the parent company and its subsidiaries depends on company objectives. Subsidiary pricing depends on parent company objectives and local market prices.

Sales Promotion Strategies

Once a firm has decided what markets it will enter, which products it will supply to each market, and how it will price those products, the firm must develop a sales promotion strategy. The objective of sales promotion is to inform prospective customers about the availability and features of the firm's products, and to convince the buyer to purchase them. The sales promotion strategy requires a mix of advertising, personal selling, and other promotional methods.[22] (See Figure 14.3.)

Advertising

Advertisements will be most effective in countries with well-developed media and a population that is responsive to the mass media. Such is the situation in the United States, where advertising is more highly developed and where per capita expenditure on advertising is greater than that of any other country, exceeding 2 percent of the nation's GNP.[23] In developing an advertising strategy, firms are most concerned with the costs versus the benefits.

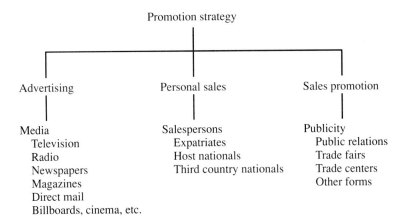

Figure 14.3   Promotional Strategies of Multinational Firms

The costs of advertising will vary greatly, according to the degree of standardization of the advertisement and the media that are selected. Standard advertisements are preferred by most companies from the point of view of cost and control. Thus, the question arises as to whether advertisements should be standardized or should be developed specifically for each market.[24] There is no set answer for every product and every country. There is no assurance that an advertisement that is effective in one country will be effective in another. Only through research and testing can the effectiveness of an advertisement be determined and the decision be made to standardize, modify, or develop a new advertisement. Usually, standard advertisements may be used effectively in many countries with only minor local modifications.

The most effective advertising medium will vary from country to country. For example, radio and television advertisements might not be effective if only a small percentage of the population owns sets. The ownership of both television and radio stations by the government will limit their use for advertising purposes. Some countries control time segments for advertisements, while others control the audiences that may be reached and the products that may be advertised. Even in the United States, advertising some products is prohibited. Where illiteracy rates are high and radios and televisions are available, advertising can be especially effective. On the other hand, in countries where radios and television ownership is limited, viewing might take place in shops or other places of public gathering.

A communications medium found in all countries is the newspaper. However, in many countries, newspapers are limited in size, restricting the space allotted to advertising. In other countries, daily newspapers have limited coverage, reaching only a small portion or select segments of the population. In multilingual countries or countries with a high level of illiteracy, this can be a particularly difficult problem.

A problem common to many countries where newspapers have a large circulation is the existence of a waiting list of several months for those desiring to advertise. Cultural and linguistic differences within countries often require adaptation of advertisements for the different regions or population groups. Every effort should be made to avoid offending the customs or culture of the people in the target group. Translation of the text is a common problem of advertising in another language. A literal translation of advertisements without considering the idioms and local differences can create interpretations that are completely inaccurate or embarrassing.[25]

Magazines are readily available in highly developed countries and among the more sophisticated elements of the population. Technical and industrial magazines are especially effective in the sales effort and are used by international advertisers, but the availability of advertising space is a problem. However, the use of magazine advertisements among international advertisers is limited because few magazines have the desired national circulation. Direct mail advertising can be used on a selective basis where an advertisement is directed toward users of a particular product.

Billboard advertisements are common in countries where they are permitted. In many less developed countries, cinemas are a major form of recreation and, therefore, a good place to advertise. Neon lights are a common sight in large metropolitan areas for the advertisement of certain products. Sound trucks equipped with loudspeakers are used in many countries. This medium is especially effective among countries where the illiteracy rate is high and where ownership of radio and television sets is limited.

Especially effective for industrial advertisers are the trade centers and trade fairs. For example, in the People's Republic of China, trade fairs are an important means of advertising a firm's products, but have been primarily limited to those who have been been invited to display their products.[26]

Problems in Advertising   The lack of an appropriate medium to carry the message is one of the major problems faced by advertisers. Another problem is the high cost of certain media. Spot advertisements on television during prime time cost thousands of dollars. Only if the desired coverage can be achieved is the benefit worth the cost.

Customs and cultural differences often result in a message being misunderstood. The lack of reliable market data or demographic data (income, age, ethnic background, geographical distribution, and other factors) in some countries makes it difficult to assess the target market. Thus, it might be difficult to determine how the majority of the population can be reached through advertisements.

Advertising strategy calls for the use of a medium that will be most effective for a given product in a given country.

Personal Selling

Personal selling informs prospective customers of a firm's products through personal contact. Personal selling has a number of advantages over advertising. Using nationals as salespersons eliminates the problems that often

This kiosk or advertising pole is the European equivalent of the American billboard and fits well into the smaller, more narrow streets that are typical in older European cities.

arise because of the differences in language, culture, and customs. It overcomes the problem of reaching people in the less developed countries where many of the media are unavailable, or where the illiteracy rate is high. Many buyers prefer to have direct contact with those selling particular products because they can observe the demonstration of the product and can ask questions on points with which they are uncertain. Segmented markets can be covered more effectively through personal selling. The costs of salepersons might be lower than those for other modes of advertising, and their use will overcome any regulations that restrict advertising.

Personal selling of industrial products generally requires the development of an international sales staff. This involves recruiting sales personnel, and deciding as to nationality preference: home country nationals (expatriates), host country nationals, or third country nationals.[27] The problems in the recruitment, selection, training, and management of home country expatriates, third country nationals, and local nationals for sales positions are equally applicable to managerial positions. Although these problems will be discussed in greater depth in Chapter 19, "Human Resource Management," some of the major advantages and disadvantages of each are covered here from the point of view of the sales effort.

Expatriates, if employees of the parent company, generally have greater technical training and are more familiar with the product line, the corporation, and its policies. They have proved their effectiveness and reliability as employees of the firm. However, they have some major disadvantages. An expatriate is more costly than either host country or third country nationals. Differences in customs, language, and cultural problems face the expatriate. Many qualified individuals from the home country are unwilling to spend extended periods abroad because it means uprooting the family and cutting familial or social ties. Some feel that their chances of moving up the corporate ladder are impeded by foreign assignments ("out of sight, out of mind").

Using host country nationals has a number of advantages. They are completely familiar with the language, customs, and culture of the country. The cost of employing such an individual is much less than using an expatriate. There is no need for moving the individual nor will it be necessary to uproot the family. Nationals are more familiar with the local politics and methods of getting around the bureaucracy. However, these advantages must be weighed against the disadvantages. The local national might be unfamiliar with the company and its products, and also might not act in the corporation's best interest on matters of conflict with local attitudes.

Many corporations have found third country nationals suitable for sales positions abroad. If they are recruited from geographic regions near or similar to the host countries, they are likely to be familiar with the language, customs, and culture of the host country. They will be less costly to employ than home country expatriates. Usually such nationals are internationally minded and are more familiar with foreign companies and their products. The cost of moving such individuals will probably be much less. However, third country nationals are more commonly used for management than for sales positions.

Personal selling is especially effective in countries where the illiteracy rate is high and where personal contact is important.

Sales Promotion

"All marketing activities other than advertising, personal selling, and publicity that stimulate consumer purchases and improve retailer or middlemen effectiveness and cooperation are sales promotions," states Cateora.[28] Indeed, sales promotions include any activity directed at the consumer or retailer to achieve such specific sales objectives as (1) trying or purchasing a product, (2) learning about the store, (3) getting permission for a point-of-purchase display, (4) encouraging stores to stock the product, or (5) supporting a retailer's advertising and personal selling effort.[29] In addition, high-profile public relations activities that benefit the citizens in the host country can also be a form of sales promotion. Sales promotion strategies are often more of a communications problem than one of promoting sales directly. Communicating a feeling of interest in the welfare of the population by maintaining a high profile in activities beneficial to the public can prove advantageous in the sales effort. Foreign firms often contribute to educational and other causes within a community.

Trade fairs are a means of introducing a firm's products. For centuries, the countries of western Europe have had trade fairs to display and demonstrate the products of many producers. The Canton (now called Guangzhou) Trade Fair represents an effort on the part of the People's Republic of China to view or even place orders for foreign products that are displayed at these fairs. The U.S. Department of Commerce participates in trade fairs in industrial, less developed, and communist nations by booking space where American manufacturers may display their products. The United States has also established trade centers in major industrial cities on a permanent basis where products from manufacturers are exhibited periodically.

Sales promotion employs any method that a firm feels will be effective in creating the atmosphere to make a manufacturer's product more acceptable.

SUMMARY

In developing a market strategy, a firm must carefully consider the product that is to be marketed, the location of the market, the prices to be charged, and the method to promote the sale of the product. The strategy that is adopted will have a direct effect upon the success and profitability of the international operation.

Unlike domestic marketing, selling abroad requires careful consideration of the various factors that make foreign markets different from the domestic market. The population's positive reaction toward a product cannot be taken for granted because human and cultural factors differ from country to country.

A different course of action must often be adopted in the marketing of consumer goods as compared with industrial goods. Maximum utility in relation to price is of major importance to the end users of consumer products, while performance of a particular task will be of primary concern to the purchaser of industrial goods.

Various factors will affect the prices at which the goods are sold. The cost of production is only one of the factors that must be considered in setting prices. Import duties, distribution costs, fluctuations in foreign exchange rates, rate of inflation, and other external factors that are beyond the control of the firm must be considered in determining the end prices of goods. However, the most important factor is the average price of comparable goods in that market.

The prices that parent firms charge their subsidiaries and the prices subsidiaries charge for their products are affected by various factors. Thus, the pricing strategy that a multinational firm adopts will vary from country to country and from product to product.

Trade promotion as a part of the marketing strategy is adopted to influence buyers to purchase a particular product or service. The method selected will depend upon the nature of the product, the media available, the cost, the governmental regulations, and various environmental factors. Advertising is commonly used for most products, but personal selling might be the only way to reach individuals in areas of high illiteracy or in the sale of technical products. Trade fairs and trade centers that are supported by many countries provide excellent opportunities for firms to display their products in different markets.

In order for a multinational enterprise to come up with an optimal marketing strategy, coordination and control are essential. A well-suited organizational structure can facilitate marketing decisions, while performance evaluation will be an appropriate method for controlling strategy. ☐

KEY TERMS AND CONCEPTS

Ad valorem duty	Sales promotion
Arms-length pricing	Standardized products
Consumer goods	Tax haven
Industrial goods	Trade centers
Product adaptation	Trade fairs
Repatriation of profits	

REVIEW QUESTIONS

1. Why is the development of a market strategy so important for a firm that is planning to engage in international business? Explain.

2. Briefly explain the meaning of product planning.

3. Explain the advantages and disadvantages of marketing standard products abroad.

4. Is product adaptation generally necessary for sales to countries with like cultures? In countries with dissimilar cultures? Why?

5. What is the relationship between the demand for industrial goods and the stage of economic development?

6. Describe the foreign channels that may be used in the distribution of industrial goods.

7. Who in a multinational firm is largely responsible for developing the pricing strategy for products being sold overseas? Why?

8. What factors generally influence the prices of goods abroad?

9. When might a firm price its products below the average market selling prices? Above the market average? Equal to the average price?

10. What is meant by arms-length pricing? When might a parent firm charge its subsidiaries prices that differ from arms-length pricing? Why?

11. What is meant by sales promotion? Explain the meaning of sales promotion mix.

12. What factors determine the media used in foreign advertising?

13. Explain the problems that firms face in advertising abroad.

14. What are the advantages of personal selling in overseas markets?

15. Describe the problems involved in coordinating and controlling marketing strategy.

DISCUSSION CASE

Gateway Manufactures, Ltd.

Gateway Manufactures, Ltd. (GML), is a medium-size producer of kitchen cabinets in Brampton, Ontario, Canada. The company sells kitchen cabinets through retail establishments and on contract bids. The company's retail sales have been growing at 6 percent per year for the last five years. The major thrust of the company's business is through its contract bids division, which has an average growth rate of 10.5 percent. GML had sales of $8.9 million (Canadian) in 1987, with 89.7 percent coming from contract bids.

Gateway operates two plants near its corporate offices. The smaller plant in Robertstown produces components (doors, box supports, and so forth). The larger plant (in Kilroy) is primarily a final assembly operation and distribution center. Of the 42,000 square feet of the Robertstown plant, more than 12,000 square feet are devoted to storage and staining operations. Of the 58,000 square feet in the Kilroy plant, 17,000 are used for storage of raw materials inventories.

Gateway's products are all European style, frameless cabinets with a variety of different doors and frame faces. The boxes are made of pressed wood with melamine laminated covers. Because the boxes are assembled with dolls and presses, they are nearly three times as strong as the traditional

By Don R. Beeman, 1989.
This case was developed for class discussion purposes only and is not intended to represent good or bad management or decision-making.

framed cabinets and cost about 7 percent less to produce. Furthermore, these types of cabinets tend to be more popular in Canada.

Gateway produces five different styles of wall-hung cabinets and three different styles of base cabinets. Each wall-hung and base cabinet was available in both melamine and wood veneer finish. About 40 percent of all cabinets sold by Gateway have melamine doors and frame faces, while 60 percent have wood veneer faces to give a more traditional look. About 95 percent of the contract sales of base cabinets were of style 100, a slightly scaled down, no-frills model. Contract sales of wall-hung cabinets were limited to only two models and were almost equally divided among these two: 303 and 303-W. Model 303 was a slightly scaled down, no-frills model, while 303-W was merely the wood veneer version of 303. There was, however, no real pattern to which wood veneers were requested or the stain desired. The costs varied on the basis of the type of wood selected but not with the type of stain. These wood veneer models were available in five different types of wood and 15 different stains, thus, creating 75 different looks. All of Gateway's cabinets are metric sized and tailored to Canadian tastes, which tend to follow European trends. This means flat and smooth surfaces with few ridges, sharp corners, bright colors, recessed (cut-out) handle grips as opposed to screw-mounted protruding handles, and so forth. Although GML produces counter tops, these are essentially a loss leader, marketed primarily as a service to its contract customers.

Most of Gateway's contract sales are for apartment and condominium developments in Ontario and western Quebec, with the greater Toronto area being the largest market. Its retail sales are made primarily through lumber company retail stores. In 1987 the contract bids division sold 4,312 kitchen packages at an average price of $1,825 Canadian. If "do it youself" consumers had purchased a comparable package in a retail store it would have cost them about $2,500; in fact the retailer would have had to pay $2,000 for the package if purchased in the normal lots (10 complete packages). Thus, condominium and apartment developers were receiving a substantial discount below both wholesale and retail prices. This degree of discounting has developed over the last five years. Although developers constantly talk about quality, they purchase almost exclusively on price.

Gateway has five competitors, all Canadian firms, each with about equal sales levels, although Gateway is more heavily into the contract market. None of the other five companies has more than two thirds of its sales through contract bids by developers. In 1987 there was essentially no foreign competition due to a variety of Canadian laws and production requirements.

By early 1987 it was becoming increasingly clear that Canada and the United States were moving closer to a free trade agreement. Such an agreement would surely remove the protection that Gateway had from competition from the larger U.S. cabinet manufacturers. On the other hand, such an agreement might open to Gateway the chance to compete in the U.S. market.

In January 1988, Prime Minister Brian Mulroney and President Ronald Reagan signed the Canadian-U.S. Free Trade Agreement. The President of Gateway, Art Guillane, hired two marketing consulting firms: the La Tour Group of Toronto and Quebec, and Walter H. Banks and Associates of Buffalo. La Tour was to develop plans for maintaining market share and profitability in Canada in the face of U.S. competition; Banks and Associates was to develop a marketing strategy for entering the U.S.

Questions

1. Assume that you are the La Tour group, and develop a plan for maintaining market share and profitability in Canada in the face of U.S. competition.

2. Assume that you are Banks and Associates, and develop the marketing strategy for entering the United States.

NOTES

1. Warren J. Keegan, "Multinational Product Planning: Strategic Alternatives," *Journal of Marketing*, January 1969, p. 58.
2. Thomas Hout, Michael E. Porter, and Eileen Rudden, "How Global Companies Win Out," *Harvard Business Review*, September-October 1982, pp. 98–108.
3. Colin Gilligan and Martin Hird, *International Marketing: Strategy and Management* (London: Croon Helm, 1986), pp. 292–296.
4. Ibid., pp. 292-293.
5. Simon Majaro, *International Marketing: A Strategic Approach to World Markets* (London: George Allen & Unwin, 1977), p. 223.
6. Ibid., p. 229.
7. Subash C. Jain, *International Marketing Management* (Boston: Kent Publishing Co., 1987), p. 662.
8. Majaro, pp. 233–242.
9. Ibid., p. 231.
10. Vern Terpstra, *International Marketing* (New York: Holt, Rinehart and Winston, 1972), pp. 492–494.
11. Jain, pp. 675–679.
12. Ibid., p. 675.
13. Endel J. Kolde, *International Business Enterprise*, 2nd ed. (Englewood Cliffs, N.J.: Prentice-Hall, 1973), pp. 394–398.
14. Philip R. Cateora, *International Marketing* (Homewood, Ill.: Richard D. Irwin, 1983), p. 408.

15. Robert D. Buzzell, "Can You Standardize Multinational Marketing?" *Harvard Business Review*, November-December 1968, pp. 102–113.

16. W. J. Keegan, "Multinational Product Planning: Strategic Alternatives," *Journal of Marketing*, January 1969, p. 58.

17. Everett M. Rogers and F. Floyd Shoemaker, *Communications of Innovations* (New York: Free Press, 1971), pp. 22–23.

18. Cateora, pp. 425–426.

19. José de la Torre, "Product Life Cycle as a Determinant of Global Marketing Strategies," in Subash C. Jain and Lewis R. Tucker, Jr., eds., *International Marketing: Managerial Perspectives* (Boston: CBI Publishing Co., 1979), pp. 278–279.

20. Cateora, pp. 433–434.

21. Ibid., pp. 575–576.

22. Ibid., p. 470.

23. Ibid., p. 467.

24. Jacob Hornik, "Comparative Evaluation of International vs. National Advertising Strategies," *Columbia Journal of World Business*, Spring 1980, pp. 36–46.

25. Vern Terpstra, *The Cultural Environment of International Business* (Cincinnati: South-Western Publishing, 1978), chap. 1.

26. J. A. Brunner and George M. Taoka, "Marketing and Negotiating in the People's Republic of China: Perceptions of American Businessmen Who Attended the 1975 Canton Fair," *Journal of International Business Studies*, Fall/Winter, 1977, pp. 69–82.

27. Cateora, pp. 508–518.

28. Ibid., p. 488.

29. Ibid.

REFERENCES AND SELECTED READINGS

Albaum, Gerald, and Robert A. Peterson. "Empirical Research in International Marketing, 1976–1982." *The Journal of International Business Studies* 15:1 (Spring/Summer 1984).

Boddewyn, Jean J. "Comparative Marketing: The First Twenty-five Years." *The Journal of International Business Studies* 12:1 (Spring/Summer 1981).

Brunner, J. A., and George M. Taoka. "Marketing and Negotiating in the People's Republic of China: Perceptions of American Businessmen Who Attended the 1975 Canton Fair." *The Journal of International Business Studies* (Fall/Winter 1977).

Buzzell, Robert D. "Can You Standardize Multinational Marketing?" *Harvard Business Review* 36 (November/December 1968).

Cateora, Philip R. *International Marketing*, 5th ed. Homewood, Ill.: Richard D. Irwin, 1983.

De la Torre, José. "Product Life Cycle as a Determinant of Global Marketing

Strategies." In Subhash C. Jain and Lewis R. Tucker, Jr., eds., *International Marketing: Marginal Perspectives*. Boston: CBI Publishing Co., 1979.

Douglas, Susan P., and C. Samuel Craig. "Examining Performance of U.S. Multinationals in Foreign Markets." *The Journal of International Business Studies* 14:3 (Winter 1983).

Gilligan, Colin, and Martin Hird. *International Marketing: Strategy and Management*. London: Croon Helm, 1986.

Hout, Thomas, Michael E. Porter, and Eileen Rudden. "How Global Companies Win Out." *Harvard Business Review*, September-October 1982, pp. 98–108.

Hornik, Jacob. "Comparative Evaluation of International vs. National Advertising Strategies." *Columbia Journal of World Business*, Spring 1980.

Jain, Subash C. *International Marketing Management*. Boston: Kent Publishing Co., 1987.

Jain, Subash C., and Lewis R. Tucker. *International Marketing: Managerial Perspectives*. Boston: CBI Publishing Co., 1979.

Johansson, Johny K., and Hans B. Thorelli. "International Product Positioning," *The Journal of International Business Studies* 16:3 (Fall 1985).

Keegan, W. J. "Multinational Product Planning: Strategic Alternatives." *Journal of Marketing*, January 1969.

Keegan, Warren J. *Multinational Marketing Management*, 3rd ed. Englewood Cliffs, N.J.: Prentice-Hall, 1984.

Kirpalani, V. H., and N. B. Macintosh. "International Marketing Effectiveness of Technology-Oriented Small Firms." *The Journal of International Business Studies* 11:3 (Winter 1980).

Kolde, Endel J. *International Business Enterprise*, 2nd ed. Englewood Cliffs, N.J.: Prentice-Hall, 1973.

Lee, Kam-Hon, and Thamis Wing-Chun Lo. "American Businesspeople's Perceptions of Marketing and Negotiating in the People's Republic of China." *International Marketing Review*, Summer 1988.

Leff, Nathaniel H., and John U. Farley. "Advertising Expenditures in the Developing World." *The Journal of International Business Studies* 11:2 (Fall 1980).

Majaro, Simon. *International Marketing: A Strategic Approach to World Markets*. London: George Allen & Unwin, 1977.

Rogers, Everett, and F. Floyd Shoemaker. *Communications of Innovations*. New York: Free Press, 1971.

Samiee, Saeed, and John K. Ryans, Jr. "Advertising and Consumerism in Europe: The Case of West Germany and Switzerland." *The Journal of International Business Studies* 13:1 (Spring/Summer 1982).

Sethi, S. Prakash, and Jagdish N. Sheth. *Multinational Business Operations III*. Pacific Palisades, Calif.: Goodyear Publishing Co., 1973.

Suzuki, Norihiko. "The Changing Pattern of Advertising Strategy by Japanese Business Firms in the U.S. Market: Content Analysis." *The Journal of International Business Studies* 11:3 (Winter 1980).

Terpstra, Vern. *The Cultural Environment of International Business*. Cincinnati: South-Western Publishing, 1978.

Terpstra, Vern. *International Dimensions of Marketing*. Boston: Kent Publishing Co., 1982.

Terpstra, Vern. *International Marketing*. New York: Holt, Rinehart and Winston, 1972.

Terpstra, Vern, and Nizam Aydin. "Marketing Know-How Transfers by Multinationals: A Case Study in Turkey." *The Journal of International Business Studies* 12:3 (Winter 1981).

Walters, Peter G. P. "International Marketing Policy: A Discussion of the Standardization Construct and Its Relevance for Corporate Policy." *The Journal of International Business Studies*, 17:2 (Summer 1986).

CHAPTER

15

Exporting, Importing, and Financing International Trade

INTRODUCTION

The purpose of this chapter is to describe the methods of direct and indirect exporting and importing practiced by firms engaged in international trade, and to discuss the various problems that firms face in financing this international trade.

METHODS FOR REACHING FOREIGN MARKETS

Organizational Structures for Direct Exporting

If a firm decides to engage in exporting, it must first decide on the type of organization it will establish to handle its export operations. Figure 15.1 provides the alternative methods that may be used to reach the foreign market.

Built-in Export Department

When a firm decides to engage in direct export, it must establish an organization within the firm to handle the details involved in foreign sales and getting the goods to the foreign customer. The simplest form of organization is the built-in export department, with an export manager and one or more

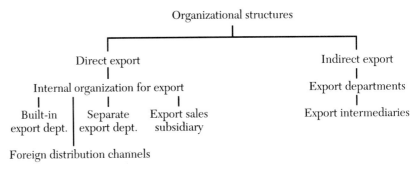

Figure 15.1   Forms of Organization Used in Exporting

clerical assistants. The export manager works closely with those involved in domestic sales since all support activities (such as advertising, accounting, credit and collections, traffic and shipping) must be supplied by the domestic departments.

The major advantages of a built-in export department is the flexibility and economy of this structure that result from using existing facilities and personnel. There are, however, disadvantages. Domestic personnel might be unfamiliar with many requirements of overseas sales, and domestic methods must be adapted to meet international business needs. Therefore, cooperation with domestic departments is absolutely essential for export success.

Separate Export Department

As the export business increases, the built-in export department might become inadequate. At this point, a firm usually sets up a separate export department that is divorced from domestic sales. Such a department is usually headed by a high-ranking corporate official with a title such as vice-president for export marketing. Reporting to this executive will be various units, some of which are comparable to those found in domestic situations while others are specialized to meet the needs of exporting.

As foreign sales grow in importance for the firm, the export department may be expanded to an export division, usually divided into product or geographic divisions. Establishing separate divisions according to product lines or geographic regions provides the opportunity to develop each independently as a part of the overall business strategy.

Export Sales Subsidiary

Some firms set up an export sales subsidiary rather than an export division. Export sales subsidiaries are corporations that are wholly owned by a parent company. Export sales subsidiaries are not involved in manufacturing; they merely obtain products from the parent company or elsewhere for export. The subsidiary president is usually an officer of the parent firm. Below this president will be other officers with responsibilities similar to those in the domestic organization.

Subsidiaries may be established in the home country to coordinate all of the firm's export business, or they may be established abroad to operate distribution facilities. Chapter 19 discusses the tax advantages provided by the various types of export sales subsidiaries, such as the foreign sales corporation (FSC).[1]

A firm engaging in direct export must establish a built-in export department, separate department, or export sales subsidiary to handle the details of exporting.

Foreign Distribution Channels

If shipment is not made directly to the end user, the exporter must entrust the distribution and sales of its products to intermediaries. These intermediaries may include jobbers, wholesalers, or others who function as retail agents setting resale prices on the basis of landed costs (purchase price, insurance, and freight) plus a markup.

Another type of intermediary is the sales agent, often called an indent agent, manufacturer's representative, or resident sales agent. Sales agents facilitate entering new markets by calling on dealers within their exclusive territory. They handle samples and catalogs as well as take orders; however, shipment is usually made directly from the exporter to the customer with no involvement by the sales agents. The selection of the intermediary is influenced by factors such as the type of business, products handled, method of distribution, location of branches, and the general reputation of the firm.

An exporter may sell goods directly to the end user or through an intermediary abroad.

The contract between the exporter and the agent prescribes the length of the agreement, the terms of sales, compensation, method of advertising, the sales territory, and other matters dealing with the distribution of the product. If the firm wants aggressive sales from its agent, it must ensure that the agent does not handle competing lines or too large a variety of other goods.

Indirect Exporting

Indirect export means that an intermediary located in the manufacturer's home country will handle the details involved in selling and distributing the goods to a foreign market. There are various intermediaries to whom firms may turn if they are unwilling or unable to engage in direct export. These intermediaries may act on behalf of the manufacturer, act on their own account, or act on behalf of the foreign buyer. Regardless of their method of operation, they carry out an important function in the export cycle. Figure 15.2 presents the major types of intermediary.

Intermediaries Acting on Behalf of the Manufacturer

Export Management Companies   One of the most effective intermediaries for handling all of the details involved in reaching the foreign market is the export management company (EMC) or combination export manager

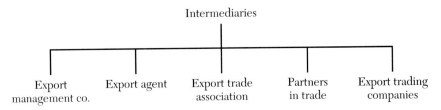

Figure 15.2   Major Types of Indirect Export Intermediary

(CEM). These firms act as the export department for small, medium-size, and even some large firms. Many EMCs even use the letterheads of the firms they represent, giving to the importer the impression of dealing directly with the manufacturer. They sign correspondence and export documents in the name of the principal. Thus, for a commission of $7\frac{1}{2}$ to 20 percent of the wholesale price, the manufacturer is relieved of all aspects of the exporting function except for filling the order. The major functions of the EMC are listed below:

1. Researching foreign markets for the manufacturer's products
2. Determining the best methods of distribution
3. Appointing distributors or other representatives
4. Exhibiting products at trade fairs and at U.S. trade centers
5. Handling the documentation involved in the shipping process
6. Making sales demonstrations and providing technical training
7. Granting finance terms to customers and assuring payment
8. Preparing and adapting advertising and sales literature
9. Corresponding in the language of the buyer
10. Ensuring the suitability of goods for local conditions
11. Advising on patent and trademark protection[2]

For many firms, using an EMC is less costly than becoming involved in direct export. There is no need for the manufacturer to hire specialists or even to send its own personnel abroad. The financial risks and other problems that are involved in setting up an export organization are eliminated. The costs of sales promotion and advertising for specific goods are arranged between the manufacturer and the EMC. The EMC consolidates shipments from different manufacturers to a given destination on a single bill of lading, thereby providing considerable savings to the manufacturer. Usually, the manufacturer bills the customer directly and carries any financing (supplier credit) that might be required. Some EMCs even relieve the manufacturer of credit risks by paying the manufacturer before the shipment is made. The EMCs may also provide credit information on foreign buyers.

Some EMCs are specialists that handle a particular product line such as pharmaceutical products or automotive parts and represent only a few companies. Others handle a more diversified product line and represent 40 or 50 principals. Large export management companies divide their operations into departments, each headed by its own manager.

Export Agents   Export agents are similar to EMCs except their services are less complete. The export agent is an individual or firm that represents manufacturers of allied but noncompetitive products. It is common for export agents to work through a foreign resident agent in countries where the export agent has a substantial level of business.

The manufacturer may place its entire product line with one export agent or parcel out different items to different agents. It may grant exclusive selling rights to one agent for certain geographical areas while shipping directly to resident agents in other areas. Compensation for the export agent is almost always in the form of a commission from the manufacturer based upon sales volume.

Export Trade Associations   Export trade associations may be used by producers who want to cooperate in exports on an industry-wide basis. The Export Trade Act of 1918 (the Webb-Pomerene Association) permits American exporters to improve their competitive position abroad by joining an export trade association. Participants in export trade associations are not subject to antitrust violations for these activities. Although export trade associations would seem to offer an attractive option, especially for small firms, they account for less than 5 percent of the total U.S. trade.

Partners in Trade (Piggyback)   Under the partners in trade program of the U.S. Department of Commerce, large companies engaged in international trade offer to distribute products of smaller noncompeting firms. The services provided by these large firms enable small manufacturers to market their products abroad without setting up their own export departments.

Intermediaries Representing Buyers

EMCs and export agents perform the export functions for indirect exporters. Export trade associations and partners in trade also aid indirect exporters.

Resident Agents   The most important of the buyers for foreign customers are the resident agents. These agents are not true intermediaries since they are actually employees of foreign governments, large foreign importers, and other large firms. They are sent abroad to buy specific products for their employers and handle all of the details involved in getting the goods to their destination. One of the best examples of a resident agent is the New York-based Amtorg Trading Company of the Soviet Union.

For the manufacturer, its products are handled as in any domestic sale except for the export regulations that may require licenses or permits on certain types of shipments. For a firm that is interested in establishing a

When the manufacturer sells to a foreign agent, it is like a domestic sale.

permanent market abroad, resident agents do not help to develop ties with potential customers.

Export Commission House   Export commission houses are similar in function to resident agents except they work for more than one buyer. In some cases, commission houses act on behalf of the seller and function similarly to export agents. Their primary source of income is from the commissions they collect from the buyers. Although export commission houses are still common in many European countries, they have largely disappeared from the American scene.

Export and Import Brokers   The major function of a broker is to act as an intermediary in bringing the buyer and seller together on the basis of standard description. Export-import brokers generally work in staple products such as grain, cotton, sugar, wool, and coffee. They do not take title to or possession of the goods. Sometimes brokers go beyond the brokerage function and dispose of goods that are consigned to a particular market. In such cases, they are often called sales expediters and collect their commission from the seller.

Export commission houses act on behalf of the buyer, whereas export and import brokers act as intermediaries in uniting sellers and buyers.

Intermediaries Acting on Their Own Behalf

Export Merchants   Export merchants are actually in the business of exporting. Some of the large export merchants operate as both exporters and importers and often have affiliates, offices, or branches abroad. Export merchants relieve the manufacturer of all of the details involved in getting the goods to the market. They may even take over the functions of packing, crating, and labeling, especially if they are interested in consolidating small shipments to a particular destination to save on freight charges. They handle all of the necessary documentation and the logistical aspects of the shipment. Large export merchants handle foreign advertising and sales promotions. The export merchant usually extends credit to a buyer and is responsible for any risk or other problems involved in the sale. Thus, for a small manufacturer, selling to an export merchant will provide exposure for its products in overseas markets without involvement in the intricacies of direct export. However, there is no assurance that the merchant will actively promote the sale of the product.

Export merchants buy and sell on their own account.

Export Trading Companies (ETCs)   Although there are trading companies in the United States, they are of minor significance compared with those in Japan and in some of the countries of western Europe. In Japan, ETCs account for 40 to 60 percent of all exports and imports. Furthermore, Japanese trading companies handle 20 percent of the wholesale trade within the country.[3] The importance of trading companies in Japan is not surprising since they have been in existence for more than 300 years. Currently, there are more than 6000 Japanese trading companies but only the largest are highly diversified in such activities as banking, finance, transportation, distribution, wholesaling, insurance, contracting, real estate, and other services. The only activities that the general trading companies do not perform are production and retailing. Figure 15.3 presents the organizational structure of Mitsubishi Corporation, illustrating the extensive activities of Japan's largest trading companies. For firms interested in developing the Japanese market, the general trading companies are invaluable in penetrating the cumbersome distribution system and in helping to overcome cultural and institutional differences.

Trading companies in the United States are of recent origin. In 1982, export trading company legislation was passed to improve the export performance of small and medium-sized firms. Bank participation was authorized to provide ETCs with better access to capital and financing. Antitrust provisions were relaxed to enable firms to engage jointly in export efforts without violating antitrust laws. The legislation permits various forms of operation, such as general or regional trading companies. They may be product-oriented, geographically oriented, or industry-oriented. In spite of

Figure 15.3   Mitsubishi Trading Company: Organizational Chart
Source: Adapted from Simcha Ronen, *Comparative and Multinational Management* (New York: John Wiley and Sons, 1986), p. 473.

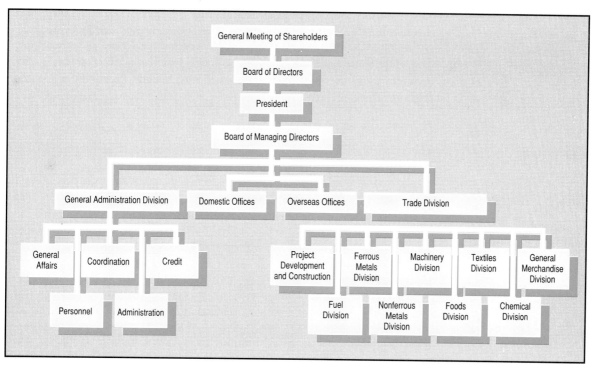

Trading companies provide a variety of functions in the international movement of goods and services.

the possible benefits, through 1987 only 82 ETC certificates had been issued by the U.S. Department of Commerce, with 684 firms participating.[4]

Export Jobbers and Wholesalers   Export jobbers resemble export merchants since they buy goods outright for their own accounts; however, unlike the merchants, they purchase in job lots. Generally, the jobbers do not stock merchandise or have exclusive sales rights. They operate best in a seller's market, as after the two world wars; they locate job lots of goods not readily available, contract to purchase the merchandise within a stated period of time, find a customer, and deliver the goods. Many exservicemen who were given priority in purchasing government surplus products after the war acquired goods, sold them for a profit, and then discontinued operations. The most successful jobbers are those who locate sources of supply for regular customers on a permanent basis.

Export jobbers and wholesalers function like export merchants, but deal in large quantities.

Intermediaries Providing Specialized Services

Freight Forwarders   Freight forwarders are intermediaries who provide specialized services for both exporters and importers. They are generally located at port cities, where they are in a better position to provide logistical services in the export cycle. They relieve the exporter of many of the details regarding transportation, reservations for space, storage, and routing. They often consolidate small shipments and issue their own bills of lading. They renew letters of credit, obtain export licenses or permits, prepare shipping documents, and even get involved in packing, labeling, and repacking damaged goods. Some foreign freight forwarders also act as customs house brokers on imports and frequently perform the same functions as a commission merchant.

Freight forwarders are specialists who are used by both direct and indirect exporters to handle the logistical functions of the export cycle.

Documentary Requirements

Documentation is an integral part of every international transaction. Various documents are required, some by the exporter's country, others by the importer's country.

There are six major documents that are used in every export shipment. These are the commercial invoice or bill of sale, export declaration, certificate of origin, consular invoice, marine insurance policy or certificate, and the bill of lading. Packing lists, export and/or import licenses, special certificates, and other documents may also be required, depending upon the country of destination. The absence of a specific document might mean the violation of a customs regulation prohibiting the import of a product, confiscation, or possible fine. Accuracy is very important; even typographical errors may be interpreted as attempts to evade regulations or to defraud the government.

Commercial Invoice

In every sales transaction, a bill of sale is issued. This is referred to as a commercial invoice. The commercial invoice provides all the pertinent information regarding the sale of the goods and its complete description. It shows the names and addresses of the seller and buyer, the date, the port of shipment and the name of the carrier, terms of sale, invoice and purchase order number, unit price and total price, charges and fees, quantities, weights and measurements of packages, marks, numbers, and insurance coverage. All of this information is important to the bank financing the transaction and the insurance underwriter.

Export Declaration

The U.S. government requires filing an export declaration on all shipments leaving the country. This declaration contains all the information pertaining to the shipment. On mail shipments, the export declaration is required if the value exceeds $25 or if an export license is required. The original copy of the declaration must be verified under oath by the exporter or its authorized representative before a customs officer, notary, or other person authorized to administer oaths, and must be filed with the Collector of Customs at the port or point of exit. Its major purpose is for export control and for the collection of statistical information. If the shipment is subject to an export license, the export declaration must be presented with the license before the goods may be delivered to the pier. The carrier will generally require a certified export declaration before a delivery or shipping permit will be issued.

A vessel is not granted clearance until the ship's manifest with a certified export declaration for each shipment has been verified and submitted to the customs authorities.[5] Violation of these customs regulations may subject the vessel operator to heavy fines.

Certificate of Origin

Many countries, including the United States, require a certificate of origin. This is especially important when shipments are made to certain countries that prohibit the import of goods originating in a particular country. The U.S. Chamber of Commerce issues this document for goods originating in the United States.

Consular Invoice

The consular invoice is issued by the consulate of the importing country in the language of the country to which shipment is being made. The shipper provides the information for the document that is almost identical to that included in the commercial invoice and swears to its accuracy before it is certified by the foreign consul of the importing country. Accuracy is extremely important because any error may subject the buyer to fines that must be borne by the exporter. This invoice is necessary for clearance of merchandise through customs in the importing country.

Ocean Bill of Lading

A bill of lading (B/L) is a document acknowledging the receipt of goods by a carrier for transport to a particular destination. It states the conditions under which the carrier accepts the goods. The carrier provides the blank forms of the bills, which are prepared by the shipper (exporter). The number of copies prepared depends on the requirements of the seller, the steamship line, and the consular authorities.

Bills of lading take different forms and serve different functions (see Table 15.1). The ocean bill of lading is either a straight or an order bill of lading, depending on the requirements of the country to which shipments are made.

A *straight bill of lading* has two functions: as a receipt from the steamship line and as a contract to transport the goods to a particular destination. It is a nonnegotiable document; the title to the goods is in the name of the one to whom shipment is being made (consignee). Thus, the exporter loses control of the goods unless the goods are consigned to a local agent of the exporter, to a customs house broker at the port of entry, or to a foreign correspondent bank. A straight bill of lading is generally used only when a country does not permit the use of an order bill of lading.

The *order bill of lading*, the most commonly used, serves three major functions: as a receipt from the steamship line for the goods, as a contract to transport the goods to the port of entry, and as title to the goods. Negotiability of the bill of lading depends upon its being made out to the order of the shipper (exporter), signed by the shipping company, and endorsed in blank by the shipper. If these conditions are met, title passes to the bearer (holder) of the bill.

The use of an order bill of lading gives the exporter complete control over the goods. The exporter may not transfer the bill to the buyer (importer) until the attached draft is paid or accepted. It may transfer the original order bill of lading to a bank or an agent with instructions as to the

Table 15.1 **Types and Characteristics of Ocean Bills of Lading**

Types	*Functions*
Order B/L	Receipt from the carrier
	Contract to transport the goods to a destination
	Title to the goods is held by the holder of the bill of lading; thus, it becomes a negotiable instrument.
Straight B/L	Receipt from the carrier
	Contract to transport the goods to a destination

conditions under which the bill will be released to the buyer. The carrier will not release the goods to the importer until the importer is in possession of the original copy of the order bill of lading.

Other forms of bills of lading that serve a particular function are also used in export transactions. These are the *through bill of lading, on-board bill of lading,* and *received for shipment bill of lading.*

Marine Insurance Policy or Certificate

On shipments outside the United States, the freight charges do not include premiums for insurance coverage. It is necessary to take out marine insurance because the steamship line will disclaim responsibility for loss or damage to the goods unless these arise from negligence on the part of the carrier. Marine insurance policies and certificates are described in greater detail in Chapter 16, which deals with transportation and logistics.

Other Documents

Some countries require other documents or modifications of the above-mentioned documents. A visaed certificate of origin in place of or in addition to a consular invoice may be required. Some countries require packing lists. Special certificates issued by the Department of Agriculture, the Food and Drug Administration, export and import licenses and permits, and other documents may be required by various departments or agencies of the exporting or importing country. Even ocean carriers require certain documents, such as the delivery or shipping permit that authorizes delivery of the goods on the docks for shipment. Thus, there are great variations in the requirements, depending upon the type of goods exported or imported, and the country with which trade is conducted.

Each exporting document serves a particular purpose. Documentary requirements vary with the type of shipment, and the carrier's and countries' requirements.

CHANNELS FOR IMPORTING

A firm may handle all details of purchasing goods from a foreign supplier (direct importing) or may contract with an intermediary to handle those details (indirect importing). The latter route is taken when a firm knows that international sourcing is necessary or desirable but lacks the necessary skills within its own organization.

Direct Import

When the purchase of foreign products is a regular part of the business of a firm, it will usually establish an import office as an adjunct to its domestic purchasing department or as a separate foreign purchasing department. Direct importing is advisable when a large volume of imports is required or when there are other advantages.

Merchandise from abroad may be purchased directly from producers, through intermediaries, or through foreign brokers or agents. The buyer must maintain constant communications with the seller to make sure that the necessary documents are completed and all aspects of the packing, shipping, and insurance are handled as required. When the goods arrive at the port of debarkation (entry), they must be cleared through customs by the importer unless the task is turned over to an import broker or other intermediary.

If a firm's purchases are of sufficient volume and are evenly distributed throughout the year, it might even be advantageous to establish a branch office abroad to handle the details of purchasing and shipping. This can greatly reduce the cost of the imported goods and will ensure continuous supply. The branch office serves as the headquarters for the importer when abroad. It prepares market reports and handles the details of purchase. It supervises the grading, sorting, and packing for shipment, and arranges for the international transportation.

An alternative to the branch office for large importers is to assign traveling buyers to foreign countries; these are generally employees of the importer. They are completely familiar with the customs, culture, and language of the country where they are stationed and are specialists in a limited line of products. They inspect the goods before shipment to make sure they are acceptable. The degree of authority given to these buyers depends on the customs of trade and the ease with which communications can be maintained between the employer and the buyer. Maintaining a traveling buyer is an expensive proposition; therefore, only firms that import large quantities can afford such employees.

When a firm engages in direct importing, it must handle all of the details involved in getting the goods into the country.

Indirect Import

Indirect importing occurs when the seller handles all arrangements for the shipment of the goods to the buyer, or when the buyer engages intermediaries to take care of the details. The most important intermediaries are import merchants, foreign agents, indent houses, import commission houses, foreign commissionaires, wholesalers or jobbers, and brokers or factors.

Import Merchant

An import merchant purchases products from abroad and makes them available to buyers. All functions of financing the foreign purchases and all risks of possible loss due to the fluctuations in currencies, changes in import duties, and delays between purchases and sales are the responsibility of the import merchant. Among the products that are normally handled by import merchants are spices, coffee, tea, raw wool, linen, and the like. The import merchant stores the goods, thereby providing the buyer with a domestic source of supply. Since the buyer does not perform any of the importing functions, the buyer is, in reality, only a user of imported products and not an importer.

Exclusive Agents

When import merchants act as the sole selling agent of the foreign firm or manufacturer, they are known as exclusive agents. In almost every respect the exclusive agent functions as an import merchant.

Foreign Agents

A more accurate term for foreign agent is a manufacturer's representative or sales representative who resides in the country of the importer but sells products of a foreign manufacturer to wholesalers, jobbers, and retailers in specified territories. These foreign agents may represent many firms that produce noncompetitive goods. They may receive and stock goods, but do not take title or assume any financial responsibility. They often advertise or otherwise promote goods to help the manufacturer establish a permanent market. Shipments are generally made directly to the buyer, who makes payment to the foreign supplier. The foreign agents get goods through customs, thus relieving the buyer of many of the technicalities of importing.

Because of differences in service of various agents, the specific rights and obligations of the agent are enumerated in the contract with the manufacturer, from whom the agent receives a commission.

Indent House

An *indent* is an order for goods. An indent house, therefore, is an importer that buys on orders received from a domestic buyer. The foreign supplier will ship the goods to the indent house, which quotes a CIF (cost, insurance, and freight) price to the domestic firm. The amount of income earned by the indent house is determined by its skill in buying, negotiating lower transportation charges, fluctuations in the rate of exchange, and the markup.

Import Commission House

An import commission house is often the recipient of shipments made on consignment. A commission is received from the foreign producer who shipped the goods. Some import commission houses function as import merchants, purchasing goods for a domestic buyer, who pays the commission.

Foreign Commissionaire

An importer may make use of a foreign commissionaire who acts on behalf of the importer in seeking, purchasing, assembling, and shipping goods to the importer. The commission is paid by the importer.

Import Wholesalers and Jobbers

Wholesalers and jobbers may import directly from foreign suppliers, although they generally make their purchases through import merchants, brokers, and resident agents. Wholesalers and jobbers serve the independent retailers who are too small to import directly, even extending credit to them. Some of them carry an inventory of nonperishable commodities and products that are not subject to wide price fluctuations. Larger wholesalers and jobbers have their own importing departments and maintain direct contacts with foreign sources. They may even send out traveling buyers to locate what they need.

Import Brokers and Factors

Import brokers and factors are located in the country of import. They attempt to consummate sales by bringing buyers and sellers together. They may buy goods for the account of a client, but they never take title to the goods. Usually, the seller ships the product directly to the buyer, who makes payment. The brokers collect their fees from either the domestic buyer or the foreign seller. The major advantage in using brokers is that they are familiar with various sources of supply, differences in product grades, and other technical features of a product.

A *factor* is a broker who helps to finance a particular transaction. For example, in shipments on consignment the factor may advance to the seller a part of the funds until the consignee has sold the goods. Factors even advance funds to domestic buyers to make purchases for resale. Thus, a factor may function as an export credit company.

In indirect import, intermediaries are used to get the goods into the country, relieving the importer of the details of importing.

Clearing Imports Through Customs

Goods that originate in a foreign country must go through customs upon their arrival in the importing nation. The following section describes clearing imports through U.S. customs.

Filing the Entry

The carrier notifies the importer when a shipment arrives at the port of entry. The importer or an agent must file the customs entry to prevent a delay in obtaining the goods. If the importer is unable to prepare and file the entry, a customs house broker, who has been licensed by the Treasury Department, may be used. If the importer does not enter the goods through customs within five days of arrival, they are shipped to a bonded warehouse and held as being unclaimed. If the goods are not claimed within one year, they are sold.

The importer or a broker must prepare an invoice that describes the merchandise, its value, and other data. The importer must also indicate the tariff classification for duty purposes. These documents are delivered to the Commodity Team (customs officials) for processing. If the Commodity Team approves the entry, the importer must pay the estimated duty and post a surety bond, which guarantees payment of any additional duty that may be due after regional liquidators review the entry.

The shipment is taken to a warehouse or left on the pier for examination by import specialists. If everything is in order, including quantity verifica-

A tired U.S. customs officer questions returning travellers at the Los Angeles International Airport.

tion, a release is sent to the Commodity Team. Permits for entry with the manifest and other documents are forwarded to the regional liquidators, where determination is made as to the assessment of the final duties.

Protest

Importers may challenge the duty assessed by filing a protest with the customs officer within 60 days. If disagreement continues and the problem cannot be resolved, the matter is sent to the U.S. Customs Court. If either the government or the importer is dissatisfied with the decision of the lower court, either may appeal to the Court of Customs and Patent Appeal. The findings of this court are usually final and binding.

Shipment in Bond

It is possible to ship goods from the port of entry to a customs port. The shipment containers are sealed and placed under bond until their arrival, when the goods go through customs. Often such shipments are made to a foreign or free trade zone (FTZ), where the goods may be inspected, stored, processed, repaired, remarked, and packaged for resale. The goods do not formally go through customs until they are removed from the FTZ; therefore, duties are not paid until that time. Foreign trade zones can be used to facilitate the distribution and servicing of the imports before delivery.

Imports may also be destined for warehouse entry. Bonded warehouses store goods for up to two years. Theoretically, the goods have not entered the country, so they do not go through customs until they are removed from the facility. In the United States, goods stored in the bonded warehouses may not be processed, repaired, remarked, and so forth, although some foreign countries do permit such activities.

Mail Shipments

Mail shipments that do not exceed $250 in value are entered under a mail entry prepared by a customs officer after the post office submits the package for customs examination. The post office will deliver the merchandise to the addressee if the goods are not prohibited. If there is a duty payable, it will be so indicated on the mail entry accompanying the package. Upon payment of the duty and the postal fee, the item will be surrendered to the addressee.

Mail shipments exceeding $250 in value will be forwarded to the customs office nearest the addressee. The post office will notify the addressee of the arrival of the item and the location of the customs office. Customs clearance will require filing an entry in the same manner as on a shipment that has arrived at a port of entry.

Examination and Appraisal

When a traveler debarks from a carrier, one of the first officials encountered is the customs inspector. The baggage of the traveler is examined to prevent the import of illegal or harmful articles. The inspector has the authority to search, detain, and even arrest those who are violating customs or other laws.

Customs inspectors are assigned to inspect cargo arriving by way of air, land, or water carriers. When a seagoing vessel arrives at the port of entry, the inspector will board the vessel to examine the ship's manifest and other documents before passengers and cargo may be unloaded. Certain items must be weighed, gauged, or measured. Casks of liquor must be unloaded to permit sampling for laboratory analysis. Other parcels may be designated for comparison with invoices or for examination. Discrepancies will be noted and the importer will pay a duty on only what has actually arrived.

On small shipments and when certain classes of goods such as bulk commodities are imported, the examination may occur on the docks. Once examined, the goods are released to the importer. In other shipments, random packages may be retained by the examiner and the remainder released to the importer. After the examination has been completed and everything has been determined to be in order, those packages that were withheld will be released to the importer.

After going through the required formalities to clear goods through customs, an importer must pay any duties owed before removing the goods.

Mail shipments must also formally go through the customs.

Appraisal of the value of the goods being imported is often necessary. This occurs when some product does not fall within one of the classifications in the schedule of duties. The appraiser must then determine the value of the goods for duty purposes. Often, customs service specialists are called upon to settle intricate technical or legal problems. Usually, precedent aids the customs official in making judgment, although some of these precedents seem to defy common sense. The following examples cited in the *United States Customs and You*, issued by the Commissioner of Customs, illustrates the difficulties of interpreting the classifications of imports for duty purposes. Are Chinese gooseberries berries? Yes, says your common sense. No, say Customs! Why? Because they are too large—the size of cherry tomatoes. They will not fit into the tariff concept of a berry—a small soft fruit. The duty naturally varies according to the tariff classification. Is rhubarb a vegetable or fruit? A vegetable, shouts the botanist. A fruit, declares Customs—because of its use. Is soap manufactured in the shape of lemons considered to be artificial fruit or soap? It is obviously soap, right? Wrong again! To the Customs people soap in the shape of a lemon is artificial fruit; whereas, cherries made of glass may not enter as artificial fruit. Tariff Schedules specifically provide that glass articles cannot be classified as artificial fruit.[6]

Some commodities not specifically named in the Tariff Schedule are considered for customs purposes under other classifications: components of chief value, chief use, similitude, and so on. This often results in conflicts between the importer and customs. Once the problem has been resolved, all field offices are notified so that the practice will be uniform. This is important because different tariff classifications can result in considerable differences in the amount of duties assessed.

The uncertainty of tariff classification makes it difficult for the importer to plan a sales strategy. Higher duties could make the goods noncompetitive in the domestic market. To minimize the uncertainties of importers and exporters, application may be made to the Commissioner of Customs in writing for a ruling on the tariff classification of any item. The decision will be binding and will not be changed until it is published in the Federal Register and hearings have been held.

All goods entering a country are subject to examination and appraisal by the customs service.

Restricted Merchandise

Although U.S. customs laws do not require licenses or permits to import merchandise from any country, other agencies of the federal government do. Since enforcement is easier for the Customs Service than it is for other agencies, this task also falls to the customs officials. Examples are such products as animals, certain drugs, cotton, firearms and ammunition, fruits, gold bullion, gold coins, gold coin jewelry, gold medals, liquor, meat and meat products, milk, plants and plant products, trademarked articles, and vegetables. Other merchandise must be examined for fitness for use, freedom from contamination, and import quotas. Customs will not permit the

The Customs Service acts on behalf of other agencies of the government to seek out restricted imports.

release of merchandise unless the import requirements of other agencies have been met.

Foreign Assets Control

The purchase abroad or the importation of merchandise originating in countries with which the United States does not have diplomatic relations is prohibited without a Treasury license. Although the restrictions of these licenses seem clear enough, the bureaucratic language of government agencies enters the picture to complicate matters: For example, "a general license has been issued authorizing persons subject to the jurisdiction of the U.S. to purchase and import into the U.S. for noncommercial purposes any merchandise of mainland Chinese origin or of a type or kind which was traditionally imported from mainland China."[7] No one is quite sure what this means, but the customs officials must enforce the restrictions.

Trade with countries with which the United States does not have diplomatic relations is closely regulated.

FINANCING INTERNATIONAL TRADE

The terms of payment that a firm extends to its customers are affected by business and nonbusiness factors. The buyer and seller will negotiate the method of financing that is to be used once the terms have been determined. The purpose of this section is to make familiar the most common methods of financing international trade.[8] This will involve the remittance of funds to the seller through a bank by way of mail transfers, cable transfers, or drafts either in the importer's, the exporter's, or third country's currency.

Terms of Payment

Cash in Advance

Cash with the order or in advance of shipment means that the buyer must pay for the goods when the order is placed. Usually a sight draft is drawn by the seller (drawer) on the buyer (drawee) calling for payment upon presentation. When this method is used, the buyer (payer) is actually financing the transaction days, weeks, or even months before receiving shipment. This means that working capital is tied up until the goods are received and sold or utilized in the buyer's operation. The buyer has no opportunity to inspect the goods prior to making payment to the seller (payee). If the wrong goods are shipped or the goods are damaged during shipment, the buyer will incur considerable time and expense returning the goods or negotiating settlement with the carrier or underwriter. If the seller were to file for bankruptcy before the goods are shipped, the buyer could lose what had been advanced. The only possible advantage to the buyer is that some sellers provide a discount for paying cash in advance.

Because there is little risk, cash in advance is the seller's preferred method of financing trade.

Open Account

Open account sales are used in international trade only when the seller has had long-standing relations with the buyer or the buyer is a branch or subsidiary of the selling firm. For buyers, open account sales are the most advantageous method of financing a purchase; however, for the seller there are many dangers:

1. The buyer is merely promising to pay for the goods.
2. There is no documentary evidence of the debt and no assurance that the buyer will make payment on the due date.
3. In the event of a bankruptcy, the seller is merely another creditor with claims against the assets of the firm.
4. Conditions beyond the control of the buyer might prevent payment.
5. The entire burden of financing is borne by the seller.

If an open account buyer does not pay within the stipulated period, the seller has little recourse. The seller may try to charge interest on overdue accounts but this is usually ineffective. The buyer may decide to owe the supplier rather than to borrow money at a higher interest charge to make payment. Relatedly, short-term or working capital loans might not even be available in the buyer's country; thus, supplier credit becomes the buyer's source of working capital.

If the buyer refuses to make payment, the seller's only alternative may be to bring a lawsuit. This might not be a viable option because of the time and costs involved and the ill-will it might create.

The open account method of financing is generally limited to related entities or to regular customers.

Mercantile Credit

Mercantile credit involves the use of a time draft or bill of exchange that is drawn by the seller (drawer) on the buyer (drawee), obligating the buyer to pay the seller or a third party holder of the draft a given sum of money upon maturity. If the seller holds the draft until maturity, the seller is financing the transaction. If, however, the drawer sells (discounts) the draft to a bank, the financing is transferred from the seller to the bank. The bank will pay the seller the face value of the draft less the interest charge until maturity for the use of its funds until the bank collects from the importer. (See Figure 15.4 for a sample draft.)

Parties to the Draft   The major parties to a draft are the seller (exporter), the buyer (importer), the importer's bank, and the correspondent bank (the bank's agent located in the country of export). The seller is the drawer or maker of the draft, while the buyer is the drawee or the one on whom the draft is drawn. By accepting a draft, the importer (payer) becomes liable and must honor the draft when it matures. Thus, the accepted draft becomes

02-035   TOLEDO, OHIO,_____19_____

ON_____SIGHT PAY TO THE

ORDER OF_____$_____

_____DOLLARS

DOCUMENTS ATTACHED:_____

_____

VALUE RECEIVED, AND CHARGE TO ACCOUNT OF

TO_____   _____

_____

_____   BY_____

_____   _____

Figure 15.4   Sample Draft
Source: Courtesy of Ohio Citizens Bank, Toledo, Ohio. Reprinted by permission.

a negotiable instrument and may be sold (discounted) by the exporter to a bank or anyone (payee) who is willing to buy the document.

Steps in the Use of a Time Draft   If mercantile credit is used to finance international trade, either the exporter or a third party is financing the transaction. The following describes the steps involved in the use of a time draft.

1. The exporter (drawer) draws a draft on the importer (drawee) and mails it to the exporter's correspondent bank in the importer's country.
2. The bank presents the draft to the importer for acceptance.
3. The importer accepts the draft by signing it and receives documents to claim the goods from the carrier (documents against acceptance).
4. The bank mails the draft to the exporter via its correspondent bank in the exporter's country.
5. The exporter may hold the draft until maturity and collect the amount of the draft from the importer or sell it to a bank (discount) and collect the money immediately.
6. If the bank discounts the draft, it will collect the amount of the draft from the importer at maturity.

Value of the Draft   Several factors determine the value of a draft:

1. The face value of the draft.
2. The credit standing of the buyer (acceptor of the draft). The bank will

not readily discount or purchase a time bill (draft) unless it is certain the due amount can be collected at maturity.

3. The credit standing of the exporter. When the seller discounts the draft, it endorses the draft over to the bank. The seller promises that if the buyer does not honor the draft upon maturity, the bank has recourse against the seller.

4. The maturity date of the draft. The later the maturity date, the less a draft is worth since factors beyond the control of the importer might prevent payment when the draft becomes due.

5. The goods that are being financed. Perishable commodities have a limited repossession life.

6. The currency on which the draft is drawn. Some currencies are unstable or difficult to convert.

Mercantile credit involves the use of a time draft drawn on a buyer for acceptance, creating an obligation to pay on maturity.

Commercial Letters of Credit (L/C)

One of the most important methods in financing international trade is the use of a commerical letter of credit. Although there are many types of L/Cs, one may think of a letter of credit as a financial instrument that authorizes the exporter to draw a draft on a bank when certain stipulated conditions stated in the letter of credit have been met. The letter may authorize the drawing of either a sight draft or a time draft. (See Figure 15.5 for a sample L/C.)

The popularity of commercial letters of credit among U.S. exporters developed after World War II, when many nations adopted exchange controls. American exporters were in the enviable position of commanding a seller's market and were able to dictate financial terms. Since there was no assurance that buyers would be able to convert their domestic currencies into U.S. dollars, the use of letters of credit meant that dollars had been set aside and were available for specific purchases.

Types of Letters of Credit   Four major types of letters of credit are commonly used:

1. An *irrevocable letter of credit* issued by the importer's bank is a promise by that bank that a draft drawn upon it will be honored when certain conditions stipulated in the letter of credit are met, and that the letter of credit will not be revoked or amended without the consent of the beneficiary.

2. An *irrevocable and confirmed letter of credit* issued by the importer's bank is a promise by that bank that the credit will not be revoked or amended without consent of the beneficiary. The correspondent bank in the exporter's country also adds its guarantee (confirmation) that if the issuing bank does not honor the draft drawn by the exporter, it will honor the draft.

APPLICATION FOR COMMERCIAL LETTER OF CREDIT

Ohio Citizens Trust Company

TO: P.O. BOX 1688
TOLEDO. OHIO 43603

Attn: International Division

Date _____

GENTLEMEN:

I/WE HEREBY REQUEST YOU TO ISSUE BY ___CABLE___ YOUR IRREVOCABLE LETTER OF CREDIT AS FOLLOWS:
                           AIR MAIL

IN FAVOR OF _____

FOR ACCOUNT OF _____

UP TO THE AGGREGATE AMOUNT OF _____

AVAILABLE BY _____DRAFTS DRAWN AT YOUR OPTION, ON YOU OR YOUR CORRESPONDENTS
               Tenor

FOR_____PER CENT AMOUNT OF INVOICE.

WHEN ACCOMPANIED BY THE FOLLOWING DOCUMENTS: (CHECK DOCUMENTS REQUIRED)

☐   FULL SET OF _____BILLS OF LADING DRAWN TO THE ORDER OF SHIPPER. BLANK ENDORSED

    NOTIFY _____

    EVIDENCING SHIPMENT FROM _____TO _____

☐   COMMERCIAL INVOICE IN TRIPLICATE STATING THAT IT COVERS _____
_____
_____

☐   PACKING LIST IN TRIPLICATE

☐   U.S. CUSTOMS INVOICE #5515 IN DUPLICATE

☐   INSURANCE POLICY OR CERTIFICATE COVERING ALL RISKS

☐   PARTIAL SHIPMENTS   ☐ PERMITTED   ☐ NOT PERMITTED

☐   AIRWAY BILLS OF LADING _____

☐   OTHER DOCUMENTS _____

INSURANCE TO BE EFFECTED BY   ☐ SHIPPER (SELLER)   ☐ US

BILLS OF LADING TO BE DATED NOT LATER THAN _____

LETTER OF CREDIT TO EXPIRE ON_____

TERMS: FOB _____ CIF _____ C&F_____ OTHER _____
      (port or city)   (port or city)   (port or city)   Please specify
                                                         (port or city)

OTHER INSTRUCTIONS:

IN CONSIDERATION OF YOUR ISSUING A LETTER OF CREDIT SUBSTANTIALLY CONFORMING WITH THE ABOVE REQUEST, WE HEREBY AGREE WHEN REQUESTED BY YOU TO SIGN AND DELIVER TO YOU AN INDEMNITY AGREEMENT IN A FORM SATISFACTORY TO YOU, AND WE FURTHER AGREE THAT EACH AND ALL OF THE PROVISIONS OF ANY GENERAL INDEMNITY AGREEMENT HERETOFORE SIGNED AND DELIVERED TO YOU BY US, OR ANY OF US, RELATING TO LETTERS OF CREDIT ISSUABLE BY YOU, IN THE ABSENCE OF WRITTEN AGREEMENT TO THE CONTRARY, SHALL BE DEEMED TO BE INCORPORATED AS A PART OF THE ABOVE REQUEST.

VERY TRULY YOURS,

_____

_____
AUTHORIZED SIGNATURE

02-304

Figure 15.5 Commercial Letter of Credit
Source: Courtesy of Ohio Citizens Bank, Toledo, Ohio. Reprinted by permission.

3. An *irrevocable unconfirmed letter of credit* means that the importer's bank promises not to revoke or amend the letter of credit without the consent of the beneficiary, but the correspondent bank in the exporter's country does not add its guarantee to that of the importer's bank.

4. A *revocable unconfirmed letter of credit* means that neither the issuing bank nor the correspondent bank promises to honor a draft that is drawn by the exporter. This type of letter of credit is little more than a guide for the preparation of shipping documents.

Figure 15.6 outlines the types of letters of credit that are issued by the importer's bank.

Figure 15.7 outlines the steps in using an irrevocable confirmed letter of credit. (Note: This example assumes that the correspondent bank is also the exporter's bank.) See Figure 15.8 for an example of an L/C application.

With an irrevocable and confirmed L/C, the seller is assured of receiving payment because both the issuing bank and the confirming bank promise to make payment.

Bank Credit

Commercial banks become involved in financing international trade in several ways. An exporter (seller) may draw a draft on a bank, creating a bankers' bill. When the bank accepts the draft, it becomes a banker's acceptance. These are generally easier to discount than those that have been drawn upon and accepted by merchants because of the generally favorable perception of banks and their credit worthiness.

A bank may accept a draft to create dollar exchange during periods when there is a shortage of that currency in a particular country. A foreign bank will draw a dollar draft on an American bank (a banker's bill), which accepts the draft (banker's acceptance). The drawer bank will then discount the draft and obtain dollars. These dollar exchange drafts, which are unsecured transactions, have a maximum maturity of 90 days and are commonly used in transactions with South America.

Unsecured loans may be given by a bank to foreign government agencies, foreign banks, or foreign corporations, usually with the endorsement of a foreign bank. An unsecured loan may be given to a foreign subsidiary

Figure 15.6   Types of Letters of Credit

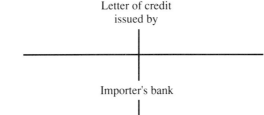

Letter of credit
issued by

Importer's bank

| Irrevocable confirmed | Irrevocable unconfirmed | Revocable unconfirmed | Irrevocable L/C |

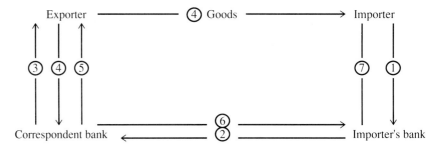

1. The buyer (importer) goes to his or her bank and applies for an irrevocable and confirmed letter of credit to be issued in favor of the seller (exporter).

2. The bank will process the application, issue a letter of credit in favor of the exporter, then mail the L/C to its correspondent bank for confirmation. (The bank may request the importer to put up collateral, or require the documents be delivered to the bank so that it may claim the goods when they arrive, store them, and issue them to the importer on a trust receipt.)

3. If the correspondent bank approves the transaction, it will confirm the letter of credit and send the original copy (notify) to the exporter.

4. The exporter makes the shipment according to the conditions that are stipulated on the L/C and presents to his or her bank the documents and a draft drawn on his or her bank (correspondent bank).

5. If all the conditions on the L/C have been met and if a sight draft is called for, the bank will pay the exporter and debit the account of the issuing bank (importer's bank). If a time draft is called for, the exporter's bank will accept the draft and discount it in behalf of the importer's bank.

6. The bank will mail the documents to the issuing bank in the importer's country.

7. The importer's bank will provide the documents to the buyer when payment is made so that the goods may be claimed.

Figure 15.7   Steps Involved in the Operation of a Letter of Credit

of a multinational corporation with the guarantee of the parent company. Lines of credit may be granted to foreign correspondent banks for the purpose of confirming letters of credit, acceptance financing, or short-term overdraft privileges.

Consignment Shipments

Shipments on consignment occur when the seller (consignor) ships products to a designated consignee in hopes that these goods will be sold by the latter. The consignee may be a foreign branch or subsidiary of a multinational firm, a foreign representative, or a certain type of import house. Title does not pass to the consignee. Consignment shipments may be made to a foreign trade zone or a bonded warehouse so that the consignee is not required to pay the import duties until the goods are removed from the premises.

TELEX: 286044
ANSWER BACK:
OHIOCIT TOL
CABLE ADDRESS: OCIT BANK

OHIO CITIZENS BANK

ORIGINAL
INTERNATIONAL DIVISION
P.O. BOX 1688
TOLEDO, OHIO 43603 U.S.A.
TELEPHONE (419) 259-6566

☐ THIS CREDIT IS FORWARDED TO THE ADVISING BANK BY AIRMAIL

☐ THIS IS A CONFIRMATION OF THE CREDIT OPENED BY CABLE UNDER EVEN DATE

DATE _____

This credit is subject to the "Uniform Customs and Practice for Documentary Credits (1983 Revision), International Chamber of Commerce Brochure No. 400"

Irrevocable Documentary Letter of Credit
—————— Advising Bank ——————

ISSUING BANK'S NUMBER
OC-

ADVISING BANK'S NUMBER

Applicant

—————— Beneficiary ——————

Amount

EXPIRY DATE

IN THE

COUNTRY OF THE BENEFICIARY UNLESS OTHERWISE INDICATED

We hereby issue in your favor this documentary letter of credit which is available for payment/acceptance of your draft(s) drawn
at _____ sight on Ohio Citizens Bank, Toledo, Ohio
accompanied by the following documents (at least in duplicate unless otherwise specified)

☐ Beneficiary's Commercial Invoice in   Copies

☐ Airway Bills of Lading

☐ Marine and War Risk Insurance Policy or Certificates

☐ Terms:
Evidencing Shipment of

☐ Full Set Clean on Board Ocean Bills of Lading made out to Order of

☐ Notify:

☐ Packing List in Triplicate

☐ U.S. Customs Form No. 5515 in Duplicate Signed by Shippers.

Special conditions:

To

From

INSURED BY   ☐ Buyer   ☐ Seller

Partial shipments   permitted.
Transshipments   permitted.

All negotiation charges are for your account. Documents to be forwarded to issuing bank by one air mailing.

WE UNDERTAKE THAT DRAFTS DRAWN AND PRESENTED IN CONFORMITY WITH THE TERMS OF THIS CREDIT WILL BE DULY HONOURED   DRAFTS MUST BE MARKED AS DRAWN UNDER THIS CREDIT
<u>INSTRUCTIONS TO THE NEGOTIATING BANK</u>
The amount of each drawing must be endorsed on the reverse hereof.
Drafts accompanied by a certificate from the negotiating bank that all terms and conditions of this credit have been complied with, are to be forwarded to the drawee bank

Advising bank's notification

Very truly yours,

_____
Authorized Signature

_____
Place, date, name and signature of advising bank

02-134

Figure 15.8   Application for Letter of Credit
Source: Courtesy of Ohio Citizens Bank, Toledo, Ohio. Reprinted by permission.

427

The consignee will, upon the sale of the goods, pay the storage charges and import duties and retain a commission before remitting the balance to the exporter. If the consignor utilizes the services of a correspondent of its bank in the foreign country, the goods will be shipped to a warehouse and released to the consignee upon the directions of the correspondent. Title to the goods will remain in the name of the exporter or the designated bank. When the goods are sold, the consignee will deduct the duties, commission, and other charges before turning the remainder over to the designated bank, which will remit these funds to the exporter's bank so that payment can be made to the exporter.

Uncertainty and risk characterize consignment shipments. The seller's assets are tied up while the goods remain unsold. Political instability might result in loss of the goods, or exchange controls might prevent taking the proceeds out of the country. There is no assurance that the goods will be sold and if they are sold, that a profit will arise. Unsold goods may be returned to the consignor without liability to the consignee. In fact, it is all too common for unethical consignees to sell the goods and never pay the consignor. Nevertheless, exporters resort to such shipments to break into a market or to ensure that goods are available along with those of a competitor.

When goods are shipped on consignment, there is no assurance that the goods will be sold or that payment will be received from the consignee.

Countertrade

Countertrade is essentially a form of barter.[9] In its simplest form, goods are exchanged for goods rather than for money. This usually occurs when a country lacks the foreign exchange or gold to make payment, or because the seller is unwilling to accept payment in soft currency. This method of paying for purchases gained prominence in the 1950s when the Soviet Union paid for essential imports with goods because of its inability to earn sufficient hard currency to replace its depleted gold supply.

Countertrade often occurs when a firm seeks to capture a larger share of a market by accepting payment in goods rather than foreign exchange. American firms, for example, are known to have received payment from abroad in such products as butter and hazelnuts for machinery when the importing country was experiencing a period of dollar shortage. Peru, for example, has proposed servicing its foreign obligations with products.[10] Some countries have sought to further their bilateral relations with certain countries or to gain entry into new markets through countertrade.

Countertrade has been increasing steadily in recent years. This has been especially true among the less developed countries, but has not been limited to these countries. See Global Insight on countertrade in Peru. Bussard found that the number of countries requesting countertrade has increased from 15 in 1972 to 27 in 1979, and reached 88 in 1983.[11] It is estimated that in 1986, more than three fourths of the International Fortune 1000 companies had some sort of countertrade department.[12] (See Figure 15.9 for forms of countertrade.)

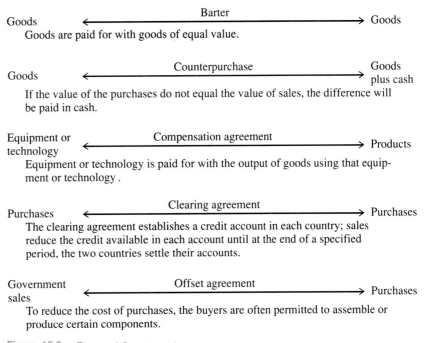

Figure 15.9   Forms of Countertrade

Countertrade can take the form of *counterpurchase* or *parallel barter* agreements where contracts are signed specifying the goods or services to be exchanged. At the end of the stipulated period, if the value of the goods or services is not in balance, the difference will be settled with cash. In a *buy-back* or *compensation agreement,* one of the parties will supply technology or equipment and receives payment in the goods produced with that equipment (see Chapter 13). *Clearing agreements* may be signed by nations where credit accounts are provided to the other country. Each promises to purchase a given amount from the other, resulting in a balance over the stated period of time. The type of goods to be purchased from the other must be clearly stipulated. The agreement may provide for *switch trading* so that one party may sell or transfer its credit account to a third party.

Another form of countertrade is referred to as *offset,* where the cost of large purchases, usually government transactions, is reduced by permitting the buyer to participate in the production. For example, a nation will make a contract to purchase aircraft provided the production or assembly of certain parts will occur in the purchasing country to lessen the negative effect on the current account of the nation's balance of payments. The agreement may call for coproduction, licensing, subcontracting, or joint venture.

Countertrade is a particular type of trade transaction that is actually a form of barter.

Countertrade Helps Peruvian Trade Despite Foreign Exchange Shortages

Peru's foreign trade institute (ICE) has long advocated countertrade (CT) as a method of minimizing foreign exchange outflows, encouraging nontraditional exports, and penetrating new markets. ICE's expectations have proven true since the foreign exchange shortages became severe in 1987.

In 1987, there were 45 CT deals totaling more than $231 million; however, when oil-related products are excluded the total was only $12.3 million. In 1988 the story was very different. There were 119 CT transactions involving exports of $152.2 million and imports of $107.4 million. Not considering petroleum-related products, the exports were still $135.3 million and imports $91 million. Furthermore, these transactions were increasingly from private sector organizations. In 1988, private firms accounted for 78 percent of CT-financed exports and 75 percent of CT-financed imports. These figures are all the more impressive when one

realizes that they do not include any of the debt-for-goods deals that Peru has used to try to reduce its foreign debt levels.

Countertrade transactions have been conducted with more than 40 countries (mainly Andean Pact countries, the United States, and the EEC) and have involved exports of everything from iron ore and sawed timber to canned asparagus and finished clothing. Of perhaps greatest importance is that CT has allowed the continuation of imports that would otherwise have been nearly impossible due to foreign exchange rationing, the cumbersome Peruvian import approval process, and the excessive governmental red tape. Among the goods that Peru has imported through CT transactions are sugar, computers, tractors, pharmaceutical and chemical products, and livestock.

Source: Adapted from Vivianna Prochazka, "Profile of CT in Peru," *Business Latin America*, May 1, 1989, p. 131.

Terms of Payment to Meet Foreign Competition

Many foreign firms are provided with very favorable credit insurance or guarantees by their governments. Since the U.S. government does not provide its firms with as attractive credit insurance or guarantee programs, American firms are unable to provide the same liberal terms of payment as their competitors, placing them at a competitive disadvantage.

Credit-related aid provided by the U.S. government to exporters is of recent origin. It was not until October 1961 that the Export-Import Bank embarked upon a program to provide commercial banks and other institutions with export credit guarantees to finance medium-term export sales without recourse to the exporters. The Eximbank was further authorized to extend credits directly to exporters and credit insurance to them through the Federal Credit Insurance Association. Initially, credit insurance was provided only on short-term credit (180 days); however, in July 1962, this was extended to medium-term credits (1 to 5 years). These programs enable exporters to shift the greater portion of their credit risks and allow them to grant more liberal credit terms. However, many exporters are critical of the coverage provided, the necessity of insuring all shipments to a given area, and the relatively high premiums charged. Thus, the adequacy of government credit guarantees and insurance will have a great impact on the future competitiveness of U.S. exports, especially to countries with a shortage of hard currency.

U.S. exporters have attempted to meet the liberal credit terms granted by their competitors through the development of variations in the orthodox methods of financing export transactions. Without violating domestic laws and regulations, many exporters cooperate with importers who are faced with a shortage of foreign exchange. For example, at the request of the importer, the exporter may quote prices at more than the regular rate. The buyer makes application for dollar exchange at the central bank or other designated financial agency on the basis of such price quotations. When the application is approved and domestic currency is deposited, a dollar draft is drawn in favor of the exporter. The exporter will then credit the importer's account with dollars equal to the amount of overpayment. The existence of this dollar balance provides the importer with greater flexibility in future purchases. The ethics of such a transaction may be questioned, but from the American exporter's point of view no law or regulation has been violated. The buyer rationalizes that the government has profited because the ad valorem duty on the higher prices provided more than the expected revenues.

The use of bank acceptances as a means of financing exports has been growing at a rapid rate. This is a time draft that is drawn by the seller on the bank and is accepted by the latter. The exporter or drawer can wait until the draft matures for payment, or discount the acceptance prior to the maturity date and realize the proceeds from the sale immediately. The buyer has time to sell the imported goods and repay the bank at the maturity of the draft. This procedure enables the exporter to make sales on more liberal credit terms than if it were to finance the transaction without the use of bank credit.

Another variation in the use of banker's acceptances to finance an export transaction is for the buyer to make an acceptance agreement with its bank rather than to apply for a loan to make a purchase. The buyer draws a time draft on the bank. If the bank accepts the draft, it becomes a banker's acceptance and may be sold on the open market to provide funds to pay for imports. From the bank's point of view, the use of acceptances may be preferable to granting loans because they will not affect the statutory loan limit of the bank.

When exporters feel confident of the buyer's credit standing, they may extend the maturity date of the draft drawn upon the buyer. When exporters do this, they are essentially financing the transaction. If this puts pressure on their cash flow, they will try to discount the draft with a bank. It becomes more difficult to discount these bills when bank holdings of such papers increase. Exporters then turn to factors. Unfortunately, factors will pay only a percentage of the face value of such drafts; therefore, many firms have discontinued the practice of extending the maturity dates of drafts drawn on importers.

A unique method of financing used by some firms may be referred to as combination financing. With this method, the exporter jointly finances a transaction with a commercial bank. Terms as long as five years are granted. The commercial bank often finances the first $1\frac{1}{2}$ years (earlier maturity), while the exporter finances the last $3\frac{1}{2}$ years (later maturity). However, if for any reason the buyer defaults on the obligation to the bank for the earlier maturities, the exporter will be liable and will have to reimburse the bank.

The noticeable decrease in the use of irrevocable and confirmed letters of credit within the last two decades indicates that international competition will dictate the method for financing international trade transactions. Specific data are not available to indicate the relative importance of each of the other methods of financing exports, but the consensus among those engaged in international business is that the use of mercantile credit and open account financing is increasing in importance. In the face of the increasing trade competition and the growth of nations with both shortages of hard currency reserves and rapidly expanding needs, it would seem that large multinational firms will become increasingly important in exporting since they are better able to meet the competition and grant more liberal credit terms. They can avail themselves of the Export Import Bank credit guarantees and the services of the Federal Credit Insurance Association. The extent to which the smaller exporters have the opportunity to participate in such guarantees and insurance will probably determine their willingness to extend liberal credit terms and to compete in the export markets.

> Competitive success in world export markets is often determined as much by credit terms as by price as product quality.

SUMMARY

A firm that decides to export its products abroad has the alternatives of reaching that market through direct export or indirect export. If it decides to engage in direct export, it must establish an organization within the firm to handle all details of getting the goods to the foreign market. This may be accomplished through a built-in export department that utilizes the domestic sales departments to handle the details. The firm can establish a separate export department with an international staff handling the various functions, or it may establish an elaborate export division with various departments, comparable to the domestic sales division. Some firms find it advantageous to establish an export sales subsidiary to conduct the export functions of the firm.

If a firm decides to engage in indirect export, it must make use of intermediaries to handle the export functions. Various types of intermediary are available. Some of these act on behalf of the manufacturer, such as the export management company or the export agent, while others, such as the commission houses and resident agents, represent the buyers. Still others, such as the individual export merchant or the huge trading companies of Japan, carry on all functions related to the movement of goods, and act in their own behalf purchasing and selling products abroad. Finally, there are those who carry out some specialized functions in the export cycle, such as freight forwarders.

Various documents are required for every export shipment. The six most commonly used are the commercial invoice, consular invoice, certificate of origin, export declaration, ocean bill of lading, and the marine insurance policy or certificate. The number and type of documents required will vary with the type of shipment, the needs of the carrier, and the requirements of the exporter and importer countries.

Low cost, efficient delivery, and maximum quality are of prime concern to the overall strategy of a firm. Thus, understanding the details of importing is of major importance. An importer has the alternative of using direct or indirect importing when it makes a purchase from abroad. If it engages in direct import, it must handle all of the details involved in getting the goods into the country. If it turns to indirect import, the details of getting the goods into the country are turned over to an intermediary. What seems the least costly and most efficient method will be used by an importer.

Governments adopt controls to regulate the import of commodities into a country. The customs service is assigned this task. In the United States, the major functions of the Customs Service are to examine imports, appraise and collect duties, prevent the import of illegal and contraband goods, and protect the health and welfare of the American public. Many of the regulations are implemented in the name of other federal agencies.

The countries and the customers to whom sales are made determine the terms of payment that are used. When sales are made to unknown customers or to countries of extreme political instability, sellers usually want cash payment before making shipments. When sales are made to customers of long standing or to branches and subsidiaries, firms may use open account sales. Because of increasing international trade competition, more and more firms are extending credit on open accounts or mercantile credit. Other than cash in advance, the safest method of financing a sale is to insist upon the use of an irrevocable and confirmed letter of credit. As long as the seller meets the conditions stipulated on the letter of credit, collection is assured.

Countertrade has gained importance in recent years as a method of paying for imports. In reality, it is a form of barter that is used most often by buyers who do not have access to sufficient foreign exchange to make payment, or by sellers who see countertrade as a competitive weapon for improving their position abroad. International competition has also resulted in the granting of more liberal credit terms, especially among exporters from countries that provide liberal credit insurance or other forms of support for exporting. ☐

EXPORTING

Bill of lading

Built-in export department

Certificate of origin

Commercial invoice

Consular invoice

Direct export

Export agent

Export declaration

Export sales subsidiary

Export trade association (Webb-Pomerene Association)

Freight forwarder

Jobber

Marine insurance policy or certificate

Partners in trade (piggyback)

Resident agent

Retailers

Separate export department

Trading company

Wholesalers

IMPORTING

Bonded warehouse

Customs declaration

Direct importing

Exclusive agent

Exclusive buying agent

Foreign agent

Foreign assets control

Foreign broker or factor

Foreign commissionaire

Foreign export merchant

Import brokers and factors

Import commission house

Import merchant

Import wholesalers and jobbers

Indent house

Indirect importing

Liquidation of entry

Mark of origin

Protest

Traveling buyers (resident buyers)

FINANCING TRADE

Bank acceptance

Barter

Bill of exchange or draft

Clearing account barter

Correspondent bank

Counterpurchase or parallel barter

Countertrade

Discount a draft

Documentary draft	Hard currency
Documents against acceptance	Payee
Documents against payment	Payer
Drawee	Sight draft
Drawer	Soft currency
Endorsee	Switch trading
Endorser	Time draft
Factors	Trust receipt

REVIEW QUESTIONS

1. Explain the differences between direct and indirect export, and briefly describe the forms that organizations use to conduct direct export.

2. What are the major functions of an export management company? Is their operation limited to small firms?

3. What are the major functions of trading companies?

4. If you are engaged in direct import, who will aid you in locating foreign sources of supply? Explain.

5. List the intermediaries that may be used in indirect importing and describe how each operates.

6. What are the responsibilities of the U.S. Customs Service?

7. Describe the documents used in clearing goods through customs.

8. What are some of the problems that might be encountered in examination and appraisal of goods for import?

9. Under what conditions might an exporter insist on cash in advance? Accept open account sales? Utilize mercantile credit?

10. Describe the types of drafts and the parties involved.

11. What is a commercial letter of credit? Define the functions of each of the parties and the steps involved in the use of an L/C.

12. What is a consignment shipment?

13. Why and how does foreign competition determine the terms and methods used in financing an export sale?

14. What is meant by countertrade? What are the various forms? Explain the major reasons for the increasing use of countertrade.

15. Should multinational firms engage in countertrade?

DISCUSSION CASE

Spectrum Speakers, Inc.

In 1979, two undergraduate students at the University of Toledo decided to quit school and take a shortcut in making their first million dollars. Eric Johanson and Larry Perault were both interested in sound engineering, but since no such program was offered at the University of Toledo, they decided to develop stereo speakers that were based on their own theories. This led to the establishment of a partnership, Spectrum Speakers. As might be expected, the initial capitalization was minimal.

The major objective of this new business was to manufacture speakers that would outperform other speakers but could be sold at prices below those of established competitors. Considerable research went into speaker development, eventually resulting in the manufacture of a product that received raves at electronics trade shows in Reno, Nevada, and Chicago, Illinois. Spectrum's speakers also received excellent reviews in national audiophile magazines. The price for a pair of speakers was set between $200 and $800, depending on the model. The ability to produce speakers at a highly competitive price was in part because many of the components in Spectrum's speakers were purchased from Europe and were thus available at very low dollar prices. Although Spectrum's management did not realize it, the high U.S. interest rates that created the "King Dollar" were in fact subsidizing the cost of components. The future for the fledgling firm seemed bright.

Inquiries began to come in from various dealers in the United States and some from foreign countries. Exclusive dealerships were granted to firms in several states as well as Sweden, the Netherlands, Taiwan, and Indonesia.

With these initial successes, family members of the two founders provided additional capital to develop the business. Then in 1982, the business was incorporated as Spectrum Speakers, Inc. Unfortunately, this successful growth was short-lived.

Orders grew faster than expected. Spectrum lacked sufficient inventories to manufacture enough speakers to fill the orders and lacked the funds necessary to purchase the needed components. Spectrum found itself unable to purchase component parts until it was paid on previous sales. Part of Spectrum's production advantage, using foreign components, became a liability as these suppliers demanded cash in advance or irrevocable letter of credit payment.

By George M. Taoka, 1989.

This case, developed with the assistance and permission of Eric Johanson and Larry Perault, is for class discussion only. It is not intended to represent good or bad management or decision-making.

Spectrum had been quite successful in developing export sales. Unfortunately, this too became a disadvantage. Some customers were lost because of Spectrum's insistence on the use of letters of credit. The combination of cash in advance payment for speaker components and loss of customers resulted in a cash flow crisis.

Adding to this problem was the company philosophy of wanting to keep profit margins to a minimum. The desire of Spectrum's management to undersell the speakers of competitors became a millstone around the financial neck of the firm. Despite the seriousness of these problems, they were viewed as temporary.

With no systematic effort at marketing Spectrum speakers, orders continued to increase rapidly. This was especially true for orders from abroad. In fact almost all of Spectrum's orders were unsolicited. People seemed to be hunting for Spectrum's speakers. Sales to Sweden alone amounted to more than one third of the total sales. Indeed, a marketing consultant estimated that sales should double annually until ultimately reaching $5,000,000 in 1990.

Before the firm could reach its potential, a number of factors had a negative effect on its operation. The decrease in the value of the U.S. dollar in the mid-1980s increased the costs of imported components. As costs increased, profit margins dropped to such an extent that it became difficult to hold prices to the original objective, substantially below the prices of competitors. Increases in sales did not materialize as expected. Several other factors have plagued the operation of the firm. The two founders may have been able to make an excellent speaker but neither had any knowledge or experience in operating a business. Relatedly, the lack of working capital prevented their employing someone who could have kept them informed of the status of the business. In fact the record-keeping was so bad that the firm could barely determine its current financial position.

As a result of these problems, the firm's gross income for 1989 was only $200,000. The firm could no longer support the two owner-managers. One left the employment of his own firm and the other is taking no income from the business. In spite of excellent product ratings, massive demand, and enormous effort, Spectrum's future is uncertain at best.

Questions

1. What options are available to this firm, if it is to survive?

2. Because of the reputation the product has gained in the limited overseas market, suggestions have been made that the firm manufacture the product specifically for export. Is this a viable option? Why?

3. How might Spectrum finance the international sales potential that is obviously there?

NOTES

1. Robert North, and Robert Feinschreiber, "From DISC to FSC: What, Why and How," *Export Trade*, Spring 1985, pp. 59–64. Also see John J. Korbel and Charles M. Bruce, "Shared FSCs: An Innovative, New Benefit for Small- and Medium-Size Exporters," *Business America*, January 20, 1986, pp. 11–14.

2. U.S. Department of Commerce, *Channels for Trading Abroad* (Washington, D.C.: U.S. Government Printing Office, 1954), pp. 5–7.

3. Kung-Ming Lin and W. R. Hoskins, "Understanding Japan's International Trading Companies," *Business*, September/October 1981, pp. 20–31.

4. John E. Stiner, "The Future of the Export Trading Company Act," *Business America*, October 12, 1987, pp. 3–9.

5. The ship's manifest provides a detailed summary of the total cargo of a vessel, a list of passengers, and their baggage. The ship's stores are listed on a separate manifest.

6. U.S. Treasury Department, Customs Service, *Tariff Schedules and the U.S.* (Washington, D.C.: U.S. Government Printing Office, 1970), p. 7.

7. The Commissioner of Customs, *U.S. Customs and You* (Washington, D.C.: U.S. Government Printing Office), p. 26.

8. George Ghareeb, Vice President, International Department of Ohio Citizens Trust Corporation of Toledo, Ohio, and David Kaczala, Director of the International Division, Trustcorp of Toledo, Ohio, provided insight into the use and purposes of the various financial documents.

9. Michael R. Czinkota, Pietra Rivoli, and Ilkka A. Ronkainen, *International Business* (Chicago: Dryden Press, 1989), pp. 493–513.

10. "Peru Devises Novel Plan to Pay Debt with Products," *Wall Street Journal*, March 26, 1987, p. 24.

11. Willis A. Bussard, "Countertrade: A View from U.S. Industry," *Countertrade and Barter Quarterly*, May 1984, p. 54.

12. Czinkota et al., p. 510.

REFERENCES AND SELECTED READINGS

EXPORTING AND IMPORTING

Bauerschmidt, Alan, Daniel Sullivan, and Kate Gillespie. "Common Factors Underlying Barriers to Export: Studies in the U.S. Paper Industry." *The Journal of International Business Studies* 16:3 (Fall 1985).

Bello, Daniel C., and Nicholas C. Williamson. "Contractual Arrangement and Marketing Practices in the Indirect Export Channel." *The Journal of International Business Studies* 16:2 (Summer 1985).

Bilkey, Warren J. "An Attempted Integration of the Literature on the Export Behavior of Firms." *The Journal of International Business Studies* 9:1 (Spring/Summer 1978).

Bilkey, Warren J. "Variables Associated with Export Profitability." *The Journal of International Business Studies* 13:2 (Spring/Summer 1982).

Brady, Donald L., and William O. Bearden. "The Effect of Managerial Attitudes on Alternative Exporting Methods." *The Journal of International Business Studies* 10:3 (Winter 1979).

Brasch, John J. "Export Management Companies." *The Journal of International Business Studies* 9:1 (Spring/Summer 1978).

Cooper, Robert G., and Elko J. Kleinschmidt. "The Impact of Export Strategy on Export Sales Performance." *The Journal of International Business Studies* 16:1 (Spring 1985).

Czinkota, Michael R., and Wesley J. Johnston. "Exporting: Does Sales Volume Make a Difference?" *The Journal of International Business Studies* 14:1 (Spring/Summer 1983).

Czinkota, Michael R., Pietra Rivoli, and Ilkka A. Ronkainen. *International Business*. Chicago: Dryden Press, 1989.

Davies, Gary J. "Developments in the Role of Exporter and Freight Forwarder in the United Kingdom." *The Journal of International Business Studies* 12:3 (Winter 1983).

Korbel, John J., and Charles M. Bruce. "Shared FSCs: An Innovative, New Benefit for Small- and Medium-Size Exporters." *Business America*, January 20, 1986.

Lin, Kung-Ming, and W. R. Hoskins. "Understanding Japan's International Trading Companies." *Business*, September/October 1981.

Moustafa, Mohamed E. "Pricing Strategy for Export Activity in Developing Nations." *The Journal of International Business Studies* 9:1 (Spring/Summer 1978).

North, Robert, and Robert Feinschreiber. "From DISC to FSC: What, Why and How." *Export Trade*, Spring 1985.

Rabino, Samuel. "Tax Incentives to Exports: Some Implications for Policy Makers." *The Journal of International Business Studies* 11:1 (Spring/Summer 1980).

Reid, Stanley D. "The Decision-Maker and Export Entry and Expansion." *The Journal of International Business Studies* 12:2 (Fall 1981).

Rosson, Philip J., and I. David Ford. "Manufacturer-Overseas Distributor Relations and Export Performance." *The Journal of International Business Studies* 13:2 (Fall 1982).

Sarathy, Ravi. "Japanese Trading Companies: Can They Be Copied?" *The Journal of International Business Studies* 16:2 (Summer 1985).

Stiner, John E. "The Future of the Export Trading Company Act." *Business America*, October 12, 1987.

Young, Alexander K. *The Sogo Shosha: Japan's Multinational Trading Companies*. Boulder, Colo.: Westview Press, 1979.

U.S. Department of Commerce. *Channels for Trading Abroad* (Washington, D.C.: U.S. Government Printing Office, 1954).

U.S. Department of Commerce. "Development Banks Offer Opportunities to ETCs." *Business America* 7:6 (March 19, 1984).

U.S. Department of Commerce. "Export Trading Companies." *Business America* 7:6 (March 19, 1984).

U.S. Treasury Department. *Tariff Schedules of the U.S.* (Washington, D.C.: U.S. Government Printing Office, 1970).

FINANCING TRADE

Alexandrides, C. G., and B. L. Bowers. *Countertrade*. New York: Wiley and Sons, 1987.

Bussard, Willis A. "Countertrade: A View from U.S. Industry." *Countertrade and Barter Quarterly*, May 1984.

Czinkota, Michael R., and Anne Talbot. "Countertrade and GATT: Prospects for Regulation." *International Trade Journal I* (Fall 1986).

Czinkota, Michael R., Pietra Rivoli, and Ilkka A. Ronkainen. *International Business.* Chicago: Dryden Press, 1989.

Huszagh, Sandra M., and Hiram C. Barksdale. "International Barter and Countertrade: An Exploratory Study." *Journal of the Academy of Marketing Science* 14 (Spring 1986).

Korth, Christopher M. *International Business Environment and Management.* Englewood Cliffs, N.J.: Prentice-Hall, 1985.

Mirus, Rolf, and Bernard Yeung. "Economic Incentives for Countertrade." *The Journal of International Business Studies* 17:3 (Fall 1986).

Wall Street Journal. "Peru Devises Novel Plan to Pay Debt with Products." March 26, 1987.

16

Transportation and Logistics Management

- Learn the role of transportation in international trade

- Become familiar with the commodity categories used by ocean carriers

- Learn the various types of services and charters

- Understand the various types of price quotations

- Become familiar with the types of coverage provided under marine insurance

- Become familiar with the roles of air and surface transportation in the international movement of goods

INTRODUCTION

Since historic times, the primary concern of international trade has been selecting a dependable mode of transportation that would ensure the shipment's safe arrival at its destination within a reasonable period of time at reasonable costs. Shippers depended on ocean carriers to provide them with such services. Thus, it is not surprising that ocean carriers served as the backbone of international trade; therefore, until recently the concept of logistics was limited largely to the physical movement of goods. Today, logistics includes not only transportation but also the most efficient use of the storage and warehousing facilities, the control of inventory levels and flows, the packaging and marking of containers, and efficient materials handling.

This chapter describes the various modes of transportation utilized in international trade. Emphasis is placed on marine transportation because the patterns of world trade are primarily intercontinental. Air transportation is discussed because of its increasing importance in transporting international cargo in recent years, although the market share of this transport mode is still quite small. Railroad and motor transportation are used primarily in intraregional trade. This chapter covers price quotations where transportation charges and marine insurance premiums are included. It also includes the description of various marine insurance terms and coverages.

SEABORNE CARGOES

Categories of Seaborne Cargo

The cargoes entering seaborne trade fall into two broad categories: general cargo and bulk cargo. General cargo consists mainly of high-valued manufactured goods, such as consumer products. Bulk cargo consists of liquid and dry cargo. Of the bulk cargo in liquid form, crude oil is the most important. Iron ore, coal, grain, bauxite/alumina, and phosphate rock are the most important dry forms of bulk cargo. These five dry-bulk commodities are often referred to as *major bulks* because they account for a very large percentage of dry cargoes entering seaborne trade. Other dry bulk cargoes are referred to as *minor bulks* that are also transported by shiploads.

The majority of bulk cargoes are in free-flowing form. They can be poured, piped, or handled by suction in or out of a ship without any packaging. There are a small number of commodities that are not physically free-flowing but are increasingly transported by shiploads, such as automobiles, timber, and steel. Their growing trade tonnage makes their carriage by shiploads economically attractive. They are referred to as *neobulks*.

The primary factor differentiating general cargoes from bulk cargoes is their shipment size rather than their physical characteristics. General cargoes are normally transported in small consignments and are referred to as *liner cargoes* because they depend almost entirely on the services provided by cargo liners. Bulk cargoes are transported in shiploads, either by contract carriers or private carriers, on specially built tankers or dry-bulk carriers.

Ocean transportation is unique in that the size of the shipment rather than the general characteristics of the cargo usually determines the type of carrier used.

Types of Shipping Service

There are several types of seaborne shipping service. The type used by cargo owners depends on the size of their shipments and other shipping requirements such as sailing frequency and regularity, special cargo handling facilities, ports of call, and so forth.

Tramp Shipping

Tramp shipping services are provided for single-commodity shipments by shiploads. Each shipment is arranged separately through shipping brokers for a particular voyage or series of successive voyages. The freight rates for tramp services are negotiated between individual cargo owners and ship operators.

Tramp shipping services are characterized by almost total flexibility with regard to itinerary, scheduling, and cargoes. Balanced two-way flows of bulk cargoes between two ports rarely exist. For instance, Japan is the destination of many bulk trades (e.g., crude oil, iron ore, and grain) but offers very little bulk cargo for outbound voyages. The country exports mainly manufactured goods, which are ordinarily handled by liner service.

A tramp ship must, therefore, continually search for new business opportunities. For example, it may carry coal from the east coast of the United States to Japan and sail in ballast (that is, carrying only ballast) to South Korea for a shipment of cement destined for Brunei. The ship may then sail in ballast to India and acquire a load of manganese ore for shipment to Germany. Therefore, tramp ships are relatively small in size, normally less than 15,000 deadweight tons. They are designed with several cargo holds and equipped with versatile cargo handling equipment that give them the needed operational flexibility.

Tramp shipping services resemble closely the model of pure competition postulated in economic theory. There are virtually no effective barriers to entry into this business. The cost of vessel acquisition by prospective shipowners is not prohibitive. There is little need for an elaborate and costly marketing organization because tramp shipping services are arranged through brokers. Information regarding tramp freight rates are widely reported, making it possible for shipowners and shippers to take into account market conditions in their rate negotiations. In such a competitive market, freight rates are determined primarily by supply and demand.

Generally, only a small percentage of commodity production enters world trade, thereby limiting the demand for shipping. Many commodities can be economically produced almost anywhere worldwide. Other commodities that are considered vital to a nation's survival and essential for economic development are encouraged to be produced domestically and are often protected from foreign competition as a matter of public policy. Imports are intended only to make up for any shortfalls in domestic production. For instance, a country may produce 90 percent of its grain requirement and meet the remaining 10 percent through imports. A decrease in domestic grain production by 5 percent will mean a 50 percent increase in the demand for shipping capacity to serve that country's grain imports. This incremental change in demand for shipping means that tramp freight rates are very volatile. It is not unusual for tramp rates to rise or fall three- or fourfold within a few months.

Tramp rates are also quite unpredictable because the demand and supply for shipping are affected by other variables. An announcement by the U.S. government to embargo grain exports to the Soviet Union, for instance, might cause a drop in tramp rates as shipowners anticipate lower levels of grain shipments. However, if the USSR is subsequently able to make up for the shortfalls in U.S. grain imports with supplies from other sources such as Argentina, Australia, or Canada, tramp rates might rise sharply. Not only does the total volume of grain shipments to the USSR recover but the average shipping distance gets longer, thus causing higher demand for shipping capacity.

Ocean transportation provides different types of transportation services to different shippers. Those desiring greatest flexibility make use of tramp shipping.

Specialized Bulk Shipping

Traditionally, ocean transportation of raw materials was handled by tramp ships. Since the mid-1950s, rapid economic growth among industrial coun-

Oceangoing oil tankers are enormous in size and in their importance to international business.

tries has created some regular, high-volume, intercontinental flows of certain dry and liquid bulks such as iron ore, coal, and crude oil from distant sources. Such regularity and large volume of shipments make it economically attractive to employ very large tankers and dry-bulk carriers. These specialized vessels can provide transportation services at much lower unit costs than tramps. They are, however, much less flexible than tramps because their designs are suitable for the carriage of only a limited variety of commodities. Besides, there are very few trade routes with port facilities and cargo volume sufficient to support these vessels. Growing world trade in certain commodities with special cargo-handling requirements such as liquefied natural gas (LNG) and automobiles have also stimulated the development of specialized vessels (LNG tankers and pure car carriers) that are capable of transporting only a single type of cargo.

As with tramp shipping, specialized bulk shipping services handle ship-load-size consignments. Ideally, these specialized or industrial carriers should be deployed under long-term contracts between shipowners and cargo owners because they lack the operational flexibility of tramp ships. In other words, specialized ships should be built only after shipowners receive long-term employment commitments from cargo owners. In practice, however, many of these vessels are built speculatively in anticipation of rising demand for shipping capacity. Should such anticipations fail to materialize, the resulting surplus tonnage puts heavy downward pressure on freight rates. Some of these vessels have to be laid up or sold for scrap metal at great losses to shipowners. During the 1979–1981 period, for instance, fast-rising oil prices increased the demand for thermal coal. In anticipation of booming coal exports, shipowners placed orders for many large dry-bulk carriers. These ships have been delivered to the market in recent years when the level of coal exports is hard hit by declining oil prices. The dry-bulk shipping market has yet to recover from this massive tonnage surplus.

Industries generally own or charter specialized carriers to transport shipload lots of bulky commodities.

Liner Shipping

Liner services are characterized by regular, scheduled sailings between designated ports on a trade route. Liners are common carriers that handle many small cargo consignments in each sailing. Their cargoes have a higher per unit value than bulk cargoes and are able to withstand higher costs of transportation. Shippers using liners are, therefore, willing to pay higher freight rates in return for better shipping service. They emphasize the importance of the quality-related factors such as timeliness of service (short transit time, frequent and reliable sailing schedule), convenience in use (adequate port coverage, low rate of cargo loss and damage), and other marketing "touches" (being responsive to shippers' needs and complying with their requests).[1]

Liner shipping is dominated by steamship lines belonging to conferences. These are associations of ocean liner companies formed for the purpose of eliminating competition among shipping lines. Members of each conference collectively set freight rates and conditions of service. They may also undertake other collective measures to limit competition among themselves by agreements on sharing cargoes and/or revenues, limiting the number of sailings by each member, and so forth. There are about 400 conferences worldwide, with each covering a particular trade route or a single direction on a trade route.

Not all shipping lines wish to join conferences, nor are all those that desire to join admitted by existing conference members. Independent (nonconference) shipping lines normally have to penetrate trade routes by undercutting conference freight rates. Historically, nonconference lines have been only marginal operators, holding insignificant market shares. They were simply unable to offer frequent sailings and wide port coverages that would match conference service quality, nor could they withstand the occasional heavy rate cuts and other retaliatory measures by conferences aimed at driving potentially important independent lines out of the trade routes. In recent years, financially strong and competitively aggressive independent shipping lines have emerged, many of them from the newly industrialized countries in the Far East, which compete quite successfully with conference lines.

Since supply is controlled, liner freight rates are generally demand based. High-value cargoes, which can withstand high freight costs, are charged higher rates. Low-value cargoes, which cannot withstand high freight charges without losing out in the market, are charged low freight rates. Freight rates are also modified so as to take into consideration some cost-related factors such as charging low-density cargoes on the basis of their volume rather than their weight. Liner freight rates are, therefore, very complex. A major multinational corporation such as Dupont, which ships a variety of cargoes to worldwide destinations using some 400 different ocean carriers, has to deal with thousands of rates.[2]

The liners are common carriers whose rates vary, depending on the conference to which they belong and the routes they serve.

Charters and Contracts of Affreightment

Arrangement for bulk shipping service are made under various forms of charter. Short-term arrangements include single-voyage and trip charters. They commit a charterer (cargo owner) and a shipowner to a single cargo movement.

Single-Voyage Charter

Under a single-voyage charter, a shipowner agrees to transport a specified quantity of cargo between named ports and is paid a lump sum amount per cargo ton carried.

Trip Charter

A trip charter is quite similar to a single-voyage charter, except that the freight rate is expressed as a monetary sum per day instead of a lump sum per cargo ton. In essence, the charterer pays for the time it takes to complete a voyage. This arrangement is more appropriate than a single-voyage charter when the duration of a voyage cannot be estimated because of possible delays in loading or unloading in congested ports.

Long-Term Freighting

Long-term freighting arrangements involve multiple cargo movements. They include consecutive voyage charters, time charters, bareboat charters (see below), and contracts of affreightment.

Consecutive Voyage Charters   This is an extension of a single-voyage charter. A shipowner agrees to transport a specified quantity of cargo in a number of "shuttle" voyages that follow consecutively between named ports.

Time Charters   Under this arrangement, a shipowner makes available a vessel for a period of time, leaving the charterer free to use the ship and its crew for such cargoes and voyages as the charterer wishes.

Bareboat Charter   A charterer hires only the vessel without its crew. The charterer is responsible for the costs of manning, provisioning, maintaining, and managing the vessel.

Contract of Affreightment   Quite different from the foregoing arrangements, a contract of affreightment does not specify any vessel. It only specifies the cargo to be transported between named ports over a fixed period of time, as well as the timing and the size of the individual shipments. Vessel assignment and scheduling are left to the shipowner's discretion.

The choice among the various types of carriage arrangements depends on several factors. Among these are the shipping needs of cargo owners with regard to the trading volume, the regularity of shipments, and the geographical pattern of cargo movements. Large and regular cargo movements make long-term freight arrangements more economical for cargo owners. International oil companies, for instance, control large tanker fleets through ownership and long-term charter arrangements; single-voyage charters meet less than 10 percent of their shipping needs. Similarly, large proportions of iron ore and bauxite imports by major steel and aluminum producers, respectively, are transported in producer-controlled vessels. Erratic cargo movements, on the other hand, necessitate single-voyage and trip charters. The grain trade, for instance, is quite vulnerable to political and weather factors. As a result, the shipping volume between specific exporting and importing countries fluctuates widely from year to year. Grain shippers, therefore, rely heavily on voyage charters.

Consecutive voyage charters are particularly suitable for shuttle-type cargo movements in which charterers are willing to have the vessels sailing in ballast for about half of the time. Contracts of affreightment leave the task of finding employment for the vessels to shipowners. A shipowner who has a contract of affreightment for a large volume of iron ore from Brazil to Japan is free to schedule cargo from the Middle East to Brazil under another contract of affreightment. The ships will have to sail in ballast only between Japan and the Middle East, or for less than one-third of the time.

Shippers may charter a vessel for a particular voyage, trip, or time or make other arrangements with the owner or operator of a vessel.

Price Quotations and Freight Rates

Transportation costs are an important part of the total price that is quoted by exporters. The amount of service provided by the carrier determines the transport charges. Except when goods are moved by tramps or industrial carriers, the most common methods of price quotation that include transportation charges are FOB vessel, named port; CIF vessel, named port; and FAS vessel, named port.

FOB Vessel, Named Port

FOB always refers to the port of shipment, according to the Revised American Foreign Trade Definitions of 1941. Under this method of price quotation, the price of the goods includes the freight charges for transporting the goods to the designated port of shipment. The actual placement of the goods on board the vessel is the responsibility of the seller (exporter). The seller must also provide a clean ship's receipt or on-board bill of lading indicating that the goods were delivered to the carrier free of damage. Any loss or damage to the goods until they are placed on board the vessel is, therefore, the seller's responsibility. The buyer (importer) is responsible for any loss or damage thereafter. The buyer is responsible for the subsequent movement of the goods and must pay the insurance premiums and ocean and other transportation charges. Title passes at the point where the responsibility of the seller ends.

CIF Vessel, Named Port

The cost of the goods, the ocean freight charges to the port of destination, and the marine insurance premiums are included in the price that is quoted. The seller must pay for the freight charges and the marine insurance premium, but is not responsible for any loss or damage to the goods after they have been delivered to the carrier. The seller must deliver a clean bill of lading and a marine insurance policy or certificate to the buyer, and must take out war risk insurance if applicable. The buyer pays for the discharge of the goods, customs duties, and other charges after the arrival of the goods at the port of debarkation. If the buyer requests to take out marine insurance, the C&F (cost and freight) price quotation will be used, indicating that the price quoted does not include the marine insurance premium.

FAS Vessel, Named Port

This method of price quotation (*free alongside ship*) means that the seller is responsible only for placing the goods on the dock alongside the vessel at the port of shipment. The price quoted includes the freight charges to that point, and any loss or damage to that point is the responsibility of the seller, who must provide a clean dock or ship's receipt. The buyer must incur any charges that might be necessary to load the goods on the vessel (for example, the cost of special equipment to load a locomotive on board a vessel). The buyer must pay for the marine insurance premiums and the freight charges to the destination.

Exporters normally include shipping costs in the price charged; however, the buyer may pay the shipping charges directly to minimize foreign currency outlays.

Various other methods of price quotation may be used, for example, FOB point of origin, FOB destination, ex factory, ex point of origin, and so forth, but these methods are uncommon compared with the three methods described above.

Marine Insurance and Marine Insurance Terms

A unique feature of ocean transportation is that the carriers are not responsible for loss or damage to the goods unless negligence on its part can be proved. Perils of the sea, for example, are beyond the control of the carrier. Therefore, it is essential that shippers take out marine insurance.

A shipper may take out an open policy with an underwriter to cover all shipments for a specified period of time, in which case a certificate is made out for each shipment. It is a printed standard contract with attached riders covering specific needs of a shipment. The shipper may negotiate with an underwriter each time a shipment is made, in which case a separate policy is issued for each shipment.

Marine insurance policies make use of many archaic and obsolete words and phrases. It is extremely difficult for nonexperts to determine the precise definition of words and phrases since they have not been "translated" to modern language because changes might affect the interpretations that have been established by numerous precedents and court decisions. However, there are some basic terms with which one engaged in international trade should become familiar.

Marine Insurance Terms

The term *assured* refers to either the shipper or the consignee—the one who has an insurable interest in the shipment—who benefits from the safe arrival of the goods and is injured by its loss or damage. *Average* is the term used for loss or damage to the goods. *Free of particular average* means free of partial loss. *General average* refers to voluntary loss for the benefit of the ship and its remaining cargo; such loss might result when cargo is thrown overboard to save the ship, burning cargo to make port when the ship's fuel has been exhausted (coal burners), costs incurred to maintain a crew when forced to seek shelter from a storm, and any other loss that is undertaken voluntarily for the benefit of the ship and the majority of the shipment.

Maritime law and bill of lading clauses distribute the losses into three equal shares: the shipowner whose vessel was saved because of the voluntary loss, the ship operator who collected the freight charges, and the shippers whose cargo was saved.[3] If the shipowner and operator are the same, that party will bear two thirds of the total loss. It is only fair, therefore, that the shipper whose cargo was voluntarily jettisoned should not have to bear the total cost of the loss. As a precaution against this eventuality, the shipper will take out marine insurance with an underwriter. All marine insurance policies cover general average losses.

Free of particular average, American condition, means that only partial losses caused by sinking, stranding, burning, or collision will be covered by insurance. Partial losses from other causes will not be covered. If total loss occurs, the shipment will be covered by insurance. *Free of particular average, English condition*, means that any partial loss will be covered by insurance as long as sinking, stranding, burning, or collision is encountered by the vessel or lighter. Thus, its interpretation is more liberal than the American condition.

The term *with particular average* (W.P.A.), often abbreviated *with average* (W.A.), means that the insurance covers partial loss over and above a given percentage of the value of the shipment. *Five percent with particular average*, therefore, means that any loss exceeding 5 percent of the value of the goods due to the perils of the sea will be covered by insurance. If total loss occurs due to the perils of the sea, 100 percent of the loss will be covered despite the 5 percent particular average. Each package insured separately means that losses to any single package rather than the total shipment over and above a given percentage will be covered by insurance. The purpose of this clause is to cover the loss of a single case that might be less than 5 percent of the value of the total shipment. With average coverage is generally taken out on shipments of perishable items, when a given percentage of damage is expected due to deterioration.

Average, irrespective of percentage, means that losses due to the perils of the sea are paid regardless of the percentage. To this may be added special claims to cover possible losses or damages due to theft, pilferage, nondelivery, sweat damage, and so forth. *Theft* means loss of a complete case or package, whereas *pilferage* means partial loss of the contents of one or more cases.

Against all risks covers any loss or damage regardless of the cause, including theft, pilferage, and nondelivery. This might be comparable to full coverage in automobile insurance, wherein any damage to the car will be covered by insurance. Naturally, such coverage requires higher premium payments, but it might be worthwhile on shipments to some areas where theft and pilferage are common. Premiums on this type of coverage may be reduced by careful packing and marking to discourage possible losses.

Marine insurance may be extended to cover parcel post and air shipments. Usually all risk coverage is taken out on such shipments.

> In ocean transportation, the shipping charges do not include the insurance premiums to cover loss or damage to the goods unless negligence can be proved.

CONFLICTS IN INTERNATIONAL SHIPPING

Shipping is an integral component of the international trade practice. It may be used for promoting national political and economic interests such as supporting national defense, earning foreign exchange, and so forth. Measures taken by governments to support their merchant marines have raised major trade issues. Among them are the conduct of liner conferences and the registration of ships under the flags of convenience.

> Conflicts occur in international shipping because of its competitive nature.

UNCTAD Code of Conduct for Liner Conferences

Liner conferences were established on most trade routes during the late nineteenth and the early twentieth centuries, before many less developed countries gained their independence. Conference membership and practices have naturally reflected the economic interests of shipping companies from developed market economy countries (DMECs). Liner conferences are often viewed by the LDCs as instruments for preserving a status quo under which shipping lines from DMECs continue to dominate the liner shipping sector. Through the forum of the United Nations Conference on Trade and Development (UNCTAD), LDCs have successfully passed a code of conduct for liner conferences.

The UNCTAD Code requires that membership in individual conferences be open to the shipping lines from those nations whose trade is covered by conferences. The code contains a controversial provision widely referred to as the "40-40-20" cargo reservation formula. This means that national shipping lines from each of two trading nations shall have equal rights to participate in the liner trade being carried between them by a conference. Shipping lines from third-party countries shall be allowed to compete for up to 20 percent of this trade. Through these provisions, LDCs hope to strengthen their bargaining positions against liner conferences and to gain sufficient cargo to support the development of their merchant marines.

DMECs have generally opposed the UNCTAD Liner Code, particularly its cargo reservation formula. The strongest opponent has been the United States, which regards the code as anticompetitive, leading eventually to higher freight rates and lower quality of service. The European Economic Community has adopted the "Brussels package," which requires member nations to ratify the code only with specific procompetition reservations.

In the EEC-LDC liner trade, national shipping lines from LDCs are entitled to carry their 40 percent cargo share. The corresponding 40 percent to which shipping lines from the EEC countries are entitled under the code will be made available to all EEC members and other reciprocating countries on the basis of commercial considerations.

Though the industry is open to all, the influence of steamship conferences often impedes independent owner/operators from operating on any established route.

Flags of Convenience

International law has traditionally adhered to the principle that every vessel must have a nationality. This nationality is conferred upon the vessel through registration. Vessels are not always registered in the countries in which the beneficial owners hold their nationality. This practice of operating under foreign flags is known as "flags of convenience" (FOC), or "open registry."

The FOC phenomenon began in the early 1920s. It was, however, the intense competition in the world shipping market after World War II that caused the tremendous growth of FOC fleets from 1.2 percent of the world fleet tonnage in 1939 to about 30 percent in recent years. FOC registry offers shipowners several advantages. They are able to avoid the high taxes of operating under their national flags. They may freely employ crew members of any nationality, pay low wages, and provide minimum benefits. They can conceal their nationalities for political reasons. Among those who benefit most from the operation of FOC fleets are shipowners from the United States, Hong Kong, Greece, and Japan.

Countries that permit foreign shipowners to register their vessels within the country are usually small LDCs whose foreign trade and national security do not depend on their ability to control large fleets of ocean carriers. They offer FOC registry only as a means to generate income in hard currencies from vessel registration fees and annual tonnage dues. Because they lack the ability to enforce safety and pollution standards, foreign vessels flying their flags generally ignore such regulations. Among the major FOC countries are Panama, Liberia, Honduras, Bermuda, and Cyprus.

FOC registry has had many proponents and opponents. Among the proponents are shipowners from traditional maritime countries that are able to maintain competitive merchant fleets under convenience flags. Among the opponents are the maritime labor unions and LDCs. Through the forum of UNCTAD, LDCs have pressed for an international agreement on ship registration that would gradually phase out FOC registry. As the LDCs see it, FOC registry has enabled shipowners from DMECs to take advantage of their low-cost labor supply and neutralize any potentially competitive edge in shipping they might achieve.

Flags of convenience make it difficult for many LDCs to compete in ocean shipping.

INTERNATIONAL AIRFREIGHT SERVICES

Airfreight is the fastest-growing mode of transportation. Its growth is attributable to the growth of high-value manufactured goods in world trade. In tonnage, airfreight still accounts for less than 1 percent of international cargo movements. In value, however, it accounts for 10–20 percent of such movements, depending on the trade routes involved.

Competitive Advantages of Airfreight

Airfreight offers superior transit time not only in terminal-to-terminal movement but also in door-to-door movement, particularly on medium and long hauls. First, the average speed of an airplane is more than 20 times that of a containership. Second, the frequency of international flights available at most trading centers is many times greater than the sailing frequency of liner shipping. Third, airports are often located nearer to markets than are seaports. Transfer of cargo between one flight and another is faster than the equivalent between two liner vessels. This is attributable to higher flight frequency, reducing layover time, and the smaller volume of cargo being handled by the airlines. Speedy cargo transfers benefit shipments between pairs of cities where direct service is not available.

Demand for Airfreight Services

Airfreight services offer superior transit time only at freight rates higher than other modes of transportation. Freight cost is, however, only one of the several elements of distribution costs. From a total distribution cost standpoint, airfreight could be economical because it saves inventory holding costs through shorter transit time, lowers warehousing costs through less inventory holding, reduces packaging costs through more delicate cargo handling, lowers insurance costs because of less exposure to pilferage, and so forth. Airfreight is therefore suitable for certain types of shipments and commodities.

Time-sensitive commodities such as perishable products and goods with short economic lifespans such as newspapers and style goods must reach their market promptly so as not to lose their market values. Emergency shipments may be needed so as to meet unanticipated increases in market demand to avoid costly interruptions in production operation. The cost of airfreight is more than compensated for by the avoidance of lost sales or shutdowns in operation. High-value commodities benefit the most from potential cost savings in inventory holdings and may thus find airfreight economical. Shipments to isolated locations where highways, rail lines, or waterways are not available may have to rely on airfreight. There are available certain types of aircraft that are capable of landing and taking off from primitive airstrips.

Provisions of Airfreight Services

Airfreight services are performed on either a scheduled or charter basis. Scheduled services utilize all-cargo or passenger flights. On the latter, cargo is carried in the belly-holds of aircrafts. The needs of passengers determine the aircraft type, time schedule, and destinations of passenger flight. Belly-hold freight services are, therefore, usually considered a by-product of passenger operation. They have two competitive advantages over all-cargo flights. On most international routes, there are more scheduled passenger flights than scheduled all-cargo flights because the volume of passenger flight is much higher. Belly-hold services are, therefore, the backbone of time-sensitive shipments. Furthermore, as an incremental business, belly-hold services can be priced so as to recover only the costs directly attributable to cargo operations—that is, cargo-handling, extra fuel, insurance, sales, and promotion. The passenger flights must be performed regardless of the availability of such cargoes. In contrast, all-cargo services must recover the full cost of the operation.

Scheduled all-cargo service is offered on routes where the volume of cargo reaches a level at which all-cargo operation becomes competitive with belly-hold services. When airlines offer passenger nonstop flights on long distance routes, extra fuel is needed; therefore, the aircraft's payload available for cargo is reduced. Large-size consignments and outsized and hazardous cargoes may be technically and legally carried only on all-cargo flights.

Charter cargo service is offered as a premium specialty service for large-size consignments. Small cargo consignments usually find scheduled services more economical. Charter cargo services are suitable for shipments to isolated destinations where scheduled services are not available or for shipments requiring special cargo-handling.

On some routes there is a demand for additional cargo capacity beyond that provided by the belly-holds of the scheduled passenger flights, but insufficient to support all-cargo flights. To meet such demands, some air carriers operate what is known as combi-airplanes, which carry both passengers and cargo on the main deck.

International Air Transport System

Air transportation is an innovation of the twentieth century, a time when governments take an active role in guarding and promoting their national interests. International air transport services are, therefore, governed by a complex system of bilateral agreements among nations. Through such bilateral agreements, each government hopes to negotiate arrangements for air transport services to or from its country that best serve its national interests, such as protecting its national airlines, gaining political and/or economic concessions from other governments, and so forth. This represents a break from the long-held tradition in the maritime field. Generally, vessels of one nation are allowed free access for peaceful purposes to ports in another country except when the two nations are in a state of hostility toward each other.

Air transportation provides major advantages in the movement of time-sensitive commodities, emergency goods, high-valued commodities, and shipments to isolated locations.

SURFACE TRANSPORTATION

Rail and motor carriers are relatively unimportant in international transportation. Their uses are, however, quite important in the intracontinental movement of goods in North America and in continental Europe.

The railroad is used primarily for the transportation of high-density and low-value products of the forests, mines, and agriculture. It is becoming increasingly important in intermodal transportation for both transcontinental shipments and to and from inland points. Intermodal transportation means the use of several different forms of transportation: truck, rail, ship, and so forth. Its major disadvantage is that there is a scarcity of border crossing points, and different track gauges are used among different countries.

International highway transportation is most widely used when goods are being transported to an adjacent country. Highways are especially important in connecting the small communities and rural sections with the large cities and communities among different countries. This is a very effective mode of transportation in continental Europe, where the distances to be traversed are relatively short. In the United States and Canada, highway transportation has played an important role in intermodal shipments.

Motor transportation is used primarily for the movement of manufactured goods of high per unit value over relatively short distances. Its major advantages are speed, safety, reliability, and accessibility to the delivery site.

Transportation of petroleum by pipeline is used primarily in conjunction with water transportation. Some pipelines cross international boundaries to reach tankers at ports of export. Transport of natural gas by international pipelines occurs between gas-surplus areas and gas-deficit areas. The Soviet Union ships natural gas by pipeline to western Europe, and Canadian natural gas enters the United States by pipeline.

Surface transportation is important in intracontinental shipments.

OTHER LOGISTICAL FUNCTIONS

In logistics management, firms must give careful consideration to the inter-relationships among those activities involved in the physical movement of raw materials—in process inventory and the finished goods inventory.[4] Efficient logistics management requires more than the use of the most efficient form of transportation. Production, marketing, and finance must work together in order for the logistics system to be more effective.

Storage and warehousing facilities are required to hold goods that are being shipped. They provide an essential service when the shipment waits to be loaded or unloaded from a vessel, or is awaiting further transportation. Warehousing performs five major functions: receiving goods from outside suppliers or from the warehouse's own production facilities; identifying goods; sorting goods according to their characteristics; assembling the goods upon the receipt of orders; and dispatching the shipment to the appropriate carrier after packing as necessary.

The control of inventory levels and flows in international logistics is determined largely by the overall policy of the firm that is based on customer service standards and the inventory investment needs to meet these standards. The objective of inventory control is to maintain the optimum inventory level that is consistent with the customer service and manufacturing goals. The achievement of these goals requires in-transit inventory control. Inventory control might mean ordering amounts in excess of immediate requirements because of unexpected delays in receipts or to maintain safety or buffer stocks. The availability of quantity discounts might also encourage ordering more than the needed amount.

Consideration must be given to special packaging and marking requirements. Climatic conditions, the danger of pilferage, damage to the contents, primitive transportation facilities, and other environmental conditions require special care in packaging. All countries have customs regulations specifying the marking and labeling of containers. Noncompliance can result in severe penalties. In addition, marks facilitate the handling of containers in countries where dock workers might not understand directions written in a foreign language.

There are four elements in the global aspect of materials handling. First is the physical movement of the goods. They must be transferred into and out of the storage facilities as efficiently as possible. Second, there is the time element involved in global material handling. The products must be delivered when needed to prevent production delays or the accumulation of unneeded inventory. The third involves quantity. That is, the products must be transferred in the right quantity to meet the logistical requirements of the recipient. The final element of material handling is space, which must be utilized as efficiently as possible to minimize costs, whether in the warehouse or in the holds of an ocean carrier.

Logistics deals with various services pertaining to the transportation of goods and materials handling.

SUMMARY

The physical movement of commodities from one country to another is primarily a function of ocean transportation. Different types of carriers transport these goods, depending upon the size of the shipment, the per unit value of the goods, and other characteristics. Bulk cargo such as grain, iron ore, and petroleum is generally shipped in shipload lots, hence making use of dry bulk carriers or tankers, respectively. Manufactured goods that have a high per unit value make use of the services provided by liners.

Bulk carriers and tankers may be further classified according to the specialized services they provide. Some are capable of transporting different types of dry cargo while others, such as oil tankers and refrigerated vessels, are restricted in the type of goods they carry.

The operation of the bulk carriers is unlike any other form of transportation in a number of respects. If the vessel is not owned or under contract by a particular corporation, the rates are negotiable. Liners charge a common rate and the rates depend upon the conference to which a steamship line belongs. Peculiar to ocean transportation is the fact that marine insurance premiums are not included in the transportation charges. Therefore, it is essential that the shipper takes out marine insurance and indicate the type of coverage desired.

Water transportation is the dominant form of transportation for the movement of goods among countries located in different continents. The particular vessel might be owned by nationals of a country other than that in which the vessel is registered.

Although air transportation, like water transportation, is not restricted to a particular continent, its widespread use at the present time is restricted by its high cost. Hence it is used primarily for the movement of passengers and high-valued freight. Surface transportation, on the other hand, can be used only in countries with adjoining land masses.

Logistics management includes more than the physical movement of the goods. It involves other activities that have an impact on the overall production, marketing, and financial strategies of a firm.   ☐

KEY TERMS AND CONCEPTS

Against all risks	**Average**
Assured	**Average, irrespective of percentage**

Bareboat charter

C&F vessel, named port

CIF vessel, named port

Consecutive voyage charter

Contract of affreightment

Dry bulk carriers

FAS vessel, named port

Flag of convenience (FOC)

FOB vessel, named port

Free of particular average

General average

Jettison

Liners

Major bulk carrier

Neo-bulk cargo

Shipping conference

Single voyage charter

Special bulk carrier

Tankers

Time charter

Trip charter

With average

REVIEW QUESTIONS

1. Describe briefly those commodities that are classified as bulk cargo. How do they differ from liner cargo?

2. Describe the major characteristics of tramp shipping. Compare them with the characteristics of liner shipping.

3. Why are tramp rates subject to wide fluctuations?

4. What is a steamship conference? Who belongs to these conferences? What are the purposes of the conferences?

5. Do all water carriers belong to a conference?

6. Differentiate among voyage charter, time charter, and bareboat charter.

7. Define FOB vessel, named port; CIF vessel, named port; FAS vessel, named port.

8. Define average, free of particular average, and with average marine insurance coverage.

9. Why is it necessary for shippers to take out marine insurance on an overseas shipment?

10. What is meant by *flags of convenience?* What are the major advantages of registering a vessel in a country such as Panama or Liberia?

11. What are the major characteristics of airfreight service?

12. For overseas shipments, why is it advantageous to use scheduled passenger airlines rather than a scheduled all-cargo flight?

13. What are the forms of surface transportation that are used in the international movement of commodities? Why might they be considered less important than water transportation in international trade?

DISCUSSION CASE

The Trouble with Insurance: L&E International

Lawrence & Erausquin, Inc. (L&E International) was an export management company that operated in Toledo, Ohio, for nearly 50 years. L&E management knew their business well and handled even complex orders routinely. In addition to the standard EMC functions, L&E purchased and stocked some standard products, and in some cases operated as an importer for products with substantial demand in their geographic area.

In January, Dennis Lawrence, son of the founder of L&E and its president, received a request for a C&F quotation for automotive parts from a Turkish company. This was a new customer but the request for a C&F quotation was typical of most received from Turkey. Since automobile parts were the largest sales volume line carried by L&E, a quotation as per the customer's request was routinely prepared and mailed to the customer. In June, L&E received a purchase order and covering letter of credit.

L&E proceeded to purchase the required parts from eight different vendors, consolidated these with items that L&E had in their own inventory, and packaged the products for export. Next L&E contacted a freight forwarder to book space on a vessel bound for Turkey and obtained all of the proper documentation necessary for cashing the letter of credit. The vendors' charges for the parts, domestic transportation charges for the delivery of the parts to L&E's warehouse, transportation charges for shipment to the port, the freight forwarder's fees, and the ocean freight charges had all been paid. Upon presentation of the documents, the bank had even honored the letter of credit and paid L&E. The sale seemed complete.

In October, Dennis Lawrence received a telex from the customer in Turkey advising L&E that the merchandise was not aboard the vessel. Upon checking with the forwarder and the steamship line, it was discovered that although L&E had in their possession an on-board bill of lading signed by the captain of the ship, the shipment had never been loaded onto the vessel. What finally emerged from all of the confusion was that the pier in New York had caught fire. The ship, partially loaded, had sailed away to escape and had simply resumed its scheduled itinerary without going back to check the status of any cargo that might have been still on the dock. All unloaded merchandise was left on the pier and was destroyed by the fire.

To further complicate the matter, the customer had not insured the merchandise under its own marine policy as was implied in the request for a C&F quotation. Whether out of ignorance or merely to save what

By Don R. Beeman (Professor of Management and International Business, The University of Toledo) and Dennis Lawrence (president of Winner Freight Company and former president of L&E International), 1989.

This case was developed for class discussion only and is not intended to represent good or bad management or decision-making.

amounted to $\frac{1}{4}$ of 1 percent of the value of the merchandise, the customer had lost more than $100,000 worth of automotive parts. The customer blamed L&E for not checking to see whether insurance had been purchased and did not use L&E for any future orders.

Questions

1. Did L&E do anything wrong?
2. How could this problem have been avoided?
3. If you were the president of L&E, would you change your methods for handling all orders? Orders from first-time customers?
4. What chance does the Turkish company have of collecting from the pier operators or the steamship line?

NOTES

1. Frederick M. Collison, "Market Segments for Marine Liner Service," *Transportation Journal*, Winter 1984, p. 43.
2. W. B. Jackson, "Shippers' Point of View on Redesigning of Liner Tariffs," *The Future of Liner Shipping*, a report on an international symposium held at Bremen, West Germany, September 1975, p. 196.
3. The York-Antwerp rules determine the distribution of losses.
4. John Gattorna, ed., *Effective Logistics Management* (Bradford, W. Yorkshire, England: MCB University Press, 1988), p. 41.

REFERENCES AND
SELECTED READINGS

Collison, Frederick M. "Market Segments for Marine Liner Service." *Transportation Journal*, Winter 1984.

Davies, Gary J. "Developments in the Role of Exporter and Freight Forwarder in the United Kingdom." *The Journal of International Business Studies* 12:3 (Winter 1981).

Gattorna, John, ed. *Effective Logistics Management*. Bradford, W. Yorkshire, England: MCB University Press, 1988.

Jackson, W. B. "Shippers' Point of View in Redesigning of Liner Tariffs." *The Future of Liner Shipping*, a report on an international symposium held at Bremen, West Germany, September 1975.

CHAPTER

17

International Financial Management

- Become familiar with the role of the international financial manager

- Learn about the management of cash at the subsidiary level including the determination of transactional and precautionary balances

- Understand the effects of high inflation on the financial accounts

- Understand why subsidiaries keep a portion of their cash holdings in a currency different from that of the host nation

- Learn why multinationals pool subsidiary precautionary cash reserves

- Explain how the "netting" of intrasubsidiary transfers reduces the firm's overall exchange transaction expenses

- Understand the three most common methods of international capital budgeting: payback, net present value, and internal rate of return

- Be able to explain the complicating effects on capital budgeting of currency of analysis, repatriations, and risk differences

- Learn the differences among translation, transaction, and economic exposure

- Be able to calculate the cost of foreign debt

- Learn the Purchasing Power Parity and International Fischer Effect theories

462

OUTLINE OF TOPICS

INTRODUCTION

The purpose of this chapter is to describe the functions of international financial management: the management of cash and working capital under normal as well as high-inflation conditions, capital budgeting, and foreign exchange exposure management.

INTERNATIONAL CASH MANAGEMENT

One of the major responsibilities of international money management is the management of the current assets (including cash) and current liabilities of the firm at both the subsidiary and corporate level to help the firm achieve its long-term objectives. International money management also involves the cross-national collection, distribution, and transfer of funds arising from international transactions.

One of the first decisions of international financial management is whether to allow subsidiaries to manage their cash holdings and cash needs as if they were independent corporations or whether to rationalize these on a global basis.

Managing Subsidiary-Level Cash and Cash Flows

Managing cash and near-cash items for a subsidiary of an international firm that has opted to decentralize the cash management function is similar to cash management in an independent firm. First, the financial manager needs to decide on the necessary level of cash holdings. Second, the manager must decide the amount to be kept in each of the available forms: cash, demand deposits (checking accounts), time deposits (interest-bearing bank deposits), certificates of deposit (C.D.s), and marketable securities. Third, the financial manager must decide on the appropriate characteristics for each of the forms in which the "cash" is to be held: maturities, yields, and so forth.

Determining Cash Holdings

The first of these three decisions, concerning the amount of cash to be held, is perhaps the most significant of the three. In determining cash balances required by a subsidiary for a period of time, there are two primary considerations or motives. The first is the cash needs to be managed in anticipation of day-to-day cash disbursement needs, the *transaction motive*. Second, cash balances are maintained as protection against unexpected fluctuations in the level of cash inflows from those expected, the *precautionary motive*.[1]

Transactional Considerations   The cash holding of a firm must cover the difference between expected cash receipts (inflows) and expected cash disbursements (outflows). The following example and Table 17.1 illustrate this consideration.

Assume for simplicity that a U.S. firm makes its cash need determinations on a monthly rather than weekly or daily basis and that it has subsidiaries in three countries: Mexico, the Netherlands, and Japan. To reduce confusion and exchange rate complications, the figures in Table 17.1 are presented in U.S. dollars.

This situation requires that both Mexico and Japan plan for a monthly cash flow deficit. Thus, the financial manager of the Mexican subsidiary would need to hold pesos equal to $20,000 to cover this deficit. Conversely,

Table 17.1   **Expected Cash Needs of Three Subsidiaries— Transactional Motive***

Country	Inflows	Outflows	Cash needs
Mexico	10	30	20
The Netherlands	30	20	(10)
Japan	90	150	60

* In thousands of U.S. dollars.

the financial manager for the Netherlands could anticipate a cash surplus of guilders equal to $10,000.

If a firm was able to forecast cash flows with perfect accuracy, then the Mexican and Japanese subsidiaries could maintain cash balances of exactly $20,000 and $60,000, repectively, and be sure that they would be able to cover all cash disbursements during the month. Relatedly, the Dutch subsidiary could make investments of longer than one month's duration or purchases of $10,000, and still be confident that it had cash holdings sufficient to cover its disbursement requirements. Unfortunately, cash flow forecasts can never be perfectly accurate; therefore, every firm must take precautions to ensure that it does not find itself unable to meet cash obligations.

Precautionary Considerations The *precautionary* motive in determining the level of cash holdings is really nothing more than keeping on hand cash in excess of forecast needs. In the example presented in Table 17.1, the Mexican subsidiary could hold pesos equal to $40,000, $60,000, or more. Obviously, the larger the cash holdings, the greater the probability of having a sufficient amount to cover unexpected cash demands or shortfalls of cash inflows. However, it is equally obvious that excessive quantities of cash represent an inefficient use of that resource. The real questions in determining the precautionary cash reserve are how much is enough and how much is too much.

Although these questions may be answered by managerial intuition, it is perhaps best to utilize statistics. If one were to assume that the forecast cash needs (the difference between cash inflows and cash outflows) can be represented by a normal probability distribution around the most likely estimate of cash needs, then one can calculate a standard deviation for that distribution and use probability estimates to determine the amount of cash needed to create the desired level of certainty. For example, if the amount of cash the subsidiary decided to hold was set at a level equal to the forecast cash shortfall plus an amount equal to three standard deviations, then there would be a 99.87 percent chance of having sufficient cash on hand. Stated differently, there would be only a 0.13 percent chance of not having enough cash on hand (see Table 17.2).

From Table 17.2 it is obvious that there is a cost associated with the protection achieved by increasing subsidiary cash holdings by a precautionary reserve equal to three standard deviations. First, $45,000 of additional funds are tied up in cash, and are thus not available for long-term investments either in the firm's operations or elsewhere.

Currency Considerations for Subsidiary Cash Holdings

In addition to determining the amount of cash needed, the form of investment of these cash holdings, and the appropriate characteristics of those investments, the international financial manager must decide how much of the subsidiary's cash and near-cash accounts will be kept in the host national

Subsidiaries need to maintain transactional cash balances sufficient to cover the difference between expected cash inflows and expected cash outflows.

Besides cash for transactional needs, subsidiaries also must maintain a precautionary balance.

Table 17.2 **Expected Cash Needs of Three Subsidiaries—Precautionary Motive***

Country	Transactional cash needs (A)	Precautionary reserves (3 SDs) (B)	Cash needs with protection (A + B)
Mexico	20	15	35
The Netherlands	(10)	12	2
Japan	60	18	78
	70	45	115

* In thousands of U.S. dollars.

Adapted from D. K. Eiteman and A. I. Stonehill, *Multinational Business Finance*, 3rd ed. (Reading, Mass.: Addison-Wesley, 1983), p. 605.

currency and how much will be kept in other currencies. One reason for keeping a portion of the subsidiary's cash holding in a currency other than that of the host nation is the potential loss of value resulting from local inflation or an expected devaluation of the host national currency. For example, an American firm operating in a country that has rampant inflation and a rapidly deteriorating exchange rate may want to keep the precautionary component of its "cash" balances in some hard currency such as U.S. dollars, Japanese yen, or Swiss francs.

Economic problems are not the only reasons for a firm to keep a portion of its "cash" reserves in a nonlocal currency. Some countries have poorly developed short-term debt markets; therefore, the financial manager has few good choices for the subsidiary's cash investments. A third reason for keeping cash in a different currency is to ensure its availability for paying cash obligations owed outside of the host nation. Payment of these debts could become a problem if the host nation were to adopt exchange restrictions.[2]

For a variety of reasons, subsidiaries should hold a portion of their cash balances in currencies other than that of the host nation.

Cash Management Under Conditions of High Inflation

Protecting the firm's assets against the effects of inflation, especially in countries with extremely high inflation rates, is one of the most important and most challenging aspects of the international financial manager's job. Cash and accounts receivable are particularly vulnerable to the depreciating effects of inflation. In countries with high inflation, the financial manager must ensure that the firm takes the following steps. First, minimize those local-currency-denominated accounts that are negatively affected by inflation (cash, accounts receivable, and debt denominated in stronger currencies). Simultaneously, maximize those accounts that are resistant to the effects of inflation or are affected by inflation in a manner that results in gains for the firm (inventory, assets denominated in stronger currencies, and other inflation-resistant assets such as land, precious metals, and so forth). Relatedly, the subsidiary should delay payment on fixed-price, non-inflation-affected liabilities so that the firm is actually paying less because it is making payment in a less valuable currency—that is, accounts payable or short-term notes payable. The firm may also wish to borrow long or short term in the high-inflation country if interest rates are fixed or adjusted at a rate that is not likely to increase as rapidly as inflation (i.e., debt with ceilings or caps). Cash in excess of what is required could also be converted into hard currencies, transferred to the home country, or converted into inventory. Receipts from low-inflation countries should be delayed as long as possible. See Global Insight on cash management in Brazil.

In nations with high inflation, one of the financial manager's key tasks is to minimize the eroding effects of inflation.

Managing Corporate-Level Cash and Cash Flows

From the perspective of the entire international firm, the basic purpose of cash management is to reduce the total amount of cash held in the corporate system without encumbering the activities of the firm or decreasing its ability to meet cash obligations. Additionally, a firm seeks to minimize its cash holdings so that excess funds can be profitably invested.

Frequently, this can best be accomplished by the centralization of many aspects of cash management. To these ends, financial managers initiate corporate-level *cash management plans*. These involve developing highly specific budgets that not only show the level of liquidity at key future dates but also forecast cash inflows and outflows for days, weeks, and even months in advance for each subsidiary and the corporation as a whole. These plans also include specific strategies and policies to decrease the number of days the firm has to wait for funds coming to the firm and to increase the amount of time it takes for payments by the firm to actually result in a cash outflow. The latter not only includes avoiding early payments (unless discounts offered by vendors make early payment desirable) but also maximizing the time it takes for checks to clear the firm's bank. Cash management also involves plans for investing excess cash and establishing lines of short-term credit for borrowing during periods of cash shortfall. Finally, these plans deal with globally managing cash balances at different subsidiaries and ensuring the mobility of funds among various organizational units.

Cash management plans are implemented in many ways from simply requesting payments by cable rather than mail, to globally centralizing cash management through techniques such as *pooling*. The concept of pooling in a central account can also be used to eliminate differences in liquidity among affiliates. Using this procedure, cash deficits in one affiliate are offset by surpluses in another.[3]

Centralizing cash holdings allows for an equal level of protection with lower corporate cash holdings. Because variances among independent probability distributions are additive, the equivalent standard deviation for the three subsidiaries presented in Table 17.2 when taken as a whole would be less than the sum of the three standard deviations of the three subsidiaries

GLOBAL INSIGHT
Inflation in Brazil Makes Cash Management Critical

As pressure begins to build on the new cruzado, rising interest rates and prices will make it increasingly difficult for money managers to keep corporate assets safe from inflation and devaluations. Furthermore, the situation is being made doubly difficult by the Sarney administration's continuing flip-flopping on monetary policies.

Despite an absence of indexation and a government clampdown on prices, inflation for the first four months of 1989 was 100.8 percent. This is 10.6 percent higher than for the same period of 1988. Analysts project that inflation will in fact get worse over the next several months. The projections are based upon several facts:

1. Indexation is being phased in.

2. Widespead labor walkouts are resulting in higher wage settlements.

3. The government price freeze is being lifted.

Local executives expect the inflation rate for all of 1989 to be in the 550 to 625 percent range.

The local borrowing rates are staggering. Commercial bank rates during April were 22 percent per month. Working capital loans on amounts of over 1 million new cruzados (NCz) carried rates of 12.1 to 16.1 percent per month, and 18.1 to 20.1 percent per month on amounts under 1 million NCz.

Source: Adapted from Axel de Tristan, "Money Management in Brazil Grows More Critical As Inflation Moves Upward," *Business Latin America*, May 15, 1989, p. 150.

treated independently (see Table 17.3). Thus, centrally pooling subsidiary cash holding reduces total system cash holdings by approximately 16 percent, from $115,000 to $96,000.

A system called *netting* is also used when there are a large number of separate foreign exchange transactions among subsidiaries, branches, or affiliates of a firm. Netting of transactions reduces the number of exchange transactions and the associated costs. The netting procedure essentially replaces actual foreign exchange transactions with bookkeeping rectification. Settlement is made periodically on the basis of the net debt or credit position.[4] (See Table 17.4.) Obviously the total number of transactions would be reduced from the number actually taking place among the four nations to only four transactions, each between the central netting fund and the national affiliate.

Successful netting and pooling require the centralization of cash deposits or at least centralized (home office) control of cash balances rather than decentralized control among the affiliates.

Centralizing international cash management can reduce the total amount of cash holdings. Similarly, netting intracompany transactions can reduce total system exchange costs.

CAPITAL BUDGETING AND FINANCING INTERNATIONAL INVESTMENTS

Capital budgeting and the financing of international investments are areas of substantial importance for both the international financial manager and

468

Table 17.3   **Cash Needs of Three Subsidiaries—Pooled Precautionary Reserves***

Country	Transactional cash needs (A)	Precautionary reserves (3 SDs) (B)	Cash needs with protection (A + B)
Mexico	20	15	35
The Netherlands	(10)	12	2
Japan	60	18	78
Subsidiary total	70	45	115
Centralized system	70	26.325†	96.325

* In thousands of U.S. dollars.

$$† = (3) \times [(5)^2 + (4)^2 + (6)^2]^{\frac{1}{2}}$$
$$= (3) \times [77]^{\frac{1}{2}}$$
$$= (3) \times 8.775$$
$$= 26.325$$

the firm's top management. Although these issues have been addressed briefly in earlier chapters, it is important that they also be treated from a financial perspective.

Capital budgeting, also called capital allocation, is the process whereby a firm decides whether to invest in a business venture or project. This is done in the face of a limited quantity of investable funds called the *capital constraint*. A variety of different methods can be used to determine whether a venture or project should be funded. These range from the simple payback

Table 17.4   **International Payments Netting***

Receiving affiliate	United States	Mexico	The Netherlands	Japan	Total receipts
United States	—	300	1,000	1,100	2,400
Mexico	500	—	100	500	1,100
The Netherlands	1,200	100	—	2,000	3,300
Japan	4,000	600	1,500	—	6,100
Total payments	5,700	1,000	2,600	3,600	12,900
	Payments	Receipts	Net payments		Net receipts
United States	5,700	2,400	3,300		—
Mexico	1,000	1,100	—		100
The Netherlands	2,600	3,300	—		700
Japan	3,600	6,100	—		2,500

* In thousands of U.S. dollars.

Adapted from D. K. Eiteman and A. I. Stonehill, *Multinational Business Finance*, 5th ed. (Reading, Mass.: Addison-Wesley, 1989), p. 570.

period calculation to the more complex discounted cash flow analysis. Whichever method is employed, a number of complicating factors need to be addressed.

1. Currency: Which currency will be utilized for the analyses?
   a. If analyses are done in the local currency, how will the firm consider such issues as inconvertibility of currency, exchange rate changes, taxes on repatriations, local inflation rates, and nonrepatriable (blocked) funds?
   b. If the capital investment evaluations are calculated in the investing country's currency, how will the firm forecast exchange rates over the life of the investment?

2. Repatriations: If a firm wants to globally rationalize its financial management, then the repatriation policies of the host nation come into play.
   a. Will the firm give special weight to projects or investments in countries with few barriers to the repatriation of profits or equity?
   b. How will the firm differentiate between projects in countries that levy a graduated tax on repatriations versus countries that put limits on the amount of repatriations?
   c. Will the evaluation system differentiate among funds it plans to repatriate, funds it could but does not plan to repatriate, and funds that are blocked?
   d. Since there could be income tax rate differences between repatriated and nonrepatriated funds, what tax rates will be utilized?

3. Risk differences: Different types of investments and different countries carry with them differences in risk.
   a. Will the firm's analyses reflect business and country risk differences?
   b. How will the risk differences be included in the evaluations?
   c. Will the evaluations indicate the effects of a particular investment on the overall level of corporate risk?

All types of capital budgeting processes must address the complicating issues of which currency to use, repatriations, and risk differences.

The following sections demonstrate various methods and illustrate the aforementioned concerns of currency, repatriations, and risks. The analyses and decision-making tools presented in each of the sections will utilize the data presented in Table 17.5.

Payback Period Analysis

As in domestic business, international capital budgeting is usually accomplished by comparing expected cash inflows from a proposed project with expected cash outflows. Perhaps the simplest of these methods is the payback period analysis, which shows how many years it will take the firm to generate net cash inflows equal to the net cash outflows (including the initial investment).

Table 17.5   **Projected Cash Flows from Alternative International Capital Investments**

Year	Brazil (cruzado 000's)			France (franc 000's)			Korea (won 000's)		
	Projected Inflows*	Projected Outflows	Projected Exchange Rates†	Projected Inflows*	Projected Outflows	Projected Exchange Rates†	Projected Inflows*	Projected Outflows	Projected Exchange Rates†
1989(0)		100			150			11,000	
1990(1)	(7)		6.8	(5)		6.2	(1,000)		670
1991(2)	120		11.0	3		6.5	(200)		675
1992(3)	130		18.2	12		6.4	1,000		675
1993(4)	150		28.0	65		6.5	3,000		670
1994(5)	185	25	45.5	85		6.9	4,000		660
1995(6)	200		75.5	85		7.3	5,000		650
1996(7)	250		125.0	45		7.5	7,000		650
1997(8)	310		200.0	25		7.5	8,000		655
1998(9)	450		355.5	15		7.8	8,000		645
1999(10)	600		500.0	5		8.4	7,000		625

* Projected inflows from funded project.
† Forecast exchange rates are presented in terms of the number of local currency units per U.S. dollar.

Payback in Local Currency Terms

The easiest method of payback evaluation is merely to determine the number of years of local cash inflows required to equal the local currency value of the initial investment and any other outflows. The payback periods for investment alternatives are then compared with a preestablished standard and with one another. Table 17.6 presents an example using a required local currency payback of five years or less. In this example the Korean investment would be rejected because it would not pay back the investment within five years. Both the French and the Brazilian investments exceed the standard by paying back the investment within five years: The French investment has a payback of 4.9 years and the Brazilian investment, 1.9 years. Thus, these two investment proposals would make it to the second level of analysis; they would be compared with one another, and funded or rejected on the basis of whether sufficient funds were available for both investments. If the amount of investable funds was not sufficient to fund both investments then management would have to decide. Even though the Brazilian investment has a much shorter payback period, management might still opt for the French investment. Since both investments meet the minimum standards, management might use other than purely financial considerations in making the final decision.

Table 17.6 Payback Analysis of Alternative International Capital Investments

Year	Brazil (cruzado 000's)			France (franc 000's)			Korea (won 000's)		
	Projected Inflows*	Projected Outflows	Net Cash flows	Projected Inflows*	Projected Outflows	Net Cash flows	Projected Inflows*	Projected Outflows	Net Cash flows
1989(0)		100	(100)		150	(150)		11,000	(11,000)
1990(1)	(7)		(107)	(5)		(155)	(1,000)		(12,000)
1991(2)	120		13	3		(152)	(200)		(12,200)
1992(3)	130		143	12		(140)	1,000		(11,200)
1993(4)	150		293	65		(75)	3,000		(8,200)
1994(5)	185	25	453	85		10	4,000		(4,200)
1995(6)	200		653	85		95	5,000		800
1996(7)	250		903	45		140	7,000		7,800
1997(8)	310		1,213	25		165	8,000		15,800
1998(9)	450		1,663	15		180	8,000		23,800
1999(10)	600		2,263	5		185	7,000		30,800

* Projected inflows from funded project.

472

Translated Payback Analysis

A second approach to payback analysis that considers the effects of exchange rate changes is to forecast exchange rates and then translate the cash flows into the home country currency. Table 17.7 shows the effect of translation on the three investment alternatives presented in Table 17.5.

When the payback analysis is conducted using translated (dollar value) cash flows, the results are very different. Only Brazil (3.7 years) meets the payback standard. France and Korea pay back the investment in the sixth year. It is interesting to note that the payback period for the Brazilian investment using translated dollar cash flows was double the local-currency-determined payback due to the effects of the declining value of the cruzado.

Other Factors in Payback Analysis

When one recognizes that only translation effects were included in the above analysis with no consideration of the time value of money, these investments look even worse. Clearly, these translated (dollar value) cash flows could have been adjusted (discounted) by some factor, such as the parent company's cost of capital or even the U.S. inflation rate, to determine the current value of the projected cash inflows. Those translated, current value cash flows could have been used to determine the payback period. Clearly, this would make these investments look even less attractive.

Furthermore, in the above examples of local currency and translated payback analyses, the same payback standard (five years) was used. In reality it is quite possible that there would be substantial differences in risk among these three investments. The firm might forecast high levels of political risk in one country, currency inconvertibility risks in a second, and market-competition risks in the third. These differences in the level of risk associated with the industry or country might necessitate using different payback standards—that is, three years for Brazil, five years for Korea, and seven years for France. If these differing payback standards had been used, the Brazilian and Korean investments would have been rejected and the French investment accepted.

Payback period analysis (local currency or dollar terms) calculates the number of years required to generate cash flows equal to the original investment.

Discounted Cash Flow Analyses

One of the most common methods of international capital budgeting is comparing the current value of expected cash inflows from the proposed project with the current value of expected cash outflows. This is accomplished by discounting future cash flows to determine their current value. If the present value of expected cash inflows exceed the present value of expected outflows, the firm has a positive indication that the investment will pay off. If the reverse is true, the indications are that the firm should not invest in a particular project.

The complicating factors presented earlier (currency, repatriation, and

Table 17.7 **Translated Payback Analysis of International Capital Investments***

Year	Brazil			France			Korea		
	Projected Annual Net Inflows (local currency)	Projected Exchange Rate†	Translated (U.S. Dollar Value) of Projected Net Inflows‡	Projected Annual Net Inflows (local currency)	Projected Exchange Rate†	Translated (U.S. Dollar Value) of Projected Net Inflows‡	Projected Annual Net Inflows (local currency)	Projected Exchange Rate†	Translated (U.S. Dollar Value) of Projected Net Inflows‡
1989(0)	(100)	6.7	(14.93)	(150)	6.1	(24.59)	(11,000)	670	(16.42)
1990(1)	(7)	6.8	(15.96)	(5)	6.2	(25.40)	(1,000)	670	(17.91)
1991(2)	120	11.0	(5.05)	3	6.5	(24.94)	(200)	675	(18.21)
1992(3)	130	18.2	2.09	12	6.4	(23.06)	1,000	675	(16.73)
1993(4)	150	28.0	7.45	65	6.5	(13.06)	3,000	670	(12.25)
1994(5)	160	45.5	10.97	85	6.9	(0.74)	4,000	660	(6.19)
1995(6)	200	75.5	13.62	85	7.3	10.90	5,000	650	1.50
1996(7)	250	125.0	15.62	45	7.5	16.90	7,000	650	12.27
1997(8)	310	200.0	17.17	25	7.5	20.23	8,000	655	24.48
1998(9)	450	355.5	18.43	15	7.8	22.15	8,000	645	36.88
1999(10)	600	500.0	19.63	5	8.4	22.74	7,000	625	48.08

* In thousands of U.S. dollars.
† Forecast exchange rates in local currency units per U.S. dollar.
‡ Projected net cash flows translated into thousands of U.S. dollars.

risk differences) are as important in discounted cash flow analysis as in payback analysis. For example, will the analysis of cash flows be calculated in the currency of the country of investment (local currency) or in the currency of the home country? If the firm opts to use translated cash flows, then the issues of what exchange rate to use and the forecasting of future exchange rate comes into play. Some firms use the current exchange rate for translating future cash flows; however, this rewards investments in countries with a high inflation rate since no consideration is given to the fact that host country inflation would probably result in a declining exchange rate. Equally important is the question of whether to include as cash inflows the translated value of all local cash flows or only those cash inflows that are actually to be repatriated to the home country. This calls into question the issue of taxes on repatriations as well as differences in income tax rates and taxing policies among the countries involved. Finally, and perhaps most importantly, is the question of what discount factor will be used. In domestic capital allocations, it is common to use the firm's cost of capital; however, for a foreign investment, different risks (business, foreign exchange, and political) must be considered.

When using a local-currency-denominated, discounted cash flow form of international investment analysis, many firms will first adjust the local-currency-denominated cash flows for the expected levels of inflation and then adjust for risks. This is called deflating the cash flows or putting them in "real," current terms. If a country is projected to have an inflation rate (i) of 10 percent per year for the next five years, then the real, current value of 100 pesos of annual income (I) for each year (n) can be calculated using the following formula:

$$\text{Current Value of } I = I/(1 + i)^n$$

The current value of the 100 pesos for each year would be: year 1—90 pesos, year 2—83 pesos, year 3—75 pesos, and so forth.

Once the local cash flows have been adjusted for inflation, the projects can then be analyzed in either of two methods: net present value (NPV) or internal rate of return (IRR).

Some firms wish to avoid having to deflate local cash flows and instead translate the cash flows into home currency terms using projected exchange rates to create home-currency-denominated cash flows for NPV or IRR analyses. Since forecasting long-term exchange rates depends on forecasts of both home and host country inflation rates, this makes local cash flow inflation adjustments unnecessary. For a clarification of this point see the section on purchasing power parity in Chapter 4, "Foreign Exchange," and the later section in this chapter on forecasting exchange rates.

Unfortunately, forecasting both host country inflation and exchange rates is both risky and difficult. For this reason firms often make two assumptions. First, they assume that after the second year the current value of cash inflows from an investment will remain constant. In other words, they assume that inflation will affect their revenues and expenses in an identical manner. Second, they assume that these level cash flows can accurately be translated into home currency terms at the third exchange rate. This makes the investment calculation substantially easier.

Net Present Value Analysis

The net present value (NPV) of a project is the present value of a stream of net cash flows from a project minus the project's initial investment. For domestic investments, future cash flows are discounted at the firm's cost of capital, the minimum acceptable rate of return for projects of average risk. Since international investments are often substantially more risky than domestic projects, some form of adjustment is required. In dealing with the added risks associated with many foreign operations, firms often use one of two methods for modifying their standard corporate discounted cash flow analysis procedure: (1) decrease the level of expected cash inflows, or (2) increase the discount factor above the domestic cost of capital.

Cash inflows can be adjusted by multiplying these by a coefficient between 0 and 1, with larger coefficients indicating lesser added risk. For example, a firm may account for country risks by reducing expected cash inflows by 10 percent (a coefficient of 0.9). Discount factors are adjusted by adding some amount to the discount rate that would be used if the investment being considered were in the home country. For example, a firm may account for added risks in countries by increasing the discount factor by 2 percent over the U.S. rate in one country but by 6 percent in another. This modification is generally made based upon management's subjective assessment of the levels of business, foreign exchange, and political risk in the host country as well as consideration of this investment's impact on the total corporation. Tables 17.8 and 17.9 illustrate NPV analysis of the translated cash flows for a Brazilian investment using the cash flow adjustment, while Tables 17.10 and 17.11 illustrate NPV analysis using discount factor adjustment procedures.

NPV analysis determines whether for a predetermined discount factor the present value of the inflows from a project equals the present value of the outflows.

Net Present Value Analysis Using Cash Flow Adjustments   Table 17.8 shows a NPV analysis of the Brazilian investment previously cited using a 20 percent cash flow adjustment and the translation of the cash flows into dollars based on 10 years of exchange rate forecasts. In this example the Brazilian investment shows a positive net present value. Table 17.9 uses cash flow adjustments but assumes level cash inflows after the third year and translates those cash flows into dollars at the third year rate. This simplified process also yields a positive NPV but a substantially greater present value for the life of the project.

Net Present Value Analysis Using Discount Rate Adjustments   This project could have been analyzed by adjusting the discount factor and not adjusting the local currency cash flows. Table 17.10 uses the discount factor adjustment along with 10-year exchange rate forecasts, while Table 17.11 uses

Table 17.8 **NPV Analysis of International Capital Investment—Brazil with Adjusted Local Currency Cash Flows**

Year	Cash flows			X-rate*	Trans. CF†	PV coef. (discount = 10%)	NPV
	L.C.‡	RF§	Adj. L.C.				
1989(0)	(100)		(100)	6.7	(14.93)	1.000	(14.93)
1990(1)	(7)	0.8	(7)	6.8	(1.03)	0.909	(0.94)
1991(2)	120	0.8	96	11.0	8.73	0.826	7.21
1992(3)	130	0.8	104	18.2	5.71	0.751	4.29
1993(4)	150	0.8	120	28.0	4.29	0.683	2.93
1994(5)	160	0.8	128	45.5	2.81	0.621	1.75
1995(6)	200	0.8	160	75.5	2.12	0.564	1.20
1996(7)	250	0.8	200	125.0	1.60	0.513	0.82
1997(8)	310	0.8	248	200.0	1.24	0.467	0.58
1998(9)	450	0.8	360	355.5	1.01	0.424	0.43
1999(10)	600	0.8	480	500.0	0.96	0.386	0.37
Total	2288		1809		12.51		3.71

* Forecast exchange rates: local currency units per U.S. dollar.
† Translated annual cash flows (000's U.S. dollars).
‡ Local currency (000's cruzados).
§ Risk adjustment factor to reduce cash inflows to reflect risk levels.

477

Table 17.9 Simplified NPV Analysis of International Capital Investment—Brazil with Adjusted Local Currency Cash Flows

Year	Cash flows			X-rate*	Trans. CF†	PV coef. (discount = 10%)	NPV
	L.C.‡	RF§	Adj. L.C.				
1989(0)	(100)		(100)	6.7	(14.93)	1.000	(14.93)
1990(1)	(7)	0.8	(7)	6.8	(1.03)	0.909	(0.94)
1991(2)	120	0.8	96	11.0	8.73	0.826	7.21
1992(3)	130	0.8	104	18.2	5.71	0.751	4.29
1993(4)	130	0.8	104	18.2	5.71	0.683	3.90
1994(5)	130	0.8	104	18.2	5.71	0.621	3.55
1995(6)	130	0.8	104	18.2	5.71	0.564	3.22
1996(7)	130	0.8	104	18.2	5.71	0.513	2.93
1997(8)	130	0.8	104	18.2	5.71	0.467	2.67
1998(9)	130	0.8	104	18.2	5.71	0.424	2.42
1999(10)	130	0.8	104	18.2	5.71	0.386	2.20
Total							16.52

* Forecast exchange rates: local currency units per U.S. dollar.
† Translated noncumulative cash flows (000's U.S. dollars).
‡ Local currency (000's cruzados).
§ Risk adjustment factor to reduce cash inflows to reflect risk levels.

Table 17.10   **NPV Analysis of International Capital Investment—Brazil with Discount Factor Adjustment**

Year	Cash flows (000's cruzados)	X-rate*	Trans. CF†	PV coef. (discount = 30%)	NPV
1989(0)	(100)	6.7	(14.93)	1.000	(14.93)
1990(1)	(7)	6.8	(1.03)	0.769	(0.79)
1991(2)	120	11.0	8.73	0.592	5.17
1992(3)	130	18.2	5.71	0.455	2.60
1993(4)	150	28.0	4.29	0.350	1.50
1994(5)	160	45.5	3.52	0.269	0.95
1995(6)	200	75.5	2.12	0.207	0.44
1996(7)	250	125.0	1.60	0.159	0.25
1997(8)	310	200.0	1.24	0.123	0.15
1998(9)	450	355.5	1.01	0.094	0.09
1999(10)	600	500.0	0.96	0.073	0.07
Total	2263		13.22		(4.50)

* Forecast exchange rates in local currency units per U.S. dollar.
† Translated net annual cash flows (000's U.S. dollars): not cumulative.

discount factor adjustments but with the simplified assumptions about cash flows and exchange rates. In each case the discount factor has been increased from 10 percent to 30 percent.

Using this method of NPV analysis, we find that the Brazilian investment ends up with a negative net present value using both procedures; therefore, it would be rejected. This leads to the obvious question of why the investment would be accepted when cash flows are adjusted for risk but rejected when the discount factor is adjusted for the higher risk. The answer is that cash flow adjustment procedures tend to reward projects that have greater levels of cash inflows in the later stages of project, whereas discount factor adjustment penalizes projects that have later cash flows and rewards projects with earlier cash inflows.

> In NPV analysis the level of risk is included by either lowering projected inflows or increasing the discount factor.

Internal Rate of Return Analysis

Internal rate of return analysis is similar to NPV except that instead of calculating the present value of the inflows and outflows for a predetermined discount rate, one calculates a discount rate such that the present value of the outflows will exactly equal the present value of the inflows. In this process, one begins by guessing a discount rate and conducts a net present value calculation similar to that in Table 17.10 or 17.11. If the net present value is negative then one selects a lower discount rate and continues the process until the net discounted cash flows become positive. At that point one must interpolate to determine the IRR. For example, if at a discount factor of 10 percent the net present value of the cash flows were −50 and

Table 17.11   **Simplified NPV Analysis of International Capital Investment—Brazil with Discount Factor Adjustment**

Year	Net Annual Cash flows (000's cruzados)	X-rate*	Trans. CF†	PV coef. (discount = 30%)	NPV
1989(0)	(100)	6.7	(14.93)	1.000	(14.93)
1990(1)	(7)	6.8	(1.03)	0.769	(0.79)
1991(2)	120	11.0	8.73	0.592	5.17
1992(3)	130	18.2	5.71	0.455	2.60
1993(4)	130	18.2	5.71	0.350	2.00
1994(5)	130	18.2	5.71	0.269	1.54
1995(6)	130	18.2	5.71	0.207	1.18
1996(7)	130	18.2	5.71	0.159	0.91
1997(8)	130	18.2	5.71	0.123	0.70
1998(9)	130	18.2	5.71	0.094	0.54
1999(10)	130	18.2	5.71	0.073	0.42
Total					(0.66)

* Forecast exchange rates in local currency units per U.S. dollar.
† Translated cash flows (000's U.S. dollars): not cumulative.

at a discount factor of 9 the discounted cash flows were +50, then through interpolation the IRR can be determined to be 9.5 percent. As with NPV analysis, IRR calculation may be done in either local currency terms or in translated terms.

Once the IRR has been determined it needs to be compared with a predetermined acceptable level called the *hurdle rate*. If the hurdle rate had been 8 percent and the IRR of a project was 9.5 percent then the project has passed the first hurdle. This does not mean that the project will be funded but only that it has arrived at the stage wherein it will be compared with other projects that have IRRs in excess of their hurdle rates. It is important to note that risk differences, based upon differences in industry or country, are reflected in different hurdle rates for the projects. Thus, a proposed plant to produce glass wine bottles in Argentina may have to exceed a hurdle rate of 25 percent, while an identical facility in the United Kingdom may be subjected to a hurdle rate of only 15 percent.

For all proposed capital expenditures that exceed their hurdle rate, the final decision will be based upon such strategic concerns as meeting competition, following large customers, or expected market growth rates. Finally, the number of funded projects will be predicated upon the capital constraint, the available investable funds.

IRR calculated the discount rate that creates a zero net present value. This is compared with a predetermined "hurdle" rate that is required for project approval.

The Capital Constraint in International Capital Budgeting

Since no firm has an unlimited supply of investable funds, it must make decisions among alternatives. With luck, the firm will generate many more good investment alternatives than it has the capital to fund. If this is the case then management has the difficult but pleasant task of selecting projects to fund from among good choices. Table 17.12 presents a list of projects all of which have exceeded the hurdle rate established for that project; however, the total cost of all five projects exceeds the total investable funds available to management.

If the firm is to spend all or nearly all of its investable funds and not sell stock, float bonds, borrow, or sell assets to generate additional funds it will have to make choices among these five attractive alternatives. If the firm wants to fund project 4 it has only three choices: project 4 alone ($40M), projects 4 and 1 ($50M), or projects 4 and 2 ($45M). If, however, the firm will forego project 4 or hold it for next year then it could fund all of the other projects.

Continuation Investments

Not all capital expenditures by firms are subjected to capital budgeting analyses. The exceptions are termed continuation projects, and are capital expenditures that are required to maintain a going concern. For example, if a firm such as Owens-Illinois, the multinational glass and packaging firm, had a wine bottle producing plant in Brazil, it would ultimately have to rebuild the furnace used to melt the glass. Despite the fact that a furnace rebuild may cost tens of thousands of dollars, it will not be analyzed in any of the aforementioned ways. If the original capital expenditure evaluation, when the plant was first constructed, was done properly, it would have included periodic outflows reflecting these required expenditures. Look at Table 17.6; note that for the Brazilian investment there is shown an outflow of 25,000 cruzados during 1994, the fifth year of the project. This anticipated fifth year outflow of cash was included to indicate a continuation investment. If this project were to be funded, the commitment to the continuation investment would have already been made. Thus, before any new investment alternatives are even considered in 1994, the 25,000 cruzados will have been removed from the firm's stock of investable funds.

Certain capital projects called continuation investments are not subject to capital investment analyses because they are necessary to the continued operation of a business.

Table 17.12   **The Effects of the Capital Constraint on Project Funding***

Project no.	Rank	Hurdle rate	IRR	Capital cost
1	1	25	26	$10M
2	5	12	15	5M
3	4	20	22	20M
4	2	15	15	40M
5	3	15	19	15M

* Capital constraint: $50M.

Despite the apparent objectivity of net present value, internal rate of return, or any of the other discounted cash flow analysis procedures, the adjustments necessary to deal with international and host country risks are more of a subjective art than an exact science. In the face of this subjectivity, many firms have opted for inherently less complex procedures such as payback period. Many firms use local currency payback with a maximum acceptable payback of three to five years. Some firms like the simplicity of the payback method but want to include expected exchange rate changes in their analysis. This is done because it is the translated value of earnings or cash streams that will ultimately appear on the financial statements of the parent firm. Furthermore, since the source of the funds originally invested was the parent company and home country (retained earnings, a stock issuance, or debt), the project should have an acceptable payback in terms of that same currency. Firms often use a minimally acceptable payback period that is at the short end of what might be used for similar domestic projects, seven to ten years. Whether the firm selects a complex and detailed method of analysis or a rather simple one, the method of analysis can strongly influence the investment decision.

Sources of Capital to Finance Foreign Operations

Once a decision is made to invest, the firm must decide on the method for financing the project: equity or debt. If a firm decides to finance its overseas investments with equity, it must decide where to issue the stock. Should the stock be purchased by the parent company, or be sold in the host country, home country, or any country where buyers can be found? If the parent firm purchases all of the stock, it retains managerial control over that firm unless the laws of the host country restrict majority foreign ownership. Earnings will provide local-currency-denominated dividend income to the firm. The parent company will have to deal with foreign exchange risks for any dividends it intends to repatriate. If stock is issued in the host country, some of the policy decision-making will be controlled by local nationals. This eliminates foreign exchange exposure risks on dividends paid to local national stockholders; nevertheless, the parent company still has to deal with foreign exchange risks for any dividends it repatriates. If the stock is issued in the home country or some third country, the dividends must be denominated in that currency, thus creating exchange risks on all dividends.

A firm can rely on debt to finance its international operation. This debt may consist of loans from financial institutions, floating bonds, or loans from third parties (governments, other corporations, or individuals). If the firm opts to float bonds, these may be denominated in the home currency, the host currency, or some third currency, depending on where the bonds are sold (floated). Many firms make use of Eurobonds for financing international projects because lower rates of interest are generally available.

This photograph reminds us that international business is not limited to manufacturing but also includes services such as banking. It further serves to illustrate that Japan is a major global power in banking as well as manufacturing.

Care must be taken to ensure that any savings in interest rates are not more than offset by exchange rate changes. Consider the following simplified example. Company X needs $10,000,000 for expanding its manufacturing operations in New Jersey. Assume that the going interest rate on a five-year loan of $10,000,000 in the United States was 10 percent, and for simplicity assume that the entirety of the principal is not due until the end of the five years. Also assume that a comparable loan could be obtained in Switzerland with a rate of only 3 percent. Where should the company borrow the money? It would seem that the Swiss loan would be a real bargain, but maybe not because of exchange rate effects.

The U.S. loan would involve borrowing $10,000,000 and paying back $15,000,000. The firm would have to pay $5,000,000 of interest ($1,000,000 per year for five years) and then repay the entire $10,000,000 it had originally borrowed. If the dollar cost of the Swiss loan is expected to be less than $15,000,000, then the firm should borrow there. (See Table 17.13.)

Thus the total cost of the 3 percent Swiss-franc-denominated loan would

Table 17.13   **Effects of Exchange Rates on the Cost of Foreign-Currency-Dominated Debt***

Year	Interest at 3% (Sw. Fr)	Expected X-rate	Interest ($)
1	600,000	$1 = 2.0 Sw. Fr	300,000
2	600,000	$1 = 1.8 Sw. Fr	333,300
3	600,000	$1 = 1.6 Sw. Fr	375,300
4	600,000	$1 = 1.4 Sw. Fr	428,600
5	600,000	$1 = 1.2 Sw. Fr	500,000
Total	3,000,000		$1,937,200

* Amount borrowed at ($1 = 2.0 Sw. Fr): 20,000,000 Sw. Fr = $10,000,000.
Amount of principal repaid at ($1 = 1.2 Sw. Fr): 20,000,000 Sw. Fr = $16,666,667.
Total cost − Swiss loan = $1,937,200 (interest) + $16,666,667 (principal)
= $18,603,867

International financial managers must determine how much debt and equity to use in financing a foreign operation, and the source of that capital.

be approximately $18.6M compared to only $15M for the 10 percent U.S. loan.

FINANCIAL MANAGEMENT OF FOREIGN EXCHANGE

Many of the major topics associated with the financial management of foreign exchange were addressed in Chapter 4, "Foreign Exchange." However, the significance of foreign exchange management to international financial management warrants treating these issues in even greater depth here.

Forecasting Exchange Rates

It should be clear from the sections of Chapter 15 pertaining to financing international trade and the earlier sections of this chapter that the international financial manager needs to understand the factors that affect both long- and short-term exchange rate movements. Two of the most important theories for this understanding are the Purchasing Power Parity theory and the International Fischer Effect theory.

Purchasing Power Parity (PPP)

The Purchasing Power Parity theory states that, in the long run, inflation differentials (differences in inflation rates between two countries) will be equal and opposite to the exchange rate differentials between the two currencies. To illustrate this point, assume that Germany had an inflation rate of 3 percent while the United States had an inflation rate of 5 percent. The inflation differential would then be 2 percent. According to PPP, the exchange rate stated in terms of deutsche marks per U.S. dollars would decline by an average of 2 percent per year—that is, each year a U.S. firm would get approximately 2 percent fewer marks for each dollar exchanged.

The change in the exchange rate is necessary so that parity (equality) of purchasing power is maintained. For example, if a market basket of goods sells for $10 in the United States and the same basket of goods would sell for 20 marks in Germany, then the exchange rate should be $1 = 2 DM. As inflation in each country changes the cost of that market basket of goods, the exchange rate should change to maintain a parity of purchasing power. An inflation rate of 5 percent in the United States but only 3 percent in Germany would have the effect of devaluing the dollar relative to the mark (see Table 17.14).

If you perform the mathematics accurately you will see that the change in the exchange rate is not exactly the difference in the inflation rates; however, using the difference between countries' inflation rates serves as a good approximation when inflation rates are relatively low.

Table 17.15 demonstrates the PPP effect for a country such as Brazil with its dollar-denominated long-term debt. Assume that the United States has an inflation rate of 5 percent while Brazil has an inflation rate of 205 percent.

> The PPP theory states that exchange rates between two currencies will change such that equality of purchasing power is maintained.

The International Fischer Effect

Whereas the Purchasing Power Parity theory helps explain long-term exchange rate changes, the International Fischer Effect helps explain short-term exchange rate changes. The International Fischer Effect theory states that exchange rates between two countries will change in relation to changes in the nominal interest rates of those countries. In other words, if the interest rates of a nation increase relative to those of another nation, the exchange rate between the currencies of those nations will change to reflect the new difference in interest rates. For example, in the early 1980s interest

Table 17.14   **A Simplified Example of the Purchasing Power Parity Theory**

Year	United States Cost of goods ($) (inflation 5%)	Germany Cost of goods (DM) (inflation 3%)	Exchange rate (DM/$)
1	$10	20 DM	2 DM
2	$10 × 1.05	20 × 1.03 DM	2 × (1.03/1.05)
3	$10 × (1.05)^2	20 × (1.03)^2	2 × (1.03)^2/(1.05)^2
4	$10 × (1.05)^3	20 × (1.03)^3	2 × (1.03)^3/(1.05)^3
		.	
		.	
		.	

Table 17.15   **Purchasing Power Parity Effects on Brazilian Debt Service**

Year	Exchange rate (cruzados/$)	Debt service (U.S. dollars)	Debt service (Brazilian cruzados)
1	7	$100M	700M Cr.
2	21	$100M	2100M Cr.
3	63	$100M	6300M Cr.
4	189	$100M	18900M Cr.
5	567	$100M	56700M Cr.
		.	
		.	
		.	

The International Fischer Effect states that the currency of a country with higher interest rates will appreciate relative to those of countries with lower interest rates.

rates in the United States increased to a level that was higher than interest rates in the Netherlands. As a result the value of the dollar increased relative to the guilder. Thus, it took more guilders to buy one dollar.

Exposure Risks

Responding to anticipated fluctuations in foreign exchange rates is one of the most important challenges faced by multinational corporations. The task of the financial manager is to minimize losses that might result from changes in exchange rates.

Translation Exposure

There are three types of exchange risks to which the firm is exposed. The first is *translation exposure*. Income from foreign subsidiaries must be translated into domestic currency terms before the financial statements can be combined (consolidation). According to the Financial Accounting Standards Board Ruling No. 52 (FASB) of 1982, U.S. corporations are required to translate the results of most financial statement items into the currency of the home country at the current exchange rate. Balance sheet items must be translated at the rate existing at the end of the reporting period. Income statement items must be translated at the rate when the revenues or expenses were incurred or at a weighted average exchange rate for the period of the report. For example, if a British subsidiary of a U.S. firm owned equipment totaling £1,000,000 when the rate of exchange was £1.00 = $2.00, the value of the equipment in dollars would be $2,000,000. However, if at the end of the reporting period the pound sterling had depreciated to £1.00 = $1.50, the value of the asset in dollars would have declined to $1,500,000, a *translation loss* of $500,000.

The financial manager may attempt to reduce this "paper loss" through a *balance sheet hedge*. This may be accomplished by having the firm borrow from a London bank £1,000,000 at the same time that it paid out the $2,000,000 to purchase the equipment. Under this situation, the loss in value of the equipment due to the depreciation in the pound sterling will be offset by the decreased dollar value of the outstanding loan—that is, the £1,000,000 loan can be repaid with $1,500,000 rather than $2,000,000. As a result the translation loss would be offset by a translation gain.

Transaction Exposure

Second, the firm is exposed to *transaction risks*. These risks arise because the exchange rate between the buying and selling currency might change between the time of the sale and that of the payment. As was explained in an earlier chapter, this risk can be minimized through a hedge in the futures or forward market. Because there are costs involved in the hedging operation, the firm must weigh the hedging costs against the losses that might occur through the depreciation in the currency's value.

The financial manager may adopt alternative measures to reduce the exposure risks. These include financing transactions that are repayable in the buyer's home country currency or other hard currencies, discounting foreign notes and bills, and credit swaps. (Note: These concepts were explained in Chapter 4, "Foreign Exchange.")

Economic Exposure

The third risk to which the foreign investing firm is exposed is *economic risk*. This is the possible long-term effect of the changing value of the currency on the firm's profitability. The rapid appreciation in the value of the yen relative to the U.S. dollar in recent years provides an excellent example of the problem faced by the financial manager of a Japanese firm exporting to the United States. Should that firm quote the same dollar price for merchandise exports, thus reducing profits, or should the firm increase its prices to reflect the declining dollar and possibly lose unit sales volume? In the case of the Japanese automobile industry, export prices were increased, but by an amount that was less than the increase in the value of the yen. This increase in price resulted in the loss of some sales and smaller unit profit margins. To offset economic losses, firms often invest in the country with the depreciating currency or find an alternative production site whose currency is linked to the depreciating currency. Many Japanese auto firms established assembly plants in the United States. In other industries, Japanese firms began sourcing the U.S. market from South Korea, whose currency is tied to the dollar.

One of the major functions of the financial manager is to minimize losses from foreign exchange: translation, transaction, and economic exposures.

SUMMARY

Effective financial management is essential for the success of any business operation. This is especially true for international firms. The financial manager is largely responsible for the management of the firm's cash, for taking advantage of investment opportunities abroad, and for helping the firm deal with the risks associated with exchange rate changes.

International cash management has four important dimensions. First, the international financial manager must ensure that the firm and each of its foreign operations have sufficient cash reserves to cover expected and unexpected cash needs. These are generally called transactional and precautionary reserves. Second, the financial manager needs to protect against excessive cash levels resulting from duplication of precautionary reserves by subsidiaries. This is often accomplished by centrally pooling these precautionary balances. Third, the international firm must closely manage its current assets and liabilities to prevent the erosion of value reflecting the high levels of inflation found in many nations. Fourth, the financial manager needs to minimize the foreign exchange costs associated with an excessive number of transactions among members of the corporation.

In addition to involvement with cash management, the international financial manager will play an important part in capital investment analysis. Thus, the financial manager needs to be familiar with the various methods for investment analysis: payback, net present value, and internal rate of return are the three most widely used.

The third major dimension of international finance involves understanding the factors that affect exchange rate changes and the types of risks that this creates for the firm: translation, transaction, and economic exposure. This requires understanding theories such as the Purchasing Power Parity and International Fischer Effect theories.

KEY TERMS AND CONCEPTS

Capital allocation	Net present value analysis
Capital budgeting	Netting
Continuation investments	Payback analysis
Discounted cash flow analysis	Pooling
Discount factor or rate	Precautionary cash reserves
Economic exposure	Purchasing Power Parity theory
Exposure risks	Transaction exposure
Hurdle rate	Transactional cash reserves
Internal rate of return analysis	Translation exposure
International Fischer Effect theory	

REVIEW QUESTIONS

1. Explain the problems involved in international cash management.

2. What is meant by transactional reserves?

3. What is meant by precautionary reserves?

4. How does the "pooling" of precautionary reserves benefit the international firm?

5. How can a firm protect its assets during a period of rapid inflation?

6. Explain the concept of "netting."

7. What is international capital budgeting?

8. Explain payback analysis. Explain NPV. Explain IRR.

9. Why are repatriation taxes or limits an important consideration in international investment analysis?

10. Explain the concept of a hurdle rate.

11. Why would a firm use different payback period standards for different countries?

12. Why are some projects not subjected to capital investment analyses?

13. Explain PPP and the International Fischer Effect.

14. Explain the terms of translation, transaction, and economic exposure.

15. How does a firm deal with the situation of having more good investment alternatives than it has investable funds?

DISCUSSION CASE

Why International Financial Managers Suffer from Stress

David Drapcho is the Chief Financial Officer (CFO) of Western Electrical Equipment Products, Inc. (WEEP). He is well trained for his job, with two master's degrees: one in electrical engineering and one in finance. During his 15 years at WEEP he has had a string of successes in both technical and financial jobs. His rise to CFO has surprised everyone including himself, but he now suspects that the successes are about to come to an end because of the economics of two Latin American governments.

By Don R. Beeman

This case was developed for class discussion only and is not intended to represent good or bad management or decision-making. The facts for the case are drawn from Stephen Graham, "MNCs React Calmly To Brazil's New Clamp on Profit Remittances," *Business Latin America*, September 4, 1989, pp. 275 and 278, and Gary Newman, "MNCs in Mexico Rejigger Financial Strategies," *Business Latin America*, September 18, 1989, pp. 289–290.

WEEP manufactures electronic control equipment for industry. Originally, when the machines were relatively simple and manually controlled, WEEP's products were also simple. With the development of increasingly complex, computer-controlled equipment and industrial robots, the electronic controls have also become more complex. WEEP was up to the technical challenges and found itself with an increasing market share of more expensive equipment. Thus, sales increased doubly fast and profit margins skyrocketed.

Five years ago WEEP needed to expand operations. In light of rapidly increasing labor costs at WEEP's Dallas plant and increasing labor relations problems at its Portland, Oregon, plant, the company decided to invest abroad. The first foreign plant was put in Mexico and a year later a second plant was built in Brazil. Drapcho has never really understood what was going on with those economies but as long as the local managers made a profit he was prepared to leave them alone. Now things have changed.

Sitting on his desk are two reports prepared by two of the bright young MBAs who work for him. Each is sitting on top of a pile of supporting documentation.

Brazil—September 4, 1989

In recent weeks clamp-downs on remittances by foreign firms have increased. Since early July, all remittance applications have required high-level approval by the Central Bank. It has been taking 30 to 45 days to get these applications examined, and another month or more to get approval. The cause for the delays in remittance approval is a weakening of Brazil's foreign exchange position due to a slowing of funds from international lenders. Most local executives believe that the current situation will last at least until the November elections.

Arnim Lore, Central Bank External Area Director, told the *Financial Times* that the remittance blockage would last "indefinitely." I have spoken with Marcio Orlandi from the São Paulo office of Arthur Andersen, who thinks that the blockage will last only until Brazil's foreign exchange reaches $7 billion; it is now back up to $6.5 billion. He says that most of his clients are not reacting strongly to this situation for two reasons.

1. The high interest rates in Brazil have allowed for excellent returns on the nonrepatriated funds.

2. In light of the coming election, many firms anticipated something like this so they remitted more than usual in the first half. [I guess I blew it by not recommending early repatriation of profits.]

Despite Orlandi's position we still need to be concerned about what this does to our exchange exposure!

Dave, I took the initiative to contact some other firms to see what they are doing or have done. Here is what I found out. Alexander Ho, financial and administrative director for Rohm & Haas Brazil says that they used early remittances in anticipation of something like this. Furthermore, he says that they are putting money into fixed assets like land and buildings.

Maria Goldsmith of Giant Global Chemical says that they are submitting numerous, small dollar-value remittance applications. She argues that smaller and more frequent remittances are more likely to be approved than larger and less frequent ones. Furthermore, she says that remittance applications will be processed in the order received so we should submit them ASAP.

Mexico—September 18, 1989

In light of the new financial policies of Mexico we should take a new look at the way we are operating. Interest rates are down sharply and the risk of devaluation is substantially diminished. The new economic environment would seem to call for us to take a renewed look at long-term peso financing options and reconsider using dollar-denominated financing.

Since Mexico concluded its new foreign debt arrangement, the whole ball game has changed. Since July 1st, the 28-day Cetes (treasury certificate) has fallen by 24 points—a 40 percent drop. Most firms operating in Mexico seem optimistic but many are taking a wait-and-see approach. The magic date for them seems to be March 1990, when the current economic plan officially ends.

A few firms are reacting now. One U.S. firm is looking for new investments because "interest rates are nearly affordable." Another firm is looking to replace its dollar financing with long-term peso financing if it can convince a Mexican bank to fix it to something other than the 28-day treasury certificate. Another firm is doing the opposite—converting to dollar financing because it no longer fears the exposure of a devaluation. Numerous U.S. and Mexican brokerage houses and investment bankers are offering dollar financing packages for a 3 to 5 percent fee.

Some firms are even hunting for more pesos because the risks have decreased and the returns are still good. For example, the Cetes is paying a 33.1 annual percentage interest. Even when we adjust for the expected devaluation (14 percent), we still have a yield of nearly 20 percent. In the long term, there are still concerns. Consumer goods prices have been frozen for 20 months while inflation has gone up over 60 percent.

Questions

1. What should Drapcho do in Brazil? What steps can he take to deal with exchange exposure and the hyperinflation?

2. What should Drapcho do in Mexico? Should he be seeking peso financing, dollars financing, or both—or what?

3. How should Drapcho prepare for the various possible futures of these two economically attractive but unpredictable countries?

4. Should WEEP have stayed in the United States? Invested somewhere else, for instance, in a Pacific Rim NIC?

NOTES

1. D. K. Eiteman and A. I. Stonehill, *Multinational Business Finance*, 5th ed. (Reading, Mass.: Addison-Wesley, 1989), pp. 565–568.

2. Ibid., p. 566.

3. Stefan H. Robock and Kenneth Simmonds, *International Business and Multinational Enterprises*, 4th ed. (Homewood, Ill.: Richard D. Irwin, 1989), p. 550.

4. Ibid., p. 551.

REFERENCES AND
SELECTED READINGS

Batra, Raveendra N., Shabtai Donnenfeld, and Josef Hadar. "Hedging Behavior by Multinational Firms." *The Journal of International Business Studies* 13:3 (Winter 1982).

Choi, Jongmoo Jay. "A Model of Firm Valuation with Exchange Exposure." *The Journal of International Business Studies* 17:2 (Summer 1986).

Daley, Lane, James Jiambalvo, Gary Sundem, and Yasumasa Kondo. "Attitudes Toward Financial Control Systems in the United States and Japan." *The Journal of International Business Studies* 16:3 (Fall 1985).

Eiteman, David K., and Arthur I. Stonehill. *Multinational Business Finance*, 5th ed. Reading, Mass.: Addison-Wesley, 1989.

Gentry, James A., Dileep R. Mehta, S. K. Bhattacharya, Robert Cobbaut, and Jean-Louis Scaringella. "An International Study of Management Perceptions of the Working Capital Process." *The Journal of International Business Studies* 10:1 (Spring/Summer 1979).

Gernon, Helen. "The Effect of Translation on Multinational Corporations' Internal Performance Evaluation." *The Journal of International Business Studies* 14:1 (Spring/Summer 1983).

Jacque, Laurent L. "Management of Foreign Exchange Risk: A Review Article." *The Journal of International Business Studies* 12:1 (Spring/Summer 1981).

Kohlhagen, Steven W. "A Model of Optimal Foreign Exchange Hedging Without Exchange Rate Projections." *The Journal of International Business Studies* 9:2 (Fall 1978).

Michel, Allen, and Israel Shaked. "Multinational Corporations vs. Domestic Corporations: Financial Performance and Characteristics," *The Journal of International Business Studies* 17:3 (Fall 1986).

Rhee, S. Ghon, Rosita P. Chang, and Peter E. Koveos. "The Currency-of-Denomination Decision for Debt Financing." *The Journal of International Business Studies* 16:3 (Fall 1985).

Robock, Stefan H., and Kenneth Simmonds. *International Business and Multinational Enterprises*, 4th ed. Homewood, Ill.: Richard D. Irwin, 1989.

Sarathy, Ravi, and Sangit Chatterjee. "The Divergence of Japanese and U.S. Corporate Financial Structure." *The Journal of International Business Studies* 15:3 (Winter 1984).

Shaked, Israel. "Are Multinational Corporations Safer?" *The Journal of International Business Studies* 17:1 (Spring 1986).

Shapiro, Alan C. "Payments Netting in International Cash Management." *The Journal of International Business Studies* 9:2 (Fall 1978).

Vinso, Joseph D. "Financial Planning for the Multinational Corporations with Multiple Goals." *The Journal of International Business Studies* 13:3 (Winter 1982).

Wall Street Journal. "Peru Devises Novel Plan to Pay Debt with Products." March 26, 1987, page 24.

Wihlborg, Clas. "Economics of Exposure Management of Foreign Subsidiaries of MNCs." *The Journal of International Business Studies* 11:3 (Winter 1980).

18

International Supply Strategies: Production and Sourcing

- Become familiar with production strategies in foreign operations
- Understand the competitive advantages of a technology-directed strategy
- Understand how standardization to minimize costs per unit can be used as a production strategy
- Learn how to adapt production strategies to less developed countries
- Become familiar with the major impediments to standardization
- Understand why firms move to low-wage-rate countries
- Become familiar with the use of international sourcing

INTRODUCTION

Increasing global competition has made the development of production and sourcing strategies among the most important concerns of domestic as well as multinational firms. Even smaller firms can no longer treat international production and sourcing strategy as secondary to marketing or financial strategy. This chapter addresses two critical aspects of this important topic. First, production strategy is analyzed from global, regional, and individual country perspectives. Second, international sourcing is discussed from both intracompany and intercompany perspectives.

Any firm that markets abroad must "consider off shore as well as domestic production."[1] The strategy of maintaining all production in the home country and exporting to foreign markets is increasingly being met by protectionist policies that force consideration of foreign production. Once the decision has been made to establish manufacturing operations abroad, the focus of production strategy shifts to determining the degree of integration among these operations and the relationships among these units. This involves deciding which products or components will be produced in which plants as well as where the assembly of finished goods will take place. This integration and coordination is called *rationalization*. The firm has basically three choices: rationalization on a national, regional, or global level. In addition to determining the countries in which production will be located, the products to be manufactured in each plant, and the interplant relationships, the international firm must also select a specific site within each country, decide on the operational and technological design of each plant, and choose between acquiring an existing facility or constructing a new one. Finally, other market, organizational, competitive, and technological factors need to be considered in the development of production strategy.

The issue of internationalization of sourcing is usually considered for manufacturing firms since the make-buy decision is essentially the most basic production strategy decision. However, even for manufacturing firms, sourcing decisions amount to much more than choosing suppliers for raw materials; they may include decisions about purchasing component parts, subassemblies, and even finished goods. For example, Chrysler Corporation purchases finished automobiles from Mitsubishi to complement its line of small cars. To understand the importance of sourcing in international business, one cannot limit oneself to manufacturing firms; one must also consider international buying for domestic sales by retailers, wholesalers, or importers. Whether one considers shoes from Brazil, dried beef from Argentina, "boom boxes" from Japan, men's suits from Venezuela, or wine from Yugoslavia, one must recognize that international sourcing of finished goods is a major dimension of the international supply strategies of retailers, wholesalers, and importers. Stated simplistically, purchasing and buying are important aspects of an international supply strategy.

Finally, the tremendous quantity of goods that are sourced internationally, whether from affiliated or nonaffiliated firms, requires the international executive to have an in-depth understanding of techniques and processes of importing. See Chapter 15 on importing, exporting, and trade financing.

PRODUCTION STRATEGIES

Multinational firms adopt production strategies as a part of their overall strategy to achieve or retain their competitive position. These production strategies are an integral part of both worldwide and subsidiary business strategies. Once the firm has decided that international production is called for, it must address five key aspects of manufacturing strategy.

1. Deciding the location of facilities and the degree of integration among these operations
2. Developing manufacturing strategies that are consistent with the firm's overall business unit strategy
3. Selecting a specific site within each country
4. Deciding on the technological design of each plant
5. Choosing between acquiring or constructing the facility

Location and Integration of International Manufacturing

The first component of a production strategy is determining the location of international production facilities and the means of coordination or integration among worldwide manufacturing activities. One alternative is to maintain production in one location and to supply all other markets through exports. This can be viewed as the ultimate type of centralized control. With this type of strategy, there is obviously no need for integration among international manufacturing centers. There might, however, be problems of coordination between international and domestic manufacturing. This approach is typical of the way many large Japanese firms exploit foreign markets. Recently, even these firms have had to deviate from this approach because of protectionist barriers by importer nations. Overall, this strategy would seem most appropriate for smaller firms or for a firm just entering international markets. When larger firms follow this approach, the effects on the economy of the importing nation are largely negative: jobs are lost in both local manufacturing and the associated supplier chain, personal and corporate income tax revenues are reduced, trade deficits develop, and so forth. As a result, nations seek to limit market access.

A second alternative is to locate production operations in or accessible to markets of high or potentially high demand, and then to allow these plants to operate with little if any integration. This approach is the ultimate in decentralization of production strategy. Each production facility produces goods exclusively for that market. Such production operations resemble purely domestic firms because they tend to produce a range of products. International firms that operate in this manner are often called *multidomestic* rather than multinational. Multidomestic firms also tend to have more and smaller manufacturing operations abroad.

Between these two extremes of location strategy is a third approach that establishes foreign manufacturing operations but operates these as components of a globally or regionally integrated system. Firms adopting this approach tend to follow one of two procedures: Each plant may specialize in a product that it exports to all global or regional markets in which the firm competes, or each facility may specialize in the production of some component that is shipped to assembly plants in third countries.

Developing an Overall Production Strategy

The production strategy of a firm needs to be consistent with the business unit strategy as well as the realities of the firm's organization, markets, competition, and technology. Porter defines two generic types of business unit strategy that are of significance for the development of a production strategy: product differentiation and cost leadership.

With a strategy of product differentiation, the business unit attempts to create goods that are uniquely beneficial to customers and therefore command higher market prices, resulting in higher corporate profits. As a result, firms develop more diversified and complex product lines. Traditionally, this meant higher production costs due to the underutilization of specialized machinery and shorter production runs. The development of manufacturing equipment and systems with a greater range of product

In the quest for improved product quality and production efficiency, manufacturing jobs like welding are increasingly being done by computer-controlled robots instead of skilled workers. Scenes like the one above may soon be as rare as horse-drawn plows and ones like the one below may stop reminding us of science-fiction movies.

possibilities has greatly reduced this disadvantage of a differentiated product strategy. Therefore, when firms opt for a production strategy of differentiation or when there is rapid and frequent change in markets, competition, or customer demands, firms often utilize flexible manufacturing systems (FMS) to facilitate this continuing product adaptation.[2] This flexibility permits the creation of a variety of products at a low cost; such an approach is known as *economies of scope*. The ultimate extension of this push toward increased flexibility in the manufacture of a diverse and complex line of products is the development of computer-integrated manufacturing (CIM), which involves computer-aided design and engineering, cellular manufacturing, just-in-time inventory control, robotics, and a variety of other component technologies.[3]

With a cost leadership strategy, firms emphasize the reduction of labor, material, energy, and processing costs as well as cost controls to achieve above-average returns even at low market prices.[4] This generally results in low product-line complexity and manufacturing processes that are typified by continuous runs, machine-paced materials flows, and low levels of work-in-process inventories. Manufacturing processes of this type represent a production strategy of cost leadership and *economies of scale*.

When these business unit strategies and the production strategy components of each are extended into the arena of international business, it becomes evident that a strategy of product differentiation can be accomplished without highly technological and complex flexible manufacturing processes. The establishment of numerous and often smaller manufacturing operations, each with products developed and manufactured for a specific market, allows the same end result. From a worldwide perspective, these products represent a total corporation production strategy of product differentiation. These production processes are flexible not because of their technical complexity, but rather by their size, proximity to local markets, and technical simplicity. Manufacturing processes of this type represent a production strategy of product differentiation through *market intensivity*. Nevertheless changing technologies are of substantial importance for MNFs; see the following Global Insight. Thus, there are three production strategies, which Stobaugh and Telesio have labeled *technology-driven*, *low-cost*, and *marketing-intensive*, respectively.[5]

Technology-Driven Strategies

Firms using technology-driven production strategies are essentially using technology to create product and service differentiation. Technology-driven strategies seek to develop or utilize technologies that result in competitive advantages of quality, flexibility, and cost. Additionally, firms with a technology-driven production strategy generally wish to offer a continuing flow of technologically improved, high-performance, and high technology products to their customers. This is accomplished by the development and implementation of production processes that stress primarily production quality and flexibility and, secondarily, cost minimization. Such firms generally serve the large, high-income markets of advanced industrialized nations, which demand frequent changes in both production volume and products. Because accurate sales projections are difficult for such products, volume flexibility is important. Since the product's features and performance are the major competitive weapon, manufacturing costs are not of primary importance.

Good communication with and swift response to market changes are essential. The initial plant will ordinarily be located in a highly industrialized country because of the availability of a well-educated and skilled labor work force. This pattern is slowly changing because of the rapid spread of technology and the proliferation of foreign subsidiaries, which permit the simultaneous introduction of products in different markets.

Firms with a technology-driven production strategy generally do not attempt to substitute labor for capital even in low-wage-rate countries. Such firms often adopt identical processing, tooling, and equipment throughout the world except where there is a need to accommodate variations in the grade of local raw materials.

Stages of Foreign Manufacturing Investment In the early stages of foreign investment, technology-driven firms tend to establish only assembly plants abroad. As demand increases, the assembly operations are replaced by full-scale manufacturing. Plants serving local or regional markets are generally limited to assembly. In still smaller markets, production may be limited to component parts intended for assembly elsewhere. In larger market areas, plants generally include all phases of production. IBM's manufacturing strategy, cited by Stobaugh and Telesio, illustrates these points.

> Market considerations determined the order in which the company established its foreign operations (1925 in Germany, 1935 in Italy and 1950 in Brazil) and the type of products each turns out (the more advanced goods being produced first in the larger, higher-income markets). In the mid-1970s, for example, IBM used about half the capacity of its German facility to build central processing units but only a quarter of its Italian facility and none of its Brazilian facility.[6]

Managing Technology For firms using a technology-driven strategy, research and development play an extremely important role since they are the source of both product and process development. Technology management is, therefore, an important concern of production strategy. Policy decisions pertaining to R&D tend to be centralized at the corporate headquarters, while normal manufacturing decisions are handled in a more decentralized manner. Despite the essentiality of technology, R&D units may be associated with foreign plants to assist in the transfer of complex technology, the adaptation of products to the local market, or the modification of processes to facilitate the use of local materials.

Technology Trends Change MNF Production

The rate of technological change presents a complex challenge for the way multinational firms manufacture their products. Among these are 13 trends and developments that will continue to reshape the face of worldwide manufacturing for decades to come.

1. *Production Flexibility.* The continuing development of computer-based production technologies and information systems is making possible flexibility in manufacturing that was unheard of in the past. These combined with techniques such as just-in-time inventory or materials control, total quality control, MRP, CIM, and robotics are allowing the rapid changes of production volume, product mix, and retooling that allow firms to "turn on a dime."

2. *Merging Telecommunications and Computing.* The more rapid communication and utilization of data further facilitate flexible manufacturing.

3. *Cross-Functional and Cross-Organizational Ties.* Computer-based information systems allow business functions (finance, marketing, manufacturing, and so forth) within organizations to integrate their activities and facilitates ties with suppliers and customers.

4. *Computer Obsolescence.* Today's computers will be obsolete within 10 years. In the complex task of mechanical design, we will see increased use of "super computers."

5. *New Ways to Measure Success.* Traditional accounting methods do not properly assess the payback of advanced manufacturing technologies or the cost of falling behind competitors in the world of high tech, flexible manufacturing.

6. *More Cooperative Ventures.* In areas of basic research and new product or process introductions, there will be increased levels of corporate alliances and private/public initiatives.

7. *Upgraded Skills Required.* Increased engineering and information systems skills will be required of both workers and managers.

8. *Reorganization of Production.* The increasing importance of technology and automation will require that management reorganize the very nature of production activities.

9. *New Division of Labor.* Fewer employees will be needed in production supervision and production planning, while more people will be employed in sales, R&D, engineering design, and information systems.

10. *Microfactories.* Manufacturing facilities will be developed for use by several companies on a time-share basis. These will be continuously reprogrammed to make differing products without losing their scale economies.

11. *"Designer" Materials.* Technological advances will allow the development of materials that are designed to have properties that precisely fit a firm's cost and properties specifications.

12. *Artificial Intelligence.* By the year 2000, most companies and governments will use computers with artificial intelligence to assimilate data and solve problems.

13. *High Tech Growth Industries.* The growth industries of the next century will be biotechnology, computers, electronics, industrial materials, superconductivity, and transport equipment.

Source: Adapted from Ann Blumberg, "Technology-Based Trends That Will Change the Way MNCs Make Their Products," *Business International*, January 23, 1989, p. 22.

Another technological concern is the issue of the licensing of technology. Although some firms are quite liberal in their licensing policies, this might be unwise since it could stimulate price competition or create problems in the establishment of a worldwide manufacturing network. (See the section on licensing in Chapter 13.)

Eventually, product technologies mature and markets for those products become more competitive. This maturity manifests itself in lower unit profit margins and causes firms to seek ways to lower manufacturing costs and generate other revenues. In these situations, firms tend to move away from a technology-driven strategy and toward cost minimization.

Marketing-Intensive Strategies

Firms following a marketing-intensive strategy also seek to prosper from differentiated products but do so by decentralizing operations to specific country markets. Marketing, not low cost, is the source of competitive advantage for firms following this strategy. Nevertheless, manufacturing plays a vital role. Establishing numerous production plants, each dedicated to a market, lets the firm respond quickly to changes in the volume of market demand, facilitates product adaptation to local tastes, and allows for the use of local ingredients. This market responsiveness outweighs the benefits that would come from centralized production. In fact, reductions in cost usually have little effect on profit margins or on sales because differentiated products are usually priced well above manufacturing costs and are relatively insensitive to price changes.[7]

For firms following a strategy of market-intensive product differentiation, little R&D is conducted abroad, although products are adapted to local tastes and specifications. Licensing is not a significant issue for such firms since they seldom possess technologies that are attractive to licensees or they are not willing to accept the loss of market control. For example, Colgate-Palmolive has virtually no licensing agreements.[8]

Since there are few intracompany shipments, centralized manufacturing control is not necessary. Major decisions regarding location and capacity may receive the attention of headquarters, but the day-to-day operations are left to local managers.

Technology-driven production strategies emphasize production flexibility and quality to achieve competitive advantage, while market-intensive strategies rely on product differentiation.

As these markets expand and mature, the scale and scope of productive activities broaden to more complete operations, competition becomes more intense, and cost minimization becomes a more significant concern. This cost competition can result in the firm having to shift its production strategy to one of cost minimization.

Low-Cost Strategy

A low-cost production strategy is usually required when the product market is mature or price competition is intense. A firm in this situation will have to either compete in a niche of the market or seek to maximize its profits through cost reduction. Cost reduction can be accomplished in several ways:

achieving economies of scale through standardization and large-scale operations, or locating operations in countries with low labor, raw material, and
energy costs. Economies of scale in production normally result in substantial
production process complexity: larger, automated plants with greater specialization in work force and equipment. These, together with greater intracompany flows of components, make the manufacturing system more
predictable and make centralized control more desirable.

Economies of Scale   Establishing economies of scale is an important method
for reducing production costs. There are two components for establishing
economies of scale. First, economies of scale can be achieved at the subsidiary level by establishing large-scale operations so that the subsidiary can
purchase in larger quantities and therefore at lower prices, making the most
efficient use of human resources. Second, the firm can achieve economies
of scale on a regional or global basis by standardizing the design and
operation of production facilities. The advantages and disadvantages of standardization, methods for implementing standardization, and alternative production strategies are discussed later, in the section on production design.

Whether through large-scale operations or standardization, economies
of scale are strongly dependent on the well-understood advantages of specialization. In the EEC, many American firms have used standardization
and the mass production of components in specialized plants to achieve
economies of scale. High freight costs can be offset and the tailoring of final
products to market or customer needs can be achieved by assembling final
products in the markets where they are sold. Economies of scale discourage
the substitution of labor for capital since in high-volume operations, labor
costs are a relatively small portion of total costs. R&D is not necessary in
overseas operations since products are standardized.

Low-cost strategies through economies of scale require centralized control by corporate headquarters to ensure minimum costs. When shipments
are made among the various subsidiaries, control must be exercised over
shipping schedules and product quality to ensure smooth operations in the
various facilities. Corporate or regional headquarters often set quantities
and prices on intracompany shipments and issue instructions for production
scheduling, quality, cost standards, inventory, transportation of products,
and materials storage. Under such conditions, it is advantageous to license
technology only when the technology owner does not enjoy a dominant
position in the industry and when competing technologies have a number
of different sellers.

Low-Cost Labor   Some firms attempt to achieve low-cost production strategy by locating their facilities in low-wage-rate countries. In such situations,
the scale of operation and the span of production should be limited. Such
operations are usually labor-intensive; however, the firm should not ignore
the possibility of automating some aspects of production. The production of
electronic products in newly industrialized or developing countries such as

Singapore, Hong Kong, South Korea, Costa Rica, or Haiti provides an example of this type of approach.

As with other low-cost strategies, corporate headquarters must exercise control where integration among subsidiary operations is involved.

Minimizing Other Input Costs   Low-cost strategy also calls for minimizing the cost of other manufacturing inputs. Access to a reliable and abundant source of low-cost energy is often important. Locating operations in countries containing critical raw materials can result in savings in transportation charges and ensure an abundant supply—as, for example, when a petrochemical firm invests in Saudi Arabia. Unless the final market for the product is in the same country, it makes sense to limit the span of operations to the stage of production that makes use of the low-cost input. Plant size will follow an industry's economy of scale just as the choice of technology will follow the varying quality of the raw materials.

The extent of integration with other plants in the system will determine the degree of corporate involvement by the corporate headquarters. Centralized control becomes less important if the end product is primarily sold in the local market.

A low-cost production strategy can be achieved through economies of scale and standardization, or by seeking areas of low labor and other input costs.

Site Selection Within the Host Country

Firms often spend more time selecting a location within a country than selecting the country itself.[9] This is easy to understand when one thinks of the substantial internal differences that can exist in large countries regarding energy cost, labor (availability, skills, wages, and attitudes toward management), infrastructural development, land costs, transportation considerations, tax rates, and so forth. These considerations may be further complicated by the availability of government incentives for firms to locate in particular regions. In addition to the standard business or economic factors, many firms consider the quality-of-life implications for their expatriates: schools, health care systems, acceptance of foreigners, and so forth. High technology firms also look for areas that have major universities nearby. These not only provide highly educated employees but also can serve as a source of technical expertise and contract services.

Although there is no universally applicable formula for selecting a location within a country, such decisions can usually be explained by several variables.

Economic Issues

Labor availability, skills, costs, and attitudes

Taxes and incentives

Land and construction costs

Energy and utilities, availability, and costs

Business Issues

Accessibility to markets

Availability of materials and components

Transportation systems

Level of industrialization

Employee Issues

Living conditions

Health care availability and quality

Educational opportunities

Economic, business, and employee issues influence the selection and location of plants.

Plant Design: Operational and Technological Factors

In designing foreign production operations, management has two dimensions to consider. The first concerns the overall strategy: technology-driven, market-intensive or low-cost, each of which calls for a different process design. Technology-driven strategies call for a production process that provides economies of scope and flexibility. Market-intensive strategies require processes that are small, localized, and flexible. Low-cost strategies usually demand economies of scale, standardization, and rationalization on a regional or global basis. The second factor to be considered in deciding on a production design is the level of development and size of the host market or the accessibility of the market to be served from the production facility. The combination of corporate strategy and the nature of the host market determines whether management should transfer an existing production design, develop a hybrid design, or engineer an entirely new and country-specific production process.

For firms following a low-cost strategy, one of the most important considerations is that of standardizing operations across subsidiaries.

Advantages of Standardization

Standardization of production processes and procedures results in a number of cost savings at both the subsidiary and corporate headquarters levels. First, it simplifies the production organization at corporate headquarters. Plant design is simplified since each new facility is a scaled-up or scaled-down version of the existing one. Fewer technical experts are required to assist overseas operations. Technicians from domestic operations can be used for temporary foreign projects. The uniformity in production methods eliminates the need for separate specifications for each plant. Equipment change notices can be given with one standard mailing, thus reducing costs and errors. The purchasing can be consolidated to generate quantity discounts.

Second, standardization enables management to rationalize the production of components among subsidiaries to achieve economies of scale and lower production costs on a global or regional scale. Thus, the firm can move toward the production of identical products globally or regionally. Boorstin states that the "supreme law" of our age is convergence of products and global commonality of markets.[10] Successful firms have reacted to this trend by increasing the sale of standardized products in all parts of the world.[11] Global rationalization generally will not work when consumer tastes and preferences differ markedly.

Third, standardization also results in economies in logistics (see Chapter 16). Savings can be achieved by organizing all production facilities into one logistical supply system, thus controlling the movement of raw materials, parts, and finished inventory. Fourth, standardization of production facilitates the control of quality and maintenance. When production equipment is similar, all plants can be expected to adhere to the same standards. Manufacturing reports can be quickly analyzed and deviations spotted. After allowing for differences in human and environmental factors (culture, dust, humidity, temperature), standard machinery should have the same frequency of maintenance. Fifth, production control is also easier. The same machinery should produce at a similar rate; thus, it is easier to estimate production levels. Sixth, the construction of new plants is greatly facilitated: planning, design, and engineer time is reduced. Design engineers need only copy existing drawings and lists of materials. The same equipment can be purchased from the same vendors. Manufacturing specifications from other facilities can be used with little or no alteration. Accurate forecasts can be made regarding construction time. In essence, standardization eliminates many of the difficulties inherent to new operations and allows cost savings in existing operations.

In designing operations abroad, consideration must be given to the type of strategy that is adopted to compete in a given market.

Obstacles to Standardization

Although standardization would seem to be the answer to many of the production problems of global multinationals, it is not without its drawbacks, especially in developing nations. Because infrastructure is lacking and the markets are segmented in many less developed countries, standardization might be all but impossible. The labor-intensiveness of general purpose machines can actually be more productive than capital-intensive equipment. Automation does not increase productivity if the machines are operated only a fraction of the time; production costs can be very high despite low labor costs.

Cultural factors also influence standardization. Where there is a lack of skilled workers, specialized machinery might be favored because unskilled workers can be more quickly trained. Highly automated operations are highly efficient only if they are used uninterruptedly. Absenteeism by production workers, the setup crew, or the maintenance crew could shut down an entire line.

Political factors can force management into a no-win situation. Countries may emphasize job creation that favors labor-intensive operations but for reasons of prestige insist on the most modern, automated equipment, which requires fewer workers. Labor-intensive operations are generally more appropriate for developing nations since these would create more employment, require less capital, result in a wider distribution of purchasing power, have shorter setup and breakdown times, and require lower skills in maintenance, equipment operation, and management.[12]

Deficiencies in supplier capabilities also impede standardization. In developing nations suppliers often depend on the buyers to provide them with tooling and technical assistance, whereas in industrialized nations, suppliers often provide the technical know-how and even design component parts or processes and tooling for their customers.

Technical or legal factors can also inhibit standardization. For example, motor vehicles must be designed with consideration as to horsepower, road speed, weight, longevity, reliability, and driver convenience. Local standards must be considered such as the use of the metric system and safety standards.

Cultural, economic, political, legal, and other factors act as impediments to standardization as a production strategy.

Developing Hybrid and New Production Designs

Although many managers see a production plant and its operation as a fixed constant, those who would be successful internationally must view production design as a variable. In other words, to be successful internationally one cannot view a production operation as a set of machines tended by individuals performing tasks. This view leads to the conclusion that these machines can be put anywhere and staffed by any individuals, and they will work the same as at home. This orientation is particularly troublesome for the firms that need to standardize as a means to achieve a low-cost strategy. It tends to diminish managerial ability to see the possibilities for developing new or hybrid production systems that can still be integrated into a global or regional system.

There are many steps management can take to implement some degree of standardization. Hybrid forms of production design can be developed making use of degrees of automation and standardization. For example, automated welding rather than hand welding might be used, while painting, packaging, and materials handling might be performed manually. Many less developed countries prefer this kind of production process and the associated intermediate technologies that are transferred to the host nation. This approach requires that multinationals develop manufacturing methods to suit environments rather than transfer older technologies. In these hybrid systems, capital-intensive methods should be maintained where reliable delivery and consistent quality are important or where components are shipped for further assembly.

If one views the production process as a variable to be adapted to the environment in which it operates, then the machines, work flow, workers, and activities themselves become variables. Management becomes aware of the need to question the correctness and propriety of what goes on in the plant. Not only are machines reexamined but also the levels of worker training, the nature of compensation, the specifications of materials, the nature of labor-management relations, and so forth are scrutinized. The results of such redesign could result in more effective and efficient functioning of the plant and more amicable relations with local national employees. In many cases management can also reduce its capital costs substantially.

Nowhere is the need for reassessment of plant design more important than with the degree of automation and the associated capital versus labor trade-off for production operations in less developed countries. On this important question, management must recognize that automation versus handcraft is not an either/or issue. Indeed, management can automate the production of some components and not others; automation is a matter of degree. The best approach is to adapt the production technology to the specifics of the local situation. There are seven criteria for deciding on the degree of automation that is most appropriate:

1. Scale of production
2. Quality requirements
3. Sophistication of suppliers
4. Technical and managerial skills of production management
5. Wage rates relative to capital costs
6. Labor considerations
7. Employment goals of the host nation[13]

This adaptation generally involves scaling down the size of operations and modifying production techniques to use less sophisticated equipment. See Table 18.1 for alternative production designs.

Table 18.1   **Production Plant Design Alternatives**

	Corporate Production Strategy		
Level of country development	*Technology-driven*	*Market-intensive*	*Low-cost*
Advanced industrialized	Economies of scope (flexible systems)	Localized	Economies of scale (large-scale operations, standardization)
Large, developing	Modified-scope economies (flexible systems, industrial goods)	Localized	Modified-scale economies (large-scale, hybrid technology)
Small, developing	Localized or new (flexible systems technology)	Localized	Localized or new (flexible systems technology)

Acquiring an Existing Facility or Constructing a New One

A question that must be answered for each country in which a firm wants to establish operations is whether to construct a new facility or acquire an existing one. Obviously, an important consideration is whether an appropriate facility can be found and purchased, but there are also other factors. First is the relative costs of the two options. Second, when the new firm acquires an existing firm, competition is simultaneously eliminated. Third, an acquisition usually brings with it an experienced management team and work force. Fourth, acquisition usually provides an established distribution system. Fifth, acquiring an existing operation can save time. Sixth, acquiring an operation prevents one's competitors from acquiring that production capacity.

> A hybrid form of production design adapted to a particular environment might be the most suitable, especially in less developed countries.

The negative factors include acquiring old equipment and perhaps labor or management problems. If the firm being acquired is currently locally owned, one should not ignore the reaction of the local government to having productive capacity passing into the hands of foreign nationals. In fact, many countries have laws regulating, restricting, or prohibiting "alien takeovers." If the acquisition involves a merger or joint venture, then there are numerous possible problems. (See Chapter 13.)

Production Problems in LDCs

Less developed countries present unique problems for firms from large and highly developed nations. Countries in the early stages of industrialization, with limited market size and small-scale production operations, are characterized by high unit costs because of the use of less specialized machinery and processes. Less specialized techniques raise direct labor inputs and the smaller-scale plants increase indirect overhead costs. These considerations result in a squeeze on profits.

Manufacturing in diverse cultural environments brings a new dimension into many conventional decisions in production management. There is often an inadequate supply of managerial and technical personnel to plan and carry out the production programs. Training managers is one of the basic problems that firms must address in developing countries. Professionalism in management must be put in the place of paternalism. Decisions must be based on ability and productivity rather than kinship and personal relations.

INTERNATIONAL SOURCING AND PROCUREMENT STRATEGIES

For the remainder of this century, both domestic and international firms will face increasingly intense competition. In contrast to the situation in past decades, raw materials now are becoming less important, while component parts and subassemblies are becoming more important.[14] In their attempt to remain competitive, firms will have to find lower-cost and better quality sources for finished goods and component parts. The rapid development of manufacturing capacity throughout the world, especially in the newly industrialized countries of the Pacific Rim, presents not only new competitors but also new sources for these components.

Three basic strategies guide this new quest for international sourcing. These new strategies can involve both intercompany and intracompany transfers of goods. The first involves finding suppliers, the second forming joint ventures, and the last establishing wholly owned operations. Where a firm's requirements are short term, vender relationships may suffice. Larger firms with long-term requirements will usually opt for an equity relationship, either joint ventures or wholly owned operations. These two equity involvement sourcing strategies are especially attractive because of the savings possibilities associated with intracompany sales of components and the control over quality and availability.

In less developed countries, sourcing is also a major concern that often leads to international purchasing of components. Procurement is one of the most critical problems in these countries. Scarcity of the production factors as well as problems of cost, quality, and delivery are major considerations in the design and management of production systems in LDCs. When these problems are amplified by local content legislation requiring the use of domestic materials and parts regardless of quality or costs, companies might even be forced to temporarily or permanently shut down operations.

As a result of inadequate procurement sources, considerable managerial talent has to be devoted to cultivating domestic suppliers, instructing them in industrial techniques, and developing quality control and other aspects of the productive process. This is in marked contrast to the case in industrial countries, where much of the technical know-how comes from parts suppliers who even advise manufacturers on product design and production techniques.

Retail firms also source globally. The convergence of product style and performance characteristics as well as global competitiveness means that goods produced in Korea or Sweden may well satisfy market needs in the United States or Egypt. From automobiles to tableware, examples of the increasing importance of global purchasing are everywhere.

In all aspects of sourcing, some common questions play a role in determining whether to source locally or internationally:

1. Are there local shortages?
2. Are foreign exchange controls a significant concern?
3. What are the cost differences after considering tariffs, subsidies, insurance, freight, and so forth?
4. Does the firm have the available importing skills and if not, what are the costs and inconveniences of using outsiders?

Globally competitive success requires that both retailers and manufacturers source globally for high quality and low-cost components and finished goods.

5. Is there a significant antiforeign bias among the customers?

6. How sensitive is organized labor to the firm's importing foreign goods or components, and what is their likely reaction?

7. Do foreign goods have an appeal to customers?[15]

SUMMARY

Production strategy constitutes one component in the overall operational strategy of a multinational enterprise. Firms may adopt different production strategies to gain a competitive edge over rival manufacturers. Some firms use technology as a means of achieving their production strategy. Research and development are important to such firms, whether they are developing new products or adapting existing ones to the market. Firms emphasizing technology usually establish their initial production facilities in highly developed countries.

Other firms use a marketing-intensive production strategy in which they build numerous smaller factories in end-user markets and adopt highly localized production processes. Still other firms employ a low-cost strategy. With such strategies, the firm may stress standardization and large-scale production, resulting in economy of scale. One of the problems of standardization is its application in the less developed countries. Under these circumstances, a firm may attempt to overcome this disadvantage by developing a hybrid production system—that is, automate some aspects of production while using labor-intensive methods in others.

A low-cost production strategy can also be achieved by establishing plants in low-wage-rate nations. A related approach is to locate operations in countries with an abundance of low-cost raw material and energy.

The site for a production plant within a country can be as important as the country selected. Thus, management must weigh costs and other criteria for in-country site selection. Sourcing is also an important dimension of an international supply strategy. Increasingly, both manufacturers and retailers or wholesalers are sourcing globally for the best cost, quality, and delivery. ☐

KEY TERMS AND CONCEPTS

Economies of scale	Production strategy
Economies of scope	Rationalization
Capital-intensive process	Standardization
Labor-intensive process	Technology-driven strategy

REVIEW QUESTIONS

1. Discuss briefly why process flexibility is considered more important than cost of production in technology-driven strategies.

2. In a marketing-intensive strategy, are low costs essential for such product lines to survive? Explain.

3. Why are economies of scale important for a low-cost production strategy?

4. When a U.S. multinational firm moves to a low-wage-rate country, is the firm exploiting the foreign workers? Is it hurting American workers?

5. Briefly describe critical inputs, other than labor, that might enable a firm to achieve a low-cost strategy.

6. Discuss briefly some of the problems that arise in the management of production systems in the LDCs.

7. Explain what is meant by economies of scope.

DISCUSSION CASE

Production Strategy Changes at Minolta

Minolta Camera Company, Ltd., had sales in 1988 of $2.3 billion; nearly 75 percent of these were outside of Japan. Originally Minolta followed the standard Japanese practice of producing in Japan and exporting to markets overseas. Later they shifted production overseas to developing countries in search of lower costs. For example, Minolta currently manufactures camera parts and assembles cameras in Malaysia. Minolta believes that today that is not enough. Minolta believes that companies have to localize their operations and integrate with the local economies and communities. They must offer technical services, tailor their products to their local customer needs and even develop software.

These changes are part of a rethinking of Minolta's overall production and supply strategy. Hideo Tashima, president of Minolta, has come to the conclusion that changes in the global business environment require the successful integration of business operation on a global scale. "The world, in a business context, is shrinking," says Tashima. "Companies can no longer take a single-market approach to overseas business." A combination of a maturing industry and trade tensions in Minolta's key markets of Europe and North America have necessitated this strategic redirection.

Minolta hopes that this new localization will help avoid trade criticisms and restrictions in the United States, where protectionism seems to be on the rise. As a result of this new strategy, Minolta has plans for the construction of a toner plant in the United States, which may ultimately produce other products. Relatedly, it will be substantially more difficult to do busi-

By Don R. Beeman, 1989.
Source: Adapted from "Global Japan," *Fortune*, July 31, 1989, p. S-61.
This case was developed for class discussion only. It is not intended to represent good or bad management or decision-making.

ness in Europe after 1992 for firms without production sites within the EC. Duties and local content legislation could make exporting to the EC prohibitively expensive or impossible. As a result, Minolta plans to expand its European operations; it currently has a copier plant in West Germany. This strategy of localization is also under way for large markets in developing nations. Minolta recently opened a copier plant in Manaus, Brazil.

According to Tashima, Minolta is "optimistic about future business prospects not only in the U.S. but in global market as a whole."

Questions

1. Describe Minolta's evolving global production strategy in terms of the Stobaugh and Telesio framework.

2. Do you think Minolta's new strategy is the result of market dynamics or trade barriers?

3. What are the downside or potential negative consequences of Minolta's new strategies?

4. What are the implications of these new strategies for Minolta's domestic (U.S.) competitors?

5. If you were one of Minolta's competitors would you need to reassess your own production strategies?

NOTES

1. Heidi Vernon Wortzel and Lawrence H. Wortzel, *Strategic Management of Multinational Corporations: The Essentials* (New York: John Wiley & Sons, 1985), p. 313.

2. Suresh Kotha and Daniel Orne, "Generic Manufacturing Strategies: A Conceptual Synthesis," *Strategic Management Journal* 10 (1989), 225.

3. William J. Doll and Mark A. Vonderembse, "Forging a Partnership to Achieve Competitive Advantage: The CIM Challenge," *MIS Quarterly* 11:2 (June 1987), 207–209.

4. Kotha and Orne, pp. 224–225.

5. Robert Stobaugh and Piero Telesio, "Match Manufacturing Policies and Product Strategies," *Harvard Business Review* 2 (March/April, 1983), 113–120.

6. Ibid., pp. 114–115.

7. Ibid., pp. 117–118.

8. Ibid., p. 118.

9. Richard D. Robinson, *International Business Management*, 2nd ed. (Hinsdale, Ill.: Dryden Press, 1978), p. 156.

10. Daniel J. Boorstin, *The Americans* (New York: Random House, 1973), p. 284.

11. Ibid., p. 284.

12. S. B. Prasad and Y. Krishna Shetty, *An Introduction to Multinational Management* (Englewood Cliffs, N.J.: Prentice-Hall, 1976), pp. 125–129.

13. Jack Baranson, "Automated Manufacturing in Developing Economies," *Finance and Development* 8:4 (1971), 12.

14. Daniel F. Hefler, "Global Sourcing: Offshore Investment Strategy for the 1980s," *Journal of Business Strategy* 2:1 (Summer 1981), 7.

15. Robinson, p. 140.

REFERENCES AND SELECTED READINGS

Boorstin, Daniel J. *The Americans*. New York: Random House, 1973.

Baranson, Jack. "Automated Manufacturing in Developing Economies." *Finance and Development* 8:4 (1971).

Doll, William J., and Mark A. Vonderembse. "Forging a Partnership to Achieve Competitive Advantage: The CIM Challenge." *MIS Quarterly* 11:2 (June 1987).

Hefler, Daniel F. "Global Sourcing: Offshore Investment Strategy for the 1980s." *Journal of Business Strategy* 2:1 (Summer 1981).

Kotha, Suresh, and Daniel Orne. "Generic Manufacturing Strategies: A Conceptual Synthesis." *Strategic Management Journal* (1989).

Prasad, S. B., and Y. K. Shetty. *An Introduction to Multinational Management*. Englewood Cliffs, N.J.: Prentice-Hall, 1976.

Robinson, Richard D. *International Business Management*, 2nd ed. Hinsdale, Ill.: Dryden Press, 1978.

Starr, Martin K. "Global Production and Operations Strategy." *Columbia Journal of World Business*, Winter 1984.

Stobaugh, Robert, and Piero Telesio. "Match Manufacturing Policies and Product Strategy." *Harvard Business Review* 2 (March/April, 1983).

Wortzel, Heidi Vernon, and Lawrence H. Wortzel. *Strategic Management of Multinational Corporations: The Essentials*. New York: John Wiley & Sons, 1985.

CHAPTER

19

Human Resource Management

LEARNING OBJECTIVES

- Learn the major problems in recruiting personnel for overseas operations

- Become familiar with the sources of expatriate managers and the criteria for selection

- Explain predeparture orientation of expatriates and spouses

- Understand the purposes for training and development programs

- Learn how and why expatriate training is different from host training

- Explain the methods of compensation used by most multinational firms

- Understand how firms evaluate the performance of overseas managers

- Understand labor relations problems and the role of labor unions in overseas operations

- Describe the role of the host government in the management of both local nationals and expatriates

- Become familiar with some of the problems and decisions a subsidiary manager must make in hiring, training, and compensating workers

INTRODUCTION

In international business, as in domestic business, people are the most important asset of the firm and the key ingredient for success. A firm will succeed or fail on the basis of its ability to manage effectively its human resources in the headquarters and subsidiaries.

The objective of this chapter is to introduce the problems a human resource manager faces when placed in charge of recruiting, hiring, training, assigning, supervising, compensating, evaluating, promoting, and dealing with overseas personnel, both managerial and nonmanagerial, in the extraordinarily complex environment of the multinational corporation. Furthermore, this chapter discusses the various options available to the multinational firm for growth and development through the intelligent management of people.

RECRUITMENT AND SELECTION OF MANAGERS

A multinational firm can follow one of three policies regarding the recruitment and selection of employees. It may follow an ethnocentric policy, using home country personnel to staff its positions at home and abroad. It may follow a polycentric policy by staffing home country positions with personnel from the home country and foreign positions with host country nationals. Finally, it may follow a geocentric policy by staffing key positions at home and abroad without regard to the nationality of the person. Whichever policy the firm follows, the first step is still finding those persons with the right mix of attitudes, knowledge, and skills, and this is not as simple as it seems.

Sources of International Manager Personnel

Sources for the recruitment of managerial personnel vary with the firm and the practice within a country. If a firm is entering the international arena for the first time, chances are that a foreign manager will be recruited from within the firm—perhaps an export manager with little or no overseas experience but with a general understanding of international business. If the firm has acquired an existing subsidiary, the executive of the acquired firm will probably be left in charge. Another source is someone who has held such a position with another firm.

If the firm is a well-established multinational, sources for recruitment will vary from country to country. In societies where the social class of the individual determines economic position, managers generally come from the upper classes. In Britain and the United States, there is no elite class from which managers come. In Japan, the educational elite (graduates of top universities) customarily dominate the top and middle-management positions of major corporations and government. Similarly, in France most top positions in government as well as industry come from very few key schools. Robinson lists six additional sources of prospective employees:

1. Recruitment of foreign students or alumni of domestic schools of engineering, business, and management

2. Recruitment of students and alumni from recognized management development schools abroad

3. Application to the files of such organizations as the Institute of International Education in New York City

4. Development of a company-sponsored management training program for foreign nationals

5. Reference to the Home Country Employment Registry of foreign students in the United States, located at Tulane University

6. Utilization of one or more management recruitment organizations operating in the countries of interest.[1]

Seeking candidates for international management positions from among university graduates is more common in Europe and Japan than in the

United States. A potential source that is currently underutilized by American firms are the foreign students who are enrolled in American universities to study business administration, engineering, or related areas. Some companies recruit these individuals for subsidiary positions in their home country and even pay to fly them there for interviews with subsidiary management; however, very few firms recruit these students for employment in the parent corporation. After hiring, these students are often exposed to the environmental conditions of the parent company to complement their university training. Through such exposure, they will better understand the operations of the headquarters and be better able to communicate with the parent firm.

Despite the rapid increase in the number of female managers over the past ten years, women have made little headway in getting foreign assignments. Affirmative action has helped many achieve top positions in the United States and western Europe, but those desiring foreign positions with MNCs are generally excluded, either explicitly or implicitly. Although some do not make the effort to apply for overseas positions or reject an offer when tendered, many more are turned down during the selection process.[2] The reason generally given is that they will not be able to function effectively due to sex discrimination and sexist attitudes in the host country.

Cultural biases do exist against women in many countries of the Middle East, Latin America, and Asia. When women are assigned to managerial positions in these countries, the immediate reaction is negative. Local nationals in many countries have the attitude that women will have less influence at headquarters. There are, however, a number of countries where women have had quite an impact in managerial positions, especially in the northern European countries. There would seem to be no valid reasons for excluding women from these countries. Furthermore, it would seem to be in managements' best interests to recruit and develop minority candidates for international management positions. There is no doubt that in many countries black, Hispanic, and Asian-American managers would have some inherent advantages as subsidiary managers.

Because of the limited sources for qualified overseas managerial candidates and to minimize the future problems of recruitment, some firms keep detailed records of potential candidates for such positions. Employees are categorized under such characteristics as adaptability, motivation, job satisfaction, technical competence, travel, and family flexibility.

American MNCs generally seek international managers from within the corporation, while the MNCs of many other countries recruit graduates of leading universities.

Selecting Top Managers for a Firm's International Operations

Most top executives at the headquarters of U.S. multinational corporations are home country nationals. Their selection is based on past performance in top management positions. Unfortunately, many of these key executives have few cross-cultural experiences. Generally, they are less familiar with the types of decision that might be most appropriate in their dealings with subsidiaries. On the other hand, employing home country nationals in international management positions at headquarters will eliminate many of the intrafirm communication problems.

Selecting Managers for Overseas Assignment

The selection of a manager who is capable of making decisons without consulting corporate headquarters might well determine the success or failure of a foreign operation; therefore, the first task facing the multinational corporation when it establishes a subsidiary in a foreign country is to staff that operation with the most qualified individuals.

Business International reports that American MNCs have failure rates between 10 percent and 50 percent.[3] A part of this high failure rate can be attributed to inadequate human resource management. There is clearly a need for improvement in the recruitment, selection, and training of managers of foreign operations. Greater emphasis must be placed on the candidates' adaptability and other characteristics. The candidate with the most relevant expertise and the greatest technical competency might be least suitable if the individual's family is unable to adapt to living abroad or if the individual is unable to deal with the host nationals as equals.

The type of government and its attitude toward foreign operations, the stage of economic development, and the social or business customs often make it difficult to apply domestic management practices to the foreign operation. For an expatriate, these difficulties are compounded by unfamiliarity with the language, beliefs, superstitions, expectations, and other factors in the host country. For example, in most countries customs generally determine the relationship between management and labor, so the role of the superior toward the subordinate varies from country to country. Using a supervisor's given name is strictly taboo in many countries. Formality is often carried over to the dress code. Participative management may be encouraged in some countries and discouraged in others. The commonly accepted American concepts of equal opportunity and merit promotions are not universally accepted. Seniority, age, or social class often determines who becomes a manager, while competence regardless of age or social status may be the determining factor in others.

Managers might be expected to become directly involved in the personal affairs of their employees, or to maintain an impersonal and formalized attitude away from the place of employment. In many Arab countries, the manager is expected to provide counsel to employees with personal problems such as illness, marital difficulties, or financial concerns. In Japan, large corporations take a personal interest in the welfare of their employees and provide such fringe benefits as housing, recreation, vacation cottages, educational opportunities, and lifetime employment, and even serve as "go-betweens" in marriages.

Recruitment Policies

The responsibility for recruiting a staff for the different international business positions may be centered at the home office or it may be decentralized, with the final decision given to the foreign subsidiary. Whatever the location of this function and the types of policies used, they must be appropriate for the particular firm and the country of operation.

According to Ronen, the type of recruiting policy that a firm adopts is influenced by three factors. First are the characteristics of the company, including the ownership of the subsidiary, the industry, the level of technology, market factors, age of the investment, organizational structure, commitment to international business, cost factors, and the corporate management style. Second are the characteristics of the available individuals. What is their experience and record of previous performance? What is their attitude toward international business and their dedication to the field? Are they adaptable to international business? What is the level of family commitment? Third are the characteristics of the host country. What are the levels of economic development and technological sophistication? Is the country politically stable? How nationalistic is the country? What type of policy has the country adopted regarding the rules and regulations for foreign investments and immigration? Are qualified and experienced management personnel available within that country? How difficult would it be for an employee from outside of the country to adjust to the sociocultural setting?[4]

The recruitment policy of a MNC is determined largely by the characteristics of the firm, the individuals, and the host country.

Nationality Considerations

Most less developed countries resist the appointment of expatriates to managerial positions. An increasing number of these countries insist that nationals be trained to take over key managerial positions. This development in recent years reflects a number of factors, such as the growth of nationalism. This is especially true for countries that have gained their independence since World War II. They feel that local nationals should play a more dominant role in the development of their economies. They also believe that expatriates will force the managerial style of the home country upon the host country rather than adapting to the new environment. And above all, they want the subsidiary corporation to operate in the best interest of the host country rather than of the home country or the multinational enterprise.

To ensure the hiring and training of local nationals, many countries have passed laws dictating the use of local nationals and placing limits on the percentage of foreign managers. Therefore, most firms use expatriates only long enough to train local nationals.

In the absence of host country laws restricting foreign nationals, the manager may be from the home country (expatriate), a third country, or the host country. Where area expertise is important, local or third country nationals are used. Where product expertise is important, home country nationals are used. Robinson lists such factors as company "experience, technical competence, language and area expertise, health, marital relations and the attitude of the spouse to living abroad, career plans, personal preference, age, social acceptability, sex, and personality attributes" as being generally considered important.[5]

A survey of the practices among multinationals of different countries indicates that most firms use a mixture of nationalities to staff all levels of management in their foreign operations.[6] Most American MNCs favor hiring local nationals for foreign subsidiaries, home country nationals for headquarters, and a mix of foreign and home nationals for regional organizations. Banks use more home country nationals in foreign operations because serving the financial needs of the home country multinationals is often the bank's prime operation abroad. In general, American and European MNCs employ a greater percentage of host country nationals in more developed countries (MDCs) than in the less developed countries (LDCs). In the LDCs, U.S. firms tend to use more host country nationals in management than do the European firms. Japanese multinational corporations generally staff their subsidiaries with home country managers in both MDCs and LDCs. They rarely use third country nationals at higher levels of subsidiary management.

Home Country Nationals   Selecting a home country national for the overseas assignment enables the firm to employ an individual of known experience, qualification, and competence. Furthermore, the individual is familiar with the company policies and procedures, management techniques, and technical methods. This person will also have the background to train local managers according to the objectives of the firm and will have little difficulty communicating with headquarters. An expatriate manager also facilitates control of the subsidiary since this individual will clearly have the parent company's interest in mind.

There are, however, disadvantages to using home country nationals. Most expatriate managers will not be familiar with the language, the culture, and the local business environment. Two of the major areas of difficulty faced by American expatriates are adapting to different cultures and mastering the local language. Using expatriates is also a very costly approach. Allowances for housing, cost of living, children's education, travel home, and other benefits will add at least 25 to 100 percent to the base salary.[7] In addition to these are the cost of relocation, tax equalization, and the eventual repatriation of the manager.

A loss of productivity is common when an expatriate is assigned to a position abroad. According to estimates, it generally takes a year to achieve the level of production that the manager enjoyed at home. There is the danger that negative cultural, racial, or ethnic attitudes might surface and adversely affect the performance of subordinates. These can disrupt the effectiveness and the integration of the entire subsidiary. Opposition might also arise if there is the feeling that the management style of the parent company and its home country cultural biases are being forced upon the subsidiary.

Finally, as an unproven outsider, the expatriate will have to build a relationship with government agencies, the public, customers, and employees. The manager must also be socially acceptable to associates. In many countries, managers are expected to possess certain social graces, including an in-depth knowledge of the arts, history, politics and etiquette. Many American managers have difficulty learning or even accepting the importance of these "nonbusiness" interests.

Third Country Nationals   A second source of candidates for overseas assignment is third country nationals. They are usually individuals from the region near the host country who are currently employed at one of the subsidiaries of the firm. For example, a firm may send an employee from its Mexican subsidiary to Panama. Third country nationals generally possess abilities and experiences that are relevant for the host environment. They have demonstrated their ability to adapt to a particular environment, and chances are that they will have less difficulty in adapting to a new environment, especially if the language, customs, culture, economy, politics, and other pertinent characteristics of the host country are similar to those of their home country. They often demand lower salaries and fringe benefits, especially if the manager's salary is tied to the pay scale in the third country.

Offsetting these advantages is the fact that third country nationals from a subsidiary will be less familiar with the policies and procedures of the home office and might lack the depth of product knowledge. Furthermore, there is the danger of national hostilities being involved. For example, Argentine citizens generally feel superior to Chileans; there is still some anti-German feeling in Belgium; and many older Koreans still resent the treatment they received when they were a colony of Japan.

Host Country Nationals   A third source of managers for foreign operations is nationals of the host country. There are a number of advantages in using a local national as manager. The language barrier is completely eliminated, which facilitates communications with the local staff and employees. There is no cross-cultural adjustment problem. Interpersonal problems are avoided and more positive local public opinion might be generated. Management is more stable since the manager's home is in the country. Although relocation within the host country could be a problem, it will probably be less of an issue. The foreign image of the company will be minimized. This is especially important in highly nationalistic countries. The individual is familiar with the political situation and might have contacts with government agencies that could prove beneficial.

Making use of a local manager also offers clear cost advantages. There will be no need for the long distance transfer of the individual and family. Base wages are generally lower in most countries than in the United States, so it might be possible to attract talented personnel by paying a small premium over salary. The payment of related fringe benefits will be minimized or eliminated.

These advantages must be weighed against the disadvantages. It might be difficult to coordinate the subsidiary with the rest of the system because of cross-cultural problems experienced by the local manager in dealing with the home office. The manager might have difficulty fitting into the multinational enterprise because of differences in education, customs, and cultural background. The local national will almost certainly have a different concept of what it means to be a manager than what is prevalent in the United States. The local national's knowledge of management techniques, products, and technology as practiced in the parent country might be inferior to that of the expatriate. Of prime concern is that the local national manager will side with policies of the host government against the corporation. Local managers often conclude that there is no place for them to go once they reach the top. This can result in problems of morale.

Local national workers, especially those from an agrarian background, often have difficulty adjusting to the mechanized pace, routines, and standard operating procedures of industry. As a result, the company might have to deal with absenteeism, high turnover, and an unwillingness to accept responsibility. Managers from some traditional or authoritarian cultures have difficulty being trainers because they are accustomed to taking orders. In hiring host country nationals as managers, the issue of integrating different social classes or religions must be anticipated.

One of the key decisions of any international firm is the selection of a subsidiary manager.

Processes and Criteria for Selecting International Managers

Once the source has been identified and the recruitment process is under way, the firm must establish criteria on which to base the selection decision and the processes for making that decision. These criteria will vary with the company, but most attempt to identify general qualities or characteristics (see Table 19.1).

Early Identification   Early identification programs, which utilize questionnaires and interviews of both the candidate and spouse, are designed to determine the compatibility of the candidate for the foreign assignment. To determine compatibility, management tries to assess certain personal qualities: adaptability, flexibility, intellectual capacity, problem-solving ability, decision-making ability, results orientation, professionalism, and communication skills, including teaching and listening. Determining the candidate's level of technical expertise is usually easier since this is primarily firm-specific know-how. The assessment also tries to ascertain the candidate's level of economic and managerial understanding. To these factors the

Table 19.1   **The Criteria 70 Companies Use in Selecting Executives for Overseas Operations**

Criteria	No. of times mentioned	Percentage of companies citing
Experience	30	42.9
Adaptability, flexibility	28	40.0
Technical knowledge of business	24	34.3
Competence, ability, past performance	24	34.3
Managerial talent	16	22.9
Language skill/ability	8	11.4
Potential	7	10.0
Interest in overseas work, executive ambition	7	10.0
Appreciation of new management, sensitivity	5	7.1
Education	4	5.7
Initiative, creativity	4	5.7
Independence	3	4.3
Communication	3	4.3
Maturity, emotional stability	2	2.9
Same criteria as for comparable jobs	2	2.9

Source: Business International, *Compensating International Executives* (New York: Business International Corp., 1970), p. 2.

firm must add the candidate's managerial competence as reflected in past performance.

Nationality Mix in Subsidiary Management   The selection process also needs to take into consideration company policies regarding the desired national composition of the employees. The desired nationality mix within a subsidiary depends on five factors:

1. The nature of the firm's business and product strategy
2. National laws and regulations that favor hiring local nationals
3. Laws and regulations regarding transferring personnel
4. The supply of managerial talent within the host country
5. Costs considerations[8]

Steps in Expatriate Manager Selection   Once the national mix has been determined and the criteria have been established, the next step is considering potential candidates for the position. Selection is usually accomplished through a series of stages. First, those who are interested only in short-term assignments or are unwilling to accept positions in certain locales can be eliminated. This is followed by in-depth interviews before the next decision stage. Firms favor interviews because they have often been found to reveal more about the attitudes of the candidate and spouse than psychological tests.

One should not underestimate the importance of the expatriate manager's spouse. The success or failure of foreign assignments is often determined by the spouse. Adapting to the sociocultural environment can be very difficult. The adjustments can be extremely demanding because of lower or at least different living standards, inadequate medical and health facilities, inferior educational institutions, climatic discomforts, and physical dangers including terrorism. These are compounded by the disorientation and cultural discord of living away from home, and the inability to communicate with others in one's own language. Living abroad is often frustrating for the whole family, especially for the spouse, since the spouse must handle the bulk of interaction with the local community. An unhappy spouse and family often cause an expatriate manager to fail.

During or before these interviews, the candidate must be told of the location of the assignment and length of stay. The company must also describe the requirements of the job, work schedules, vacations, and so on. The candidate must be given information regarding compensation, taxes, allowances, and details regarding housing, transportation, and schools. It is also important that this interview be used to discuss the specifics of repatriation when the foreign assignment is completed or if the manager asks to be repatriated before that time.

After these interviews, some firms make the final decision. Other firms actually finance visits to the locale by both the candidate and the spouse before the final decision is made.

> Most MNCs select expatriate managers for experience, adaptability, and technical competence. Knowledge of the language and culture are seldom major factors.

Problems After Assignment

Multinational enterprises regularly transfer personnel across national and cultural boundaries for short durations to meet a particular need, as a part of the career development program or for a permanent assignment. Those involved are likely to encounter problems in the new culture. They must deal with different languages, customs, beliefs, superstitions, attitudes, values, and religions. Social adaptation for the manager and family is usually more difficult than job adaptation. Language barriers will limit social interactions. To add to the problems, the spouse may have too much free time because servants are hired. Boredom and loneliness can lead to serious problems. Excessive drinking and money-spending are not uncommon under such conditions. The expatriate manager's satisfaction and performance is to a great extent determined by the family's ability to adjust to the new environment.

The failure rate of expatriate employees is high. Thus, firms should be keenly aware of the need to select culturally adaptable individuals, to provide extensive language and culture training, and to help the expatriate's family develop a social support structure. Management should also be aware of excessively strong family group attachments, health problems, marital instability, and other potential problems. It is critically important that corporate management in the home office realizes that its responsibilities to

The high failure rate of expatriate managers is due largely to their inability to adapt to the new environment.

the expatriate manager do not end when the transfer has been made, because that is the very time when the expatriate's problems begin.

REPATRIATION OF MANAGERS

Although most multinational corporations have discontinued the use of career expatriates, some executives are still sent abroad for permanent assignment. Under these conditions, the problem of repatriation does not arise. Such people adopt the customs and culture of the country and are at home in the new environment, where they expect to spend their careers. Neither does the problem of repatriation arise when executives are sent abroad as a planned part of a management development program. After serving in some managerial capacity in a foreign subsidiary, they return to corporate headquarters, where they are placed in other positions of responsibility. However, when expatriates are sent abroad for an unspecified period of time to manage some aspect of the foreign subsidiary, repatriation problems can occur. Thus, many firms have developed specific and detailed repatriation programs.

To prepare the expatriate for the expected reverse cultural shock, many firms provide six months of counseling and orientation prior to returning to the home country. They prepare the expatriate for a new assignment that might not be comparable to the overseas assignment. In comparison with foreign assignments, most domestic jobs have less responsibility. The expatriate who expected to use the foreign assignment to move rapidly up the corporate ladder might be disappointed. Less than one-half of the expatriates receive a promotion after returning to corporate headquarters.

If the firm does not have plans and policies, expatriates are left alone to deal with the problems of repatriation. If they are not provided with suitable jobs, returning expatriates might feel that they would have had greater promotions if they had not accepted a foreign assignment. The movement of peers up the corporate ladder often confirms these suspicions. Even when assigned to comparable jobs, many returning managers find that they have less responsibility than before they left. Furthermore, upon returning home, the expatriate is no longer provided with the various allowances and perquisites, making it difficult to maintain the same standard of living enjoyed abroad. It is not uncommon for returning managers to find that due to inflation, they cannot afford to purchase a home comparable to the one sold before leaving.

In addition to job-related problems, returning managers must adjust to the cultural changes that have occurred. Such individuals are facing reverse cultural shock. They must adjust to the fact that they are not looked upon with the respect that superiors often receive abroad. Ironically, the more successful the individual is in adapting to a foreign culture, the more difficult it is to readapt to the home culture.

The high failure rate of American expatriate managers indicates that many are repatriated before they have completed their tour of duty. If the individual is unable to adjust to the foreign environment and must return prior to completing the assignment, the experience might be even more traumatic. Facing one's peers and explaining why you were unable to complete the assignment is not pleasant. Having such individuals return to their former positions is quite costly to the firm, which must pay for their transfer home and find a replacement for the overseas position. If the individual leaves the firm, there will be the loss of talent.

Repatriation often results in reverse cultural shock for those not provided with adequate counseling and orientation before leaving the overseas assignment.

TRAINING AND DEVELOPMENT OF INTERNATIONAL MANAGERS

Each organization must design a training and development program for all of its employees. For managers who are to be sent abroad, this training needs to focus on foreign assignments. For foreign nationals at the subsidiary level, this training is aimed at improving business and technical skills. In both cases, training and development programs need to be tailored to meet individual as well as organizational needs and objectives. Any combination of a number of methods may be used to achieve the goals.

Orientation and Training for Expatriates

Once the individual has been selected for a foreign assignment, the individual and family must be provided with an orientation to the host country. Some firms limit the orientation to a brief survey of the host country and its people, usually through lectures by outside consultants. Others have a more formal program that provides greater detail about the foreign environment including information on housing, educational and medical facilities, shopping, social relations, and so forth. These "familiarization" programs can help reduce ethnic prejudices but generally do not adequately prepare the expatriate manager for life abroad.

Inadequacy of Orientation and Training

Few companies provide adequate predeparture training. Of those that do provide some kind of training, few offer anything beyond simple language and culture classes, and this seldom includes the spouse and other family members.[9] This absence of training is particularly surprising because of continuing statements from overseas managers about the importance of language, customs, living conditions, economic environment, business law, government and political structure, geography, and especially spouse and family attitudes.

There are, however, reasons that predeparture training is not emphasized: (1) many assignments are temporary, (2) the employee is needed immediately, (3) firms increasingly use local nationals to fill long-term needs, (4) many firms still do not believe training is necessary, and (5) firms doubt the effectiveness of training programs.[10]

Most European and Japanese firms take such training much more seriously than do American firms; 69 percent of European companies and 57 percent of Japanese companies have formalized training programs as compared to only 32 percent of U.S.-based multinationals.[11] Many Japanese make use of the Institute of International Training and Studies near Fuji, Japan, which was established specifically to improve the development and effectiveness of international managers. This institute provides a one-year program including English language training, U.S. culture studies, general and international management, a second language, and the culture of a second country. The program is capped with a two-month study tour of some part of the world. Young corporate executives are sent to this program by their employers, usually after they have completed a rotation through various departments of the firm. Although spouses are not provided with the same training, firms like Mitsui send spouses through language and culture training provided by independent organizations.

Inadequate orientation and training of expatriates and their families are partly responsible for the difficulties and dissatisfaction with assignments abroad.

Categories of an Expatriate Training Program

Expatriate training can be segmented into three categories: cultural, job-specific, and continuing development.

The cultural sensitization aspect of an expatriate training program should be divided into three stages. The first stage involves relaying general information on climate, housing, health conditions, education, and politics. Training in the host country language should be provided for the expatriate and family for as long as necessary. The second stage provides more in-depth understanding of taxes, home sales, perquisites, and job upon repatriation. The final stage occurs during the relocation process, when the expatriate is made aware of housing arrangements, support services, salary distributions, and legal advice. The best approach to cultural training is actually sending the candidate and family to the country for "on-the-ground" training.

The second component of expatriate training is job-specific. In this training, the expatriate is taught details of the tasks to be performed, including policy, lines of communication, competition, government relations, and the legal environment, as well as the technical dimensions of the job.

The training for expatriate managers involves cultural sensitization, job-specific skills, and problem-specific developmental activities.

Finally, some firms provide development programs after the individual is on the job. The expatriate is given specific training to gain competencies and skills to perform the tasks more efficiently. This includes information on problems that arise and the most effective methods for dealing with them.

Training Local Nationals

Technical training should be provided for those on the staff with deficiencies in this area. Management development programs teach the manager how to maximize individual and subordinate performances by utilizing "management by objectives" and other tools of modern management. "On-the-job-training" is especially important in the less developed countries because it provides for "hands-on" instruction under the supervision of an experienced manager. One shortcoming of this method is that it does not provide opportunities to learn higher skills. Technical or vocational schools, which are often supported by the local government and industry, provide a source of such training. One deficiency of such "off-site" training is that since no direct contact is made with the actual workplace, training might become too abstract. Actually, the best method is a combination of "on-the-job" and classroom training. In many MNCs, training may also take place outside of the country in a plant of comparable size, complexity, and technical sophistication. Thus, the worker or supervisor will have the opportunity to see how the job is done in a more sophisticated plant. This is a practice used by many European firms when a plant is being constructed in a developing country. Once the plant is built, experienced workers and supervisors are ready to step in. The following Global Insight provides an example of how one corporation, Motorola, recruits, trains, and develops both technical and managerial employees.

COMPENSATING INTERNATIONAL MANAGERS

It is essential for a firm to adopt a compensation policy that meets the following four objectives:

1. To effectively attract and retain qualified employees
2. To facilitate transfers among foreign affiliates and the home office
3. To establish and maintain a consistent and reasonable relationship among the compensation levels of all employees of an affiliate and between affiliates
4. To arrange competitive compensation in the various locations[12]

Without such objectives, compensation differences among employees will be a source of dissatisfaction and managerial problems instead of a reward for past accomplishments and a motivator for future performance.

American multinational corporations generally include in their international compensation package for expatriate managers and technical personnel three components: base pay, premiums, and cost of living allowances. This combination generally amounts to about $2\frac{1}{2}$ times the base salary.

Executive-Level Salaries

Levels of executive salary vary among countries because of the different bases that are used to determine the worth of the individual and because of different customs. In Japan, salaries are determined largely by seniority while in the United States accomplishment, regardless of age, determines salaries. Because of these differences in customs and bases for compensation determination, American chief executives generally receive salaries that are enormously higher than their European or Japanese counterparts.[13] Stock options are generally included in the salaries of American executives, adding greatly to the base salaries, while Japanese executives are provided with generous fringe benefits that are not considered as a part of the salaries. (See Table 19.2.)

Although the difference in salaries among executives tend to decrease as one goes lower in the organization, there remain substantial differences between firms of different nationalities. As a result, the higher the level of executive being transferred, the greater the likelihood of substantial salary differential and dissatisfaction.

Base Salaries

Expatriates must receive a base pay that is comparable to that offered by competitors within the country, but must also receive a total compensation that does not decrease the standard of living to which the expatriate had

531

Table 19.2   **A Comparison of 1987 Executive Compensations**

Industry	Executive, firm, country	Salary (U.S. dollars)
Electronics	Jack Welch, General Electric, U.S.	12,631,000
	Karlheinz Kaske, Siemens, W. Germany	930,000
	Anders Scharp, Electrolux, Sweden	437,000
	Ichiro Shinji, JVC, Japan	290,000
Automotive	Lee Iacocca, Chrysler, U.S.	17,656,000
	Edzard Reuter, Daimler-Benz, W. Germany	1,200,000
	Jacques Calvet, Peugeot, France	250,000
	Tadashi Kume, Honda, Japan	450,000
Banking	John Reed, Citicorp, U.S.	950,000
	Alfred Herrhausen, Deutsche Bank, W. Germany	1,500,000
	Herve De Carmoy, SGB, France	1,300,000
	Kenichi Kamiya, Mitsue Bank, Japan	280,000
Petroleum	Lawrence Rawl, Exxon, U.S.	5,523,000
	Sir Peter Walters, British Petroleum, Britain	582,000
	L.C. Van Wachem, Royal Dutch/Shell, the Netherlands/Britain	500,000

Source: Shawn Tully, "American Bosses Are Overpaid . . . ," *Fortune*, November 7, 1988, pp. 121–136.

become accustomed prior to the transfer. This is accomplished by providing a compensation package that includes a base salary, premiums, and allowances. If the going rate in the host country is higher than the home country base, some companies will raise the base salary. If the host country has a lower base pay rate than the home country, the firm will usually give the expatriate the home country base salary. Some firms deviate from this method by retaining the home country base wherever the expatriate is sent. This facilitates salary determination when repatriation occurs. When third country nationals are involved in the organization, there is the problem of aligning salary rates with still another country. Thus, different nationalities might find themselves receiving different compensation for doing similar work in a country. For local nationals, most multinational enterprises follow or marginally exceed local salary patterns in order to attract top local managers.

Other factors unrelated to performance also affect salaries. The constantly changing exchange rates can increase or decrease the salary of an expatriate. The firm may, however, make adjustments for the discrepancies in the salaries between the home and host countries by utilizing various forms of compensation as described below. There is no standard method for compensating expatriates. Each firm needs to design a compensation package specifically tailored to meet the needs and policies of the organization and its members.

Premiums

One form of compensation is the use of premiums. Premiums are a fixed percentage of the expatriate's base salary that are paid for the duration of the foreign assignment. They are provided for two reasons: to encourage mobility to foreign countries, and as compensation for the hardship that may be involved in living in less desirable areas.[14] For example, the overseas premium for assignment in western Europe may be zero, but assignment in parts of Africa or the Middle East may carry a premium as high as 100 percent of the base salary. Such bonus payments create problems because the additional income over and above the base salary encourages some managers to remain abroad even if their services are required elsewhere. Companies have tried to correct this situation by either incrementally phasing out the premiums after a few years or by providing a single payment tied to the move rather than to the assignment.

Cost of Living Allowances

An allowance for cost of living is a major supplementary payment that enables expatriates to continue living in the manner to which they are accustomed. This allowance is intended to cover expenses for housing, utilities, taxes, and insurance. In addition, allowances are provided for the payment of social security taxes in the host country, which the expatriate will rarely collect, educational expenses for children under college age, travel, and other expenses that are incurred because of the foreign assignment. The U.S. State Department indices of living costs abroad enable firms to determine the differences in costs of living in different geographic areas. The allowance for someone assigned to Tokyo, for example, will be greater than the allowance for someone assigned to London, which in turn will be greater than the allowance for Santiago, Chile.

Other Perquisites

Various other perquisites ("perks") may be provided to the expatriates. Firms often pay the membership fees for social or country clubs, and provide cars and drivers. They often provide special insurance to protect against political hazards such as kidnapping. Continuing language and cultural training for the expatriate and family is often encouraged and paid for by the firm.

U.S. firms generally provide expatriate managers with a base salary plus premiums, cost of living allowances, and perquisites.

PERFORMANCE APPRAISAL AND EVALUATION

Evaluative Process

The forms and appraisal techniques used by multinationals vary in several ways. Who makes the appraisal? How many people are involved in making the appraisal? Should the results be made known to the employee? How often should the appraisals be made?

To retain objectivity, more than one supervisor or a team is commonly involved in the evaluative process. Organizations strongly disagree on whether to inform the employee of the results of the appraisal. Some feel it is necessary so that the employee can correct weaknesses and learn more about the process in appraising the performance of others. Others feel that the appraiser is put in a difficult position if he or she must make all of the results known.

Most companies do not adhere to an exact performance appraisal schedule. Usually, appraisals are made every 12 to 18 months, but this may be lengthened to 24 months, especially if an employee has been with the company for a long time. The logic seems to be that the capabilities of experienced managers are well known, whereas more frequent evaluations must be conducted to determine progress of a newcomer.

Different appraisal formats are used by multinationals, often several by the same company. Emphasis may be placed on managerial ability, potential for advancement, readiness for advancement, actual job performance, and so forth. Because of the differences in emphasis, divisions within a company may be allowed to design their own formats.

Promotion

Regardless of the performance of foreign subsidiary managers, the current practices of many multinational enterprises limit the opportunities for foreign nationals to become top executives at corporate headquarters. This is especially true among Japanese companies because of the nature of the country's culture (closed). American-based multinationals also have few non-U.S. nationals in top corporate positions, although the trend seems to be toward greater numbers of foreign national executives. Both Japanese and American multinational firms tend to follow the policy of promotion from within at headquarters.

Most multinational corporations evaluate their staff every 12 to 24 months, often using differing appraisal formats.

LABOR RELATIONS AND WORK FORCE MANAGEMENT

A policy problem that must be settled before a foreign subsidiary begins operations is that of work force management. Should coordination be centralized at headquarters or decentralized to the subsidiary? The answer depends on several factors. When local management is new and inexperienced in labor relations, or when agreements made in one country affect negotiations or set precedents for others, it may be necessary for international management to centralize coordination. While centralized coordination of employees might be important, it is essential that subsidiary management be involved as much as possible. Many firms authorize managers of foreign subsidiaries to negotiate agreements and to manage under the terms of these agreements. This granting of autonomy to subsidiary management strengthens their position in the eyes of their subordinates and facilitates their ability to manage effectively.

The expectations of workers vary among countries. A paternalistic attitude is expected by workers in a traditional society where belonging to a particular social class is an accident of birth. This might create difficulties for an expatriate manager who is unaccustomed to the role of "benevolent father." Most American managers are more familiar with a formalized and impersonal attitude that is generally more appropriate and expected in highly developed countries.

The expectations of labor, especially pertaining to its role in decision-making, vary among different countries. In the more highly developed countries, labor is usually more questioning of hierarchical corporate control and demands a larger role in decision-making. It is somewhat of a paradox that greater labor participation in decision-making often results in a reduction of tensions and the adversarial relationship between labor and management, thus weakening the position of labor unions. Nevertheless, the trend worldwide is toward increasing worker participation.

Labor Union Structures

The structure of unions varies from country to country. There are national unions, local unions, industrial unions, and company unions. There may be several unions in the same company or only one union representing all workers in a company. In the United States, the union selected by the majority in a plant has a monopoly bargaining right. This is not true in western Europe. The amount of union influence on company policies also varies from country to country. Generally, unions have greater influence in the more highly developed countries than in the less developed countries.

Forms of Worker Participation and Labor-Management Cooperation

Substantial differences exist among countries in the form of worker participation. *Self-management* refers to the situation wherein labor's position is predominant to that of management, as in the case of Yugoslavia. Next is the situation of *codetermination* wherein there is a 50-50 representation of labor and management on the board of directors. The principal example is the Federal Republic of Germany, which in 1951 adopted codetermination for the iron, coal, and steel industries, and since 1976 extended the policy to all firms employing more than 2000. For firms employing between 500 and 2000 employees, *minority board* participation is required, providing for a $\frac{1}{3}$ labor representation on boards of directors. *Work councils* are bodies through which labor-management relations have been institutionalized at the enterprise level. They have the right to be consulted on matters dealing with working conditions, training, methods of payment, hiring and firing, promotion, transfers and regrouping, and all work allocation. These work councils are required by German law of all firms employing 5 or more people. Although *job enrichment* is actually a group of management methods used by firms to enhance the motivational character of an individual's job, in some countries it actually serves as a mechanism for worker participation. With job enrichment, individual workers determine their own daily and weekly work schedule. The best example of this is the Saab automobile plant in Sweden, which scrapped the assembly line and permits a team of 3 to 10 people to determine its own division of work and job rotation.[15]

There are four types of relationship that may exist between unions and management. These are competition, arbitration, sharing, and cooperation.[16] When the relationship is one of competition or arbitration, there is an adversarial relationship between the two. The expiration of a contract without agreement for renewal could result in a strike that could close down operations, as has occurred in many U.S. manufacturing plants. In the sharing and cooperation type of relationship, both parties desire to work together for the overall benefit, thus minimizing the importance of unions to represent labor as an adversarial force. This has applied in Japan, where unions often call a strike for only an hour to show their displeasure. These four forms of relationship can be viewed as stages on a continuum (see Figure 19.1).

The amount of union-management cooperation varies from country to country. In Great Britain, the lack of cooperation is largely due to there being little mobility between labor and management. In Germany and Sweden, greater cooperation can be traced to labor's representation on the boards of directors, mandated by law. This enables labor to influence managerial policies in such matters as foreign investments, plant acquisitions, and closures.

The formation of quality circles to improve output is an outward manifestation of labor's attempt to cooperate with management on productivity matters. These circles, although not of Japanese origin, have been in existence in Japan for many years and are becoming increasingly popular in the United States and western Europe. In Sweden, labor-management cooperation has resulted in an increase in worker morale through job rotation, job enlargement, and job enrichment. Stated more simply, cooperation has allowed greater worker determination regarding the what, how, and when of each job.

Figure 19.1   Continuum of Labor–Management Relations

Adversarial competition   Arbitration   Shared decision-making   Cooperative decision-making

Strikes for economic issues such as wages, benefits, and job security are far more common in the United States than in other countries. Foreign labor unions often have very different motivations.

Although cooperation is becoming increasingly evident in labor-management relationships in most countries, there are still deep-rooted adversarial attitudes in some countries—for example, the United States, Brazil, Switzerland, Great Britain, and others. This antagonism surfaces when unions attempt to win the loyalty of workers by emphasizing the preservation of jobs at the expense of technological progress or increased productivity. A union's push for higher wages often results in increasing the specific job classifications or defining job descriptions more narrowly. This is often detrimental to the international competitive position of the firm and, therefore, to the long-term security of the workers' jobs. Many unions are powerful enough to influence elections to the extent that politicians who are sympathetic to union causes are elected to promote legislation that is prolabor and antimanagement. However, legislation contrary to the interest of labor is often promoted by elected officials who have the support of management.

In the less developed countries, firms soon discover that labor unions generally have less clout than in the industrialized nations. The major weakness of unions in these countries reflects unfavorable economic conditions: high labor mobility, low employment, low per capita labor income, and lack of labor homogeneity. Since the income from dues is inadequate to finance union activities, the influence of unions is limited. Thus, many enter into alliances with political parties, religious organizations, or government groups that are more interested in national politics than in shop floor economics and welfare of the workers. This leads to one of the essential differences between labor unions in the LDCs and the MDCs. LDC unions tend to be more interested in issues of national politics, whereas MDC unions are more concerned with economic matters. In the case of North American unions, the economic focus is directed at issues of salary, fringe benefits, and job security; in Europe it is targeted at corporate decision-making from the plant level to the board room. Recent trends indicate increased militancy among labor unions in South Korea and other Pacific Rim countries as they move to increasingly higher levels of economic development.

The role of labor unions, the degree of labor-management cooperation, and the laws governing labor activities differ substantially among countries.

A characteristic peculiar to many LDCs is that collective bargaining is restrained since many countries have adopted restrictions on the rights of labor to strike, enacted comprehensive labor codes, and adopted legal provisions for compulsory arbitration.

Recruitment and Employment of Unskilled Labor

The composition of the work force in a foreign subsidiary is determined largely by the policies of the host government since many have laws that control the hiring and firing of nationals and require the employment of local nationals if they have the qualifications necessary to fill a particular job. The hiring of nationals is further assured by the adoption of strict immigration laws that regulate the temporary and permanent movements of foreign nationals. Quantitative restrictions are often placed on the number of expatriates who may be hired and trained.

Most countries grant work permits only to technical and managerial personnel. Even the United States restricts the employment of foreign nationals if citizens are available. An exception to this is the seasonal Mexican work force allowed to enter the United States to harvest agricultural crops. Although there may be sufficient workers in the United States to do these jobs, they are generally unwilling to work for the same wages or are unavailable during the harvest season. In the EEC, where freedom of movement among member nations is permitted, labor shortages in West Germany and the Benelux countries are often met by migratory workers from labor surplus countries such as Italy or Spain.

Because subsidiaries of foreign corporations are under the complete jurisdiction of the host government, the practice of hiring and promoting local nationals will minimize business-government friction, and the employment of nonnationals is not recommended unless special circumstances require it.

The hiring practices of foreign subsidiaries depend largely upon the country of operation. The subsidiary manager has few alternatives to conforming to the accepted standards for employment even though these may be contrary to what the firm would do at home or may be personally objectionable to the individual manager. For example, in a given society it may be improper for those considered social inferiors to supervise their social superiors. Similarly, in some countries, certain minority groups, whether based on sex, race, religion, or ethnic background, may not be placed in key positions without creating problems regardless of the individual's competence. The same general principles would be equally applicable to promotions and wages in these societies. This might create a serious ethical or moral problem for the expatriate manager.

In the face of these issues, many corporations have taken the burden from the subsidiary management by enacting policies mandating that the subsidiary managers not discriminate on any of these bases. In these cases, the corporation accepts the costs and consequences of deviating from local norms or customs.

Training and Development of Labor

The problems associated with training will vary depending on the country in which the subsidiary is established. If the foreign operation is in a developed country, there might be little necessity for long-term training of employees. For example, the Mazda automobile plant that began operation in Flatrock, Michigan, in 1987 is manned primarily by former factory workers from the area. Most had been unemployed and were pleased to find the type of job with which they were familiar. Training consisted more of introducing the Japanese technical processes and work methods: wearing uniforms, arriving early enough to participate in exercises prior to working, and so forth. Those who were willing to accept the Japanese management philosophy encountered no difficulty in adapting to the new requirements.

The training program will differ markedly if the subsidiary is located in a less developed country. Complete orientation to the job may be necessary, especially if host nationals are recruited directly from nonbusiness employment positions. It will be necessary to train the worker to perform a specific task while on the job, with someone providing assistance when necessary. Firms with subsidiaries in different parts of the world have found that it is not difficult to provide such training to the local workers. It is only when an individual is asked to change life styles and habits that some difficulties might arise.

The effectiveness of the training will depend partly on the motivational effectiveness of monetary and nonmonetary rewards as well as the methods used in the training. The primary reward that has been used is money; however, recently greater emphasis has been placed on nonmonetary factors such as improved health and dental insurance coverage, better working hours, limited overtime work, longer vacations, and guaranteed job security. There is no assurance that any single factor will motivate a worker in a particular society. Some individuals will be motivated by the opportunity to gain social status, while others may seek money. Some individuals are

The stage of economic development of the host country influences the recruiting and training of the work force.

motivated by a promise of promotion to a cleaner job, while others are motivated by such things as greater responsibility, better hours, greater self-actualization, greater opportunity for recreation, greater freedom, less supervision, or greater job security. In essence, anything that directly or indirectly enhances the self-image of individuals in that culture ought to be considered a potential motivator.

Wage Rates and Compensation Systems for Unskilled Labor

Various factors should be considered before adopting a local pay scale. The optimum strategy should be a function of the local law, custom, and company objectives. Multinational corporations often find it necessary to pay more than the going rate in a particular region. Even these higher wage rates in the less developed countries are still only a fraction of what American labor is paid, though the productivity differential is not anywhere near the wage differential. Paying wages abroad that are lower than those in the home country often evokes charges of exploitation. Quite frankly, these are absurd; the concept of equal pay for equal work is not applicable when comparing wage levels among nations, because of differences in buying power. Even within a country the concept of equal pay for equal work may not be applicable. In countries where wage rates are often determined by social status, seniority, age, race, and ethnic background, equal pay could create enormous problems for subsidiary management. For example, the highest-paid workers in Saudi Arabia are the nationals. The pay scales of foreign nationals doing similar work vary widely, depending on whether they are from the United States, Lebanon, South Korea, Pakistan, or other countries.

When deciding on a local pay scale, the firm has basically three choices. It can pay lower than, at, or above the average market rate in the country. Assuming that local laws do not specify the rates, a firm should pay sufficient wages to retain workers of the desired level of competence. If the firm is willing to have workers with a low level of competence and will accept problems of turnover, absenteeism, and so forth, then it may well choose to pay below-average wages. If, on the other hand, the firm wishes superior workers and low turnover, then it will probably want to pay higher than average wages.

The actual wage level selected by a firm will be determined by a number of factors: the influence of labor unions, wages paid by competitors, the attitude of local firms toward the wage scale of the subsidiary, and the type of worker sought. If the firm believes that the workers are underpaid, yet realizes that the wages cannot be increased without creating community tensions, premiums over and above wages may be paid. This may serve to improve the morale of the workers and encourage greater productivity.

Many firms pay higher wages in the form of fringe benefits to silence criticisms that the subsidiary is luring the best workers away from their current jobs and disrupting the local economy. These fringes may include health insurance, retirement, educational aid for the children, interest-free loans, low-cost living quarters, company stores for food and clothing for employees, and year-end bonuses. The value of the fringe benefit in terms of the basic wage or salary can vary widely among countries as well as among firms within a country. In Japan, bonuses amounting to several months' wages are often paid to full-time employees at the end of June and at the end of December, depending upon the profitability. Workers appreciate these payments because they serve as a method of forced savings.

In addition to the compensation system of paying a rate per hour, many firms use a piece-rate system that pays the worker on the basis of the amount produced. This method serves as an incentive to individuals since their income can be increased through an increase in productivity. Agricultural workers, for example, are often paid a given amount for each bushel of tomatoes harvested.

Some firms have a profit-sharing method of fringe benefits, but these might be politically intolerable in some countries if profits fluctuate from year to year. Furthermore, profit sharing creates problems because there are questions as to who should participate, how the profits should be shared between labor and management, who determines the allocation, and so on.[17]

The pay scale must be competitive to retain workers and to rebut the charges of exploitation, yet low enough to prevent disrupting the economy.

SUMMARY

When a multinational corporation establishes operations abroad, it is faced with the problem of staffing the subsidiary with the best possible candidates. It must recruit individuals who can best fill the positions. The firm must seek out the source and select the candidate from among home country, third country, or local nationals. The firm must weigh carefully the advantages and disadvantages of each before making the final selection.

Although less developed countries generally discourage the assignment of expatriates for managerial positions in the subsidiaries, MNCs have found that most local nationals do not initially have the experience or the managerial know-how that is required to operate a sophisticated plant. The alternative is to assign an expatriate to train local talent, then terminate the assignment after the training has been completed. This practice will be in accord with the regulations that require the training of local nationals for managerial positions.

The manager of a foreign subsidiary is responsible for managing human resources abroad. For an expatriate from the home country, this task might require a great deal of learning and the utmost in diplomacy. For example, the recruitment of workers from an agrarian economy will require training in a completely different type of activity. In compensating employees, the manager must take into consideration local wages because compensation cannot be overly generous nor can it be so low as to raise the charge of exploitation. Promotion might create problems because factors other than competence might be more critical in the relationship between superiors and subordinates. The structure of the labor unions and the labor-management relationship differ among countries. These and other problems are certain to create difficulties in the management of human resources.   ☐

KEY TERMS AND CONCEPTS

Base salary	Host country (local) national
Bonus	Incentive pay
Cultural shock	Perquisite
Cost of living allowance	Piece work
Ethnocentric policy	Premiums
Expatriate	Repatriation
Home country	Reverse cultural shock
Home (parent) country national	Subsidiary
Host country	Third country national

REVIEW QUESTIONS

1. Should recruitment policies be centered at the multinational headquarters or at the subsidiary level? Why?

2. Why are the staffing policies of U.S. firms different from those of Japanese firms?

3. Should women be assigned to a managerial position in countries that do not treat women as equals? If so, why? If not, why not?

4. What are the advantages and disadvantages of appointing a person from the home country, host country, or third country as manager of a foreign subsidiary?

5. Discuss why it is important to provide predeparture orientation to both the applicant and the spouse.

6. What topics should be covered in the training and development of a candidate for expatriate assignment?

7. What type of training should be provided to local nationals who will become managers?

8. What are some of the problems that an expatriate manager might encounter upon returning from an overseas assignment? How can an MNC minimize such problems?

9. Describe the performance appraisal that would be most effectively used to evaluate the work of an expatriate.

10. Why are labor unions less effective in gaining benefits for their membership in the LDCs than in the more highly developed countries?

11. Discuss how host governments attempt to control the subsidiary employees and employment policies.

12. List some of the difficulties encountered in training factory workers in the LDCs. Compare these with problems in MDCs.

13. What would be the criticism if a U.S. subsidiary underpaid local workers? Overpaid local workers?

DISCUSSION CASE

Mitsui K.K.

The Mitsui method of identifying and grooming potential international managers starts before a candidate leaves school. Each September, Mitsui receives a thousand or so applications from seniors in Japan's top-ranking colleges who will graduate the following March. It runs these candidates through a culling procedure which weeds out about half of them: a careful analysis of school records; a battery of "yes or no" tests that check out factual knowledge; an essay-type test that reflects both common sense and business sense; and a multi-tier personal interview system that starts with in-company peer groups—junior executives who have been with the company two or three years—and works up the corporate ladder to a designated senior executive who puts his final "chop" on a candidate's eligibility.

Five to Ten Years of Rotation

The process also produces the first indications of what direction the candidate's career path in the company should take. That direction, however, is not final. For five to ten years after these carefully screened candidates are hired, they are rotated within the company and systematically monitored to make sure they wind up in slots that best conform to their abilities.

The monitoring system includes an annual evaluation by the supervisor in direct daily contact with the executive, which is checked by the section chief and double-checked by the general manager of the department. In addition, an elaborate written report provides detail under two headings: business ability and work attitude. The former contains such items as ability to administer staff, decisiveness, prejudices, perception, judgment, concentration, planning and negotiating ability, and business knowledge. Work attitudes are measured by such criteria as following proper reporting procedures, keeping apart personal and professional matters, accepting respon-

Source: "Mitsui's Big Machine for Choosing, Grooming Its International Managers," *Business International*, July 18, 1975, pp. 228–229. Reprinted by permission.

sibility, maintaining required office hours, and obeying company regulations.

As a general rule, home-base executives are not moved into international jobs until they have been thoroughly pretested within the Mitsui system, i.e., at the middle management level. Three general criteria are applied: character—a combination of strength of character and adaptability; professional rating (Mitsui rates its executives on an A through D scale; candidates for service abroad must rank C or higher and for the major overseas posts B or higher); and language ability.

In addition, personal characteristics are put into the selection hopper. Example: Is the executive's temperament right for the post? (Under Mitsui rules, a quick-tempered executive may be sent to North America but would not be assigned to a post where he might have to deal with "mañana" attitudes.)

Finally, physical factors are weighed. Can the executive adapt to the food patterns of the country to which he is sent? Can he adapt to the lack of oxygen if the place of assignment is located at elevations of 5,000 feet or higher, such as Mexico City or Bogotà?

Having met all criteria, the executive is put through a concentrated training and briefing process. He takes a three-month intensive language course at corporate expense and is briefed by in-house experts—staff and line—on political, economic and business conditions in the country to which he has been assigned.

At the same time, the executive's wife is put through an appropriate language and culture course. A number of independent organizations offer such courses in Japan, with varying degrees of intensity and comprehensiveness. Mitsui picks the course and pays for it.

Once the executive is in his overseas post, Mitsui insists on intensive language training for another year. In some locations, the company finances university training, combining exposure to language with substance of valid interest to the firm. In the past, Mitsui has allowed its executives to choose these courses and take them on an audit basis. The new trend is to have executives take MBA degrees where the academic facilities are available.

Mitsui also takes care of the special schooling needs of executives' children. In Japan, high schools and universities are sharply competitive and inordinately decisive in shaping careers. Japanese executives are therefore particularly anxious to channel their children into the school system early and under the best auspices. Mitsui provides dormitory facilities for children of its executives, boys and girls, at both the high school and the university level. These facilities are situated in the company's residential quarters at various locations in Tokyo and Osaka, and are tightly supervised. Room and board are subsidized, but students pay their own transportation costs (daily travel can be two hours and more) and provide for tuition out of their own resources.

Two Routes to Overseas Duty

At Mitsui, the assignment process for service abroad has two channels. Requests can initiate from the field, with specific requirements, or can be "self-initiated" with specific motivation. A typical example of the first would be Mitsui's North American manager, foreseeing substantial growth in the petrochemical industry in Houston, asking corporate headquarters for a candidate who knows the petrochemical industry, has a workable base of English, and is temperamentally suited to function in Texas. Such a request is fed into the Mitsui personnel computer, which currently has a pool of some 600 executives considered eligible for international service. Once the computer comes up with its choices, a negotiating-selecting process is set in motion between headquarters and the field. Depending on the urgency of filling the slot, this works by letter, telex, or telephone.

An example of self-initiated assignment is the executive who asked for—and quickly got—a post in Saudi Arabia. His main argument was that the country represented an important opportunity for the company.

Most Mitsui executives return to Japan—and the computer pool—after assignments of three years' duration. Hardship posts have shorter stints, and some of the plum assignments tend to last longer; but the general policy is to pull executives back to headquarters regularly to make sure they do not lose touch with how things are done at Mitsui and to make certain they continue to feel part of the mainstream. Occasionally, a particularly adaptable and well-regarded executive, especially at the higher echelons of middle management, is transferred directly from one overseas post to another international assignment, but that is rare.

The new concept at Mitsui—still very much in an embryonic state—is to "nationalize" expatriate executives, i.e., leave them in a post in which they are effective and which they find congenial for as long as they like.

At the senior management level, selected executives are sent each year to advanced management courses in the U.S. and Europe to such institutions as Harvard, the Sloan Management School at M.I.T. and IMEDE in Switzerland.

The "Inbound" Program

Mitsui also has a training system for "inbound" executives, i.e., non-Japanese executives with upward corporate mobility. That system has three channels. In one, candidates are selected from their home country's top universities and rotated in various departments of the local Mitsui subsidiary. London-based Mitsui & Co. Europe, for example, gets graduates from Oxford and Cambridge and, for about three years, trains them in-house, focusing at the same time on plotting long-term career paths. Career opportunities include staff and line positions, as well as the more specialized managerial activities in the commodity divisions of the Mitsui Trading Company.

A second channel sends promising foreign executives to the Mitsui office that commands a particular expertise. For example, a German executive with a career path in Mitsui's production division is sent to the New York office for a training stint of two to three years.

The third Mitsui channel for foreign managerial talent is reserved mainly for young executives from the developing countries, who are pulled into Tokyo for two to three years of training before a career path is plotted for them, preferably in their own countries or contiguous areas.

Mitsui pays particular attention to these young executives from the LDCs because it knows that LDC governments will increasingly insist on local managers as well as on local equity. As a Mitsui executive put it, "Sooner or later, we'll have to ask them to hold our company shares."

For its non-Japanese senior managers, Mitsui organizes a two-week in-house seminar once a year in Tokyo, at which key employees are immersed in company policies and techniques. Some 30 to 50 executives attend these seminars each year. English is the working language, with executives chosen from any and all of Mitsui's global operations, including its 230 joint ventures.

Mitsui policy in managing joint ventures is to recruit top local management wherever possible. In the U.S. and Canada, for example, the policy is to have an American or Canadian serve as president of the venture, with a Japanese vice-president. In countries with fewer top managerial resources, the pattern is reversed. The newest trend at Mitsui is to look for top non-Japanese executives to serve on the boards of Mitsui companies in Japan.

Questions

1. What are the strengths and weaknesses of the Mitsui system?

2. Would you recommend the adoption of this system for an American corporation? If so, why? If not, why not?

3. Discuss fully the advantages and disadvantages of nationalizing expatriate executives.

4. Do you foresee any problems that Mitsui might be faced with in following this personnel policy? Explain.

NOTES

1. Richard D. Robinson, *International Business Management: A Guide to Decision Making*, 2nd ed. (Hinsdale, Ill.: Dryden Press, 1978), p. 297.

2. Julie Solomon, "Women, Minorities and Foreign Postings: Few Go Abroad; Many Challenge Reasons Why," *Wall Street Journal*, June 2, 1989, p. B1.

3. Business International Corporation, "Worldwide Executive Compensation and

Human Resource Planning," July 23, 1982 (New York: Business International Corporation), pp. 235–236.

4. Simcha Ronen, *Comparative and Multinational Management* (New York: John Wiley and Sons, 1986), pp. 506–507.

5. Robinson, pp. 304–305.

6. Ibid.

7. L. G. Franko, "Who Manages Multinational Enterprises?" *Columbia Journal of World Business* 8:2 (1973), pp. 30–42.

8. Ronen, pp. 505–555.

9. Robinson, p. 313.

10. Ibid., p. 314.

11. Rosalie L. Tung, "Selection and Training Procedures of U.S., European, and Japanese Multinationals," *California Management Review,* Fall 1982, pp. 57–71.

12. S. H. Robock and K. Simmonds, *International Business and Multinational Enterprise*, 4th ed. (Homewood, Ill.: Richard D. Irwin, 1989), p. 585.

13. Shawn Tully, "American Bosses Are Overpaid . . .", *Fortune*, November 7, 1988, pp. 121–136.

14. Robock and Simmonds, p. 586.

15. Robinson, pp. 205–206.

16. Ibid., p. 257.

17. Ibid., p. 257.

REFERENCES AND SELECTED READINGS

Business International Corporation. "Worldwide Executive Compensation and Human Resource Planning." New York: Business International Corporation, 1982.

Copeland, Lennie, and Lewis Griggs. *Going International.* New York: Random House, 1985.

Desatnick, Robert L., and Margo L. Bennett. *Human Resource Management in the Multinational Company.* Hants, England: Gower Press, 1977.

Franko, L. G. "Who Manages Multinational Enterprises?" *Columbia Journal of World Business* 8:2 (1973), 30–42.

Robinson, Richard D. *International Business Management: A Guide to Decision Making,* 2nd ed. Hinsdale, Ill.: Dryden Press, 1978.

Robock, Stefan, and Kenneth Simmonds. *International Business and Multinational Enterprises,* 4th ed. Homewood, Ill.: Richard D. Irwin, 1989.

Ronen, Simcha. *Comparative and Multinational Management.* New York: John Wiley and Sons, 1986.

Tung, Rosalie L. "Selection and Training Procedures of U.S., European, and Japanese Multinationals." *California Management Review,* Fall 1982, pp. 57–71.

CHAPTER

20

International Accounting and Taxation of Foreign Source Income

LEARNING OBJECTIVES

- Understand the problems arising from different accounting systems
- Learn how foreign currency transactions can result in gains or losses for a firm
- Explain why local currency financial statements must be translated into home currency terms
- Describe the role of the accounting profession in establishing standards
- Review the efforts to harmonize international accounting systems
- Understand the impact of the IRS code on the international earnings of U.S. firms
- Learn how multinational corporations can minimize the payments of taxes on income earned abroad
- Become familiar with the taxes levied on income earned abroad
- Describe the impact of U.S. taxes on foreign individuals and firms operating in the United States
- Learn the differences in tax rates among countries

548

INTRODUCTION

Major developments in recent decades have increased the importance of international accounting. The rapid growth in foreign direct investments, the increasing contributions of foreign operations to the total revenues of multinational corporations, the volatility of exchange rates, and other changes require a better understanding of the role of international accounting in the management of multinational corporations.

For multinational enterprises (MNEs), the differences in accounting systems among different countries create problems that are generally absent in the domestic market. First, MNEs must be able to analyze and interpret the information from different countries so that management can make sound decisions. Second, they must prepare reports that are acceptable to their stockholders, their creditors, and the different users of their financial statements. Third, they must submit reports to governments of the various countries in which they operate.

This chapter describes some of the problems arising from differences in accounting practices and procedures among countries. Furthermore, this chapter explains why harmonization of accounting is of major concern to international businesses and describes some of the efforts that have been made at harmonization on regional, national, and international levels.

THE IMPACT OF DIFFERENT ACCOUNTING SYSTEMS

National Differences in Accounting Systems

Since multinational corporations operate in many different countries, their activities cut across several accounting systems. They must collect, analyze, and interpret financial statements that are issued by firms in countries that make use of different accounting practices and procedures. Understanding the terminology, format, and disclosure practices is essential. The use of different languages and currencies requires translation, adjustment, and consolidation. The currency used and the degree of inflation must be considered in valuation and income determination. For example, in Brazil, the statements are prepared in Portuguese, in cruzados, and according to the nation's accounting procedures and laws. In the United States, the statements are prepared in English according to "generally accepted accounting principles" (GAAP), in dollars, and in accordance with the nation's tax regulations. Germany, France, the Netherlands, Chile, Japan, and all other countries have their own requirements. Thus, without some knowledge of foreign accounting practices, MNCs will encounter difficulties in analyzing and interpreting statements prepared in any country.

Each country may use its own method of inventory valuation, resulting in different values. Some countries make use of last in-first out (LIFO), first in-first out (FIFO), replacement cost, weighted average cost, or appraised valuation. Fixed assets may be valued differently in different countries. In the United States and Japan, the value of fixed assets is based on acquisition cost or construction cost less accumulated depreciation. In France, such assets are valued according to the appraised value. Similarly, different methods may be used in the treatment of leases, long-term debt, share valuation, and research and development costs.[1]

In the evaluation of foreign operations, ratios are often used. By American standards a high debt to equity ratio, low cash levels, and high inventory might be frowned upon; yet in a country with rampant inflation the same conditions might be considered good management and a hedge against inflation.[2]

The task of the MNC is made difficult because of the differences in national accounting systems.

Transactions in Foreign Currencies

Transactions occur when payment is to be made or received in terms of foreign currencies. Foreign-currency-denominated transactions create major problems in accounting for the value of assets, liabilities, revenues, and expenses. Fluctuations in exchange rates result in gains or losses through no effort of the firm. As was discussed in Chapter 15, if a purchase is made on credit in terms of a foreign currency, the amount payable in domestic currency will vary with the rate at which foreign currency can be acquired at a future date. If, for example, a credit purchase of £1000 is made in

London when the rate of exchange is £1.00 = $1.70, the dollar value of that purchase is $1700. However, if the rate of exchange is £1.00 = $1.60 when payment is due at a future date, it will take only $1600 to acquire £1000 to make payment, resulting in a windfall profit of $100. How is this to be recorded in the financial statement? According to U.S. GAAP, the $100 must be recorded as gain (income) to the firm at the end of the accounting period. If the rate of exchange had been £1.00 = $1.80, the transaction would have been recorded as a loss on the financial statement.[3] Similarly, a loss or gain might occur if money is borrowed that is repayable in foreign currency. To protect themselves against possible losses from fluctuations in exchange rates, firms may enter into hedging contracts, as was discussed in earlier chapters.

> When foreign currencies are used in an international transaction, the gain or loss from the transaction must be reflected in the financial statement.

Translation of Foreign Currencies in Financial Statements

Translation is the process of converting the foreign currency balance sheet and income statement into U.S. dollars. The first step in the process requires the firm to restate its foreign financial statements into those of the generally accepted accounting principles. Once this has been done, the foreign currency amounts must be converted into U.S. dollars using the current rate method.[4]

> The foreign currency balance sheet and income statement must be translated into the domestic currency according to the current rate method.

The current rate method requires that all assets and liabilities, other than net worth, be translated at the current rate of exchange. Once this is done, the income statement is translated into dollars using the average rate of exchange during the period, including depreciation and cost of goods sold.

EFFORTS AT HARMONIZATION OF ACCOUNTING STANDARDS

The Role of the Accounting Profession

The development of the accounting profession and its role in setting standards are influenced by a number of factors. The economic, legal, cultural, and political environments influence the philosophy, postulates, concepts, and standards for accounting. Accounting standards in a free enterprise environment are different from those in a central command economy, where financial statements may be used as a tool to facilitate achieving national objectives. In an agricultural society, simple financial statements might suffice, while in a sophisticated economy, the statements usually reflect the complexity of the economy.

Where accounting is highly developed, the accounting profession usually takes the leadership on policy formulation, but where it is not highly developed, the government often passes legislation regulating the profession. Where neither dominates, the government and the accounting profession cooperate in determining policy.

In the United States, the accounting profession plays a major role in recommending accounting standards. The American Institute of Certified Public Accountants (AICPA) and the Financial Accounting Standards Board (FASB) are largely responsible for setting standards for regulating accounting and auditing practices. The U.S. Uniform Commercial Code and state laws determine minimum requirements for record keeping. The Securities and Exchange Commission (SEC) specifies the form and content of financial statements of publicly held corporations, including income statements, balance sheets, and statements of changes in financial position. Under Section 19(a) of the Securities Act of 1933, the SEC can standardize accounting terminology, measurement, and reporting. It requires that financial statements of publicly held corporations be prepared in accordance with the U.S. generally accepted accounting principles. It also requires that an auditor's report accompany the detailed supplementary statements to support financial statements that are filed with the Securities and Exchange Commission.

In France and the United Kingdom, the accounting profession takes the leadership in developing standards and procedures and in recommending government legislation, while in Germany the profession plays a lesser role in establishing standards and is more concerned in complying with accounting principles that are prescribed by law. In Japan, the Ministry of Finance sets the accounting standards. The accounting systems of other countries show wide variations.

The role of the accounting profession in establishing standards for accounting in a country is determined largely by its relative importance in that country.

Current Harmonization Efforts

Many scholars and practitioners support the worldwide harmonization of accounting standards and procedures.[5] To this end, various attempts have been made to develop and implement international accounting standards. The first such attempt was made in 1904 when the First International Congress of Accountants was held in the United States. This was followed by other conferences in different countries without any significant progress toward standardization. In the Tenth International Congress of Accountants held in Sydney, Australia, in 1972, the International Accounting Standards Committee (IASC) was established with the primary objective of formulating international accounting standards for the preparation of financial statements. Standards were introduced and agreed to by representatives of different countries, but member nations have been reluctant to adopt the recommendations.

The International Coordination Committee for the Accounting Profession (ICCAP) was established with the objective of developing auditing standards. It was replaced in 1977 by a more permanent body called the International Federation of Accountants Commission (IFAC), with the objective of establishing standards in auditing, ethics, education, and training, leaving the formation of accounting standards to the IASC. The United Nations has also been actively involved in an effort to establish international accounting standards that emphasize increased disclosure in financial statements.

At the regional level, the Organization for Economic Cooperation and Development (OECD), a group of 24 nations committed to achieving economic growth, employment, and a rising standard of living, in 1976 proposed a code of conduct for MNEs dealing with financial disclosure. The European Community has issued directives for harmonizing accounting standards among the member countries. These directives narrow the alternatives for the conduct of accounting rather than set standards.

> Despite widespread agreement on the need to standardize or harmonize the accounting systems among the different countries, only moderate progress has been made.

TAXATION OF FOREIGN SOURCE INCOME

Since taxes are a significant part of overall costs of doing business abroad, the legal minimization of taxes is a major objective of management. The taxation of income from international business can be perplexing because income earned from different sources is taxed differently.

The purpose of this section is to describe the different methods that are used to tax income earned abroad and how the impact of taxes will differ, depending on the source from which the income is derived.

There are three major sources of income from international operations.

1. Exporting goods or services to buyers in a foreign country
2. Establishing a branch office in a foreign country to receive and sell goods or services imported from the home country
3. Founding a subsidiary company or engaging in a joint venture or other type of partnership operation in a foreign country to vend goods or services, and to manufacture goods in that country

Tax planning by domestic corporations engaged in international business necessitates investigation of the impact of taxes assessed on earnings by the home country and by each foreign country in which the international company is doing business. The changing political, economic, and competitive climates in developed and less developed nations create changing tax environments in those countries. In the United States, Congress passes tax legislation to place restrictions on or provide benefits to companies doing business in particular locations throughout the world. This creates an unending challenge for firms that wish to earn adequate economic benefits without excessive taxation on income and investments from international business. Therefore, it is important for businesses to plan to minimize the taxation of income and investments as well as to diminish the impact of various taxes on overall income from sources around the world.

Table 20.1 provides a general summary of the method used by the United States government to tax income earned from major foreign sources.

National sovereignty permits various countries to assess taxes on foreign businesses within their political jurisdictions. These may be called income tax, transfer tax, value added tax, import duty, sales tax, vendor tax, disallowance in the expatriation of earnings or cash, and so forth.

Since the tax system of each country is somewhat different, the following pages are limited to discussing some effects of the U.S. Internal Revenue Code on international earnings of domestic businesses, taxation of U.S. nationals working in foreign locations, taxation of foreign businesses operating in the United States, and various taxes imposed against those United States and foreign businesses operating in foreign countries. The foreign countries selected represent developed and less developed countries on different continents, but they are not necessarily representative of all countries at these stages of economic development. They only illustrate some of the taxes that companies operating abroad might encounter. Because of the significance of tax considerations, executives should evaluate taxation advantages and disadvantages as part of their location selection process.

Taxation of U.S. Businesses

The complex and extensive rules and regulations of the Internal Revenue Code are too technical and cumbersome to explain fully in this text. Persons seeking further knowledge of these tax details may refer directly to the Internal Revenue Code or to one of the many professional tax services available in libraries and in the offices of CPA firms, and corporate tax planners. The discussion in this chapter excludes details and exceptions and may be regarded as general rules with which one should become familiar to understand the possible effects of foreign taxes on international business.

Table 20.1   **Taxation of Foreign Source Income**

Type of business	*Income source*	*Taxable when earned*	*Deferral principle*
U.S. corporation	Subsidiary	No	Yes
U.S. corporation	Controlled foreign corporation	No	Yes
U.S. corporation	Branch	Yes	No
U.S. corporation	Partnership	Yes	No
U.S. corporation	Joint venture	Yes	No
U.S. corporation	Franchise	Yes	No
U.S. corporation	Tax haven	Yes	No
U.S. corporation	Royalties	Yes	No
Individuals	Wages and salaries	Yes	No

Foreign Subsidiary Income

U.S. taxpayers may elect to take a credit against the U.S. income tax for foreign earnings taxed in foreign countries up to a ratio of foreign earnings to total U.S. taxable earnings from all sources. Let us take a hypothetical case.

Bizmuth Corporation has subsidiary corporations Carthage and Duvall operating in two different foreign countries, such that in 1989, the data in Table 20.2 were generated from corporate operations.

The amount of the U.S. income tax credit on taxes paid to a foreign country would be calculated as follows:

$$\text{Tax credit} = \frac{\text{Foreign earnings}}{\text{Total taxable earnings}} = \frac{\$100,000 + \$100,000}{\$600,000} = \frac{1}{3}$$

Since the tax credit for foreign income is in a ratio of 1 to 3 to total taxable income, the maximum credit allowable would be $\frac{1}{3}$ x $192,250 = $64,083.

Since the foreign tax paid is $87,000 ($40,000 + $47,000) and the income ratio of 1 to 3 limits the credit to $64,083, then Bizmuth Corporation's U.S. tax is $192,250 less $64,083 = $128,167, and total income tax paid to both countries would be $215,167 ($128,167 + $87,000). Congress has thus limited double taxation on foreign earnings of U.S. corporations. The U.S. corporation must file a form 1118 to get tax credit. The difference between the $87,000 foreign tax paid and the $64,083 allowed, amounting to $22,917, may be carried back as a tax credit for the two preceding years and forward for the five succeeding years until used.[6]

If losses are incurred from foreign operations, they reduce U.S. source taxable income. However, such losses must be recaptured in succeeding years if the foreign operation becomes profitable. The amount recaptured

Table 20.2   **Example—Taxation of Foreign Subsidiary Income (Bizmuth Corp.)**

	Bizmuth Corp.	Subsidiary Carthage	Subsidiary Duvall	Total taxable income
Corporation income	$400,000	$100,000	$100,000	$600,000
Foreign taxes paid		40,000	47,000	87,000
U.S. tax on $600,000		192,250		

U.S. corporate tax rate on taxable income for 1989 was:

15% on first $50,000	15% × 50,000 = 7,500
25% between $50,000 and $75,000	25% × 25,000 = 6,250
34% over $75,000 ($600,000 − 75,000)	34% × 525,000 = 178,500
Total U.S. tax on $600,000	$192,250

Source: *Prentice-Hall Federal Taxes, 1989*, Vol I (Englewood Cliffs, N.J.: Prentice-Hall, 1989), p. 3201.

against foreign income is the lesser of the prior year's loss or 50 percent of the foreign taxable income. This process must continue until the loss is recaptured.[7]

Corporations will find that the taxes payable vary from year to year as foreign income increases or decreases. In their tax planning, managers should take these factors into consideration to determine (1) tax effects on foreign earnings, (2) foreign subsidiary locations for tax benefits, and (3) return on investment of foreign operations.

A U.S. firm may take a credit against its U.S. income tax liability for a portion of the foreign income taxes paid.

Controlled Foreign Corporations (Sub-part F Income)

A controlled foreign corporation (CFC) is usually a paper corporation in which more than 50 percent of the stock is owned by U.S. shareholders, each of whom has at least a 10 percent interest, and is set up in a country different from the country of production, sales, or service.[8] Foreign corporations are usually not taxed on foreign source income, and U.S. persons who are shareholders pay U.S. taxes only on dividends received. This is according to the deferral principle.[9]

Unfortunately, some countries have purposely implemented tax laws that encourage firms to use them as tax havens for the avoidance of U.S. taxes. Since these countries impose little or no tax on income brought into that country, income earned in other foreign countries would be held in the tax haven. Some U.S. corporations have tried to make use of these tax havens by manipulating their transfer prices. The domestic corporation will accomplish this by allowing a controlled foreign subsidiary to acquire goods at costs below arms-length pricing. The lower profits incurred by selling to its subsidiary at lower profit margins are offset by higher profits for the controlled subsidiary when the products are resold. This results in the accumulation of profits in the controlled subsidiary rather than in the United States. Since earnings are taxed at lower rates by that foreign country, the domestic corporation avoids higher U.S. taxes on profits that are held in the controlled subsidiary through the "passive" transfer price manipulation.

If an item that is normally priced at $10,000 is sold to the CFC for $8,000, the sale would be below arms-length pricing. When the CFC resells the goods to a third party for the regular selling price of $12,000, the profit will be $4,000 rather than $2,000 normal profit because of the lower costs. Thus, the parent company's income is lower by $2,000, but is offset by the $2,000 additional profit in the controlled foreign corporation. In other words, the parent company does not report the $2,000 that is held by the subsidiary as income until it is repatriated as dividends because of the deferral principle. Meanwhile, the $2,000 that the subsidiary declares as its earnings will be taxed at a lower rate in the tax haven. Since the parent corporation owns the subsidiary, it makes little difference where the profits are held. Thus, the non-U.S.-taxed profits that are accumulated in the CFC may be used to meet the capital requirements of the parent firm. This situation is presented graphically in Figure 20.1.

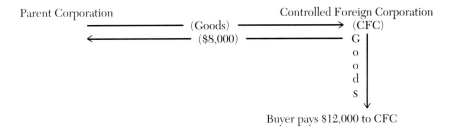

Parent Corporation

Controlled Foreign Corporation

(Goods) ⟶ (CFC)

($8,000) ⟵

Buyer pays $12,000 to CFC

Figure 20.1   Transfer Pricing and the Controlled Foreign Corporation.

Since the tax haven company is often only a paper company without warehouses, factories, offices, and so forth, it seldom takes possession of the goods. It only has title of ownership. In other words, the title of ownership to the goods may go from the parent corporation to the controlled foreign corporation to the buyer, but the actual shipment of the goods is directly to the buyer from the parent corporation.

Section 482 of Sub-part F of the Internal Revenue Code prevents domestic U.S. corporations and individuals from using controlled corporations as a tax haven. It states that

> in any case of two or more organizations, trades, or businesses . . . owned or controlled directly or indirectly by the same interests, the Secretary [of the Treasury] may distribute, apportion, or allocate gross income, deductions, credits or allowances between or among such organizations, trades, or business, if he determines that such distribution, apportionment, or allocation is necessary in order to prevent evasion of taxes or clearly to reflect the income of any such organizations, trades, or businesses.

Owners of CFCs are not permitted to defer payment of taxes on the earnings of these companies if they serve as tax havens.

The I.R.S. taxes owners of controlled foreign corporations that are functioning as tax havens on their annual earnings even though such earnings are not distributed, thus voiding the deferral principle. Such features of the Internal Revenue Code attempt to prevent improper avoidance of taxation by U.S. taxpayers on their income from international operations.

Specialty Exporting Companies: WHTC, DISC, and FSC

Of academic interest are the efforts on the part of Congress to promote U.S. exports by passing legislation granting tax concessions to American exporters. The first such effort was made in 1939 when the Internal Revenue Code authorized the reduction of taxes on income earned from exports through a Western Hemisphere Trade Corporation (WHTC). This act was modified in 1954 but remained operative until the Revenue Act of 1971 provided for the phasing out of the WHTC after 1976. The act permitting the operation of the WHTC was repealed in 1979.[10]

The Revenue Act of 1971 provided for the replacement of the WHTC with a broader-based Domestic International Sales Corporation (DISC).[11] The incentive to establish a DISC as an export arm of U.S. corporations was a concession in the form of corporate income tax deferral for an indefinite period on one half of the earnings until the earnings were distributed to the stockholders. The undistributed earnings could thus be used to meet various capital requirements of the parent corporation.[12]

In 1976, as a result of the Foreign Corrupt Practices Act, the tax law was modified, so DISCs could no longer defer taxes on export sales resulting from illegal payments for bribes to officials of foreign governments. Furthermore, DISCs could not receive tax benefits if engaged in the Arab boycott.[13] However, the the end of DISC came about because members of the General Agreement on Tariffs and Trade (GATT) regarded the tax deferral on DISC income as an export subsidy by the U.S. government, contrary to GATT provisions. GATT signatories requested that retaliatory action be taken against the United States.

To alleviate the situation, Congress passed the Tax Reform Act of 1984. The tax deferral rules were changed to avoid possible retaliation and to enable the GATT countries to get on with other business important to the United States.[14] In 1985, DISCs were replaced by a new, less favorable type of corporation known as a Foreign Sales Corporation (FSC). As a transition rule in the elimination of DISC, the corporation's deferred income was considered as previously taxed and, therefore, exempt from taxation.[15]

In order to qualify as a FSC for export income tax purposes, the firm must meet the following requirements:[16]

1. It must be a foreign entity incorporated under the laws of a foreign country or a U.S. possession that meets certain exchange of information requirements; 23 countries and 4 U.S. possessions meet these requirements.

2. The FSC may have no more than 25 stockholders at any time.

3. More than one class of stock may be outstanding, but no preferred stock that is limited and preferred to dividends and distributions is allowed.

4. Permanent accounting records must be maintained at a non-U.S. office and, under IRS Section 6001, records must be kept at a U.S. location during the tax year.

5. The corporation board of directors must include at least one individual who is not a U.S. resident and must operate under the laws of the country in which the firm is incorporated.

6. The corporation must elect to be a FSC on Form 8279 for a taxable year within a 90-day period prior to the beginning of the year. A failure to qualify as a FSC for five consecutive years results in revocation of the election.

The gross receipts from exports of certain goods and services to unrelated parties or at an arms-length pricing method constitutes the foreign trade income of the FSC. Only foreign trade income is subject to tax exemption for FSCs, and this is subject to pricing rules. If foreign trade income is from arms-length pricing, 30 percent is tax exempt. If foreign trade income is subject to special administrative pricing rules, about 65 percent ($\frac{15}{23}$) of that income is exempt from taxation. The Internal Revenue Code provides related rules on costs and investments.

The U.S. government continues to try to stimulate the nation's exports by offering tax concessions.

Foreign Branch Income

U.S. corporations must include foreign branch income as part of total corporate earnings just as if it were income from a domestic branch. But since the income earned abroad is taxable by the foreign government, credit for the taxes paid is allowable. However, income is not favored with the deferral principle even if it is not remitted during the year in which it was earned.

Income Earned Abroad by U.S. Individuals

U.S. corporations often send employees abroad to perform duties such as sales, purchasing, engineering, consulting, auditing of subsidiaries, and legal and executive decision-making. Such short-term visits are treated by the corporation as operating expenses in their determination of taxable U.S. income. The individuals involved regard compensation as normal earnings, and such reimbursable costs of travel, meals, and lodging as company expenses.

Individual taxpayers are generally taxed on all income earned from U.S. or foreign services. U.S. tax laws permit certain credits and exclusions from taxes of residents working outside of the country if proper conditions are met. A "qualified individual," in order to receive foreign residence tax credits and exclusions, must meet the following requirements:[17]

1. Be a citizen of the United States and be a bona fide resident of a foreign country or countries for an uninterruped time period including an entire taxable year, or
2. Be a citizen or resident of the United States who resides in a foreign country over a period of 12 consecutive months and is present in a foreign country at least 330 days of this 12-month period.

As a "qualified individual," a person may exclude from U.S. taxable income "foreign earned income" computed on more than $80,000 per year from 1983 through 1987; $85,000 in 1988; $90,000 in 1989, and $95,000 in 1990 and the years following.[18]

In addition, a "housing cost amount" may be excluded from taxable U.S. income. This includes reasonable expenses such as rent, utilities, and insurance for the individual and dependents. It does not permit phone, interest, and taxes as housing expenses. The exclusion of the "housing cost amount" is the excess of housing costs over an amount equal to 16 percent of the salary of a Government Service (Grade GS-14, Step 1) employee, computed on a daily basis, times the number of days of that taxable year within the applicable period.[19]

If the employer provides housing cost, the employee may exclude only the lesser of what the employer provides or the individual employee's foreign earned income for the year as a maximum amount.[20] As with many issues of the Internal Revenue Code, this can be quite complicated.

Employees such as skilled construction workers, geologists, and surveyors, living abroad in locations where reasonable housing is not otherwise available, do not have to include housing or meal costs as income if supplied by an employer since such housing is at the employer's convenience and is necessary to complete extended work at the site. Such housing must not be available to the public and must be in an enclave accommodating 10 or more employees.[21] For example, if a construction company contracts to build a tunnel through a remote mountain in Chile for rail passage, it will provide housing and meals to the heavy equipment operators and technical personnel at company expense near the construction site. These costs are not taxable to the employees and may be deducted as part of the project expense by the employer.

There are other special rules for self-employed individuals, married couples, and federal employees that can be found in Section 911 of the Internal Revenue Code.

American citizens working abroad are permitted to exclude from U.S. taxes a portion of their foreign earned income.

Taxation of Foreign Corporations and Individuals

The numerous foreign corporations that operate with factories, sales offices, service facilities, and distribution centers and those "nonresident aliens" in their employ within the U.S. borders are subject to federal income tax. The amount of tax levied on these foreign corporations depends on whether their income is "effectively connected" with U.S. business. That is, does the foreign corporation have a branch operation or a subsidiary in the United States? Therefore, two types of foreign corporation are specified by IRS regulations: those that *are not* engaged in U.S. business at any time within the taxable year, and those that *are* engaged in U.S. business at any time within the taxable year. "A foreign corporation not doing business here continues to be taxed at 30 percent (or lower treaty rate) on all U.S. source income."[22]

The 1984 Tax Reform Act attempted to remove tax avoidance by foreign corporations and U.S. corporations operating through tax havens such as the Netherlands Antilles, Guam, or the Virgin Islands. Special rules provided in Section 881(b) and 7651(5)(b) of the Internal Revenue Code are efforts to close any loophole. According to these rules, "effectively con-

Foreign firms and individuals are required to pay taxes on income earned in the United States, but the rate depends on the nature of such income.

nected" income of foreign corporations is taxed at regular U.S. corporation tax rates.[23]

TAXATION OF CORPORATE EARNINGS IN SELECTED COUNTRIES

In their financial planning for foreign operations, managers of U.S. corporations should take into consideration the possible long-run impact of foreign country taxes on business. Major differences in the tax systems exist among countries in different stages of economic development and in different geographic areas.

In some less developed countries, especially in Africa and Asia, which have less well-developed political systems, taxes are often adopted to meet the whims of short-term government programs rather than to improve the long-term economic environment of the country. As a result, greater risks for business ventures exist than in the more highly developed countries. However, because such countries need investment capital, they are more likely to adopt general and specific tax incentives to encourage foreign investments that will provide jobs and stimulate the growth of foreign-exchange-earning industries.

If a U.S. corporation is considering the industrialized countries of western Europe as a location for a manufacturing or marketing operation, it will find that each country has a different tax structure. Accounting standards for reporting taxable corporation income vary for such things as inventory valuation, depreciation methods, and deductibility or nondeductibility of certain expenses. These factors must be taken into consideration in comparing the tax impact of one country with another.

The following section will discuss some common taxes that are levied by most countries and that have a bearing on the operation of firms in these countries. The value added, corporate income, and individual income taxes are levied by many countries. The application and the levels of these taxes vary among the countries.[24]

Value Added Tax

All European Community nations and many other countries of western Europe assess a value added tax (VAT). Taxes are collected at each step of business production, distribution, or service, usually based on the invoice value. The total amount is eventually paid by the consumer as part of the final price of the good or service. This type of tax is usually regarded as regressive because lower-income consumers pay a higher proportion of their income for this tax. Different countries use different methods to make the tax less regressive, such as charging lower rates on necessities and higher rates on luxury goods or by exempting or partially exempting items such as food and medicines from the value added tax. The level of VAT rates for selected countries is summarized in Table 20.3; a brief explanation of these taxes follows here.

Denmark levies a value added tax of 22 percent on all sales and services except real estate, medical, banking, and insurance services. The taxpayers pay the difference between the tax on their own sale and the tax that was paid on purchases from other producers or distributors. The tax is not charged on exports of goods or services rendered outside of the country, but is applicable to imports.[25]

The 14 percent turnover tax of Germany that is levied on most goods and services is actually a value added tax. Norway, a non-EC country, levies a valued added tax of 20 percent. A 10 percent investment tax is levied on some items where the 20 percent VAT tax is refundable.

Greece makes use of three VAT rates: 6 percent for basic commodities and services such as food and dairy products, hotel accommodations, professional services (doctor and lawyer fees are exempt), transportation, and agricultural services; 36 percent for services and luxury products such as perfumes, clocks and watches, TV sets and VCRs, photographic equipment, tobacco products, alcoholic beverages, leather goods, and similar products; and 16 percent for all other categories not included under the 6 and 36 percent rates. The VAT is levied on all imports as well as domestically produced goods.[26]

Finland levies a turnover tax similar to a VAT. It imposes this tax on all imported and most domestic goods. For imports, the rate is 19.05 percent of the CIF value plus import duty, which includes a 16 percent sales tax. This tax differs from most European VATs in that the valuation of fixed assets, fuels, and other goods intended for consumption by business are not deductible. Exports and certain domestic items are exempt from the turnover tax. The only services that are taxed are hotels and restaurants.[27]

Many of the developing nations have adopted the value added tax and have modified the tax to fit the local situation. Bolivia is such an example. It levies a 10 percent value added tax on all sales, imports, and services.

Table 20.3 **VAT Rates for Selected Countries**

Country	Rate of tax
Denmark	22%
West Germany	14%
Norway	20%
Greece	6%, 16%, 36%
Finland	19.05%
Bolivia	10%

Excluded are interest payable to or by financial institutions, sales or transfers of shares or titles, the sale or transfers of assets, and exports. The VAT is payable on the total purchased amount listed in the billed sales price (termed *fiscal debt*). The taxpayer may discount, against this fiscal debt, 10 percent of all purchases and imports as a fiscal credit. There are no exemptions. However, a 10 percent complementary tax is payable by all citizens and estates for income from Bolivian sources such as salaries, fees, rents, interests, royalties, patents, trademarks, commissions, dividends, and so forth. The VAT payments are deductible from the complementary taxes.[28]

Corporate Income Tax

All governments levy corporate income taxes. The bases for these taxes vary from country to country and are often levied at the federal, state, and local levels. Corporate income taxes for selected countries are summarized in Table 20.4; an explanation of their application follows.

In Finland, a 33 percent corporation tax is levied on taxable income that is based on actual net income. Business expenses that are deductible are rents, raw materials, wages and benefits, pension payments, repairs of plant and equipment, interest on borrowed capital, and depreciation based on the declining balance method. Other deductions from gross income include profits on land and buildings held more than 10 years, profits on sale of shares held more than 5 years, and transfers to investment reserves of up to 20 percent of net profits. Companies may also deduct up to 40 percent of distributed dividends. Dividends transferred from one Finnish company to another are not taxable. In addition, there is a municipal tax ranging from 14 to 18 percent and a church tax of 1 percent.[29]

Norway's federal income tax rate on corporations is 27.8 percent. In addition, there is a municipal income tax of 23 percent. Accounting for tax reporting requires the use of FIFO (first in-first out) inventory valuation. Depreciation is based on a reducing balance method applied to the asset

Table 20.4   **Corporate Income Tax Rates for Selected Countries**

Country	Tax rate
Finland	33%
Norway	27.8%
Greece	46%, 40%, 35%
West Germany	36%, 56%, 50%
Israel	40% + 8.53%
Singapore	33%
Bolivia	2% of net assets
Peru	35%
Zaire	See explanation in text

value at 35 percent for machinery and equipment, 30 percent on ships and aircraft, and 9 percent on new construction. Donations and subscriptions, investment losses, and entertainment costs are not deductible as expenses, but dividends received from other Norwegian companies are not regarded as taxable income to the recipient corporation.

Payments to foreign affiliates are regarded as operating expenses if paid at arms-length transaction rates. Consolidated corporation tax returns are disallowed. A special tax credit of 22 percent of pretax profit is allowed for firms investing in a special fund for future investment in fixed assets in prescribed geographic areas. The withholding tax on dividends paid to foreign persons range between 9 and 50 percent. The federal income tax is not imposed on annual profits distributed as dividends.[30]

In Greece, corporations and other business organizations are subject to the corporate income tax, but other types of Greek companies or partnerships are not taxed as such. However, their members are taxed. Corporate profits are taxed either as retained earnings of the corporation or as dividends in the hands of the stockholders. When retained earnings that have already been taxed are distributed to shareholders, the corporations may apply for a refund. Corporations that are incorporated in Greece are taxed on their income earned both domestically and abroad. Nonresident corporations are taxed on income derived from a permanent establishment in Greece or from other Greek sources. The general rate is 46 percent. Industrial, handicraft, mining, and quarrying companies are taxed at 40 percent. Certain companies qualify for reduced rates under investment incentives and are taxed at the rate of 35 percent. For dividends, the shares not registered on the Athens Stock Exchange are taxed at 47 percent and bearer shares are taxed at 50 percent. For shares listed on the Athens Stock Exchange the rate is 42 percent for registered shares and 45 percent for bearer shares.[31]

West Germany has one of the most complicated tax systems among the industrialized countries. The corporate income tax rate is 36 percent on distributed profits (dividends) and 56 percent on undistributed profits. Branches of foreign corporations are taxed at 50 percent of total income. A municipal trade tax ranging from 11.1 to 20 percent is assessed by various municipalities. This tax is a deductible business expense for national income tax determination. Additional taxes include a 0.6 percent tax on 75 percent of all business assets exceeding 125,000 DM ($71,176) which is not deductible for income tax purposes. A 1 percent tax is imposed on new capital entering the business. This tax is deductible as a business expense before taxes. Payments to foreign affiliates for royalties, services, and interest are permitted as deductible expenses if at arms-length pricing. Inventories must be valued at either replacement cost or net realizable value, whichever is lower. Depreciation may be straight-line or declining-balance (at three times the straight-line rate, not to exceed 30 percent) over the asset life.

U.S. branches in Germany are subject to the same rates as corporations.

Consolidated tax returns are permitted for nonresident companies only if a registered branch is maintained in the country. Withholding taxes are imposed on corporations for dividends, royalties, rents on moveable assets, and interest on convertible bonds and certain secured loans. Tax rates on dividends range from 15 to 25 percent, royalties from 0 to 25 percent, rents from 0 to 25 percent, and interest from 0 to 50 percent. U.S. recipients of dividends are subject to a tax of 15 percent.[32]

In Israel, the corporate tax is computed in two stages. First, most corporations pay 40 percent on taxable income. The balance, after deductions of tax and distribution of cash dividends, is subject to an income tax of 8.53 percent.[33]

The corporate tax rate in Singapore is a flat 33 percent after deductions for allowable expenses such as direct and overhead expenses incurred in the business operation (interest on loans; dividends declared; rent; repairs of building and equipment; bad debts; pensions; depreciation of building, equipment, and machinery; and trading losses and donations to approved charities). Various tax exemptions are available to companies engaged in certain manufacturing, services, and export trade activities.[34]

In Bolivia, all public and private corporations, including individual corporations, must pay a 2 percent tax based on the net assets at the closing of each taxable year on the assumption of corporate profits.[35]

In Peru, the rate on taxable corporate income is 35 percent that is based on "gross revenue less total expenses, charges and losses necessarily incurred in the trade or business and recorded in the legal books of account." Taxes on subsidiary profits are calculated as for local corporations. The nation does not levy a tax on dividends, but assesses a tax of 15.4 percent on the whole of the profits whether or not they are remitted to the head office after deduction of the normal tax on profit and other charges. Capital gains are taxed as ordinary income. Fixed assets are revalued periodically after accumulated depreciation using government specified percentages. Dividends paid to nonresident shareholders are subject to withholding tax of 15.4 percent. Recipients must pay taxes on royalties, patent fees, and income from leasing equipment. Fixed assets are depreciated according to the straight line method, varying in rate from 3 percent for buildings to 20 percent for machinery, equipment, and vehicles.[36]

In Zaire, corporations are subject to a 15 percent employment tax on gross wages of non-Zairian employees and an educational tax of 1 percent of gross wages of all employees. Property taxes of 0.15 zaire to 0.40 zaire ($1.00 = 187.07 zaire) per square meter are charged on land and buildings. Registration duties are assessed at rates of 2.5 to 6 percent on transfers of real property to new owners. Foreign branches of corporations are taxed at 50 percent of the Zaire income tax rate.

For tax purposes, inventory methods are not specified. Depreciation is straight line with allowable rates of 3 to 5 percent for buildings, 10 to 15 percent for furniture and equipment, 20 to 25 percent for machinery and vehicles, and 33 percent for small tools. Payments to foreign affiliates are allowed for fees and royalties at arms-length rates only if the service is not available in Zaire. Home office costs may not be allocated against branch income as an expense. Consolidated tax returns are not permitted.[37] The following Global Insight illustrates how one country, Venezuela, is attempting to reform its taxing system to aid business and economic development.

Individual Income Tax

The methods used to determine personal income tax vary from country to country. Time of residence and other factors cause variations in tax rates. Furthermore, the central government is not the only one that levies duties on income, as is indicated by these few examples.

People who maintain a residence in Denmark or who remain in the country for more than 6 months are considered residents and are subject to full tax liability. Expatriates who are sent to Denmark for less than 3 years receive special deductions for 2 years. Taxes on personal income are progressive, but county and local taxes are proportional. At the state level, the tax rate is 22 percent, but local rates vary, with an average of about 28 percent.[38]

Residents of Greece are taxed on their worldwide income regardless of their nationality. The rates range from 18 percent to 50 percent; tax is payable in four bimonthly installments. If the tax due is paid in full on the due date of the first installment, the taxpayer is allowed a 10 percent discount. A 2 percent monthly penalty, but not exceeding 75 percent of the tax liability, is charged for late payment.[39]

The individual tax rate in Finland is progressive and ranges between 6 and 51 percent. In addition, individuals are subject to municipal taxes ranging between 14 and 18 percent, church taxes of 1 percent, and a 3 percent tax for national pension and sickness insurance premiums. Deductions from taxable income include old age and disability rebates, business travel expenses, most interest, and certain costs of child care and schooling. Some of these may also be deductible from the municipal taxes.[40]

In Israel, the personal income tax is levied on gross income from employment, trade, business, dividends, interest, pension, rents, or royalties. Taxes are withheld from wages of salaried employees when they are paid. Certain deductions are permitted for payments into pension funds, national insurance, and medical insurance. Credits also exist for personal exemptions, life insurance premiums, charitable contributions, medical and dental expenses, and alimony. The individual tax rates range between 20 and 48 percent, with the highest rates applicable for income over $25,000 per year.[41]

Two thirds of the national revenue of Singapore is derived from income taxes. Temporary residents of Singapore are exempt from the income tax if they have not resided in Singapore for a period of 6 months in 1 year.

Corporate Tax Reform—Venezuelan Style

Venezuela's finance minister has put the finishing touches on its new income tax law. This law will simplify filing procedures, reduce the number of brackets, lower tax rates, and generally bring Venezuela more in line with international levels. The following are the key provisions to this law.

1. All corporations will be taxed at a single rate and that rate will decline over the next 3 years: 45 percent in 1990, 40 percent in 1991, and 35 percent for 1992 and thereafter. This is a substantial change from the current situation in which taxes vary from 15 to 50 percent, with most MNFs at the top of that range.

2. Off-shore earnings will no longer be taxed.

3. The consolidation of the earnings of related firms will be eliminated.

4. Automatic deductions for expense accounts will be eliminated.

5. Dividends, except those paid to nonresidents, will not be taxed.

6. Tax exemptions established by decree would remain in effect until the stated expiration date.

Of perhaps greatest significance for corporations, the bill revokes the controversial consolidation requirements of the 1986 law. These mandated the consolidation of earnings of firms whose stockholders were related in such far-flung ways as blood or marital connections. It seems that at last these nightmare regulations will end.

Furthermore, the bill seeks to close loopholes that numerous corporations exploited to reduce their tax burdens.

Source: Adapted from Juan F. Rodriguez, "Venezuela Readies Tax Reform," *Business Latin America*, October 2, 1989, p. 307.

However, directors of companies are liable for a flat income tax rate of 30 percent regardless of the length of stay in Singapore. Short-term visiting employees who stay in Singapore for less than 60 days in one year are exempt from income tax. Persons residing in Singapore for more than 60 days but less than 183 days in a year are considered nonresidents and pay a flat tax of 15 percent, provided the tax payable is not less than that payable by a resident in the same circumstance. Income from most other sources is taxed at 40 percent. Permanent residents and those who reside in Singapore more than 183 days in one year are subject to a tax that ranges between 4 and 30 percent after deductions.[42]

Other Taxes and Tax Incentives

In addition to the value added tax, business related taxes, and income taxes that are common to most countries, various other taxes are levied by most countries. Brazil levies a sales tax on goods ranging from 9 to 17 percent, and a municipal service tax of 5 percent is charged against gross service revenues. Its withholding taxes on interest, dividends, and royalties paid to foreign recipients vary from 10 percent to 25 percent. For nontreaty countries, such as the United States, the rate is 25 percent.

Denmark has a special hydrocarbon tax on foreign firms engaged in surveying, exploring, or extracting hydrocarbons from Danish territory or firms that provide service to such firms. Credit and tax benefits are also granted for investments made in the less developed regions of the country.

Greece levies a tax on nonagricultural imports from outside of the EEC. It also levies a consumption tax on many imported goods, ranging from 10 to 150 percent. Subject to tax levies are immovable property, real estate transfer, and banking transactions. Stamp duties are based on each transaction or document, and a proportional duty may be levied based on the value of the transaction.

Excise taxes are levied by Finland on such products as tobacco, alcoholic beverages, fertilizers, and sugar products. A 144 percent tax is levied on the import of motor vehicles.

Israel imposes numerous indirect taxes on expenditures, business transfers, and various fees for licenses. A purchase tax is levied on certain goods for local consumption whether they are domestic or imported. In addition, different excise taxes are levied on various goods produced for local consumption such as alcoholic beverages and tobacco, fuel taxes on gasoline and kerosene, and an entertainment tax. Israel also requires the payment of a revenue stamp tax on documents such as contracts, mortgages, debt certificates, powers of attorney, and insurance policies. License fees are charged for private automobiles, trucks and taxicabs, driver's licenses, television sets, radios, and licenses for certain trades. A 15 percent tax is levied on the purchase of foreign currency.

Singapore levies a stamp tax on certain legal documents such as contracts, affidavits, conveyances, bills of sale, receipts, and securities. The rate of tax varies with the type of document and the amount involved. Some business forms are subject to such taxes.

Bolivia levies a tax on transactions by firms or individuals engaged in trade, and professional or business activities that result in a transfer of any asset or right. It also has a special consumption tax on alcoholic beverages and cigarettes and other tobacco items, and levies a tax on precious stones and hydrocarbons.

Many of the developing countries provide business tax incentives in the form of exemption from duties and excise taxes on imported equipment for certain projects. Many have adopted major tax incentive programs to encourage outside capital investment for economic development and for the stimulation of export-related industries.

Although Peru levies a tax on holders of mining concessions, it also provides tax incentives to stimulate investment in various sectors of the economy. Approved projects are allowed accelerated depreciation on equipment produced in Brazil, and approved projects receive selected income, excise, and sales tax reductions.[43]

A number of tax incentives are available in Zaire. In certain areas of the country, new businesses are exempt from income taxes for five years.

An investment code of the government allows exemption from registration duties, a five-year tax holiday (no tax is levied on profits during this period), reduced taxes on profits that are reinvested, exemption from dividends tax, exemption from import duties and sales taxes on imported equipment not locally available, and exemption from employment tax while the new enterprise is in the development state. Additional tax benefits are available to firms located in a special tax-free zone.

Malaysia exempts "pioneer status" corporations from income taxes for two years. This term may be extended for up to eight additional years. Dividends from these corporations to Malaysian recipients are also tax-free during the exemption period. For approved projects, capital expenditures for manufacturing are tax-exempt for five years on income of 25 percent to 100 percent of the capital invested. Dividends paid from the tax-exempt income are tax-exempt to shareholders. Additional tax incentives to businesses include special double expense allowances for export promotion and marketing, accelerated depreciation on factory modernization for export products, export allowance tax deductions of 5 percent of the value of export sales, and income tax exemption for Malaysian shipping businesses using Malaysian registered ships.[44]

Most countries levy VAT taxes, corporate and personal income taxes, and other income-related taxes.

SUMMARY

The differences in accounting systems among different countries create problems for firms with foreign operations. They must be able to interpret and analyze accounting statements prepared abroad and translate these into statements to meet the requirements of the shareholders and the governments involved.

The accounting profession is aware of the difficulties created by different accounting standards and procedures; thus, efforts are being made at the regional, national, and international levels to harmonize the accounting systems. However, progress has been slow.

This chapter analyzed the tax impact of foreign source income and of foreign employee income. Of the special U.S. tax-incentive corporations, the FSCs were described. In addition, foreign corporations operating in the United States were reviewed for U.S. tax implications.

Countries at different stages of economic development were selected at random in order to see the variations in tax systems that international corporations face abroad. In spite of the countries' different levels of economic development, taxation among them is quite similar. Most countries make use of value added taxes, sales taxes, corporate and individual income taxes, and withholding taxes on foreign payments of interest, royalties, and services. However, there are major differences in tax rates.

Generally speaking, as political and economic conditions change, so do the taxation rules. In the EEC, a conscious effort is being made to standardize member nation taxes through agreements. In the United States, Congress responds to changing conditions abroad by making agreements and concessions and adopting various tax measures. Therefore, changes in tax law are frequent in the world business community, so corporations must investigate and plan the financing of foreign branches, subsidiaries, and exports to minimize taxes relative to expansion, profit, and marketing goals.

All countries levy taxes affecting the operation of businesses. The value added tax is added at each stage of the production or distribution of a product or service. The height of the corporate income tax varies among countries. In addition, firms must pay various other taxes related to business operations with no specific pattern among nations. Many less developed countries provide tax incentives for economic development. Most countries levy a personal income tax.

KEY TERMS AND CONCEPTS

Arms-length pricing

Controlled foreign corporation

Declining balance depreciation

Income deferral

Domestic International Sales Corporation

Double taxation

Excess profits tax

Federal excise tax

First in-first out inventory valuation

Foreign Sales Corporation

GAAP

Last in-first out inventory valuation

Municipal trade tax

Straight line depreciation

Tax credit

Tax haven

Temporal method

Turnover tax

Value added tax

Western Hemisphere Trade Corporation

REVIEW QUESTIONS

1. What is meant by tax credit? Why is it important for a firm to take advantage of the tax credit when filing corporate taxes?

2. What is a controlled foreign corporation? What was the purpose for establishing controlled foreign corporations?

3. What is the Domestic International Sales Corporation? Why was there opposition from other countries to its establishment?

4. What are the requirements for qualifying as a Foreign Sales Corporation?

5. Describe how income earned abroad by U.S. citizens is taxed by the U.S. Internal Revenue Service.

6. How is the income earned by foreign firms operating in the United States taxed?

7. Describe the value added tax as levied by the members of the European Economic Community.

8. Briefly describe the tax system of West Germany.

9. Describe the tax systems of the developing countries of Brazil and Peru.

10. Briefly describe the tax system of Malaysia.

11. Briefly describe the tax system of Zaire.

DISCUSSION CASE

Operating in the Grey, or How You Can Afford a 300-Foot Yacht

Bob and Jack had been college friends. Both had majored in secondary education and played on the college baseball team. Jack had gone on to minor league baseball but never made it to the majors; he finally gave up, becoming a high school history teacher and baseball coach. Bob had decided that he could never make it in baseball, so he got an MBA, specializing in accounting. Their friendship continued even after college and marriage. The two couples vacation together each year.

In 1988, the two couples took a tour to Greece. As Bob and Jack waited on the hotel room balcony, a 300-foot yacht glided smoothly out of Athens harbor. "What a beauty!" Jack said. "How much do you think it costs to operate that yacht? It must have a crew of 60."

"64," Bob commented almost casually. "One of our subsidiaries holds the insurance policy on it. The annual costs of operation are more than $10 million."

"Is it owned by a corporation?"

"No, some guy with a name no one can pronounce."

Jack shook his head in disbelief and muttered half to himself. "How could any private citizen afford something like that? It has got to be old money."

Bob answered without looking at Jack; his eyes were fixed on the older man sipping coffee and the two beautiful young women sunbathing on the rear deck. "He arrived in New York a penniless immigrant from the Balkans about 35 years ago."

"Then he must be a crook," Jack snapped.

By Don R. Beeman, 1989.
Source: Adapted from "How Can You Afford a Twenty Million Dollar Yacht?" by Richard N. Farmer, *Incidents in International Business*, 3rd ed. (Bloomington, Ind.: Cedarwood Press, 1980), pp. 100–103.
This case was developed for class discussion purposes only and should not be viewed as representative of good or bad management practices or decision-making.

Bob looked back to Jack and continued, "Jack, he seems totally honest, in his own way. Well, at least no country is after him."

"It is not possible today."

Bob called over his shoulder into the hotel room, "Sharon, Jack and I will meet the two of you down in the cafe in about 30 minutes, okay? We have a few things to talk about."

As they ordered cool drinks, Bob began. "Listen, Jack, and I'll tell you how it is done. You can make $50 million a year legally and never pay a penny of tax."

"You begin by buying a couple of old freighters on borrowed money. I mean the kind that are ready for the scrap metal yards. Then you register them in Liberia. The taxes are low, safety requirements almost nonexistent, and operating laws the most flexible in the world. It is all perfectly legal; lots of major and reputable companies operate out of Liberia. Get your ship's officers from a country with highly skilled but relatively low-cost merchant marines, Norway or Finland. Then assemble crews from wherever you can get cheap labor, South Korea or Malaysia. Put no money into safety equipment because no one will ever look. Oh, an insurance carrier might, so keep away from ports where insurance inspectors tend to be active. Take any cargo from any shipper of any country to any country. Remember, you are a Liberian business and Liberia boycotts no one."

"Go to Liechtenstein and set up a holding company that will own your Liberian shipping business. You do this because Liechtenstein has no personal or corporate income tax. Next, you change your citizenship to one of the Caribbean Island countries that have little or no income tax; the Cayman Islands might be a great place. The climate is great but you don't have to stay there. When you are making $50 million a year, you can keep apartments in Toronto, Paris, and New York if you wish."

Jack half smiled, "Go on."

Bob was really rolling now. "You will have the freighters paid off in a few years. So you go and borrow against them and buy, in your own name, a few small businesses in rapidly growing developing economies: Brazil, Singapore, and South Korea, for example. Remember, only small companies so that the local government agencies and especially taxing authorities will basically leave you alone. They audit big firms all the time but who cares about a small firm with 50 employees that exports doormats to the United States and Canada. Never locate in a tax-incentive area or make use of any special investment incentive plans; these will only attract attention. Now remember, Jack, report all of your income and pay all of the required taxes; they won't be much anyway."

Jack was really puzzled now. "If I won't make much income, why bother with the investments?"

Bob didn't like being interrupted. "Jack, listen! Next you incorporate an international management services company in Andorra; they also have no taxes. Staff this firm with some bright, young MBAs. Your small manufacturers then contract with your Andorran firm for the services of these professionals. As a result, profits will accumulate in Andorra (no tax) and your small manufacturing firms will show a minimal profit but learn to do business better. Just to be safe, make sure that each small business earns about 1 to 2 percent on capital. If anyone questions these expenditures you have the highly professional reports developed by these consultants and glorious reports of rapidly increasing exports to the United States."

"Now what?" Jack asked.

"Now you are ready to play the old transfer pricing games on products as well as services. Buy machinery or machine tool companies in industrialized countries with trade deficits. Then sell your ownership position down to less than 50 percent; however, make sure that enough of those shares are purchased by dummy broker accounts in Switzerland or Lebanon where company secret laws favor the companies. Use these broker accounts to ensure that you maintain a controlling interest."

"And, Jack, don't worry about government tax authorities being tough on transfer pricing. First, they worry about Ford and IBM, not little guys. Second, when your Ajax Textile Machinery Company of Coventry, England, sells to your Hong Kong Hosiery Company, it will not, strictly speaking, be an intracompany sale. Furthermore, the British government will probably give you a medal for exporting. No one will ever notice that the profits of Ajax are only 2 percent of capital due to the export marketing consulting charges from Andorran Marketing Services, Limited, and the expensive component parts purchased from Technological Components, Ltd., a Bahama-based trading company. It goes without saying that all of these products get transported on your ships. And so it goes with you adding new businesses and layers of interconnectedness."

"Bob, that can't be legal."

"What is wrong with amassing wealth, making investments, creating jobs, having the company of beautiful young women, and owning 300-foot yachts?"

Jack looked out at the yacht, which had almost disappeared into the blue of the Greek waters. "Is that what old what's his name did?"

Questions

1. Will Bob's plan work?
2. Is it legal? Is it ethical?
3. Is this legal tax avoidance or illegal tax evasion?
4. Should the owner of the 300-foot yacht be given a medal for job and export creation?
5. If you were a government official, would you try to create tax laws to stop this kind of business or at least tax the profits? Try to develop such regulations.

NOTES

1. Jeffrey S. Arpan and Dhia D. AlHashim, *International Dimensions of Accounting* (Boston, Mass.: Kent Publishing Company, 1984), pp. 60–64.

2. Ibid., pp. 91–92.

3. Ibid., pp. 122–128.

4. Ibid., pp. 129–131.

5. Ibid., see Chap. 2, pp. 18–56, for a complete description of the efforts at harmonization.

6. Prentice-Hall *Federal Tax Course*, 1985 (Englewood Cliffs, N.J.: Prentice-Hall, 1984), pp. 1,162–1,163 (3703b).

7. Prentice-Hall *Federal Taxes*, 1985, vol. 7 (Englewood Cliffs, N.J.: Prentice-Hall, 1984), Sec. 904, pp. 30,464–30,465 (30536 [e]).

8. *Complete Internal Revenue Code of 1984*, January 1, 1984 Edition (Englewood Cliffs, N.J.: Prentice-Hall, 1984), pp. 25,760A–25,771, Sec. 951–964.

9. According to the U.S. tax system, the deferral principle applies to income earned by an American subsidiary abroad in a given year.

10. Prentice-Hall *Federal Taxes*, 1985, vol. 7 (Englewood Cliffs, N.J.: Prentice-Hall, 1984), pp. 30,666–30,773.

11. Ibid., pp. 30,927–30,998.49.

12. *Federal Income Tax Text*, 1985 (Englewood Cliffs, N.J.: Prentice-Hall, 1984), pp. 1,043–1,044.

13. *DH + S REVIEW*, 85–14, July 8, 1985 (New York: Deloitte Haskins and Sells), p. 7.

14. Prentice-Hall *Federal Taxes*, 1985, vol. 7 (Englewood Cliffs, N.J.: Prentice-Hall, 1984), pp. 30,681–30,700.43.

15. Ibid., pp. 30,700.43–30,700.45 [30681].

16. Ibid., Sec. 911, p. 30,650 [30607].

17. Ibid., p. 30,647 [30607].

18. Commerce Clearing House, *Federal Tax Course*, 1986 (Chicago: Commerce Clearing House, 1985), p. 3,111 [3109].

19. Ibid., p. 3,112 [3109].

20. Prentice Hall *Federal Taxes*, 1985, Vol. 7, Sec. 911, p. 30,645 [30606].

21. Ibid., Sec. 881, p. 30,301 [30311].

22. Foreign corporations are required to file Form 1120f to pay their taxes.

23. Price-Waterhouse, *Corporate Taxes, A Worldwide Summary*, 1985 edition (New York: Price-Waterhouse Center for Transnational Taxation, 1985), pp. 120–127.

24. For a description of the VAT tax, see Price-Waterhouse *Information Guide, Value Added Tax* (New York: Price-Waterhouse Center for Transnational Taxation, 1979), p. 6.

25. U.S. Dept. of Commerce, *Marketing in Denmark*, OBR 89-04, May 1989.

26. U.S. Dept. of Commerce, *Marketing in Greece*, OBR 88-12, Oct. 1988, p. 43.

27. U.S. Dept. of Commerce, *Marketing in Finland*, OBR 89-05, May 1989.

28. U.S. Dept. of Commerce, *Marketing in Bolivia*, OBR 89-01, Jan. 1989.

29. *Finland*, OBR 89-05, pp. 28–29.

30. Price-Waterhouse, *Corporate Taxes*, 1985 edition, pp. 266–271.

31. U.S. Dept. of Commerce, *Marketing in Greece*, OBR 88-12, Oct. 1988, pp. 40–44.

32. Price-Waterhouse, *Corporate Taxes*, 1985, pp. 120–127.

33. U.S. Dept. of Commerce, *Marketing in Israel*, OBR 88-11, Sept. 1988, pp. 31–32.

34. U.S. Dept. of Commerce, *Marketing in Singapore*, OBR 89-07, May 1989, pp. 32-33.

35. *Bolivia*, OBR 89-01, pp. 28–29.

36. U.S. Dept. of Commerce, *Marketing in Peru*, OBR 88-07, May 1988, pp. 36–39.

37. Price-Waterhouse, *Corporate Taxes*, 1985, pp. 393–396.

38. *Denmark*, OBR 89-04, pp. 35–36.

39. *Greece*, OBR 88-12, pp. 40–44.

40. *Finland*, OBR 89-05, pp. 35–36.

41. *Israel*, OBR 88-11, pp. 31–32.

42. *Singapore*, OBR 89-07, pp. 32–33. Income is defined as gains or profits from any trade, business, profession, or vocation; earnings from employment; dividends; interest and discounts; pensions and annuities; and rents, royalties, and earnings from property.

43. Price-Waterhouse, *Corporate Taxes*, 1985, pp. 225–229.

44. Ibid.

REFERENCES AND SELECTED READINGS

Arpan, Jeffrey S., and Dhia D. AlHashim. *International Dimensions of Accounting*. Boston, Mass.: Kent Publishing Company, 1984.

Commerce Clearing House. *Commerce Clearing House Federal Tax Course*. Chicago: Commerce Clearing House, 1985.

Department of Commerce. *Commerce America*, November 22, 1976.

Deloitte Haskins and Sells. *DH + S Review*, 85/14. New York: Deloitte Haskins and Sells, 1985.

Price-Waterhouse. *Price-Waterhouse Corporate Taxes. A Worldwide Summary*. New York: Price-Waterhouse, 1985.

Price-Waterhouse. *Information Guide. Value Added Tax*. New York: Price-Waterhouse, 1979.

Prentice-Hall. *Federal Tax Course 1985*. Englewood Cliffs, N.J.: Prentice-Hall, 1985.

Prentice-Hall. *Federal Taxes 1985*, vol. 7. Englewood Cliffs, N.J.: Prentice-Hall, 1985.

Prentice-Hall. *Complete Internal Revenue Code of 1984*. January 1, 1984 edition. Englewood Cliffs, N.J.: Prentice-Hall, 1984.

Prentice-Hall. *Federal Income Tax Text 1985*. Englewood Cliffs, N.J.: Prentice-Hall, 1985.

PART FIVE

Trends and the Future of International Business

CHAPTER

21

Prospects for the Future of International Business

LEARNING OBJECTIVES

- Understand the difference between evolutionary change and revolutionary change

- Understand how and why changes in the environment can affect the operations of international business firms

- Become familiar with technological, ecological, sociocultural, political, and economic trends that might affect the future of international business

- Understand the problems arising from the increase in population and a decrease in resources

- Understand why actions of the government influence international business

- Discuss why international firms of the future will have to adopt newer and more flexible forms for international involvements

INTRODUCTION

All history can be summed up by saying that it is an unpredictable mixture of evolution and revolution. The *evolution* is the gradual change that is both understandable and predictable on the basis of clearly observable trends. Unfortunately, these trends are often interrupted by *revolutionary* changes: radical shifts and discontinuities in trends. Even in biological terms, the gradual changes of evolution do not fully explain all of the major and dramatic changes that have occurred. Catastrophes have occurred that resulted in more biological change in a few million years than in the previous hundred million years. The same is true in the social, political, and economic worlds.

War, famine, natural disaster, new political leadership, or technological developments often result in rapid radical changes that dwarf the gradual changes of many decades. Although this chapter focuses on the trends that seem to be in place to shape the next several decades, we must accept the fact that revolutionary change is both possible and probable, albeit impossible to forecast. Who among us even in 1987 could have forecast the radical political and economic changes in Eastern Europe and the Soviet Union? The trends from 1947 through 1986 gave little indications of what was to come.

For understanding the future, one must also recognize that in addition to the evolution-revolution dichotomy, the rate of change in human society is increasing. For at least the last 400 years, the rate of creation of new knowledge, new inventions, new social and political systems, and so forth has been increasing at a geometric rate. In fact at no time in human history have the lives of one generation been so dramatically different from those of the next. For most of the thousands and millions of years of human existence, the life of one generation was extremely similar to that of the one preceding and the one following. This is no longer the case and as a result, the relevance of one generation's knowledge to members of the next generation is declining—thus, the famous "Generation Gap."

As the remainder of this chapter discusses the significant trends of the 1990s, it must be remembered that the rate of these changes is increasingly rapid and yet they are also subject to immediate and abrupt endings or new directions.

GLOBAL TRENDS AND INTERNATIONAL BUSINESS

Historical Trends

The historical trends of international business provide some bases for predicting the prospects for international business. Until the 1950s, the environmental conditions within which business firms operated were relatively stable. Firms were able to adapt to the conditions without difficulty, primarily because international trade and international business were almost synonymous. The future of international business could be predicted with relative certainty. Unlike past prognostications, however, attempts to predict the future of international business in the year 2000 become more difficult. The field of international business is much broader and changes in the environment of business are occurring with greater rapidity. Not since 1848 have there been as many momentous political and economic developments as in recent months. In Eastern Europe, the old order has been overthrown, while the new one has not yet been installed. These conditions create uncertainty for multinational firms until the direction of the changes and their permanency are determined.

Political Trends

Of the various factors influencing international business, the changing political environment is one of the most important. Various factors account for these changes. New policies adopted by governments have a direct influence on the commercial and economic relationships among nations. If diplomatic relations are severed, it may be impossible for the countries involved to do business.

Cuba is still politically and commercially isolated from the United States because of U.S. opposition to the policies that were adopted when Fidel Castro overthrew the Batista regime more than three decades ago. U.S. firms were forced to leave the country and their assets were expropriated. Relations with Iran remain at a standstill because of the continuation of the policies adopted by the Ayatollah Khomeini. The deterioration of U.S. business in Panama was due largely to the political policies of Noriega. His removal from power is providing American firms with an opportunity to reassess the situation. The change of leadership in the People's Republic of China resulted in cultural exchanges, the resumption of diplomatic relations with the United States, and the granting of the most favored nation treatment. These relations have been set back because of the 1989 events in Tiananmen Square in Beijing and the suppression of the democratic movement. Examples of the significant impact of political changes on international business are to be found in great abundance.

The Soviet Union and Eastern Europe

The installation of Mikhail Gorbachev as Premier, his election as President of the USSR, and his policies of *perestroika* (restructuring of the economy) and *glasnost* (openness) have encouraged the overthrow of the single-party communist regimes in most of the countries of Eastern Europe. Gorbachev has also opened the gates for political and economic reforms in the Soviet Union with the call for a multiparty system.

Current political trends may have far-reaching economic implications. Already we are seeing situations that were not dreamed possible a few years ago—for example, the opening of a McDonald's franchise in Moscow early in 1990. Because the Soviet Union has had difficulty meeting the demand of its consumers for goods that are found in abundance in the free world, pressures are being put on the Soviet leaders to reduce the military budget and shift resources to the consumer sectors. The thawing of relations between the United States and the USSR will provide many opportunities for firms engaged in international business.

Unless the USSR reverses its policy of economic self-sufficiency and resistance to importing manufactured goods from abroad, and follows Gorbachev's February 1990 suggestion of free convertibility between the dollar and the ruble, trade will continue to be constrained. If these changes are made, the USSR will be able to purchase capital goods and highly sophisticated products, and implement more rapid economic development.

East-West commercial relations will continue to improve as long as the new political environment continues to develop. As opportunities for investments and export markets open up, competition will increase. Initially, competition will be among multinationals from various countries vying for a share of the huge yet latent market; however, ultimately local enterprises will begin to challenge for these markets.

Western Europe

In western Europe, the single-Europe 1992 movement is also adding a radical new dimension to the political and economic environment. The Single European Act, an amendment to the Treaty of Rome, will fulfill to a large extent the original vision of the EEC in the free movement of goods, services, capital, and people. It will mean the establishment of the world's largest single open market, with a population of some 320 million.

To take advantage of the business opportunities, many U.S. and Japanese multinationals are in the midst of planning to set up additional operations in anticipation of the free movement of goods within the EEC. Elimination of the customs delays at border crossings will result in tremendous savings in intercommunity transportation charges. Mutual recognition of educational qualifications and diplomas will enable EEC citizens to work in any country of the community without challenge. Harmonization of the VAT and indirect taxes will prevent large distortions in the levies among different members. The harmonizing of technical standards for television and satellite technology will eliminate different specifications among the countries. The telecommunications industry will be open to all members of the community, eliminating the existence of monopolies in equipment and services. Increased efficiencies will result in lower costs of production.

However, 1992 will probably witness a single approach to the rest of the world with the possibility of increased protectionism. In anticipation of such a policy, there has been an increase in direct investments by multinational firms from the United States, Japan, and non-EEC countries of Europe as well as negotiation at the current Uruguayan Round of GATT.

Countries in other areas of the world are closely monitoring the developments in the European Community. If complete integration proves advantageous, countries on other continents will probably follow suit.

The People's Republic of China

The resumption of diplomatic relations between the United States and the People's Republic of China (PRC) had resulted in increasing business contact between the two countries, which was growing at a rapid pace until the political suppression of the democratic movement in the spring of 1989. The People's Republic of China had been wooing private industry to make direct investments for the manufacture of such products as automobiles, fast foods, and even golf courses. Now some firms are waiting to assess the impact of the political crackdown. Furthermore, the development of the PRC as an international market and as a site for foreign direct investments is now somewhat uncertain.

Pacific Rim Nations

One of the most rapidly developing regions in the world is the Pacific rim. Most of the countries in this region are highly dependent on international trade. Government policies have been directed toward the export market. According to the Selected Information Retrieval Company, U.S. exports to this area surpassed those to the European Community. Excluding the PRC, there are 11 countries included in this category—Japan, Thailand, Hong

Kong, Taiwan, the Philippines, Australia, Indonesia, Singapore, Malaysia, Korea, and New Zealand. Their total population is 508 million. Of these countries, South Korea has the greatest trade potential, with its population of 43 million and a continuing 10 percent GNP annual growth rate. Business leaders around the world will increasingly be dealing with Pacific rim nations as competitors, partners, and customers.[1]

Japan will continue to be a major competitor, especially in the U.S. market. This partly reflects its huge trade surplus with the United States, encouraging Japanese firms to make foreign direct investments. One can expect new start-up investments as well as mergers and acquisitions in the United States to continue.

Latin America

Democracy, despite laboring under economic problems, seems to be alive and growing throughout Latin America. Although the long history of military intervention in the political process continues to cast its shadow over new democracies, we at last have reason to dream of a totally democratic Western Hemisphere.

Africa and the Middle East

Africa continues to try to deal with immense problems of economic development, overpopulation, and internal ethnic divisions; nevertheless, negotiations have upstaged violent revolution. The next 20 years of African development will require substantial economic assistance if these nations too are to become viable democracies.

Because of the continuing importance of Middle East crude oil reserves, the OPEC cartel maintains its importance as a quasi-political organization as well as an economic entity. Beyond the geopolitical significance of this region for its oil reserves, the political story is both sad and distressing. In a world of increasing political "good news," the Middle East is the most significant exception.

National and religious violence is still the dominant way of life from Israel's West Bank to the Persian Gulf. The future is by no means clear. In part the continuing turmoil results from the complex struggle between Israel and its numerous neighboring states. This struggle has remained intractable over more than four decades because it is rooted in three major bases of nationalism and international violence: blood, earth, and religion. The Arab-Israeli conflict is rooted in blood lines, with each group seeing the other as ethnically or racially different. It also grows from conflicting claims to a piece of land as "their home." The Palestinians can correctly argue that the territory in question was theirs for more than a thousand years. Conversely, the Israelis can substantiate claims that date back more than two thousand years. If blood and earth claims were not sufficient to ensure continuation of the conflict, there is also at issue the millennia of religious animosity and struggle. The Israelis can claim that this "homeland" was, in fact, given to them by God himself as their promised land. On top of this are a myriad of U.N. resolutions and lands taken in wars and so on. The net effect is conflict, varying from war to terrorism and reprisal, that simply will not go away.

The political instability and turmoil of the region has been amplified in recent years by the rise of Islamic fundamentalism, as typified by the overthrowing of the Shah in Iran and the coming to power of the Ayatollah Khomeini. This led directly to the Iran-Iraq war. Despite the death of Khomeini, Islamic fundamentalism would still seem to make Arab-versus-Arab conflict a possibility.

Through its political policies and intergovernmental cooperation, the government is in a position to influence the patterns and direction of trade.

Unless this internal and international strife can be ended, the international business contribution of this region will become little more than that of a customer for arms.

Economic and Financial Trends

While East-West relations are dominated by political concerns, North-South relations are most directly influenced by economic and financial matters. The international debt crisis overwhelms other problems. Total debts to lenders around the world are estimated to be more than $1 trillion, with some $90 billion owed to U.S. financial institutions. The $1.1 billion reported loss by Chase Manhattan Corporation during the third quarter of 1989 was largely due to a write-off of uncollectable LDC loans. How to resolve the debt crisis is of major concern to both creditor and debtor nations.

Many debt-ridden nations have been attempting to restructure their loans. They have been negotiating with the International Monetary Fund and the World Bank for loan guarantees to keep from defaulting on their obligations. Some have adopted austerity programs and have cut back on essential imports in an attempt to accumulate sufficient foreign exchange to service their foreign obligations. Although some nations have made substantial progress, the problem is tenacious.

The United States is also involved in a debt crisis of its own. The international debt position of the United States could not have been anticipated under the most pessimistic conditions a few decades ago. The nation's budgetary deficits have been financed largely by capital imports, resulting in the accumulation of large amounts of government obligations to foreign investors. The United States is now the world's greatest debtor nation. This means that an increasing amount of future U.S. export earnings will have to be earmarked for servicing these obligations. This will no doubt place greater emphasis on the importance of international trade for the nation's welfare. The U.S. federal budget deficit and trade imbalance have reached such levels that one must forecast relatively stringent activities. These could come in the form of tax increases (visible or hidden), some form of controls on imports, or both.

Sociocultural Trends

The converging of cultural values across countries is having a significant influence on international business. Simultaneously, the task of adapting business to foreign cultures becomes easier. Japan after World War II is a good example of the effects of exposure and immersion of a population in an alien culture. The Japanese adopted many of the cultural characteristics of the American society. Their demands for consumer goods, for example, are very similar to what is demanded in the United States. These range from foodstuffs to clothing to country and western music. This cultural convergence has affected the patterns and direction of trade and investments.

Changes in the environment within a country will have tremendous influence on the operation of a multinational firm.

The development of global mass media and multinational firms have contributed to this cultural convergence. Although many dislike the idea of having Paris become more like Washington or Tokyo, these same people are exceedingly happy to be able to use their MasterCard or Visa in most countries.

Population and Resource Trends

Among the most significant trends influencing international business are population pressures and declining resources. An understanding of these issues is critical for any attempt to predict international business in the year 2000. Changes in population size, composition, density, distribution, education, or income level will profoundly affect the patterns and directions of trade and the conduct of international business.

Malthus argued that if unchecked, the world's population would increase exponentially while the means of subsistence would increase only arithmetically, with the obvious conclusion of starvation on a global scale. Whether Malthus's theory is completely correct or not, it is becoming increasingly difficult to provide sustenance for the ever-increasing population. Somalia and Ethiopia provide examples of countries without the capacity to feed their citizens.

The population of the world totaled only 1 billion in 1830. However, 100 years later in 1930, it had doubled to 2 billion. In 1960, only 30 years later, it had reached 3 billion, and 16 years later in 1976 it had reached 4 billion. In 1987 the world's population totaled more than 5 billion and by the year 2000, it will be well in excess of 6 billion. Projections suggest that the world population will exceed 8 billion before the year 2020.

The greatest increases are occurring in countries that can least support a large population. The U.S. Census Bureau states that 80 percent of the growth in world population between 1950 and 1975 occurred in the less developed countries. Various estimates indicate that by the year 2000, between 85 and 90 percent of the world's population will be in the less developed countries. This projection is based on the fact that the annual population growth rate in the LDCs is higher than in more developed countries. For example, in the 1970s, the annual growth rate was 2.6 percent for Africa and 2.7 percent for Latin America, while the world growth rate averaged 1.9 percent (0.9 percent for the United States and 1.0 percent for the Soviet Union).[2]

An additional population concern for LDCs is the rural-to-urban migration of the poor. In India, Mexico, Brazil, and other countries with population explosions, large numbers of people are migrating from the rural to the urban areas to seek employment, creating problems associated with rapid growth in areas that are not prepared to absorb the increase. Mexico City and Rio de Janeiro are examples of large metropolitan areas with severe problems associated with overpopulation.

The concern in developed countries is the increasing age of the population. The percentage of people in the older age groups in the more highly industrialized countries will continue to rise as life expectancies increase (see Table 21.1).

The world's population is increasing at a rapid rate, putting pressure on the world's diminishing resources.

The world's resources are unevenly distributed over the earth's surface and many are exhaustible. Allocation of the available resources to meet the needs of the ever-increasing population is of primary concern and will become more serious with time.

Even wealthy nations are feeling the resource problems. The United States is an example of a country that is no longer self-sufficient in many

Table 21.1   **People Aged 55 and Over as a Percentage of Total Population***

	1980	1990	2000	2010	2020	2025
West Germany	25.0	26.7	30.7	33.0	37.6	39.6
Switzerland	24.0	26.0	30.0	34.0	38.0	39.5
Netherlands	21.0	22.0	24.5	30.0	36.0	38.0
Denmark	26.0	25.0	27.0	31.7	35.7	37.6
Sweden	28.0	28.0	29.4	33.0	35.0	37.0
Austria	25.0	25.0	27.0	29.0	33.4	35.3
Italy	23.0	26.0	27.6	29.0	33.0	34.4
Belgium	25.0	26.0	26.0	29.0	33.0	34.0
United Kingdom	26.0	26.0	26.0	28.0	31.5	33.0
France	23.0	24.0	24.4	28.0	31.4	32.6
Canada	18.6	20.0	22.0	26.0	31.0	32.0
Japan	17.6	23.0	28.0	32.0	32.0	32.0
East Germany	24.3	23.5	26.6	28.0	31.0	32.0
United States	21.0	21.0	21.0	24.5	29.0	29.0
Australia	19.0	19.4	20.4	23.5	27.0	28.3
USSR	17.3	20.0	21.4	23.5	25.6	26.0

* Rank order according to the year 2025.

Source: *Business International*, October 30, 1989, p. 331.

essential minerals. Fifty years ago, the United States had one of the largest reserves of iron ore in the world and it was the world's leading producer of low-cost steel. Today, little remains of these reserves; the United States is now largely dependent on imported ores or on scrap metal. The U.S. steel industry can no longer compete with imported steel without government assistance.

Petroleum is another example. For 100 years after the discovery of oil in Titusville, Pennsylvania, the United States was the world's leading producer of petroleum; today the country must import large quantities. The United States is dependent upon foreign sources for about 50 percent of its petroleum requirements. Other essential products continue to be added to the nation's deficiencies.

The uneven distribution of the world's resources emphasizes the necessity for future cooperation among nations. Without the movement of goods, services, and factors of production from surplus areas to areas of deficiency, the world will be in a state of chaos. This relationship between the population and resources must be given serious consideration in any prediction of the direction that international business will take.

The implications of world population growth and resource deficiencies are several. There will be greater interdependence among nations. No longer will nations be able to follow an economic policy of isolation and economic nationalism. This will call for greater economic cooperation and coordination among highly industrialized, newly industrialized, and less developed countries. It might require modifying the rules of GATT to meet the challenges of the ever-changing environment or the establishment of some other institution to ensure cooperation and coordination. Furthermore it seems clear that multinational firms will become increasingly important in the transfer of both goods and technologies.

Both population and resources are unevenly distributed over the earth's surface. Unfortunately, countries with a large and dense population are often resource-poor.

Technological Trends

Technological developments associated with computer technology will continue to alter the way we make products and, through artificial intelligence, to change the way we make decisions. Technological trends such as bioengineering will result in the creation of new products that are unthinkable today. These new, high technology products together with services will be the new international growth industries. Indeed, technology and innovation will be the drive-wheel of the next several decades.

Since technology is a consequence of research and development, and most of the world's inventions occur in the more developed nations, trade will continue to flow primarily among developed nations and secondarily from developed to developing nations. The only way this cycle will be broken is by the transfer of technology. The more rapid the transfer of technology, the more rapid the economic development of the world's LDCs. The transfer of product and process technologies will have to be accompanied by the transfer of managerial know-how. If these skills are transferred, the future of trade could involve greater participation by countries at different stages of economic development.

Transportation and Communication Trends

Developments in the areas of transportation and communications have reduced the time involved in shipping goods great distances. The first transcontinental flight from New York to Los Angeles took 48 hours; soon we may see flights from Washington to Tokyo in 3 hours. The implications of more rapid transportation are tremendous for the movement of perishable or urgent goods. Even today, florists in American cities get daily shipments of fresh flowers from the Netherlands. During the season, daily shipments of fresh clams are made from the U.S. East Coast to San Francisco.

Developments in the areas of technology, transportation, and communications will further change the patterns and direction of trade.

Rapid communications influence foreign exchange rates in the financial markets of the world, add to the international mobility of capital, and make the location of the reservoirs of capital less significant. Rapid international communications also can have a major effect on the patterns and directions of trade and investments. With satellite-linked computer-to-computer communications and international fax transmissions, the whole world is almost literally just next door.

Ecological Trends

Ecologically, there are several major trends that could be of greater long-term significance than anything discussed so far. The "greenhouse effect" and the deterioration of the ozone layer have the potential to fundamentally alter, if not end, all life on the earth. When these two issues are combined with the destruction of tropical rainforests, hazardous chemical and nuclear waste, and massive erosion of topsoil, the picture looks somewhat frightening. Indeed it should.

From the perspective of multinational firms, these ecological concerns will result in fundamental changes in the way commodities are produced. For still other firms, these problems represent tremendous new business opportunities. In either case, international businesses will increasingly be at the center of the global ecology issue.

FORMS OF BUSINESS ORGANIZATION FOR THE NEXT DECADE AND BEYOND

These major trends will create numerous and challenging business opportunities in the years ahead for the firms that can maintain effectiveness and efficiency while becoming increasingly flexible and adaptable. Firms will be faced with the challenge of developing business methods that are different from those currently used.

The trends of the last four decades have produced an increasing array of corporate forms; however, this is only the beginning. Licensing, franchising, management contracts, turn-key operations, and so forth will become increasingly common, while wholly owned subsidiaries will probably decrease. Current trends also indicate that overseas investments will increasingly be made through mergers and acquisitions or contractual agreements. The least objectionable types of agreement will be those that aid the host countries in the establishment of productive facilities, or enable them to participate in the management of those operations. For this reason one can expect an increase in the number and forms of cooperative ventures, especially those involving governments. An example of this cooperation even among competitors is the Chrysler operation in the PRC. Following the 1989 civil disobedience, Chrysler stated that there was no interruption in production. The implications of Chrysler's statement was that the lack of anti-American feeling was due to the fact that the manufacturing was a joint venture with the Chinese government.

As discussed in an earlier chapter, the characteristics of some business firms permit them to enter into franchise agreements. Such contractual agreements are especially appropriate in the fast food industry and other outlets or services that have well-established trademarks. The rapid growth of this form of foreign operation indicates that there will be an increasing number of franchise agreements with outlets worldwide.

The extent of confrontation or cooperation among nations will probably determine largely the future growth of international business.

SUMMARY

For at least the next decade, multinational firms will be operating in a world of increasing uncertainty but also increasing opportunity. If nations maintain friendly political relations with one another, even with changes in the environment, their tasks will be much easier. However, there is no assurance that the ideal political situation will exist. North Korea and South Korea in Asia, Ethiopia and Somalia in Africa, Honduras and Nicaragua in Central America, and Iran and Iraq in the Middle East are examples of nations having difficulty getting along with one another. Some less developed countries have antiimperialistic feelings toward industrialized countries, which could adversely affect political and economic relations. The adoption of retaliatory measures to adjust trade barriers could cause a substantial reduction in international commerce.

On the other side, the complete integration of the EEC in 1992, the policies of *perestroika* and *glasnost* in the USSR, the relaxation of political repression in the PRC, and the democratization in Eastern European countries could result in an explosion of international economic activity.

In the economic arena, the debt crisis of the less developed countries and the continued deficit in the U.S. balance of payments are of primary concern to many countries. What type of policy the United States adopts in an attempt to solve its problem is being watched by many. If it follows a policy of protectionism, as some in Congress recommend, retaliation is bound to result and adversely affect international business.

REVIEW QUESTIONS

1. Discuss how political trends affect international business.

2. What is meant by the "debt crisis" of less developed countries? What are the prospects for its solution?

3. The United States is faced with a debt crisis. How does this differ from that of the less developed countries? Explain.

4. Is it possible for changes in the sociocultural environment to affect international business? How?

5. What role can MNFs play in alleviating the problem of starvation in some of the less developed countries of Africa?

6. Is transfer of technology the only solution for the more rapid economic development of the less developed countries? Explain.

7. What is the Single European Act? When does it go into effect? What effect will it have on international business firms operating inside and outside of the EEC? Why do some firms fear new protectionist policies?

8. Explain what impact the political liberalization of the Eastern European countries will have on international business.

9. What forms of business organization are likely to dominate the international business scene in the year 2000? Give reasons for your answer.

10. Explain the major ecological problems facing the planet, and the role you believe MNFs could play in solving these problems.

NOTES

1. Louis Kraar, "Korea: Tomorrow's Powerhouse," *Fortune*, August 15, 1988, pp. 75–81.

2. United Nations, Statistical Bureau and Worldwatch Research Institute cited in Reader's Digest Almanac and Yearbook, 1978, p. 193.

REFERENCES AND SELECTED READING

International Monetary Fund. *International Financial Statistics Yearbook.* Washington, D.C.: IMF, 1989.

Moyer, Reed. "The Futility of Forecasting." *Long Range Planning* 17:1 (February 1984), 65–72.

Naisbitt, John. *Megatrends: Ten New Directions Transforming our Lives.* New York: Warner Books, 1982.

Naisbitt, John, and Patricia Aburdene. *Megatrends* 2000. New York: William Morrow and Co., 1990.

Owen, Richard, and Michael Dynes. *The Times Guide to 1992.* London: Times Books Limited, 1989.

Pearson, John, and Leslie Helm. "For Multinationals, It Will Never Be the Same." *Business Week*, December 24, 1984, p. 57.

Speth, James Gustave. "Questions for a Critical Decade." *Columbia Journal of World Business* 19:1 (Spring 1984), pp. 5–9.

"Technologies for the 80's." *Business Week*, July 6, 1981, pp. 48–56.

A Strategic Alliance Even Chickens Could Love

A judicious blend of Mexican labor, Japanese know-how and US "raw" materials is the driving force behind a new strategic alliance among four major players—C. Itoh (Japan), Provemex (Mexico), Promociones Industriales Banamex (Mexico) and Tyson Foods (US). The venture—Citra—capitalizes on the competitive strengths of each partner to surmount obstacles and win a share of the challenging, but conquerable, Asian market for chicken products. The partnership also highlights how some firms increasingly eye Mexico not only as a springboard to the US, but also as a base for exports to other regions.

MEETING FOUR DIFFERENT OBJECTIVES

The four corporate participants in Citra had different, yet complementary, needs that they found could be met by an innovative alliance. Their respective goals were:

• *C. Itoh* wanted to diversify its supplier base for chicken yakitori, a popular Asian treat in which bits of chicken are threaded onto a bamboo stick, marinated and grilled. Production of yakitori—that is, the cutting, skewering and marinating of chicken morsels—is highly labor intensive, making it increasingly costly and uncompetitive for C. Itoh to do in Japan. The firm was also having problems with quality and unauthorized use of antibiotics by some of its Asian suppliers.

From Mimi Cauley de la Sierra, "A Strategic Alliance Even Chickens Could Love," *Business International*, December 4. 1989. pp. 369–371, 376.

- *Provemex*, the second largest chicken producer in Mexico, wanted to expand into higher-value-added products. Before joining the venture, Provemex's only business was raising and slaughtering chickens. By acquiring the know-how for deboning chickens for products such as yakitori, the firm's management could secure a foothold in more lucrative markets and vertically integrate its operations.

The Mexican firm also wanted to expand internationally. The burden of Mexico's debt crisis on the local economy has meant that local companies must export if they want to grow appreciably. However, Provemex was uncertain how best to test the international waters. Highly competitive labor costs were, in effect, Provemex's trump card, which drew the other participants to the firm.

- *Promociones Industriales Banamex (Promociones)*, the venture capital arm of Mexico's largest bank, saw an attractive investment opportunity in the strong profit potential of Provemex's emergence as an exporter to Asia. Promociones specializes in joint ventures between Mexican and foreign firms. Its knowledge of world markets and its corporate partnering skills put it in a good position to develop a long-term strategy and made it an attractive ally of Provemex. Moreover, the two Mexican companies knew they could work well together because of their long-standing banking relationship.

- *Tyson Foods* sought new markets for its dark chicken meat. According to David van Bebber, legal counsel for Tyson Foods, the company had (and has) a huge US market for white chicken breasts, but US customers do not have a similar appetite for dark meat, which comes from chicken legs. Tyson was able to export some of its excess dark meat to the Far East, where dark meat tends to be more palatable. However, Asian demand did not nearly match US chicken consumption, resulting in a huge surplus of chicken legs. Many of these legs ended up being crushed and processed as inexpensive animal feed.

Tyson, which already had a strong supplier relationship with C. Itoh, was well aware of the Japanese firm's interest in broadening its yakitori supplier base. In fact, Tyson was eager to provide the chicken bits, but faced the same problem of steep labor costs for processing as C. Itoh. By selling its surplus chicken legs to the yakitori venture in Mexico, the US company could get more value and money for a marginal product. It would also increase Tyson's share of the Asian market by broadening its product offerings to include yakitori.

IRONING OUT OPERATIONAL DETAILS

As Citra began operating in earnest, the partners faced the usual gamut of joint venture start-up kinks. Among the stickiest issues, according to Jorge Carrillo, director at Promociones, were the following:

The Mexican-US-Japanese Connection*

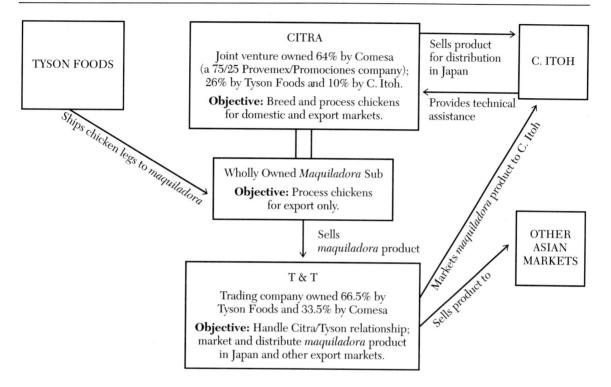

• *Adapting Japanese technology to a Mexican environment*. Carrillo and Gabriel Monterrubio, Citra's president, identified several important steps the partners implemented to facilitate the technology transfer. Very early in the process, key executives from Provemex and Promociones visited C. Itoh to obtain an overview of the operation, including the technology, the mechanics of deboning and yakitori processing, plant layout and expected output per person. Next, Citra sent 11 employees to Japan to work and train at C. Itoh for several months. After returning to Mexico, these people trained and supervised the other employees. (Citra currently has 900 employees in the deboning operations and plans to expand to 2,000 workers over the next 14 months.) Finally, C. Itoh sent two engineers to Citra's production site to provide additional technical assistance and oversee the installation of equipment.

• *Developing a suitable wage and incentive program*. Carrillo finds that handling the delicate human side in a technology transfer can often be more difficult than the actual learning of unfamiliar technical procedures. In fact, how well corporate leaders manage and organize employees to make the technology compatible with local idiosyncrasies often determines the ultimate success of the transfer. "C. Itoh did a remarkable job in providing the operational and technical specifics for processing chickens," says Carrillo.

The real test, though, came in organizing and motivating employees so that the process worked effectively. Through trial and error, Citra is streamlining the process. For instance, "Citra first offered employees the minimum wage," says Carrillo. "However, management soon faced a labor turnover problem. It quickly became evident that the task of deboning the chicken and complying with rigorous sanitary and quality standards was not a minimum wage job. By adjusting the pay scale slightly upward, labor turnover dropped."

Similarly, Citra has raised its output-per-person to meet Japanese standards and demand with a wage incentive program. Citra also reorganized workers in teams to boost quality control. With these changes, Citra is making headway in reaching its production and quality targets. After only a few months, production already tops 750,000 chickens per month. Monterrubio says the venture will reach the two million mark within the next 12 months.

• *Properly pricing the product*. Citra is currently undertaking rigorous analyses to identify a sound pricing strategy. Like other alliances, Citra has experienced unforeseen costs that required management to revise its pricing, cost and revenue projections. For instance, Citra was unaware that the Japanese require food suppliers to include an extra 2% in weight at no cost. The Japanese argue that 2% is needed to ensure that the customer is not cheated. The cost of 2%, when applied to millions of chickens, adds up, but Citra's management has been able to make up the cost difference with savings in other areas. In fact, the venture is on track to turn a profit next year.

QUESTIONS

1. What key elements seem to account for the success of this venture? Identify and explain each.

2. Why did Tyson need the Mexican firms? Why didn't Tyson and C. Itoh simply establish their own joint venture (JV) in Mexico?

3. What are the implications of Tyson's participation in this JV on US stockholders? On US employees?

4. Analyze the accompanying chart; why do you think there was the need to establish T&T (the trading company) as well as Citra? Note that T&T does not include C. Itoh!

The Rhone-Poulenc Company

In July of 1986, Union Carbide announced that it was selling its agricultural chemical division. This provided Rhone-Poulenc (RP), France's largest chemical company, with a great opportunity to enter the agricultural chemical market in the United States; however, Mr. Fourtou, Rhone's CEO, had many questions to answer before a decision could be made. Fourtou called a meeting of his top divisional managers to discuss the possible acquisition of Union Carbide's agricultural chemical division. In attendance were

Philippe Désmarescaus—agrichemical division
Jean-Marc Bruel—chemical division
Mogens Andersen—fiber division
Igor Landau—health division
François Quarre—corporate strategy and planning
Jean-Pierre Tirouflet—finance
Jean-Claude Ailleret—operations support
Xavier du Bernardi—human resources
Gerard Vuillard—quality, safety, environmental protection
Peter Neff—officer representative for the United States

Fourtou started the meeting by stating that "the opportunity to pur-

By Don R. Beeman with the assistance of Joy Navarre, Mohammad N. Anwar, and Jean-François Villard, 1989.

This case was prepared from a variety of published sources (listed at the conclusion of the case) as the basis for class discussion only. It is not intended to illustrate either good or bad management or decision-making.

chase Union Carbide's agricultural chemical division doesn't come very often. Union Carbide has been in business since 1876 and has a fully developed U.S. distribution system. The division would probably be undervalued because of Union Carbide's recent tragedy and the stigma attached to it. Therefore, we could acquire the division for far less than it's worth. However, many questions must be answered before a decision can be made. I will expect your initial comments to these questions within three weeks."

1. Would the acquisition of Union Carbide complement our strategic policy?
2. Can we afford the acquisition, or should we try to capture the U.S. market by using another strategy?
3. What organizational changes need to be made in order to fully realize the synergies created by acquiring the division?
4. Is the economic environment conducive to such an acquisition?
5. What is the health of the chemical and agricultural industries?
6. How would exchange rates and interest rates affect the decision to acquire the division?
7. Will the acquisition of the division eliminate or weaken competition within the U.S. agricultural chemical industry?
8. How would the political climate in France and the United States affect the acquisition?

COMPANY BACKGROUND

Rhone-Poulenc started in 1858 in Paris when Etienne Poulenc, a pharmacist, opened a small drugstore. Poulenc's interests were many and, apart from practicing pharmacy, he began to produce photographic products.

The firm's multinational activities began in 1922 when it acquired the British May and Banker Company to expand its pharmaceutical activities. Despite acquiring a foreign company, RP failed to develop an international strategy, the lack of which would later cause problems.

The company continued to grow and develop new products such as nylon and penicillin. These products proved especially profitable. After World War II, RP increasingly focused its attention on research and development, spending as much as 5 percent of its sales. At the same time RP reorganized into five broad divisions: chemistry, health, textiles, agricultural chemicals, and films.

In the 1960s, Rhone-Poulenc began an aggressive acquisition campaign, buying two pharmaceutical laboratories: Laboratoire Roger Bellon, and the Institut Merieux. The latter specialized in the production of vaccines. In 1969, Progil and Pechiney Saint Gobain were also acquired, strengthening the company's position in basic and agricultural chemicals. By 1969, as a result of the many acquisitions, Rhone-Poulenc was France's largest chemical producer.

The 1970s were a period of numerous difficulties for RP. The gradual decrease in French tariffs due to the European Economic Community's various treaties allowed greater international competition. Furthermore, Rhone-Poulenc's attitudes were far more provincial than those of its European competitors. While RP focused only on the European market, its competitors were penetrating the North American market and thereby achieving greater economies of scale. Only 5 percent of Rhone-Poulenc's sales came from the United States, compared with Ciba-Geigy's 39 percent, ICI and Hoechst's 25 percent, and Bayer and BASF's 20 percent. RP's international position was not only underdeveloped, but many of its foreign operations were unprofitable. As a result, the company started to retreat from international markets. RP lost potential profits by excess use of licensing agreements, especially in the U.S. market. RP had additional difficulties because of the gradual but painful dismantling of its textile division.

RP's lack of an international strategy, industry crisis, and restrictive economic policies by the French government caused the rapid deterioration of the company, and by 1981 Rhone-Poulenc was virtually bankrupt.

THE 1980s: STRATEGIC POLICIES IN THE CONTEXT OF STATE OWNERSHIP

Direct state intervention in economic matters has been a French tradition for almost four centuries, so the socialist nationalization program of 1981 did not break with tradition; however, it was extreme even by French standards.

The government had several objectives for nationalizing all the major firms of the country, ranging from the rescue of hopeless industries (coal, steel, shipbuilding) to the takeover of successful industries in order to rebuild France's industrial structure. This particular national industrial policy was the broadest in scope and the most coercive of all industrial policies implemented since the 1950s.

In 1982, all major companies in the chemical industry were under government control. To accelerate the restructuring, many corporate officials were forced by the government to resign and were consequently replaced by bureaucrats. Surprisingly, the CEO of Rhone-Poulenc, Jean Gandois, was asked to stay and pursue the policy he had initiated in the latter 1970s. This policy focused the company's attention on more rewarding products such as pharmaceuticals and agricultural chemicals. But RP's CEO Gandois, who was strongly disliked by the unions for the layoffs that had occurred under his leadership, decided to resign. His successor, Loïc le Floch Prigent, was an unknown bureaucrat who had been a technical counselor at the Ministry of Industry.

The socialist government drastically reorganized the chemical industry because it felt that the major problems within the industry were the disorganized and inefficient cross-ventures among major French chemical companies: Rhone-Poulenc, Elf Aquirtaine, Cdf Chimie, ATO Chimie, Produits Chimiques Ungines Kulhmann (PCUK), and Chloe Chimie. The government decided to redistribute assets among the firms; the result was that two firms disappeared entirely.

Rhone-Poulenc was among the remaining firms. As a consequence of the restructuring, Rhone inherited PCUK's urethane intermediates and polyurethanes, pharmaceuticals and fine chemicals, agricultural chemicals, phosphoric acids, phosphates, and other assorted products. In exchange, Rhone abandoned all fertilizer activity to Cdf Chimie and the remains of its petrochemical business to Elf Aquirtaine. In this process, RP lost its position as France's largest chemical company to Elf.

All things considered, the government's efforts to reorganize the chemicals industry around three large companies was successful at the international level. According to Stuart Wamsley, chemical analyst with Greenwell Montagu (London), Rhone-Poulenc, despite its precarious financial situation, "emerged with one of the most attractive product portfolios in the European chemical industry."

Rhone's CEO, le Floch Prigent, although a socialist, was more pragmatic than ideological. He chose to initiate Gandois's policies emphasizing long-term strategies. The nationalized status of the firm proved useful in several ways. According to le Floch, the nationalization "allows us to establish a coherent group strategy based on something other than the perpetual desire to sell something to improve the short-term results. Only a stockholder like the government, capable of looking at the return over the long-term, can do that. We are now capable of deciding a strategic plan for three, five, and ten years."[1]

The government's help was substantial. In 1983, it provided Rhone-Poulenc with $268 million—$74 million in equity and the rest in 15-year subordinated debt at preferential interest rates. With government support RP's capital spending budgets averaged $400 million per year from 1982 to 1985. Furthermore, RP continued substantial research and development expenditures. Despite state ownership, le Floch emphasized that Rhone-Poulenc must function as a competitive company.

Three of Rhone's businesses were chosen as its strategic focus: pharmaceuticals and health, agricultural chemicals, and fine and specialty chemicals. The company's broad objectives were to make the company less dependent on its home market and capable of becoming a world-class competitor. In order to fulfill these objectives, RP would have to catch up with the rest of its competitors by expanding its presence in the United States, Japan, and West Germany. The company set a goal of capturing a 2.5 percent market share in every country in which it operated. Additionally, the company decided to abandon its traditional international licensing strategy and seek acquisitions. Le Floch stated that "it is always the licensee that makes money from our research."[2] RP quickly realized that the best way to enhance company returns in the Health Division was to own U.S. facilities. This would greatly facilitate the registration of new drugs with the U.S. Food and Drug Administration.

Entering the U.S. drug market wasn't as easy as it sounded. Rhone-Poulenc had suffered a serious setback in its previous attempt to enter the U.S. market. In 1978, the company purchased a part of the Morton Norwich Company to profit from its pharmaceutical division. But in 1982 when Proctor & Gamble bought Morton Norwich's drug operations, RP was forced to sell its interest in Morton Norwich. It was the opinion of industry experts that Rhone's poor financial condition would prevent it from participating in any new deals. An appropriate-sized acquisition would be at least $400–$500 million—much too high for a company as overborrowed as Rhone-Poulenc. Other analysts felt that the socialist government would not allow a deal that would endanger France's fragile balance of payments situation. These arguments led to prediction that RP would be left with no alternative but to establish a joint venture.

The company's top officials had a different view. As Igor Landau, member of the executive committee, said, "If we can't find the right company, and admittedly the potential candidates are few, we'll continue to invest in our own subsidiaries, we'll continue to lose money if we have to in order to take a position in the U.S."[3]

Rhone's situation outside the U.S. didn't look much brighter (see Tables 1 and 2). In West Germany the company's subsidiary, Pharma, had sales of only $20 million and lacked the critical resources necessary to compete successfully in that market. The situation in Japan was slightly better due to joint ventures with Showa Denko and Chugai Pharmaceuticals.

Agricultural chemicals were also in RP's strategic plans. In 1981, Rhone-Poulenc acquired Mobil's agricultural chemical division for about $35–$40

TABLE 1
Rhone-Poulenc's Financial Position by Sector (December 31, 1985)*

	Chem	Fibers	Health	Agrochem	Other	Consolidated
Net sales	28,336	10,529	11,745	6,506	3,315	54,712
Depreciation	(894)	(515)	(337)	(121)	(135)	(2,002)
Operating margin	2,625	532	1,202	648	(374)	4,628
Assets	17,330	6,929	8,492	4,541	5,544	43,222
Capital expenditure	2,081	744	581	243	491	4,140

* Millions of French Francs.

Source: Rhone-Poulenc's 1987 *Annual Report*.

TABLE 2
Rhone-Poulenc's Financial Position by Geographic Area (December 31, 1985)*

	France	Europe	Brazil	U.S.	Others	Consolidated
Net sales	36,886	17,394	6,624	2,893	1,799	54,712
Depreciation	(1,207)	(431)	(298)	(50)	(16)	(2,002)
Operating margin	2,417	819	1,142	8	223	4,628
Assets	27,556	8,847	4,109	1,812	1,167	43,222
Capital expenditure	2,714	707	596	79	44	4,140

* Millions of French Francs.

Source: Rhone-Poulenc's 1987 *Annual Report*.

million, giving the company its first direct access to the huge U.S. agricultural market. The products acquired in that deal were mainly insecticides, herbicides, and defoliants. Rhone-Poulenc started to take full advantage of its nationalized status by establishing links with the Institut National de Recherche Agronomique (INRA), a government institute of more than 2000 researchers, in order to increase its research results.

RP's long-term efforts started to pay off in 1983. After three years of large deficits, the net income turned positive in 1984 and 1985. Profits were growing faster than sales, thus restoring the net profit margin above the 4 percent average for the entire chemical industry.

RHONE-POULENC TODAY

Rhone-Poulenc is France's largest chemical producer and one of the major multinational chemical companies in the world. It is also Europe's third-largest pharmaceutical group. Rhone-Poulenc is a world leader in rare earths, gallium, lactic acid, fluorinated derivatives, and vanillin. RP's business activities are organized into three major areas:

1. Health sciences applied to human beings, animals, and plants
2. New materials and specialty chemicals
3. Organic and inorganic intermediates

Operationally, Rhone-Poulenc is organized along four broad sectors: chemicals, fibers, health, and agricultural chemicals. The fibers business focuses on polyamide; polyester fibers and yarns used for stockings, hosiery, and sportswear; specialty PVC fibers, noninflammable aramides; acetate tow for cigarette filters; and monofilaments for industrial weaving. Rhone's health sector is organized around six activities: pharmaceutical specialties, consumer health products, active agents, vaccines, blood derivatives, and veterinary pharmaceuticals and animal nutrition products. The agricultural chemicals sector provides the company with a strong position in herbicides and fungicides. It also manufactures growth regulators. But this sector's main weakness is that it doesn't manufacture insecticides.

In 1985, RP's consolidated sales amounted to 54,712 million FF (see Tables 1, 2, and 3). The company's chemical sector contributed 52 percent of corporate sales, fibers 19 percent, health 21 percent, and agricultural chemicals 12 percent. The contribution to operating margin per sector was 52 percent for chemicals, 10.6 percent for fibers, 24 percent for health, and 13 percent for agricultural chemicals.

In 1985, RP operated in 140 countries and generated more than 60 percent of its sales from outside of France. This was accomplished through exports and foreign production. Despite the substantial international involvement, the company's four sector headquarters and main headquarters were still located in Paris.

Rhone-Poulenc's main competitors were Bayer, BASF, Hoechst, Imperial Chemical Industries (ICI), and Ciba-Geigy. Financial data for all these companies are given in Table 4.

Table 3
Rhone-Poulenc's Consolidated Income Statement
(December 31, 1985)*

Net sales	54,712
Operating expenses	(50,084)
Operating margin	4,628
Other income (expense)	(992)
Income from continuing operations before taxes and minority interest	3,636
Income taxes	(1,586)
Income from continuing operations before minority interest	2,050
Minority interest	(186)
Income from continuing operations	1,864
Discontinued operations	(252)
Net income before extraordinary credit	1,612
Extraordinary credit	515
Net income before priority dividends	2,127
Priority dividends	(69)
Net income available for distribution	2,058
Stockholder's equity:	
Common stock A	3,664
Nonvoting preferred shares B	366
Capital equity notes	—
Participating shares	620
Additional paid-in capital	3,311
Retained earnings	135
Translation reserve	616
Total stockholders equity	8,712

* Millions of French francs.
Source: Rhone-Poulenc's 1987 *Annual Report*.

TABLE 4
Financial Data of Major European Chemical Companies: 1980–1985*

	1980	1981	1982	1983	1984	1985
Rhone-Poulenc						
Net sales	7,139	6,599	5,611	5,658	5,858	6,240
Net income	(77)	(45)	(128)	(129)	(227)	(257)
Net profit margin (%)	—	—	—	2.28	3.89	4.12
Capital spending	611	448	330	365	395	460
R&D spending	354	289	267	286	282	318
Employees (000)	95	89	82	81	80	78
Exchange rate (FF/$)	4.23	5.44	6.57	7.62	8.74	8.99
Bayer						
Net sales	15,838	14,930	14,335	14,641	15,099	15,621
Net income	401	229	26	296	412	448
Net profit margin (%)	2.5	1.5	0.2	2.0	2.7	2.9
Capital spending	1,461	1,123	847	734	646	700
R&D spending	682	622	638	664	686	726
Employees (000)	182	181	179	175	175	176
Exchange rate (DM/$)	1.82	2.26	2.43	2.55	2.85	2.94
BASF						
Net sales	15,237	14,056	13,369	13,769	14,175	15,094
Net income	197	162	113	203	314	339
Net profit margin (%)	1.3	1.2	0.8	1.5	2.2	1.2
Capital spending	1,011	911	824	639	720	950
R&D spending	546	484	483	466	436	488
Employees (000)	117	117	116	114	116	130
Exchange rate (DM/$)			same as above			
Hoechst						
Net sales	16,467	15,237	14,937	14,584	14,546	14,531
Net income	305	188	130	356	474	499
Net profit margin (%)	1.9	1.2	0.9	2.4	3.3	3.4
Capital spending	1,054	870	851	733	725	804
R&D spending	715	670	642	634	638	708
Employees (000)	187	185	182	180	178	180
Exchange rate (DM/$)			same as above			
Imperial Chemical Industries						
Net sales	13,291	13,349	12,886	12,528	13,247	13,910
Net income	302	389	254	602	809	716
Net profit margin (%)	2.3	2.9	2.0	4.8	6.1	5.1
Capital spending	1,684	838	511	548	590	822
R&D spending	493	464	427	419	400	453
Employees (000)	14	132	124	118	116	119
Exchange rate (BP/$)	0.43	0.493	0.571	0.659	0.748	0.771

TABLE 4
Financial Data of Major European Chemical Companies: 1980–1985* *(continued)*

	1980	1981	1982	1983	1984	1985
Ciba-Geigy						
Net sales	7,134	6,938	6,802	7,019	7,436	7,407
Net income	183	266	304	369	505	598
Net profit margin (%)	2.6	3.8	4.5	5.3	6.8	8.1
Capital spending	511	446	428	395	428	493
R&D spending	561	549	579	594	620	680
Employees (000)	81	80	79	79	81	81
Exchange rate (SF/$)	1.67	1.96	2.03	2.1	2.35	2.46

* Millions of U.S. dollars unless otherwise specified.

In March 1986, national elections brought the conservatives back to power. Le Floch left soon thereafter and was replaced by Jean-René Fourtou, a man close to the *Rassemblement pour la République* (RPR), the party of new Premier Jacques Chirac. In late July, the news came that Union Carbide, in the wake of its problems after the catastrophic accident in Bhopal, India, was selling its agricultural chemical division.

THE RISE AND FALL OF UNION CARBIDE

In 1876, the first carbon arc street light changed night into day in Cleveland, Ohio. As a result of this invention, Union Carbide was formed in 1886 to make street light carbons and later, carbon electrodes for electric furnaces. Soon, the Everready trademark became part of the company. Four years later, it produced the first commercial dry cell battery, and in 1894 built one of the first industrial research laboratories in the United States. By 1900, its capital stock was $6,000,000.

The government's need for ethylene during World War I regenerated interest in hydrocarbon by-products. Union Carbide anticipated the future need for synthetic organic chemicals and in 1920 the company's chemical business was established.

With the outbreak of World War II, Union Carbide focused its attention on developing raw material resources and utilizing by-products. Union Carbide created a synthetic rubber and constructed three plants for treating uranium ores with newly developed processes. Following the war, Union Carbide expanded into other products such as polyethylene, the plastic used in squeeze bottles, films, and sheeting, which became the company's largest dollar volume product.

Union Carbide's international operations were restructured in 1966 to accommodate new subsidiaries. During the late 1960s and early 1970s, the firm restructured in order to devote more resources to expansion into newer industries. The Agricultural Products Division was developed in 1976 and began producing insecticides and pesticides.

All was going well until 1984, when Union Carbide's Bhopal, India, subsidiary had a massive disaster that led to the death of 2500 people and to permanent disability of thousands of others. This occurred despite a previously good safety record. In addition to the human toll, the tragedy effectively halted business at this $9 billion company. Union Carbide had to shut down production of methyl isocyanate, the product responsible for the disaster, at its plant in Institute, West Virginia. The accident put the company in a terrible position. As the Chairman of the Board conceded, "We have a stigma and we can't avoid it."[4] The losses incurred in 1985 amounted to $582 million, which included restructuring costs, plant write-offs, and a reserve of about $100 million to cover legal costs.

In addition to the Bhopal tragedy, Union Carbide had to resist a spirited takeover effort by GAF Corporation. In winning that battle, Union Carbide incurred a $5.5 billion debt. As a result Union Carbide's debt to total capital ratio soared to nearly 80 percent. The company decided to sell some of its most profitable businesses to retire debt. Three consumer product units were sold for $2.24 billion, and then Union Carbide announced that it would sell an additional $1 billion of assets, including its corporate headquarters. In July 1986, the company announced that its agricultural division was for sale.

Union Carbide Agricultural Chemical Division

The decision to sell the agricultural chemical division was regarded by experts as an economic necessity. Union Carbide, suffering weak sales and facing huge debt payments, was no longer able to effectively compete in the global market for its insecticides and agricultural chemicals. Robert D. Kennedy, Carbide's President, stated: "The real growth of our business can best be realized if it is allied with another company that has a strong commitment to agricultural products."[5]

Assets for sale included

Carbide's complex in Institute, West Virginia
Its laboratories in Research Triangle Park, North Carolina
Domestic pesticide plants in Woodbine, Georgia; Clinton, Iowa; St. Louis and St. Joseph, Missouri; and Ambler, Pennsylvania
Foreign operations as well as plants in India (Bhopal), Brazil, France, and Canada

Analysts expected Carbide's agricultural products units to attract offers but some say that the units would not command a high price because of their maturity, lack of glamorous products, and the Bhopal stigma. Paul Leming, a chemical industry analyst at Kidder, Peabody & Co., explained that "if the [annual] revenue from agricultural products is $500 million, they should be able to get at least that in a sale. Shell recently sold its agricultural chemical business for at least two times revenue, but I don't think Carbide will get an attractive multiple because it mostly makes insecticides. That's where the greatest toxicity and environmental problems lie—more so than with herbicides and fungicides."[6] Furthermore, the division was expected to lose $50 million in 1985 due to the shutdown of the Institute complex.

Companies such as Bayer, Ciba-Geigy, and Monsanto were considered potential buyers. In order to win the bid for Union Carbide's agriculture division, Rhone-Poulenc would have to bid higher than the other strong competitors. A successful bid would enable the company to become the third-largest agricultural chemical producer in the world, behind Bayer and Ciba-Geigy and ahead of BASF, Hoechst, and ICI.

AN OVERVIEW OF AGRICULTURAL CHEMICAL MARKETS IN THE UNITED STATES

Agriculture is the number one business in the United States, employing more than 22 million people. Agriculture generates 20 percent ($610 billion) of the U.S. GNP. Approximately one third of the agricultural production is exported. Except for business taxes, agricultural chemicals have the lowest input cost in the agriculture industry. Furthermore, these costs are increasing slower than the inflation rate. Agricultural chemicals significantly minimize the cost of world-scale agricultural production. The benefits that agricultural chemicals provide to producers translate into benefits to consumers. The average American family spends 15 percent of its disposable income on food, the lowest of any nation.

The agricultural chemicals industry consists of nearly two dozen producers worldwide that are engaged in the discovery, development, and marketing of proprietary agricultural chemicals. These manufacturers, formulators, distributors, and dealers participate in a worldwide end user market estimated to be in excess of $20 billion in 1985. Detailed figures representing the growth in agricultural chemicals consumption are provided in Table 5.

This industry has a very narrow profit margin, making it difficult to justify expenditures for marketing activities. The industry is, however, strongly R&D-dependent. The introduction of new products drives the industry. Products that have been discovered within the last 10 years generated over 25 percent of current sales. The main producers spent approximately 7 percent of their sales on R&D. This represents twice the chemical industry average and is substantially above the 1.5 percent found with the fibers industry.

The agricultural chemical industry, like the pharmaceutical industry, is among the most highly regulated in the private sector. The major law

TABLE 5
U.S. and World Production of Agricultural Chemicals, 1980–1985

	1980	1981	1982	1983	1984	1985
United States (in millions of pounds)						
Herbicide	80€	839	623	604	716	756
% change	22.68	4.09	−25.74	−3.05	18.54	5.59
Insecticide	506	448	379	306	350	370
% change	−17.99	−11.46	−15.40	−19.26	14.38	5.71
Fungicides	156	14፡	111	106	123	109
% change	.65	−8.33	−22.38	−4.50	16.04	−11.38
Total	1,468	1,430	1,113	1,016	1,189	1,235
% change	2.73	−2.59	−22.17	−8.72	17.03	3.87
World (in thousands of metric tons)						
Africa	58.1	69.7	52.1	40.9	46.5	41
United States	665.9	674.7	685.9	697.2	708.4	719.7
South America	95.6	83.3	72.9	80.5	91.5	100.4
Asia	818.4	743.6	728.1	669	679.1	521
EEC	437.2	466.9	563.7	562.9	609	583.5
EFTA	66.1	61.4	62.7	55.5	57.4	57.9
USSR and all	506.4	529.7	557.0	589.2	611	606.4
Total	2647.7	2629.3	2722.4	2704.2	2802.9	2629.9

regulating agricultural chemicals is the Federal Insecticide, Fungicide and Rodenticide Act (FIFRA), which came into existence in 1947. FIFRA requires approval from or registration with the Environmental Protection Agency (EPA). In addition, residues on food crops are regulated under the Food, Drug and Cosmetic Act (FDCA). The EPA administers the portion of the FDCA that deals with judging the safety of trace amounts of chemical residues on food crops. Under the combined authority of FIFRA and FDCA, agricultural chemical producers are required to provide considerable pre-market test data.

TABLE 6
Projection of Long-Term Annual Interest Rates for the United States and France, 1985–1989

	1985	1986	1987	1988	1989
France	11.7%	8.8%	9.6%	9.7%	9.7%
United States	10.8%	8.1%	8.6%	9.0%	9.6%

Source: *OECD Economic Outlook Historical Statistics,* 1960–1987 and *OECD Economic Outlook,* June 1989. (Paris, France: OECD Publication Service, 1989), p. 21; Board of Governors, *Federal Reserve Bulletin* (Washington, D.C.: Publications Service, April 1990), p. A24.

TABLE 7
Projected Annual Inflation Rate for the United States and France, 1986–1990

	1986	1987	1988	1989	1990
France	5.1%	2.9%	3.2%	3.25%	2.75%
United States	2.7%	3.3%	3.4%	5.0%	5.25%

Source: *OECD Economic Outlook*, June 1989. (Paris, France: OECD Publication Service, 1989), p. 131.

The development and introduction of new products are complicated and expensive. When a compound is first synthesized, the company starts charging costs against the venture. The cash flow turns positive after the plant is built and the production has been registered. The company breaks even a few years later. Only then do profits on the investment start to accrue.

The opportunity to recover an investment depends on good patent protection and on prompt product registration with government officials around the world. Spending an extra million dollars to secure high quality data for registration has a minimal effect on cash flows, but a delay in the EPA's registration decision can cause serious financial problems. A delay usually sends a company further into the red because of the additional work required, the postponement of the break-even point, and the decrease in the rate of return. This situation can be catastrophic for a company. Thus, firms tend to avoid high-risk ventures.

EPA registration for each new agricultural chemical costs well over $20 million and takes 7 to 10 years to complete. This expense, which has become the major factor associated with the increased costs of new products, is primarily due to the increase in both the number and complexity of the tests and research required. There is a strong built-in incentive for companies to do the best possible job on safety evaluations; otherwise, a new product may be delayed or stopped in the registration process.

The resources required to deliver a competitive portfolio of new com-

TABLE 8
Balance of Payments Position of the United States and France, 1980–1986
(in billions of U.S. dollars)

	1980	1981	1982	1983	1984	1985	1986
France	−4.17	−4.75	−12.06	−4.69	−0.84	−0.35	2.96
United States	0.87	6.89	−8.69	−46.25	−107.08	−115.10	−138.83

Source: *OECD Economic Outlook*, June 1989. (Paris, France: OECD Publication Service, 1989), p. 184.

TABLE 9
Unemployment Rate for the United States and France, 1980–1986
(percentage of total population)

	1980	1981	1982	1983	1984	1985	1986
France	6.3	7.4	8.1	8.3	9.7	10.2	10.4
United States	7.0	7.5	9.5	9.5	7.4	7.1	6.9

Source: *OECD Economic Outlook*, June 1989. (Paris, France: OECD Publication Service, 1989), p. 182.

pounds are increasing in cost. Many experts believe that R&D costs alone amount to over $100 million, and for this reason many companies are getting out of the business or consolidating.

THE U.S. ECONOMIC OUTLOOK

The economic projections over the next few years look favorable. Real GNP is expected to grow on an average of 3.3 percent annually through 1993. The unemployment rate is expected to decline steadily, to about 5.2 percent of the available work force by 1993. Government policies are expected to encourage growth in the economy. Through government efforts, research and development exenditures are expected to increase in real terms, thus encouraging innovative and technological discoveries that will increase productive efficiencies. Tax reform will continue and provide extra income to some sectors of the economy. The push to eliminate production inefficiencies should result in increasing productivity. Finally, stable inflation rates and energy prices will enable businesses to forecast more accurately the allocation of capital. Forecasts of relevant U.S. economic statistics are presented in Tables 6 through 9.

FRANCE'S ECONOMIC OUTLOOK

France will continue to abide by policies of curbing public expenditures and easing taxation. Inflation is likely to slow down to a rate of 3 percent. Household and corporate incomes will continue to grow, and domestic demand is expected to rise to the European average of 2.25 percent. Unemployment will continue to rise but at a slower rate. The French government is keeping a tight control over its spending, determined to keep it at 3.2 percent of GDP.

All in all, the demand for French-manufactured products will continue to grow by approximately 4.5 percent per year. Corporate demand, however, will remain limited by high debt levels. Forecasts of relevant French economic statistics are presented in Tables 6 through 9.

QUESTIONS

1. If you were the CEO of RP, would you make this acquisition? Why or why not?

2. If you were the CEO of Union Carbide, would you make this divestiture? Why or why not?

3. What will be the long-term impact of this divestiture on the global competitiveness of Union Carbide in the agricultural chemicals industry?

4. Do you believe that this sale is in the long-run best interests of the United States? Justify your answer.

Notes

1. "Rhone-Poulenc's Uphill Route to World Class," *Chemical Week*, April 27, 1983, p. 40.
2. Ibid., p. 41.
3. Ibid., p. 42.
4. *International Directory of Company Histories*, ed. Thomas Derdak, vol. 1 (Chicago: St. James Press, 1988), p. 401.
5. "Carbide Planning to Sell Farm Product Division," *The New York Times*, July 23, 1986, p. D2.
6. Meg Cox, "Carbide Acts to Sell Farm Chemical Units, Biggest Maker of Methyl Isocyanate," *The Wall Street Journal*, July 23, 1986, p. 5.

The New Boss Meets His First Crisis

Bob Schmidt had been appointed as the general manager in charge of western European operations of a U.S. manufacturing firm (Universal Stamping), which was listed by *Fortune* magazine as one of the second 500.

He closed his eyes and listened to the engines of the big jet as it reached cruising altitude. Bob could not help but reflect on the circumstances of his life. His wife Betty and two daughters—Amy, 11, and Julie, 13—were still in the United States trying to sell their house and finishing the school year. They would join him in about six months. Bob would live in a hotel until the company-owned house in a suburban area west of Paris had been remodeled.

Bob Schmidt had grown up in a working-class home in Turtle Creek, Pennsylvania. He was the second son and one of eight children of a first-generation German-American father and an Italian-American mother. His father had worked in the steel mills of Pittsburgh. Bob had gone into the army after high school; then after serving his tour of duty in Korea, he did a business degree part-time. After completing his B.B.A. with a marketing major, he took a marketing research position with Universal Stamping and went to law school in the evening. Although it took him nine years, Bob Schmidt finished his J.D. Bob had been with Universal Stamping for 25 years. His career had been filled with challenges; it often seemed to him

By Don R. Beeman, 1989.

This case was prepared as the basis for class discussion rather than to illustrate either effective or ineffective management.

that he had jumped around to so many different positions that he knew everything "sort of" and nothing completely. From marketing research he had gone to customer service, to sales, to sales management, to product manager for the aluminum automotive parts division. Then 10 years ago, top management had taken him out of the sales and marketing area and made him the manager of one of the oldest and least productive plants in the system. From there his career had been all production, moving to ever-larger plants. Two years ago he had been made vice-president for all aluminum products. Now he had to take on what he perceived to be his toughest challenge—trying to turn around the entire European operations of Universal. It was common knowledge in the company that the European operations were a real "snake pit" that seemed to eat good managers.

A combination of mergers, acquisitions, and direct investments had resulted in a loose confederation of nearly autonomous operations, each of which acted as if it was still an independent firm. Most of the key managers of the various subsidiaries were persons who had held those jobs before Universal entered the picture. Furthermore, there was a great deal of nationalistic rivalry among the subsidiaries and no common management systems. Universal had tried on several occasions to rationalize and integrate these operations but had never really succeeded. In the past 15 years, Universal had had several different general managers. The first was an American, who lasted two years. Next came an Englishman, who lasted eight years and although he had not done a good job, in hindsight he had probably been the best of a bad lot. Next came a Frenchman who was in the job for almost four years. In Bob's opinion, after extensively studying the record, those four years had probably set back the practice of management at least 400 years. For the last 15 months the European operations had been run by a German who had done a good job of improving production quality at most of the European plants. Unfortunately Hans had done such a terrible job on all other aspects of running the businesses that he had recently been demoted to the position of director of production operations. Bob had his doubts about whether Hans would stay with Universal.

Although the management of the European operations had been so bad that it would be hard for Bob to be worse, he was not thinking about how not to fail but rather how to succeed. Bob Schmidt was totally unprepared and he knew it. He spoke no language other than English and sometimes he doubted his skill in even that language. His sole international experience was with a rifle in his hand near the DMZ in Korea. He had no training in the languages or the cultures in which he would have to function. All he knew was what he had been able to learn from the mountain of reports and data that he had read over the last two months. Now he had to try to turn around the European operations, which had never run well. He had to make eight wholly owned subsidiaries—each with its own nearly independent production and marketing operations (11 plants and 27 sales offices in all)—three minority joint ventures, and one licensing arrangement begin to work as a unified whole.

As Bob sat on the plane he hoped that there would be no major crisis in the next six months.

Bob had been in Paris three weeks, during which time he had been trying to visit the subsidiary offices and the major plants. On his first day back in the European headquarters office after a four-day trip to three major plants, he was greeted by a line of 10 managers each of whom was holding what looked like 1000 pages of paper under each arm. There were the presidents from four different subsidiaries, the president and the vice-president of marketing from a fifth subsidiary, the president and the vice-president of sales from a sixth subsidiary, and two of his top people from the headquarters. The vice-president of marketing and the director of auditing were there. Obviously something major had happened while he was away.

Bob Schmidt's first thought was to wonder what could get all of these "self-important heavyweights" into the Paris office at 7:30 A.M. and why he had not been informed of the problem, whatever it was. In fact the latter seemed to Bob to be of greater concern than THE PROBLEM, whatever it might be.

After listening to each of the managers, Bob was able to begin to unravel the essence of the problem, at least as they saw it. It seemed that Universal's subsidiaries had been secretly competing with each other for the business of one of Europe's largest multinational corporations. This firm had been designated as a global account, which meant that it was to be handled directly and exclusively from the Paris office so that coordination could be maintained with other world regions. To make matters worse, this account had been using the price, delivery, and credit terms quoted by the various subsidiaries as justification for bargaining concessions from the head of sales in the Paris office on both regional and export purchases.

Each of the 10 executives waiting for Schmidt was there to defend himself and to try to explain why someone else was to blame. Schmidt listened to each and wondered why no one even mentioned solving the problem to which each of them had contributed. Each manager was told to go back to his own business and to meet back in Schmidt's office in one week. When they had all left, Schmidt called in his secretary and asked whether she had known about the problem and why she had not bothered to call him or to tell him when he had called in. Indeed she had known about the problem but had not informed him because she had been told not to by the head of marketing in the Paris office, Jean-Claude Boisé. Boisé had told her that he and others would be fired on the spot because that was the American way, and besides Schmidt was only going to be in Europe temporarily because he was what the Americans call a "hatch man."

When the secretary had gone, Schmidt sat in his office reflecting on the situation and wondered what his options might be.

QUESTIONS

1. List and explain the problems as you see them.

2. If you were Schmidt, what additional information would you want and why would you want it?

3. Prioritize these problems as to importance for the long-term success of Schmidt and of Universal Europe.

4. What are Schmidt's options for each problem? For each problem select the option that you would follow and justify that selection.

5. What does this incident tell you about the management at Universal Europe?

6. What should Bob Schmidt's long-term goals be for these managers and the operations that they control?

7. What kinds of training should Schmidt have been given that would have prepared him better for his new job and for this type of problem?

Wickstan Toy Company, Inc.

American labor unions are upset by runaway plants and the jobs they take with them. American toy manufacturers with only U.S. production plants are upset because they are losing market share and profits to competition. This competition comes from Asian firms, especially those from Japan, Taiwan, South Korea, and Singapore, as well as American toy manufacturers who have production operations in low-wage-rate areas. The labor unions argue that when a company invests in a low-wage-rate area for the production of components or finished goods to be shipped back to the United States, they are actually exporting U.S. jobs. Management counters that the lower-cost components and products that can be sold at lower prices allow the company to stay in business and, if successful, to increase market share. Thus, offshore production might actually create more jobs than are temporarily lost.

In the face of offshore sourcing of components by some American firms and increasing competition from foreign firms, some toy manufacturers have shifted their product line away from the standard, low technology products to more complex, computer-controlled toys. Thus, they have given up on the mature and price-competitive segments of the market in favor of the quality-oriented, higher-price segments.

What one country considers a runaway plant, another views as an

By Don R. Beeman, 1989.

Adapted from Richard N. Farmer, "THE RUNAWAYS," *Incidents In International Business: Third Edition,* Bloomington, Indiana: Cedarwood Press, 1980, pp. 84–86.

This case was developed for class discussion only. It is not intended to represent good or bad management or decision-making.

opportunity to create economic development. Many countries, having few assets other than cheap labor, encourage such plants with a variety of incentives. A job at 50 cents per hour is better than being unemployed or working on a farm at 50 cents per day. While the work force might be poorly educated and unskilled, many of these individuals work remarkably hard, learn fast, mind their business, and do not agitate too much.

The experiences of many U.S. firms is that if the plants are properly designed for the host environment, productivity levels approximate those of a domestic plant. There are, however, additional costs: greater transportation and logistics costs for shipping and handling materials and components sent to the host country and finished goods or subassemblies returned to the United States. Additionally, there are generally higher managerial and technical costs from having expatriate managers and temporary technical personnel.

Among the countries trying to attract such operations is El Palo in Central America. It has changed its laws to allow for free labor mobility for skilled persons, which means that the firm could bring in any skilled managers or technicians needed. Taxes are low—only 20 percent—and profits can be repatriated without special repatriation taxes or limits. These incentives combined with the low wage rate of 75 cents per hour including fringes have resulted in investments by numerous American firms from a variety of industries.

The Wickstan Toy Company is a medium-sized toy manufacturer with gross sales in 1987 of nearly $200 million. It currently operates three production facilities: one in New Jersey, built in 1923; one in New York, built in 1939 by Yankee Toys, Inc. and acquired by Wickstan in 1955; and the newest plant, opened in Jackson, Mississippi, in 1978. In the New York and New Jersey plants, the average worker has 21 years with the firm and an average wage rate of $9.50 per hour, with fringes totaling 35 percent of that figure. In the Mississippi plant the worker force has less seniority (seven years) and is not unionized. The average wage rate is $5.50 per hour with fringes totaling 30 percent. The Mississippi plant now employs 1200 people compared with only 900 in the two other plants combined. Over 95 percent of all Wickstan employees are unskilled labor.

The last three years have been increasingly tough financially for Wickstan: in 1985, profits of $25,000 on sales of $192M; in 1986 a loss of $50,000 on sales of $185M; and in 1987 a loss of $5.1M on sales of $178M. Management has realized that it cannot continue to be a high-cost and average-quality producer in what is increasingly a commodity industry.

Wickstan's director of manufacturing has proposed that they establish a production facility in El Palo employing about 2000 people. He believes that such a plant could eliminate the need for all three U.S. facilities. He proposes that the three domestic plants be closed, the buildings sold, and all equipment moved to El Palo. Even with estimates of 5 percent higher management costs and 15 percent higher transportation and related costs, he concludes that labor cost saving would have resulted in 1987 profits of $6.8M.

Wickstan's labor union leaders have been putting pressure on Congress to pass legislation prohibiting this type of investment. Furthermore, production output in the two Eastern plants is down more than 30 percent since the news that Wickstan might move to El Palo was first presented to the workers by their union leadership. Congress is unlikely to pass any laws prohibiting offshore investments or sourcing since El Palo is a relatively stable social democracy in an increasingly unstable area.

There is another nasty question involved here. The United States has trade agreements with numerous governments that tend to keep import duties low. If the American government bans "runaway" foreign investment, then European and other Asian firms could invest in El Palo and market their products in the United States. If this were done, the American firm might lose out totally.

QUESTIONS

1. Develop a production and sourcing strategy for Wickstan.

2. Should Wickstan move to El Palo and close its American plants?

3. What other alternatives does Wickstan have? Evaluate each of these.

4. The toy industry has always been known to have low-paying jobs. Is it really in the best interests of the United States to ensure that low-paying production line jobs stay in the United States?

Glossary

Absolute advantage   one nation has an advantage in the production of one commodity and the second nation has an advantage in the production of another product due to the differences in natural endowments or acquired efficiencies

Acculturation   the process by which the culture of a particular society is instilled in a person from infancy onward

Acquired advantage   those advantages that are acquired through a nation's own efforts, such as education, skills, capital, infrastructure and the like, that are not native to a country

Adaptation strategies   the strategy of the firm is to adapt its operations so that it is perceived as promoting the interests of the host country

Ad valorem duty   a duty that is levied as a percentage of the value of the product being imported

Against all risks   an insurance policy term meaning that coverage is provided against loss or damage from any external cause except war, strikes, riots and civil commotion, or other specifically excluded risks

Agency for International Development (AID)   an agency of the U.S. government that provides economic aid to developing countries

Alliance for Progress   the U.S. promise to provide financial assistance to 19 Latin American republics for the development of schools and infrastructure

Anti-dumping duty   a duty levied on goods imported at prices below the cost of production or below the selling price in the country of export

Arbitrage   a type of transaction wherein a profit arises from the simultaneous purchase at one price and sale at another of commodities, including foreign exchange, in different markets

Arbitration   parties to a conflict, often union and management, agree to abide by the decision of an independent third party, the arbitrator

Arms-length pricing   the price that a firm charges its related entities for goods or services that is the same as that charged to nonrelated entities

Assured   either the shipper or the consignee who has an insurable interest in the shipment

Autocracy   dictatorial power is in the hands of one person

Autonomous items   transactions that occur independent of a nation's balance of payments

Average   a term in a marine insurance policy meaning loss or damage due to the perils of the sea

Average, irrespective of percentage   losses due to the perils of the sea are paid regardless of the percentage of expected damage that is normally excluded from coverage

Avoidance strategies   to reduce political risks, firms should avoid those countries where the risks seem greatest, or divest where risks are increasing or projected to increase

Balance of payments   the itemized account of the commercial and financial transactions for a stated period of time of all the people of one country with the combined peoples of all the other countries

Bank acceptance   a draft that is drawn upon a bank and is accepted by the bank

Banker's acceptance   a bank promises to honor upon maturity a draft that is drawn upon it

Bareboat charter   the responsibility of manning, provisioning, maintaining, and managing the vessel is that of the charterer

Barter   the exchange of goods or services for goods or services without the use of a medium of exchange (money)

Barter economy   an economy wherein goods are exchanged for goods without the use of a medium of exchange

Base salary   the salary that is paid to an employee exclusive of other benefits

Bilateral agreement   a formal agreement that is made between two countries binding the parties to the provisions of the treaty

Bill of exchange or draft   an unconditional order in writing addressed by one party to another requesting the latter to pay on demand or at a stated future date a specified sum of money to order or to the holder of the document

Bill of lading   a document issued by a carrier that serves as a contract between the carrier and shipper, receipt for goods delivered to the carrier, and title to the goods if it is an order bill of lading

Bonded warehouse   a place where goods may be stored without going through customs until they are withdrawn; generally, bonded warehouses do not allow goods to be processed, marked, etc., as in a foreign trade zone.

Bonus   supplemental payments that are made by some firms to enable employees to share in the profits

Boycott (of imports or exports)   an unofficial act on the part of some country or group within the country to discourage the import or export of goods

Buffer stock   products stockpiled during periods of surplus are used to supply the market when there are shortages, thereby preventing wide fluctuations in prices

Built-in export department   department established within a company to handle the details involved in export sales

Buy-back agreements   agreements usually associated with management contracts or turn-key operations in which the foreign partner agrees to take payment for its expertise, assistance, equipment, or technology in the form of products from the operation

C&F vessel, named port   price quoted includes the cost of the goods and the freight charges to the port of destination

Cable rates   the rate that is charged to transfer funds to another country by cable

Capital account   short- and long-term capital movement from one country to another

Capital-intensive process   capital equipment is used in a manufacturing process to reduce the use of labor

Capital subscriptions   the quota that is assigned to member countries as a means of raising capital for international institutions such as the IMF

Cartel   a form of business organization or agreement among a limited number of producers to control output and prices; it can be thought of as a monopoly on an international scale

Certificate of origin   document provided by the Chamber of Commerce certifying the origin of goods being exported

Clearing account barter   a credit account is created to pay for purchases by two contracting parties with the provision that at the end of the stipulated period, funds will be transferred to balance the two accounts

Codified law (Roman law)   a legal system based upon the principles of law in ancient Rome; this system is organized into commercial, civil, administrative, and criminal statutes

Commercial bills of exchange   bills that are drawn by a merchant on another requesting payment of a given sum of money upon presentation or at a specified future date

Commercial drafts   (see *bill of exchange or draft*)

Commercial invoice   a bill of sale providing a complete description of the goods, the exporter and importer, and other details of the shipment

Commercial risk   a credit risk that arises when a buyer does not or is unable to make payment because of some business-related event

Commitment letter   letter that describes the terms under which the Eximbank will grant a loan

Commodity agreement   agreement among producers or between producers and consumers to adopt measures to stabilize prices

Commodity Credit Corporation (CCC)   an agency of the U.S. Department of Agriculture whose purpose is to promote the sales of surplus agricultural products

Common law   the legal system that is based on precedents or past decisions of the courts

Communism   the theory that advocates the elimination of private property and the common ownership of all assets

Comparative advantage   one nation is more efficient than a second country in the production of two or more products but it is relatively more efficient in the production of one of those products

Compensatory duty   a duty that is equal in amount to the duty that was levied on the import of some raw material used in the manufacture of the product

Compensatory items   transactions that are carried out to compensate for the disequilibrium in a nation's balance of payments

Compound duty   a combination of ad valorem and specific duties

Consecutive voyage charter   a shipowner agrees to transport cargo in a number of shuttle voyages that follow consecutively between named ports

Consular invoice   document required by an importing country clearing goods for import

Consumer goods   goods produced for sale to end users

Continental shelf   the underwater extension of the land mass off the coast of a country

Contract of affreightment   contract that specifies the cargo to be transported between named ports over a fixed period of time

Contractual agreement (international)   an agreement that is made between a domestic firm and a foreign firm, individual, or government to produce or provide goods, services, or know-how according to specific terms

Controlled Foreign Corporation (CFC)   a corporation in which more than 50 percent of the stock is owned by U.S. shareholders, each of whom has at least a 10 percent interest

Counterpurchase or parallel barter   participating parties sign two separate contracts specifying the goods or services that are to be exchanged over a period of time

Countertrade   the financial settlement of a transaction without the use of a medium of exchange (money)

Convectional rains   when warm air rises it cools, thus reducing its ability to hold moisture, causing it to fall as rain

Cooley Amendment funds   foreign currencies received from the sale of surplus agricultural products are allocated to AID. These may be used to make loans to U.S. firms and their related entities or host governments if they result in the economic development of the country and the expansion of markets for U.S. agricultural products

Copyright   exclusive right that is given by law for a certain number of years to reproduce, publish, and sell copies of one's original literary, musical, or artistic work

Correspondent bank   the bank that acts as the agent of a bank located abroad

Cost of living allowance   allowances that are provided to overseas employees to cover the additional costs of housing, utilities, taxes, etc., to enable them to maintain their customary standard of living

Countervailing duty   duties that are levied on imports to offset an advantage that is granted by a country to its exporters

Credit and currency swaps   method of raising capital in foreign markets without paying a currency premium through the exchange of currencies between two companies or governments

Credit and debit items   credit items in the balance of payments of a country (A) are claims by that country (A) against another country (B); debit items are claims by the other country (B) against the first (A)

Creditor nation   a nation whose investments abroad are greater than foreign investments in that country

Credit tranche   members of the IMF may draw, in convertible currencies, an amount up to their paid-up subscriptions of their allotted quota

Creeping expropriation   the intentional actions of a government to expropriate through incremental takeover of foreign-owned private property or to establish conditions that make it unprofitable for the foreign firm to continue operations

Crusades   military expeditions under the auspices of the Christian church to recover the Holy Land

Culture   a pattern of behavior or guideline for behaviors that are acquired and transmitted by individuals through symbols

Culture shock   the psychological inability of a person to adapt to the customs and culture of the foreign environment

Currency depreciation   the value of the currency of one country decreases in relation to the currency of another country

Customs declaration   a form that is filed with customs describing a product being imported and its value

Customs value   the valuation that is placed on imports to determine ad valorem duties

Debenture   an unsecured bond whose holders have a claim on a firm's assets after the claims of all secured creditors have been satisfied

Debtor nation   total foreign investments in a country are greater than that country's investments abroad

Declining balance depreciation   a particular asset is depreciated on the basis of a stated percentage of the remaining balance each year

Deferral (of income tax)   incomes earned abroad by subsidiaries of American firms are not taxable until they are brought back to the United States

Deflation   when the amount of money in circulation in a country is inadequate to cover the increasing need for currency, prices for goods and services will decline

Demand or sight rates   rates that are charged on sight drafts that call for payment upon presentation

Democracy   a system of government wherein the people exercise political power

Dependency strategies   a firm seeks to maintain control over certain key aspects in the operation so that the host country will not be able to continue operations even if it were to take over the subsidiary

Depreciation   when a country's currency decreases in value because of market or other conditions

Devaluation   when a country takes official action to decrease the value of its currency

Direct export   when the manufacturer is responsible for handling most of the details involved in getting goods to a foreign country

Direct importing   the buyer handles most of the details involved in importing goods from a foreign country

Direct investment   a company's stock ownership position allows the firm to exercise some degree of managerial control

Dirty bill of lading   notation on bills of lading indicating the goods were delivered to the carrier in damaged condition

Discontinuous innovation   when completely new products are introduced to a culture

Discounting a draft   when a holder of a draft sells the instrument to a third party and receives the face value of the draft less the cost of interest until maturity

Discounting a note   a firm raises funds by selling a note and receiving the face value of the note less the interest charge until maturity

Discount rate   the rate of interest that is charged by the Federal Reserve System to its member banks on loans secured through a pledge of securities

Disequilibrium in the balance of payments when a nation's overall claims against others do not equal the claims of others aginst that country

Diurnal range in temperature the changes in temperature between day and night

Documentary draft a draft that has collateral attached to it

Documents against acceptance the various trade documents that are transferred to the importer at the time a draft is accepted

Documents against payment the international trade documents transferred to the buyer when payment is made for the shipment

Doldrums the equatorial belt of variable winds and calms

Dollar gap when the amount of dollars in the world markets are insufficient to cover all the dollar payments

Domestic International Sales Corporation (DISC) subsidiaries established by American firms to promote their export business were granted tax benefits by the U.S. government if they met certain requirements

Double taxation if a firm or individual is forced to pay taxes on the same income to both foreign and domestic governments

Drawee the one on whom a draft is drawn, usually an importer of the goods

Drawer the maker of the draft (usually the exporter) who draws a draft on the importer

Dry bulk carriers vessels that have been constructed to transport shipload lots of cargo such as iron ore and coal

Dry farming a type of agriculture that depends upon the annual rainfall to grow crops

Dumping when a product is imported into a country and sold at a price below the cost of production or the selling price in the country of origin

Dynamically continuous innovations products are altered or new products are introduced to meet the change in lifestyle of the population

East coast continental climate short summers and long cold winters characterize this climatic zone

Economic diversification the economy of a country is based upon the production of a variety of products

Economic exposure the long-term effect of a change in value of a currency on the value of a firm's investment

Economic nationalism a type of economic policy that a country adopts to foster the development of its economy without relying on others

Edge Act Corporation corporations that are established by commercial banks to engage in equity and long-term financing that they themselves may not engage in

Embargo an official act on the part of the government to prohibit the export or import of a product

Emigration to leave one's country to seek residence elsewhere

Empathy identification with and understanding of another's situation, feelings, and motives

Endorsee the recipient to whom the draft has been endorsed

Endorser the one who endorses a document over to another party

Enervating climate a hot and humid climate that saps one's energy

Equal advantage when one nation is equally efficient in the production of several products

Equity financing when a firm issues stock to raise capital or purchases a stock ownership position in another firm

Equity foreign investments a firm commits capital to purchase productive assets abroad

Errors and omissions a balancing item in the balance of payments statement to equalize credits and debits

Escape clause a concession may be withdrawn if it results in serious injury to a domestic industry

Ethnocentric policy a type of policy wherein home country nationals are selected for positions in both home and host countries

Ethnocentrism the belief in the superiority of one's own ethnic group or cultural unit

Eurocurrency market the European financial centers where foreign currency is deposited

European Community (EC or EEC) an economically

integrated area of 12 countries located in western Europe (West Germany, France, Italy, Belgium, the Netherlands, Luxembourg, Britain, Denmark, Ireland, Greece, Spain, Portugal)

European Monetary System   countries of the EC fixed the rates of their currencies to each other and permitted them to float as a block against other currencies; called the *European Currency Unit* (ECU)

Excess profits tax   when profits exceed a given percentage, the government may levy a tax on the excess

Exchange controls   controls that are adopted by governments to restrict the inflow and outflow of foreign exchange, and the conversion of its currency into the currency of another country

Exchange hedging   method to protect one from possible loss due to the fluctuation in the rate of exchange by transferring the risk to a third party

Exclusive agent   one who acts as the sole selling agent of a foreign manufacturer

Exclusive buying agent   an agent located in the country of import who acts on behalf of the importer

Expatriate   a person who has taken up residence in a foreign country

Expatriate employees   individuals from the home or a third country who are sent abroad to perform certain tasks for an enterprise

Export agent   an intermediary who represents different manufacturers that produce related but noncompetitive goods

Export declaration   document required by an exporting country that provides all the information pertaining to a particular shipment

Export duty   a duty that is levied on goods leaving a country

Export-Import Bank   a U.S. government agency whose major purpose is to aid in financing U.S. exports

Export sales subsidiary   corporate form of organization that is set up by a parent corporation to conduct its export business

Export trade association (Webb-Pomerene Association)   an association that competing firms may join to strengthen their marketing position abroad without violating U.S. antitrust laws

Exposure risks   risks from fluctuations in the rates of exchange to which firms are exposed

Expropriation   discriminatory seizure of property by a government, usually without prompt and adequate compensation

External sources of capital   nondomestic sources of capital

Extraterritoriality   a nation's imposition of its rules and regulations on branches and subsidiaries of domestic firms operating in another country

Factor   a financial institution or individual who purchases at a discount the accounts receivable of business firms

Factor proportions or endowments theory   the theory that a country will export commodities produced with its abundant resources and import those produced with scarce resources

Factors of production   land, labor, capital, and entrepreneurship that are used in the production of goods and services

FAS vessel, named port   a price quotation that includes the cost of goods and freight charges up to the vessel at the port of shipment

Fatalism   the doctrine that all events are predetermined by fate and therefore cannot be changed by human beings

Federal excise tax   an internal tax that is levied on the manufacture, sale, or consumption of certain commodities

Federal Reserve Bank (FRB)   25 regional banks constitute the central banking system of the United States that is referred to as the *Federal Reserve System*

Feudalism   the system of political and social organization prevailing in Europe during the Middle Ages

First in-first out inventory valuation (FIFO)   a method of inventory valuation such that for the calculation of taxable income, it is assumed that those materials purchased first are also used or sold first

Flag of convenience   some shipowners register and operate a vessel under a foreign flag to take advantage of lower operating costs, lower taxes, and fewer or less stringent regulations

Floating exchange rates   the exchange rate of a currency with respect to another is free to change (float) on the basis of supply and demand

Floating of funds when funds have been dispatched by a payer, but are not in a form that can be spent by the payee

FOB vessel, named port a price quotation that includes the cost of the goods and freight charges to the port of shipment

Foreign assets control the U.S. government has control over the types of goods that may be imported from unfriendly countries

Foreign broker or factor an intermediary who brings a seller and buyer together in an attempt to consummate a sale

Foreign commissionaire one who acts on behalf of an importer in seeking out the goods and shipping them to the importer

Foreign Credit Insurance Association (FCIA) an association of independent insurance companies that was established to work with the Eximbank in providing commercial and political risk insurance to American exporters

Foreign direct investments investments that are made abroad for profit that allow the investing firm some degree of managerial control

Foreign exchange the liquid financial instruments (usually currency) representing claims against foreigners that are used in international transactions, or the exchange of money or credit of one country for money or credit of another

Foreign exchange markets financial centers where banks and other dealers in foreign exchange deal in foreign currencies

Foreign export merchant a merchant who buys products and sells them on his or her own account

Foreign manufacturer's agent an agent who acts on behalf of a manufacturer desiring to sell its products abroad

Foreign Sales Corporation tax incentives are provided on income earned from exports for firms incorporated in certain foreign countries and U.S. possessions

Foreign trade zone or free trade zone (FTZ) an enclosed area usually within a port where goods may be stored, processed, repaired, remarked, etc.,

without going through customs until the goods are withdrawn

Forward rate rate of exchange quoted at the close of the day for some specific date in the future

Franchise agreement the right to a sale or service formula that is granted to a firm or individual (franchisee) for a fee by a franchisor

Free float exchange rates are permitted to reach their levels through the market forces of supply and demand

Free gold standard a monetary standard that uses gold as the basis for the value of a currency and is characterized by free coinage, circulation, and convertibility

Free of particular average a marine insurance term indicating that partial losses due to perils of the sea will be covered by the underwriter regardless of the percentage of expected loss

Free trade a type of policy placing major emphasis on the elimination of barriers that interfere with the free movement of goods and services across national boundaries

Freight forwarder an intermediary used by both direct and indirect exporters to handle the logistical details of the export cycle

GAAP generally accepted accounting principles of the United States

General Agreement on Tariffs and Trade (GATT) a multilateral agreement among nations to set up rules of conduct for international trade

General average voluntary loss that is incurred for the benefit of the ship and remaining cargo

General cargo high per unit value manufactured goods with low trading tonnage that are shipped on liners

General-conventional tariff general rates are applicable to goods from all countries unless modified by a convention

Geocentric policy a type of policy appointing the best qualified for positions at home and abroad regardless of their nationality

Global quota the total amount that may be imported from or exported to all countries during a given time period

Gold exchange standard   when a nation's currency is backed by the currency of another country that is backed by gold

Gold points   upper and lower limits in the fluctuations of exchange rates before it became cheaper to make payment in gold rather than in foreign exchange

Hard currencies   currencies that are stable, in demand, and easily convertible

Hedging contracts   buying or selling foreign exchange in the futures market as protection against possible loss due to the fluctuations in the rates of exchange

Hedging strategies   as protection against political risks, a firm could take out political risk insurance or finance its operations through the heavy use of local debt

Home country   the country in which the multinational corporation's headquarters is located

Home country national   an individual from the home country of a multinational corporation

Host country   the foreign country where the multinational enterprise has its foreign direct investments

Humid continental climate   located between 35 and 65 degrees north and south latitudes in the interior of a continent, typified by hot rainy summers and cold snowy winters

Indirect export   the manufacturer employs intermediaries to handle the details of exporting

Industrial or producer's goods   those products that are used for the production of other goods

Infrastructure   the underlying foundation or basic framework of a country in the form of transportation facilities, power sources, warehouses, bridges, etc.

Illegal aliens   those who enter a country in violation of immigration laws

Immigration   to enter a country where one is not a native to take up permanent residence

Import brokers   intermediaries located in the country of import who bring buyers and sellers together

Import commission house   acts as the consignee when goods are imported

Import duty or tariff   a duty that is levied on goods entering a country

Import merchant   one who imports products from abroad and sells them on his or her own account

Import quotas   quantity or value limits placed on imported goods

Import wholesalers and jobbers   intermediaries who import directly from foreign sources and distribute the goods to retailers who are too small to import directly

Incentive pay   workers are provided monetary incentives to produce in excess of a given standard

Indent house   one that buys from abroad on order from a domestic buyer

Indigenization laws   laws of a country that define the percentage of ownership that must be held by citizens of that country

Indirect importing   when intermediaries are used to handle most of the details involved in getting the goods into the country

Indirect or portfolio investments   investments that are made in bonds and stock for the purpose of yield rather than managerial control

Intangible capital   capital assets that consist of such nontangible things as technology, know-how, competencies, etc.

Intellectual property   intangible assets or property such as patents, trademarks, processes, etc.

Inter-American Development Bank   a hemispheric version of the IBRD that was established by the United States

Interest rate differential theory   the flow of funds occurs from areas of capital abundance and low interest rates to areas of capital scarcity and higher rates of interest

Internalization   controlling the intermediate stages of the productive process through foreign investments; this might be compared to vertical integration on a global scale

Internal source of capital   the generation of capital from economic activities that are conducted within a country

International Bank for Reconstruction and Development (IBRD)   the World Bank, whose major purpose is to provide infrastructure loans to the less developed countries

International Development Association (IDA)   a subsidiary of the IBRD whose major purpose is to make loans to the poorest countries that cannot meet the loan standards of the IBRD

International Finance Corporation (IFC)   a subsidiary of the IBRD that makes loans to or invests in firms

International Monetary Fund (IMF)   the international financial institution that was established to provide financial assistance to member nations that have difficulties stabilizing their currency and are experiencing balance of payments problems

International trade (commerce)   the movement of goods and services across the political boundaries that separate nations

Investment climate   the nature of the political and economic environment in a host country that might influence foreign investments

Invoice   a bill of sale provided by the seller describing the goods and their weight, value, etc.

Jettison   throw cargo overboard voluntarily to save the ship and the remaining cargo

Jobbers   usually a firm that buys goods in job lots from importers or producers and sells to dealers

Joint venture   an agreement between two parties to invest equity in a business engaged in the manufacture and distribution of a product in the host country with managerial control vested in each

Kanban   a Japanese term that is used to describe a condition where goods are delivered to the factory "just in time" to meet the needs for productive purposes, eliminating the necessity of storage

Labor-intensive industries   those industries that place emphasis on labor rather than machines for the production of goods

Labor-intensive process   a process in which labor is the major production factor

Last in-first out inventory valuation (LIFO)   goods or materials that were the last to enter inventory are assumed to be the first withdrawn

Leaching   when rainfall dissolves minerals, causing them to soak into the ground beyond the reach of the roots of plants

Lend-lease shipments   shipments of military and other supplies to the allies by the United States during World War II

Leontief Paradox   the effort of Leontief to support the factor endowments theory by using the United States as an example of a country that exports capital-intensive goods because of its abundant capital resources. This did not agree with the actual U.S. export-import figures. The seeming contradiction was explained by stating that the United States was an exporter of labor-intensive goods because it is a producer of high technology products, which required large quantities of highly skilled people

Less developed country (LDC)   a country whose economy is in the early stages of development; also called *developing country* or *Third World country*

Letter of interest   the letter of interest does not commit the Eximbank to grant a loan; it only provides information on the exporter

Licensing agreement   a foreign firm is authorized to produce a patented product in exchange for royalty payments

Liners   regularly scheduled vessels between designated ports that generally transport high-valued cargoes and passengers

Liquidation of entry   when the goods are released to an importer after meeting all the requirements for entry

Local content legislation   laws of a country that define the percentage of the materials or components of a product that must be produced within that country

Local national   a citizen of the particular country in which a subsidiary of the multinational corporation is located

Long transaction   a contract to buy foreign exchange that is made in expectation of a future rise in its value

Low-latitude deserts   areas located in the low latitudes that get little rainfall

Low-latitude steppes   areas in the low latitudes typified by a long dry period and a short rainy season

Major bulk cargo   iron ore, coal, grain, bauxite-alumina, and phosphate rock are referred to as major bulk cargoes

Majority ownership position joint venture   a joint venture in which the investor owns more than 50 percent of the stock

Managed float   government interference through its central bank to influence that country's rate of exchange

Management contract   an agreement between a firm and foreign enterprise or government in which the firm supplies technical or managerial assistance for a fee

Margin   when the purchaser of stocks, bonds, or foreign exchange is not required to deposit the full amount of the transaction

Marine insurance   insurance that is taken out to cover loss or damage due to the perils of the sea; may be in the form of a policy or certificate

Marine west coast climate   between 35 and 60 degrees north and south latitudes along the coast are the areas where the westerlies blow from the sea onto land throughout the year

Market potential   the size of a market in terms of the number of units of a particular product that are sold or might be sold there

Mark of origin   a stamp on the product indicating the origin of the product

Maximum-minimum tariff   both maximum and minimum rates are determined by statute, with the minimum rates being granted to countries receiving preferential treatment and the maximum rates being applicable to all others

Mercantilism   a type of commercial policy of the Middle Ages that emphasized manufacturing and commerce as a means of accumulating precious metals through a favorable balance of trade

Middle-latitude steppes and deserts   climatic types located inland from the humid continental climates

Minor bulk cargo   all cargoes other than the five major bulk cargoes are placed in this category

Minority ownership position joint venture   a joint venture in which the foreign investor owns less than 50 percent of the stock

Monetary correction rate   a country's currency is pegged to the inflation rate during a given period to provide constant purchasing power

Monopolistic/oligopolistic advantage   the multinational firm is in possession of an exploitable factor that others do not have, thus providing the firm with monopolistic or oligopolistic advantages in its operations abroad

Most favored nation clause   a clause in commercial agreements stating that any concession granted to one country will be granted to other countries with which similar agreements have been made

Most favored nation status (MFN)   a status granted by the U.S. government to a foreign country stating that concessions granted to any MFN country will be granted to all other nations with the same status

Multilateral agreement   agreement among more than two countries that binds the signatory parties to its provisions

Multinational corporation (MNC)   a business that produces and distributes its products or services globally without regard to political boundaries

Multinational enterprise (MNE)   see *multinational corporation*

Multinational firm (MNF)   see *multinational corporation*

Multiple-column tariff   different rates of duty are levied on imports depending on the country of origin of the product

Multiple exchange rates (sliding scale)   the rate at which a currency may be converted into the currency of another country depends upon the essentiality of the import.

Municipal trade tax   a trade tax that is levied by various municipalities in West Germany

National culture   a set of beliefs, values, and norms shared by the majority of the inhabitants of a country

Natural or native advantage   those advantages that are the result of the generosity of nature, such as mineral resources, soils, forests, etc.

Neo-bulk cargo   bulky commodities that cannot be poured, piped, or handled by suction but are transported by shiploads

Nepotism favoritism shown or patronage granted by persons in high office to relatives or close friends

No-equity foreign investment a firm commits to foreign firms technical know-how or some other non-capital asset through licensing, franchising, or other form of agreement

Noncommodity agreement those agreements that cover matters of intangible nature such as patents, trademarks, antitrust, etc.

Norms a standard, model, or pattern regarded as typical for a specific group

Offset generally related to major purchases when a nation contracts to purchase equipment (e.g., defense) from another country on condition that certain components will be produced or assembled in the buying country to offset the effects on its current account

Oligarchy a type of political system wherein control is in the hands of a small group

On-board bill of lading a bill that is issued by the carrier indicating that the goods have been loaded on board the vessel

Open market operations buying and selling foreign exchange in the market in an attempt to influence exchange rate by increasing or decreasing the supply of a currency

Organizational culture common and accepted patterns of behavior shared by members of a formal organization

Organization of Petroleum Exporting Countries (OPEC) a cartel formed by the thirteen major petroleum-producing and -exporting countries for the purpose of controlling supply and world market prices. The member countries are Saudi Arabia, Kuwait, Libya, Iran, Iraq, Venezuela, Ecuador, Algeria, Gabon, Nigeria, Qatar, the United Arab Emirates, and Indonesia

Orographic rain rainfall that occurs when moisture-laden winds are forced over mountains and cooled, thus reducing their ability to hold moisture

Participative management a firm actively solicits the involvement of the host government, nationals, and labor in the operation of the subsidiary even though this is not legally mandated

Partners in trade large firms in international trade assume the distribution and marketing functions for small companies, relieving them of the burden and cost of setting up their own export departments

Patent a government grants to an inventor the exclusive right to make, use, or sell the invention for a term of years

Patriarch the male leader of a family or tribe

Pax Romana law and order under Roman rule and administration that resulted in a peaceful period for the development of commerce

Payee the holder of the draft is the one to whom payment is made when the draft matures

Payer the one who is to make payment on the draft when it matures

Payment and clearing agreements when nations make agreements to settle their trade payments without the transfer of funds by setting up an account into which funds are received and paid

Pegging when a nation fixes the value of its currency to the value of another currency

Penalty duty a duty that is levied on imports for the violation of some customs rule or regulation

Perquisite benefits ("perks") over and above the base salaries that are provided to employees

Piecework a compensation system in which the amount that an employee earns is determined by unit output or productivity

Political risk the probability of some politically induced governmental action that would be detrimental to the future of a firm's operations in a country or exports to that country

Polycentric policy a type of policy wherein local nationals are appointed to manage foreign operations and home country nationals are appointed to domestic positions

Population explosion the greater-than-average growth of population in a country

Portfolio investments see *indirect investments*

Preferential duties duties that are levied on products from countries that receive preferential treatment

Premiums a percentage of the base salary that is paid to employees who are assigned to geographic areas that are physically or climatically undesirable

Price band the upper and lower limits in prices of commodities agreed to by participants before action will be taken to stabilize prices

Primary goods products of agriculture, forest, mines, and fisheries that are in the first stage of the productive process

Product adaptation making changes so that a product will conform to the customs, culture, or physical requirements in a particular society

Production strategy a strategy for goods production that seeks to help a firm increase or retain its competitive position

Product life cycle theory in foreign direct investment new products are introduced in a domestic market, but when the domestic market becomes saturated, firms set up manufacturing operations abroad in order to remain competitive in those markets (defensive) or to develop new markets (offensive)

Product life cycle theory in international trade new products that are introduced to a market go through different stages: introduction, growth, maturity, and decline; international trade is most likely in the later three stages

Profit margin or markup the difference between the production cost or wholesale buying price and the selling price of the goods

Protectionism a commercial policy advocating the adoption of various barriers to prevent imports from competing with domestically produced goods

Protest an importer's appeal of the duty levied on a shipment

Public Law 480 the law provides for the sale of surplus U.S. agricultural products to foreign countries payable in that country's currency

Quotas quantity or value limits placed on the import or export of goods

Rate of exchange the value or price of one currency in terms of another currency

Rationalization the process of standardization and the use of economies of scale among manufacturing subsidiaries to improve efficiency

Reference price when commodity prices fall within a specific price band, participants agree to intervene in the market

Repatriation of employees the return of employees to their home country after completing a foreign assignment

Repatriation of profits transferring overseas earnings back to the home country

Required reserves the amount of liquid reserves a bank must maintain in relation to its loans outstanding

Reserve tranche the 25 percent of the subscription quota that was paid to the IMF in gold, SDR, or foreign currency that is available to the member nation without the payment of interest

Resident buying agents foreign employees of large firms and governments who are sent abroad to buy products and handle all the details of getting the goods to the importing country

Resident selling agent one who is located in the country of import and whose task is to represent a foreign manufacturer

Retaliatory duty a duty that is levied on imports from countries in retaliation for the discriminatory treatment of a country's products

Return on investment (ROI) a measure of the profitability of a business, which is calculated by dividing the after-tax profits of an operation by the total amount invested in that operation

Revaluation to increase the value of a currency through official action of the government

Reverse cultural shock when an employee returns from an overseas assignment and is unable to adapt to the home culture

Risk the probability of the occurrence of some detrimental event

Royalty payments received by the licensor from the licensee

Sales promotion a marketing strategy used to familiarize consumers with the product; it supplements the efforts of salespersons, advertisements, or publicity

Separate export department a department that is established within a company to handle the export functions of a firm

Shipment in bond goods shipped under bond from a port of entry to an inland port or bonded warehouse

Shipping conferences associations of shipping line companies formed for the purpose of eliminating competition

Ship's manifest a descriptive summary of the cargo, passengers, and their baggage on board a named vessel

Short transaction a contract to sell foreign exchange in the expectation of a fall in its value

Sight draft a draft that calls for payment when it is presented (upon sight) to the drawee

Signatory a government that has signed a convention is bound with other participants to the provisions stipulated in the agreement

Silent trade one party leaves goods in an area and retreats; a second party comes and takes what is wanted, leaving articles in exchange

Single-column or unilinear tariff one rate of duty is applicable on like imports regardless of the country of origin

Single-voyage charter agreement between a charterer and a vessel owner to cover a single trip

Sliding scale of foreign exchange see *multiple exchange rates*

Smithsonian Agreement the agreement of December 1971 that called for the devaluation of the U.S. dollar and the revaluation of the German mark and the Japanese yen

Socialism government ownership of the factors of production and distribution

Soft currency currency that is unstable, is not readily convertible, and offers no assurance that it will hold its value

Special bulk carrier industrial carriers that are designed to carry only specialized types of commodities

Special Drawing Rights (SDR) artificial deposits created by the IMF and allocated to member nations on the basis of the capital subscribed to provide them with additional reserves. An SDR is a unit of account whose value is determined by the exchange rates of the deutsche mark, French franc, Japanese yen, British pound sterling, and U.S. dollar

Specific duty a duty that is levied on the basis of some unit of measurement

Speculation an attempt to make a profit by making

a contract to buy or sell foreign exchange in the futures market

Spot rate the daily rate that is quoted when buying or selling foreign exchange

Spread the difference between the buying and selling rates of foreign exchange

Standardization the process whereby goods or components are made to be interchangeable

Sterilizing gold when gold is set aside or earmarked so that it will not be used as reserves for the issuance of more currency

Straight-line depreciation assets that are depreciated a stated amount each year until totally depreciated for tax purposes

Strategy the unique and purposeful match of the competencies of a business (strengths and weaknesses) with its environment (threats and opportunities)

Structured assessment (of political risks) the establishment of some unit within the corporate organization to collect, evaluate, and assess information on a systematic basis that will provide an indication as to risks arising from the political situation

Subarctic climate areas bordering the Arctic circle

Subculture a cultural subgroup differentiated by status, ethnic background, residence, religion, or other factors that functionally unify the group

Subscription quotas the amount of capital each member nation is required to subscribe as a member of an international financial institution such as the IMF

Subsidiary a business incorporated in a foreign country in which the parent corporation holds an ownership position

Subsidy (of exports) a grant provided by a government to producers that enable them to compete more effectively in export markets

Subtropical climate the type of climate that is found on either side of the tropical climatic zone that is further classified as dry, Mediterranean, or humid subtropical

Surtax a tax over and above a regular tax collected for a specific purpose

Switch trading when the credit in the clearing account is sold or transferred to a third party

Tankers   tank vessels that take on cargo of a liquid nature for the account of the shipper

Tariff   duties that are levied on imports or exports on the basis of the value of the goods

Tariff quota   a limit on the quantity of goods that may be imported at a given rate of duty

Tax credit (foreign)   a credit provided by the U.S. government for taxes paid to a foreign government

Tax haven   countries with low tax rates where firms accumulate income, avoiding the payment of U.S. taxes until it is brought back to the United States

Technical assistance   any one of numerous contractual arrangements in which the foreign corporation sells technical expertise and intellectual property to another firm for a fee

Technology-driven strategy   a particular type of strategy that places major emphasis on technological advances as a method of gaining a competitive advantage

Temporal method   the translation of foreign currencies into dollars at the current rate of exchange

Theocracy   a type of government wherein the head of state is also the nation's religious leader

Third country national   a national of a country other than that of the investing nation or the host country

Through bill of lading   a single bill of lading that covers the shipment from the point of origin to the destination, even on different carriers

Tie-in buying and selling agreements   assets of a firm, such as stock ownership or patent rights, are exchanged for raw materials

Time charter   the cost for leasing the vessel is based on the time that the vessel is put at the charterer's disposal

Time draft   a draft that calls for payment a certain number of days after the drawee has seen it

Tokyo Round   the GATT negotiations that began in Tokyo in 1973 and concluded in 1979

Trade centers   permanently established foreign industrial centers where firms display their products

Trade fairs   periodic exhibits where firms are invited to display and demonstrate the use of their products

Trademark   a distinguishing characteristic or feature firmly associated with the origin or ownership of merchandise, legally reserving exclusive use to the owner as maker or seller

Trading company   large concerns that are involved in the various aspects of international business relating to the worldwide distribution of products

Transaction exposure   risks of loss arising from the change in value of a currency between the sale and the receipt for payment

Transfer pricing   the price charged by a firm to related organizations; under Section 486 of the Internal Revenue Code, American firms must use arms-length pricing when selling goods to their related entities to discourage the accumulation of profits in tax havens

Translation exposure   risks resulting when a currency is translated into the currency of another country in a financial statement

Traveling buyers (resident buyers)   employees of a firm who are sent abroad to seek out and purchase products for a principal

Trip charter   a contract between the charterer and the shipowner to cover a single trip or a round trip

Tropical climate   climates that are found between 23½ degrees north and 23½ south latitudes

Tropical highlands   highland areas in the tropical climatic zones that have mild climates because the nearness to the equator is offset by the elevation

Tropical rainforests   the area of the tropics where the rainfall is in excess of 100 inches per year

Tropical savannas   areas in the tropics that are located on either side of the tropical rainforest; they have long rainy and short dry seasons

Tropical steppes   tropical areas characterized by a short rainy season and a long dry season

Trust receipt   a document, signed by a buyer, on the strength of which a bank releases merchandise for the purpose of sale, while the bank retains title to the goods

Turnkey operation   a contractual agreement whereby a firm promises to construct some facility (factory, bridge, harbor, etc.) and place it in satisfactory operating order before turning it over to the foreign customer

Turnkey plus contracts   a combination of a management contract and a turnkey project wherein a firm constructs a facility and operates it for a fixed period of time while training local nationals in all of the managerial and technical aspects of its operation

Turnover tax   see *value added tax (VAT)*

Tying clause   a loan is extended to a buyer on condition that the proceeds will be spent in the country that grants the loan

Underwriting   investment banker's function of guaranteeing the issuer of a security that it will receive at least a specified minimum amount for the issue

Unrequited transfers   the unilateral transfer of funds from one country to another

Unstructured assessment (of political risk)   the collection of political information on a sporadic and fragmented basis that is used as a basis for evaluating and assessing the political risks of a country

Value added tax (VAT)   a tax that is levied on the value that is added at each stage of the productive process and assessed when the goods change ownership

Voluntary agreement   a nonbinding agreement that a nation enters into to limit the export of products

Western Hemisphere Trade Corporation (WHTC)   lower taxes were provided for these corporations, which were established to promote the trade of the United States in the Western Hemisphere

Wholesalers   merchant intermediaries who sell in large quantities to retail, industrial, or commercial customers

Wholly owned operation   an operation that is 100 percent owned by the foreign parent company

With average   covers partial loss over and above a given percentage of the value of the shipment where a given percentage of damage is expected

Without recourse   when a holder discounts a draft that has been accepted, the holder is not liable if the drawee does not honor the draft upon maturity

Xerophytic vegetation   type of vegetation that is found in areas of scant rainfall, as in the desert

Name Index

Abudene, Patricia, 590
Adler, Nancy J., 315
Aggarwal, Raj, 51, 55, 105
Agodo, Oriye, 55
Ahmed, Ahmed A., 194
Albaum, Gerald, 399
Alexander, J. W., 216
Alexandrides, C. G., 439
AlHashim, Dhia D., 574, 575
Allende, Salvador, 232
Anderson, Erin, 371
Ansoff, H. Igor, 54, 55, 325, 326, 348, 349
Anwar, Mohammad N., 595
Arnault, Bernard, 347
Arpan, Jeffrey S., 36, 349, 350, 574, 575

Babb, John, 158
Baker, James C., 335, 349
Baldrige, Malcolm, 531
Ball, Donald A., 36
Baranson, Jack, 514
Bardi, Edward J., 216
Barksdale, Hiram C., 440
Barnett, Andy H., 350
Basek, John, 247
Batista y Zaldivar, Fulgencio, 580
Batra, Raveendra N., 492
Bauerschmidt, Alan, 438

Baughn, William H., 104, 105
Bearden, William O., 438
Beeman, Don R., 193, 245, 246, 347, 368, 396, 460, 489, 512, 571, 595, 611, 615
Beh-Horim, Moshe, 105
Behrman, Jack N., 36
Bello, Daniel C., 438
Bennett, Margo L., 547
Bergsten, C. Fred, 117
Bhattacharya, Anindya K., 161
Bhattacharya, S. K., 492
Bilkey, Warren J., 438
Billon, William R., 316
Blank, Stephen, 247
Blumberg, Ann, 501, 531
Blumbert, Aryeh, 105
Boddewyn, Jean J., 36, 349, 371, 399
Boorstin, Daniel J., 513, 514
Bourne, Leslie, 46
Bowers, B. L., 439
Brady, Donald L., 438
Brasch, John J., 439
Brooke, Michael Z., 315
Bruce, Charles M., 438, 439
Brunner, J. A., 399
Buckley, Peter J., 49, 55
Bush, George, 244, 245
Bussard, Willis A., 438, 439

Butler, Joseph H., 216
Buzzell, Robert D., 399

Calderon-Rossell, Jorge R., 105
Calvet, A. Louis, 55
Calvet, Jacques, 532
Carey, Henry C., 170
Carey, H. C., Jr., 170
Casson, Mark, 49, 55
Castro, Fidel, 232, 580
Cateora, Philip R., 257, 286, 287, 393, 398, 399
Caves, Richard E., 49, 54, 55, 349
Chang, Rosita P., 492
Channon, Derek F., 349
Chase, C. D., 349, 371
Chatterjee, Sangit, 492
Chin-Lor, Daisy, 314
Cho, Kang Rae, 161
Choi, Jongmoo Jay, 492
Chrystal, K. Alec, 105
Clay, Henry, 173
Cobbaut, Robert, 492
Collison, Frederick M., 461
Columbus, Christopher, 167
Conkling, E. C., 216
Contractor, Farok J., 55, 371
Cooper, Robert G., 439
Copeland, Lennie, 547

635

Subject Index

Nation and Region Index

Company Index

657

Western Europe: Political

International boundaries

⊛ National capitals

• Other cities

Members of the European Economic Community

IRELAND
UNITED KINGDOM
NETH.
BELG.
LUX.
FRANCE
DEN.
EAST GERMANY
WEST
PORT.
SPAIN
ITALY
GREECE

ARCTIC OCEAN

ICELAND
• Reykjavik

Arctic Circle

NORWEGIAN SEA

Faeroe Is. (Den.)

Shetland Is. (U.K.)

NORWAY
SWEDEN

• Bergen
⊛ Oslo
⊛ Stockholm

Orust I. (Sweden)

Hebrides Is. (U.K.)
Orkney Is. (U.K.)

SCOTLAND
• Glasgow

ESTONIA
LATVIA
LITHUANIA

NORTH SEA

BALTIC SEA

DENMARK
• Copenhagen

NORTHERN IRELAND • Belfast
UNITED KINGDOM
Dublin •
REPUBLIC OF IRELAND
ENGLAND
• Manchester
WALES • Birmingham
London ⊛

• Hamburg

Elbe

WEST GERMANY
Essen • Dortmund
• Dusseldorf
• Cologne
• Bonn
EAST

POLAND

UNION OF SOVIET SOCIALIST REPUBLICS (SOVIET UNION)

Vistula

Oder River

Volga

NETHERLANDS
The Hague • Amsterdam ⊛

Brussels ⊛
BELGIUM
LUXEMBOURG
Luxembourg ⊛
⊛ Paris

CZECHOSLOVAKIA

Dniester River
Dnieper River

ATLANTIC OCEAN

50°North Latitude

Loire River

Seine River

Rhine River

Danube River
• Munich
⊛ Vienna

Rhone River

LIECHTENSTEIN
Zurich • • Vaduz
Bern ⊛ SWITZERLAND
AUSTRIA
HUNGARY

ROMANIA

BLACK SEA

Bay of Biscay

10°West Longitude

FRANCE

• Bordeaux

• Lyon

Garonne River

Milan •
• Turin
• Genoa
Po River

YUGOSLAVIA

Danube River

BULGARIA

PORTUGAL
Madrid ⊛
40°N
Tagus River
• Lisbon
SPAIN

Ebro River

Marseille •
• Monaco
MONACO
⊛ Andorra la Vella
ANDORRA
Corsica (Fr.)
• Barcelona

SAN MARINO
• San Marino

ITALY
VATICAN CITY ⊛⊛ Rome

ALBANIA

GREECE

ASIA

Guadalquivir River
• Córdoba

Balearic Is. (Sp.)
Sardinia (It.)

• Naples

⊛ Athens

Gibraltar (U.K.)

Palermo •

Sicily (It.)

N
W ⊛ E
S

Crete (Gr.)

AFRICA

MALTA • Valletta

MEDITERRANEAN SEA

0   200   400 Miles
0   200   400 Kilometers

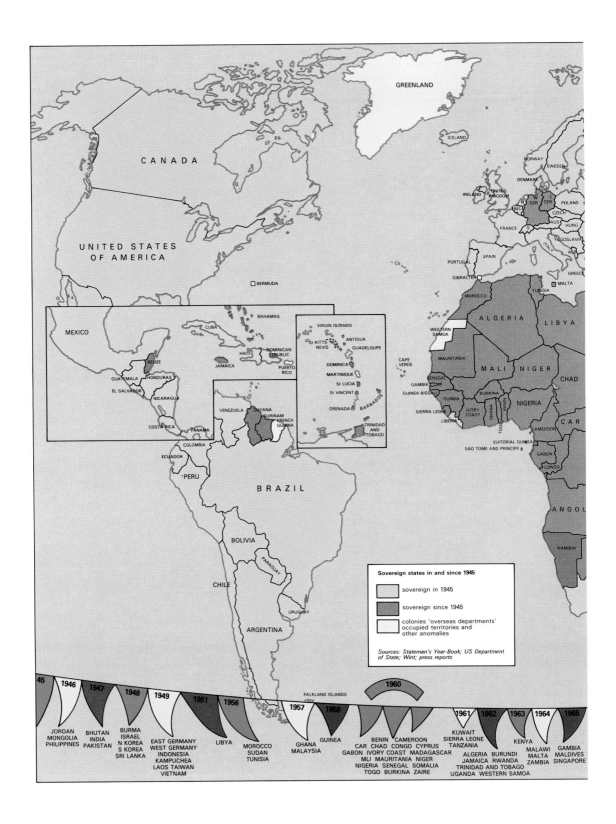

GREENLAND

CANADA

ICELAND

NORWAY SWEDEN

DENMARK

IRELAND

UNITED
KINGDOM

N W GER
GER

POLAND

CZECH

BEL AUS HUNG

UNITED STATES
OF AMERICA

FRANCE

S

YUGOSLAVIA

ITALY

ALB

PORTUGAL SPAIN

GREECE

GIBRALTER

MALTA

□ BERMUDA

MOROCCO

TUNISIA

A L G E R I A

L I B Y A

WESTERN
SAMOA

MEXICO

BAHAMAS

CUBA

HAITI

JAMAICA

DOMINICAN
REPUBLIC

PUERTO
RICO

VIRGIN ISLANDS

St KITTS
NEVIS

ANTIGUA

GUADELOUPE

MAURITANIA

M A L I

N I G E R

CHAD

CAPE
VERDE

SENEGAL

GAMBIA

GUINEA-BISSAU

BURKINA

NIGERIA

DOMINICA

GUATEMALA

BELIZE

HONDURAS

MARTINIQUE

St LUCIA

GUINEA

SIERRA LEONE

IVORY
COAST

EL SALVADOR

St VINCENT

LIBERIA

GHANA

BENIN

TOGO

C A R

NICARAGUA

GRENADA

BARBADOS

CAMEROON

COSTA RICA

PANAMA

VENEZUELA

GUYANA

SURINAM

FRENCH
GUIANA

TRINIDAD
AND
TOBAGO

EUITORIAL GUINEA

SAO TOME AND PRINCIPE

GABON

CONGO

COLOMBIA

ECUADOR

PERU

B R A Z I L

A N G O L A

BOLIVIA

NAMIBIA

PARAGUAY

CHILE

URUGUAY

Sovereign states in and since 1945

sovereign in 1945

sovereign since 1945

colonies 'overseas departments'
occupied territories and
other anomalies

*Sources: Stateman's Year-Book; US Department
of State; Wint; press reports*

ARGENTINA

FALKLAND ISLANDS

1960

45 | 1946 | 1947 | 1948 | 1949 | 1951 | 1956 | 1957 | 1958 | 1961 | 1962 | 1963 | 1964 | 1965

JORDAN
MONGOLIA
PHILIPPINES

BHUTAN
INDIA
PAKISTAN

BURMA
ISRAEL
N KOREA
S KOREA
SRI LANKA

EAST GERMANY
WEST GERMANY
INDONESIA
KAMPUCHEA
LAOS TAIWAN
VIETNAM

LIBYA

MOROCCO
SUDAN
TUNISIA

GHANA
MALAYSIA

GUINEA

BENIN CAMEROON
CAR CHAD CONGO CYPRUS
GABON IVORY COAST MADAGASCAR
MLI MAURITANIA NIGER
NIGERIA SENEGAL SOMALIA
TOGO BURKINA ZAIRE

KUWAIT
SIERRA LEONE
TANZANIA

ALGERIA BURUNDI
JAMAICA RWANDA
TRINIDAD AND TOBAGO
UGANDA WESTERN SAMOA

KENYA

MALAWI
MALTA
ZAMBIA

GAMBIA
MALDIVES
SINGAPORE

The World of States

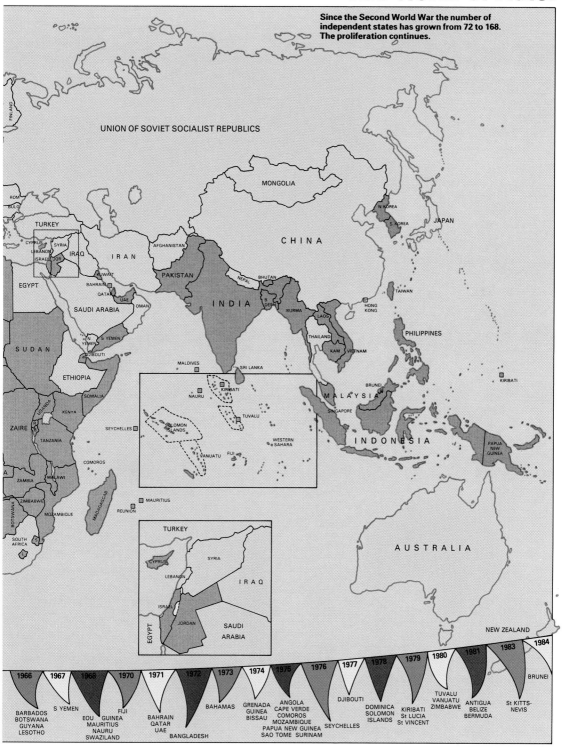

Since the Second World War the number of independent states has grown from 72 to 168. The proliferation continues.

UNION OF SOVIET SOCIALIST REPUBLICS

FINLAND

ROM
BULG

TURKEY

CYPRUS
LEBANON
ISRAEL JOR
IRAQ

SYRIA

EGYPT

KUWAIT
BAHRAIN
QATAR
UAE
OMAN

SAUDI ARABIA

IRAN

AFGHANISTAN

PAKISTAN

MONGOLIA

CHINA

N KOREA

S KOREA

JAPAN

NEPAL BHUTAN

I N D I A

B
DESH

TAIWAN

HONG KONG

BURMA

LAOS

THAILAND

KAM VIETNAM

N
YEMEN

S YEMEN

DJIBOUTI

SUDAN

ETHIOPIA

SOMALIA

UGANDA

KENYA

ZAIRE

TANZANIA

COMOROS

ZAMBIA

MALAWI

MADAGASCAR

MOZAMBIQUE

ZIMBABWE

BOTSWANA

SOUTH AFRICA

MALDIVES

SRI LANKA

NAURU

KIRIBATI

TUVALU

SEYCHELLES

SOLOMON ISLANDS

WESTERN SAHARA

VANUATU FIJI

KIRIBATI

BRUNEI

M A L A Y S I A

SINGAPORE

I N D O N E S I A

PAPUA NEW GUINEA

REUNION

MAURITIUS

PHILIPPINES

A U S T R A L I A

NEW ZEALAND

TURKEY

CYPRUS

SYRIA

LEBANON

ISRAEL

JORDAN

IRAQ

EGYPT

SAUDI ARABIA

| 1966 | 1967 | 1968 | 1970 | 1971 | 1972 | 1973 | 1974 | 1975 | 1976 | 1977 | 1978 | 1979 | 1980 | 1981 | 1983 | 1984 |

BRUNEI

BARBADOS
BOTSWANA
GUYANA
LESOTHO

S YEMEN

EQU GUINEA
MAURITIUS
NAURU
SWAZILAND

FIJI

BAHRAIN
QATAR
UAE

BANGLADESH

BAHAMAS

GRENADA
GUINEA
BISSAU

ANGOLA
CAPE VERDE
COMOROS
MOZAMBIQUE
PAPUA NEW GUINEA
SAO TOME SURINAM

SEYCHELLES

DJIBOUTI

DOMINICA
SOLOMON
ISLANDS

KIRIBATI
St LUCIA
St VINCENT

TUVALU
VANUATU
ZIMBABWE

ANTIGUA
BELIZE
BERMUDA

St KITTS-
NEVIS

World: Climate Regions

Tropical climates
- Tropical rainforest
- Savanna

Dry climates
- Steppe
- Desert

Mild climates
- Marine west coast
- Humid subtropical
- Mediterranean

Continental climates
- Humid continental, warm summer
- Humid continental, cool summer
- Subarctic

Polar climates
- Tundra
- Ice caps

High altitudes
- Highlands
- Uplands

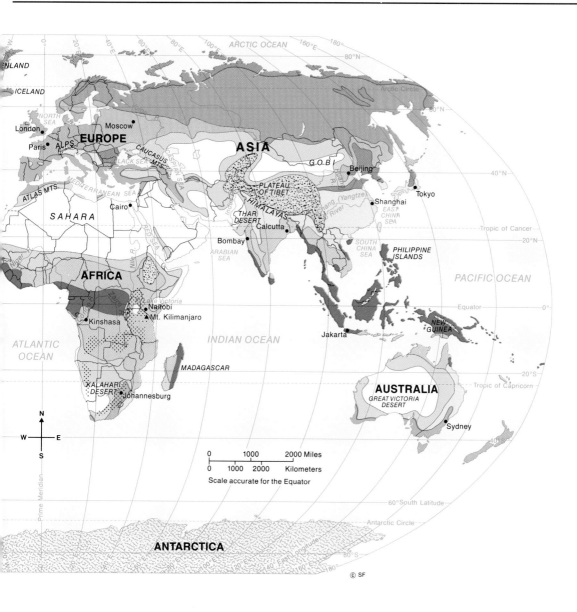

ARCTIC OCEAN

GREENLAND
ICELAND
NORTH SEA
London
Paris • ALPS
EUROPE
Moscow •
CAUCASUS MTS.
BLACK SEA
CASPIAN SEA
MEDITERRANEAN SEA
ATLAS MTS.
Cairo •
SAHARA
RED SEA
Niger R.
Nile R.

ASIA
GOBI
Beijing •
Tokyo •
PLATEAU OF TIBET
HIMALAYAS
Chang (Yangtze) River
Shanghai •
EAST CHINA SEA
Huang R.
THAR DESERT
Calcutta •
Bombay •
Indus R.
ARABIAN SEA
Tropic of Cancer
20°N
SOUTH CHINA SEA
PHILIPPINE ISLANDS

AFRICA
Zaire R.
Lake Victoria
Nairobi •
Mt. Kilimanjaro ▲
Kinshasa •
ATLANTIC OCEAN
INDIAN OCEAN
PACIFIC OCEAN
Equator
0°
Jakarta •
NEW GUINEA
MADAGASCAR
KALAHARI DESERT
Johannesburg •
20°S
Tropic of Capricorn

AUSTRALIA
GREAT VICTORIA DESERT
Sydney •

N
W E
S

| 0 | 1000 | 2000 Miles |
| 0 | 1000 | 2000 | Kilometers |

Scale accurate for the Equator

Prime Meridian

60°South Latitude
Antarctic Circle

ANTARCTICA

80°S

© SF

Groups of economies

Countries are colored to show their income group; for example, all low-income economies (those with a GNP per capita of $545 or less in 1988) are colored yellow. The groups are those used in the tables that follow.

☐ Low-income economies
☐ Middle-income economies
☐ High-income economies
☐ Data not available

Canada

United States

Bermuda (UK)

The Bahamas

Mexico

Cuba
Jamaica
Haiti
Belize
Honduras
Guatemala
El Salvador   Nicaragua
Costa Rica   Panama

Venezuela   Guyana   Suriname
Colombia   French Guiana (Fr)

Ecuador

Peru   Brazil

Bolivia

Paraguay

Chile   Argentina   Uruguay

Tokelau (NZ)

Western
Wallis and   Samoa
Futuna   American Samoa
(Fr)   (US)
Niue (NZ)
Tonga

Cook Islands (NZ)

French
Polynesia
(Fr)

Dominican
Rep.

Puerto Rico
(US)

St. Kitts and Nevis

Antigua and Barbuda
Montserrat (UK)
Guadeloupe (Fr)

Virgin Islands
(US)

Dominica
Martinique (Fr)

Netherlands Antilles
(Neth)

St. Lucia
Barbados
St. Vincent and the
Grenadines

Grenada

Trinidad and Tobago

Venezuela

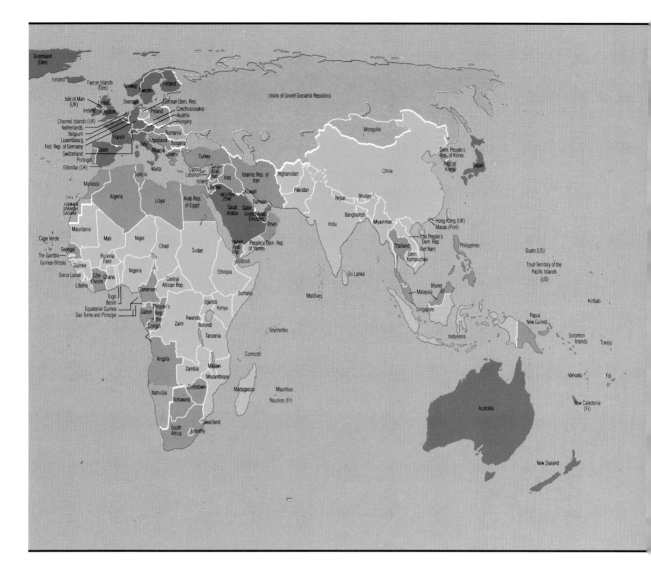

Greenland
(Den)

Iceland

Faeroe Islands
(Den)

Isle of Man
(UK)

Ireland United
Kingdom

Channel Islands (UK)
Netherlands
Belgium
Luxembourg
Fed. Rep. of Germany
Switzerland
Gibraltar (UK)
Portugal

Norway

Sweden

Denmark

Finland

German Dem. Rep.
Poland
Czechoslovakia
Austria
Hungary
Romania
Bulgaria
Yugoslavia
Italy Albania
Greece

Union of Soviet Socialist Republics

Mongolia

Dem. People's
Rep. of Korea
Rep. of
Korea

Japan

Spain

France

Malta

Tunisia

Morocco

FORMER
SPANISH
SAHARA

Algeria

Libya

Cyprus
Lebanon
Israel

Syrian
Arab
Rep.
Jordan

Turkey

Iraq

Islamic Rep. of
Iran

Afghanistan

China

Pakistan

Kuwait

NEUTRAL
ZONE

Saudi
Arabia

Qatar

Bahrain

United Arab
Emirates

Oman

Nepal

Bhutan

Hong Kong (UK)
Macao (Port)

Mauritania

Cape Verde

Senegal
The Gambia
Guinea-Bissau

Sierra Leone

Liberia

Mali

Guinea

Côte
d'Ivoire

Niger

Burkina
Faso

Ghana

Nigeria

Chad

Cameroon

Arab Rep.
of Egypt

Sudan

Central
African Rep.

Yemen
Arab
Rep.

People's Dem. Rep.
of Yemen

Djibouti

Ethiopia

Somalia

India

Bangladesh

Myanmar

Sri Lanka

Maldives

Thailand

Lao People's
Dem. Rep.
Viet Nam

Dem.
Kampuchea

Brunei

Malaysia

Singapore

Philippines

Indonesia

Guam (US)

Trust Territory of the
Pacific Islands
(US)

Kiribati

Papua
New Guinea

Togo
Benin
Equatorial Guinea
Sao Tome and Principe

Gabon

People's
Rep.
of the
Congo

Zaire

Uganda

Rwanda

Burundi

Kenya

Tanzania

Seychelles

Comoros

Solomon
Islands

Tuvalu

Vanuatu

Fiji

Angola

Zambia

Malawi

Mozambique

Zimbabwe

Namibia

Botswana

South
Africa

Swaziland

Lesotho

Madagascar

Mauritius

Réunion (Fr)

Australia

New Caledonia
(Fr)

New Zealand

Population

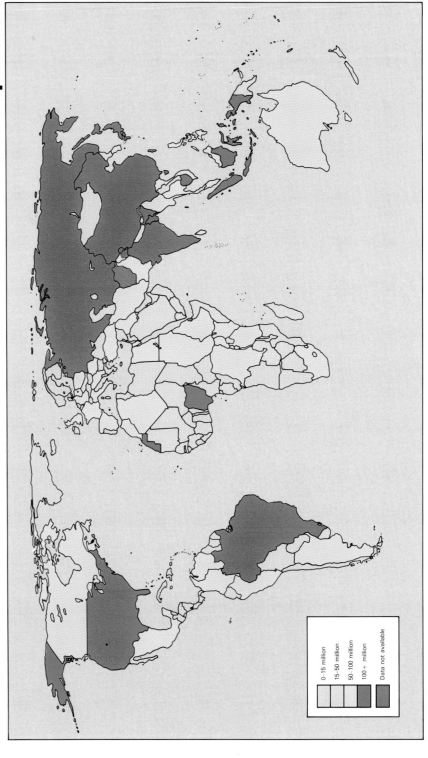

	0 - 15 million
	15 - 50 million
	50 - 100 million
	100 + million
	Data not available

The World

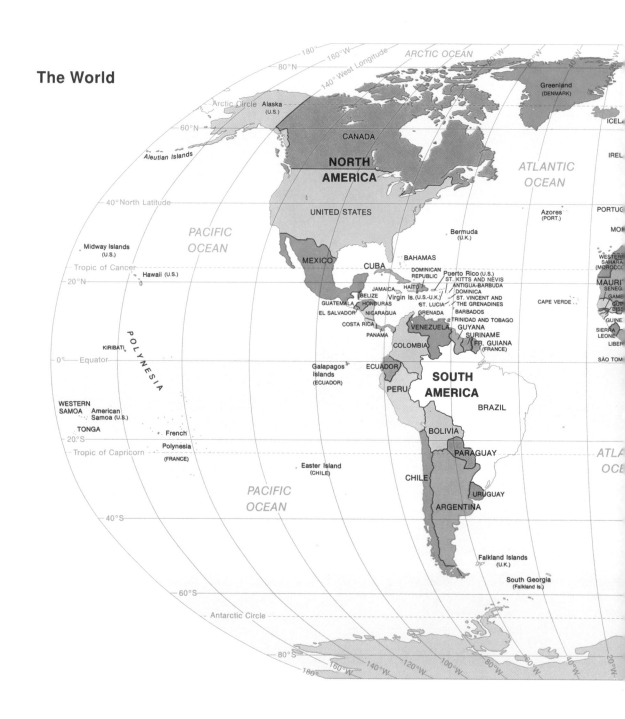

ARCTIC OCEAN

180°
160°W
140° West Longitude
80°N
60°N
40°North Latitude
Tropic of Cancer
20°N
0° Equator
20°S
Tropic of Capricorn
40°S
60°S
Antarctic Circle
80°S
180°
160°W
140°W
120°W
100°W
80°W

Arctic Circle
Alaska (U.S.)

Aleutian Islands

Midway Islands (U.S.)

Hawaii (U.S.)

PACIFIC OCEAN

KIRIBATI

WESTERN SAMOA
American Samoa (U.S.)
TONGA
French Polynesia (FRANCE)

Easter Island (CHILE)

PACIFIC OCEAN

P O L Y N E S I A

NORTH AMERICA

CANADA

UNITED STATES

MEXICO

CUBA
BAHAMAS

Bermuda (U.K.)

DOMINICAN REPUBLIC
Puerto Rico (U.S.)
HAITI
ST. KITTS AND NEVIS
ANTIGUA-BARBUDA
DOMINICA
JAMAICA
Virgin Is. (U.S.-U.K.)
ST. VINCENT AND THE GRENADINES
BELIZE
ST. LUCIA
BARBADOS
GUATEMALA
HONDURAS
GRENADA
TRINIDAD AND TOBAGO
EL SALVADOR
NICARAGUA
COSTA RICA
VENEZUELA
GUYANA
PANAMA
SURINAME
COLOMBIA
FR. GUIANA (FRANCE)

Galapagos Islands (ECUADOR)

ECUADOR

PERU

SOUTH AMERICA

BRAZIL

BOLIVIA

PARAGUAY

CHILE

URUGUAY

ARGENTINA

Falkland Islands (U.K.)

South Georgia (Falkland Is.)

ATLANTIC OCEAN

Greenland (DENMARK)

ICEL

IREL

PORTUG

MO

Azores (PORT.)

WESTERN SAHARA (MOROCCO)

MAURI

SENEG
GAMB
GUI
BISS
GUINE
SIERRA LEONE
LIBER

CAPE VERDE

SÃO TOM

ATLA
OCE